ELUSIVE VICTORY

Books by Trevor N. Dupuy

To the Colors
with R. Ernest Dupuy

Faithful and True

Military Heritage of America
with R. Ernest Dupuy

Campaigns of the French Revolution and of Napoleon

Brave Men and Great Captains
with R. Ernest Dupuy

Compact History of the Civil War
with R. Ernest Dupuy

Civil War Land Battles

Civil War Naval Actions

Military History of World War II (19 vols.)

Compact History of the Revolutionary War
with R. Ernest Dupuy

Military History of World War I (12 vols.)

The Battle of Austerlitz

Modern Libraries for Modern Colleges

Ferment in College Libraries

Military History of the Chinese Civil War

The Encyclopedia of Military History from 3500 b.c. to the Present
with R. Ernest Dupuy

Military Lives (12 vols.)

Revolutionary War Land Battles
with Gay M. Hammerman

Revolutionary War Naval Battles
with Grace P. Hayes

Holidays

Documentary History of Arms Control and Disarmament
with Gay M. Hammerman

Almanac of World Military Power
with John A.C. Andrews and Grace P. Hayes

An Outline History of the American Revolution
with R. Ernest Dupuy

A Genius for War: The German Army and General Staff, 1807-1945

Elusive Victory: The Arab-Israeli Wars, 1947-1974

Numbers, Prediction, and War

ELUSIVE VICTORY
THE ARAB-ISRAELI WARS, 1947-1974

Colonel Trevor N. Dupuy
U.S. ARMY, RET.

HARPER & ROW, PUBLISHERS

NEW YORK, HAGERSTOWN, SAN FRANCISCO, LONDON

ELUSIVE VICTORY: THE ARAB-ISRAELI WARS, 1947–1974. Copyright © 1978 by Trevor
N. Dupuy. All rights reserved. Printed in the United States of America. No part of
this book may be used or reproduced in any manner whatsoever without written
permission except in the case of brief quotations embodied in critical articles and
reviews. For information address Harper & Row, Publishers, Inc., 10 East 53rd Street,
New York, N.Y. 10022. Published simultaneously in Canada by Fitzhenry & Whiteside
Limited, Toronto.

FIRST EDITION

Library of Congress Cataloging in Publication Data

Dupuy, Trevor Nevitt, date
  Elusive victory.
  Bibliography: p.
  Includes index.
  1. Israel—History, Military. 2. Arab countries—
History, Military. 3. Jewish-Arab relations—1949–
I. Title.
DS119.2.D86   956'.04   78–2119
ISBN 0–06–011112–7

78 79 80 81 82 10 9 8 7 6 5 4 3 2 1

This book is dedicated to my Middle East travelling companion,
my beloved wife, Jonna.

Contents

LIST OF MAPS AND DIAGRAMS

MAPS

1948

1956

1967

1968-1972

1973

DIAGRAMS

Acknowledgments

It is literally impossible to acknowledge all of the assistance in preparing this book that I have received from a very large number of people. I feel however, that I have an obligation to some that is so great that I would be negligent and ungrateful if I were to fail to mention their names, and acknowledge my debt to them. But, because the number of those who have helped me is so great, once I include some names I am certain that my all-too-fallible memory will cause me to omit some who should be mentioned prominently. If my worst fears prove justified, and I fail to give proper mention to one or more of those who should be mentioned, I hope they will be tolerant and forgive me.

First, I must acknowledge the hundreds of pages of notes and comments provided to me by two people who aided greatly in documentary research. James Bloom provided much material to me on the 1947-1948 War, and on the naval operations for all of the wars. Vivian Lyons provided similar compilations of data and notes for the October War of 1973, and indeed helped on all of the wars.

In the sequence in which I first visited their countries, let me acknowledge the assistance of the many friends I have made in the Middle East in the course of writing this book.

The welcome I received in Jordan in 1971 will never be forgotten. In subsequent years Amman and Um al Jimal, the old Byzantine ruin and tribal headquarters of my dear friend Sheikh Hail Srour and his wonderful family, have seemed like homes away from home. Without effort to distinguish among them by rank, distinction or the extent of their assistance, let me list other Jordanian friends who helped: Field Marshal Habis al Majali, Colonel Fathi Abu Taleb, Major General Shafiq Jumean, Fouad Tahboub, Colonel Yahyah Rifai and his charming wife Kariman, General Amer Khammash, General Zaid ben Shaker, Major General Ma'an Abu Nowar, Brigadier Ata Ali, Anton Attallah, Brigadier Abdul Rahim Saber (who treated my pneumonia), Brigadier Haj Houj Majali, and Pakistani Brigadier Said Azhar. As coordinators of my travels and meetings in Jordan, as well as pleasant social companions, particular mention must be made of Colonel George Hanna and Major Sultan al Adwan and their gracious wives.

The list in Israel is equally long. Again, with only one or two exceptions, let me merely list them; I think each knows how appreciative I am of his help. Colonel Avraham Ayalon, Dr. E. Oren, Dr. Mordechai Gichon, Brigadier General Dov Sion, Brigadier General Yoel Ben Porath, Major General Avrahan Adan, Major General Ariel Sharon, Major General Shmuel Gonen, the late Lieutenant General David Elazar, Major General Dan Laner, Lieutenant General Haim Bar Lev, Major Yonah Gazit, Lieutenant Colonel A. Simon, Captain Danny, Louis Williams, and Abraham Rabinovich. As to the generals listed, particularly those who went far out of their way to be helpful, I hope they will feel that I have treated them fairly and objectively in my comments upon their operations. Again I must mention two people particularly. One of these is Ze'ev Schiff, military correspondent of the daily newspaper *Haaritz*, who arranged several important meetings for me, who made many useful suggestions, and who also commented very helpfully on an early draft of the book. Dr. Meir Pa'il, respected soldier, controversial politician, lecturer in history, and probably the most brilliant military scholar in Israel, also provided numerous useful suggestions, as well as valuable commentary on an early draft of the book.

Unquestionably the most extensive official assistance which I received in any of the Middle East countries was in Egypt. Three men in particular are responsible for that: the late Field Marshal Ahmed Ismail Ali; his successor as Minister of War, General Mohommed el Gammasy; and the Military Spokesman, Major General Hassan el Kateb, whose cordiality and assistance, however, far transcended the requirements of official hospitality. Others who were extremely helpful include the following: Major General Taha el Magdoub, Vice Admiral Fuad Zekry, Major General Fuad Aziz Ghali, Major General Ahmad Badawy, Lieutenant General Mohommed Fahmy, Major General Goneim, Major General A. M. Halluda, Major General Mustafa el Gamal, Major General Lotfi el Said, Major General Mohammed Abou Ghazala, Dr. M. Yehia Eweis, Dr. Mustafa Manialawi (who cured my pneumonia) and Brigadier Nabil Yousef. Two Egyptian officers were particularly helpful and have become close friends. Major General Hassan el Badri, Professor of Military History at the Nasser High Military Academy, spent many hours with me, and reviewed the first draft manuscript of this book. Major General M. D. Zohdy, who was my first military escort in Egypt, also accompanied me in most of my travels and interviews in subsequent visits to Egypt; he and his charming Russian-born wife, Vera, also introduced Jonna and me to the varied night-life potentialities of Cairo.

In Syria my contacts were less extensive. This was in part due to the cooler political climate in Syria, so far as the United States and Americans are concerned, and the related tendency of Syrians to be somewhat more formal and less relaxed than their Arab brethren in dealing with foreigners. I must, however, express my great appreciation for cordial and extensive assistance by the Minister of Defense, Major General Mustafa Tlass, his Deputy, Major General Yousef Chakkour, and Lieutenant Colonel Anwar Sakbani of the General Staff. Particularly cordial, and extremely helpful was Major General Jibrael Bitar, who carefully read my preliminary manuscript, and then spent many hours with me in reviewing that and in providing me with additional useful information. I must also mention the extreme cordiality of Major Hashim Ismail who went with me to Kuneitra, and Lieutenant Nazih Khudary, who took Jonna and me on a tour of Mount Hermon. Another fast friend is Tarek Mousleh, our unofficial escort through much of Damascus.

I cannot fail to mention the assistance and advice I received from American officials in these various countries. In Jordan I am indebted particularly to Colonel Clarence C. Mann, the Defense Attaché, and to Staff Sergeant Louis A. Novacheck. In Israel it was Colonel (now Brigadier General) Billy B. Forsman, Colonel Bruce Williams, and Lieutenant Colonel Mark Gatanas. In Egypt Colonel William R. Graham was particularly helpful. So too was our Defense Attaché to Syria, Colonel Angus Mundy, his boss, Ambassador Richard W. Murphy, and Mr. Edward Gnehm of the Embassy staff.

A number of officers of the United Nations Truce Supervision Organization were also helpful to me. Outstanding among these were Captains L. F. S. Nielsen, Toren Kruger, and Paul Jacobsen of Denmark, Major George Mayes of Australia, and Captain P. J. McDonald, USMC.

In Britain I was able to consult at some length with an old friend and comrade in arms from World War II Burma campaigning, General Sir Hugh Stockwell, who played a major role in the British withdrawal from Palestine, in 1948, and who was the commander of the Anglo-French invasion force in the 1956 War. I also received help from Major General J. D. Lunt, who had served with the Arab Legion in Jordan.

During the process of preparing the book I received very useful commentary on draft manuscripts from five distinguished American historians: Dr. J. Bowyer Bell, Professor Martin Blumenson, Dr. Hugh M. Cole, the late Professor Louis Morton, and Dr. Theodore Ropp. I am extremely grateful to all of them.

Among my associates on the HERO staff, I have already mentioned Vivian Lyons. Colonel John A. C. Andrews, USAF, Ret., has assisted me in force analyses, air operations analyses, and some of the quantitative analyses reflected in Appendices A and B. Gay M. Hammerman has provided editorial comment to the extent her other editorial and writing tasks would permit. Grace P. Hayes has provided similar editorial comment far beyond the requirements of duty. Administrative aspects of the project (of which there are astonishingly many) have been handled with typical aplomb by Billie P. Davis, who has also done much of the typing, and supervised the additional excellent transcription and typing work done by Peggy Paxton, Virginia Rufner, and Alicia Boyd. For the maps I am indebted for the assistance of Bill Dunn, Gloria Saberin and particularly Ruth Sloan and Grace Hayes.

All of these people must share with me anything that is worthwhile in this book; obviously I alone am responsible for any of its shortcomings.

—T. N. DUPUY

Introduction

Probably the principal difficulty for a historian of the Arab-Israeli Middle East Wars is to obtain reliable data. There is information in abundance—most of it based on guesswork or propaganda. There is very little official information available from any of the major participating nations, although persistent and intelligent inquiries can unearth a number of individual facts. The problem, then, is to attempt to put together this mass of information in a way that will make it consistent with the general outlines of events as they can be gleaned from contemporary news accounts and apparently reliable memoirs or secondary sources. It is a kind of detective process, requiring (this author believes) professional military knowledge and combat experience.

For a number of reasons, there is more data available from Israel than there is from the Arab nations. Most official Israeli information (and informal commentary from Israeli combatants) is truthful—but not necessarily the whole truth. Arab data is not only less abundant, but what is available is less reliable. Arabs are as trustworthy and as reliable as Israelis, and they are not as proficient in the manipulation of information for propaganda purposes. But they tend to be more emotional. No Arab official or military man seems to have told me a deliberate untruth—but I have unquestionably been misled by information or interpretations that Arabs want to believe is the truth, and which they have therefore come to believe themselves. There are, of course, many exceptions to these sweeping generalizations about information and about Arabs, but the problems of relating Arab and Western thinking and perception have been well presented by Raphael Patai in *The Arab Mind* (New York, 1976).

On the other hand, Israeli observations and assertions of facts cannot be accepted without question or corroboration any more than can similar observations, assertions, or interpretations of participants in other wars. All memories are subject to error; there can be misleading reports, gaps in information, and the distortions of human nature, to which Israelis are no more immune than other peoples.

What to do, then, when absolutely contradictory information is received from Arab and Israeli sources? There is no good solution. In such instances, this author has usually—but not always—assumed the Israeli version is more likely to be factually reliable, but the possible motives for distortion, and particularly for biased interpretation by either side, must be considered. The only sure thing about making decisions is that in each case the author will undoubtedly displease one or more Arab or Israeli friends.

Prologue

A land of darkness, as darkness itself; and of the shadow of death, without any order and where the light is as darkness.—Job. 10:22.

All wars have political causes, all have historical origins. However, the series of conflicts between Israelis and Arabs since 1948 have their roots farther back in history than most of the wars of recent times, and their causes are a complicated mixture of political, ideological, and religious differences that are not easily susceptible to negotiation and resolution.

The opposing cases can be presented quite simply.

The land of the modern state of Israel has throughout much of history been known as Palestine; during antiquity the Jewish people were frequently the principal inhabitants and during several periods were political masters of most of the region. However, they were neither the first nor the sole inhabitants, and while their domain sometimes included all of modern Israel, and neighboring regions as well, the Jewish lands were often landlocked, with the coastal areas controlled by the earlier inhabitants: Philistines, Canaanites and Phoenicians. These, like other ancient tribes—such as Ammonites, Moabites, Arameans, and Edomites—most of them in Palestine before the arrival of the Jews from Mesopotomia and Egypt—were intermingled with the ancient Jews after they came to dominate the region. These other peoples, also Semitic in racial origins and characteristics, are generally considered to be the forebears of the modern Arabs of Greater Syria, as the region between the Euphrates and the Sinai Desert was frequently called.

The tides of conquest flowed frequently across the ancient "Fertile Crescent," and at various times the lands of the Jews and their neighbors were incorporated in the empires of Egypt, Assyria, Babylonia, Persia, Macedonia, and the Seleucids. In the first century B.C., Pompey the Great brought Roman power into the region, where it would remain supreme for the next seven centuries. But although supreme, that power was not unchallenged, and one of the most determined of these challenges was made by the Jews of Judea. After two years of bitter warfare that would today be called counterinsurgency, in 71 A.D. the Romans completely suppressed the Jewish uprising, and the subsequent oppressive rule of the conqueror hastened an ongoing process of Jewish emigration from Palestine to other parts of the Roman Empire; this is the phenomenon known to history as the Diaspora.

This dispersion of the Jews from Palestine, however, did not eliminate the feeling of Jewish identification with the ancient lands of Israel and Judea. Jews, no matter where they lived, continued to think of Jerusalem as their Holy City and of their ancient lands in Israel and Judea as their homeland. Not only their aspirations, but also their prayers, focussed on the time when they could return.

This was not the first time that the Jews had been driven or enticed away from the area which had become their traditional homeland. First, in the time of Joseph, was the major migration to Egypt, followed by the long and painful return to the "Promised Land" under the leadership of Moses. Then later there had been the Babylonian Captivity, and the subsequent return of the Jews to Palestine to reestablish a Jewish state. It was not unreasonable, then, for many Jews to continue to think of still another eventual return of "God's Chosen People" to the land He had not only promised to them, but had actually given to them, a land from which many felt their absence was only temporary.

There has been no more protracted "temporary" period in history. During the 1800-odd years of the Diaspora the Jewish population of Palestine dwindled, until in 1893 there were only about 10,000 Jews in all of Palestine; most of these were in Safad, many of the remainder in the Jewish Quarter in Jerusalem.

During those centuries the Arabs remained the principal inhabitants of the region, although invariably under the rule of foreigners: Roman-Byzantines; their Bedouin-Arab Moslem cousins from Mecca; Seljuk and related Turks; Christian Crusaders; Mamelukes; and Ottoman Turks. In the middle of the 19th Century the Arab population of Palestine was about half a million, of whom some 90% were Moslems and about 10% Christians.

Nonetheless, Jerusalem—the site of the ancient Temple of the early Jews—remained the Holy City of all Jews, and the "Promised Land," the region which God had decreed should belong to Abraham "and his seed."[1] It was this promise, combined with the persecutions meted out around the world to the scattered but close-knit Jews, who refused to be absorbed into the religions and cultures of their new homes, that was a major stimulus to the Zionist Movement begun in the latter part of the 19th Century.

In the late 19th Century the Zionist Movement initiated a slow return

---

[1] Genesis 12.

of Jews to their "Promised Land." Despite occasional friction with prior Arab owners and neighbors, the Jews were able to acquire homes and land peacefully, and to look forward to the possibility that, when the universally hated Turks were driven out, they might be able to share political control of Palestine with the Arabs. By the end of World War I the population of Palestine was about 700,000, including 568,000 Moslem Arabs, about 70,000 Christian Arabs, and about 58,000 Jews. It was during World War I—in November 1917—that the British Foreign Secretary, Arthur Balfour, gave further hope to the Jews that Palestine would again become their "national home." This "Balfour Declaration," as it was called, included a provision that "nothing shall be done which may prejudice the civil and religious rights of existing non-Jewish communities in Palestine."[2]

The Balfour Declaration, and subsequent authorization of substantial Jewish immigration by the British Government (which, under the provisions of the Treaty of Versailles and a League of Nations Mandate, had replaced Turkey as the colonial ruler of Palestine), aroused alarm among the Arabs. They noted with particular concern the fact that the terms of the British Mandate referred to the political, civil, and religious rights of the Jews, but only to civil and religious rights of the non-Jewish communities. The Arab reaction touched off a three-way dispute among the Jews, Arabs, and the frustrated British Government. This dispute continued with fluctuating violence and fortunes for the next quarter of a century. The story of that struggle has been fully related in many other books. Its essence is as follows.

The Palestinian Arabs, fearful that they would be displaced from the lands on which they and their forebears had lived for centuries, were alarmed and furious at the Jews, who posed such a threat to the land which they had considered theirs since the departure of the Jews eighteen centuries earlier. The Arabs believed that their historical rights to Palestine were at least as good as those of the Jews. They believed their ancestors had been on the land when Abraham arrived from Ur, as well as when Joshua and his followers invaded and conquered the country several centuries later. They were particularly disturbed by Zionist reference to the "Promised Land." Since Arabs consider themselves as much the "seed of Abraham" as the Jews, they believe that their occupancy of

---

[2] The second paragraph of the Balfour Declaration reads as follows: "His Majesty's Government view with favour the establishment in Palestine of a national home for the Jewish people, and will use their best endeavours to facilitate the achievement of this object, . . ." The wording was obviously deliberately ambiguous. Article 2 of the British Mandate for Palestine stated: "The Mandatory *shall be responsible* for placing the country under such *political, administrative* and economic conditions as will *secure the establishment of the Jewish national home*. . . . and the development of self-governing institutions, and also for safeguarding *the civil and religious rights* of all the inhabitants of Palestine. . . ." (Emphasis added.)

the land is already a fulfillment of God's promise. Most worrisome of all to the Arabs, however, was their fear that Zionism's geographical objectives were those of God's promise: from the Nile to the Euphrates.[3]

Thus the Arabs were furious at the British for permitting and even encouraging this threat. Lacking both tradition and experience in self-rule, however, the Arabs were generally disorganized and virtually leaderless.[4] They exploded into occasional outbursts of violence against both the Jews and their British colonial rulers. The first of several large-scale Arab attacks against the Jews came in 1929. The worst of these outbursts was the Arab Riots of 1937-1938, which resulted in collaboration between British military authorities and the underground security forces being created by the Zionist Movement.

The Arabs were not mollified when the British amplified and explained the Balfour Declaration, and made explicit the policy that the establishment of a national Jewish home was not intended to displace any Arabs from their land in a region that could support several times the existing population. Nor were the Arabs satisfied when the British separated and excluded from Jewish immigration the region east of the Jordan River, under the name Transjordan, bringing in to rule its mixed population of Palestinian Arabs and Bedouin a homeless Bedouin prince —Abdullah of the Hashemite family.[5] It was only right, said the Arabs, that the region east of the Jordan should remain Arab; so, too, they insisted should the region west of the river, on both historical and ethnographic grounds.

The Jews of Palestine and of the Zionist Movement were fearful of the threat posed to their very existence by the growing hatred and opposition of the far more numerous Arabs, and by the terrorism that took so many Jewish lives in the 1920s and 1930s. There were two obvious responses to this threat: to organize themselves as effectively as possible for defense, and to offset as quickly as possible the numerical imbalance by encouraging migration of more Jews to Palestine. They were also fearful of the apparent weakening of the British determination to make

[3] Genesis 15, 21.

[4] It is perhaps significant that Article 4 of the Mandate authorized the establishment of a "Jewish agency" to be "recognized as a public body for the purpose of advising and cooperating with the administration of Palestine in such . . . matters as may affect the establishment of the Jewish national home and the interests of the Jewish population in Palestine. . . ." There was no comparable Arab agency mentioned in the Mandate, or otherwise established to represent the majority Arab population. There were enough Palestinians of ability to provide leadership—outstanding among them Haj Amin el Husseini, the Mufti of Jerusalem. But without such an Arab Agency to provide an institutional focus, more of their efforts were devoted to debilitating power struggles than in united opposition to the common Zionist foe.

[5] The Hashemites had recently been driven from western Arabia by Ibn Saud, and the British owed them a substantial debt for World War I assistance.

good on the Balfour Declaration, manifested by limits placed upon Jewish immigration, and by the exclusion of Transjordan from the promised Jewish national home. (After all, the eastern side of the Jordan Valley had always been an integral part of the ancient Jewish kingdoms.) Consequently the Zionist Movement's official machinery—the Jewish Agency—kept up constant pressure upon the British Government, not only through the influential Jewish community in Britain, but also indirectly with the assistance of the at least equally influential Jewish communities in the United States and France.

In Palestine itself Jewish policy fluctuated during these years. At times the Jewish community, and the official Jewish Agency leadership, cooperated closely with British governing authorities. At other times objections to British pro-Arab policies and actions were manifested by organized protest. Toward the end of the Mandate these protests often took the form of terrorist violence designed to increase British frustrations to the point where they would simply abandon Palestine and let the Jews and Arabs settle their own problems. By the mid-1940s the Jews were confident that, for a variety of reasons, foreign political support combined with their own remarkably increased strength in Palestine would enable them to establish the long-sought Jewish state.

The Zionists do not appear originally to have had any intention of driving the Arabs from Palestine—despite strongly-held Arab opinions that this was their intention from the outset. They seem to have recognized the potential of Palestine to support a much larger population than it had under the Turks and the British, and they believed that with unlimited immigration (particularly from Europe) the Jewish population would soon outnumber the Arabs. To achieve a numerical superiority, however, was an important objective, because of their centuries of experience as minorities in the lands of other peoples where they had, for the most part, been persecuted and victimized. If they were to have a true national home, as the Balfour Declaration promised, it was important that they be the political masters of their own fate, and not once more subject to the whims of an alien, and increasingly hostile, people.

The British sincerely but vainly sought to reconcile two fundamentally-opposed elements of their policy in the government of Palestine. They felt obligated to carry out the provisions of the Balfour Declaration in some form or other. At the same time they not only felt a humanitarian responsibility to protect the interests of the Arabs who were under their governmental authority, they also recognized a responsibility to prepare the region for self-government, and the Arab population majority meant that they would dominate any democratic government. Not until the period after World War II did the British Government recognize that these two contradicting policies, while in theory not inherently irreconcilable, could not in fact be reconciled. Neither Jew nor Arab would permit it. So, with Jewish-Arab disorders growing in Palestine, and with British military and civil administrators being killed and maimed by terrorists of both sides—mostly Jews at that time, however—they made the move which the Jewish Agency had hoped for. They shifted the burden of settling the Palestine problems to the United Nations. And when that deliberative body dawdled in considering the thorny issues, in 1946 the British Government put a practical deadline on the deliberations by setting a target date for withdrawal in 1948.

There had been two major developments affecting the future of Palestine in the previous decade or so. The first of these was the persecution and massacre of Jews by Hitler's Nazi government of Germany. The massacre of six million Jews[6] had two important effects upon the peoples of the Free World, particularly in North America and Western Europe. First was a feeling of sympathy for the Jewish survivors of the holocaust, and an understanding of the natural desire of many of them to get to a new land where the future—despite Arab opposition—was at least brighter for the Jews than it was in Europe. Second, and reinforcing the sympathetic support for the Jews, was the realization that anti-Semitism had flourished in their pre-war societies, just as in Germany, and the prevalent feeling that at least indirectly all such societies shared to some extent the guilt of the Nazi murderers.[7] Sympathy and assumed guilt combined to assure that Jewish interests in Palestine would be popularly supported by many peoples and governments of the Western world. (Arabs have noted, somewhat ruefully, that these feelings of shame and guilt were not strong enough for Britain, or other western nations, to establish a Jewish homeland inside their own national boundaries, rather than in territories already owned by Arabs.)

On top of this the Jews of Palestine had loyally supported the British in the war, had contributed fighting and support units, and had developed a small munitions industry which supplied weapons to the British war effort. They had thus earned the support of the World War II Allies, who were still the dominant element in the UN.

The other development resulted from discoveries confirming that the Middle East contained the richest reserves of oil in the world; most of this oil was in Arab-controlled lands. There was a dim but growing recognition in Europe and the United States that the future energy requirements of Europe and much of the rest of the world might become dependent upon this Middle East oil. Since all of the Arab peoples of the

[6] Some Arabs have suggested that the actual number was less; that the total was inflated by Zionist propaganda. It matters not whether the figure is three million, four million or six million; the horror is the same.

[7] In Britain, also, this feeling of guilt was enhanced by the thought that not so many Jews would have been murdered by the Nazis had there been a way for them to escape to Palestine; this, however, had been impossible because of the British limitation on Jewish immigration into Palestine.

region were wholehearted supporters of the cause of the Palestinian Arabs in achieving political self-rule in Palestine, it was obvious that a United Nations decision which was not acceptable to the Palestinian Arabs would not only be strongly opposed by the Arabs and their sympathizers among underdeveloped nations of the world, it might also alienate oil-rich Arabs from oil-hungry countries supporting such an anti-Arab solution. Even in 1946 the possibility of an Arab oil boycott was recognized by some elements in Western governments.[8]

By this time there were 1,269,000 Arabs (about three-fourths Moslem and one fourth Christian) and 678,000 Jews in Palestine.[9] The Jews, however, owned only about eight percent of the land area. A solution which would be not only equitable, but acceptable, to all of these people seemed impossible to realize. In fact, as the British had already discovered, it *was* impossible. But, spurred by the British withdrawal ultimatum, the United Nations made an effort.

The result, in a resolution approved November 29, 1947, was a plan to partition Palestine into two independent Arab and Jewish states, joined only by an economic union. The boundaries of the states were based primarily on ethnographic considerations.

The Jews were to get most of the west coastal areas, from Haifa south to Ashkelon, with a small coastal enclave for the essentially Arab city of Jaffa, adjacent to the new all-Jewish city of Tel Aviv, which had already grown to a population of 150,000. The Jews were also to receive the rich farmland region they had long been developing in eastern Galilee and northern Samaria, near Lake Tiberias. Finally, the largely unsettled region of the Negev Desert was to be Jewish; this, when developed, could take the hundreds of thousands of additional Jewish immigrants expected from Europe when British limitations on immigration were lifted.

The Arabs were to receive most of central Samaria and Judea, western Galilee, the southern coastal region from Ashkelon to Rafah, and the northwestern Negev Desert. The Jerusalem area, where the old, primarily Arab, city was abutted by a modern Jewish city of 100,000 people, was to be under international control. Nearby Bethlehem would also be in this international enclave. This would assure that the places so holy to the three major religions—Christian, Jewish, and Moslem—would be preserved for all without dominance by any.

There were two anomalies in the plan, which Arabs, then and since, have pointed out. In the first place the Jews, owning less than 10% of the land, and comprising a bare third of the population, were to get

[8] This was a major factor in 1948 Pentagon opposition to the establishment of an independent Jewish state in Palestine. President Truman, however, ignored this policy recommendation.

[9] According to a Mandate census in early 1947. There were 150,000 "others," including about 10,000 Druzes.

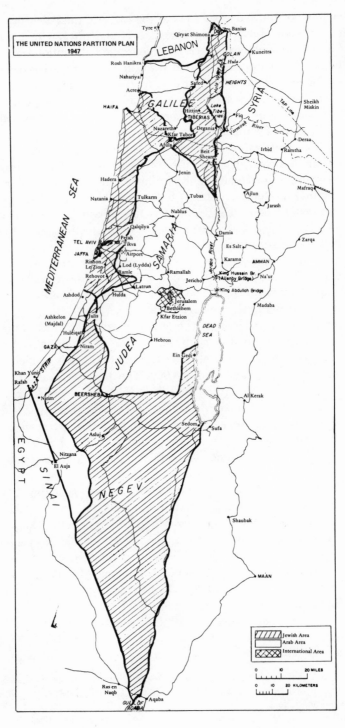

THE UNITED NATIONS PARTITION PLAN
1947

Jewish Area
Arab Area
International Area

55% of the land area of Palestine. Second, the Arabs pointed out that even though the ancient Jewish kingdoms provided a major basis for the Jewish claim to new national status in Palestine, the partition boundaries gave most of the territory which had been in those ancient states to the Arabs, and to the Jews most of what in ancient times had been non-Jewish.

However, these were not the major bases for Arab refusal to accept the partition plan. They insisted that for political, economic, and historical reasons—principally the history of the last 1,800 years—the small region of Palestine could not and should not be partitioned. It should be one political entity, governed democratically, with constitutional guarantees to the Jewish minority.

The Jews, on the other hand, while regretting that the plan kept from their control Jerusalem and much of the traditional land of the ancient Jewish states, accepted the plan in principle. They felt that they could live with it. Furthermore, since many of them recognized that Arab acceptance was unlikely, it may be assumed that many Jews felt that it was not only politically good sense to accept the plan, but that there might well be opportunities for the efficient Jewish underground government and military system they had created to expand the territory under Jewish control should the Arabs force the issue to be tested by war.

BOOK ONE

The First Arab-Israeli War
(1947-1949)

1

The Soldiers of Zion

At the time the United Nations announced the partition plan for Palestine, there were in existence in the Jewish community in Palestine —the Yishuv (the settlement), or Eretz Israel, as the community referred to itself—three distinct, efficient, and operational military organizations. One of these—the Haganah—was the underground army of the Jewish Agency, and thus was the official armed force of the Zionist Movement. The other two were essenitally paramilitary terrorist organizations: The *Irgun Zvai Leumi* (National Military Organization), and the *Lohamei Herut Israel* (Fighters for the Freedom of Israel; better known to the Yishuv by its acronym, *Lehi*, but to most of the rest of the world as the "Stern Gang").

There had been a number of contingents of local security guards in Jewish settlements in Palestine since the early days of the Zionist Movement. There had also been some Jewish military contingents in the British Army during and immediately after World War I. However, the first formal Zionist military organization was the Haganah, established in December 1920 as a nationwide underground militia, a branch of the newly-organized *Histadruth Haklalit shel Hoavdim Hairriim* (General Federation of Jewish Workers, or Federation of Labor). To control and direct this militia, the Executive Committee of the Histadruth appointed a five-man "Central Committee of the Haganah." In fact, for the next ten years the Haganah was essentially a non-centralized collection of local paramilitary militia units controlled directly by the local Yishuv administrative bodies, with only nominal coordination by the Central Committee, or "Centre."

In 1929, however, the need for improved readiness and coordination between the scattered militia units was revealed by the outbreak of a new wave of bloody Arab violence against the Palestinian Jews, resulting from a clash near the Western ("Wailing") Wall and the Arab holy places in the Temple Mount. Who was responsible for the original disorders is not clear. The Zionists blamed it on Haj Amin el Husseini, the Grand Mufti of Jerusalem since his appointment by the British mandate authorities in the early 1920s; but a later British investigation could not

3

find conclusive evidence. As a result of this traumatic experience,[1] responsibility for the coordination and control of the Haganah was transferred from the Histadruth to the National Committee of the Zionist Executive, whose administrative arm was the Jewish Agency—the quasi-official body which, under Article 4 of the Mandate, the British authorities recognized as the responsible spokesman for the Jewish community in Palestine.

The Jewish Agency established a new committee as the controlling body for the Haganah: the Political Supreme Paritetic Headquarters (PSPH), a six-man body, three from the Histadruth and three from more conservative political organizations, which was called "Paritetic" because there was parity between Histadruth and conservatives.

In the following six years the PSPH took a number of steps to assure higher standards of Haganah efficiency, and greater responsiveness to centralized control. A Technical Department of selected officers was created, to establish common standards and to supervise the training and planning of the local units; this was the genesis of a Haganah General Staff. Within the Technical Department a Provisional Planning Department was created in the mid-1930s. A radio communications network was established to link all of the local units with each other and with the PSPH and the Technical Department; this was the beginning of a Signal Corps. To facilitate control and coordination, PSPH established seventeen Rural Districts and three Urban Districts (Haifa, Tel Aviv, and Jerusalem). Professional military staffs, modelled on the Technical Department, were created in each of the three Urban Districts.

In 1936 a new series of Arab riots, sometimes called the Arab Rebellion, broke out, possibly stimulated by the Mufti of Jerusalem. This led to the establishment of a mobile "Patrol" force in the Jerusalem District by Yitzhak Sadeh, an immigrant from Russia, who had been an officer in the Red Army during the Russian Civil War. Sadeh's concept was to carry the war to the Arabs by seeking out and ambushing their guerrilla bands, rather than waiting apprehensively for attack.

Sadeh's work was unexpectedly facilitated by the British Government's reaction to the Arab violence. Determined to restore order, the British sent two divisions to Palestine to bolster the small garrison already in the country. At the same time, early in 1937, the Mandate authorities established a kind of constabulary organization, called the Jewish Settlement Police (JSP). In addition to this force—paid, trained, and equipped by the British authorities—Jewish communities were authorized to have additional unpaid local guards, who could also carry guns. Not surprisingly, practically all of the men who joined the JSP and the local guard units (collectively called *notrim*) were members of the Haganah. The

[1] Called the "Al Bouraq" uprising by the Arabs, since it began near the place where Mohammed was traditionally called up to Heaven.

PSPH thereupon authorized Sadeh, assisted by Eliahu Cohen, to recruit additional mobile units around the country from among the *notrim,* and to train them in the same hit and run tactics that he had been using so successfully in and near Jerusalem. These units—organized as squads, platoons, and companies—comprised the first standing force of the Haganah, and were called FOSH (field companies). By early 1938 Sadeh had recruited more than 1,000 men to these units.

At about this time a British Intelligence officer—Captain Orde C. Wingate—was assigned to Palestine. He soon became friendly with Jewish leaders, and established an especially close rapport with Sadeh. Although not Jewish, Wingate had become a fervent Zionist, and was able to obtain permission from British authorities to establish still another organization to deal with the Arab guerrillas. These were called Special Night Squads (SNS), consisting mostly of *notrim* and including some British soldiers. (The *notrim,* of course, were all Haganah men.) Wingate's operational concepts of hit, run, and ambush were essentially the same as Sadeh's. By 1939 Wingate's strong pro-Zionist public statements became embarrassing to the British Government, and he was posted to Africa. He is still remembered warmly in Israel.

Wingate's contributions were not new or original tactical concepts. After all, Sadeh had been doing the same kind of things for more than a year before Wingate established the SNS. But the political leaders of the Haganah had been much impressed that these concepts had been endorsed and successfully tested by a professional British officer. So they adopted the "Wingate concept" as a basis for development of the Haganah as an elite guerrilla military force. It did not occur to the Jewish politicians that this was just as much a "Sadeh concept," and that he had an equally professional background.[2]

In 1939 the Jewish Agency took another important step to enhance the growing professionalism in the Haganah, their underground army. A Chief of the PSPH was established, a virtual War Minister. At the same time, a kind of unofficial taxation policy was established. Money was collected from the local communities throughout the Yishuv, then made available to the Chief of the PSPH, as the basis for a military budget. This increased his authority, since he controlled the distribution of these funds to the local units. At the same time, the district system was reorganized; the twenty existing districts were consolidated into seven larger districts, each with a regional commander.

The existence of FOSH, the JSP, and SNS, meant that the Haganah now had, in addition to the local militia, respectable standing forces (even though nominally British-controlled) numbering more than 2,000

[2] Since Sadeh's performance later as a battlefield brigade commander was not outstanding, this may to some extent have influenced the manner in which Israeli historians, and military men, also, have subsequently assessed his pre-war activities.

trained and armed men. To perform the necessary staff functions the Technical Department was enlarged. In January 1939, a Department for Training and Instruction was also established.

In September 1939, the logical next step was taken; a Supreme General Staff (SGS) was established in Tel Aviv, under a Chief of the SGS: Ya'acov Dori. Under him were four departments: (1) a Technical Department, which exercised staff functions not specifically allocated elsewhere, (2) a Planning and Organization Department, (3) a Training and Instruction Department, and (4) a Control Department. By 1947 this underground GHQ of an underground army had been functioning and preparing itself for probable conflict with the Arabs for more than eight years. During those eight years there had been many opportunities to expand the base of professional military experience throughout the Haganah.

In 1939, as the Arab Riots subsided, the British Government withdrew its support of the *notrim*. The PSPH and the Jewish Agency thereupon decided in February to disband FOSH, but to expand its operational concepts throughout the Haganah. Accordingly the younger men—aged 18 to 25 years—were concentrated in an organization established in December and known, as usual, by its Hebrew acronym: HISH (from *Hel Sadeh*, or field corps). While the HISH men were not full-time soldiers like the FOSH, JSP, and SNS, they were given much more training (weekends and summers) than the Haganah rank and file had formerly received, and were organized so as to be available for immediate mobilization.

The outbreak of the Second World War, while resulting in tragedy for world Jewry, was a godsend to the Haganah and its leadership, who were becoming concerned over their inability to provide trained and experienced soldiers as a leavening for HISH. For several years after the outbreak of the war the British Government turned down Zionist suggesitons for the formaiton of Jewish armies and divisions. But they accepted individual Jewish recruits, and most of the Haganah members volunteered. In late 1944 the British Government finally established a Jewish Brigade Group in Italy, but it saw little active service. Nevertheless, the creation of this unit had provided further organizational training and operational experience to a substantial number of Jewish officers and men. By the time the war ended, more than 20,000 men of the Yishuv had served in the British and Allied armies. Most of this trained and experienced manpower was soon ready and available to fight again in Palestine.

Meanwhile, with much of the Haganah serving in combat theaters outside Palestine, there came a sudden new need for full-time soldiers in the Yishuv. In 1941 German General Erwin Rommel and his Afrika Korps were within striking distance of Alexandria and were threatening to drive the British from Egypt. The possibility of a German invasion and occupation of Palestine had to be considered by the Haganah SGS. In May 1941, a revitalized PSPH authorized the establishment of another full-time military organization, under the Haganah, the Palmach (from *Plugot Machatz,* striking companies). Yitzhak Sadeh was placed in command of the new organization. He quickly built six companies around a core of FOSH and SNS veterans.

Again the British unofficially recognized the existence of the new Jewish organization. Two companies of the Palmach were with the British forces based in Palestine when they invaded Syria in August 1941, to end Vichy-French control of that French mandate. By the time the British withdrew their support from Jewish military activities in Palestine—after the defeat of Rommel, in November 1942—nine (later eleven) active and about six reserve companies of the Palmach, organized in four battalions, were ready for combat. Although forced to return to an underground existence, the Palmach continued as a standing, ready force of more than 2,000 trained men.[3] In 1944 a naval company (Palyam) and an air platoon were established within the Palmach organization.

By January 1947 the outbreak of war with the Arabs of Palestine and the neighboring regions had become more and more probable. The Jews recognized that they must be ready to fight the regular armies of the surrounding Arab states; mere guerrilla capability would not be enough. The efficient chairman of the Jewish Agency's Political Department—David Ben Gurion—was also appointed head of the Defence and Security Department of the Jewish Agency Executive, with the mission of readying the Haganah for the expected war. (In other words, he became the virtual Minister of Defense, as well as Prime Minister, of the underground government of the Palestine Yishuv.) Under Ben Gurion, the Chairman of the PSPH—Yisrael Galili—served as a kind of Deputy Defense Minister.

During mid-1947 Ben Gurion sought advice from the PSPH, from Ya'acov Dori and his SGS, and also from a number of Jewish ex-regular officers who had fought with the British in World War II. On the basis of not-always-consistent recommendations, Ben Gurion directed a reorganization which was just beginning when the U.N. Partition Plan precipitated Arab determination to go to war against the Jews.

By this time HISH had grown to an active militia of some 12,000 reasonably well-trained troops—many with recent combat experience in World War II as well as in guerrilla warfare against Arabs and British. Fifteen of these companies—totalling about 7,500 men—were to be organized into four fully armed regional reserve brigade groups, ready for instant deployment primarily in their own regions, but to other parts

[3] According to Edward Luttwak and Dan Horowitz, *The Israeli Army* (New York, 1975), p. 24, and Zeev Schiff, *A History of the Israeli Army* (San Francisco, 1974), p. 28, there were 3,100, including 2,000 reserves.

of Palestine as well, if there was need. The remainder of HISH (about 5,000 men) was to remain in local militia company organizations, for essentially regional defense tasks. Backing them up were some 32,000 additional members of the Heil Mishmar (HIM, or home guard) reservists, most of these aged 26 or older, with less training and experience. An auxiliary youth organization—Gadna—had also been established, and would become the principal source of manpower for HISH and the Palmach in the coming struggle, providing about 9,500 youths from 15 to 18 years of age.[4]

The Palmach was to be reorganized as a brigade group of 4,500 men, its battalions ready for immediate action anywhere in Israel, either independently or as a single, cohesive unit. By November 1947, however, the Palmach had only 2,100 men (plus 1,000 reservists), with few of the planned heavy infantry weapons—mortars and machine guns—and no artillery. One of its four battalions was in the Jezreel Valley, another in eastern Galilee and the Jordan Valley, a third in the Judean Hills and northern Negev, and the fourth was a headquarters unit in and around Tel Aviv. This latter battalion included the naval and air units and a special commando unit.

By November 1947 there were about 4,000 members of the Haganah mobilized (2,100 Palmach and 1,800 HISH), with another 1,000 of the Palmach ready for immediate mobilization. A force of about 12,000 active duty troops was to be formed by early 1948 (4,500 Palmach and 7,500 HISH). Behind these, ready for quick mobilization, were another 5,000 members of HISH, plus the 32,000 members of the HIM home guard; these 37,000 reservists, of course, also served as a militia and were alert and on call for immediate local security functions. The most serious problem was weapons. The sources are conflicting, but for this active and militia force of nearly 49,000 men there were between 14,000 and 20,000 modern small arms, about 800 light machine guns, more than 200 medium machine guns, about 700 2-inch mortars, and perhaps 100 3-inch mortars. This meant that most of the members of the HIM organization were equipped with any of a wide variety of obsolete military weapons or hunting guns.[5]

An Air Service was established around the nucleus of the Palmach air platoon. Although there were as yet no combat aircraft, nine light reconnaissance planes had been acquired, and orders had been placed in western and central Europe for several war-surplus fighter-bombers. These, however, like all other weapons and equipment ordered by the

[4] Schiff, *op. cit.*, p. 28.
[5] These figures are based upon interpretation, and reconciliation, of inconsistent figures, primarily from Luttwak-Horowitz, Schiff, and Nathaniel Lorch, *The Edge of the Sword* (New York, 1951).

Jewish Agency, could not be delivered since the British had placed an embargo on the shipment of military supplies into Palestine.

Although it was in the throes of reorganization, and lacked the heavy weapons needed for a modern army—and indeed was short in modern small arms as well—the Haganah by 1947 had become an efficient organization of trained, ready, combat troops. It had a mission, it had a doctrine, and its actions were controlled by an experienced group of military professionals in a General Staff that had been planning and operating for eight years. Despite its weaknesses, particularly its shortage of weapons, it was (with the possible exception of the withdrawing British divisions) the most formidable military force in the Middle East when the United Nations 1947 Partition Plan heralded the outbreak of full-scale war between Jews and Arabs.

It was not the only military force available to the Jews, however.

The Irgun Zvai Leumi (also known as IZL or Etzel), made up of disgruntled members of the Haganah initially under the leadership of Zeev Jabotinsky, and later of Menachem Begin, had been established as a politically conservative counterpart to the Socialist-controlled Haganah in 1931, during the political debates that led to the establishment of the PSPH. Jabotinsky, Begin, and their adherents were unwilling to accept the policy of "self-restraint" which the Jewish Agency had adopted toward both the Arabs and the British. The Irgun initiated a campaign of sporadic, initially small-scale, terrorism, primarily directed against known anti-Zionists among the Arabs, but also designed to harass the British.

The IZL leaders hoped that reaction against Jewish Agency self-restraint would attract a large popular following to the Irgun. However, this did not turn out as they expected. The small popular base they did succeed in establishing eroded considerably during the period of British-Jewish Agency cooperation in 1937-1939. Irgun efforts to attract new adherents, after the British withdrew their support early in 1939, had barely begun when British-Jewish Agency rapport was reestablished by the beginning of World War II.

After the outbreak of the war the Irgun announced an end to its anti-British campaign, and agreed to join with the Haganah in a policy of cooperation. However, in January of 1944, when Allied victory had become inevitable, the Irgun resumed its anti-British activities with a series of terrorist attacks on British police posts and other government and army installations.

After the end of World War II, when the Jewish Agency became frustrated by continuing British controls on immigration, the Haganah also initiated a campaign of sabotage against the British. This led to some cooperation between the Haganah and the Irgun and also with the other terrorist organization, the Lehi, or Stern Group (or Stern Gang, as the British called them). This cooperation ended on July 22, 1946, when the Irgun blew up a wing of the King David Hotel in Jerusalem, killing 95 people, mostly British. The Haganah had participated in planning the sabotage operation against the hotel, but had insisted that a warning be given so that the building would be evacuated before the explosion. The Irgun, however, had ignored this, and had blown up the building prematurely.

By November 1947, the Irgun had about 2,000 men in its ranks. All were experienced terrorists, and some had had combat experience during the war.

The Irgun had broken away from the Haganah in 1931 because Begin and his associates believed that the Haganah was "soft" on the British and on the Arabs as well. Similarly, when the Irgun agreed to drop its anti-British campaign at the outset of World War II, several of its members, led by Avraham Yeir Stern, refused to comply. Complaining that the Irgun was now "soft" on the British and Arabs, they broke away to form Lehi. Despite Haganah use of force as well as persuasion to bring these dissidents back in line with Jewish Agency policy, the Lehi, or the Stern Group, remained consistently anti-British throughout the war, but active terrorism was not renewed until late 1945, after World War II.

This terrorism intensified and became ever more brutal in 1946. By the time of the U.N. Partition Plan, Lehi—now under Nathan Friedmann-Yellin—numbered 800 men. Its members were convinced that they were the only ones steadfast in the pursuit of Zionist principles; they were somewhat bitter about what they considered the pious, double-faced expressions of disapproval which their activities elicited from the Jewish Agency, which was at the same time benefitting from the pressures created by the anti-British terror.

The impartial historian must note that, even though the Jewish Agency and Haganah were from time to time embarrassed by Irgun and Lehi, these two terrorist agencies did indeed contribute to the Zionist cause by the pressures they placed on the Arabs and the British. Arab historians are convinced that despite Ben Gurion's surface disapproval of Irgun and Lehi terrorism, those two organizations were, in fact, following his orders. The *Altalena* incident (see p. 70) and other crises support the contention of Israeli historians that Ben Gurion was sincerely opposed to both terrorist groups, but there is no solid proof that the Arab historians are wrong.

2

The Forces of the Jihad

During the so-called "Arab Rebellion" of 1936-1939, there were two Arab factions waging guerrilla warfare against the Jews and British. Haj Amin el Husseini, the Mufti of Jerusalem, had a loose and ineffective organization endeavoring to coordinate Palestinian opposition to the Jews. The other faction, which included Syrians and Lebanese as well as Palestinians, was led by a former officer of the Ottoman Turkish Army—Fawz el Din el Kaukji, a Syrian. To some Arabs who served with him, Kaukji is remembered as a courageous and inspirational leader; others have called him "an unprofessional clown."[1] There seems to be truth in both thumb-nail descriptions. However, on balance his performance was generally poor.

Whatever Kaukji's combat experiences with the Turkish Army may have been in World War I, they had certainly not equipped him to be the organizer, administrator, or strategic planner of a guerrilla army. He seems to have been intelligent, personally brave, and reasonably well aware of the deficiencies of his troops and the sketchy organization into which he tried to fit them. He was unable, however, to instill discipline in, or impose order on, a collection of highly individualistic Syrian, Palestinian, and Bedouin Arabs. In fairness to Kaukji, it must be recognized that his efforts were repeatedly thwarted by the rival guerrilla groups who had responded to the Mufti's call to arms. The disorderly, disorganized guerrilla bands of both factions suffered defeat after defeat at the hands of the British and the Jewish FOSH and Special Night Squads.[2] By early 1939 the revolt had been suppressed and Kaukji had disappeared into the obscurity whence he had emerged three years earlier.

THE ARMIES OF LIBERATION AND SALVATION

In November 1947, after the announcement of the U.N. Partition Plan, the Mufti proclaimed a Jihad—Holy War—against the Jews of Palestine.

[1] From various interviews the author has had with Arabs who fought under or near Kaukji in 1947-1949.

[2] The loss statistics of the Rebellion (taken from the *Encyclopaedia Britannica* 1969, XVII, p. 170) tell the story: Jews, 329 killed, 827 wounded; British, 135 killed, 386 wounded; Arabs, 3,112 killed, 1,775 wounded.

11

He seems also to have entered into secret negotiations with King Abdullah, the ruler of the British protectorate of Transjordan, who was principal rival for leadership of the Palestinian Arabs.[3] Upon the expiration of the British Mandate, of course, Transjordan also would become independent, and Abdullah unquestionably was eying the possibility of uniting Palestine (or at least Arab Palestine, if the state of Israel were to become a reality) with Transjordan in a new Palestinian or Jordanian kingdom.

The leaders of all of the other Arab states—who could find few bases for united action—were at least unified in their opposition to Abdullah's ambitions. This was true not only of the republican leaders of Syria and Lebanon, but also of King Farouk of Egypt, and even of the government of Abdullah's 12-year-old nephew, King Feisal II of Iraq.[4] To offset the possibility of combined action by the Mufti and Abdullah, therefore, the other Arab governments quickly recalled Fawz el Kaukji from retirement to lead an irregular Arab army against the Zionists, and at the same time prevent Abdullah from gaining control over all of Palestine. This irregular force, called the Arab Army of Liberation, or ALA, was to be made up of volunteers from the other Arab countries, as well as from the Arab population of Palestine.

Headquarters of this new ALA was established in Damascus, and weapons and supplies were to be provided mostly by Lebanon and Syria. Remembering Kaukji's haphazard approach to organization, the Arab leaders appointed an Inspector General, virtually an administrative commander in chief, General Taha Al-Hashimi, an officer of the Iraqi Army provided by the Hashemite Government of Bagdad. An Assistant Inspector General also was provided by the Iraqi Government: General Ismail Safwat. The Administrative Officer was Syrian Colonel Mahmoud Haridi. Kaukji, however, had nominal command authority over the operational field forces of this "army" in Palestine.

The Mufti, meanwhile, had set up his own irregular army, the Army of the Jihad el Mukadis (Holy War of Salvation) which is generally known either as the Arab Army of Salvation, or the Army of the Jihad. To command this AAS—made up mainly of volunteers, members of an informal militia which had grown up within the Arab community of Palestine—the Mufti appointed his cousin, Abd el Kader el Husseini, who had no military experience, but whose strong personality seems to have made him the most effective of all of the irregular Arab leaders during the few remaining months of his life. Husseini apparently hoped to be able to cooperate with the ALA, and went to Damascus to seek weapons

---

[3] This is firmly asserted by Egyptian sources in personal interviews; Israeli historians tend to doubt it.

[4] Egyptian historians assert this privately; Israeli historians doubt it.

from General Al-Hashimi. The Iraqui general, however, rudely rejected Husseini's appeal, saying (in Turkish), "We don't provide weapons to *bashi bazooks* (militia)." Husseini returned to Jerusalem empty-handed and bitter.

Not only was the existence of these two rival Arab armies divisive, there was further fragmentation in each, so that there was little or no coordination of Arab effort against the extremely well-organized Zionists. The results of this disorganization and confusion would be disastrous to the Arab cause, and from the outset negated whatever theoretical numerical advantage they had over the highly organized Jewish military forces and civil administration. The only compromise between them was a general division of areas of responsibility: the ALA in the north, and AAS in the south.

The size and command structure of Kaukji's Arab Liberation Army fluctuated constantly. However, in early 1948 Kaukji himself was the field commander of the Northern Front,[5] and more or less responsive to his orders were the following battalions: First Yarmuk Battalion, under Muhamad Safa, a Syrian; Second Yarmuk Battalion, also under a Syrian, Adib Shishakly; Hittin Battalion, commanded by an Iraqi, Madlul Abas; El-Hussein Battalion, commanded by Abd el Rahim Sheikh Ali, also an Iraqi; Lebanese or Druse Battalion, under the Druse leader Shakib Wahab; the Ajnadin Battalion, Druses and Palestinians, under Michael el Issa, a Palestinian, and the Qadisier Battalion, led by Iraqi Lieutenant Colonel Mahdi Saleh.[6] After the fall of Jaffa, El Issa went home, and the Qadisier Battalion was incorporated in the Ajnadin Battalion, under Saleh.

The ALA approached its planned strength of 8,000 men only briefly, in early May 1948, when its strength was about 7,700. The planned contribution of forces from participating Arab nations was as follows:

---

[5] The "Volunteers" under Egyptian control comprised the forces of the Southern Front; see below.

[6] There was later a 3d Yarmuk Battalion, and for a while the three Yarmuk Battalions were combined in a brigade under Shishakly. Also there was briefly an Alawis Battalion, near Safad, commanded by Captain Ghassan Shdeed of the Syrian Army. Smaller units included: an artillery battery of four French 75mm guns, commanded by Lt. Fayez Qasri, a Syrian; an Acre Task Force, commanded by Captain Fouad Tahboub; a Bedouin company, later a small battalion, commanded by Captain Saadun; a Yugoslav Moslem Company commanded by Major Shawki; a Jerusalem Company, commanded by Iraqi Lieutenant Fadel Rashid; an independent Yemenite Company; and an independent North African company. Among battalion commanders who served in the ALA from time to time, Syrian Shishakly, Iraqi Saleh, and Jordanian Lieutenant Colonel Wasfi Tell would all attain political prominence in their respective countries after the war. The Surgeon General of the ALA was Dr. Amin Ruwaha.

Syria, 1,000 men, plus 1 battery of 75mm guns
Lebanon, 500 men
Iraq, 2,000 men, plus 2 artillery batteries
Jordan, 500 men, plus 1 artillery battery
Saudi Arabia, 2,000 men
Egypt, 2,000 men, plus 1 artillery battery

Within the Army of Salvation there were two principal guerrilla contingents, each less than 1,000 strong: the Central Contingent, in the Lydda Area, under Hassan Sallame; and the Jerusalem Contingent, directly commanded by Abd el Kader el Husseini. Local militia organizations could mobilize most of the male populations of the Arab communities for raids or defense, but there was no real centralized organization.

Complicating the situation in the Arab Liberation Army was the nominal participation of a semi-illegal group of Egyptian revolutionaries, called the Moslem Brotherhood. King Farouk and his government found it slightly embarrassing to have this anti-monarchical group of Egyptians participating in the covertly anti-Abdullah and overtly anti-Zionist effort which Egypt was officially sponsoring. It seemed like a good idea, however, to have these revolutionaries devoting their attention outside the country, rather than on plans of regicide, and so the Egyptian Government supported them and their leader, a Sudanese named Tariq el Afriqi, a supporter of the Mufti. By a stroke of diplomacy the Egyptian Government was able to persuade the Moslem Brotherhood that they needed a trained regular officer as their combat commander. So Colonel Ahmed Abd el Azziz, an efficient, spit-and-polish cavalry officer, replaced el Afriqi and unexpectedly found himself commanding several hundred radical, ragamuffin revolutionaries in southern Palestine. Nominally el Azziz and his men were under Kaukji, and as such were called "the Southern Contingent," of the ALA. However, they respected the unwritten geographical compromise between ALA and AAS and maintained nominal liaison with the Mufti. For all practical purposes, however, they were completely independent. To distinguish them from the Egyptian regular army units that would soon be engaged in the conflict, el Azziz and his men were usually called "the Volunteers" by other Egyptians.

ARMIES OF THE ARAB LEAGUE

On April 25, 1948, the Arab League agreed that its member states would intervene in Palestine as soon as the British had withdrawn, to prevent by force of arms the planned partition of Palestine, and to assure Arab supremacy in the new Palestinian state. Although small, the best-organized military force in the Arab world was generally acknowledged to be the British-led Arab Legion of Transjordan. Partly because of this military asset, but mainly because he was less unacceptable politically to Arab League members than either the corrupt government of Farouk or the radical government of Syria, King Abdullah of Transjordan was officially invited by the Arab League to be head of an Arab Defense Council and the commander in chief of the Arab armies that would invade Palestine upon the departure of the British. Since most of the other Arab leaders generally mistrusted Abdullah, however, even though they could not agree on other issues, at least a part of their motivation in committing forces to Palestine was to grab as much of the country as possible before he did. Consequently the Arab armies included those of Lebanon, Syria, Jordan, Egypt, and Iraq, as well as Transjordan's Arab Legion and Kaukji's Arab Liberation Army and el Husseini's Army of Salvation.

The Jewish Agency believed that it might be able to reach an agreement with Abdullah, whereby the Transjordanian monarch would agree to peace if he were to be declared the ruler of the Arab portions of Palestine as established by the UN Partition Plan. There seems little doubt that Abdullah tried to achieve just such a peaceful settlement, but could get no support from his mistrustful Arab neighbors. Such a solution was particularly abhorrent to Abdullah's old enemy, Mufti Husseini of Jerusalem, who made sure that other Arab leaders would not agree.

In an effort to try to reach an agreement with Abdullah, and to seek ways of quietly supporting him without arousing the fears of other Arabs, the head of the Political Department of the Jewish Agency—Mrs. Golda Meir—twice met with him secretly in the stormy months before the outbreak of war. The first time was in November 1947 at Naharayim (just east of the Jordan, where it is joined by the Yarmuk), the second time on May 10, 1948, in Abdullah's palace at Amman. Despite cordial conversations, agreement was impossible. The Jews understandably would not postpone their independence—indeed, could not, in the light of the British withdrawal. And Abdullah could not act in defiance of the rest of the Arab world. War was inevitable.[7]

TRANSJORDAN'S ARMY—THE ARAB LEGION

The Arab Legion was an indirect descendent of the Arab Revolutionary Army that Hashemite Prince Faisal of the Hejaz had led—with the assistance of T.E. Lawrence—in the 1917 and 1918 campaigns that drove the Turks out of their Arab empire. That was followed in the Middle East by a complex drama of power politics, desert warfare, and Anglo-French colonial duplicity in dealing with Faisal and other Arabs. When the Middle East settled to something like stability in the early 1920s,

[7] See Golda Meir, *My Life* (Tel Aviv, 1975), pp. 175-180.

King Ibn Saud of Saudi Arabia had displaced Faisal and his father from their Hejaz kingdom. Faisal had also been ejected from Syria by the French but had been installed by the British as king of the British Mandate-Protectorate of Iraq, and Faisal's brother, Abdullah, had become King of the Transjordanian portion of the British Palestine-Arabian Mandate. The British-sponsored and -led force of Bedouin that supported Abdullah on his new throne had become the embryo of the Arab Legion of the Kingdom of Transjordan.

Captain John Glubb, a thrice-wounded veteran of World War I, had served in Arabia after the war, and in 1930 joined the Arab Legion as a "contract" officer (as opposed to a "posted" officer, on assignment from the British Regular Army). At that time the Legion was essentially a camel-mounted constabulary force of desert cavalry. In 1939 Glubb, by now known among the Arabs as Glubb Pasha, became the commander of the Legion, and began its gradual transformation into a modern fighting force. He retained a few camels and horses for desert operations, but most of the Legion became a light mechanized force of infantry and armored cars, with supporting motorized field artillery. By early 1947 the strength of the Legion had grown to about 8,000 troops, and by the beginning of 1948 it had become more than 10,000, organized into three brigade groups, four armored car battalions, and a number of independent infantry companies. The field artillery batteries with the brigade groups were armed with either 25-pounders or mountain howitzers, 3.7-inch caliber.[8] This was a modern, cohesive force, roughly equivalent to a light mechanized division organized on British lines, and proud of the traditional British discipline which had transformed its fierce, individualistic Bedouin warriors into formidable soldiers.[9] There were 37 British officers, including Glubb, with the Legion.

EGYPT'S ARMY

Modern Egypt's independence nominally dates to February 28, 1922, when the British Government—which had declared a protectorate over Egypt when Turkey (then nominal suzerain of Egypt) joined the Central Powers in World War I—announced this independence. In fact, however, the British protectorate continued, and Egypt remained under British protection until early 1947, when British troops in Egypt were withdrawn to the "Canal Zone" adjacent to the Suez Canal.

During the British protectorate, lip service was paid to Egypt's long

[8] This was the famous "Screw Gun," so called because its barrel consisted of two portions, easily carried by pack animals, that screwed together to provide an artillery tube.
[9] Although Bedouin predominated, there were also Jordanians, Circassians, Palestinians, Druzes, and Armenians in the ranks of the Legion.

and honorable military tradition, but in fact the Egyptian Army during those years was a small colonial appendage of the British Army. There was little opportunity for Egyptian officers to obtain command experience above company and battalion rank, and then only in routine, garrison duties. A partial exception to this rule came during World War II, when Egypt's anti-aircraft artillery had considerable experience in protecting British port facilities and lines of communications from German aircraft.

Thus, for all practical purposes, the Egyptian Army in 1947 was a brand-new army, with officers generally inexperienced in command and administration, its units equipped mainly with cast-off British weapons. On paper the army was 55,000 strong, but most of these troops were scattered in garrisons through the Delta, and southward in the Nile Valley for hundreds of miles. When King Farouk decided, early in 1948, to thwart Abdullah's ambitions by participating in the joint invasion of Palestine, Egypt could barely scrape together an expeditionary force of 5,000 troops in a brigade group, including an armored contingent.

Colonel Azziz was supposed to have 2,000 Volunteers, mostly Egyptians but including some Sudanese and Libyans. However, the full strength of the Volunteers was never mustered in the fighting element in Palestine. Although theoretically this was part of Kaukji's ALA, in practice Azziz operated under the authority of the Egyptian commander in chief. His force had a few mortars and heavy machine guns and some old trucks.

SYRIA'S ARMY

Syria became independent of French colonial rule in April 1946. During the French Mandate a small number of Syrian units had been raised as elements of the French colonial army, and these became the nucleus of a new Syrian Army. The Syrians, however, had had even less military experience than the Egyptians, and when Syria prepared to send an expedition into Palestine, two years after independence, most officers and non-commissioned officers were little more prepared for field operations than were their newly-recruited soldiers. The army consisted of about 8,000 troops organized into two infantry brigades, a mechanized battalion (including a company of French tanks) and miscellaneous scattered units. The Syrians also possessed an air force of about 50 planes, but only 10 of these were modern combat fighter-bombers.

LEBANON'S ARMY

It would have been difficult in early 1948 to find an army in any independent nation less ready for war than that of Syria. Difficult, that is, unless neighboring Lebanon is considered. Lebanon, which had been part of the French Mandate of Syria, shared all of the military shortcomings of Syria—plus some that were uniquely Lebanese.

Since antiquity the people of Lebanon have been traders, renowned for mercantile skill and acumen, but with little interest in, or capability for, war. Few Lebanese, for instance, had served in the French army or constabulary units during the Mandate period. Thus the Lebanese Army, 3,500 strong, was even less prepared for war than was that of Syria. It comprised five infantry battalion groups and small tank, armored car, and horse cavalry units. The Lebanese force to enter Palestine was four infantry battalions and two artillery batteries, plus small armored and cavalry contingents.

IRAQ'S ARMY

Of all the Arab states involved in the "Liberation of Palestine," Iraq had been independent longest. Under King Faisal I, Iraq obtained independence from British Mandate on October 3, 1932. Thus the Iraqi Army had long been established, and was not so seriously inexperienced in coping with problems of organization and administration as were the forces of Egypt, Syria, and Lebanon. It was, however, an army without much confidence in itself. Its only combat experience had been a brief and somewhat inglorious conflict with Britain in 1941. Then, under German influence, the Iraqis had attempted to drive the British out of their Habaniyah base, near Mosul, which they had retained under treaty at the time of independence. The minuscule British garrison held the position against overwhelming Iraqi odds, and the early arrival of more British troops by air and overland from Palestine resulted in quick subjugation of the Iraqi Army.

In early 1948 this army numbered 21,000 men, well-equipped with British 25-pounders, antiaircraft and antitank guns and armored cars. The air force included at least 100 planes. An expeditionary force of about 5,000 troops was planned to join the other Arab armies in Palestine.

With both the competence and the morale of the Iraqi forces questionable, there was an even more serious practical problem. The long lines of communication, over the desert from the Euphrates River to the Jordan, would have created difficult problems for even the most sophisticated and competent modern army. Offsetting this serious problem, however, was the fact that some logistical support could be expected from Jordan, whose Hashemite king, after all, was the great uncle of Iraq's youthful monarch, Faisal II. On the other hand, thinly-populated, economically inviable Jordan could hardly support its own army, even with substantial British subsidies.

If the Iraqi Army contingent—four infantry brigades, an armored battalion and supporting troops—was to perform well in the coming hostilities, it would be despite extremely serious handicaps.

SUMMATION

In early 1948 the combined total of Arab forces about to be committed to "liberate" Palestine from the Jews was at most 40,000 men, including less than 5,000 men then under arms in the two irregular Arab armies. Of these, barely 10,000—Jordan's Arab Legion—could be considered to be at least a match for the Jewish soldiers. Yet at this time the Jews, with the advantages of defensive posture and interior lines, numbered about 30,000 men under arms, another 10,000 (admittedly short of modern small arms, but nonetheless armed) ready for immediate mobilization in local defense, and behind them about 25,000 more trained men in a home guard that combined both defensive effectiveness and a manpower pool for the active forces. Serious, however, was the Jews' almost complete lack of heavy weapons, armor, and combat aircraft. As it was, the possession of modest amounts of these necessities of modern warfare, by Arab armies that were for the most part otherwise totally unprepared for modern conflict, barely served to offset the Jewish advantages of numbers of trained men, organization, doctrine, planning experience, combat experience, and all-around efficiency.

The Jews, with their population outnumbered more than 50-to-1 by the surrounding Arabs, are fond of making much of the David and Goliath comparison. The Arabs, pointing to the size of effective forces the two sides were able to bring into this and subsequent conflicts, respond that it was really a Jewish Goliath against an Arab David. There is, in fact, something to this Arab comparison; but one can only admire the combination of efficiency and dedication which has enabled the vastly outnumbered Jews to mobilize such a large proportion of their manpower.

3

The Preliminaries I—
North and West

THE BATTLEGROUND

The land of Palestine, about to become the battleground between the Jews and the Arabs, is naturally divided into four major regions. A coastal plain extends from north to south, varying in width from 8 to 40 kilometers, except at Haifa, where the mountains come almost to the shore. Inland, a chain of mountains and plateaus extends from the Lebanese border in the north through Galilee, central Samaria, and Judea, with a central spine ridge extending southward from Nazareth through Nablus, Jerusalem, and Hebron. Farther east are the interior lowlands, west of the northern Jordan River, Sea of Galilee (also variously known as Lake Tiberias, Lake Kinneret, Lake Jenet and Lake Genazereth), then southward through the Jezreel and Central Jordan valleys. Southward from the Judean Hills and the Dead Sea a large desert known as the Negev extends to the upper tip of the Gulf of Aqaba.

The region is generally arid. From November through March there is a rainy season along the coastal plain, and some rain and dampness extend inland through most of the rest of the country, except for the Negev.

The road network in 1948 was little changed from ancient times, but many of the roads were hard-surfaced and readily traversible. The Negev was virtually roadless. There was only one major airfield, near Lydda (Lod), but there were a number of strips scattered throughout the country capable of handling the light aircraft.

THE WAR BEGINS

No single incident marked the transition from uneasy peace to outright hostilities. In reaction to the United Nations partition resolutions, Haj el Husseini, the Mufti of Jerusalem, ordered a three-day general strike of all Palestinian Arabs on November 30, 1947. That day a Jewish bus was ambushed near Lydda. On December 2 Arab rioters in Jerusalem attacked the main Jewish shopping center, beating shop owners and

20

customers and starting fires which burned down most of the buildings. At the same time, fighting broke out between Arabs and Jews throughout much of Palestine. It was particularly intensive in Haifa. The Jews complained that the British occupation force did little or nothing to restore order or to protect life and property. However, in the two previous years 127 British soldiers had been killed and 331 had been wounded by Jewish terrorists and guerrillas. It was therefore easy to understand why the British troops were in no hurry to rush to the defense of the Jews.

From the beginning the Jews thought of the war in terms of three major operational aspects: (1) the Convoy War, to keep open the lines of communications in order to maintain contact between the far-flung Jewish settlements and the center of the Yishuv in and around Tel Aviv; (2) Defense of the Settlements, partly to hold on to as much territory as possible, and partly to assure control of key points of strategic and tactical importance; and (3) War of Reprisal, to discourage the Arabs, and to punish them for actions against either convoys or settlements.

The importance of the lines of communications, and of the Jewish convoys sent to support the outlying settlements, was well appreciated by the Arabs. Groups of Arabs, with little or no central direction, positioned themselves in areas dominating the main roads, where they could interfere with Jewish communications from Tel Aviv, Jerusalem, and the various settlements scattered throughout the country. Their principal attention was focused on the Jerusalem-Tel Aviv and the Jerusalem-Hebron roads.

Ben Gurion made a decision, fully endorsed by the entire Yishuv, not to evacuate a single settlement. Recognizing that the survival of the scattered settlements depended on the delivery of supplies and ammunition, the Jewish Agency Executive attempted to supply them by trucks convoyed by improvised armored cars. These convoys, although well organized, were not uniformly successful. However, the convoy operations became the focus of the Arab-Jewish struggle during December 1947 and the early months of 1948.

Convoys supplying the outlying, and often isolated, settlements repeatedly came under Arab attack. Loss of life was heavy among the Jews, and relatively light among the Arabs. The Haganah was mobilized but operated with extreme caution, fearing that any major operations against the Arabs would force the British into direct opposition to the Jews. Some attacks were made on Arab settlements in retaliation against attacks on the convoys, but all these actions were carefully limited in scope and in intensity.

During these weeks—despite British efforts to maintain order—terrorist activity mounted on both sides. Booby-trapped cars and remotely controlled barrels of explosive were particularly popular with both Arab and Jewish terrorists. In retaliation against the Arab convoy attacks, on

January 5, 1948, two members of the Irgun drove a truck full of dynamite into Jaffa, and parked it next to a building in the center of the city which was being used as a headquarters by the local Arab militants. When the truck exploded, it caused over a hundred casualties.

The next day, in the Katamon section of Jerusalem, the Arab-owned Semiramis Hotel was blown up with a loss of twenty more Arab lives. The Haganah claimed responsibility for this incident, stating that the hotel had been the headquarters for an Arab terrorist organization.

EARLY ALA OPERATIONS

On January 10, Fawz el Kaukji led the first Arab invasion into Palestine. With a force of some 900 irregulars, he crossed the border from Syria to attack the Jewish village of Kfar Szold. Although the British had been neutral and relatively inactive during the terrorist and guerrilla activities in previous weeks, they could not condone this overt invasion. An armored unit rushed to the border from the nearby British base at Safad, and assisted the Jewish settlers in repelling the attack and driving Kaukji and his irregulars back over the border into Syria.

Although he had been unsuccessful, Kaukji had given the signal for an initiation of overt hostilities. Four days later, in a completely unrelated operation, his AAS rival, Abd el Kader el Husseini, led a force of about a thousand Palestinian irregulars in attack against the settlement of Kfar Etzion, a Jewish settlement about fifteen miles south of Jerusalem. However, the Jews had been alerted to the possibility of this attack, and a platoon of about 30 Palmach soldiers ambushed the Arabs, then helped the local settlers drive the attackers off. Worried about the dangerously exposed situation of the settlement, which was short of supplies as a result of the Arab blockade of the Hebron road, the Jewish high command sent another platoon of about 35 men with a convoy of supplies to reinforce the settlement. They left Hartuv on the evening of January 15, but were ambushed during the night by the Arabs and in a desperate nighttime fight were completely wiped out. The defenders of Kfar Etzion continued their grim existence under the sporadic attack of the nearby watchful Arabs.

Late in January, Kaukji again crossed from Syria into Palestine. He attempted to capture the settlement of Tirat Tzva. Again unsuccessful, on February 16 he withdrew southward to Nablus in the heart of Arab Palestine, where he set up his headquarters.

During the next several weeks terrorist activities by both Arabs and Jews became more intensive. The Arabs had recruited a number of foreigners—mostly British deserters, Yugoslavs, Germans, and Poles—whose fair complexions enabled them to pass either as British soldiers or as Jewish immigrants. On February 1 a group of British deserters, driving

British vehicles, blew up the Jerusalem offices of the Jewish-owned *Palestine Post*. On February 22 several apartment buildings in Jerusalem were demolished, and 50 Jews were killed and more than 70 injured. On March 11, part of the Jewish Agency building in Jerusalem was demolished, with 12 Jews killed and 90 injured. Jewish terrorists were at least as destructive as the Arabs, hitting at Arab-owned facilities and causing equivalent bloodshed and damage.

By the end of March, Palestine was a land of terror, and Arabs had halted traffic on most of the main roads of Palestine. The Jews had suffered more than 1,200 casualties since the end of November. Arab casualties, unreported, must have been at least as great.

THE HAGANAH GIRDS FOR WAR

In the Executive of the Jewish Agency, Ben Gurion had full responsibility for defense matters, but he entrusted detailed supervision of military planning and operations to his deputy, Yisrael Galili, Chief of the PSPH. The Chief of Staff of the Haganah, who had held that post since 1939, was Ya'acov Dori, but his increasingly poor health thrust ever-increasing responsibility upon Haganah's Chief of Operations, Yigal Yadin, who was virtually Dori's deputy. These four men, and the small General Staff supervised by Dori and Yadin, comprised Haganah's "High Command."

During March this High Command completed, and issued to the Palmach and the principal regional commands, a detailed plan of operations for the war that was already beginning. This plan—called Plan D, since it replaced previous plans A, B, and C—recognized that, once the British withdrew, the war would both spread and intensify.

Under Plan D, Haganah's mission was stated as follows: "To gain control of the area allotted to the Jewish State and defend its borders, and those blocs of Jewish settlements and such Jewish population as are outside those borders, against a regular or para-regular enemy operating from bases outside or inside the area of the Jewish State." Within this overall mission, the major objectives included: protection of the State from invasion; assuring freedom of communications within the State and to Jewish population centers outside its borders by gaining control of the major arteries of Palestine; capturing hostile forward bases (presumably, whether within or outside the frontiers of the State); applying economic pressure on the Arabs by various means, including siege of their towns; seizure of likely Arab guerrilla operational centers; gaining control of government installations to ensure their normal and effective operation.[1]

By the end of March the mobilized strength of the Haganah was

[1]Netanel Lorch, *The Edge of the Sword* (New York, 1961), pp. 87-88.

21,000 men between the ages of 17 and 25. Most of these were deployed to protect those settlements that appeared to be most threatened by the Arabs, while the remainder were responsible for guarding the convoys. About 30 light planes had been acquired for the Palmach's Air Service, and most of these were being used to carry emergency supplies to isolated settlements.

The weapons for the 21,000 mobilized Jewish soldiers were motley and inadequate for any sustained military operations. However, on April 1, 1948, the first foreign arms shipment—rifles—arrived by transport plane from Czechoslovakia, at a secret airstrip south of Beit Darass. On April 3 a ship from Poland arrived at Tel Aviv with more weapons from Czechoslovakia; in addition to rifles there were a number of badly needed light machine guns. This was the beginning of a flow of weapons—at first a trickle—for the Jewish troops. After the end of the British Mandate and embargo, heavier weapons would arrive: mortars, artillery pieces, tanks, and combat aircraft. For the time being, however, the shortage of weapons seriously limited the ability of the Haganah to equip its trained reserves.

KAUKJI ON THE OFFENSIVE

By early April Kaukji had sufficiently consolidated his position in and around Nablus to feel prepared to take the offensive again. On April 3 he moved west from Nazareth with about 1,000 men in two battalions. His force included seven field guns, which had been provided by the Syrian Army and were the first artillery employed in the war. His plan was to cut Jewish communications between Tel Aviv and the north; his immediate objective was the capture of the settlement of Mishmar Haemek. The Jewish garrison of the town consisted of armed settlers and a small Haganah detachment. In addition to assorted small arms, the Jewish defenders had one light machine gun and a few 2-inch mortars.

By early afternoon of April 4, Arab forces loosely surrounded Mishmar Haemek, positioning themselves on the hills dominating the village. A brief artillery bombardment was followed by an infantry assault. Jewish defenders were ready, however, and intensive small arms fire drove the attackers back. Rather inaccurate artillery fire continued through the night, becoming more intensive in the morning. However, although the settlers were expecting it, the infantry attack was not renewed.

During the morning a small British force arrived, and the British commander called for a 24-hour ceasefire to enable the settlers to evacuate their children and their wounded. During this truce Jewish reinforcements—the 1st Battalion of the Palmach, commanded by Major Dan Laner—arrived from Ein Hashofet. When the truce expired, Laner counterattacked, surprising the Arabs. For the next five days, a series of guerrilla engagements erupted around the settlement, with both sides

seeking to control villages and positions in the hills. Fighting was particularly heavy east of Ramat Yohanan. On April 12 Kaukji made another
major, unsuccessful assault on Mishmar Haemek. As several Haganah
contingents closed in and threatened to cut his line of communications,
Kaukji decided to give up his campaign, and withdrew to Jenin. In spite
of the continuing jealousy between ALA and AAS, when the Arab irregulars in Jerusalem and Jaffa asked for help, Kaukji responded promptly,
in one of the few instances of Arab cooperation in the war. He sent some
of his artillery to Jerusalem, and sent Michael el Issa's contingent to Jaffa.

TIBERIAS

Soon after this the scene of action shifted north to Tiberias. The Jews
there outnumbered the Arabs, but they were divided in two communities,
separated from each other by Arabs who were congregated in most of
the lower old town, just above the shores of the Sea of Galilee. The only
otherwise secure Jewish road from the coast to the fertile farming country
of the Huleh Valley, in eastern Galilee north of the Sea of Galilee, passed
through Tiberias, but the Arabs had blocked all passage through the
lower town.

Upper Tiberias, on the hillside overlooking the lower town and the
lake, had become the headquarters of Nahum Golan, commanding the
local Haganah HISH unit. This force would eventually become the 1st
Brigade of the Israeli Army, but it has always been known as the Golani
Brigade, after its first commander.

On April 18, the Golanis struck down the hillside into the Arab
quarter, while Palmach troops from the Huleh Valley cleared the lake-
front and then turned west up the hill. In a few hours the two forces
met, completely bisecting the Arab areas and reopening the road to the
north. The Arab population decided to evacuate their portion of the
city, and were able to do this with British assistance.

HAIFA—OPERATION "MISPARAYIM"

In Haifa, meanwhile, both sides had been preparing themselves for a
struggle. As in Tiberias, most of the Arabs inhabited the older part of
the city on the lower slopes of Mt. Carmel, while the more numerous
Jews were concentrated on the heights in a section known as Hadar
Hacarmel. The situation in Haifa was further complicated by the fact
that, as the major seaport of Palestine, it was also the principal British
supply base. In addition to the strongly fortified base area in the lower
city, there was another strong British installation on the mountainside,
near the Jewish quarter; this was the headquarters of the British 6th
Airborne Division, the principal element of the British garrison of north-

ern Palestine. British military traffic was heavy along the road from division headquarters to the supply base. For several months this contributed to a three-way guerrilla war, because British vehicles were frequently fired at by both Jews and Arabs, who of course were also firing at each other.

The Arabs in Haifa were better organized than in some of the other Arab communities, and in January they had selected Mohammed el Hemed el Huneiti to be the commander of their AAS contingent. The principal element of the Jewish military contingent in Haifa was a Haganah brigade, commanded by Colonel Moshe Carmel, and thus known as the Carmeli Brigade.

Apart from sniping, minor skirmishes and frequent running gun battles of Jews and Arabs with British trucks and convoys, four major incidents took place in the Haifa area, which served to elevate tensions before the final battle for the city. After a bomb was thrown by Jewish terrorists in the lower town on December 30, killing 6 Arabs and injuring 47, an Arab riot broke out at the oil refinery near the seaport where both Arabs and Jews were employed. In this violence 41 Jewish workers were killed.

On January 14, Arab terrorists blew up a post office vehicle in the Jewish community, injuring 45 Jews. On March 18 an Arab convoy bringing arms from Lebanon was ambushed by the Jews at Kiryat Mozkin, outside Haifa. Huneiti, who was traveling with the convoy, was killed. This loss of their leader seriously demoralized the Haifa Arabs until, on March 27, Amin Azaddin arrived with a group of irregular reinforcements, and he was appointed the new commander. The fourth incident occurred in late March, when a Jewish convoy carrying supplies to Kibbutz Yehiam was ambushed and most of its drivers and guards killed.

The British commander in northern Palestine, who was also the commander of the 6th Airborne Division, was Major General Hugh Stockwell. He had earned the enmity of both Jews and Arabs by even-handedly maintaining order in and around all areas where his troops were concentrated. As the appointed day for British withdrawal—May 15—came closer, Stockwell completed plans to concentrate his troops in the Haifa area in preparation for evacuation to the port. To do this would require him to carry out an orderly withdrawal from the various British posts further east in Galilee and northern Samaria. On the morning of April 21, he informed both the Arabs and the Jews of his intentions, and stated that his whole concern centered on the safe withdrawal of his forces. His announcement was interpreted by both sides as an indication that he would no longer interfere in local disorders, and therefore was the signal for major hostilities in the Haifa area.

Sometime before this, the Haganah high command had prepared a plan to seize control of the Arab portion of Haifa. Operation "Misparayim" (Scissors) was designed to cut the lower city into three sections. One Jewish force was to cross the Rushmiyah Valley to set up a bridgehead on the far side; a second force would descend Mt. Carmel directly into the Arab quarter, while a third force would move up to meet this from the port area.

The operation began at dusk on April 21, a few hours after Stockwell's announcement. As planned, a small Haganah detachment crossed the Rushmiyah, but after the initial success it was surrounded and isolated by a much larger Arab force. After desperate fighting, the Haganah unit was able to seize a large concrete office building, which the Jews held through the remainder of the night and the next day despite repeated Arab assaults.

While this was going on, the two major contingents of the Carmeli Brigade were carrying out the main thrusts. By dawn the two columns had united, successfully splitting the Arab city. Shortly before noon, the situation of the Arab defenders became obviously hopeless, and Amin Azaddin and a portion of his irregular force withdrew from the city. Resistance from the local Arabs at once began to collapse.

Meanwhile General Stockwell was trying to arrange a truce. He was able to set up a meeting in the early afternoon between the Arab mayor and Colonel Carmel. Carmel bluntly stated that his terms for a ceasefire required that all Arab forces surrender with their arms, submitting to Jewish control of the city. All non-Palestinian Arab soldiers and foreign mercenaries were to be surrendered to the Jews, and a curfew was to be established. The Arab leaders asked for time to consider the proposals, and left the meeting.

During the ensuing Arab caucus Kuakji's representative assured the mayor and the other civic leaders that the ALA was planning an offensive toward Haifa from Nablus, and also that there would soon be an invasion of Palestine by the armies of the surrounding Arab states. He urged them, therefore, to leave their homes in Haifa so that they would not be in the middle during the subsequent battle for the city; they could return to their homes after the Jews had been driven out. Some Jews, sincerely seeking racial harmony, tried to persuade their Arab neighbors to remain. However, the mayor and his advisors decided to evacuate the city. They returned to General Stockwell's meeting and informed him and Colonel Carmel that they would not surrender, but they would abandon the city.

Stockwell and some of the leading Arab citizens attempted to dissuade the mayor, but these efforts were unsuccessful. A five-day truce was arranged and a mass evacuation was soon begun. Only a few thousand Arabs, out of a population of 100,000, stayed in their homes.

SAFAD—OPERATION "YIFTACH"

The town of Safad, which in early 1948 had a population of more than 10,000 Arabs and 1,500 Jews, is dramatically located on a ridge 2,000 feet above sea level and almost 3,000 feet above the Sea of Galilee. It dominates the road running from the coast to northeastern Galilee, where there were many isolated Jewish settlements.

Fighting in Safad began in December 1947, but because of the presence of a British garrison it was limited to scattered sniping and occasional Arab attacks on Jewish convoys. By April, however, the Jewish quarter, some 150 feet below the Arab sector on the crest, was in a state of siege. All the Jewish supplies had to be brought in over mountain paths by night. In addition to about 1,000 armed local Arab irregulars, there was an ALA garrison in the town: some 600 Iraqis and Syrians in two battalions under Adib Shishakly.

The Jewish population was mostly Orthodox, and many of those of military age were unwilling to fight. As a result, the burden of defending the Jewish quarter fell upon a contingent of 200 Haganah troops. During the evening of April 14, however, a Palmach platoon—about 35 men— infiltrated into Safad from the Palmach base on Mt. Canaan. The Palmach platoon leader assumed command of the Jewish quarter.

On April 15, the British withdrew from Safad. The Arabs moved at once to seize the three strongpoints in the main town—the old fortress, the police station, and a building known as Shalva House. At the same time, they took over a nearby fortified police station in the Huleh Valley, and another in the town of Nebi Yusha to the north.

The Haganah High Command considered control of Safad essential to maintaining communications with the settlements of northeastern Galilee. Shortly after the British withdrawal, a contingent from the Golani Brigade attempted to take the Nebi Yusha police post—on a ridge dominating the Huleh Valley—as a preliminary to an attack on Safad. But the attack was repulsed by the defending Arabs, who killed five Golanis and wounded a number of others. Soon after this, the Palmach force at Mt. Canaan attempted to seize the Nebi Yusha post in a night attack. This attack also was repulsed with heavy loss of life. After British warnings, the Jews decided to postpone their planned operations against Safad.

While waiting for the British to complete their withdrawal from all of eastern Galilee, the Haganah High Command completed a plan ("Yiftach") for capturing key Arab positions there, not only to gain control of the major axes, but also to organize the region for defense in the face of an expected Arab invasion from Lebanon and Syria. Because of its location, Safad was a critical element in achieving both of these objectives. Youthful Colonel Yigal Allon, commander of the Palmach, was assigned responsibility for carrying out Operation Yiftach, with one Palmach battalion and one HISH battalion, in addition to the Haganah local defense units.

On April 28 the British withdrew from all of eastern Galilee. No longer hampered by the British curfew which had been in effect, limiting road movement, Allon was ready to begin his planned operations to secure Safad. First his forces seized the police fortress at Rosh Pina, and by May 1 they had occupied the villages of Birya and Ein Zeytim, on the northern outskirts of Safad. From these villages a corridor was opened to the Jewish quarter of Safad. On May 3 a second Palmach battalion reinforced Allon's force near Safad. Meanwhile, the Arabs girded themselves for the approaching struggle.

Allon struck during the night of May 5-6. The Jewish infantry, despite substantial mortar support, could make little headway in fierce fighting. The Arab artillery bombarded the Jewish quarter. Unable to make any headway, Allon called off the attack, and pulled back out of range of Safad in order to reorganize and make new plans.

Four days later, taking advantage of a heavy, unseasonable rainfall, Allon struck from three sides at dusk on May 10. During the night, the Israelis fought their way house-to-house up the hilly streets of the town. By morning of May 11, the three strong points of Safad were held by the Jews. The next day, May 12, a police fortress on the road to Mt. Canaan was also evacuated by the Arabs. As in Haifa, the local Arab population began a mass evacuation, joined in their flight by many Arabs from the Huleh Valley below the town.

SECURING THE NORTHERN SETTLEMENTS

On April 29 the British withdrew from Samakh and Gesher, and Golani troops promptly seized the fortified police posts in these predominantly Arab towns, in order to keep open the roads to Jordan Valley settlements. The Arab Legion attacked Gesher on May 1, but was repulsed.[2] Haganah troops then moved south to seize Beit Shean on May 12. At the same time, the Haganah was also securing the Mount Tabor and southern Carmel regions. In operation "Ben-Ami" the Carmeli unit, after securing Haifa, seized several Arab strongholds north of Haifa and east and northeast of Acre, partially isolating that Arab city. At the same time, they struck northeastward to establish overland communications with the Jewish settlements at Yehi'am and Hanitah.

---

[2] The Arab Legion at this time was wracked by divided loyalties. It was still nominally under British command, but actually General Glubb was receiving orders from King Abdullah which he felt forced to obey if not in direct conflict with British instructions. While British sentiment was by this time generally with the Arabs, the attack on Gesher was inconsistent with sincere British efforts to remain neutral.

JAFFA—OPERATION "CHAMTEZ"

In the U.N. Partition Plan, Jaffa was to be part of the Arab state. (See Map 1, p. xxiv). It was buffered on the east and southeast by several well-defended Arab localities, which constituted a wedge between Jewish areas northeast and southeast of the city. In mid-April the Haganah High Command issued orders for Operation "Chamtez," which was designed to link up the Jewish areas around Jaffa, thus isolating the city and at the same time opening a secure road to Lydda airport. No date was yet set for the operation.

However, on April 25, the Irgun independently launched an attack on Manshiya, the northern section of Jaffa, adjacent to Tel Aviv. For this effort they had assembled some 600 men, well supplied with small arms, ammunition, and 3-inch mortars. The Irgun assault was determined, but it made only small advances on April 25 and 26 in the face of stubborn Arab opposition. The Irgun leaders, therefore, requested Haganah assistance. Taking advantage of this opportunity, the Haganah insisted upon a firm written understanding whereby the Irgun was to be placed under Haganah command. Although the Irgun would be allowed to retain its own officers, all of its combat operations were to be approved by the Haganah. Reluctantly the Irgun leaders agreed, but on the understanding that the agreement would not apply to any region—such as Jerusalem—which was not yet under full Jewish control.

On April 27, with Haganah mortar and small arms fire in support, the Irgun troops renewed their attack, reaching the coast, and cutting off Manshiya from the rest of Jaffa. Meanwhile, however, a British tank battalion and artillery regiment were rushed to Jaffa, and other reinforcements came by sea from Cyprus. In an effort to maintain the status quo, the British began an artillery and air bombardment of the Jewish Bat Yam settlement, just south of Jaffa.

Also at this time Kaukji sent Michael Issa's contingent of ALA troops —including artillery—into Jaffa. They arrived just as the battle was escalating in intensity.

Despite British intervention and the arrival of Arab reinforcements, on April 28, the eve of Passover, the Haganah initiated Operation "Chamtez" under the command of Colonel Dan Even. The plan provided for complete encirclement of the city, while avoiding conflict with the British garrison. In the north, the Haganah quickly captured two Arab villages, ending all Arab threat to Tel Aviv. In the south a battalion of the Givati Brigade began a simultaneous attack on Tel Arish. This attack failed, however, in large part because of poor Haganah planning and coordination, and in part because of a combined ALA counterattack by an Iraqi unit and Michael el Issa's contingent. But next day, the towns of Salameh and Yazur, east of Jaffa, fell to the Jews, and the city was completely encircled. Nevertheless, the British insisted on keeping open the roads into Jaffa from the east and the south, and sent tank patrols out to enforce this demand. Thus, the Arabs could still get in and out of the city.

Taking advantage of this situation, early in May, Kaukji sent another contingent of ALA troops into Jaffa. By the time they arrived, however, there was little they could do. A mass flight of the inhabitants from the city had already begun. On May 11 the Arab Emergency Committee began negotiations with the Haganah, and on May 13 Jaffa officially surrendered. By this time only about 3,000 of the 70,000 Arab population remained in the town.

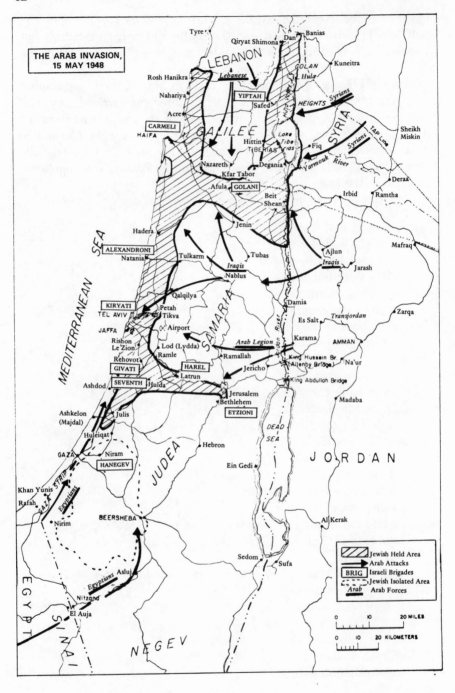

THE ARAB INVASION,
15 MAY 1948

4

The Preliminaries II—
Jerusalem

THE FIRST BATTLES FOR THE JERUSALEM ROAD

At the end of 1947, the Jewish population in the new city of Jerusalem, west of the old walled city, numbered about 100,000. There were about 2,500 additional Jews in the small Jewish quarter of the Old City. Both communities were isolated from the Jewish-controlled coastal region by intervening Arab territory and by an effective Arab blockade of the roads. In the early months of 1948, little direct communication existed between the Jews in the Old City and those in the New City.

There were two Jewish settlements north of Jerusalem on the road to Ramallah: Atarot and Neve Yaakov. These were isolated from Jerusalem and, for the most part, from each other. Near them, to the east, also cut off from the New City, were the Hadassah Hospital and the Hebrew University on Mt. Scopus.

All supplies for the New City and the nearby Jewish communities had to come from the coast along the Tel Aviv-Jerusalem highway, a tortuous route, which climbed through Arab-held terrain characterized by steep cliffs and rocky gorges. The water supply for Jerusalem came from wells at Ras el Ein, about 12 miles east of Tel Aviv. It was pumped into the city through a series of pumping stations, several of which were in Arab hands. While the Arabs had not yet cut the water supply to Jerusalem, mainly for fear of British retaliation, they had effectively blocked the road from Tel Aviv.

On April 1 the Haganah High Command decided to undertake Operation "Nachson," with the objective of opening the road between Jerusalem and Tel Aviv, and making it safe for supply convoys. A three-battalion brigade of 1,500 men was assembled from the regional commands. One battalion was responsible for the Hulda-Latrun sector, the second for the Latrun-Kiryat Anavim area, and a third was to be held in reserve. The plan was to establish a corridor one to six miles wide on both sides of the highway.

Operation Nachson was launched during the night of April 5-6 with a successful Givati battalion raid against el Husseini's headquarters, under

33

the personal command of Lt. Col. Shimeon Avidan, the brigade commander. In the western sector another battalion fought its way into the
villages of Hulda and Deir Muheisin, about a mile from Latrun. However,
on April 7 the Jews were ordered out of these hard-won positions by
British forces, who wanted the roads free for their own use. The British
promised not to allow the Arabs to return to the captured posts, and
they guaranteed the safety of the Jewish convoys.

The Jewish battalion operating further east did not have so much
success. It was repulsed from the villages of Saris and Beit Machsir,
north of the Tel Aviv-Jerusalem road, and a counterattacking Arab force
from Kolonia was able to establish itself near Notza, threatening to block
the eastern end of the axis. However, this Arab success was partially
offset by Jewish seizure of several strongpoints south of the road. During
the night of April 6-7, a convoy of supply vehicles was sent through to
New Jerusalem.

On April 7 there was a series of Arab counterattacks, led by el Husseini himself, focusing their main efforts against the recently captured
Jewish strongpoint on Kastel Hill. After two days of these attacks, the
Jewish defenders were forced to abandon the hill. Both sides suffered
heavy casualties in this battle, and el Husseini was among those killed
on April 8.

The fall of Kastel enabled the Arabs to block the Tel Aviv-Jerusalem
highway once again. Therefore, on April 9 a Haganah unit was sent to
recapture the position. When the Jews arrived, they found the strongpoint unoccupied, and then immediately moved in. Probing cautiously
northward, they met almost no resistance, and on the 11th they seized
Kolonia. Apparently as a result of the death of el Husseini, the AAS
organization in the vicinity of Jerusalem completely fell apart. Without
strong leadership, the individual Arab fighters drifted slowly back to
their villages.

The objective having been achieved, and Arab resistance having disappeared, the Haganah High Command disbanded the headquarters of
Operation Nachson on April 15.

THE MASSACRE OF DEIR YASSIN

Meanwhile, on April 9, the day of the recapture of Kastel, one of the
most tragic and most momentous events of the war had occurred. Contingents of the Irgun and of Lehi, operating out of Jerusalem under the
overall direction of the Haganah command in Jerusalem, had been given
the mission of neutralizing the Arabs northwest of the New City. While
busy with preparations for anticipated stiff resistance in the reoccupation
of Kastel, the Haganah command approved an Irgun plan to occupy the
Arab village of Deir Yassin. In their first efforts to take the village, the

Irgun and Stern soldiers were repulsed. They asked the nearby Haganah unit, preparing to attack Kastel, for fire support from machine guns and mortars. Under the cover of this Haganah support fire, the terrorist soldiers fought their way into the town. Meanwhile, the Haganah troops lifted their fire and moved on toward Kastel, and so apparently saw nothing of what was occurring in the village.

What actually did occur has never been fully described, since neither those who participated, or the few who escaped has been able or willing to provide an objective account. Apparently infuriated by the resistance which they had encountered, lacking the discipline of the Haganah soldiers, and with a callousness toward Arab lives engendered by their previous terrorist activities, the Irgun and Stern soldiers seem to have run amuck. They killed every Arab man, woman, and child they could find in the village. A few escaped by hiding and then slipping away during the night, but most of the inhabitants of the town, 245 persons, were slaughtered. Many of their bodies were thrown into the village well, before the attackers withdrew from the scene of horror.

When word of this savage incident spread, there was almost as much revulsion among the majority of Jews of the Yishuv and among most members of the Haganah as there was among the Arabs. It was, however, an event that the Arabs have never forgotten; probably more than any single incident the memory of Deir Yassin has poisoned relations between Jews and Arabs in the Middle East.

Arabs are convinced that Deir Yassin was an act of deliberate Zionist terrorism, perpetrated with the approval, if not encouragement, of Ben Gurion and the Haganah leadership. The Arabs believe that the purpose of the massacre was to arouse such fear among the Arab population that they would flee from the land in terror. There is no persuasive proof of such connivance or motivation; the incident, however, was probably the principal reason why so many Arab families fled to nearby countries in the following months whenever the Haganah approached their homes. Menachim Begin, leader of the Irgun, was later so tasteless as to boast of "heroic" acts by his men at Deir Yassin, and also to attribute the later Arab flight to this incident.

OPERATIONS IN AND AROUND JERUSALEM

The 70-kilometer length of the Jerusalem-Tel Aviv road having been reopened, the responsibility for its security was given to the Palmach. A new Palmach unit—the Harel Brigade—was established, under the command of Colonel Yitzhak Rabin. It consisted of two Palmach battalions, plus a battalion from the nearby Givati Brigade. Immediately, under the watchful protection of the Harel Brigade, a six day supply operation was begun called Operation "Harel." Three huge convoys, consisting of 250-

300 vehicles each, were sent up the mountains from Tel Aviv to Jerusalem. This massive replenishment of the dwindling stores of the New City was to prove tremendously significant a few weeks later.

Meanwhile, the Jews at the isolated Haddassah Hospital and Hebrew University on Mt. Scopus had been stubbornly holding on to their positions. Occasional convoys of supplies from Jerusalem had reached these places, but by early April the road through the Arab village of Sheikh Jarrach was completely blocked. The British, however, reopened the road and established a small post on a nearby hill dominating the Arab positions in Sheikh Jarrach, and for almost two weeks Jewish convoys were able to pass through almost unmolested to Mt. Scopus.

On April 13, however, a Jewish convoy entering Sheikh Jarrach was stopped at an Arab roadblock and attacked with intense small arms fire. At first the armored cars guarding the convoy were able to hold off the surrounding Arabs, expecting that they would soon be relieved by the British. Unaccountably, however, the British made no apparent move to interfere. There is some evidence that the Arabs had informed the British in advance that this would be an act of retaliation for the massacre at Deir Yassin. After about seven hours the Jewish convoy defenses were overwhelmed, and all of the people in the convoy—reported by the Jews to be 77 people, mostly doctors and nurses en route to the Hadassah Hospital—were killed. Obviously, in light of the protracted resistance, they had not been unarmed.

On April 18, apparently encouraged by their success against the convoy at Sheikh Jarrach, the Arabs north of Jerusalem seized Augusta Victoria Hospital on the east slope of Mt. Scopus and the village of Issawya near the Hebrew University farther to the west. This success was facilitated by artillery sent to Jerusalem from Jenin by Kaukji. With the British evacuation of Jerusalem imminent, and with additional Arab attacks forming in the area north of the Old City, the two Jewish outposts on Mt. Scopus were severely threatened, and even the New City itself seemed to be in danger.

The Haganah High Command decided to send the Harel Brigade to reinforce the garrison of Jerusalem, and Yitzhak Sadeh was sent to Jerusalem to take command of the enlarged force there. Accompanying him in a 350 vehicle convoy which left Tel Aviv on April 20 was David Ben Gurion, chairman of the Jewish Agency Executive. Upon entering the mountainous area west of the city the convoy ran into a mile-long ambush, and the road was soon blocked by damaged vehicles. A counterattack by a company of Jewish armored cars with the convoy failed to disperse the ambushing Arabs, although the firepower with the convoy was too strong for the Arabs to close in. Toward evening, however, reinforcements arrived from Jerusalem, the convoy was freed, and it continued on to the city. This was the last major convoy to reach Jerusalem from Tel Aviv in April. The road behind the convoy was again under Arab control, and Jerusalem was isolated.

In addition to a number of local defense companies and detachments, Sadeh had two Haganah brigades available to him. One of these was Rabin's Palmach Harel Brigade, the other was the Etzioni Brigade, made up of men from the Jerusalem area. Sadeh decided that he would use these troops to carry out an operation which was designed both to increase the security of Jerusalem, and to end the isolation of the beleaguered settlements on Mt. Scopus, Atarot and Neve Yaakov. To accomplish this, Sadeh issued orders for Operation "Jebussi," which involved the seizure of three key positions held by the Arabs: Nebi Samuel, to the west, to reestablish contact with Neve Yaakov and Atarot; Sheikh Jarrach, to the north, to link up with the positions on Mt. Scopus; and Katamon, to the south, to establish firm contact between New Jerusalem and the frequently isolated southwestern and southern suburbs of Rehavia, Kiryat Shmuel, Mekor Chaim, Ramat Rachel and Talpiot.

Operation Jebussi began on the night of April 21-22 with a Palmach drive to the west toward Nebi Samuel. After an auspicious beginning, the attack bogged down. Reinforcements sent to regain the momentum were ambushed by the Arabs and then strayed into an area which the British had declared off-limits, and suffered severely from accurate British fire. The attackers were forced to withdraw, and Atarot and Neve Yaakov remained isolated.

The next phase of Operation Jebussi began on April 25 with an attack on Sheikh Jarrach. After a night-long battle, the Jews occupied most of the town, but once again the British intervened. They ordered the Jews to withdraw, as Sheikh Jarrach lay along the evacuation route of British units east of Mt. Scopus. At first the Israelis refused to obey this order, but late in the afternoon of the 26th they were attacked by a British infantry battalion supported by tanks and artillery. After brief resistance, the Jews withdrew from Sheikh Jarrach, some of them moving back to Mr. Scopus, some to Jerusalem. The British commander thereupon told the Jewish commander that he would not allow the Arab forces to return to Sheikh Jarrach, and until the Mandate expired Jewish convoys were able to travel undisturbed to Mt. Scopus. Thus, while the operation had not been a success materially, it had achieved its objective. After the British departed, the Jews promptly reoccupied Sheikh Jarrach.

On April 28, in order to improve the security of their outposts on Mt. Scopus, the Jews attempted to recapture the Augusta Victoria Hospital. Rabin's Harel Brigade made the attack, but it failed to achieve surprise, and was driven off by alert Arab defenders. During the operation, however, the Jews briefly occupied the nearby Jerusalem-Jericho road, and before withdrawing they blew up several Arab installations on the road.

The next day, April 29, the third phase of Operation Jebussi was initiated. Another Harel battalion moved south against Katamon, the principal objective being to seize the Greek Orthodox monastery of St. Simon, occupied by a force of Iraqi ALA irregulars. The Harel troops seized the monastery during the night, after a short battle, but the next morning they received a series of vicious counterattacks from the Iraqis and other Arabs. With great difficulty, and despite many losses, the Jews in the monastery held out, and the position was secured when an Etzioni battalion arrived in the early evening.

The next day, May 1, the Jews were also able to secure their position in nearby Kiryat Shmuel and to reestablish contact with Mekor Chaim. The operation was halted during the day, however, when the British imposed an armistice on both sides.

OPERATION "MACCABI"

On May 9 the Jews launched a new effort to reopen the Jerusalem-Tel Aviv road. The objective of Operation "Maccabi" was to occupy the center of Arab resistance around the villages of Beit Machsir and Latrun. The Harel Brigade was ordered to operate along the corridor from Jerusalem in the east, while the Givati Brigade was to advance from Ramle in the west.

The main effort was begun on May 9 by a unit of the Harel Brigade, which attempted to seize Beit Machsir. The attackers suffered heavy casualties from Arab artillery on the 9th and 10th and failed to take the village. On May 11, however, the Harel troops succeeded in seizing the road overlooking Beit Machsir, and early the next morning they seized the village itself.

On May 12 an armored column set out from Hulda to patrol the sections of the road opened by the capture of Beit Machsir. It is not clear why this was done, since British troops were still patrolling the road, and with the Arabs were still holding Deir Ayub and Latrun. As the column passed near those positions it was met and stopped by intense, uncoordinated small arms and machine gun fire from the British and from ALA and AAS contingents. Many vehicles were hit and immobilized and the survivors could be evacuated only after dark. That night the armored column reorganized near Latrun, where it was joined by three companies of the Givati Brigade.

The next morning, before this combined infantry and armored force could continue its planned operations, it was intensively shelled by both ALA units and British troops who still occupied the Latrun police post. After suffering heavy casualties, the Jews withdrew to the west, having completely failed to open the road.

The next day, May 13, Colonel Avidan, commander of the Givati Brigade, was directed to assume responsibility for carrying out Operation

Maccabi. He immediately initiated a plan to carry out a wide circling movement to the west, to cut the Ramle-Latrun road. During the night of May 13-14 Avidan's troops took the fortified village of Abu Shosha (Gezer) and by evening of May 14, after capturing two more villages, the Givati troops threatened to isolate and encircle the Arabs in Latrun. Thus, by evening of the 14th, the last day of the British Mandate, both Latrun and Deir Ayub were about to fall. This would permit the reopening of communications along the road to Tel Aviv from Jerusalem.

BATTLE FOR THE ETZION "BLOC"

Meanwhile the beleaguered garrison of the so-called Etzion Bloc, four Jewish settlements south of Jerusalem, was still in a serious situation. The villages had been under siege for several weeks and had been receiving supplies only by airlift; some were dropped to the settlers by parachute; others landed by light plane on the Bloc's extremely hazardous runway. During April the local Arab irregulars surrounding the Bloc had moved close, but they made only two half-hearted attacks, on April 4 and 12. The Jews in the settlements, on the other hand, were quite a nuisance to Arab vehicles moving along the Hebron road, harassing traffic with small arms fire and attacking convoys. The garrison consisted of some 280 male and female settlers, reinforced by a Palmach platoon, and a HISH company—a total of nearly 500 fighters.

At the beginning of May the Jews intensified their harassment of Arab vehicles on the Hebron road. As a base, the Jewish forces used a Russian monastery which was midway between the main road and the Bloc. The British, who wished to keep open the lines of communication between Jerusalem and Hebron, considered these Jewish harassment activities intolerable. Accordingly, two companies of the Arab Legion, which was still under British command, were sent to drive the Jews from the monastery, and to reopen communications on the Jerusalem-Hebron road.

On May 4, the Arab Legion force, reinforced by a small British contingent and local irregular Arab infantry, made a general attack on three villages of the Bloc—Gush Etzion, Kfar Etzion, and Sudir—and the Russian monastery. During the day the Arabs took the monastery, but that night it was recaptured by the Jews.

Losses had been heavy on both sides. However, the Arabs were satisfied that, even though they had failed to capture any of the principal Israeli positions, they had removed the Jewish outposts and road blocks. On the other hand, the losses the Jews suffered during the fighting on May 4, combined with the fact that they could see no relief from the continuing Arab blockade, severely affected their morale.

Since the Arab Legion was under orders to be east of the Jordan before May 14, the Arabs decided to make one last assault on the Etzion Bloc before this occurred. The attack took place on the night of May 11-12, the principal objectives being the oldest settlement, Kfar Etzion, and the landing strip in the middle of the Bloc. While this operation was going on, the monastery was subjected to heavy artillery and mortar fire. Finding themselves about to be isolated, the platoon defending the monastery—having been reduced to only eight wounded men out of an initial strength of thirty-two—withdrew to Kfar Etzion. Aftere severe fighting on the 12th and the night of 12-13, the Arabs succeeded in isolating each of the four individual settlements.

Early on the 13th, the Legion succeeded in penetrating to the center of Kfar Etzion, and the Israeli area commander attempted to surrender, raising a white flag. The Legion troops in the vicinity of the white flag ceased firing, but Arab irregulars in other sections of the settlement continued firing and soon completely overran Kfar Etzion, killing most of the men, women, and children. This incident, combined with some captured orders, provided a basis for a Jewish claim that Arab leaders had ordered the destruction of the villages and the massacre of their inhabitants. However, during the afternoon, negotiations for the surrender of the other three settlements were conducted in Jerusalem with the assistance of the International Red Cross. On the basis of the agreed terms, the next day, the 14th, the surviving inhabitants of the Etzion Bloc were removed by the Arabs, the wounded being sent to Bethlehem, the remainder to Hebron as prisoners.

THE BRITISH EVACUATION

Early on May 14 the last British troops withdrew from Jerusalem. In accordance with the Haganah's previously prepared plans for Operation "Pitchfork," the Jews took over the areas in and around Jerusalem evacuated by the British. Responsibility for this was given to the Etzioni Brigade, which also occupied the British sector in the center of the city, known as "Bevingrad." The nearby King David Hotel was also seized, and contact was established with the settlement of Yemin Moshe. The Arabs took the Allenby army base, the government printing office, and the railway station. The Etzioni Brigade attacked, and after a few hours of fighting drove the Arabs out of these positions and the Abu Tur district. While all this was going on, the monastery of Notre Dame was occupied by Haganah forces and a Lehi unit operating under the orders of the Haganah. The stage was now set for a new battle.

5

The Arab Armies Converge

THE ARAB OBJECTIVES

On Friday, May 14, 1948, General Sir Alan Cunningham, the last British High Commissioner for Palestine, left the country. The British Mandate ended at midnight. The same afternoon, just before the Sabbath, the Jewish National Council, or General Zionist Council, at Tel Aviv proclaimed the independence of the State of Israel, effective at midnight, and appointed David Ben Gurion Prime Minister of the Provisional Government.

Actually, this meant no change—either in Tel Aviv or the areas of Palestine under Jewish control. Ben Gurion had for months been acting as prime minister of a *de facto* state, and on May 14 that state had in the field an army of nearly 40,000 mobilized full time troops, organized into twelve brigades. Arms, including aircraft, were arriving from overseas at a rapid rate. While there was no assurance of survival of the new state of Israel in the light of the threatening attitudes of the neighboring states, it was, at least for the time being, already viable and flourishing upon the date that it formally came into existence.

Within Palestine there were two threats to the survival of Israel. Neither was serious. The Arab Liberation Army under the command of Fawz el Kaukji had perhaps 10,000 men as its total strength, and nearly 6,000 actually in the Arab portion of Palestine. These consisted of about 2,500 Syrians, 2,500 Iraqis, 500 Lebanese and a handful of Yugoslav Moslems. There were in addition a number of bands of Arab irregulars of the Arab Army of Salvation scattered throughout the country. There were at least 50,000 armed Palestinian Arabs available for local defense, but the actual strength of AAS guerrilla contingents was between 5,000 and 10,000 men. However, the deaths of Mohammed el Huneiti and Abd el Kader el Husseini had ended any internal coherence or cohesion amongst the Palestinian fighting units.

By May 14 the military committee of the Arab League had failed to settle its internal disagreements in order to establish a united high command or a combined strategy. King Abdullah of Transjordan assumed the position of Commander in Chief of the United Arab Armies, but this was really a title without a role, since the military actions of each country

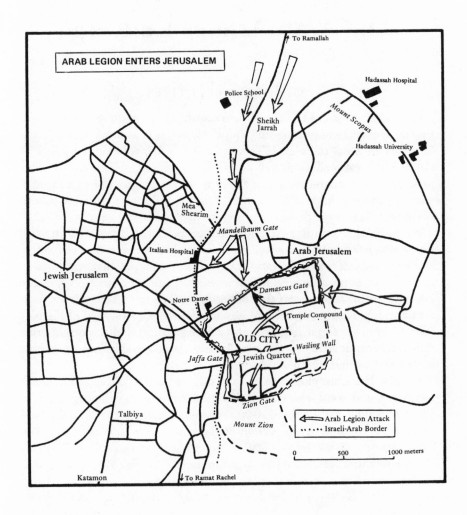

ARAB LEGION ENTERS JERUSALEM

To Ramallah

Police School

Hadassah Hospital

Sheikh
Jarrah

Mount Scopus

Hadassah University

Mea
Shearim

Mandelbaum Gate

Italian Hospital

Arab Jerusalem

Jewish Jerusalem

Damascus Gate

Notre Dame

Temple Compound

OLD CITY

Wailing Wall

Jaffa Gate

Jewish Quarter

Talbiya

Zion Gate

Mount Zion

Arab Legion Attack
Israeli-Arab Border

Katamon

To Ramat Rachel

0   500   1000 meters

were governed by conflicting national policies rather than by any coordinated common plan of campaign.

However, there was a plan of sorts, really a kind of mutually-agreed staking out of claims by each of the invading nations.

The Lebanese contingent was to advance along the coast from Nakura to Nahariya. The Syrians, crossing the Jordan above the Sea of Galilee, would strike for Zemach. The Iraqi contingent would move from its concentration area west of Irbid in Transjordan to establish a bridgehead across the Jordan south of the Sea of Galilee, and then advance to Natania on the coast. The Jordanians had two objectives: One brigade of the Arab Legion would seize Nablus in central Samaria; a second brigade would advance to Ramle in the central coastal plain; the third brigade was to remain in reserve. The Egyptians, based on El Arish on the northern Sinai coast, also had two objectives: the main body would advance along the coastal road, with naval support if necessary, to seize Gaza and be prepared to advance further north toward Tel Aviv; the other contingent—Azziz's "Volunteers"—would strike northeastward across the upper Sinai through Auja and Beersheba to secure Hebron.

In accordance with this general agreement—it would be wrong to call it a plan—on May 15 five Arab armies crossed the borders of Palestine in a concerted, if not coordinated, invasion. The invasion was heralded by an Egyptian air attack on Tel Aviv. For the next 25 days the Haganah was engaged in a desperate effort to meet all five of these invasions, any one of which, if successful, could have destroyed the new state of Israel.

It is easy to discount the strength of the uncoordinated invaders, since with one exception they were weak, poorly trained, and badly organized. On the other hand, the concentric advance of the five contingents, combined with the assistance they were receiving from Kaukji's Arab Liberation Army and the local Arab levies, posed a truly serious threat. The Haganah, about as numerous as the combined strength of its foes, was severely outmatched in military hardware. All of the invaders had ample artillery and a variety of armored vehicles ranging from armored cars to modern tanks.

ISRAELI FORCES AND DEPLOYMENTS

There are no accurate statistics of the mobilized forces of the new state of Israel.[1] There seem to have been about 40,000 Jewish troops available for battle in nine operational brigades, with three more brigades in various stages of formation. The status of these units was as follows: There were three Palmach brigades, about 2,000 men in each. The

[1] For an objective discussion of the inconsistencies among the sources, see Luttwak-Horowitz, p. 34, and footnote, and notes 71-73, pp. 404-405.

Yiftach Brigade was in eastern Galilee, facing Syria to the east, and Lebanon to the northwest. The Harel Brigade was in the Jerusalem Corridor. The smallest of these brigades, the Negev, or Hanegev Brigade, about 1500 strong, was responsible for the security of the semi-isolated Israeli Negev settlements, west and northwest of Beersheba.

Five HISH Brigades were also fully mobilized. The Golani Brigade, 2,238 men, was in southern Galilee, generally concentrated between Nazareth and Jenin. Further west, in the Haifa-Acre region, was the Carmeli Brigade of 4,095 men. Holding the thin strip of Jewish-controlled territory along the coast between Tel Aviv and Haifa were the 3,588 troops of the Alexandroni Brigade. The Kiryati Brigade, 2,504 strong, was north and northeast of Tel Aviv. The 3,229 troops of the Givati brigade were east and southeast of Tel Aviv, holding open the western approaches to the Jerusalem Corridor. In Jerusalem itself was the Etzioni Brigade, 3,166 men.[2]

Ben Gurion's diary lists the following additional forces available on May 15: Training Branch, 398; Air Force 675; Artillery 650; Engineers, 150; Military Police, 168; transport units, 1097; and new conscripts in training, 1,719.[3]

Presumably most of these new conscripts in training were members of the newly-established 7th Brigade, which was to be a mechanized unit. This brigade, commanded by Colonel Shlomo Shamir, had a cadre of veterans and was close to operational. It was already deployed west of the Jerusalem Corridor, and just south of the Givati Brigade. Also in the process of establishment in central Israel was the 8th Brigade, planned as an armored unit; commanded by Yitzhak Sadeh, consisted of an infantry battalion of former Lehi men, a tank battalion, with two tank companies of 13 mixed French, British and American tanks already at sea and en route to Israel, and a jeep commando battalion (soon to be commanded by Major Moshe Dayan). By May 15 this unit probably had close to 1500 men in training. Also assembling and training in the north was a new Oded Brigade, which also probably had about 1,500 men by this time.

Not included in Ben Gurion's figures are logistical or headquarters troops, which must have totalled at least 5,000 more active duty soldiers and officers. In addition to these 30,000-40,000 in the mobilized field forces, there were at least 10,000 additional registered HIM soldiers under partial mobilization, available for local security, and also capable of being employed in field operations in their home territory.

The sources are also conflicting in the lists of weapons available to

[2] These figures are contained in Ben Gurion's diary, *Medinat Israel,* quoted by Luttwak-Horowitz, *op. cit.,* p. 34.
[3] *Ibid.*

these troops. However, not counting the heterogeneous collections of obsolescent small arms and mortars with which the HIM units were equipped, the weapons inventory of the field forces seems to have been approximately as follows:

There were approximately 33,000 infantry small arms, of which about 22,000 were rifles of several calibers, and 11,000 were submachine guns (mostly locally produced). There were 1,550 light and medium machine guns, and 877 mortars, almost all British, of which 195 were 3-inch caliber, the rest 2-inch. There were 86 hand-carried anti-tank weapons, mostly British PIAT (a crude British non-rocket version of the American "Bazooka"), the rest relatively ineffective antitank rifles. There were five old French 65mm howitzers, recently arrived in Israel, having eluded the British blockade; the vintage of these weapons is evident from the fact that fifty years earlier they had been displaced in the French Army by the famous "French 75," model 1897. In addition, as has been noted, 13 tanks were due soon to arrive by ship at Tel Aviv.[4] There was also a handful of crudely constructed armored cars, mostly concentrated in the new 7th and 8th Brigades.

Balancing its assets and liabilities, the performance of the Haganah with these weapons in the next few weeks was to prove highly commendable, despite a number of "learning" mistakes.

THE LEBANESE FRONT

The Lebanese, wisely avoiding the possibility of isolation from the other Arab armies, and responding to "orders" from Abdullah of Transjordan, decided to make their initial move into Palestine by an advance against the western face of the finger of Galilee that extends northward up the Jordan and Huleh Valleys to Dan. This was the only instance in which Arab operations followed an overall plan, placing the Israelis under pressure simultaneously from two fronts, since the Syrians were crossing the Jordan into the eastern side of that finger, a few miles to the east and southeast.

This Lebanese invasion route lay through the Arab village of Malkiya. Having observed the concentration of the Lebanese contingent and anticipating its advance, during the night of May 14-15 a Palmach battalion from nearby Ramat Naftali attacked Malkiya and Kadesh, and had occupied both by morning. However, shortly after dawn, the Lebanese launched a counterattack eastward across the border on Malkiya with mortar support and forced the Israelis back with heavy casualties. Advancing in strength across the border, the Lebanese occupied the village,

4 *Ibid.,* p. 36.

and then began to maneuver to threaten nearby Kadesh. Recognizing the vulnerability of that position, the Palmach evacuated Kadesh the next day, and that town too was immediately taken by the Lebanese. Well satisfied with two successes in two days on Palestinian soil, the Lebanese army halted its advance and consolidated its position a few miles inside Palestine.

Not yet aware that the Lebanese advance had stopped, on the night of May 17-18 the Israelis finally took the police post at Nebi Yusha and began to organize this and nearby territory to block the road from Kadesh into the Huleh Valley.

Meanwhile, to the west and southwest the Israelis had been preparing against the possibility of a Lebanese advance down the coastal plain. The Arabs controlled the seaport town of Acre, across the bay from Haifa. The garrison of Acre not only posed a threat to Haifa but lay between it and Jewish-controlled Nahariya, first significant town on the potential invasion route. Accordingly, the Haganah High Command decided to capture Acre.

The ancient Crusader town, encircled by an old, heavy wall which had been rebuilt and modernized several times, is further protected by its position on a promontory sticking into the sea. The walls, which would be a negligible obstacle to a modern army with adequate artillery, were a major barrier to any attack by the Haganah. They were well manned by a garrison of Arab irregulars. To the north, on the coast just beyond the wall, was a fortified police post held by another Arab force.

On May 15, Colonel Moshe Carmel attacked Acre with his Carmeli Brigade. One contingent seized "Napoleon Hill," east of the city, while to the northwest another took the village of Samaria, north of Shavei Zion, and two villages north of Nahariya. The next day, the main body of the Carmeli Brigade, with mortar support from Napoleon Hill, assaulted and captured the police post north of the city. Mortars were quickly set up there and in combination with those on Napoleon Hill began to bombard the northern and eastern city walls. After a few hours of this bombardment, a messenger under a flag of truce was sent into Acre to demand the surrender of the garrison.

It was obvious to the Arabs in Acre that they were completely isolated since the Israelis had securely blocked any possibility of support from the north or east. Early on the 17th, the garrison surrendered, and Acre fell to the Israelis.

Back on the Malkiya front, after the Lebanese had remained motionless for a week, Colonel Shmuel Cohen, commander of the Yiftach Brigade, decided to take the offensive. His plan was to feign an attack on the towns of Nebi Yusha and Kadesh from the south, while attacking Malkiya from the rear through Lebanon. On the night of May 28-29, he sent a force of armored cars and infantry in trucks, moving without lights across the frontier from Manara to reach a road running parallel to the border west of Malkiya. North of the town the column encountered a small unit of Lebanese, who were taken completely by surprise and easily driven back. The noise of this engagement alerted the Lebanese in Malkiya, but before they could properly organize themselves for defense against the surprise attack, they were struck by the Israelis to their rear. The town fell after a brief battle. Kadesh was also abandoned by the Lebanese, who withdrew completely behind their own frontier.

Following this success, the Yiftach Brigade was transferred to the central front, where reinforcements were desperately needed to deal with the threat of the Arab Legion to Jerusalem. The new Oded or 9th Brigade under Colonel Uri Joffe was to maintain the defense in the north.

When a combined Lebanese, ALA, and Syrian attack struck Malkiya on June 6, the Oded Brigade was caught by surprise. The attacking forces, about the equivalent of two brigades in strength, were seriously delayed by the minefields which the Yiftach and Oded troops had laid around Malkiya. The ALA and Syrian contingents were too discouraged by this obstacle to continue the attack, but the Lebanese persisted, and by evening of the 6th they had captured the town for the second time. Encouraged by this success, they pushed ahead and the next day captured Ramat Naftali and Kadesh. This opened the way to the Huleh Valley to the south. While the Lebanese organized their newly-won positions, the ALA pushed down into central Galilee. It was a significant Arab success.

SYRIAN FRONT

On Friday, May 14, the Syrian 1st Infantry Brigade, commanded by Colonel Abdullah Wahab el Hakim, was in southeastern Lebanon, poised to attack toward Malkiya. That day Colonel Hakim was ordered to return to Syria, move south across the Golan, and advance into Palestine south of Lake Tiberias, toward the abandoned Arab village of Semakh. As ordered, Hakim began his advance across the old frontier at 9:00 a.m. Saturday, even though he had only two of his battalions, and all of his men were exhausted. Since the Israelis had apparently expected the Syrian main effort to be made north of the lake, there were no mobile Haganah units in this area. However, there was a small fortified defensive position near Semakh; this immediately opened fire on the attacking Syrians, and pinned them down shortly after they had made their crossing.

Supporting his two attacking infantry battalions, Colonel Hakim had an armored car battalion, and a company of tanks, while an artillery regiment provided support from the Golan Heights. Hakim's force was more than adequate to overwhelm or merely bypass the small Israeli force near Semakh, but the Syrian troops were inexperienced as well as tired, and they contented themselves with returning the Israeli fire. All day and through the night Syrian artillery fired sporadically at the Semakh position and also harassed Ein Gev, the only Jewish settlement on the eastern shore of Lake Tiberias.

On the morning of May 16, Semakh and other Jordan Valley settlements were subjected to Syrian aerial attacks, while the artillery bombardment continued. Two Syrian companies belatedly began an envelopment of the Israeli reserve units arriving from Tiberias. Another Syrian company, supported by armored cars, advanced toward the settlements of Massada and Shaar Hagolan. The settlers, however, were able to hold off these attacks; the Syrians dug in, while their air and artillery continued sporadic bombardment of Jewish positions and settlements.

Early in the morning of May 18, the Syrian 1st Brigade, now commanded by Brigadier General Husni el Zaim, renewed operations against the Israeli fortified camp near Semakh. Tanks and armored cars began to encircle the position, and, with their line of communication threatened, the defenders withdrew to the nearby Jewish settlement of Degania. At 8:00 a.m. the Syrians occupied the abandoned position.

The Israelis, assuming that this was to be the main Syrian thrust, had sent reinforcements from Lieutenant Colonel Moshe Mann's Yiftach Brigade, further north. These and local HIM reserves now concentrated near Degania. To coordinate the defensive effort, the Haganah High Command sent Major Moshe Dayan, from the High Command Staff, to Degania.

In fact, the Syrians had not intended any further operations south of the lake, planning to make their main effort further north, near the Bridge of Jacob's Daughters. However, on May 19, the Iraqis, about to thrust westward through Nablus toward Tulkarm, asked the Syrians to make a diversion in the Degania area, to protect their right flank. In compliance with this request, at 4:30 in the morning of May 20 the Syrian 1st Brigade began an assault on the twin settlements of Degania. Artillery and tank fire covered the assault. The principal Syrian objective was to seize the bridge across the Jordan River north of the village known as Degania A. This would block any Israeli attack from Tiberias against the Iraqi line of communications.

The Syrian attack, spearheaded by tanks and armored cars, soon pierced the settlement defense. However, the Syrian infantry was some distance behind the tanks, and the Israeli defenders were able to use Molotov cocktails and PIAT antitank missiles to destroy several of the attacking vehicles. Meanwhile, other defenders kept up small arms fire on the Syrian infantry, who halted in citrus groves several hundred meters from the settlement. The surviving tanks withdrew, and the attack failed.

The Syrians then turned their attention to the south to Degania B. Eight tanks, supported by mortar fire, approached to within 400 yards of the settlement defense, where they stopped to provide fire support for an infantry attack. However, the green Syrian troops were still unable to face Israeli small arms fire and after two abortive attempts gave up the effort. About noon two newly arrived field guns—obsolete French 65mm howitzers, the first Israeli artillery to be employed in the war—arrived from Tel Aviv. They were quickly emplaced and opened fire on the Syrians near Degania B. The Israelis attributed the subsequent Syrian withdrawal to surprise at the unexpected Israeli artillery fire.

Although the Israelis in the Semakh-Degania area did not realize it, there were two quite different reasons for the Syrian withdrawal. The first of these was a threat to their line of communications. A Palmach battalion from the Yiftach Brigade had been sent by boat during the previous night across Lake Tiberias to Ein Gev. During darkness they had climbed up the Golan Heights, and at dawn carried out a counter raid on Kaffir Harel on the Golan Heights, to threaten the line of communications of the exposed brigade.

Another reason for the Syrian withdrawal was the fact that they had run out of ammunition. General Zaim, having been promised replenishment, had begun his attack against the Deganias even though he was short of ammunition. In fact, however, the promised replenishment was being delivered to the 2d Brigade further north. When his troops ran out of ammunition, Zaim ordered a withdrawal.

Meanwhile, in the area north of the Sea of Galilee, and south of Lake Huleh, the Israelis had been awaiting another attack. On May 14, in apparent preparation for a major offensive, the Syrians established a fuel and ammunition base east of the customs house near the Bridge of Jacob's Daughters. As the Syrians had intended, this gave the Israelis the false impression that this was where they would make their first attack, and it diverted Israeli attention from the blow near Semakh. However, when the Syrians failed to do anything near the Bridge of Jacob's Daughters, the Israelis in the settlement of Mishmar Hayarden seized the initiative. On the night of May 17-18, simultaneously with an operation further west against the Lebanese near Malkiya, a company of the Yiftach Brigade crossed the river, routed the Syrian defenders of the supply base, and destroyed the collected supplies. They returned without having suffered any casualties. The loss of these supplies forced the Syrian 2d Infantry Brigade to postpone its attack, intended for May 22.

For two weeks the Syrian front was quiet, except for frequent shelling of Israeli positions in the valley from Syrian artillery on the Golan Heights. A new offensive was being planned by Major General Abdulla Alfe, the Syrian Army Chief of Staff, who was exercising overall command and direction of combat operations along the upper Jordan.

On the morning of June 6, the Syrian 2d Brigade, under Colonel Kawass, attempted a surprise assault across the river to seize Mishmar Hayarden. Its ultimate objective was to capture the nearby bridge, and then to join the Lebanese and the ALA near Malkiya. However, because of accurate Israeli machine gun and mortar fire on the river fords, the Syrian armor failed to get across the river, and the two battalions of infantry which had been harassing the settlement soon withdrew.

At the same time, further north, a reinforced battalion under Lieutenant Colonel Sami Hinawi advanced from Banias toward Dan, on the Israeli side of the frontier. After advancing a few hundred meters, Hinawi's troops were halted by Israeli small arms fire from Dan. The Syrians dug in where they were.

As the Syrian forces east of the river were reinforced, the Israeli Oded Brigade was alerted, and was largely concentrated in the vicinity of Mishmar Hayarden. On June 8 a Carmeli battalion also arrived to reinforce the defenders.

On June 10 the Syrians made their first truly effective, coordinated attack of the war. The 2d Infantry Brigade assaulted and seized all three of the fording points east of Mishmar Hayarden and this time continued to press forward despite Israeli small arms and mortar fire. Syrian armor successfully negotiated the river crossings. Working in close coordination with the infantry, the tanks overran the outer defenses of Mishmar Hayarden. A desperate battle took place, but the Syrians fought well, and their numbers were overwhelming. Shortly after noon, Mishmar Hayarden was in their hands.

That same day, as a diversion, the Syrian 1st Brigade mounted an attack against Ein Gev. Since the hills dominating Ein Gev, leading up to the Golan Heights, were occupied by Syrians, the only link from Ein Gev to the remainder of the Yishuv was by boat at night. However, Ein Gev was one of the most alert of all of the Israeli settlements, since it was the most exposed. The defenders were well dug in, and they were determined. Although most of the houses in the settlement were destroyed during this intensive attack, simultaneous assaults from both north and south were driven back. A small penetration from the east was soon contained, and the attackers were driven out by noon.

THE IRAQI FRONT

The Iraqi contingent of the Arab forces consisted of an infantry brigade and an armored battalion under the command of General Mahmud. This force had concentrated near Mafraq in Transjordan in April. Early in May the Iraqis had shifted west, between Irbid and the Jordan

River, and prepared to operate in their assigned sector: the north-central Jordan Valley and the northern Samaria "triangle" of Jenin-Tulkarm-Nablus.

Early on May 15, Iraqi troops forded the Jordan River near the oil pipeline south of Maad and occupied the high ground overlooking the settlement of Gesher.[5] When the Iraqis attacked Gesher and a neighboring police post the next afternoon, they were repulsed with heavy casualties. Next day they tried again, with infantry advancing from the north, and armored cars from the south. Again the assaults, quite uncoordinated, were repulsed. Gesher was now completely blockaded, but the Iraqis did not attack again.

The route through Gesher being blocked, the Iraqis decided to cross the Jordan farther south, at the Damiya and Allenby Bridges, which had been occupied intact early on the morning of May 15 by the Transjordanian Arab Legion. They were able to move their entire contingent across the river to Nablus, where Kaukji had his ALA headquarters. There the Iraqis concentrated and awaited reinforcements from Iraq. These arrived during the last week of May, another infantry brigade and another tank battalion, giving the Iraqis two infantry brigades and an armored brigade.

On May 25 the Iraqis struck west from Nablus past the Arab city of Tulkarm. They captured one settlement, and their armored spearheads reached Kfar Jonah and Ein Vered, between Tulkarm and Natania, and were within 10 kilometers of Natania before being halted by the Alexandroni Brigade on May 30.

In anticipation of a major Iraqi offensive, the Israeli High Command had ordered two brigades—the Golani and Carmeli—to coordinate their operations with the Alexandroni Brigade, defending the narrow coastal plain of Sharon. Now, to seize the initiative from the Iraqis, the Israelis decided to assume the offensive in central Samaria. The first objective was to be Jenin.

On May 28 the Golani Brigade began its offensive against Arab irregulars holding the Mt. Bilboa Range northeast of Jenin, and captured Zaryin. Next day the Golanis drove the local Arabs and Iraqis from their position on the Gilboa Range. On May 30 and 31 they seized Megiddo and then Lajun.

The stage was set for a major effort against Jenin. It was to be made by the Carmeli Brigade, passing through the Golanis from the north, with one Golani battalion as reinforcement. Apparently the Alexandroni

[5] The crossing was made much more difficult by a sudden and unexpected rise in the level of the river. The state of Arab cooperation may be realized by the fact that the Iraqis blamed the Transjordanians for having opened the dams on the Yarmouk River and its tributaries, which caused the sudden rise in the level of the river. In fact, however, Israeli raiders were responsible.

Brigade to the west was expected to carry out an attack through the Wadi Ara, shelling Tulkarm. The rapidly growing Israeli air force was to provide reconnaissance, and at least a pretense of air support.

The offensive against Jenin began at dusk on May 31, spearheaded by the Golani battalion, with the Carmeli battalions following behind. In the next 48 hours the Golanis occupied the villages of Sandala, Arrana, Jalma and Muqueibla, north of Jenin, opening the way for the Carmeli assault, which began on the night of June 2-3. The Carmeli objectives were two hills dominating the main road south of the city. As soon as these hills were secured, the Golani battalion was to continue south from Muqueibla, to occupy the city.

Against negligible resistance, the Carmeli battalions advanced southward slowly but steadily on June 3. They attacked during the night and seized the two hills before dawn.

However, for reasons that are not clear, there had been no diversionary action by the Alexandroni Brigade to attrack Iraqi attention toward Tulkarm. Early on the 4th an Iraqi unit southwest of Jenin counterattacked the Carmeli position. The Israelis, who had been unable to dig effective foxholes or entrenchments in the rocky soil, took heavy casualties; nevertheless, they beat off the attack. Shortly after 9 a.m. the two hill positions were again secured, and the Golani battalion occupied Jenin.

About noon, however, an additional Iraqi battalion arrived from Nablus and the reinforced Iraqis counterattacked, this time with air support. The Israelis lost some ground west of the city and the hill southwest of the city. Although they retained the other hill, Colonel Carmel decided the position was too exposed to further counterattacks, and during the night withdrew from Jenin. Both sides could claim success. The Israelis retained all the territories north of Jenin that they had taken between May 8 and June 2. However, the Iraqis had driven the Israelis out of their principal objective of Jenin, and they had outposts in striking distance of the Mediterranean coast between Natania and Tel Aviv. The new state of Israel was in danger of being cut in two.

THE JORDANIAN FRONT

On May 13 most of the Transjordan Arab Legion, under orders from the British Mandate's High Commissioner, completed its evacuation from Palestine. Early on the 14th the remainder—those that had been engaged at the Etzion Bloc—also withdrew west of the Jordan River. The following night, however, when the British Mandate expired, General Glubb sent his troops back across the river into Palestine by way of the Allenby Bridge. Their objective was to occupy positions within the agreed area of Jordanian operations, at the edge of the Arab sectors assigned under the U.N. plan. The Legion's armored vehicles, having crossed the Allenby Bridge, advanced rapidly into Samaria and Judea, and toward Jerusalem. At nightfall, one Jordanian contingent attacked the village of Atarot, which was abandoned by its inhabitants, who moved to Neve Yaakov.

During the 14th there had been considerable firing in and around Jerusalem, after the British departed. While the principal Haganah forces had focused their attention on the area southeast of Jerusalem in the King David Hotel and Railroad Station area, the newly-appointed, controversial Israeli commander of the Jerusalem area, Colonel David Shaltiel, had asked the Irgun contingent in Jerusalem to occupy Sheikh Jarrach, to reestablish communications with the Mt. Scopus settlements.

Early on May 15 the Arab Legion arrived east of Jerusalem, and began shelling Israeli-occupied New Jerusalem with 25-pounders and 6-inch mortars. The Legionnaires advanced from the Mount of Olives

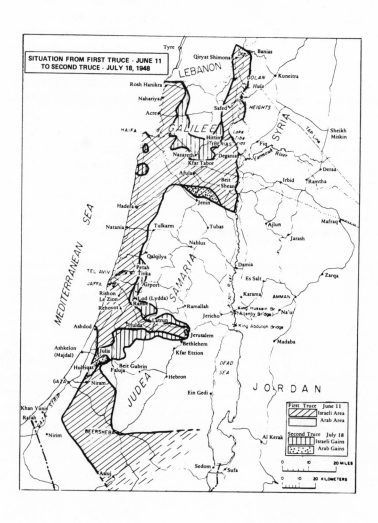

toward Sheikh Jarrach and had little trouble ejecting the Irgun. Communications between Mt. Scopus and the New City were thus again cut. The Legion then mounted attacks on New Jerusalem, from both the northeast and the southeast, while shelling the area from their newly-occupied positions in Sheikh Jarrach. The Arabs ran into strong Israeli resistance north of the large Mandelbaum Building, however, and, after a few more probes, General Glubb called off the attacks against the New City. He did not want to get his troops bogged down in street fighting against the substantially more numerous Israeli troops in the area.

Meanwhile, further east, the Legion contingent that had taken Atarot attempted to seize Neve Yaakov. They were unsuccessful in this effort, but during the night the people of Atarot and Neve Yaakov withdrew to the Hadassah Hospital on Mt. Scopus.

While one brigade of the Arab Legion was thus occupied in the Jerusalem area, the other brigade carried out its assigned missions promptly and efficiently. By May 17 the Legion had established itself securely on the ridge overlooking the Tel Aviv-Jerusalem road between Latrun and Deir Ayub. Thus, Legion outposts were within 30 kilometers of Tel Aviv. At the same time other Legion units seized Bethlehem.

To the south, the Israeli potash plant at the northern end of the Dead Sea was isolated. As the Arab Legion closed in on the potash works and the nearby settlement of Beit Haarava, it became evident to the Jewish settlers that their position was hopeless. During the night of May 19-20, therefore, the settlers were evacuated by boat to Sodom on the south shore of the Dead Sea. To the west on May 19th the Legion units seized the water pumping station near Petah Tekva (first Zionist agricultural settlement in Israel) and next day repulsed an Israeli counterattack. This was a deadly threat to the heart of the new state of Israel.

THE SOUTHERN (EGYPTIAN) FRONT

Southern Palestine had been embattled long before the formal Arab invasion. Early in 1948 Sheikh Hassan El-Bana, leader of the Moslem Brotherhood, sent two small battalion-sized contingents of his "Volunteers" from Egypt. Based in the Gaza-Khan Yunis area, they were soon raiding into the Jewish Negev settlements to the east. Their leader, Tariq el Afriqi, kept close contact with Mufti Husseini. By late April or early May, however, Colonel Azziz arrived from Egypt, and assumed command of the Volunteer contingents. He seems to have brought with him at least one battery of Egyptian artillery, and a more focussed objective than the somewhat aimless raiding and killing which had occupied the Moslem Brotherhood prior to his arrival. He clearly intended to try to assure freedom of movement for regular Egyptian forces when they arrived, while at the same time blocking communications between Tel Aviv and the Negev.

On May 10 Azziz and his Volunteers attacked the Jewish settlement of Kfar Darom, just east of the main road between Khan Yunis and Gaza. After suffering heavy casualties—as much from their own mis-directed artillery as from the Jewish defenders—the Volunteers were repulsed. This setback was soon followed by another. On May 12 elements of the Givati and Negev Brigades, approaching from north and south, captured the Arab villages of Brier, Huleiqat, and Kaukaba, thus securing an inland dirt road from the north into the western Negev.

Two days later, on October 14, however, Azziz and his Volunteers bloodlessly achieved an offsetting success. The British had held the powerful police fortress at Iraq Suwaydan, to secure their route of withdrawal from central Palestine to Rafah and thence to the Canal Zone. On the 14th, however, as the last British units marched to the southwest, they abandoned Iraq Suwaydan, which Azziz promptly occupied. This not only gave him control of the principal east-west road from Majdal to Hebron, it also bisected the Jewish supply road to the Negev through Brier and Huleiqat. With the arrival of more Egyptian forces, Azziz was in a position to isolate the Negev.

By this time the Egyptian invasion force was concentrating in the northeastern Sinai at Abu Ageila[6] and El Arish. The commander was Major General Ahmed Ali el Mawawi, his second in command was Brigadier Mohammed Naguib. The force comprised approximately 7,000 men, in five infantry battalions, an armored contingent of British Mark VI and Matilda tanks, a medium machine gun battalion, a field regiment of sixteen 25-pounder guns, a battery of eight 6-pounder (57mm) guns, an antiaircraft company, and miscellaneous supply and other supporting units. Available as air support were 15 fighter aircraft, five converted bombers as transports, and a few miscellaneous reconnaissance aircraft. The force was divided in two brigade groups of unequal size. The larger group, approximately 5,000 men accompanied by General Mawawi, and commanded directly by Naguib, moved from El Arish to Rafah on the 14th. The main element of the smaller force—less than 2,000 men—was two battalions of regular infantry, plus another contingent of Moslem Brotherhood Volunteers. Also on the 14th this contingent advanced from Abu Ageila to El Auja, four kilometers inside the frontier of Palestine.

The Jewish forces facing the invasion consisted of the armed settlers in each settlement, plus initially the Negev Brigade under Colonel Nahum Sarig. Shortly after the beginning of the invasion the Givati Brigade under Colonel Shimeon Avidan also joined the defenders of southern

---

[6] There are many spellings of this name, an obscure police post and crossroad in the northeast Sinai Peninsula; its strategic location has caused it to figure prominently in three Arab-Israeli wars.

Palestine. But the Arab hold on Iraq Suwaydan and the east-west road prevented an actual junction of the two brigades. There was little coordination between these units until August, when one commander was appointed for the entire front.

Because of the sparseness of the settlements in the area from which it was recruited, the Negev Brigade, with three battalions, was one of the smaller brigades of the Haganah, with only about 1,500 men. The Givati, on the other hand, was one of the largest, consisting of five battalions, totalling some 3,200 men. On May 14, with invasion imminent, two battalions of the Negev Brigade, consisting of about 800 men, were deployed to observe the southwestern frontier. In addition to their small arms, these troops were equipped with light mortars, two 20mm guns, and two "Davidka" heavy mortars. Shortly after the invasion began, the third battalion was moved to the front, along with a battery of 65mm guns, and two companies of jeep-mounted infantry, giving Sarig a front line strength of more than 1,500 men.

The Egyptian invasion plan provided for two divergent simultaneous thrusts northward into Palestine. The larger column was to follow the coastal road and railway toward Tel Aviv, to link up with a small contingent landed by sea at Majdal late on the 14th. The inland column was to advance by way of Beersheba and Hebron to meet with the Arab Legion in the vicinity of Jerusalem.

Early on May 15, both columns crossed the frontier, the larger brigade at Rafah, the smaller at El Auja. The larger force moved toward Khan Yunis, which was held by Arab irregulars of the Moslem Brotherhood and armed local Arabs. Just off the road, some six kilometers beyond Rafah, was the tiny Jewish settlement of Nirim, held by approximately 40 settlers. General Mawawi sent a detachment of infantry and artillery to deal with this fortified settlement, while with the main body he moved on to Khan Yunis, where he quickly occupied the airfield and prepared to continue the advance to the north.

An Egyptian bombardment of Nirim began at 7:00 a.m. Shortly after this an Egyptian column of armored vehicles[7] and a company of truck-mounted infantry approached to within 400 meters of the settlement under cover of artillery fire. At noon the infantry, covered by intense artillery and machine gun fire, assaulted the settlement, but they were stopped 150 meters from its security fence by Israeli small arms fire. The Egyptian infantry withdrew, leaving some 30 dead behind them.

There was no further effort to attack that day, but on the 16th the Egyptians again attempted to seize the settlement. This time air support was available, but the infantry failed to press its attack. On the 17th,

---

[7] There is dispute as to the amount of armor in this force; the defenders of Nirim say that there were four tanks and several armored cars; the Egyptians say there were only a few Bren gun carriers.

Haganah reinforcements arrived with arms and ammunition, and the Egyptians made no further effort to attack.

General Mawawi's main body, meanwhile, had continued its advance northward from Khan Yunis toward Gaza. In the late afternoon, some five miles south of Gaza, the Egyptians passed another Jewish settlement, Kfar Darom, which had been under siege by local Arabs for months. (The thirty armed members of the settlement's defense unit had most recently repelled an assault of the Moslem Brotherhood on the night of May 10-11.) Again Mawawi left a detachment to deal with this potential threat to his line of communications, and continued his advance to Gaza, which he entered in the early evening.

The commander of the Egyptian detachment left to deal with Kfar Darom planned an assault for the following dawn. An intensive artillery barrage was followed by an artillery and mortar smoke screen to cover the infantry assault. The screen was not completely effective, however, and as the Arabs approached the barbed wire fence around the settlement, the defending Jews opened fire with devastating effect. After several unsuccessful attempts to push through the defense—attempts marred by poorly directed artillery support—the Arabs finally withdrew. Their losses were 70 dead and 50 wounded.

In subsequent weeks Kfar Darom was to be subjected to a number of similar attacks, but none of these had been successful when the town was evacuated in July.

General Mawawi's column did not tarry to learn the results of the attacks on Nirim or Kfar Darom. Early on the morning of the 16th the Egyptians advanced from Gaza to reach Yad Mordechai, one of the oldest settlements of the Negev. This position was too strong for Mawawi to risk bypassing it. Since his supplies had not moved as fast as the main body, and having learned of the tenacity of the Israeli defense from the experiences at Nirim and Kfar Darom, General Mawawi took two days to prepare for an attack on Yad Mordechai. On May 19 the attack was begun, but after three hours of desperate fighting the Egyptians had succeeded only in seizing one small outpost and had failed in all attempts to penetrate into the settlement itself.

The attack was renewed on May 20, but four assaults were driven back by the Israelis with the help of reinforcements from Gvar Am. The Egyptians did not renew the assault until the afternoon of May 23. This was a major, coordinated infantry-armor assault. By evening the Egyptians had succeeded in taking part of the settlement, which was in a desperate situation. That night the Negev Brigade's small commando battalion, in armored cars, reached Yad Mordechai. The commander made a quick estimate of the situation and decided that the settlement must be evacuated. Just before dawn on May 24, the entire garrison at Yad Mordechai withdrew to Nirim.

Meanwhile, the inland column had been moving rapidly. Unopposed in this desolate Arab territory, the motorized advance guard of the column reached Beersheba on May 17. The main body arrived there on the 20th. That same day the advance party linked up with the Arab Legion at Bethlehem, and assumed responsibility for the control of that city the next day, on May 21. At about this time this force was joined by Colonel Azziz and the contingents he had been commanding north-east of Gaza, and Azziz assumed command of the combined force.

On the seacoast on that day, General Mawawi, having decided to leave part of his command to continue the assault on Yad Mordechai, continued on to Majdal (Ascalon) with his main body. There he met a small contingent earlier landed by ship. General Mawawi now sent a small column eastward through Iraq Suwaydan, Faluja and Beit Gubrin to establish lateral communications with Colonel Azziz and the Jordanians in the Bethlehem-Hebron area. On the 28th, Mawawi tried to secure this line of communications by an attack on Negba, supported by 25-pounders and aircraft. However, the attack was repulsed.

Moving more slowly and more cautiously, the remaining Egyptians renewed the advance northward, still without serious opposition, to enter Ashdod on May 29. Continuing to the Ashdod Bridge, three kilometers north of the city, they were only 32 kilometers from Tel Aviv, which was under frequent air bombardment by Egyptian planes.

Here, however, the Egyptians encountered Israelis in considerable force. Troops of the Givati Brigade, coming from Rehovoth, had blown up the bridge, and had taken up defensive positions just north of Ashdod in the area of Gedera-Boshit. An advance Israeli position was established in the vicinity of Kfar Warburg, southeast of Ashdod, thus threatening the line of Egyptian communications. Patrols on both sides were soon in active encounters in an arc around Ashdod. Suddenly the Egyptians found themselves attacked by four Israeli Messerschmitt fighter planes, recently arrived from Europe. (One was shot down by Egyptian anti-aircraft fire.) Soon another Israeli weapon, not previously encountered by the Egyptians, was in action: 65mm howitzers in newly-established Israeli artillery units. General Mawawi decided to dig in, correctly estimating that he was outnumbered and that further advance would be impossible without reinforcements.

The Israeli High Command determined to make a major effort to destroy the seriously depleted Egyptians at Ashdod, about 2,500 men commanded by Brigadier Naguib. The Israeli plan called for an attack by two battalions of the Givati Brigade, an Irgun battalion, and two companies of jeep infantry from the Negev Brigade. Originally planned for the night of June 1-2, the attack was postponed for 24 hours because of confusion in communications.

The Israeli attack on Ashdod began after midnight on June 2-3. The main effort, attempting a wide envelopment south of Ashdod, ran into intense fire from the Egyptians. Through lack of coordination, the other Israeli units failed to provide adequate support, and the attackers were forced to withdraw, having lost about 400 dead and wounded, considerably more than Arab losses.[8] Surprisingly, the Israelis made only one feeble attempt against the exposed Egyptian lateral line of communications through Iraq Suwaydan and Faluja. They withdrew after being easily repulsed from Iraq Suwaydan.

Satisfied that Naguib could hold Ashdod, General Mawawi turned his attention to the settlement of Nitzanin, about midway between Ashdod and Negba, which he had bypassed on the original advance to Ashdod. Nitzanin, located in a deep valley, was garrisoned by a force of 150 men. Although it was a more formidable obstacle than any of the other small settlements which the Egyptians had encountered, they had learned from these failures, and from their success at Yad Mordechai. The assault was carefully planned, and involved the cooperation of an Egyptian infantry battalion, a platoon of tanks, a company of armored cars, and most of the 25-pounder regiment. In addition, a squadron of aircraft was assigned to support the operation.

An artillery bombardment on Nitzanin began at midnight on June 6-7, and the ground assault began at 6:00 a.m. After an initial repulse, the Egyptians called in the air force, and under the cover of the air strafing the armor succeeded in penetrating into the town's defenses, closely followed by the infantry. Realizing that they could no longer hold the settlement, the defenders attempted to withdraw, only to find themselves hemmed in by surrounding Egyptians. At 4 p.m., after several unsuccessful attempts to break out, Nitzanin surrendered with 33 dead.

Egyptian morale was bolstered by two Egyptian combat successes in quick succession: Ashdod and Nitzanin. However, frequent and persistent raids against their lines of communication by the Negev Brigade allowed them little time to celebrate these successes.

---

[8] Mohammed Naguib, *Egypt's Destiny* (New York, 1955), p. 22.

6

The Battles for Jerusalem

On May 15 the Israeli High Command decided that the Givati Brigade battalion in the Jerusalem-Tel Aviv Corridor should be sent south to reinforce the rest of the brigade blocking the Egyptian advance along the coast toward Tel Aviv. First, however, it was decided to send one more convoy through to Jerusalem before Colonel Avidan's troops left the area. On the night of May 15-16 one company of the Givati Brigade seized Latrun, while the Harel Brigade was occupying Deir Ayub. On May 18, as the Givati troops were leaving, a Jewish convoy began to drive from Tel Aviv to Jerusalem. Then, to meet the Arab Legion's threat to New Jerusalem, the Harel Brigade was shifted eastward, closer to Jerusalem.

The Israeli High Command had taken a calculated risk, moving these two regular Haganah brigades from the Jerusalem Corridor. They apparently hoped that the Arabs would be too occupied elsewhere to move major forces to block the road. The gamble was almost successful.

When Kaukji learned of the coordinated Arab invasions of May 15, he assumed that his army had completed its misson. He withdrew to Lebanon from Galilee and ordered his units that had been operating north of the Jerusalem Corridor to concentrate in the Samarian "triangle," to await further instructions from the Arab League. At the same time the Arab Legion, assuming that Kaukji's troops were still in the Corridor, had not allocated any units to that sector. General Glubb, however, realized the situation when on May 18 he learned of the arrival in New Jerusalem of Jewish trucks from Tel Aviv. He promptly sent his 4th Regiment[1] to occupy Latrun, which it did without opposition on May 19. Jewish Jerusalem was again isolated; the route of the supply convoy that had started the previous day was blocked.

Meanwhile, just east of the New City, between May 16 and 22 the Arab Legion occupied itself with consolidating its positions at Sheikh Jarrach and in and around the Old City of Jerusalem. During much of this time the Transjordanians were dealing with a troublesome problem in the Jewish Quarter of the Old City.

The Jewish Quarter of Old Jerusalem was bordered on the east by

[1] A battalion in strength.

60

the Mosque of Omar, on the west by the Armenian Quarter, on the north by the large Moslem Quarter, and on the south by the Old City wall. During the last days of the Mandate, detachments of the Haganah and an Irgun unit had infiltrated into the Jewish Quarter to stiffen the resistance of the inhabitants, and to boost their morale. By the time the British left, on the evening of May 13, the garrison consisted of about 200 Haganah troops and some 100 from the Irgun.

As the British pulled out, the garrison occupied a number of nearby posts which covered the approaches to the Jewish Quarter. They also seized a Greek church in the Armenian Quarter, because they feared that otherwise its tower, which dominated the Jewish Quarter, might become an Arab observation post and strongpoint. At the request of the Patriarch, however, they evacuated the church, on the understanding that Arab troops would not be permitted to take possession of the tower. In spite of the Patriarch's assurances, no sooner had the Israelis withdrawn late on the 14th than Arab irregulars seized the church and its tower and began firing on the Israeli defenders, supporting a number of small-scale Arab counterattacks. At the same time, Arab assaults forced the Israelis from positions which they held near the Zion Gate, the only link between the Jewish Quarter and the New City.

With the Arab Legion coming up on the east, it was obvious to the Israeli commander, Colonel Shaltiel, that the defenders and inhabitants of the Jewish Quarter were in a desperate situation. He therefore prepared a plan to reopen communications with the Jewish Quarter, which could then be reinforced or, if the situation got worse, could be evacuated. Units from the Harel Brigade were to capture Mt. Zion and to enter the Armenian Quarter from the south through the Zion Gate. Meanwhile, part of the Etzioni Brigade would penetrate from the west by way of the Jaffa Gate. The operation was to take place on the evening of May 17th.

However, communications between the brigades were poor and coordination practically non-existent. Due either to an administrative failure, or to inadequate planning on the part of the Etzioni staff, it became necessary to delay the attack for 24 hours. Meanwhile, the preparations had become evident to the Arabs, and, when the four Etzioni platoons detailed to this operation did mount their attack on the evening of May 18th, the local Arab irregulars were waiting for them. All of the engineers with the attacking force were killed. Its armored cars were dispersed, and instead of pressing on with their attack the troops spent the remainder of the night evacuating their wounded.

The much better trained Harel Brigade, however, carried out its part of the operation efficiently. While some units attacked Mt. Zion, a detachment of engineers blew a breach in the Zion Gate at 3:25 a.m. on the 19th. The waiting Harel units rushed in and quickly made contact with the defenders of the Jewish Quarter. A reinforcement unit of 80 men and substantial quantities of ammunition were moved in. During the day, and into the night, there were a number of minor Arab counterattacks, striking mainly at the communication line between the Zion Gate and the Jewish Quarter. Early on the 20th, even though apparently under no great pressure, the Harel units withdrew to Mt. Zion, allowing the Arabs to regain control of the Zion Gate.

Meanwhile the Arab Legion had completed its consolidation of the rest of the Old City and was prepared to devote itself to eradicating the Jewish enclave. Although reluctant to commit his troops to city fighting, General Glubb felt it was essential to secure all of the Old City before making any further attempts against the New City.

Accordingly, a battalion of the Arab Legion concentrated its attention on the northwest corner of the Jewish Quarter. Under cover of heavy mortar fire, and with artillery support from the Mount of Olives, the Transjordanian infantry advanced from building to building. Gradually the Israelis in the Old City were forced back into two large buildings, one of them the Ben Zakkai Synagogue. There were about 1,500 Jews concentrated in this small area; of these perhaps 250 were soldiers still fit for combat. Hammered by artillery and mortar fire, however, with the Arab Legion evidently preparing itself for a final assault, the defenders of the Jewish Quarter surrendered at 2:00 in the afternoon on May 28th. The remaining Jewish soldiers, including wounded, were taken to Amman as prisoners of war. The old people and children also were kept briefly as prisoners, contrary to the capitulation agreement. But they were soon released and allowed to return to Israeli territory in the New City.

Meanwhile, by May 23 it had become obvious to General Glubb that it would be merely a question of time before the resistance in the Jewish Quarter would be overcome. Therefore, he turned his attention back toward the New City. He set as his first objective the seizure of Notre Dame, just west of the Jaffa Gate and dominating the eastern portion of New Jerusalem. The thick-walled monastery had been made into a fortress by the Israeli soldiers, and it was obvious that a major effort would be needed to drive them out.

On May 23 a coordinated infantry and armored car assault was launched against Notre Dame. An Arab Legion column advanced from the Damascus Gate toward the monastery, covered by heavy fire from infantry units on the Old City wall. It was planned that the armored vehicles, in turn, would provide support for a direct infantry assault against the monastery. However, several of the armored cars were knocked out by Molotov cocktails, blocking the advance of the column, and preventing the planned deployment of the armored vehicles. Glubb was forced to call off the attack.

After one more abortive effort at a surprise assault on the monastery, in which casualties were heavy, Glubb ordered all further attacks against the monastery to cease. He did not believe that seizure of the position warranted the casualties that would be incurred. He and his commander in chief, King Abdullah, were satisfied that by gaining control of the Old City and of most of the remaining territory around the Jewish New City, they had achieved their prime objective. Furthermore, by this time other Arab Legion troops had cut the Tel Aviv-Jerusalem road, and Glubb decided that he would wait until either the Jews were starved out of the New City or boundary lines were established by a peace settlement. Arab Legion guns continued to bombard the monastery and other Israeli positions on the perimeter of the New City defenses, but no further ground attacks were attempted.

On May 20, Egyptian forces—mostly Azziz's Volunteers—advancing through Hebron reached Bethlehem in force, to link up with Arab Legion troops there. The next day the Arab Legion, coordinating its advance with an Egyptian movement north from Bethlehem, moved south from the Old City against the village of Ramat Rachel. Early on the 21st, a coordinated infantry attack drove the Israelis—including an Irgun unit—out of the village, and by afternoon the Egyptian Volunteers had occupied the settlement. By midafternoon, however, the defenders had been reinforced by an Etzioni Brigade company from Jerusalem. That evening the Israelis counterattacked, ousting the Egyptians. By May 25 the Israelis had beaten off further Arab Legion and Egyptian counterattacks, and—after the arrival of a reinforcing Harel unit—had also seized the nearby Mar Elias Monastery. The southern flank of New Jerusalem was now secure. Except for the mopping up in the Jewish Quarter of the Old City, the battle for Jerusalem had ended. The Israelis held all of the New City of Jerusalem, the nearby settlement of Ramat Rachel, and the two isolated settlements on Mt. Scopus. Otherwise, the region was dominated by the Arabs.

The fate of Jewish New Jerusalem by this time clearly depended on the outcome of operations to the west. The 4th Regiment of the Arab Legion, under the command of Lieutenant Colonel Habis al Majali, had by May 20 established firm control over a three mile section of the road in the vicinity of Latrun, Deir Ayub, and Bab el Wad. Further east units of the Legion's 2nd Regiment also blocked the road at Biddu. Thus Jerusalem was again isolated from Tel Aviv and this time by a well disciplined force of regular soldiers, instead of the unreliable irregulars who had only sporadically interfered with road traffic in previous months.

The Haganah High Command now decided to undertake a major operation to seize Latrun and break the Arab stranglehold on the highway. The operation, called "Bin-Nun," after Joshua Bin-Nun, the biblical conqueror of Jericho, was to be a coordinated attack from east and west by two brigades. The main effort would be made from the west by the newly organized 7th Brigade, commanded by Colonel Shlomo Shamir. This brigade included a hastily-assembled armored battalion, equipped with newly-arrived half tracks, and thus became the first armored unit of the Israeli Army. Its other battalion was composed of recently-arrived immigrants from Europe. Also assigned to the 7th Brigade was a veteran battalion of the Alexandroni Brigade.

In a secondary attack, from the east, elements of the Harel Brigade would pin down as many as possible of Colonel al Majali's troops, to keep them away from the main effort. Once Shamir's brigade had achieved its initial objective of occupying the Latrun crest, the Harel troops would occupy the Latrun-Bab el Wad section of the road, then move north to secure the rugged hills between Biddin and Biddu and Ramallah.

The 7th Brigade's assault on Latrun and the nearby crest was to be executed by two battalions—an Alexandroni Brigade battalion, led by Major Zvi Germann, and a battalion of new immigrants from Europe, commanded by Major Haim Laskov. Some of the immigrants were veterans of World War II who had served in the armies of their countries of origin, but they had had only a brief training period together and with their Haganah cadre before this operation. The assault was planned for shortly after midnight on May 25th, but it was delayed by the late arrival of the Alexandroni battalion, which was not ready to begin its movement until 4:00 a.m. By this time a premature bombardment from the Israelis' handful of 65mm howitzers had alerted the Arabs. When the assault came al Majali's troops were ready. Both of the Israeli battalions suffered very heavy casualties, particularly the Alexandroni battalion. The First Battle of Latrun ended as a devastating defeat for the Israelis.

Early the following morning, before dawn on May 26, an Arab Legion company assaulted an Israeli position on Radar Hill, overlooking the road between Abu Ghosh and Biddu. This attack was successful; the Harel company on the hill, caught by surprise, was driven off. The Arab Legion immediately consolidated the position, thus securing the approaches to Latrun from the east. Despite numerous counterattacks, the Israelis were never able to recover this key position.

On May 28 Colonel David ("Mickey") Marcus, an American volunteer and a graduate of West Point,[2] was appointed commander over all the

---

[2] There has been speculation that Colonel Marcus, recently resigned from the US Army, was sent to Israel by the Pentagon in response to pressure from the White House, itself under pressure from US Jews to support the new state of Israel. It has not been possible to establish the facts.

Israeli forces operating in Jerusalem and in the Jerusalem-Tel Aviv corridor. He immediately directed another effort against Latrun.

On May 30 a second assault was mounted against the Legion defenders of Latrun. Again, two battalions were to take part in the main effort. One of these was Laskov's battalion of the 7th Brigade and the other a Givati battalion under Major Yaakov Peri, replacing the Alexandroni battalion.

The Givati battalion took Deir Ayub without opposition, but as the troops advanced toward Latrun they met intense fire and were driven back. Meanwhile, Laskov's battalion, which included an armored car company, was approaching Latrun from the other direction. Unaware of the withdrawal of the Givati battalion, Laskov attempted a combined infantry-armored assault on the village, which failed in part through poor coordination. The primary cause of failure, however, was the accuracy and intensity of the Arab Legion fire. After suffering extremely severe casualties, Laskov and his men were also forced to fall back.

This second failure to take Latrun was a severe blow to the Israelis, particularly in view of the critical supply situation in Jerusalem. To provide some of the most urgently needed supplies, Marcus organized an emergency supply operation over some mountain trails in the corridor, with supplies carried on mules, and in some cases on the backs of soldiers. The first unit to get through to Jerusalem with supplies was a company of the Givati Brigade.

On June 1 the Haganah High Command approved Colonel Marcus's recommendation that an alternate route be constructed south of the main road from Beir Muheisin to Bab el Wad. To prevent the Arabs from learning about this operation and possibly interfering with it, most of the construction was carried out at night. Also, the nearby Arab villages of Beit Jiz and Beit Susin were occupied and cleared of their inhabitants, to preserve security. All available soldiers and engineers were assembled to work on the project, and all of the bulldozers that could be collected in the Israeli-held portions of Palestine were gathered together. By June 6, with working parties approaching each other from Jerusalem and Tel Aviv, most of the road track had been cleared, except for one particularly rugged section. On that day the first supplies moved over the road, although they had to be hand carried for the short distance where the road was incomplete. The route, which was known as the "Burma Road" was traversable—although far from completed—on June 10, when the first convoy drove straight through from Tel Aviv to Jerusalem.

In spite of construction of the "Burma Road," the Haganah High Command decided to attempt one more assault on Latrun, by this time held by two Arab Legion regiments, the 2nd and the 4th. The Yiftach Brigade was moved into the corridor and placed under the command of

Colonel Marcus. The Israeli plan, code-named Operation "Yoram," provided for a large-scale pincer movement against Latrun. Two Palmach battalions, one from the Harel Brigade and one from the Yiftach Brigade, would attack Latrun from the east. Another Yiftach battalion was to assault Biddu, and thereby isolate a portion of the Legion in the eastern section of the corridor.

The operation began at midnight of June 8-9, and elements of all three battalions reached at least portions of their objectives. They could not hold their positions, however, against the intense fire and aggressive local counterattacks of the Legion. The next night the operation was tried again, but one battalion became lost, while another was forced to withdraw under intense Transjordanian fire.

On June 10 the Legion counterattacked, and captured the settlement of Gezer. Later in the evening, however, Gezer was retaken by elements of the Yiftach Brigade. While this counterattack was taking place, at 3:50 a.m. on the morning of June 11, Colonel Marcus was killed when he failed to respond to the challenge of an Israeli sentinel. The challenge was in Hebrew, a language which Colonel Marcus had not yet learned. The young sentinel tried to kill himself when he realized whom he had shot.

In its immediate consequences, the third Israeli defeat at Latrun was not so serious as the two previous disasters, nor were the losses so heavy. However, in less than two weeks in an important position of command, Colonel Marcus had demonstrated a combination of energy and ability which marked him as one of the outstanding leaders of the Haganah. His death was a disaster.

7

The First Truce

BERNADOTTE AND THE UN OBSERVERS

During the weeks following the Arab invasion of Palestine, the United Nations tried vainly to bring about a ceasefire. On May 20 the Security Council appointed Swedish Count Folke Bernadotte af Wisborg as United Nations mediator between the Arabs and the Israelis. He was assisted by a team of United Nations observers, made up of army officers from Belgium, France, Sweden, and the United States, designated as the United Nations Truce Supervision Organization, or UNTSO. After intensive efforts Bernadotte was able to persuade each side that the other was desperate for a truce, and thus by adroit diplomacy saved both from asking for the truce, which, in fact, they did desperately need.

The Arabs, although they seemed to believe that they could profit more from a short truce than could the Israelis, nevertheless, would not agree to a truce period of more than four weeks, from June 11 to July 9. The Israelis would have preferred a longer truce, but were willing to accept four weeks.

In addition to an in-place ceasefire, the principal conditions of the truce terms were that neither side would attempt to improve its military position; there was to be no movement of troops or materiel; no new fighting forces were to be introduced by either side; no immigrants of military age were to be allowed into Palestine, except with the specific approval of the UN mediator; finally, Jerusalem was to be supplied by convoy under the supervision of the International Red Cross. Actually, only the last of these additional conditions was fully adhered to, although both sides generally obeyed the ceasefire for the entire period of four weeks.

ISRAELI REORGANIZATION

Israel made excellent use of those weeks. Priority was put upon the reorganization and training of the armed forces, and the absorption of war material which was arriving from Europe, particularly from Czechoslovakia, in a steady stream. At the same time this respite provided an

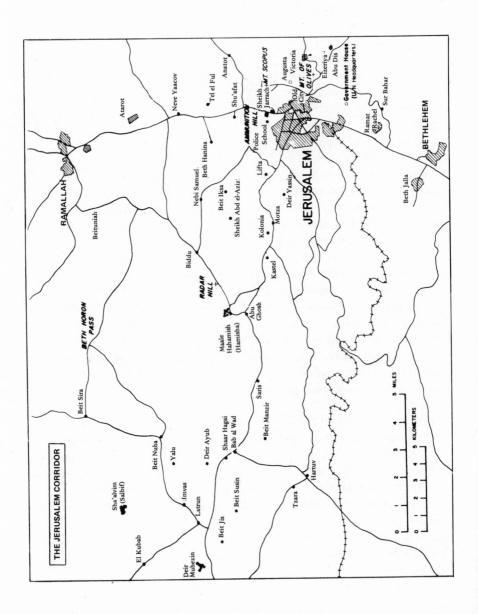

THE JERUSALEM CORRIDOR

RAMALLAH

BETH HORON PASS

RADAR HILL

JERUSALEM

BETHLEHEM

Atarot

Neve Yaacov

Tel el Ful

Anatot

Shu'afat

Beituniah

Sheikh Jarrach - MT. SCOPUS

Augusta Victoria

Eizeriya

Abu Dis

Sur Bahar

Beth Hanina

AMMUNITION HILL

Police School

Old City

Government House (U/N Headquarters)

MT. OF OLIVES

Nebi Samuel

Beit Iksa

Sheikh Abd el-Aziz

Lifta

Ramat Rachel

Biddu

Kolonia

Motza

Deir Yassin

Beth Jalla

Kastel

Abu Ghosh

Maale Hahamisha (Hamisha)

Beit Sira

Saris

Beit Nuba

Yalu

Deir Ayub

Shaar Hagai

Beit Manzir

Bab al Wad

El Kubab

Sha'alvim (Salbif)

Imvas

Latrun

Beit Jis

Beit Susin

Tzara

Harruv

Deir Muhezin

5 MILES

5 KILOMETERS

opportunity to reorganize civil administration throughout the newly established nation, and to assert central authority over the scattered settlements and the territory occupied by its armed forces.

A major element of the military reorganization was to put into effect the provisions of the Provisional Government's enactment which had formally created a national army. This was Order No. 4, promulgated on May 28, which authorized the government to institute conscription in time of emergency, and which provided for the establishment of a national army, effective on June 1, 1948. This was to be known as the Zvah Haganah Le Israel, or Israel Defense Forces, soon popularly known as Zahal, or in English, IDF.

In accordance with previously prepared plans, the new Zahal's High Command established four regional, or area "commands." This led to severe disputes between the IDF General Staff and Ben Gurion over the question of who should be appointed to these major command positions. Ben Gurion, although a socialist himself, seems to have had some doubts about the reliability of some of the socialist-oriented Haganah officers. There was no question about their loyalty to the state, but many were members of the pro-Soviet, left-wing Mapam Party, and less than enthusiastic supporters of Ben Gurion, leader of the rival Mapai Party. He felt that some of the more conservative officers who had served during World War II with the British Army were not only more experienced military professionals, but also were likely to be more sympathetic to the Mapai Party, and would be more stable and disciplined in their positions of responsibility. Important among the officers Ben Gurion favored were Colonels Shlomo Shamir and Mordechai Makleff.

Yigal Yadin, General Dori's deputy, was for all practical purposes the Chief of the General Staff during Dori's illness. He strenuously opposed Ben Gurion's proposed appointments. He felt it was important for the morale of the army, as well as for assurance of mutual understanding between commanders and subordinates, that these key positions be held by experienced Haganah officers, most of whom had seen active duty with the Palmach. While they respected them, most of the old Haganah and Palmach looked upon the British-trained officers as outsiders.

When he found that Ben Gurion was adamant in appointing the former British officers to the regional command positions, Yadin submitted his resignation. This in turn aroused concern and considerable opposition among members of the Ben Gurion's own Mapai party; so Ben Gurion also submitted his resignation. The impasse was resolved by postponing appointments to any of the commands except the crucial Central Command, where the next series of major operations was anticipated. That important position was to be given to the youthful Palmach commander, Yigal Allon. The appointment was partially a recognition of Allon's exceptional ability, but it was also an effort by Ben Gurion to appease the Palmach leaders, who were upset at having their units—once the elite of the Haganah—merged into the other units in the new Zahal. It was at about this time that the title of Aluf, or brigadier general—which up to this time had been granted only to Dori and Yadin—was given to their principal department heads; Allon also was promoted to Aluf.

The fourth clause of Order No. 4 was an explicit provision against the maintenance of any armed forces other than those of the IDF itself within the territory of the state; this provision quite obviously was directed against the Irgun and Lehi.

Under the provisions of the agreement of April 26 between the Haganah and the Irgun, the Irgun had been permitted to constitute a unique force under its own officers within the framework of the Haganah. After the proclamation of independence, both the Irgun and the Lehi remained intact as formations, and, while they acknowledged the superiority of the Haganah High Command, their subordination to this authority was only nominal. Now, however, Prime Minister Ben Gurion made it clear that he had every intention of putting into effect the provisions of the fourth clause of Order No. 4.

On June 2 representatives of the Irgun signed an agreement with representatives of the IDF that all members of the Irgun in territory under the authority of the Provisional Government would join the IDF and take the oath of allegiance; all Irgun arms and equipment would be turned over to the IDF; the Irgun would cease to exist as a separate and independent organization within the state of Israel; all separate arms purchases would cease and all supply contracts would be transferred to the IDF. It was explicitly understood, however, that this agreement did not apply to forces in areas cut off from the remainder of Israel—meaning, of course, those in the Jerusalem area.

THE *ALTALENA* INCIDENT

In the months before independence, the Irgun had collected a huge quantity of arms abroad, and its leaders now informed the Israeli government that these, together with some 900 recruits for the Irgun, would be arriving on a ship called the *Altalena*, which the Irgun had obtained in France. The Irgun representatives made it clear that they expected that these recruits and this equipment would be for the exclusive use of the former Irgun units.

Ben Gurion saw this incident as an opportunity to have a showdown on the authority of the Provisional Government. He informed the Irgun that under the terms of Order No. 4 and the agreement of June 2, the IDF would be responsible for the allocation of the equipment and the assignment of the recruits. This was unacceptable to the Irgun, and efforts at a compromise failed. Ben Gurion then simply ordered that all arms and ammunition be handed over to the IDF, which would assume responsibility for the arriving recruits.

On June 20 the *Altalena* arrived off the coast of Israel and anchored opposite Kfar Vitkin. The Alexandroni Brigade (to which a jeep company from Major Moshe Dayan's new "mechanized assault" battalion was attached) was instructed to prevent waiting Irgun units from unloading and distributing the arms. After 48 hours of tension, in which there was sporadic firing between the Irgun and Alexandroni units, the Irgun force surrendered.

Then, suddenly, at midnight on June 2, in open defiance of the government, the Irgun brought the *Altalena* into the roadstead off Tel Aviv. Ben Gurion again ordered Haganah troops to prevent the unloading of arms from the ship, and units from the Negev and Yiftach Brigades were rushed to Tel Aviv to reinforce the small city garrison in enforcement of that directive. Once again fighting broke out between the IDF and the Irgun, and 15 men were killed. To make certain that the Irgun would not obtain the equipment, the *Altalena* was sunk by 65mm gunfire during this struggle.

On June 28 the oath of allegiance was taken by the entire army and the Irgun ceased to exist as a separate force. Except for the battalion in Jerusalem, which retained its identity and some autonomy, Irgun units were broken up and the men transferred to Haganah units.

CONTINUING ARAB DISUNITY

One of the things the Arabs had hoped to achieve during the truce was to resolve their differences and to devise a unified plan of action. Despite intensive but uncoordinated efforts by Husseini and King Abdullah of Transjordan, this proved to be impossible. However, most of the Arab armies took advantage of the truce to rest, regroup, and rearm their forces.

FRICTION IN THE SOUTH

The observation of the truce was not so complete in the southern sector as in other areas of the country, primarily because of the intersection of two important lines of communication of the opposing forces. The east-west road from Majdal through Beit Gubrin to Hebron was the lateral axis connecting the two principal Egyptian forces in southern Palestine. The Egyptians considered possession of this road to be essential to their security, and they also recognized that it comprised a corridor isolating Israeli forces in the Negev from those in north and central Palestine. For the Israelis, the survival of the settlements and forces in the Negev was dependent upon a supply route from the north, which intersected the Majdal-Hebron road near Huleiqat. Thus, any action by either side to keep open its supply and communications route was automatically considered a violation of the truce by the other side.

The United Nations observers had attempted to arrange a compromise solution which allowed the Egyptians to use the east-west road during part of the day while the Israelis utilized the north-south road during other hours. However, on June 25 the Egyptians stopped an Israeli supply convoy en route to the Negev during the hours reserved for Israeli operations. As a result, the IDF (with the apparent acquiescence of UN headquarters) resumed operations in the area. By June 29, however, the UN Mediator was able to achieve another compromise, with the Egyptians promising to allow the passage of Israeli convoys. There were, nonetheless, many complaints of violations by both sides during the remainder of the truce.

THE BERNADOTTE PLAN

During the truce period, Count Bernadotte anxiously sought a formula for peace in hopes that the truce would become an armistice, and lead eventually to a peace treaty. Early in July he presented a plan which he hoped would be satisfactory to both sides. It proved totally unacceptable to either.

Since the Israelis had conquered most of western Galilee, which had been set aside for the Arabs in the original UN partition plan, and since the Negev was worthless desert, Bernadotte proposed that the original partition plan be modified to award all of Galilee to the Israelis, and most of the Negev to the Arabs. Jerusalem would be under the authority of the United Nations, but the Israelis would be allowed to keep their corridor so that they would have direct access to the internationalized Holy City without having to go through Arab territory, as would have been the case under the UN partition plan. He proposed that all of the Arab portion of Palestine be placed under Transjordan for administration.

On paper this seemed a very logical plan. It meant that both the Israelis and the Arabs would have fairly solid continuous territories instead of the peculiar and unrealistic jumble of enclaves which had been created by the United Nations. The amount of territory would still be about the same for both sides. Although the Arabs would have a little additional area, all of this gain would be useless desert.

To the Arabs, most of whom misinterpreted the results of the first phase of the fighting in May and June, it was unthinkable that they should abandon so much of their territory to the Jews. In fact, since the very concept of an independent Israeli state was unacceptable under any circumstances, it seemed to the Arabs to be adding insult to injury to compensate them for the loss of the farm and pasture lands of Galilee with the inhospitable Negev Desert. The Bernadotte Plan confirmed the Arabs in their resolution to carry the war to a successful conclusion as soon as the four weeks of truce expired on July 8.

To the Israelis, Bernadotte's proposals confirmed their suspicions that he was a tool of the British. They had evaluated the results of the first four weeks of combat much more accurately than had the Arabs. They were now confident that the state of Israel was secure and that the areas that they occupied at the time of the truce could be held against any possible Arab offensive. In fact, they saw no reason why, with weapons and equipment pouring in to Israel from abroad, particularly from the east European states, they could not take the offensive after the expiration of the truce, and establish firm control over the regions which had been awarded them under the UN partition plan, and which were still in dispute. Principal among these regions was the southern Negev.

Ben Gurion, in particular, was convinced it was of the utmost economic significance to the Israeli state that it have an outlet to the Red Sea through the Gulf of Aqaba. Thus he was determined to keep the southern Negev at least within the boundaries set by the UN partition plan. He was also convinced that the Negev had resources that would be important to Israel and might even become valuable agricultural land if water could be diverted from the Jordan, or possibly from the Dead Sea or the nearby open seas through some form of desalinization scheme.

While the Israelis would have preferred more time for military reorganization and buildup, and to await the arrival of more aircraft and heavy weapons, they were fearful that the United Nations might adopt the Bernadotte Plan and attempt to impose it upon them. They decided that they could best thwart the plan by making it unrealistic. Accordingly, they prepared to launch an offensive as soon as the truce expired. Since the Arabs had already decided on a similar course of action, there was no possibility of an extension of the truce.

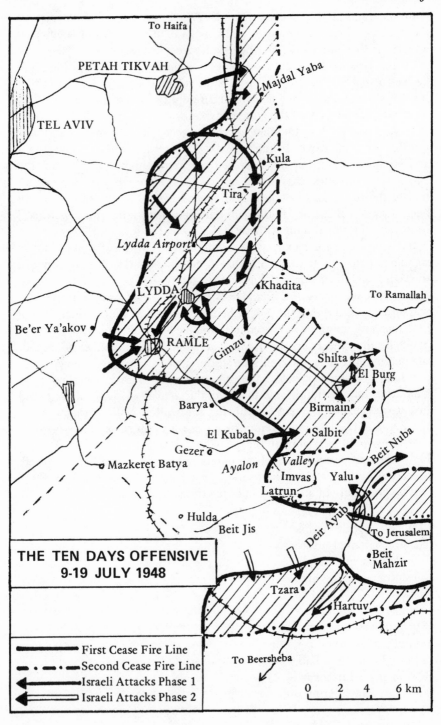

To Haifa

PETAH TIKVAH

Majdal Yaba

TEL AVIV

Kula

Tira

Lydda Airport

Be'er Ya'akov

LYDDA

Khadita

To Ramallah

RAMLE

Gimzu

Shilta

El Burg

Barya

Birmain

El Kubab

Salbit

Gezer

Ayalon   *Valley*

Mazkeret Batya

Imvas   Yalu

Beit Nuba

Latrun

Hulda

Deir Ayub

Beit Jis

To Jerusalem

**THE TEN DAYS OFFENSIVE
9-19 JULY 1948**

Beit
Mahzir

Tzara

Hartuv

First Cease Fire Line
Second Cease Fire Line
Israeli Attacks Phase 1
Israeli Attacks Phase 2

To Beersheba

0   2   4   6 km

8

The Israeli
Ten Days' Offensive

Stimulated by their desire to wreck the Bernadotte Plan, the IDF formulated a new strategy, designed to accomplish their most important objectives as rapidly as possibly. Their first priority was to secure New Jerusalem and their control over the access routes as firmly as possible. Once Jerusalem was protected, their second objective was to open secure access routes to the Negev. Elsewhere they planned to maintain a strategic defensive, but by local tactical offensives they intended to inflict as much damage as possible on Kaukji's ALA, while nibbling away at all Palestinian areas still under Arab control, and preventing the Arabs from expanding any of their current holdings.

How much time they would have to carry out their new strategy neither side knew, but the Israelis were prepared to launch attacks in all areas almost the moment the truce expired. As it turned out, they had ten days before a second truce again brought operations to a halt.

CENTRAL FRONT

When the first truce expired, the Jerusalem Corridor became the main focus of the Israeli Defense Force's activity. The Arab Legion and the ALA held Lydda, Ramle and the Lydda Airport, providing them with a base for potential attacks on Tel Aviv, barely 10 kilometers away. Two Arab Legion infantry battalions, with armor and artillery support, were concentrated in the area north and east of Latrun. Between Latrun and Ramle, the IDF held the villages of El-Baria and El-Kubab, while approximately 2 kilometers east of Latrun was the isolated fortified Jewish village of Ben Shemen. General Glubb had wanted to take Ben Shemen at the time his troops occupied Latrun in mid-May, but local Arab leaders protested that they had always been on good terms with the people of Ben Shemen; furthermore, they feared that such an attack would bring the entire Israeli Army down on them.[1]

[1] Sir John Bagot Glubb, *A Soldier With the Arabs* (New York, 1957), p. 142.

Lydda and Ramle were both held by local and irregular forces, all nominally under Kaukji's ALA. Both of these towns were well fortified, and both had small Legion contingents in support of the guerrillas.

During the truce, the IDF High Command had prepared plans for an operation called "Dani," designed to eliminate Arab pressure on Jerusalem and on the corridor by attacking the Arabs in the Lydda-Ramle-Latrun-Ramallah area generally northwest of Jerusalem. An important secondary objective of seizing this territory would be to eliminate the direct Arab threat to Tel Aviv. A substantial additional benefit would be the occupation of Lydda Airport, the only major airport in all of Palestine, although not then in operation.

During the final weeks of the truce, General Allon devoted himself to plans for the execution of Operation Dani. By July 9, when the truce expired, the plan was ready. The operation was to be conducted in two phases. First the Arab towns of Lydda and Ramle were to be seized, to secure the coastal plain and gain control of Lydda Airport. Next the corridor to Jerusalem was to be widened by the seizure of Latrun and then Ramallah.

Three brigades were assigned the principal roles for the first phase. The Harel Brigade under Colonel Joseph Tabenkin and the Yiftach Brigade under Colonel Shmuel Cohen were hardened and battle-proven. Operating with them was the newly organized 8th Armored Brigade, commanded by Yitzhak Sadeh, with its tank battalion—a number of homemade armored cars and ten French H-35 light tanks, two British Cromwell tanks, and one American Sherman M-4—a jeep and half-track commando battalion, and two infantry battalions, one assigned from the Alexandroni Brigade, and another from the Kiryati Brigade. Support was to be provided by some newly organized artillery units, equipped with 75mm and 65mm guns that had recently arrived from Europe, and also by aircraft of the rapidly growing IDF Air Force.

There were some interesting command relations here. Yigal Allon, as the commander, was giving orders to his old teacher and former commander, Yitzhak Sadeh, who still had the rank of colonel. And in Sadeh's brigade, commanding the jeep and half-track commando, or armored-infantry, battalion was Allon's former associate in the Palmach, Moshe Dayan, still a major.

The plan for the first phase of Operation Dani provided for a thrust by Sadeh's armored brigade from the west, first to seize the airport, and then to drive into the hill country north of Latrun to relieve Ben Shemen. Simultaneously, the Yiftach Brigade—near Gezer in the Jerusalem corridor south of Latrun—would advance northward through the hills northeast of Latrun to meet Sadeh at Ben Shemen. Once these two forces met, Lydda, Ramle, and Latrun would all be isolated, and could then be taken one at a time; Lydda first, Ramle next, and Latrun (the toughest nut of all) last. The Harel Brigade was assigned the responsibility of protecting the Jerusalem road and widening the southern portion of the corridor as well as providing a reserve for the other two brigades.

The Israeli offensive started at nightfall on July 9, with the expiration of the truce. During the night and the following morning, the Yiftach Brigade advanced rapidly north from the corridor, easily seizing three Arab villages in its path. The Israeli Air Force began bombing Lydda and Ramle, and a battalion from the Kiryati Brigade undertook a diversion north of the airport and east of Tel Aviv. By nightfall of July 10, the Yiftach Brigade had reached Ben Shemen, and Sadeh's Brigade had captured Lydda airport. Sadeh's troops had failed, however, in their efforts to capture Deir Tarif against fierce Arab Legion resistance. But Moshe Dayan's 89th Mechanized Assault Battalion had bypassed Deir Tarif and had reached Ben Shemen. Although communications to the west were tenuous, the pincers had closed.

Without pausing to rest or wait for artillery support, Dayan and his troops pressed on to Lydda. The mechanized battalion dashed into the town, breaking through the surprised Arabs in the outer defenses. The Israeli half-tracks and jeeps—plus one captured armored car—drove through the town, shooting at all suspected centers of resistance, then again surprised the confused defenders by turning around and driving back through Lydda again. While the Arabs were trying to reorganize themselves, the Yiftach Brigade arrived, and during the night the Israelis overwhelmed feeble and scattered resistance. This exploit attracted to Dayan the favorable attention of Prime Minister Ben Gurion.

Lydda surrendered to the Yiftach Brigade next morning. However, when an armored patrol from the Arab Legion entered the town a short time later, the Arab irregulars poured out of the houses and attacked the Yiftach units. After desperate hand-to-hand, house-to-house fighting, the city was secured by the Israelis, and most of the Arab residents left during the following night.

The next day—July 12—the Kiryati Brigade closed in on Ramle, which surrendered without a fight. Again a mass evacuation of the Arab population followed the fall of the city.

The first phase of Operation Dani had been completed successfully by the Israelis.

The loss of Lydda and Ramle, while disappointing to the Arab Legion, was not unexpected. General Glubb had not had sufficient troops to put large garrisons in those two towns and had been forced to rely upon the local inhabitants and a motley group of ALA detachments from Syria and Jordan. Calmly the Legion girded itself for another defense of Latrun. By this time there were—in addition to the battalion in Latrun—

two other battalions deployed to the north and east of the embattled town.

The Israeli plan for the second phase of Operation Dani called for one battalion of the Harel Brigade to make a diversionary attack on Radar Hill, overlooking the road west of Jerusalem, during the night of July 14-15. Under cover of that diversion, the Yiftach Brigade and one battalion of Sadeh's armored brigade were to converge on Latrun, the Yiftach Brigade from the west and the armored battalion from the south. (The remainder of Sadeh's brigade was further north, holding the Lydda airport and Ben Shemen.)

At 2:45 on the morning of July 15, the Harel Brigade attacked the ridge to the north and rear of Latrun. Here, however, the opposition was very difficult. The Israelis were unable to make any progress against the two battalions of disciplined Arab Legionnaires holding Latrun, and, after suffering many casualties, they withdrew. Simultaneously the Yiftach Brigade captured the villages of Brafalia and Saldit, but failed in its effort to take the village of Budnef.

For the next two days the fighting was intense, as the Israeli brigades continued their attacks. By dusk on July 17, the two brigades were only three kilometers apart, and during the night both renewed their efforts. However, by this time the Israeli troops were exhausted. Not only were they stopped without gain, but they were forced to yield some of the ground they had taken to spirited Arab Legion counterattacks.

A new truce was imminent, and General Allon decided to try a direct assault on Latrun by part of the Yiftach Brigade, with tank support from the 8th Brigade. But time was limited, and the poorly coordinated attack mounted shortly after midnight failed to accomplish anything. At dawn on July 18 the truce came into effect, and firing ceased.

On balance, Operation Dani was a significant Israeli success. The capture of the airport was a major achievement in itself, and the occupation of the cities of Lydda and Ramle assured almost complete Israeli control of the coastal plain in the vicinity of Tel Aviv.

On the other hand, the Arab Legion was not seriously disappointed by the results of the operation. Glubb had not had enough troops to garrison Lydda and Ramle without dangerously weakening the forces in Latrun, Ramallah and Jerusalem. He had hoped that the local Arab levies, with the assistance of irregular units from Jordan and Syria, could hold the towns.[2] But when they were lost, the Legion concentrated on the defense of Latrun and there it was completely successful.

Although the Israelis failed to take Latrun, the Harel Brigade did widen the Jerusalem Corridor to the south, and this permitted the construction of another road to Jerusalem.

2 Glubb, op. cit., p. 158.

Meanwhile, a series of secondary Israeli offensives was taking place in and around Jerusalem. These Israeli attacks had three principal goals: the capture of the villages of Malha and Ein Kerem, to the south of the Old City; the reestablishment of control over at least part of the Old City of Jerusalem; and the capture of Sheikh Jarrach. The accomplishment of the first of these objectives would strengthen Israeli control of the northern end of the Jerusalem-Tel Aviv road, and thus contribute to the major action (Operation "Dani") taking place to the west. Occupation of the Old City of Jerusalem was an important goal, in the light of the Bernadotte Plan. The achievement of the third objective—seizure of Sheikh Jarrach—would block Arab approaches to the New City of Jerusalem from the east and the north, would link up the principal Israeli positions in New Jerusalem with the outposts on Mt. Scopus, and would outflank the Old City, thus contributing to the achievement of the second objective.

On the night of July 9-10, a Gadna "youth" company (composed of soldiers aged 16 and 17 years) of the Etzioni Brigade moved south to clear the slopes of Mount Herzl, dominating the village of Ein Kerem. At the same time, a Lehi company attacked the ridge overlooking the road connecting the villages of Malha and Ein Kerem. Although the Lehi company completely failed to achieve its objective, and was forced to withdraw with heavy losses, the "youth" company was successful, and captured the villages of Hirbet el-Namame and Bet Masil. Once the Israelis were established on Mount Herzl, the Arabs began to withdraw from Ein Kerem.

On July 11 New Jerusalem suffered its first air attack. Egyptian bombers dropped a number of 100 kg. bombs on the city, but did not cause any significant damage.

On the night of July 13-14 the village of Malha was attacked by an Irgun battalion, which succeeded in gaining part of the town. On the 15th, however, the Arab Legion counterattacked and forced the Irgun troops to withdraw with heavy casualties. That night the Irgun unit was reinforced and was able to retake most of the village.

Before the second truce became effective, the Israeli High Command decided to press operations in the Jerusalem area. However, General Glubb had decided to do the same thing. On July 16 his Arab Legion forces began to shell the northern and northeastern sections of the New City, and probing attacks penetrated several sections of the Jewish defenses. Fighting was particularly severe around the Mandelbaum Building, which the Israelis succeeded in retaining, but a number of the houses near the Damascus Gate were seized by the Legion.

The IDF High Command now activated an additional battalion of the HISH forces in Jerusalem. They were to cooperate with the Irgun battalion in an operation codenamed "Kedem," which was designed to seize all or part of the Old City before the truce.

For several hours, Arab positions in and around the Old City were hit by Israeli artillery fire, but Arab Legion gunners returned the fire effectively. Finally, the Israeli attack was mounted. The new Jerusalem battalion attacked the Zion Gate in the south in coordination with the Irgun attack against the New Gate in the north. The Irgun unit was actually able to penetrate a short way past the New Gate, but was soon halted. The new battalion never succeeded in breaking through the defenses near the Zion Gate. At dawn on July 17, as the truce took effect in Jerusalem (24 hours earlier than elsewhere) both Israeli units withdrew to their former positions.

SOUTHERN FRONT

In the southern sector, two battalions of the Givati Brigade held a ring of settlements north and east of Ashdod, extending from Yavne to Galon. The other two Givati Battalions were in reserve just behind them. The Negev Brigade was assigned to the defense of the Negev settlements and was therefore widely scattered. One battalion guarded settlements south of the Gaza-Beersheba road, while the other was responsible for the security of those north of it. The third battalion, a small commando force, was involved primarily in assuring supply and communications to settlements and units.

The Egyptian forces in this region had been augmented during June and early July, and totalled four brigades when the first truce expired. One of these, with headquarters at Gaza, occupied the coastal strip from the border to Majdal; another—the 2nd Brigade, under Brigadier Mahmoud Fahmy Nemat-allah, with headquarters at Majdal—was responsible for the security of the Ashdod area; a third—the 4th Brigade, now commanded by Brigadier Naguib, with headquarters at Faluja—occupied the axis from Majdal through Beit Gubrin to Hebron; the fourth brigade —consisting mostly of Azziz's Volunteers—held Beersheba and the area north to Hebron and Bethlehem.

Both sides had plans for launching an offensive immediately upon the cessation of the truce during the night of July 9-10. The Egyptians' plan was to widen their east-west corridor; this would make their communications more secure, would effectively cut communications between the two Israeli brigades in the southern region, and would prevent further resupply of the Israeli settlement in the Negev.

The Israeli offensive was given the code name "An-Far" (for anti-Farouk). Colonel Shimon Avidan, commander of the Givati Brigade, was appointed the overall operation commander. The Givati and Negev Brigades, operating in coordination, were to clear a route to the Negev, cut Egyptian supply routes, and drive the Egyptians out of Ashdod. During the first night, July 9-10, Givati forces would distract the attention of the Arabs in the Ashdod-Gubrin area, while Colonel Nahum Sarig's Negev Brigade raided in the vicinity of Kfar Darom. The second night the Negev Brigade was to capture the Iraq Suwaydan police post at the road intersection, while the Givati Brigade continued to keep the Egyptians and their local Arab supporters occupied to the north.

Having observed the Israeli preparations, the Egyptians decided to seek surprise by attacking first. Claiming an Israeli violation of the truce (a claim which may or may not have had some foundation), at 6:00 a.m. on July 8, 36 hours before the end of the truce, the Egyptians launched their own offensive. The first surprise attack, made by Brigadier Naguib's reinforced brigade south of the road, resulted in the capture of the outpost of Kaukaba from the Negev Brigade. The Israelis withdrew to Huleiqat, but were soon forced out by pursuing Egyptian armor. At the same time the Egyptians seized Hill 113, an eminence dominating the Negev road junction, and attacked the village of Beit Daras. Although Beit Daras was able to repel four attacks by Sudanese units, the Egyptians fortified Hill 113, then attacked nearby Kibbutz Negba.

The Israeli response to the Egyptian offensive was to move the timing for Operation An-Far ahead by 24 hours. Just after dark on July 8, Negev and Givati units began to move toward their assigned objectives. Although the Givati Brigade was able to capture the villages of Beit Affa and Ibdis, and temporarily held part of the village of Iraq Suwaydan, the latter village had to be abandoned when the Negev Brigade was repulsed from the nearby police post.

Late on July 9 the Egyptians counterattacked, planning to encircle and then overwhelm the Israeli settlement of Negba. However, they made little progress in the face of stubborn Israeli resistance. After a night and a day of continuous fighting both sides rested during the night of July 10-11 and reorganized on July 11. General Mawawi and Brigadier Naguib disagreed about plans; Naguib refused to carry out Mawawi's plan, and so the general relieved him.

Three Egyptian infantry battalions, an armored battalion and an artillery regiment, with various support weapons and aircraft, took part in a renewed attack which Mawawi ordered against Negba on July 12. At dawn they began an intense artillery and aerial barrage to soften up the settlement, while diversionary attacks were mounted against Ibdis and Julis. But Negba had been reinforced by units from the Negev Brigade, and—as Naguib had predicted—the Egyptian main effort was thrown back with heavy losses. Having suffered more than 200 casualties, the Egyptians gave up the attempt. The Israelis reported 21 casualties.

The Egyptians next turned their attention to the Jewish settlement of Berot Yitzhak, near Gaza. Somewhat belatedly they were clearing up a threat to their line of communication which they had allowed to remain for two months. Berot Yitzhak was garrisoned by approximately 70 armed settlers, reinforced by a Negev Brigade platoon of approximately the same strength.

After preliminary air and artillery barrages, the Egyptians began an infantry assault on three sides of the settlement, and by noon all of these had made some penetration. At that time the Egyptians stopped the assault to reorganize and bring up reinforcements. However, Israeli reinforcements, in the form of the Negev commando battalion and an artillery battery, were also approaching. Although the Egyptian Air Force attacked this column, results were negligible. The Israeli artillery succeeded in taking up positions within range of the Egyptian forces, while the commando battalion reinforced the defenses. By 6:45 p.m. the Egyptians had abandoned their attack, after suffering another 200 casualties. Israeli losses were reported as 33.

The double failures at Negba and Berot Yitzhak, combined with the well-publicized dispute between the two senior officers of the expeditionary force, had a profound effect upon Egyptian morale. Thenceforward the Egyptians were always on the defensive; the Israelis had established a significant moral ascendancy.

Meanwhile, the Givati Brigade—reinforced by a naval amphibious company acting as infantry—had renewed its efforts to break open the road junction and reestablish communications with the Negev. This time, however, the Israelis made their assault further to the east, with the intention of establishing territorial continuity through the capture of the towns of Hatta and Karatya. The operation had the code name "Death to the Invader."

The Negev Brigade at the same time was to recapture several strongholds south of the road junction, while the Harel Brigade—in the Jerusalem Corridor—was to face south and to press the Egyptian forces in that area. In order to secure the vital element of surprise, several diversions were executed. One of the most successful of these, by the Givati Brigade, surprised the Egyptian battalion at Beit Affa, during the night of July 14-15.

The main operation began on the night of July 17-18, just before the second truce went into effect. The Negev Brigade seized an important position just south of Faluja, but the attackers were repulsed from Huleiqat and Kaukaba. The Givati also failed in their efforts to take Beit Affa, whose defenders were well alerted. Particularly heavy losses were suffered by the company of naval infantry attached to the Givati.

In contrast to these failures, however, the Israeli attacks in the east against Hatta and Karatya went quite smoothly. Hatta was captured after a brief but intense battle. Major Dayan's armored-commando battalion, reinforced, moved on to Karatya, which fell before dawn on July

18. Although the Egyptians counterattacked several times, using infantry as well as armor, the Israelis repulsed these assaults until the second truce came into effect at 7:00 p.m. on the evening of July 18. Thus, although their hold was more tenuous than they had hoped for, the Israelis had succeeded in opening a new corridor to the Negev and in blocking the east-west communications between Majdal and Hebron.

NORTHERN FRONT

One objective of Israeli forces in northern Palestine was to destroy Kaukji's ALA or at least severely reduce its effectiveness. Although this was a slight diversion from the major objective on the central front, the Israelis felt that it could be achieved with a relatively small application of force, since Kaukji's was the weakest of all the opposing armies. Simultaneously their main effort was to drive the Syrians from their positions at Mishmar Hayarden in east central Galilee.

The Syrian bridgehead at Mishmar Hayarden was held by one infantry brigade supported by tanks and artillery. A second Syrian brigade was on the heights overlooking the east bank of the Jordan River. The Lebanese Army held a line from Rosh Hanikra, on the coast, to the vicinity of Malkiya. The Israelis rightly suspected that the Lebanese would seek to avoid involvement in any operations to the east or south.

At this time the ALA in northern Palestine consisted of some 2,200 troops, including 600 men in a regular Syrian battalion. These troops were mainly concentrated in the hilly region north of the valleys of Esdraelon and Jezreel. The Iraqis, two brigades with some armored support, were concentrated in the Samarian triangle, Jenin-Tulkarm-Nablus. The Israelis in north-central Palestine included the armed guards of the several settlements, plus the Alexandroni, Golani, Carmeli, 7th, and Oded Brigades. Overall commander was Brigadier General Moshe Carmel.

The first phase of the planned Israeli offensive was code-named Operation "Brosh," and had for its objective the encirclement and destruction of the Syrians in the bridgehead around Mishmar Hayarden. The main effort in the operation was to be carried out by the Carmeli Brigade, now under the command of Colonel Mordechai Makleff. Some units of the Oded Brigade were put under Makleff's command for the operation. While the Oded units conducted a holding attack against the Syrian bridgehead from the west, the main force of the Carmeli Brigade would envelop Mishmar Hayarden from the north. An essential feature of the operation was for two of the Carmeli battalions to ford the Jordan River east of Hulata, in order to encircle the Syrians in Mishmar Hayarden, to cut their lines of communication, and to attack them from the east.

Operation Brosh was launched immediately after nightfall on July 9.

One of the two enveloping battalions was able to get across the Jordan River as planned. The other was delayed by unexpected difficulties, soon compounded by effective Syrian artillery fire from both east and west. Then when word was received of an apparent Syrian threat to Rosh Pina (seven kilometers northeast of Safad), the encirclement was called off, and the units were pulled back to their starting point, giving up several Syrian positions which had been captured. It is hard to understand why the Israelis allowed themselves to be so easily diverted from their objective as a result of a Syrian threat which should have made the Israeli task all the easier. It is not clear whether the responsibility for this failure lay with Brigadier General Carmel, the overall commander, or with Colonel Makleff, the operation commander.

At dawn the Syrians counterattacked, receiving excellent support from their air force. The rocky ground around Mishmar Hayarden had impaired the Israelis' ability to dig in, and they suffered many casualties from Syrian artillery and aircraft. By noon the Syrians had regained all of their earlier possessions west of the river and the Israelis had withdrawn to cover the approaches to Rosh Pina and Machanayim.

Meanwhile, the Syrian brigade on the heights attacked the Israeli units that had established themselves on the east bank of the Jordan River. This attack forced a complete withdrawal of Israeli troops to the west bank.

After three days of reorganization, the Israeli effort to encircle Mishmar Hayarden was repeated, but the Syrians were alert and stopped it before it got fully started. Operation Brosh had failed completely; a stalemate settled around the Syrian bridgehead and Mishmar Hayarden.

At the time of the first truce the northern units of Kaukji's ALA held most of west central Galilee from Nazareth north to the Lebanese border. However, he was hemmed in on the west by the Carmeli Brigade's control of the coastal road from Acre north to Rosh Hanikra, and in the south and east by the Golani Brigade's control of the road through Afula to Tiberias. For reasons that are not clear, Kaukji seems to have planned two simultaneous offensives at the end of the first truce, in divergent directions. With part of his force he planned to attack northward toward Sejera (Ilaniyya) presumably with the objective of retaking Tiberias and perhaps reestablishing a link with the Syrians. In the other direction —to the west—his objective was apparently to capture either Acre or Nahariya, or possibly both, to give himself a base on the seacoast. Since it must have been evident to Kaukji that his forces were inadequate for even one independent offensive, it is probable that his projected move to the west was a diversion, to help him join up with the Syrians to the east.

In any event, Kaukji's strategy of divergent offensives actually played into the hands of the Israelis, one of whose post-truce objectives was to destroy, or vitally damage, the ALA. Lieutenant Colonel Haim Laskov, with three battalions from the 7th Brigade (one of which was armored) and one battalion from the Carmeli Brigade, had the mission of securing control of the coastal road and plain of western Galilee north of Haifa, and then driving south toward Kaukji's base at Nazareth. This operation was code-named "Dekel." In support of Operation Dekel the Golani Brigade—stretched along the Afula Corridor from the coast to eastern Galilee—had the mission of keeping the ALA busy, and distracting it from the main effort to the west. This mission, of course, was facilitated by Kaukji's attack towards Sejera.

On July 9, at the expiration of the truce, Kaukji began his offensive from Nazareth toward Sejera, but he made no progress. The Arab attack was repeated each of the three following days, but failed to make any dent in the Golani Brigade's defenses covering the crossroads in the valley south of Sejera. On the 12th, the defenders of the village were subjected to a sophisticated high-burst artillery concentration carried out by the Syrian artillery attached to the ALA, but this too failed to dislodge the defenders. On the 14th, having arranged for air support from the Syrian Air Force, Kaukji tried once more. This final attack, pushed aggressively with armored cars and air support, also failed. Next day, while the Arabs were reorganizing, Golani units, reinforced from Tiberias, began a limited counteroffensive.

Meanwhile, to the west, the Israeli Operation Dekel had gone according to plan. On the evening of July 9 Laskov's troops, advancing eastward from the vicinity of Acre, had reached the inland road at the base of the foothills. On the 10th and 11th the Israelis pushed north and south and, in cooperation with Druze villagers in the vicinity, established themselves also in the hills to the east.

On July 11 the ALA units east of Acre somewhat belatedly began the offensive—or diversion—toward the coast which Kaukji had ordered in coordination with his drive on Sejera. By this time, however, the Israelis were so well established on the hills that the Arabs were easily driven back.

Laskov held his positions for another day, waiting to see if the Lebanese were going to enter the fight in support of the ALA. When it became evident that there would be no Lebanese activity, Laskov turned his full attention to the southeast, and moved towards Shefar'an on the road from Acre to Nazareth. Shefar'an was taken on the morning of July 14 and Laskov began to prepare for a drive toward Nazareth.

On July 15, as the Golani troops in Sejera were seizing the initiative from the ALA, another Golani unit further south, in the vicinity of Afula, began to probe north toward Kfar Hahoresh, further threatening Kaukji's base at Nazareth. Late that day, Laskov began his drive from Shefar'an toward Nazareth with his armored battalion in the lead.

Threatened from three directions, Kaukji withdrew from the vicinity of Sejera to Nazareth, and tried to block the Israeli thrusts from Shefar'an and Afula. However, by dawn on July 16 Laskov's advance units had reached Zipori, barely six kilometers from Nazareth. Word of this Israeli advance reached the city of Nazareth before noon, and the civilian population began to evacuate the town. By 4:30 p.m. the Israeli infantry had reached the high ground overlooking Nazareth from the northwest and from these positions easily repelled a counterattack by Arab armored cars; most of Kaukji's armored cars were destroyed. The Israeli advance then was renewed, and shortly before 6 p.m. the leading elements of the Israeli units entered Nazareth. At 6:15 the city surrendered, and Operation Dekel had come to a successful conclusion. Kaukji and the remnants of his troops were in flight to the northeast, no longer capable of any effective opposition.

AIR OPERATIONS

The Israeli Air Force was active throughout these ten days of intensive ground combat. The new fighter planes were generally successful in discouraging Arab air attacks against Israeli towns and installations, and became increasingly effective in providing close support to the ground troops. They also moved out on the offensive with a number of militarily insignificant, but symbolically important, attacks against Arab cities, in retaliation for the attacks on Tel Aviv and New Jerusalem. On July 14 three newly purchased World War II Flying Fortresses arrived from Europe to augment the IAF further. En route these planes dropped bombs on Cairo, Rafah, and El Arish. (There was quite a fuss about this in the American newspapers.) Soon after this Damascus was also bombed.

ASSESSMENT

Acceding to the strongly expressed demand of the United Nations, the Israeli 10-day offensive ended at 7:00 p.m. on July 18, and the second truce went into effect.

The first period of combat between May 5 and June 11 had been a standoff; the Israelis had been able to hold most of the areas which had been assigned to them under the UN Partition Plan, but they had been hard pressed, and the situation in Jerusalem had been particularly precarious.

The results of this 10-day campaign, however, were very different. Although not uniformly successful, the Israelis had made impressive gains on most fronts. They had secured the communications between the coastal plain and Jerusalem; they had maintained a tenuous link with the almost isolated settlements in the Negev, and they had conquered northern Galilee while virtually destroying the effectiveness of the Arab Liberation Army. They had failed, however, in repeated efforts to eject the Arab Legion from its coastal plain outpost at Latrun; they had also failed miserably in their efforts to eject the Syrians from northeastern Galilee. In the south they had retained communications with the Negev, and by taking the initiative from the Egyptians after the Battle of Neba they had set the stage for further offensive action.

During these ten days the Israelis lost 838 soldiers killed, an unknown and unreported number of wounded (estimated at perhaps 3,000), and about 300 civilians had also been killed. Arab losses are unknown but were probably at least double those of the Israelis, and most of them had been suffered by Kaukji's ALA.

9

The Second Truce

GROWTH AND REORGANIZATION OF ZAHAL

The second truce—which was ordered rather than called for by the United Nations Security Council—came into effect at 7:00 p.m. on July 18. Unlike the first truce, it was not limited in duration, and both sides were threatened with sanctions under the United Nations charter in the event of violations. Yet the truce was very quickly violated by both sides, and sanctions were never imposed. The truce was, in fact, merely an insecure ceasefire; the combatants remained on the alert in their positions, ready to resume hostilities instantly, and they often did.

There were numerous breaches in the Jerusalem area, each side blaming the other for violations or incitement. But despite many exchanges of small arms, machine gun, mortar, and artillery fire, neither side attempted to seize hostile positions. The most serious action on this part of the front was the Arab Legion's destruction of the Latrun pumping station on the water pipeline to Jerusalem. It is perhaps surprising that this had not been done before, and the Israelis were ready for it. They quickly laid a pipeline along their "Burma Road," and New Jerusalem was soon adequately supplied with water.

Violations were particularly common along the southern front, where vital lines of communications of both sides were threatened. Under the terms of the truce, both sides were again authorized to use the main north-south and east-west intersection near Huleiqat. In mid-July, however, the Egyptians accused the Israelis of attempting to widen their corridor north of the intersection near Karatya. They attacked and seized several Israeli outposts near Karatya and blocked the new Israeli road to the Negev. In response, at the end of July the IDF initiated Operation "Gis" to reopen the Karatya corridor.

The Yiftach Brigade attacked Faluja, and the Givati Brigade attempted to seize Iraq el Manshiyya, to the east. Both attacks failed. Nevertheless, on July 31 a big Israeli convoy was pushed through to the Negev, and for a few weeks things quieted down on the southern front.

On August 18 there was a flare-up just south of Jerusalem, with a skirmish between Israeli units and Col. Azziz's Volunteers. Two nights later Azziz was killed by mistake by an Egyptian sentry. His death was a serious blow to the Arab cause.

At the beginning of the uneasy second truce, full-time IDF forces numbered approximately 59,000. (There had been 49,000 at the beginning of the first truce.) Mobilization of able-bodied men continued under the conscription provisions of Order No. 4 of May 28. Men were called up to service as rapidly as the arrival of equipment and the training process would permit. By mid-October this intensive mobilization effort had produced an Israeli armed force of over 90,000 men, equipped and in uniform.

To handle this large army, organized decentralization had become essential. The plans for four major commands—which had been initiated but never completed during the first truce—were now put into effect. Ben Gurion, apparently satisfied by the manner in which Yigal Allon had handled the main effort in the Ten Days' Offensive, no longer attempted to impose his political desires upon General Yadin. In the north, Colonel Moshe Carmel, who had in fact actually been functioning as a front commander, was confirmed in that position and formally promoted to brigadier general. Brigadier General Dan Even was appointed to command the Central Region. Jerusalem and the corridor were put under the command of Brigadier General Zvi Ayalon. Yigal Allon was shifted down to command the Southern Region, which had now obviously become the principal front.

The reorganization of the Haganah into the modern and efficient framework of Zahal—the Israel Defense Forces—which had been initiated during the first truce, was continued. This involved processing and allocation of manpower, unit organization, and the creation of an effective military supply service. A regular order of military rank, which had up until this time been rather haphazard, was established. Aircraft, guns, ammunition, and all kinds of military equipment and supplies were pouring into Israel, and the training and equipping of the army went on at a furious pace.

CONFUSION AMONG THE ARABS

Confusion and lack of coordination still characterized the Arab efforts. There were recriminations among the Arab nations regarding their lack of concentrated effort during the period of the Israeli Ten Days' Offensive, but no concrete corrective measures were taken. The Syrians were bitterly resentful that they had received no assistance from either the Lebanese or the Iraqis during the fighting around Mishmar Hayarden.

Relations between Amman and Cairo became particularly cool when the Egyptians accused the Legion of having abandoned Lydda and Ramle without serious resistance, and of allowing the Israelis to operate against the over-extended Egyptian line across southern Palestine without even diversionary attacks to the north and east. The Transjordanians' were just as critical of the other Arab contingents, particularly that of Iraq, for their failure to provide diversionary actions during the time that the Israeli main effort was focused against them in the Jerusalem corridor and particularly at Latrun. As a result of this lack of coordination and cooperation, King Abdullah seems to have ordered General Glubb, some time between July 14 and July 18, to cease all offensive operations and merely to hold the areas now occupied.

Abdullah was satisfied with Count Bernadotte's proposals that the truce should be extended into a peace, with the Arab areas of Palestine being placed under the jurisdiction of Transjordan. This arrangement, quite naturally, was not satisfactory to the Egyptians, who did not believe that their military efforts in southern Palestine should merely accrue to the advantage of King Abdullah of Transjordan. As a consequence, on September 25 the Egyptians sponsored the establishment of an independent Palestinian government in Gaza. Abdullah was furious.

THE REVISED BERNADOTTE PLAN

This action of the Egyptians was nominally a response to Count Bernadotte's revised peace plan, which on September 16 he presented in more detail to the United Nations. It was similar to his first plan, but with some minor modifications. Its principal new, non-territorial provision was to establish a "union" of the entire former British Mandate with two component states: Israel and Transjordan, the latter being enlarged to include Arab regions west of the Jordan River. In addition, all Arab refugees would either be allowed to return to their homes or be compensated for the loss of their property.

The territorial provisions of the new plan were as follows: The Negev south of a line from Majdal to Faluja was to go to the Arabs. Lydda and Ramle were also to be returned to the Arabs, and their populations allowed to return. This would give the Arabs access to Lydda airport, which would then become a free airport under the United Nations' supervision. The Israelis were to have all of Galilee; this somewhat controversial provision of Bernadotte's original peace plan had been for all practical purposes confirmed by Israel's successful July offensive in central Galilee. Jerusalem, as before, would be under the control of the United Nations, and Haifa would be a free port within a United Nations' controlled enclave.

THE ASSASSINATION OF BERNADOTTE

From the beginning of his role as United Nations mediator, Bernadotte had been mistrusted by the Arabs, who considered him pro-Israeli. On the other hand, the Israelis were perhaps even more vehement in accusing him of pro-Arab and pro-British sympathies, and he was strongly denounced in the Israeli press. On September 17, the day after his plan had been presented to the United Nations, Bernadotte was assassinated by three men while he was driving to his headquarters in the demilitarized zone of Jerusalem. There is no doubt that the assassins were Israelis and that they were members of the Lehi, Stern Group. After an intensive 24-hour investigation by the Israeli government, Ben Gurion ordered the dissolution of the Irgun[1] and Lehi, and directed that Lehi members be rounded up by Israeli military and police authorities. Over 200 were arrested, including the leader, Nathan Friedmann-Yellin. The murderers, however, were never identified, and those arrested were eventually released without trial. The Arabs accused the Israeli Provisional Government of covering up and protecting the assassins. Until or unless the crime is solved, Israelis cannot prove that this is an unjustified accusation. On the other hand, Israel did accept the UN finding that Israelis were responsible, and paid an indemnity in response to this finding of culpability.

Bernadotte was succeeded in the position of United Nations Mediator by his American deputy, Dr. Ralph Bunche.

INTENSIFICATION OF EGYPTIAN WAR EFFORT

Soon after this the Egyptians agreed, in a conference with United Nations representatives in Cairo in late July, not to interfere with Israeli resupply of their southern settlements. However, in late August or early September the Egyptian Government seems to have taken a firm decision to oppose the efforts of King Abdullah to extend Transjordan's control over Arab Palestine. The Egyptians appear to have decided at least to retain control over southern Palestine, which was to be established as an independent Palestinian republic, under Egyptian domination. This meant that the Egyptian war effort would have to be intensified.

During September and early October the Egyptian forces were substantially increased. The total strength of forces deployed in Palestine rose to about 18,000 men, not only the largest, but the best supplied Arab force in Palestine. It was organized into nine infantry battalions, which in turn were combined in three brigades, all under the control of a division headquarters at Rafah. In addition, and also under the direction of the Rafah headquarters, there was a brigade of three battalions of Volunteers or Moslem Brothers, into which were incorporated a few regular Egyptian units.

By early October the Egyptian expeditionary force was deployed as follows: one brigade group was in the Ashdod-Majdal area, with head-

[1] Official dissolution came in January 1949.

quarters at Majdal; another brigade group was deployed on the Majdal-Beit Gubrin corridor, with headquarters at Faluja; the third brigade group, consisting of only two battalions, and with headquarters at Gaza, was deployed in the Rafah area. To the east a battalion of about 1,000 Egyptians and Volunteers held the area between Beit Gubrin and Bethlehem. A similar battalion was in the Hebron-Beersheba-el Auja corridor. By this time the Egyptian expeditionary force had a total of 106 antitank guns, 48 antiaircraft guns, 90 field guns (mostly 25-pounders), 139 Bren gun carriers, 132 light and medium tanks, and three heavy tanks.

General Mawawi, from his headquarters in Rafah, recognized that this considerable force was in fact totally inadequate to defend the extended area where it was deployed. He knew that he was opposed by Israeli forces which were almost twice as strong in numbers of troops, and that Israeli reinforcements were available further north. He submitted recommendations to Cairo that he should be permitted to consolidate, concentrating his forces primarily in the coastal corridor, and in the Beersheba-el Auja area. This was disapproved in Cairo, however, as it would mean the abandonment of most of southwestern Palestine to the Israelis. Since negotiations for a final armistice were being conducted by the U.N., with indications that the resulting boundaries would be negotiated on the basis of territory held, the Egyptian Government was reluctant to make such a major withdrawal.

For comparable reasons, the Israelis had decided by late August that they would have to undertake an offensive in the southern sector. On August 25 a Southern Command was established, under Brigadier Genreal Allon. His mission was to reestablish undisputed control over the semi-isolated settlements in the Negev, in order to avoid a final settlement along the lines of the Bernadotte Peace Plan. During September he devoted himself to preparation for the offensive. Thus the second cease-fire, which was never formally terminated, was obviously about to end.

10

The Israeli
October Offensives

It was obvious to the Israelis from the manner in which the different Arab forces had responded—or had failed to respond—to their Ten Days' Offensive, that none of the other Arab contingents would support the Egyptians in opposition to their proposed offensive in southern Palestine. Furthermore, with an army that was now probably twice as large numerically as the combined Arab armies in the field, the Israelis knew that they could not only concentrate overwhelming strength against the Egyptians in the south, but could maintain adequate security elsewhere along the scattered fronts. They could, in fact, even mount simultaneous offensives in other areas where Arab forces retained territorial footholds in regions which the Israelis felt they must have. Partly because of respect for the fighting qualities of the Arab Legion, and partly in hopes of reaching a political settlement with Abdullah, no further action was anticipated in the Jerusalem Corridor, except to the south and east where the opponents would be Egyptian.

SOUTHERN FRONT

The IDF General Staff's plan for a major offensive in the south against the Egyptians was codenamed "Yoav." Concentrated under General Allon in the Southern Command were three infantry brigades—the Givati, the Negev, and the Yiftach—plus the Palmach armored-commando battalion of Colonel Sadeh's 8th Armored Brigade. The Oded Brigade also was alerted for movement to the Southern Front. In support of these units were a number of contingents of the newly established Israeli artillery: four batteries of 75mm guns and four of 65mm howitzers, plus several companies of 6-pounder and 7-pounder antitank and infantry guns, as well as a number of heavy mortars. The major objectives of Operation Yoav were to defeat the Egyptian army and to end the isolation of the Negev. The first step would be to cut the Egyptian corridor between Majdal and Beit Gubrin; then operations would begin against the Egyptian LOCs through Beersheba and Gaza.

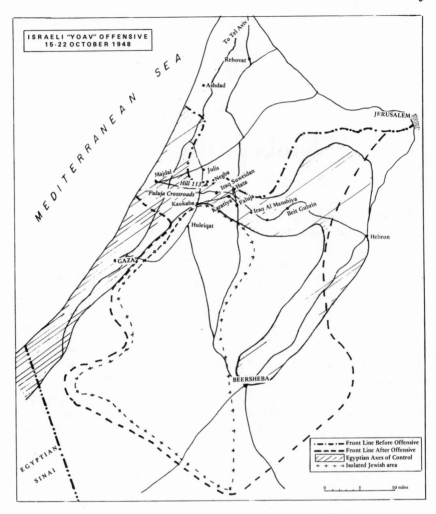

In preparation for this offensive, in September the Israelis occupied a number of small hills along the east-west road east of Faluja. On September 29 they drove Egyptian outposts from vital heights overlooking the main Faluja positions from the east. Despite several counterattacks the Egyptians were unable to dislodge the Israelis.

Then in early October the Israelis began an airlift into the Negev, shifting materiel and men of the Yiftach Brigade into the Negev, and flying out most of the exhausted troops of the Negev Brigade. This brigade was to recuperate and regroup in the north, where it would receive 1,000 replacements to bring it up to standard strength. It would then become the reserve of the Southern Front. One battalion of the Negev Brigade, however, was left in the southern region.

Allon's objective was to cut the two main Egyptian LOCs and their east-west corridor, then to defeat the isolated Egyptian forces in detail, driving them out of Palestine. He planned to begin the offensive by opening a new corridor to the south in the foothills region east of Faluja near Iraq el Manshiyya. This would be done by an armored battalion attacking from the north, while the remaining infantry battalion of the Negev Brigade attacked from the south. In preparation for this assault, the Givati Brigade was to capture a number of strongpoints on both sides of the Majdal-Beit Gubrin road. At the same time the Yiftach Brigade, in the south, was to drive a wedge between Gaza and Majdal and Beit Hanun to isolate Egyptian forces to the north from their bases in Gaza and Rafah.

At noon on October 15, the Israelis sent a convoy along the main road to their Negev settlements, in accordance with the terms which had been agreed upon under the supervision of the United Nations. Since the Egyptians regularly fired at Israeli movement on the convoy route, not unexpectedly it was attacked en route, and forced to withdraw after several vehicles were destroyed. This incident provided the spark for Operation Yoav. It had been intended to do so.

Late in the afternoon of October 15, the Israeli Air Force attacked the Egyptian airfield at El Arish and struck also at the Egyptian bases at Gaza, Majdal and Beit Hanun. The objective of these attacks was to establish complete air supremacy, and to neutralize the Egyptian Air Force in the Palestine area. Although this was accomplished, temporarily, the Egyptian Air Force was not completely knocked out, and after a delay of a few days was again able to operate, although in a limited fashion.

Just after nightfall on the 15th, a commando battalion of the Yiftach Brigade blew up the railroad line between Rafah and El Arish, and mined the road between Rafah and Khan Yunis. The commandos at the same time carried out harassing operations against the Egyptian installations and camps in this rear area. While this was going on, the remainder of the Yiftach Brigade occupied positions east and northeast of Beit Hanun, while the Palmach commando battalion and the Givati Brigade attacked southward to break through the east-west Egyptian corridor and block the road between Iraq el Manshiyya and Beit Gubrin.

Just after dawn, the Palmach battalion mounted a full-scale assault against Iraq el Manshiyya. Under the cover of an artillery and mortar barrage, an infantry battalion with armored support drove into the fortified village. Egyptian resistance was tenacious. Contributing to the determined fighting of the dug-in Egyptian infantrymen was accurate and well-controlled artillery fire, which knocked out several of the Israeli tanks and prevented effective maneuvering and adequate reinforcement of the assault elements. By mid-morning the Israeli infantry had been driven out and the Egyptians had reestablished their position. Israeli losses were heavy, and evacuation of the wounded went on until evening.

It was now obvious to General Allon that his plan to open a new route in the Iraq el Manshiyya area could be accomplished only at the price of heavy losses. He decided, therefore, that the best place to break through to the Negev would be near the main road intersection near Huleiqat. Although heavily defended, the flat terrain denied the Egyptians the commanding observation which had made their artillery so devastating in the foothills to the east. Once a breakthrough was made in this area, the Egyptians would be unable to plug the gap.

The Egyptian defenses around the road junction were based on three fortified areas, occupied by a reinforced battalion. To the north were two hills (designated 100 and 113 from their map elevations),[1] occupied by a company. To the west, at the junction itself a company was entrenched in two mutually supporting positions. To the south another company held the strongly fortified hilltop villages of Huleiqat and Kaukaba. Farther east, and also on high ground dominating the road junction, another company was based on the fortified police post at Iraq Suwaydan. General Allon decided to focus his efforts against the northern and western positions first, while the Yiftach Brigade made a holding attack against Huleiqat and Kaukaba. A battalion of the Givati Brigade was to make a frontal attack on the two hills north of the junction, while simultaneously enveloping strongpoints near the road junction.

The attack began shortly before midnight on October 17. In less than an hour, both Hills 100 and 113 had been overrun. Egyptian resistance was more determined and protracted at the two strongpoints near the road junction, but by dawn both of them also were in Israeli hands. The Yiftach Brigade now intensified its operations against Huleiqat but by dawn it was forced to withdraw. Thus Huleiqat remained the only position blocking the establishment of a corridor from the central coastal plain to the Negev.

Meanwhile to the west the main body of the Yiftach Brigade had been successful in cutting the main north-south coastal road near Beit Hanun. With their line of communications thus cut, and under the threat of complete encirclement, the Egyptians began to evacuate the Ashdod-Majdal area. It was a difficult and costly withdrawal, under constant fire from Israeli troops on high ground dominating the road from the east. To minimize their losses from this fire, the Egyptians hastily established an alternate route farther west along the sandy beaches and were able

---

[1] A common military designation of unnamed hill features is by the altitude, in feet or meters (in this case meters), as shown in standard military maps.

to get most of their brigade out of the Ashdod-Majdal area without further serious losses.

This withdrawal of the main Egyptian force from Majdal, combined with the Israeli breakthrough at the Huleiqat crossroads, left an Egyptian force of about 4,000 men, including about 1,000 in Iraq el Manshiyya, approximately a brigade, exposed and partially isolated in the vicinity of Faluja. So long, however, as the fortified post at Iraq Suwaydan remained in Egyptian hands, this "Faluja pocket" could not be completely encircled and isolated except with a far larger force than was available to General Allon. In command of this isolated contingent was able Colonel Sayid Taha, a Sudanese.

Since by this time it was obvious that the Israelis did not have to fear the intervention of the other Arab armies in the north, they decided to transfer the Oded Brigade to the southern front. This unit arrived on October 18, and was immediately committed by Allon to the vicinity of Karatya, to attempt to make a breakthrough by advancing southeastward through the hills to bypass the formidable Egyptian defenses at Iraq el Manshiyya, and to isolate further the garrison of Faluja. The operation was hastily planned, however, and the Oded units, despite the availability of guides and liaison officers from the Givati Brigade, were unfamiliar with the terrain. The Egyptian positions in the vicinity of Karatya held, and the Oded attack was driven back.

As a result of the renewed outbreak of full-scale war in Palestine, on October 19 the United Nations Security Council passed a resolution for still another ceasefire in Palestine. Fearing that this would soon force him to halt his offensive operation, Allon decided to make one more effort to force open the Huleiqat barrier. He decided to use the Givati Brigade despite its exhaustion and losses in the earlier fighting. He seems not to have had much confidence in the newly arrived Oded Brigade.

The Egyptian force in Huleiqat was approximately a battalion in strength, consisting of one Egyptian and one Saudi Arabian infantry company with a heavy weapons company in support. These units held six mutually supporting strongpoints in and around Huleiqat.

One reinforced Givati battalion initiated the assault of October 19-20, supported by all of the artillery and heavy mortars that Allon could assemble. The attack was successful, despite the fierceness of Egyptian resistance, and by midmorning on October 20 the Huleiqat position had been overwhelmed.

Simultaneous attacks by other Givati and Yiftach units against the Iraq Suwaydan fortress, however, were repulsed. A renewed assault the following night, October 20-21, was also repelled. Israeli losses were heavy in both of these unsuccessful attacks. Nevertheless, despite this failure at the police post, the Israelis had succeeded in opening a secure corridor to the Negev. Although some harassment by long-range fire from the Iraq Suwaydan post could be expected, no other real Egyptian interference was now possible.

Anticipating the capture of Huleiqat, the IDF High Command was prepared to exploit this success by seizure of the town of Beersheba. Once this place was under Israeli control, the Egyptians remaining in the Hebron Mountains and in the area south of Jerusalem would be cut off from Egypt. The isolation of the Faluja pocket—which had retained tenuous and sporadic communications with Beersheba—would be complete. To carry out this plan Allon had organized a special task force consisting of most of the 8th Brigade, plus the infantry and commando battalions of the Negev Brigade, brought south from reserve. The advance on Beersheba began shortly after dark on the night of October 20.

Beersheba was garrisoned by a force of about 500 Egyptians. The town was surrounded by an antitank ditch, with barbed wire fences southeast and northwest. On October 19 and 20, air raids on Beersheba had been mounted to soften up the defenses.

Shortly before dawn on October 21, the Israeli main body approached the town from the west. At the same time, a diversionary attack was mounted from the north. The Egyptian garrison, taken completely by surprise, fought stubbornly, but after being split into small groups surrendered at 9:15 in the morning.

As a result of the operations between October 17 and 21, the Egyptian field forces were now divided into four almost completely isolated forces. The line of communication of the brigades withdrawing from Ashdod and Majdal was still tenuously open, secured by an Egyptian strongpoint tenaciously holding the position at Beit Hanun. Less than a brigade was with the division headquarters in the Rafah-Gaza area. A brigade was isolated in and around Faluja. Approximately two battalions, mostly Azziz's Volunteers, were isolated in the Hebron-Jerusalem area.

Alarmed by this development, in late October General Glubb sent a combined arms force—about a battalion in strength—down to Hebron, with the apparent intention of driving westward to relieve the Egyptians in the Faluja pocket. This proposed operation was code-named "Damascus." When the Israeli strength in the area became evident, however, Damascus was called off. Furthermore, Abdullah in the meantime had made it clear to Glubb that he had no desire to help the Egyptians.

To the west, on October 22 the Israelis endeavored to complete the isolation of the forces withdrawing from Ashdod and Majdal. They took the village of Beit Hanun, cutting the railway and extending their hold on the road. However, they were unable to dislodge the defenders from the high ground between the road and the coast, and the Egyptians were still able to use their makeshift road along the beach to maintain communication between Majdal and Gaza. This was obviously an untenable situation, and on October 27 the Egyptians evacuated Ashdod, pulling their troops back as rapidly as possible along the threatened beach road. On November 5, Majdal also was abandoned, giving the Israelis full control of the coast as far south as Beit Hanun. This withdrawal also relieved the besieged Israeli settlements of Yad Mordechai and Nitzanin.

As a result of these disasters General Mawawi was relieved of command of the Egyptian Expeditionary Force and was replaced by Major General Ahmad Fuad Sadek. On November 19 Sadek placed Brigadier Naguib in command of the 10th Infantry Brigade Group, and a few days later placed the 4th Infantry Brigade also under his command. But the task facing Sadek and Naguib was not an easy one.

THE CENTRAL FRONT

While these operations in the Negev were in progress, an Israeli task force made up of units primarily from the Harel Brigade, with one Givati battalion attached, advanced eastward and southward in two columns from Hartuv in the Jerusalem Corridor, in a clearing operation called "Hahar." Its objective was to widen the Jerusalem Corridor, to complete the isolation of the Egyptians in Bethlehem to the east, and then to move southeast on Hebron.

The two columns joined at Beit Gubrin and turned eastward toward the Jerusalem-Hebron road. Seven kilometers east of Beit Gubrin the Israelis encountered the Arab Legion column which General Glubb had sent southward to the Hebron area. A short battle took place, in which the Arab Legion held its ground. The Israelis withdrew to Beit Gubrin, and the Transjordanians made no further move against them.

Despite this isolated setback, the Israelis managed to occupy most of the southern and southwestern Judean hills and substantially widen their area of control south of the Tel Aviv-Jerusalem corridor. This permitted them to improve their alternate route from Tel Aviv to Jerusalem, officially called "The Road of Valor." This road, which ran from the coast to Jerusalem south of the Burma Road, was officially opened in December 1948.

Late in October or early November, General Allon recommended to the IDF High Command that he be authorized to move eastward to occupy Hebron and the surrounding mountains and to reach Jerusalem from the south. However, this recommendation was disapproved, essentially for political reasons. The recent encounter with the Arab Legion near Beit Gubrin had once more demonstrated the substantial superiority of the Transjordanian Army over the other Arab forces. The Israelis did not fear the Legion, but it was clear that Allon's recommendation could be accomplished only at severe cost in casualties. Politically, furthermore, it seemed likely that if the Transjordanians were left alone they would be willing to live with the status quo in and around Jerusalem and in central Palestine. Ben Gurion hoped that this might even lead to some sort of negotiations with King Abdullah to bring about Arab recognition of the state of Israel and a permanent peace.

In November, Colonel Moshe Dayan, now in command of the Etzioni Brigade in New Jerusalem, had several truce discussions with Colonel Abdullah El-Tel, commanding the Arab Legion forces in and around old Jerusalem. As a result of these talks, on November 30 the two commanders agreed to a "sincere" cease fire, which went into effect on December 1st. A major provision of this agreement was to allow the Israelis to send regular supply convoys to their two isolated positions on Mt. Scopus.

That same day, December 1, King Abdullah was proclaimed king of Arab Palestine and on December 13 the Transjordanian Parliament approved a union of the two states, with the combined territories to be known as the Hashemite Kingdom of Jordan.

NORTHERN FRONT

After his disastrous defeat at Nazareth in July, Fawz el Kaukji had regrouped his shattered forces in Lebanon, and in the small strip of Palestine occupied by Lebanese forces. The strength of his revived army was about 3,100 men, with ten artillery pieces and about ten armored cars.

When the Israelis began their major offensive in the south against the Egyptians, and particularly after the Oded Brigade was moved south from Galilee, Kaukji was apparently the only Arab leader in northern Palestine who recognized—or at least who was willing to do something about—the opportunity which this Israeli offensive seemed to give to the other Arab forces. However, his freedom of action was limited because, since he was operating in an area administered by Lebanon, his plans had to be approved by the Lebanese regional commander, Colonel Shukeir.

On October 22, with Lebanese approval, Kaukji began a new offensive —really a raid—south into Galilee. His first objective was the settlement of Manara in the Huleh Valley, just east of the frontier.

In order to capture Manara, it was first necessary to capture the nearby strongpoint of Sheikh Abed, which dominated the settlement. This was quickly accomplished, and the surprised Israelis were driven out back to Manara. Kaukji then moved down into the valley and blocked the road between Manara and Malkiya. A small force of Israeli armored cars attempted to drive the Arabs back, but was easily repulsed. The strong defenses of Manara discouraged the Arabs, but the town was completely isolated.

Kaukji's tiny army consisted of four "brigades," each really the equivalent of about a battalion. The brigade under his personal direction had just isolated Manara. The 2nd Yarmuk Brigade was located a few miles west in the vicinity of Sasa and Gish. The 3rd Yarmuk Brigade was in the vicinity of Tarshia. The 1st Yarmuk Brigade was isolated from the others, and was operating in the hills south of the Acre-Safad road.

The Israeli High Command, which had hoped that the defeat in July had so discouraged the Arabs as to eliminate the effectiveness of the ALA, now decided to finish the job which apparently had been only half done at the time. The IDF High Command accordingly prepared plans for Operation "Hiram," which had three objectives: to knock Lebanon out of the war, to destroy the ALA, and to conquer all of upper Galilee to stabilize a defensive line across the border. Speed was of the essence in this operation, since it would be necessary to destroy the ALA before the Lebanese and Syrians could come to its assistance. Brigadier General Moshe Carmel, Chief of the Northern Command, was responsible for carrying out the operation.

Operation Hiram was to be executed in two phases. In the first place, the 7th Brigade and the Oded Brigade (brought back north from the southern front) were to encircle and isolate the separated Arab forces in the north. The 7th Brigade would advance from Safad to Sasa from the east, while to the west the Oded Brigade would carry out a diversion, moving from Nahariya through Tarshia toward Sasa, where a road junction controlled the entire road system of Upper Galilee. To the south the Golani Brigade would carry out a number of holding attacks, while guarding against possible Iraqi interference from the south or from east of the Jordan. Similarly, in the northeast, the Carmeli Brigade was to keep the Syrians off balance. Supporting these four brigades were four artillery batteries, two of 75mm guns, two of 65mm howitzers.

Once the two columns had met at Sasa, the second phase of the operation would begin. The Arabs, trapped in the pockets created in this pincer movement, could be eliminated one at a time. General Carmel then planned a general advance northward to the Huleh Valley, clearing the countryside as he advanced. The Israeli Air Force was to be available to support this attack and to deal with any interference by the Syrian Air Force.

Operation Hiram was launched at dusk on October 28. During the afternoon the Israeli Air Force had carried out heavy bombing raids on several objectives in the Arab-held territories. The Golanis' diversionary attacks in the south and southwest had attracted the Arab attention, but

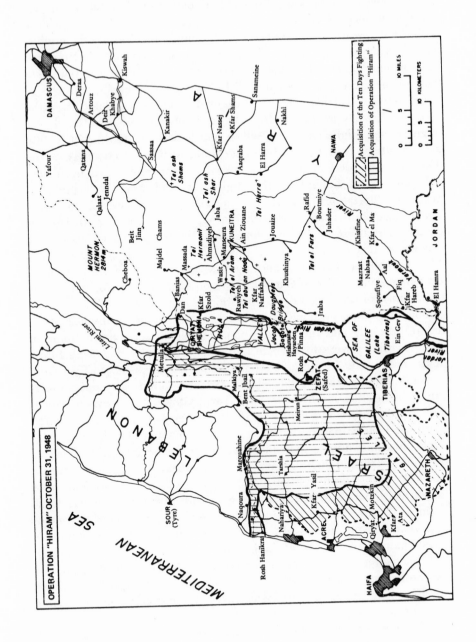

had failed to contain the Arabs adequately. As the Oded Brigade advanced from the west, Kaukji was able to withdraw his southern brigade northward over the Acre-Safad road. The Oded column advancing from Kabiri to Tarshia failed in its first effort to storm the defenses of that village. This brigade, which had yet to gain any major success, had just recently been rushed rapidly northward from the Negev, and had again been given a difficult task with insufficient time to study the terrain and make adequate plans. The result was still another failure by the Oded Brigade. Despite an intensive air bombardment of Tarshia, the column withdrew to Kabiri.

Meanwhile, a Druze company attached to the Oded Brigade had been given the task of occupying the village of Yanuh, south of Tarshia, which was occupied by pro-Arab Druzes. At first the residents of Yanuh welcomed the combined Israeli-Druze force, but news of the defeat at Tarshia, combined with reports that the ALA was marching southward toward their village, led the villagers to turn against the Israelis and the Israeli-Druze detachment. There was a local Druze and Arab militia force, and its members were secretly assembled. A surprise attack drove the Israelis and their Druze unit out of the village.

Meanwhile to the east General Carmel, accompanying the 7th Brigade column, advanced northward on the road from Safad to Meirun. The road was blocked by many obstacles and minefields, and the 7th Brigade did not reach Meirun until dawn. An assault on the Meirun defenses, however, was quickly successful, and the village was in Israeli hands by 8:00 a.m. Continuing north the column overwhelmed the ALA defenders of Safsaf, which fell shortly after noon. After a brief rest, during which he regrouped and reorganized his troops, Carmel continued his advance northward to the important road junction of Gish.

By this time, Kaukji recognized that his forces were about to be split by the 7th Brigade's advance, and he appealed for help to the Syrians to the east. In response a Syrian battalion moved to his support. But it was ambushed by the Carmelis and thrown back after losing more than 200 dead. Gish was then easily occupied. General Carmel then turned west and advanced toward Sasa. The village was on high ground overlooking the crossroads and was very well fortified.

After dark on October 29 the Israelis opened a heavy artillery barrage on the village, and under cover of this fire the 7th Brigade assaulted up the hill. The Arabs, not expecting such an attack to be mounted so quickly, were surprised. By midnight the village and the crossroads were in the hands of the Israelis. Kaukji and his brigade fled northward. As soon as the word of the fall of Gish had reached Tarshia, that village also was evacuated. On October 30, following a really unnecessary air bombardment, the Oded Brigade advanced again from Kabiri and took Tarshia without opposition.

The Oded column then continued eastward to join General Carmel, encountering a large convoy of withdrawing Arabs in the vicinity of Hurfeish. Although the Israelis captured or destroyed a number of vehicles, the Arabs were able to retreat northward across the Lebanese border with some of their supplies. But most of the heavy equipment was abandoned. Having achieved its first significant success of the war, the Oded Brigade reached Sasa and joined Carmel's force, thus ending the first phase of Operation Hiram.

Carmel next turned his attention to clearing the Huleh Valley. He decided that he would do this with the 7th Brigade, sending the Oded column back westward to clear the region between Nahariya and Sasa, and to gain control of all of the countryside south of the Lebanese frontier west of Sasa.

Carmel himself, with his 7th Brigade column, moved northeastward from Sasa, capturing first the village of Saliha and then Malkiya, which had been the scene of some of the earliest fighting of the war. Simultaneously, the Carmeli Brigade advanced northward from Safad through Rosh Pina toward the Syrian bridgehead at Mishmar Hayarden. With the 7th Brigade approaching from the west, and the Carmeli Brigade from the south, the Syrians pulled back from their outposts, but continued to hold their position in Mishmar Hayarden itself. This strongly-fortified position was closely contained by the Israelis but not attacked.

Carmel then advanced northward up the Huleh Valley with the 7th Brigade. Arab resistance faded. The positions around Manara fell without a struggle, and the Israelis crossed the Lebanese border to occupy a strip of that country from the Litani River south to Malkiya.

Thus at about dawn on the 31st, Operation Hiram drew to a close. The ALA had been totally defeated and its remnants either captured or driven out of Galilee. At the same time, the Lebanese had lost their few small footholds in Galilee, while the Syrians retained only their tiny bridgehead just west of the Jordan at Mishmar Hayarden. Both sides accepted a local ceasefire that day. For all practical purposes the war in the north was ended.

11

The Negev and Sinai

OPERATIONS IN THE EASTERN NEGEV

During the October offensive, the Israelis had begun to occupy the eastern Negev between Beersheba and the Dead Sea. At the outset of the war they had evacuated the settlement of Beit Haarava at the northern end of the Dead Sea, transferring the inhabitants to Sodom by water. Sodom, in the Amazyahu Valley just south of the Dead Sea, is 1,200 feet below sea level. The town was blockaded by the Arab Legion early in the war and had to be supplied by air. However, there were no Arab attacks on the settlement, and morale there remained high.

To the west of Sodom, the southern range of the Judean hills is extremely rugged and totally barren, inhibiting the establishment of an overland line of communications. However, the IDF High Command decided in October that a link with Sodom should be established. On November 23rd an Israeli column from Beersheba reached the garrison at Sodom after a difficult journey, most of it across roadless desert mountains, by way of Cornov and Bin Hucov. From Sodom, the column then advanced northward along the western shore of the Dead Sea, occupying Masada.[1]

OPERATIONS SOUTH OF BEERSHEBA

The military disasters in October had forced the new Egyptian commander, General Sadek, to shorten his lines and to consolidate, as General Mawawi had originally recommended. The troops that had been in Ashdod and Majdal were regrouped in the Gaza-Rafah area and some of them sent to El Auja to block a possible Israeli advance toward the Sinai from Beersheba. The Egyptian High Command had also decided to evacuate Faluja, if the force there could break its way out.

There was a reinforced brigade in the Faluja-Iraq el Manshiyya area, which had been isolated by the Israeli capture of Beersheba on October 21. This force, commanded by Sudanese Colonel Sayid Taha, was able

[1] Scene of heroic last stand of the Jews in their uprising against the Romans, 70-72 A.D.

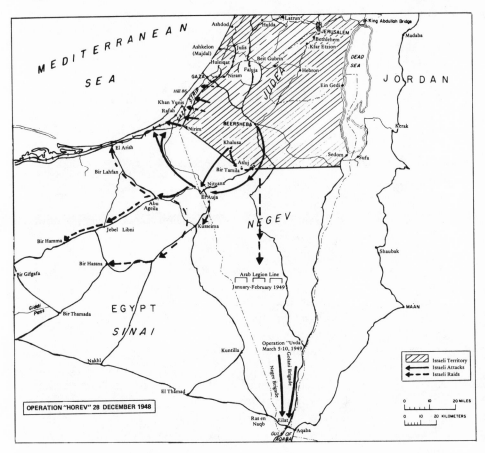

to maintain tenuous communications across the desert with Asluj. Ammunition was plentiful, but other supplies were short. Most of the brigade was concentrated at Faluja, with one battalion at Iraq el Manshiyya. The Israeli Air Force harassed the isolated Egyptians daily.

On November 9, just before Sadek took command of the Egyptian forces, the Israeli 8th Brigade attacked and finally captured the fortified police post at Iraq Suwaydan in an assault marked by massive employment of fire power. This completed the encirclement of the troops in the Faluja Pocket. Through the United Nations, the Egyptians sought to obtain permission to send supplies to the beleaguered unit in Faluja, but the Israelis refused to allow any convoys to pass through. Unable to get sufficient supplies into the Faluja pocket to give the garrison there a reasonable chance for a successful breakout, the Egyptian High Command decided to undertake a relief operation.

On November 10, while these military decisions were being made, there was an Arab League conference in Cairo. After considerable argument and disagreement, the conferees settled down to a serious discussion of the problem of Palestine. However, nothing came of the discussions except for conclusions which merely indicated Arab recognition of the obvious. The conferees agreed that they had not had adequate forces to prosecute the war; that they had failed to exploit early success when they had the opportunity; that they had been severely penalized by their failure to establish a truly unified command; and that they had failed to make adequate use of the truce periods. They promised each other that they would provide their forces with more and better equipment, mobilize their resources, and give higher priority to military considerations. Implicit in this was a decision to renew the war when they had corrected the deficiencies which caused their defeats and failures. Meanwhile they agreed to cooperate and coordinate policy.

The value of these conclusions and agreements was soon demonstrated when the Jordanians and Syrians agreed to their ceasefires with the Israelis. Lebanon had already virtually withdrawn. Only the Egyptians continued to prosecute the war vigorously. The United Nations directed Egypt and Israel to enter into armistice negotiations, but Egypt ignored this.

Meanwhile, shortly after the capture of Iraq Suwaydan, on November 9 Allon was able to persuade Colonel Taha to confer at Gat, under a flag of truce. But he was not persuasive enough to get the Sudanese officer to surrender. Allon argued that the Egyptian Army had lost everything but its honor, and that surrender after a gallant defense was equally honorable. Mindful of the defeats and disasters that the Egyptians had been suffering in past weeks, Taha gallantly responded that as long as they had ammunition, he and his men would not surrender. After this Allon assigned the Alexandroni Brigade to blockade the isolated Egyptians.

On November 19 an Egyptian column began to move northeastward from the Khan Yunis-Gaza area, apparently intending to relieve Faluja from the south. However, they advanced only a few kilometers from their base area. By November 21 they had occupied the hills of Tel Jamma and Tel Fara, which dominated several Israeli villages and outposts in the southwestern Negev, and there they stopped. On December 7 a small Egyptian force from Rafah shelled Nirim, but did not push home an attack. The next day, units from the Negev and Yiftach Brigades counterattacked to the westward, driving the Egyptians back to their starting point.

Although this Egyptian effort had been almost casual, and its threat insignificant, so long as the main body of the Egyptian army remained concentrated and undefeated in the Gaza-Khan Yunis area, the Israelis recognized that the southern front could not be considered secure. Accordingly, the IDF High Command developed a plan for clearing and securing the Negev, and eliminating the Egyptian threat to that region. General Allon, commander of the Southern Command, was given responsibility for the operation, for which he had available the Golani Brigade, the Negev Brigade (now partially armored), the Harel Brigade, and a battalion of the Alexandroni Brigade, approximately 15,000 men of whom more than half were Palmach troops. This operation, although called "Ayin" by the IDF headquarters, was given the local name of "Horev" by the Southern Command headquarters. (Horev is the Hebrew name for Mt. Sinai.)

THE SINAI CAMPAIGN

The Egyptian forces in Palestine were deployed in a roughly horseshoe-shaped arc. The left point of the arc was north of Gaza; it swung southwest and then south through Rafah to El Auja and then northeast along the road from El Auja to just north of Asluj. In the Gaza area were four infantry battalions and a motorized battalion. At Deir el Balah there was an infantry battalion plus two motorized companies. Khan Yunis was held by two infantry battalions and a motorized battalion. There were four infantry battalions at Rafah and south into the desert to El Auja. The Asluj area was held by two infantry battalions. Detachments from Rafah held the important road junction at Abu Ageila, while another battalion garrisoned El Arish. In addition to the isolated brigade in the Faluja pocket, the remnants of the two ALA Volunteer battalions were also cut off in the Hebron-Bethlehem area.

The Egyptians had learned that one of the Israelis' great advantages was their facility in making night attacks. The Egyptian commanders were all ordered, therefore, to pay special attention to keeping their troops alert at night.

General Allon's plan was to use the bulk of his available force to strike southward from Beersheba against the inland point of the Egyptian defensive line above Asluj. While this offensive was being undertaken by his main body, the Golani Brigade to the west would make a holding attack against the coastal strip, to pin down as many Egyptians as possible in the Gaza-Khan Yunis-Rafah area.

In the first phase of the operation Allon intended to capture Asluj and drive the Arabs back over the border at El Auja. Once this was accomplished he planned to initiate the second phase of the operation by swinging northwestward and threatening Egyptian communications with the base at El Arish. He hoped that this threatened envelopment would force a complete evacuation of the coastal strip by the Egyptians.

On December 22 Israel informed the United Nations that, since Egypt refused to comply with the UN demand to open negotiations, Israel felt free to initiate an offensive against Egyptian forces in Palestine. A few hours later Operation "Ayin-Horev" was initiated with Israeli air attacks on Egyptian airfields near Gaza and El Arish. Most of the Egyptian planes were destroyed on the ground, thus assuring Israeli air superiority for the rest of the war. The Israeli planes then struck troop concentrations in the vicinity of Gaza, Khan Yunis, and Rafah. Shortly after dark the Golani Brigade (which had replaced Yiftach in late November) advanced on a broad front against the coastal strip.

By dawn the Israelis had succeeded in occupying a series of small hills some eight miles south of Gaza. Brigadier Naguib reacted quickly to this apparent renewed Israeli effort to cut the Gaza-Rafah road, and sent an armored force to counterattack. The Israelis were forced to withdraw from some of the positions they had captured, but managed to hold on to several. The Golani troops, however, had accomplished their principal objective by attracting the attention of the Egyptians to the coastal area. During this fighting Naguib was severely wounded.

On December 23, General Allon and his main body advanced against the Arab positions south of Beersheba. However, the Egyptians had anticipated such an advance, and had set up a series of strong, fortified road blocks on the road north of Asluj. They were confident that the terrain would not permit any extensive Israeli maneuvers off the road.

However, General Allon and his staff had closely studied Haganah photo maps which showed the remains of an ancient Roman road running almost in a straight line from Beersheba to El Auja.[2] Allon sent staff officers to check this route, and they found it promising. A few hours of work by Israeli engineers and the road was traversable by wheeled vehicles and light armored cars. An unexpected rainstorm and flood on the 24th undid some of this work, and the advance—planned for the 24th —had to be postponed for one day. On the 25th, however, the Israeli main body pushed down the road to the vicinity of El Auja without meeting any serious opposition. A smaller column had branched off west of Asluj. Bypassing that fortified village, it reached the main road and turned southwest toward El Auja. A third column, going completely across country east and then south from Beersheba, also bypassed Asluj,

[2] General Yadin, a renowned archaeologist as well as Deputy Chief of Staff, had also noted this, and may have brought it to Allon's attention. This was no new discovery, as some historians have assumed. The old road had been used on several occasions by units of the Negev Brigade and is easily identified on the ground, as the author of this book has discovered.

and joined the other two columns outside El Auja late on the 25th. Before dark, the main column had continued past El Auja to block the El Auja-Rafah road, capturing two Egyptian strongpoints on the road by surprise attack from the rear.

During the night of December 25-26, the Israelis deployed around El Auja, completely encircling the position. At dawn on December 26 an attack was launched, immediately encountering fierce resistance. Pulling back, the Israelis tried to soften up the position with mortar and artillery fire, but the result was the same on the next attack. During the day the Israelis contented themselves with a close investment of the position, hammering at the defenders continuously with artillery and mortar fire. An effort by a column of Egyptian armored cars and infantry, pushing down the Rafah road to relieve the garrison, was repulsed. A new Israeli attack was planned for the morning of the 27th.

On radio orders from Rafah, however, the El Auja garrison withdrew quietly during the night of December 26-27, infiltrating through the Israeli lines southeast into the desert. Early the next morning, the Israelis moved in and took possession of the deserted post and its important road junction.

During the battle for El Auja, a fourth Israeli column advanced south down the Roman road, turned off below Asluj, and assaulted that position from the south on the 26th. Here the fight, although intense, was briefer. Early on the 27th the Egyptians surrendered.

During all this intensive activity in the inland desert, the Golani Brigade was maintaining constant pressure against the Egyptian positions along the coastal strip. By December 27, Gaza, Khan Yunis, and Rafah were all cut off from each other.

That night, further north, the Alexandroni Brigade launched a surprise attack against the eastern portion of the Faluja Pocket at Iraq el Manshiyya. The Egyptians fought stubbornly. Early on the 28th Colonel Taha sent reinforcements from Faluja. When this movement was spotted by Israeli aircraft, the Alexandroni attack was called off.

Once El Auja was secured, General Allon's force pushed into the Sinai in two columns. One of these went north along the road to the coast, where it joined the Golani and local Israeli forces near Rafah. The other column, under Allon's personal leadership, advanced westward 50 kilometers from El Auja into the desert on the road to Abu Ageila. Despite delays and casualties caused by a mistaken attack by Israeli fighter planes, the Israelis surprised and quickly overwhelmed the outpost garrison during the night of December 28-29. Allon sent small raiding units against the Egyptian outposts at Kusseima, Bir al Hamma, and Bir Hassna, but with his main column he turned northwestward and raced to El Arish.

After a brief skirmish with an Egyptian outpost at the road junction at Bir Lahfan, the Israelis pushed on to the airfield, between Bir Lahfan and El Arish, about fifteen kilometers from the coast. Several Egyptian aircraft were taken by surprise. Continuing on, before nightfall they had reached the outskirts of El Arish and were in sight of the sea. However, the Egyptian defenders of El Arish were prepared, and the exhausted Israelis, after a few probes of the defenses, recognized that this was too difficult a position to seize quickly.

12

Ceasefire and Armistice

STORMY FINALES

Meanwhile, at the United Nations the Israeli thrust into the Sinai—Egyptian territory—had aroused great excitement. The Security Council ordered a ceasefire on December 29. Political pressure was placed upon the government of Israel to withdraw its troops from the Sinai. On December 30 Britain announced that under the provisions of the Anglo-Egyptian treaty it would be forced to help Egypt unless Israel immediately complied with the UN ceasefire demand and withdrew from Egyptian territory. General Allon received orders to postpone a planned attack on El Arish. Next day, December 31, he was given orders to withdraw completely from Egyptian territory. He called back his raiding parties, destroyed the buildings at Abu Ageila and on January 4 began to march slowly northeast along the coastal road toward Rafah.

Rafah had been under attack by the Golani Brigade since January 2. The Harel Brigade joined the attack the next day, and on the 4th and 5th the two Israeli units slowly fought their way, against desperate resistance, toward the Rafah Junction. When Allon and his column arrived on the 6th, the Israelis had overwhelming force encircling the town and the junction. Late that night, as the Israelis were preparing for a climactic assault, the Egyptian government requested an armistice. This request was immediately accepted, and Allon was ordered to call off his planned attack. The active field combat operations of the first Arab-Israeli war had come to an end.

There was, however, one last battle to be fought. Next day a flight of five Royal Air Force planes from the Canal Zone swept over the coast north of Rafah. Israeli planes rose to meet them, and in a brief, intensive series of dogfights, all five of the British planes were shot down near Nirim. For a few hours the British government contemplated retaliation, but news of an unwarranted British intrusion into a war zone was more upsetting to the British public than was wounded British pride. The London Government, after sending reinforcements to Aqaba, contented itself with a warning—a virtual ultimatum—to the Israelis to withdraw from the Sinai. When the Israelis promptly complied, the threat of Anglo-Israeli hostilities ended.

Even as these operations were going on along the Sinai-Palestine frontier, other Israeli forces had begun to move into the Negev Desert, which now lay open before them as far as the Gulf of Aqaba. As the Israelis moved southward into the Negev and toward the Gulf of Aqaba, they carefully stayed within the boundaries of Palestine, as shown on the UN Partition map. However, King Abdullah invoked the Anglo-Jordanian Treaty. On January 8, after learning that British troops were en route to Aqaba, the Israelis immediately halted their movement into the southern Negev.

For nearly two months the Israeli troops postponed any further moves into the southern and southwestern Negev, while consolidating their positions further north, and awaiting progess in formal and informal negotiations with the Jordanians. The Israelis were anxious to avoid any incidents involving British troops, some of whom had occupied positions west of the Jordan-Palestine frontier. Finally, after exchanges of diplomatic notes, and some minor clashes between Israelis and the Arab Legion, the British and most of the Jordanians withdrew to the eastern side of the old Palestine-Transjordan frontier.

Soon after this, on March 5 Operation "Uvda" was begun, having as its objective the occupation of the southern and western Negev. Two brigades were assigned to this mission: the Negev Brigade and the Golani Brigade.

The Negev Brigade was directed to move south on existing roads and tracks through the center of the Negev toward the Gulf of Aqaba and Um Rashresh, which the Israelis were already calling Eilat. At the same time, the Golani Brigade was to move down the eastern side of the Negev, being careful to stay west of the border, exploring the condition of roads and tracks in this frontier region. On March 7 the Golanis reached the settlement of Ein Huzov, and from there continued southward across country, encountering scattered interference until they reached Um Rashresh at 5:00 p.m. on March 10. They found that the advance guard of the Negev Brigade, commanded by youthful Captain Avrahan Adan, had arrived two hours earlier down the desert track from the northwest. The Israeli flag was now planted on the shore of the Red Sea.

While this was going on, a battalion of the Alexandroni Brigade, the one which had been operating for several months with the Harel Brigade, captured Ein Gedi, on the Dead Sea, in an amphibious landing from its base in Sodom. This assured Israeli control at least of the southwest quarter of the coast of the Dead Sea. The Jordanians protested bitterly, but to no avail, that here as in the southern Negev the Israelis were settling by force of arms issues that were supposedly to be resolved at the negotiating tables.

ARMISTICE NEGOTIATIONS

On January 13, 1949, armistice negotiations began on the island of Rhodes, under the chairmanship of the United Nation's Acting Mediator, Dr. Ralph Bunche. These were bilateral negotiations, between delegations from Israel on the one hand, and from the several Arab nations on the other.

Because of the precarious situation of the Egyptian brigade isolated by the Israelis at Faluja, the Egyptians were anxious to start the talks quickly, and so they were the first to negotiate with the Israelis. With Dr. Bunche smoothly directing the discussions, and suggesting compromise drafts on thorny issues, an armistice agreement between Egypt and Israel was reached on February 24. The ceasefire line generally followed the pre-war boundary between Palestine and Egyptian Sinai, but with the small strip of southwestern Palestine held by Egyptian forces at the end of the war—the so-called Gaza Strip—remaining under Egyptian administration. Upon signature of the agreement the Israelis lifted their blockade of the Faluja Pocket, and the Egyptian troops there returned to Egyptian Sinai.

Negotiation of an armistice agreement between Lebanon and Israel was much easier, and carried out somewhat more leisurely. The agreement, which confirmed the pre-war Palestine-Lebanon frontier as a ceasefire line, was signed on March 23.

Meanwhile there had already been considerable preliminary negotiation between King Abdullah and a small Israeli team of which Foreign Minister Moshe Sharett and Colonel Moshe Dayan were the principal members. The principal problems were (1) to obtain Israeli approval of Jordanian assumption of control of the areas occupied by Iraqi troops—since the Iraqis refused to negotiate with Israel—(2) to get Jordanian agreement to Israeli occupation of the southern Negev within the pre-war boundaries of the British Mandate of Palestine, and (3) to work out satisfactory arrangements for the complicated ceasefire situation in and around Jerusalem. The first two of these were settled reasonably amicably. The third was never totally resolved until the Israelis captured Jerusalem 18 years later.

When the formal negotiations moved to Rhodes on March 1, secret meetings between Abdullah and Israeli representatives continued in Amman. A formal agreement was signed on April 3, at Rhodes.

Negotiations between Israeli and Syrian representatives were much more difficult. The principal stumbling block was to reach an agreeable compromise on the three small areas of former Palestine held by Syrian troops at the end of the war. Since these small parcels of land were extremely fertile, and would support two crops a year, practical consid-

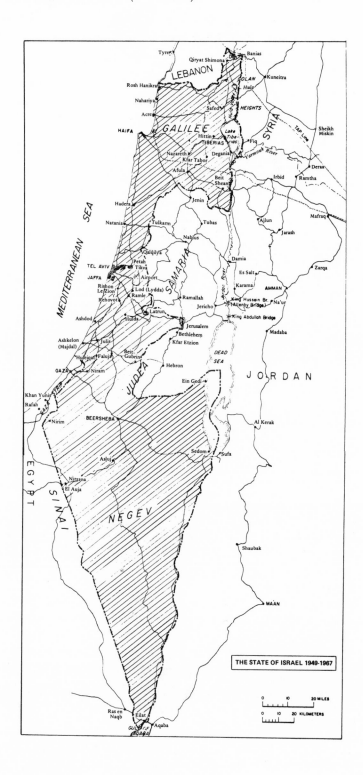

THE STATE OF ISRAEL 1949-1967

erations as well as those of pride and prestige were involved. Finally, it was agreed that these were to remain demilitarized zones, not to be controlled by either side. The Syrian troops would move out, but the Israelis were forbidden to move in. The local farmers, Jews and Arabs, were to be allowed to till their soil under the administration of a Mixed Armistice Commission of Israeli and Syrian officers, which in turn was to be supervised by the United Nations Truce Supervision Organization. The agreement was signed on July 20, 1949.

Each of the agreements provided for the exchange of prisoners of war. Each also reaffirmed the continuing role of UNTSO—originally established under Prince Bernadotte. And to resolve local disputes along each ceasefire line there was a Mixed Armistice Commission. These organizations are still nominally in existence at the time of the writing of this book, nearly 30 years later, but the MACs have not been very active. Of all of them, the Syrian-Israeli MAC has had the stormiest existence.[1]

---

[1] See E.L.M. Burns, *Between Arab and Israeli* (New York, 1963); Carl Von Horn, *Soldiering for Peace* (New York, 1967); and Odd Bull, *War and Peace in the Middle East* (London, 1976).

13

Naval Operations

THE OPPOSING NAVIES

Between 1945 and 1947 the naval branch of the Palmach—called the Palyam—was a secret force of motor boat sailors, built around a cadre of World War II veterans of the Royal Navy, including several naval commandos, or frogmen. They were principally involved in efforts to smuggle illegal Jewish immigrants into Palestine past the British blockade vessels. They were also successful in some sabotage activities against British vessels and shore installations.

By early 1948 the initial inventory of a few motorboats was augmented by Jewish Agency purchasing teams which acquired a motley collection of somewhat larger—but elderly—vessels in Europe and North America. These included a former US Coast Guard cutter, a former US Navy icebreaker, and (about May 1948) several British *Flower* class corvettes. The latter, 1,000 ton vessels about 200 feet long, became the most useful vessels of the early Israeli Navy. Just before independence, the Palyam in a daring raid seized several former immigrant vessels which the British had interned in Haifa harbor.

After the end of the Mandate the British—who retained a naval base at Haifa—permitted the Israelis to refit and recondition their new vessels in the Haifa shipyards, but would not allow the Israelis to place any armaments on these vessels while in Haifa harbor. The first seagoing vessel to be so reconditioned was the icebreaker—former U.S.S. *Bear*—which was rechristened *Eilat*, and sent to Tel Aviv, where some 65mm field guns were installed on improvised mounts, converting the ancient craft into a warship. Colonel Nachman Shulman, an immigrant from the United States, was appointed the first commanding officer of the Israeli Navy. Additional vessels were acquired during the course of the war.

Israel's only Arab adversary with a navy in May 1948 was Egypt. That navy, in fact, was even younger than Israel's Palyam, having been established in June 1946. Its original vessels were a handful of old British Coast Guard craft, plus some royal yachts. Its officers were all former Royal Navy sailors or junior officers, who had served exclusively on coastal vessels in Egyptian waters. Only a few of the officers had had formal naval schooling in Britain.

In October 1946, an Egyptian Naval Academy was established at Alexandria. At about the same time the Navy began to acquire a few warships, of which perhaps the most important were some American-built minesweepers, and to arm them with field artillery cannon, acquired from the Army. The following year a former Royal Navy frigate was added and became the flagship as the *Emir Farouk.*

INITIAL OPERATIONS

Just before the outbreak of formal hostilities, on May 14, 1948, Egyptian warships landed a small contingent of troops at Majdal. After this, however, the Egyptian Navy confined itself to transport and supply of the invasion force gathering in the Gaza Strip. Although the land communications back to the Canal had not been molested, Egypt apparently preferred to rely mainly on resupply and troop rotation by sea. In part this was due to a shortage of motor vehicles; also it was recognition of the lengthy land route's vulnerability to ambush by deep penetration Jewish commando raiders.

Not until June 2, eighteen days after the invasion began, did a lone Egyptian warship shell Caesarea, causing only light damage and no casualties. On June 4 a small Egyptian squadron of two or three vessels was observed by the Israelis moving northward along the Gaza Strip coast. The *Eilat* put out to sea with the *Hannah Senesh* standing by and back up air support allocated. Approximately two hours later the *Eilat* sighted the Egyptians approximately ten miles to the south and about four miles offshore. Upon closer examination the Egyptian vessels were identified as the large armed transport *Amura Fawzia,* followed by a minesweeper or a corvette, and a large landing craft, all steaming north parallel to the coast. The Israelis assumed that the Egyptian objective was either to support their advanced ground units near Ashdod, or to make an amphibious landing near Tel Aviv.

Since this force was obviously too great for the *Eilat* to challenge, and no air support had appeared, at 2:00 p.m. the *Eilat* was ordered to change course and turn north. The Egyptian corvette at once increased speed and soon closed to three miles, whereupon it opened fire. For about one hour the two vessels exchanged fire with few hits and little effect.

By 3:15 p.m. the *Eilat* was opposite Jaffa, when at last three Israeli fighter planes arrived. They made six passes at the Egyptian ships. Only one bomb hit was scored, and one Fairchild fighter was lost to Egyptian antiaircraft fire. However, the Egyptian ships turned south at about 5:30 p.m.

During the balance of this initial period of the war (the Invasion Phase), Israeli naval activity was confined to patrolling the entrances to

Tel Aviv harbor and escorting in-bound immigrant ships. The Egyptians, aside from occasional bombardment of coastal installations, were at the same time engaged mainly in providing logistical support to the Army.

The most intensive combat of the Israeli Navy during the war took place completely on land. A company of naval infantry was attached to the Givati Brigade during the fighting near Negba in mid-July. On July 18, at Beit Affa, this company lost more men than did the rest of the Navy during the entire war. (See p. 82.)

About the same time, at dusk on July 17, the *Eilat* and the *Wedgewood* (former British corvette) proceeded north along the Lebanese coast to Tyre, which they shelled for about 15 minutes before heading ten miles out to sea and turning south to return to Tel Aviv. The attack was evidently a surprise, since there was no answering fire from the shore. The bombardment possibly contributed to Lebanon's decision not to take a further active part in the war, since troops and guns previously employed on forays into Galilee were now tied down to coastal defense.

During Operation Yoav in October, Israeli vessels used long-range gun fire to harass Egyptian units in the coastal strip. Israeli naval vessels also tried to keep the land routes back to Port Said under interdictory gunfire and to intercept Egyptian vessels carrying provisions to their ground troops.

On October 19, a troop-laden Egyptian corvette was putting out from Gaza, when approached by an Israeli squadron consisting of the *Wedgewood* and the *Eilat*. The Egyptian vessel returned to shore, disembarked the troops and went out to fight the Israeli ships. In the ensuing exchange of fire one of the Israeli vessels was damaged. As the Egyptian vessel then retired southward, several Egyptian Spitfires, apparently summoned by the corvette, strafed the Israeli vessels, killing one sailor and wounding three. One of the planes was downed by antiaircraft fire.

This was during the period when Egyptian troops were withdrawing from the Ashdod-Majdal area. On October 20 Israeli ships shelled a line of these troops on the shore south of Majdal and harassed them all the way to Gaza. This forced the Egyptian rear guard to shift the fire of its guns from the pursuing Israeli soldiers and direct them against the Israeli vessels.

Just before a truce went into effect, two Egyptian ships, the flagship *Emir Farouk* and a minesweeper, were detected by Israelis moving out from Gaza, and a "special unit"—with remotely controlled explosive boats —was sent in to attack. Guiding the weapon from a nearby motorboat was Lieutenant Yochai Bin Nun, later commander of the Israeli Navy. The explosive boat hit the *Emir Farouk* and sank her within three minutes. Another explosive boat hit the minesweeper, which was badly damaged but stayed afloat. Yochai Bin Nun was decorated as a Hero of Israel, one of 12 men so honored during the war. Shortly afterward,

Egypt ceased seaborne supply attempts, and U.S. and British insurers reduced premiums on Israel-bound vessels.

The Israeli naval harassment begun during Operation Yoav graduated to a full blockade in Operation Horev. In Yoav the Israeli warships had waited for aerial reconnaissance reports before setting out on a mission, thereby often arriving too late or at the wrong place. In Horev, beginning on December 22, the entire fleet actively patrolled off the Sinai coast by day, and cruised closer to shore to shell the roads and beaches at night. By this time the "tacked on" field artillery had been replaced by 3-inch and 4-inch naval guns, with improved fire control.

By December, however, the Egyptians were better prepared for the naval bombardments and their blackouts prevented effective fire at shore targets at night. On the other hand, the Egyptian shore batteries were not very effective. On one occasion the Israeli ship *Haganah* was caught in the beams of two Egyptian searchlights, and fire from a coastal battery caused some damage, but this is the only such instance on record.

On balance, the Israeli naval effort during Horev was successful. Although the coastal railroad was not interrupted, the Egyptian naval supply effort was completely blocked, and not a single Egyptian vessel got through. Egyptian strength ashore was weakened, moreover, by the necessity to divert troops and guns to coastal defense.

ASSESSMENT

Under the circumstances of the conflict, the performance of both inexperienced navies was creditable. On balance the Israeli Navy had slightly the better of the encounters at sea. On the other hand, the Egyptian Navy made a greater contribution to the combined arms war effort in its support of both the Egyptian land offensive and the later Egyptian withdrawal.

Overall, however, the naval war had little effect upon the course of the war, or upon the outcome. Neither side was geared or prepared to carry out a naval blockade, the only way in which naval power could have had a decisive effect. It was, after all, a war primarily to gain control of the land, and none of the combatants had sufficient naval strength to influence the outcome significantly.

14

Envoie

The population of Jewish Palestine at the end of 1947 was about 680,000; the combined populations of Lebanon, Syria, Transjordan, Iraq and Egypt, plus the Palestinian Arabs, were well over 30,000,000: thus the Arabs had an overwhelming 45-to-1 population preponderance.

Yet the actual odds in mobilized military forces was far, far different. From the beginning the outnumbered Jews fielded mobilized forces as large as those of the Arabs. While a substantial proportion of these troops had to be deployed around the country for security, the Jews usually were able to bring to the battlefield larger forces than did the Arabs. Initially these Jewish forces were not so well equipped as their opponents, but (with one exception) they were better organized and better trained. And, by the end of the war, as weapons and equipment poured into Israel as a result of a superbly planned and executed procurement program, the Jewish superiority in mobilized numbers, organization, and training was complemented by near equality in most armament, and superiority in some categories, particularly aircraft.

In the final weeks of the war, the Israelis brought to bear a substantial numerical superiority over the Egyptians in the Gaza Corridor and the northern Negev. By this time the efficient mobilization capability of the Jews had brought 13% of the population under arms.

The great percentage of men mobilized by the Israelis was made even more significant by the disunity that characterized relations among their Arab opponents. The Jews were prompt to take advantage of this disunity. The combination of jealousy, old feuds, and an amazing inability by the Arabs to bring themselves to the coordinated action that they clearly recognized to be necessary, assured the Jewish victory.

Among the Arab units the Arab Legion stands out for its good fighting qualities. It is easy for Westerners to attribute this to the organizing and leadership qualities of General John Glubb and his British officers. There is no question that British training and the adoption of British military customs and operational and logistical procedures and doctrines did contribute to bridging the gap between the older Arab military culture and that of modern Europe. But, the gap once bridged, the Arab Legion fought as well under its own officers as under the British, and fought on even terms with the best of the Israeli Palmach units. There is a lesson here that was only partly perceived at the time, either by the participants or by foreign observers, and is perhaps not yet fully understood. It is a lesson involving the interaction of doctrine, training, organization, and leadership. It should be restudied, in the light of later developments in the Arab-Israeli conflict.

The Arab soldiers of all forces in a number of instances demonstrated stubbornness in defense. This was particularly evident under strong leadership—like that in the Arab Legion at Latrun—but was evident even in instances where leadership was less than ideal—like the performance of the Syrians at Mishmar Hayarden, and the Egyptians at Faluja and Iraq Suwaydan. Yet on other occasions Arabs in excellent defensive positions collapsed under pressure—as at Lydda—or simply dissolved, as at Kastel after the death of el Husseini. These incidents, too, warrant serious study by both Arab and Israeli General Staffs—and perhaps by others—also in relation to subsequent events in later wars.

On the other hand it must be noted that the defense was generally successful in this war—both Arab and Israeli—because both sides lacked the experience, and usually the means, to arrange adequate firepower support to forces assaulting fortifications. The final assault on Iraq Suwaydan was a notable exception.

From the beginning of the second truce, until the end of hostilities on January 7, the Israelis lost 2,133 soldiers and civilians killed. There are no reliable statistics on the wounded, but these must have totalled between six and seven thusand. This brought the total Israeli military casualties for the war to more than 4,000 dead and approximately 12,000 wounded. There are no reliable figures on Arab losses. A very rough estimate is that Arab dead were probably 15-20,000, with at least 25-30,000 wounded. (See Table, page 124.)

THE WAR ISSUE

It is simplistic and misleading to suggest that the Zionist Jews used the pretext of religion and ancient historical tradition to eject the legal occupants of Palestine from their homes by force and terror, and then illegally expropriated their land. It is equally simplistic to suggest that the sole Israeli answer to such accusations is that they made better use of the land than did the Arab former occupants. These interpretations ignore the facts that the original Zionists came legally to Palestine in the late 19th and early 20th Centuries, that they legally bought the farmlands which they caused to bloom so spectacularly, and that until the late 1930's their immigration into Palestine was a legal way for them to escape from the anti-Semitic environments of their former homes to a land where they were at first welcomed, and later at least tolerated, by governmental authorities as well as by a majority of their new neighbors.

These arguments conveniently forget also that the war was precipitated by Arabs who had as their avowed aim the extermination or expulsion of these peaceful Zionist settlers from their lawful property, and forget also that, during this war started by the Arabs, those who lost their property to Israelis fled the country voluntarily, while those that remained were allowed to keep the houses and land they owned and occupied before the war.

Unfortunately, however, these answers to accusations of critics of Israel (and the Zionism on which it is founded) are also simplistic. Because, in fact, a majority of Israelis *do* believe that the possession of much of modern Israel by their ancestors thousands of years ago is a major and valid basis for them to reclaim their ancient homeland from the modern occupants, and that their appropriation of the property of the displaced Arabs is not only legitimatized by right of conquest, but excused by the Nazi Holocaust, and further that their right to the land is affirmed by their ability to get more out of it. These answers also overlook the fact that the Arabs who fled their homes did so as civilians endeavoring to escape from the dangers and horrors of open warfare, and the sincere fear (justified or not) that they might otherwise suffer the fate of the victims of the Deir Yassin massacre.

There are, of course, logical, sincere, and reasonable Israeli responses to these reasoned rebuttals of their basic defense of their right to the land that has become the State of Israel. And there is the rub. Many of the arguments of both sides are logical, sincere, and reasonable. Both could—and do—claim that theirs is the righteous and just cause, but in fact neither can demonstrate that the issues can be resolved to anyone's satisfaction without perpetuating some past wrongs or inflicting new injustices.

The 1947-1949 War resolved the question of Israeli independence. It did not resolve the issues which led to that independence.

APPROXIMATE STRENGTHS, OPPOSING FIELD FORCES
1948 War[1]

	15 May 1948		October 1948	
Israel	34,400		45,000[2]	
Arabs	42,000		55,000	
ALA		5,500		3,000
Army of Salvation		5,000		5,000
Lebanon		2,000		2,000
Syria		5,000		5,000
Jordan		7,500		10,000
Egypt		7,000		20,000
Iraq		10,000		10,000

[1] Excluding Israeli and Palestinian Home Defense contingents.
[2] 90,000 mobilized and under arms.

ESTIMATED LOSSES
1948 War

	Killed	Wounded	Total
Israel	6,000	15,000	21,000
Arabs	15,000	25,000	40,000

ORDER OF BATTLE
Israeli Armed Forces, 1948-49

Minister of Defense	David Ben Gurion
Deputy Minister of Defense	Israel Galili
Chief of Staff	Maj. Gen. Ya'acov Dori
Deputy Chief of Staff (Operations)	Brig. Gen. Yigal Yadin
Northern Command	Brig. Gen. Moshe Carmel
Central Command	Brig. Gen. Dan Even
Eastern Command (Jerusalem)	Brig. Gen. (Col.) David Marcus
	Brig. Gen. Zvi Ayalon
Southern Command	Brig. Gen. Yigal Allon
Palmach	Brig. Gen. Yigal Allon
Brigades:	
Yiftach (Palmach)	Col. Shmuel Cohen
Harel (Palmach)	Col. Yitzhak Rabin;
	Col. Yossef Tabenkin
Hanegev (Palmach)	Col. Nahum Sarig
1st—Golani	Col. Nahum Golan
2nd—Carmeli	Col. Moshe Carmel;
	Col. Mordechai Makleff
3rd—Alexandroni	Col. Ben Zion Ziv
4th—Kiryati	Col. Michael Benzal
5th—Givati	Col. Shimeon Avidan
6th—Etzioni (Jerusalem)	Col. David Shaltiel;
	Col. Moshe Dayan
7th (Mczd)	Col. Benjamin Dunkelman
8th (Armd)	Brig. Gen. Yitzhak Sadeh
9th—Oded	Col. Uri Joffe;
	Col. Yitzhak Pundal
Air Force	Brig. Gen. Ahron Remez
Navy	Brig. Gen. Nachman Shulman;
	Brig. Gen. Shlomo Shamir

ORDER OF BATTLE
Arab Armies, 1948-49

Allied Commander in Chief	King Abdullah, Transjordan
Deputy	Maj. Gen. Nur el-Din Mahmud, Iraq
Arab Liberation Army	
Inspector General	Maj. Gen. Taha Al-Hashimi
Deputy	Maj. Gen. Ismail Safwat

ORDER OF BATTLE
Arab Armies, 1948-49

Field Force Commander	Fawz el Din el Kaukji
Galilee District Command	Adib Shishakly
Yarmuk Battalions (1, 2, & 3)	Mohommed Safa, Adib Shishakly, Wasfi Tell, etc.
Hittin Battalion	Madlul Abas
Lebanese Battalion	Shakib Wahab
El Hussein Battalion	Abd el Rahim Sheikh Ali
Qadisier Battalion	Mahdi Saleh
Ajnadin Battalion	Michael el Issa, Mahdi Saleh
Jaffa Command	Adel Nijmeddin, Michael el Issa
Acre Command	Adnin Murad, Khalil Kallas
Gaza Command	Abdulhaq Azawi
Arab Army of Salvation	
Commander	Abd el Kadr el Husseini, Khaled el Husseini
Deputy	Muni Abu Fadel
Lebanese Army	
Minister of Defense	Majid Arslan
Chief of Staff	Maj. Gen. Fouad Shehab
Syrian Army	
Minister of Defense	Ahmad Sharahati
Chief of Staff	Maj. Gen. Abdullah Atfeh
1st Brigade	Col. Abdullah Wahab el Hakim, Brig. Gen. Husni el Zaim
2d Brigade	Col. Kawass, Col. Mohommed Jamil Burhani
3d Brigade	Col. Sami Hinawi
Arab Legion (Transjordan)	
Chief of Staff	Maj. Gen. John Glubb
1st Brigade	Brigadier N. O. Lash
2d Brigade	Colonel J. O. M. Ashton
Jerusalem Command	Col. Abdullah El-Tell
Iraqi Army	
Minister of Defense	Shaker el Wadi
Chief of Staff	Gen. Saleb Sayeb Gabouri
Field Force Commander	Maj. Gen. Nur el-Din Mahmud
1st Brigade	Col. Najib Rubici
3d Brigade	
4th Brigade	Col. Saleh Zaki Tawfik
Nablus Force (Mczd Bde)	Col. Rafik Aref
Air Force	Lt. Gen. Sami Fattah
Egyptian Army	
Chief of Staff	Maj. Gen. Muhamad Haider
Field Force Commander	Maj. Gen. Ahmed Ali el Mawawi, Maj. Gen. Ahmad Fouad Sadek
1st Brigade	Brig. Mohommed Naguib
2d Brigade	Brig. Mahmoud Fahmy Nemat-allah
4th Brigade	Brig. Tawfik Radwan
Faluja Command	Col. Sayid Taha
Volunteers	Col. Ahmed Abd el Azziz, Col. Hassan Touballah

BOOK TWO

The Sinai-Suez War,
October-November 1956

1

Uneasy Tides
of War and Peace

TURMOIL IN THE ARAB WORLD

Following the overwhelming victory of the new state of Israel in the 1947-1949 Palestine War, most of the Arab states participating in that war went through one or more violent internal upheavals. In each instance local social, political, and economic conditions played a part in the crises, but a common theme was discontent with the outcome of the war, and dissatisfaction with the governments that collectively had been responsible for the Arab debacle. A related theme was determination on the part of most of the Arab peoples to gain revenge on Israel, and to assist in returning to their homes the hundreds of thousands of dislocated Palestinian Arab refugees who had fled to neighboring countries during the war.

Syria was the first of the Arab states participating in the 1947-1949 War subsequently to suffer unrest, and that unrest persisted for more than two decades. There were three coups in 1949, another in 1951, one in 1954, followed by still another in 1955. Since military leaders were major participants in each of these coups, there was something approaching administrative chaos in the armed forces; frequent purges ripped the officer corps into shreds. The one common characteristic of these successive governments was hatred of Israel.

The next "confrontation" state to be affected by the virus of upheaval was Jordan. On July 20, 1951, King Abdullah was assassinated at the entrance to Jerusalem's Al Aksa Mosque (adjacent to the Dome of the Rock, on the Temple Mount) by a follower of the king's ancient foe, Haj Amin el Husseini, the Mufti of Jerusalem. (Husseini had taken refuge in Cairo after the war.) Abdullah was succeeded by his son Talal, but that mentally-disturbed monarch was deposed by the Jordanian Parliament thirteen months later, August 11, 1952, and Talal's 17-year-old son Hussein was proclaimed King. Hussein was crowned on May 2, 1953, his eighteenth birthday.

In late December 1944, Amman, the capital of Jordan, was rocked by riots, protesting the kingdom's proposed participation in the Bagdad Pact, after the treaty had been denounced by Egypt's President Nasser. Early the next year Nasser's influence was again evident as King Hussein, under pan-Arabist pressures, dismissed General Glubb (who returned to Britain to be knighted by Queen Elizabeth II) and other British officers of the Arab Legion. During the following months, while the Legion was being reorganized as the Jordan Army, some of its units became involved in border clashes with Israel. Arab guerrilla-terrorists—mostly Palestinian Arabs—had been carrying out hit-and-run raids inside Israel, and the Israelis retaliated, provoking response from the Jordanian border troops on the eastern frontier. Although the principal support for the guerrillas came from Syria, Iraq, and other Arab League countries, most of them were active on the long, easily-infiltrated frontier between Israel and Jordan's "West Bank" region—the remnant of Arab Palestine.

While not so chaotic as the turmoil in Syria, nor so confused as the situation in Jordan, the most important upheavals in the Arab world in the years following the 1947-1949 war took place in Egypt. Much of the trouble in that country was related to the continuing presence of British troops in the Suez Canal Zone, and additional friction with Britain regarding the future of Sudan, over which Egypt exercised nominal condominium with Britain. Following armed clashes with British forces at Suez and Ismailia in early 1952, a group of Army officers seized control of the government on July 23, forcing King Farouk to abdicate in favor of his infant son, Ahmed Fuad II, and to flee the country. The coup leader was Lieutenant Colonel Gamal abd al Nasser, who had distinguished himself during the Palestine War at the siege of Faluja. One of Nasser's principal assistants was Lieutenant Colonel Anwar al-Sadat.

The young officers selected as their leader highly-respected General Mohammed Naguib, who was one of Egypt's few popular heroes of the war. Following a number of political moves to entrench its political power, on June 18, 1953, the military group overthrew the infant monarch—who had in fact left Egypt with his father—and declared a republic. Naguib, in addition to being prime minister, became provisional president. However, the driving force behind the new, reform-minded government remained Colonel Nasser. On April 18, 1954, as a result of a clash of personalities, Nasser replaced Naguib as Prime Minister, and began openly to exercise his leadership.

Nasser's popularity increased in July as a result of an agreement with Britain whereby British troops would be withdrawn from the Suez Canal Zone over a period of 20 months. (Britain faithfully adhered to the treaty.) On November 14, 1954, Naguib was dismissed from the government, shortly after a Moslem Brotherhood assassination attempt against Nasser. It is doubtful that Naguib had any involvement in the plot; this seems to have been a convenient pretext for Nasser not only to crush the Moslem Brotherhood, but also to end the embarrassment of apparently divided leadership by getting rid of Naguib.

During this period the Egyptian leaders had not forgotten the greater embarrassment caused by their defeat in Palestine. Both Naguib and Nasser were energetic in revitalizing the army; preparation for revenge against Israel was an important objective for both of them. However, Egypt did not at first become involved in frontier incidents like those which were occurring along the Israel-Syria and Israel-Jordan frontiers. In fact, during 1954, a tentative indirect dialogue between Egyptian Premier Nasser and Israeli Prime Minister Moshe Sharett was begun, through British diplomat Richard Crossman. This was halted, however, by an incident early in 1955.

On February 28, in retaliation for Palestinian guerrilla raids into southern Israel from the Gaza Strip (the small portion of Palestine held by Egyptian troops at the end of the 1947-1949 War) Israeli troops raided into Gaza, and briefly seized the Egyptian Army headquarters there. There is controversy as to the extent of the guerrilla raids which prompted this retaliation. The Egyptians claim there had been none, and apparently there had been no serious incident. Nasser was infuriated by this Israeli raid, and immediately began to recruit Arab guerrillas—or *fedayeen*—to harass southern Israel not only from the Gaza Strip, but also across the Sinai frontier. By April approximately 700 guerrillas were assembled in the Gaza Strip, under the direction of Egyptian Military Intelligence.

This intensification of Egyptian hostility against Israel had adverse effects on Egyptian relations with western countries, particularly the United States and France. Partly because of this, and partly for reasons of pan-Arab politics, Nasser refused an American offer of military assistance in return for joining the Bagdad Treaty between Turkey and Iraq. Instead, he vehemently denounced the treaty and the participation of Iran and Pakistan. His firm opposition had much to do with Syrian and Jordanian refusals to join the pact.

Soon after Nasser assumed the leadership of Egypt, he focussed his attention on means of strengthening Egypt's ever-precarious economy. The foremost economic project in his mind at this time was the construction of a new high dam on the Nile River above Aswan, which would not only provide Egypt with a tremendous supply of electricity for industrial and social development, but would also greatly improve the agricultural economy of the country by controlling the annual floods of the Nile River and, through irrigation, adding approximately 20% to the arable land.

Nasser sought funding for this project from the United States, Great Britain, and the International Bank. To avoid either the possibility or appearance of dependency on the West, however, Nasser at the same time negotiated a major trade agreement with the Communist Bloc—dealing through Czechoslovakia—whereby Egypt would obtain massive quantities of weapons and other military equipment in return for rice and cotton. He announced this agreement on September 27, 1954. Over the following year, Egypt was to receive on easy purchase terms from the Communist bloc 230 tanks, 300 other armored vehicles, 500 artillery pieces, 150 MiG fighter planes, 50 Iluyshin-28 bombers, several submarines and other naval craft, a variety of other weapons and several hundred trucks and tractors.

Things were somewhat quieter in the other two confrontation states—Lebanon and Iraq—during the seven years following the 1947-1949 War, although there were evidences of unrest that would later escalate to major violence in both countries. The uneasy truce between Moslem and Christian Arabs in Lebanon was briefly interrupted by disorders and strikes that overthrew the president on September 18, 1952.

In Iraq, two months later, riots by Bagdad mobs overthrew the government and early the following year led to the premiership of Nuri es Said, who had been a distinguished general in the Turkish Army in World War I. On May 2, 1953, on his 18th birthday, King Faisal II assumed royal authority. On February 18, 1955, a defensive alliance with Turkey was signed at Bagdad; this Bagdad Pact was to become the framework for the short-lived Middle East Treaty Organization when it was joined by Iran, Pakistan, and Great Britain. It also was to become an important focus of the efforts of President Nasser of Egypt to become the leader of Pan-Arabism; he attacked the treaty as an instrument of Anglo-American imperialism, designed to retain Anglo-Saxon hegemony over the Middle East.

ISRAELI ASSESSMENT OF ARAB INTENTIONS

In the years following the 1947-49 War, Israel devised a military system providing for a small regular army, conscription of all able-bodied males and most females, and a highly trained and ready reserve force, capable of being mobilized within 48 hours. Thus the active army, some 50,000 regular and conscript troops, could quickly be expanded to an effective combat force of nearly 200,000 soldiers.

By the beginning of 1956 it was evident to Israelis that time was not healing the wounds of the 1947-1949 War of Independence as they had hoped. David Ben Gurion, who had resigned as Prime Minister and Defense Minister in December 1953, returned to the government little more than a year later as Minister of Defense in the administration of Prime Minister Moshe Sharett. He had reluctantly come back to public life partly to restore confidence in the Defense Ministry following a peculiar crisis in political-military relations in Israel, known as the Lavon Affair,[1] and partly because he had become convinced that another war with the Arabs was inevitable. There were three principal aspects of the deepening crisis between Israel and her Arab neighbors.

The first of these, considered intolerable by most Israeli citizens, was the increasing tempo of Arab guerrilla activity along all of the frontiers of Israel. The long border of the deep Jordanian salient into the heart of Israel provided a base for many terrorist raids by Arab guerrillas who were mostly Palestinians. But there were also raids across the Syrian and Lebanese frontiers. Most serious, however, and threatening most dangerous developments for the future, was the increasing commando activity along the southern border with Egypt, particularly in the region of the Gaza Strip, beginning in August 1955. The fedayeen organizations that carried out the raids from the Gaza and Sinai borders were obviously trained, directed, and equipped by the Egyptian Army. It was these Egyptian-supported fedayeen—some of whom were Palestinians, some from other Arab countries, but most Egyptians—who inflicted most of the mounting casualties caused by these raids in Israel. According to official Israeli reports, 137 Israeli citizens were killed or wounded by guerrillas in 1951, 147 in 1952, 162 in 1953, 180 in 1954, and a rapidly rising total of 258 in 1955.

Apparently confirming the danger from Egypt as the most serious of Arab foes was President Nasser's September 1955 announcement of the arms agreement with Czechoslovakia, which was clearly functioning as a pawn of Moscow. Up until that time Israel and Egypt had something close to parity in major military weapons, each having about 200 tanks and about 50 jet aircraft. It was clear to Ben Gurion and to Army Chief of Staff Major General Moshe Dayan, that these new Egyptian weapons were intended to be used in a new war against Israel just as soon as the Egyptian Army could be adequately trained in their employment. While Major General Yehoshofat Harkabi, the new chief of Israeli Intelligence, did not think that the Egyptians would be ready to use these weapons in war before 1957, General Dayan's personal assessment was that they might be ready by late 1956.

Arab economic pressure, however, particularly from Egypt, was perhaps the most dangerous threat to the future viability of tiny, resource-poor Israel. Egypt, asserting that there was still a state of war with Israel, refused to permit the passage of any Israeli vessels, or even of goods on foreign vessels going to or from Israel, through the Suez Canal.

---

[1] It was precipitated by the failure of an ineptly handled intelligence operation in Egypt, apparently the responsibility of Defense Minister Pinchas Lavon, who attempted to blame it on Shimon Peres (Director General of the Ministry), General Moshe Dayan (new Chief of Staff), and General Benjamin Givly (Chief of Intelligence).

The ban on Israeli goods and Israeli navigation through the Suez Canal was an apparent violation of the Constantinople Convention of 1884 governing the international status of the Suez Canal. It was also a violation of the Israeli-Egyptian armistice agreement and of several decisions of the UN Security Council.

Perhaps more directly serious, however, was the effect of the blockade Egypt had imposed on the Strait of Tiran in 1953, prohibiting passage of vessels from the southern Israeli port of Eilat into the Red Sea, and thus seriously impairing Israeli plans for the future economic development of the Negev. Egypt also justified this blockade by the continuing state of war with Israel. In September 1955, Egypt blocked the flight of Israeli commercial aircraft over the Strait.

While Arabs were unquestionably thinking of revenge and the elimination of the Zionist state, Arab thinking and planning were far less concerted and coherent than the Israelis assumed. This was due only in part to the natural human tendency of the Israelis to exaggerate an apparent threat. It was stimulated also by loud and repeated warnings from Arab leaders, of whom the most outspoken and most threatening was President Nasser.

NASSER'S ASPIRATIONS FOR EGYPT AND THE ARABS

It is doubtful, in fact, that Nasser himself had any specific plans or timetable in mind for another war with Israel. It is not even certain that he looked upon such a war as inevitable, despite his many statements to this effect. Nasser seems to have been motivated by two parallel, and not completely consistent objectives in the mid 1950s. In the first place, his efforts to strengthen Egypt's economy were focussed on the planned Aswan High Dam. The United States had given Egypt encouragement in this project, although the enthusiasm of American Secretary of State John Foster Dulles had notably cooled after the Egyptian-Czechoslovakian arms deal. Nevertheless, on October 20, 1955, the United States offered to finance the dam if the project was also supported by the International Bank for Reconstruction and Development.

Nasser's other objective was to strengthen his somewhat insecure position as the leading statesman of the Arab world. He unquestionably had visions of himself uniting most of the Arab countries of the Middle East into a single Arab nation under his personal leadership. Although one motive for such unification might have been coordination of a new Arab war against Israel, in fact he used the common antipathy to Israel as a major theme in orchestrating his own personal political ambitions. Thus he evidently thought less about the specifics of his threats against Israel than he did of their effect in rallying to his support as many as possible of the Arabs of all neighboring nations.

Three of the most important of the nearby Arab states were monarchies, whose rulers were strongly suspicious of Nasser's motives. While Saudi Arabia, Iraq, and Jordan were equally outspoken against Israel in meetings of the Arab League, they were notably cool toward accepting Nasser as the Arab spokesman or strategic coordinator. Syria, whose soldier politicians were playing a kind of game of musical chairs in one coup d'etat after another, was as vociferous in its anti-Israeli statements as was Nasser, as each succeeding leader attempted to outdo his predecessor in anti-Zionist vitriol intended to rally popular support. Lebanon, whose peculiarly balanced Christian-Moslem political system was showing signs of strain, had no intention of getting involved in another war with Israel, although Beirut businessmen were eager to seize any opportunity to make an honest or dishonest pound acting as middlemen in the arms trade with other Arab states.

For these reasons, therefore, neither Israeli nor neutral observers took very seriously announcements from Cairo on October 19, 1955, about the establishment of a joint Egyptian-Syrian military command, or in March 1956 about a new plan for combined action against Israel by Egypt, Syria, and Saudi Arabia. King Hussein of Jordan, invited to join the agreement, at first declined because he would not give up British economic and military subsidies essential to the economic viability and political stability of his own poor nation. However, as tension increased along the Israel-Jordan border in October 1956, Jordan joined the Egyptian-Syrian military command.

It was, of course, unlikely that Egypt would participate in an early war against Israel as negotiations for the joint financing of the Aswan Dam by the United States and the International Bank moved forward during the last months of 1955. Early in 1956 Nasser rejected an offer from the Soviet Union to provide the financing he desired, part of it as an outright gift.

Although not directly linked to the American and International Bank's offer to finance the High Dam, Nasser's apparently firm financial commitment to the western world made it easier for Britain to complete its final withdrawal from the Suez Canal Zone in June 1956. This ended 74 years of British military occupation of all or part of Egypt.

2

The Suez Crisis

NATIONALIZATION OF THE SUEZ CANAL

Five days after final British withdrawal from the Suez Canal Zone, on June 18, 1956, the Soviet Union with much fanfare made a new offer to Egypt to finance the Aswan Dam. This time Russia agreed to provide about one billion dollars at an annual interest of only two percent. While Nasser had previously made it clear that he would prefer a deal with the United States, Britain, and the International Bank for Reconstruction and Development, rather than with the Soviet Union, he seems to have thought that this Soviet offer might be useful as a bargaining chip for getting better terms from the westerners. This was too much for Secretary of State Dulles, who had already formed a deep personal antipathy for Nasser, and mistrusted his new negotiations with the Soviet Union. Using an unfavorable economic report from the International Bank as a basis for his action, in mid-July 1956 Dulles withdrew the American offer to finance the Aswan Dam. Britain followed suit, and so the deal for western support of the Aswan Dam collapsed.

One week later, on July 26, a furious President Nasser announced the nationalization of the Suez Canal by seizure of control from the private Suez Canal Corporation, in which the British Government had majority control. Nasser said that Egypt would use the funds seized from the corporation, and proceeds from Canal toll fees, to go ahead with his plan for the Aswan Dam. At the same time he began to negotiate more seriously with the Soviets, who were probably surprised at this turn of events.

The Egyptian seizure of the Suez Canal gave rise to hot debate in and out of the United Nations. France and Britain, in particular, considered the action a threat to world peace, and—more serious from their viewpoint—a threat to their access to Middle East oil. Secretary Dulles, somewhat shocked by this unexpected reaction to the punishment he had inflicted on Nasser, took the lead in negotiations to achieve some kind of mutually acceptable international control over the Canal. This was impossible to achieve within the United Nations, however, since the Communist bloc and many unaligned nations completely supported the Egyptian move.

Early in August Prime Minister Anthony Eden of Britain decided that he would use force if necessary to restore to the Suez Canal Corporation its rightful ownership of its property in and on the Suez Canal. Although he seems not to have expected that it would be necessary to take such drastic action, he ordered preparations. On August 3 a military planning staff was hastily assembled in London, and began plans to invade and reoccupy the Suez Canal Zone. France, annoyed by Nasser's support of Algerian nationalists, was equally determined to overturn the Egyptian nationalization action, and sent liaison officers to join the British planners in London. Both the French and the British governments were still optimistic that negotiations would make it unnecessary to use force. Military planning—with a target date in early September—was undertaken solely for use in the event that diplomacy failed to cause Nasser to see the light of reason, as reason was viewed in London and Paris.

ISRAEL AND FRANCE

Totally unrelated to the Suez Canal crisis, during July and August the Israeli government had come to the conclusion that the intolerable state of affairs in its relations with its Arab neighbors could be resolved only by war. Ben Gurion—who had become Prime Minister as well as Defense Minister on November 2, 1955—shared Dayan's concern about the potential danger to Israel once Egypt had absorbed its new Soviet bloc weapons. On that date, in a speech to the Knesset he warned Egypt: "This one-sided war will have to stop, for it cannot remain one-sided forever." He authorized Dayan to start planning for seizure of the Strait of Tiran. Now, in July 1956, he gave tentative approval to planning for war that year, and Dayan and his staff began to make final adjustments to existing plans for an operation codenamed "Kadesh." An important preliminary to the plan was to hasten delivery, if possible, of military equipment on order from France.

During the previous two years there had been increasing collaboration in Mediterranean affairs between France and Israel. This was mainly due to the fact that Nasser, in his self-appointed role as leader of the Arab nations, had been providing both moral and physical encouragement and support to the rebels in the French colony of Algeria. By 1954 common enmity of Nasser had led France to provide weapons to Israel on easy terms. Particularly instrumental in establishing this relationship was young Shimon Peres, the dynamic Director General of the Israeli Ministry of Defense. A close relationship in exchange of information was also established between the French Deuxieme Bureau and General Harkabi's Israeli military intelligence organization.

The French Foreign Ministry was not happy about the close relationship which was developing between the French and Israeli intelligence agencies, or between the defense ministries of the two countries. However, even the Foreign Ministry gave reluctant approval to the French-Israeli military rapprochement in late April 1956, after a French warship stopped an Egyptian vessel off the coast of Algeria and found it loaded with arms for the Algerian rebels. One week earlier Nasser had made a formal commitment to France that he would stop all arms shipments to the Algerians.

In early August 1956, following the Ben Gurion-Dayan decision for war, Major General Meir Amit, head of the Operations Branch of the Israeli General Staff, visited Paris to try to expedite some of the agreed weapons shipments. Unexpectedly he was asked rather bluntly if Israel would cooperate with the Anglo-French allies in the event they carried out military operations against Egypt.[1] After cabling Tel Aviv for instructions, General Amit initiated negotiations leading to an agreement on a joint invasion of Egypt.

PLANNING OPERATION "MUSKETEER"

When the British Ministry of Defence started planning for a Suez Canal operation on August 3, Lieutenant General Sir Hugh Stockwell, commanding a corps of the British Army of the Rhine in Germany, was called back to London to head up the planning staff for the proposed amphibious operation. Stockwell, a veteran of several amphibious assaults in World War II, was also familiar with the Middle East, having been in command in northern Palestine during the last years of the British Mandate. Within a few days Stockwell and his planners were joined in their War Office planning room, in a subterranean chamber deep under the Thames River, by some French liaison officers. From the beginning, however, most of the planning was done by the British.

Quite early in their planning Stockwell and his staff decided against a direct thrust down the Canal from Port Said. The northern portion of the Canal for more than 40 kilometers is flanked on both sides by impassable lakes or marshes with no solid ground other than the road and railroad embankments beside the waterway. The British planners believed, therefore, that the initial airborne and amphibious landing should be made at and near Alexandria, where there are excellent beaches and a good seaport for a base. Seizure of Alexandria was to be followed by a quick thrust eastward across the Nile Delta to reach the Canal on a broad front.

Stockwell's planners decided that the earliest they could mount this

---

[1] In his book, *Story of My Life* (Tel Aviv, 1976), p. 151, Moshe Dayan suggests that General Amit was sent to Paris to explore negotiation possibilities following an initial query through the Israeli military attache.

operation would be on September 8. Air Marshal Denis Barnett, who was to be the air commander for the operation, assured Stockwell that the Egyptian Air Force would be destroyed within 36 hours. Stockwell added 12 hours for safety, and thus set D-Day for September 6, when a massive British airstrike against the Egyptian airfields in the Delta and the Canal Zone would destroy the effectiveness of the Egyptian Air Force. This would facilitate the approach of the amphibious flotilla to the Alexandria beaches two days later. The initial landing was to be made by Royal Marines and a division of the French Foreign Legion which had been trained for amphibious operations. Immediately after the landing armored spearheads would rush to the Canal Zone via the northern suburbs of Cairo, but bypassing the Egyptian capital.

Working day and night the planners finished their work by August 8, when they submitted their plan—initially code-named "Hamilcar"—to the British Ministry of Defence. The Ministry approved the plan that same day and sent orders alerting British troops in Cyprus and Malta. At the same time the French government alerted troops in Algeria. Stockwell immediately flew to Algeria, Malta, and Cyprus to make an inspection trip of the Allied forces assigned to the operation, and to give personal instructions to the troop commanders.

When the plan reached Prime Minister Eden a day or two later, however, it was accompanied by some serious Foreign Office questions about landings in the vicinity of Alexandria. Landing so far away from the Canal seemed to the diplomats to be inconsistent with the concept of a police action that was designed only to protect the Canal from the Egyptians. Even worse, the operation would require the seizure of at least part of Cairo in order to move rapidly to the Canal Zone. This was politically unacceptable. The Prime Minister agreed.

So a week later, when Stockwell returned from his trip to the Mediterranean, he was ordered to revise the plan in order to provide for an initial assault at or near Port Said. The plan was modified accordingly; the Marines were to land on the west side of the northern entrance to the Canal at Port Said, with the French Foreign Legion landing on the east side at Port Fuad. This assault was to be preceded by airborne landings to secure the Port Said airport and the beaches and their exits. Following the landings there would be a combined thrust down the road and railroad embankments to Kantara. This difficult operation would be assisted by helicopter-borne attacks to wipe out bottlenecks on the narrow corridors. Once the invaders reached Kantara, ground for maneuver could be found on both sides of the Canal, to facilitate a quick drive to Suez.

At this time British General Sir Charles Keightley was appointed overall commander of the allied combined operation. His deputy was French

Admiral Pierre Barjot. Stockwell was confirmed as land force commander, with French General André Beaufre as his deputy. The air commander was British Air Marshal Denis Barnett; the naval commander was Admiral Robin Durnford-Slater; each had a French deputy.

Also at about this time, in mid-August, another political decision was taken which seriously affected the attack planning. The planners had allowed five days for the slow-moving landing craft, steaming from Malta and Algerian bases, to reach the assault area. Thus they had provided for a D−3 departure in order to be able to make a D+2 landing. But Prime Minister Eden feared that it would not be possible to keep the embarkation a secret. He and the French Government planned to issue a twelve hour ultimatum to Nasser to withdraw from the Canal Zone, a demand which would obviously be rejected by the Egyptians. Upon the expiration of the ultimatum the allied air bombardment would begin. But if it were known that the embarkation of the assault forces had been made prior to the rejection of the ultimatum, it would be difficult for the French and British Governments to justify the operation as a policing action.

Eden's decision was essentially political, but it was apparently easier for him to make it, overriding the bitter protests of Generals Keightley and Stockwell, because he seems to have received conflicting military advice from Air Marshal Barnett. The air commander is believed to have assured Eden that the air bombardment would cause a complete collapse of the Egyptian armed forces and that the amphibious assault would really be unnecessary. In any event, the Prime Minister insisted that the invasion fleet could not even start the loading process until after the bombing began. This meant that—allowing time for loading—the landing would be on D+7, or September 13.

Finally the operation as modified—and now code-named "Musketeer"— was accepted by both the British and the French governments. Phase One called for the destruction of the Egyptian Air Force. In Phase Two a continuing air offensive would disrupt Egypt's economy and logistics and reduce Egyptian morale, while the amphibious force was at sea. Phase Three, beginning on September 13, would comprise airborne and amphibious assaults at the northern end of the Suez Canal, and then the occupation of the Canal Zone.

In the two weeks remaining before the planned embarkation time the British and French troops rushed to complete their preparations. They were ready to sail on September 6. However, the operation was postponed, without any explanation to the troops or their commanders. The reason, in fact, was to permit completion of negotiations with the Israelis, and then to allow Israel to make its own preparations to fit its plans in with those of Musketeer.[2] However, since even the senior leaders of the allied expeditionary force were not informed that their operation was to be coordinated with the Israelis, they had no idea of the reason for delay. The British and French landing craft remained combat loaded, and the participating troops were kept in military installations, isolated from their families and all outside contacts. Since there were no explanations, morale problems were severe.. There were some practical problems, as well, such as keeping the batteries charged on idle trucks and tanks on the landing craft.

In late September Dayan and a small planning staff met with French military leaders in Paris to coordinate plans. By early October D-Day was set for October 20. A few days later it was revised, and became firm: October 29 for the Israelis, October 31 for the European allies. The Israelis—by a threat to the Suez Canal—would give the British and French an excuse for initiating a police action for the purpose of preventing Israeli-Egyptian hostilities from disrupting traffic on the Canal. With D-Day set for October 31, this meant that the Anglo-French troops would land at Port Said on November 7. Stockwell hoped that by the 10th his troops would be able to fight their way south 160 kilometers from Port Said to reach Suez, the southern terminus of the Canal.

THE SÈVRES AGREEMENT

On October 16, the date that these plans were tentatively agreed on by representatives of Britain, France and Israel, Prime Minister Ben Gurion received an invitation from France to attend a secret meeting with representatives of the British and French Governments to complete the negotiations, and to assure full coordination of all aspects of the operation. Ben Gurion, who had been prepared to fight the Egyptians without the participation of the British and French, was beginning to have second thoughts about being involved in a multi-national operation, because he was afraid that the British and French might pretend to the rest of the world that Israel was the aggressor in the war, and that they were the peacekeepers, as well as the saviors of the Suez Canal. Furthermore, relations were strained with Britain, which was upset by Israeli raids against Jordan, which had an alliance with Britain.

Peres and General Dayan, however, urged Ben Gurion to attend the meeting in order to reach a clearcut understanding with the Anglo-

[2] See Moshe Dayan, *op. cit.*, pp. 151-194, and Golda Meir, *My Life* (Tel Aviv, 1975), pp. 245-246, for the Israeli version of these events. It has also been suggested that another reason for the delay was last-minute second thoughts in the British and French governments because of a speech by President Eisenhower on September 5, emphasizing that the crisis had to be resolved peacefully. In light of the circumstances here recounted, as well as Dayan's version, it is doubtful if the Eisenhower speech influenced either of the allies.

French allies and in particular to pin down the British. Ben Gurion did not trust the British in general or Anthony Eden in particular. It would also provide an opportunity for the Israelis to demand officially what had already been promised informally: French aerial defense of Israel's homeland to prevent Egyptian air attacks on Tel Aviv and Jerusalem before the allied air bombardment began.

The conference began on October 22 at Sèvres, near Paris. From the outset Ben Gurion made it very clear that he would not accept a situation in which Israel initiated the war, thus giving Britain and France an opportunity to intervene, ostensibly as peacemakers. General Dayan, however, was able to make a proposal which was acceptable to Ben Gurion and satisfactory to the British and French, and which would not involve serious changes in the overall operational plans for either Operation Kadesh or Operation Musketeer. Dayan's plan was that an Israeli paratroop battalion should be dropped near the Mitla Pass less than 40 miles from the Canal Zone, in an apparent Israeli raid in retaliation for fedayeen terrorism. If the British and French kept their promise by going into action against Egypt following this limited Israeli move, then Israel would continue Operation Kadesh according to the plan. If the British and French did not move in, Ben Gurion and Dayan would still have an opportunity to pull out the paratroop unit and explain it as merely one more punitive raid.

France agreed to provide urgently needed equipment, particularly trucks, and to send 60 planes and pilots to help the Israeli Air Force provide air cover for Israel. Some French transport aircraft would also be sent to assist in air movement of ground forces and supplies. On October 24—at Ben Gurion's insistence—a formal protocol was drawn up, specifying the agreement to go ahead with the plan; it was signed by representatives of all three governments. Ben Gurion, Dayan, and Peres then flew back to Israel. Ben Gurion, however, waited three more days— until October 28, one day before the operation was to begin—before he informed his government of the agreement with the British and French. It was a tribute to his prestige and authority that the wide and sweeping commitments that he had made without any governmental authority were approved without question by the entire Israeli Cabinet.

During those three days Dayan had been ordering extensive troop movements along the Jordanian frontier. Partial Israeli mobilization had begun on the 25th, and, while this was initiated in the utmost secrecy, the Israelis knew that some word of unusual activity would reach the outside world. The impression to be given, therefore, was of a planned raid against Jordan. Credibility to this had been provided two weeks earlier, by a major Israeli retaliation raid against Qalqilya, in Jordan, during the night of October 10-11.

One incident will demonstrate the extent and nature of the secrecy and deception which were used. On October 26 the Director General of the Prime Minister's office asked Ben Gurion what was going on. The Prime Minister, after swearing his assistant to absolute secrecy, told him that Israel was planning a possible attack on Jordan and that the troop movements were taking place to permit this in the event it became necessary.

There is no evidence that the Arab states were aware of either the Israeli or Anglo-French planning, or of their proposed collaboration. Because of the Suez crisis, of course, Nasser had long recognized the fact that British and French forces in the Mediterranean could be committed against the Canal Zone on short notice. And all of the Arabs were apparently aware of unusual activity along Israel's side of the frontier with Jordan. These facts, however, do not appear to have in any way influenced a joint decision announced on October 25 by the governments of Egypt, Jordan and Syria. They had concluded a new military agreement for the formation of a single command under an Egyptian general. On the other hand, this increasing formalization of the threat of a three-pronged invasion of Israel gave greater urgency to Israeli planning.

One indication of the effectiveness of Israeli security is that on October 26, the day after announcement of the joint military command, General Abd el Hakim Amer, the Egyptian and Allied Arab commander in chief, left on a trip to visit the Jordanian and Syrian headquarters. Early on October 30, as originally planned, he returned to Cairo; the war had begun the previous evening.

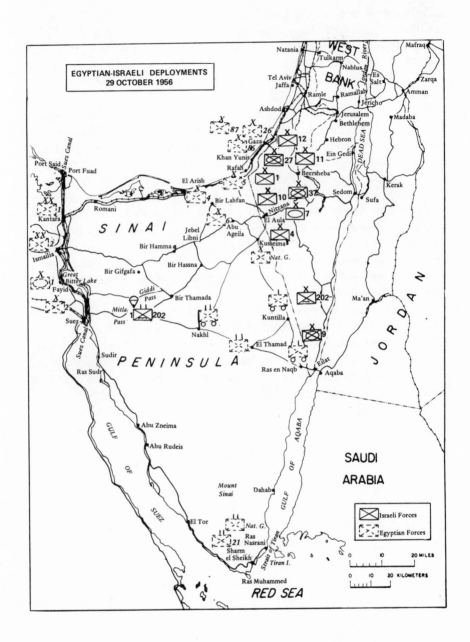

EGYPTIAN-ISRAELI DEPLOYMENTS
29 OCTOBER 1956

3

Sinai Offensive

THE TERRAIN

The Sinai Peninsula is a triangular-shaped isthmus, some 200 kilometers wide in the north between the Suez Canal and the Israeli frontier, and about 400 kilometers in north-south depth from El Arish on the Mediterranean coast to the tip of Point Muhammad jutting southward into the Red Sea between the Gulf of Aqaba and the Gulf of Suez. In the extreme north is a flat, narrow coastal band with scant vegetation; the remainder of the isthmian region, to the south, is covered by arid, rugged hills and constantly shifting sand dunes. The southern half of the peninsula is dominated by still higher, jagged mountain peaks rising to 8,000 feet. Extending northwestward from this mountain range is a ridge, some 30 to 50 kilometers inland from the Gulf of Suez coast and the Suez Canal. The only major town in this vast desolate region is El Arish, which has traditionally served as a civilian market and military supply center, and which is located near the coast on the northeastern portion of the peninsula.

Four major east-west routes traverse the northern portion of the Sinai. The northernmost is a hard-surface coastal road running westward from Gaza to Kantara by way of Rafah, El Arish and Romani. Running beside this was a narrow gauge railroad line (built by the British in World War I and torn up by the Israelis after 1967), a major supply route for the Egyptian forces in the northern and northeastern Sinai. The north central route—also hard-surfaced—runs from Auja, on the Israeli-Egyptian border, to Abu Ageila, then on across the northern tip of the western mountain ridge to Ismailia. Paralleling this second route is a road, parts of which were then dirt, starting initially in a southwest direction from El Auja, passing through Kusseima and Bir Hassna to Bir el Thamada, where the road splits; the northern fork continues westward through the Giddi Pass to reach the Suez Canal near the Little Bitter Lake; the southern fork goes through the Mitla Pass to reach the Canal just north of Suez. The fourth route, which at that time was in many places little better than a track, runs west from the southern Negev to Thamad, Nakhl, the Mitla Pass (where it joins the third route), and

Suez. The only one of these routes with some good water supply through-out the year was the northern, coastal road.

In addition to these east-west roads, there are north-south routes down both sides of the peninsula, converging at Sharm el Sheikh, just northeast of Point Muhammad, the southern tip. The western road, paralleling the Gulf of Suez through Abu Rudeis, Abu Zneima, and El Tor, was paved and easily traversable. The route down the eastern side of the peninsula followed a number of wandering, difficult tracks, several miles inland from the Gulf of Aqaba.

About 15 kilometers northeast of Sharm el Sheikh is Ras Nasrani, at the Strait of Tiran, controlling the only access by sea to the Gulf of Aqaba and the Israeli port of Eilat. Two islands in the Strait, Tiran and Sinafir, and a number of coral reefs narrow the waterway to only 600 meters at Ras Nasrani.

EGYPTIAN DEPLOYMENTS

Following the nationalization of the Suez Canal in July of 1956, it became obvious to the Egyptians that the British and French were con-templating various methods for removing President Nasser from power and returning the Canal to European control. In August Anglo-French forces began to mass on Cyprus and Malta, and although Nasser found it hard to believe that either power would intervene physically in Egypt he withdrew much of the Sinai garrison to the Delta region, in order to be better prepared to meet possible Anglo-French moves against the Canal. Thus, at the time of the Israeli attack, Egyptian forces in the Sinai Peninsula numbered approximately 30,000 men, only half of the normal Sinai garrison strength.

The bulk of the Egyptian force in the Sinai was deployed in static defense positions in the northeast triangle formed by El Arish, Rafah and Abu Ageila. There were two divisions and other miscellaneous units under the direction of the Eastern Command of Major General Ali Amer, with headquarters at Ismailia. The 3d Infantry Division had one brigade at Rafah (the 5th), one at Abu Ageila (the 6th), and one at El Arish (the 4th). The 8th Palestinian Division, stationed in the Gaza Strip, consisted of the 86th and 87th Palestinian Brigades and the 26th Egyptian National Guard Brigade; these units were poorly trained and lightly armed. Although the majority of the men in the 86th and 87th Brigades were Palestinian, all of the officers and most of the NCOs were Egyptian. There were three squadrons of Sherman tanks in the Peninsula, one at Rafah and two at El Arish. Each brigade was supported by a normal field artillery complement of 12 to 16 guns, mostly British 25-pounders. In addition a number of "Archer" self-propelled 17-pounder antitank guns were distributed among the troops. The mountain areas and the isolated border stretches southeast of Abu Ageila were patrolled by the motorized Border Patrol, which was organized on constabulary rather than military lines.

The garrison of the Sharm el Sheikh region, at the southern end of the peninsula, was not under Eastern Command, but was directly under control of General Headquarters in Cairo. This garrison consisted of the 21st Infantry Battalion, one National Guard battalion, two platoons from the Border Patrol, a battery of two six-inch coastal guns, another battery of four three-inch coastal guns, six 30mm antiaircraft guns, and four 75mm antiaircraft guns. Based also in the harbor of Sharm el Sheikh was the frigate *Rashid*. Observation outposts were established at Es-shat, Abu Zneima, El Tor, Tava, Wasil, Dahab, and both of the nearby islands. All of these posts were in radio communications with Sharm el Sheikh.

Just west of the Suez Canal were two infantry divisions and an armored division. They were under the command of General Ali Amer, and available for operations in the Sinai.

The Egyptian Air Force had some 255 aircraft. There were three squadrons (45 aircraft) of MiG-15s, three squadrons (40 aircraft) of Vampires, two squadrons (32 aircraft) of Meteors, and four squadrons (49 aircraft) of Il-28 light bombers. There were 60 transport aircraft, one squadron of eight reconnaissance planes, and one squadron of six night fighters (Meteor NT-13), and a few administrative craft. Not all of these aircraft were operational, however. Fully operational were two squadrons of MiG-15s, a squadron of Vampires, a squadron of Meteors, a squadron of Il-28s, and all 60 transports, for a total of 130 operational planes, of which 70 were combat aircraft.

ISRAELI DEPLOYMENTS AND PLAN

By the evening of October 28, just before D-Day, the Israeli Army had mobilized all 18 of its mobile field force brigades.[1] Twelve of these brigades were assigned to—or available to—the Southern Command of Brigadier General Assaf Simhoni. The other six were held in reserve in the northern and central sections of the country, ready to deal with any hostile moves from Syria or Jordan.

The units of the Southern Command totalled some 45,000 combat troops, divided into two task groups[2] and two brigade groups, each of which was assigned to one of four principal land routes or axes. The Northern Task Group (known also as Task Group 77) was commanded by Brigadier General Haim Laskov, and consisted of the 1st Infantry and

---

[1] On October 27 and again on the 28th, President Eisenhower sent messages to Ben Gurion, urging him to demobilize.

[2] Called "ugdah," approximately division-sized units.

27th Armored Brigades, with support from the 11th Infantry Brigade. Its axis of advance was the coastal road, through El Arish.

The Central Task Group (also known as Task Group 38) was commanded by Colonel Yehudah Wallach and comprised the 4th and 10th Infantry Brigades, and the 7th Armored Brigade. The 37th Mechanized (or Armored) Brigade, in GHQ reserve, was earmarked to support Wallach if necessary. This task group, or division, was to advance along one or both of the two central Sinai routes toward the Canal.

The southern axis was assigned to the 202d Paratroop Brigade under Colonel Ariel Sharon. Still further south, the 9th Mechanized Brigade, commanded by Colonel Avraham Yoffe, was to advance southward from Eilat, along the route down the Gulf of Aqaba to Sharm el Sheikh. One additional unit—the 12th Infantry Brigade—was in reserve, intially assigned a support role in the Gaza area; later it was to be available to follow troops of Task Group 38 or the 202d Paratroop Brigade advancing along the Gulf of Suez toward Sharm el Sheikh.

The objectives of operation Kadesh were:[3] to create a military threat to the Suez Canal by seizing the high ground just to its east; to capture the Strait of Tiran (and thus end the blockade of Eilat and open the Gulf of Aqaba to Israeli shipping); and to create confusion in the disposition of the Egyptian Army in the Sinai Peninsula, and bring about its collapse (and thus prevent or delay any possibility of an Egyptian attack against Israel). An implicit objective was to destroy fedayeen bases in the Gaza Strip and on the Sinai border.

The spearhead of the threat to the Suez Canal would be the 1st Battalion of the 202d Paratroop Brigade, which was to be dropped at the western entrance to the Mitla Pass, some 170 kilometers west of the Israeli frontier, and a little more than 30 kilometers from the Canal. This action was expected to create the threat which would spark and justify the Anglo-French operation. At the same time, the remainder of the paratroop brigade would advance overland by way of Kuntilla, Thamad and Nakhl to link up with the 1st Battalion west of Mitla. This operation was designed so that, if the British and French did not carry out their part of the agreement—and until the very last minute Ben Gurion had serious doubts if the British would follow through with it—the paratroopers at the pass could be withdrawn, and the whole incident could be explained as a raid in reprisal for Egyptian-fedayeen frontier activity.

Wallach's Central Task Group would not move at all on D-Day but its 4th Brigade would begin its advance that night, southwest from Nitzana

<hr>

[3] As stated in General Dayan's Operational Directive of October 25, quoted in his *Diary of the Sinai Campaign, 1956* (London, 1967), p. 197. The first of these objectives was directly related to the Anglo-French "Musketeer" operation, which would be launched as an indirect result of the Israeli military threat to the Canal.

to seize Kusseima before dawn on D + 1. The 10th Infantry Brigade would wait until that night (D + 1) before moving directly through El Auja against the Abu Ageila-Um Katef positions from the east. After a 48-hour delay, the 7th Armored Brigade was to carry out an exploitation into the central Sinai. The 37th Mechanized Brigade was to be held in reserve to be used either for reinforcements or for exploitation as needed. The 48-hour delay in employment of armor was intended to allow the Israelis time to evaluate Egyptian and world reaction and to make absolutely certain of Anglo-French involvement, before becoming irrevocably committed to a full-scale campaign. Furthermore, once the Anglo-French operation against the Egyptian Air Force had begun, Israeli armor should have much greater freedom of action in the Sinai.

Laskov's Northern Task Group was to undertake no actions until the evening of D + 2, when it would attack Egyptian positions at Rafah, and isolate the Gaza Strip. While the 1st Infantry Brigade cleared the Rafah area, the 27th Mechanized Brigade was to break through to El Arish, and then to proceed west toward the Canal.

Not until after the Gaza Strip was isolated by the Northern Task Group would the 11th Infantry Brigade start its operations against the Strip. It would expect to be supported by all or part of the 37th Mechanized Brigade, which presumably could be released for this purpose from the Central Task Group after the capture of Abu Ageila. Also available for support in the Gaza area, if needed, would be elements of the 12th Infantry Brigade, in GHQ reserve.

After the main body of the 202d Paratroop Brigade had linked up with its 1st Battalion at the Mitla Pass, elements of that brigade supported by units of the 12th Infantry Brigade—which would be flown in as they were released from operations in the Gaza Strip—would move down the west coast road toward Sharm el Sheikh, and be prepared to assist the 9th Brigade in its capture, if necessary.

Since the Anglo-French air forces were to deal with the main force of the Egyptian Air Force, and since additional French aircraft were to provide air protection for Israeli air bases and civilian centers, the Israeli Air Force was expected to be able to devote itself almost completely to ground support tasks, either interdiction or close support. In addition the Air Force was given transportation, supply, and evacuation missions. At the outbreak of war, on October 29, Israel had 155 operational aircraft, of which 69 were modern French Mystère or Ourigan or British Meteor jet fighters, and 45 were piston-engined fighter-bombers. Commanding the air force was Brigadier General Dan Tolkowsky.

The Israeli Navy was assigned service and support roles primarily in the Red Sea. The Israeli Chief of Staff, General Dayan, believed that the Anglo-French naval forces would sufficiently restrict Egyptian naval activity in the Mediterranean. Commanding the Navy was Brigadier General (or Rear Admiral) Shmuel Tankus.

As early as October 23 three squadrons of French aircraft arrived in Israel. The primary mission of one squadron—Mystère fighters—was to protect Israeli cities from possible Egyptian bombing raids before the Anglo-French attack on Egyptian air fields. A squadron of F-84 fighter-bombers was to assist the Mystères in the air protection role and otherwise be available to provide support for the Israeli Army. A NorAtlas transport squadron was given the mission of supporting the 202d Paratroop Brigade, and particularly assuring adequate resupply to the 1st Battalion dropped near the Mitla Pass.

On October 29, a few hours before the planned late afternoon H-Hour, a change was made in the drop zone of the 1st Battalion of the 202d Paratroop Brigade. Aerial reconnaissance had detected considerable Egyptian activity just west of the Mitla Pass, in the general area that had been selected as the drop area. (It later turned out that this was simply a civilian construction gang working on road repairs.) Therefore, instead of being dropped at the west end of the pass the battalion would be dropped at a site near the so-called Parker Monument[4] near the eastern end of the pass, 65 kilometers from the Canal, and thus a less direct threat to the waterway.[5]

---

[4] This small, somewhat crude, Bedouin-constructed memorial to a British colonial administrator is known to history by the name of another man. Edward Palmer reconnoitered and explored the Sinai Peninsula in 1882 for the British Government during the complicated diplomatic and military maneuvering that preceded the British occupation of Egypt. Palmer, an impecunious professor of Arabic, was recruited by the First Lord of the Admiralty, Lord Northrop, to explore the region east of the Suez Canal, and to gain the support of the Sinai Bedouin for the British. He was supplied with considerable gold, and this, combined with his facility in the language, helped him make friends with many of the Bedouin. However, after some initial success, he was killed and robbed by the Hewaitat Tribe in the region just east of Suez. When the British occupied Egypt a few months later, they sent a punitive force to avenge Palmer's death, and hanged some of the Bedouin. The Hewaitat people and some of their neighbors tried to make amends to regain British favor and built the small monument to the memory of Palmer, just east of the Mitla Pass. But about 30 years later, the best known British name in the Sinai region was that of Colonel A.C. Parker, Governor General of the Sinai from 1910 to 1923. The Arab pronunciation of these two names was such that local Britons, unaware of the story of Palmer, thought the memorial was for Governor Parker; so it became known as the Parker Monument. Dayan (*op. cit.*, p. 79) was unaware of the true origin of the name. There is apparently still confusion about this in the British Ministry of Defence, as the author learned in a conversation with the British Military Attaché to Israel in October 1975. The monument has disappeared since 1967.

[5] After the war Sharon learned that GHQ in Tel Aviv had already discovered that the Egyptians west of the pass were not a military force, but unaccountably had not changed the drop area back to that originally planned. (Interview with Sharon.)

THE PARATROOP ASSAULT

Shortly after 4:20 p.m. on October 29 the first of four flights of four Dakota aircraft crossed the Israeli-Egyptian border, carrying in each flight approximately 100 men of the 1st Battalion of the Israeli 202d Paratroop Brigade, commanded by Lieutenant Colonel Rafael Eitan. The aircraft flew at an altitude of approximately 500 feet in order to avoid radar detection, and were escorted by ten Israeli Meteors. Sixteen Mystères were patrolling across the central Sinai, looking for activity from nearby Egyptian airbases. There was none.

At 4:59 the leading Dakotas rose to an altitude of 1,500 feet, and the paratroopers began their jump. There was no opposition, there was no interference, and apparently not a single Egyptian soldier saw the operation. By dusk Eitan had assembled his 395 troops, taking care of the few minor drop injuries. Realizing that he was several kilometers east of the east end of the pass, he marched westward. By 5:30 the paratroopers had reached what they believed to be the two hills marking the eastern end of the pass, and in the gathering dark they deployed in defensive positions. In addition to digging themselves in, they established blocking positions and ambushes on the road in both directions. Electronic guidance beams for resupply aircraft were set out. These planes arrived on schedule at 9:00. The paratroopers were strengthened by eight jeeps, four 106mm recoilless guns, two 120mm mortars, ammunition, water, food and medicine, parachuted from six French aircraft.[6] Dropped with the reinforcements and supplies was an order that they should not move into the Mitla Pass itself.

Although the drop had not been observed by the Egyptians, shortly after dark three Egyptian vehicles—carrying soldiers from the Frontier Regiment going on leave—approached one of the Israeli blocking positions on the road from the east. The Israelis ambushed and destroyed one of these vehicles but the others escaped. One returned to Nakhl to report the situation; the other also soon reported the incident at El Shatt. Thus by mid-evening two Egyptian installations in the Sinai knew that there were Israelis near the Mitla Pass.

[6] Apparently there has been some controversy as to whether these were French or Israeli aircraft which brought in the resupplies. Both Kennett Love (*Suez: The Twice Fought War*) and Sylvia Crosbie (*The Tacit Alliance*) assert that they were French aircraft. On the other hand, S.L.A. Marshall (*Sinai Victory*) and Robert Henriques (*A Hundred Hours to Suez*) state that the same Dakotas which had dropped the men also dropped the supplies. General Dayan says only that the supplies were dropped. Since Henriques was certainly deceived by the Israelis, and Marshall may have been, and since the French had sent supply aircraft to Israel for just such purposes, Love and Crosbie are assumed to be correct. The Egyptians say this is confirmed by their intelligence.

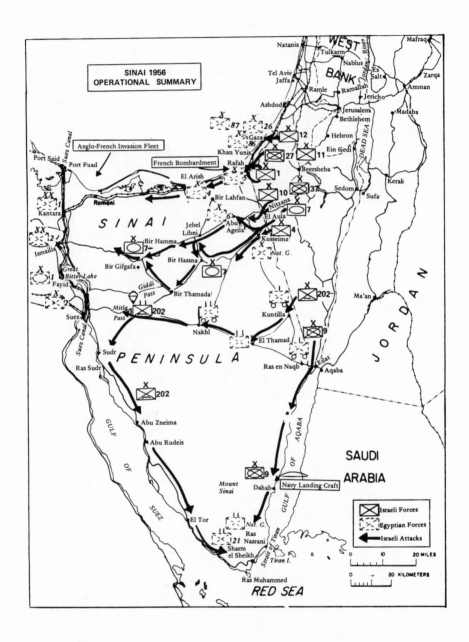

SINAI 1956
OPERATIONAL SUMMARY

Meanwhile, the main body of Sharon's paratroop brigade had been on the road for several hours. To support the impression of a possible Israeli operation against Jordan, the brigade had originally been assigned a concentration point at Ein Khussub, near the Jordanian frontier. In order to march most of the way across the Negev and to reach their starting positions on the Egyptian frontier by 4:00 p.m., they had to leave Ein Khussub at 3:00 in the morning.

In addition to the battalion near the Mitla Pass, Sharon's command consisted of his other two paratroop battalions, two Nahal (military-agricultural corps) companies, a squadron of thirteen AMX tanks, a field artillery battery of eight 25-pounders, a battery of eight 120mm mortars, two Piper aircraft (including one which joined the 1st Battalion at Mitla just before dark), and the usual support units. The total strength of the ground column was about 3,000 men.

The brigade had been allocated some 150 modern 6x6 military trucks which had recently been supplied by France (part of the Sèvres Agreement), equipped with six-wheel drive to enable them to cross difficult stretches of desert easily. These trucks did not reach Israel until October 27. Late on the 28th, Sharon was informed that he would receive only 90 of them. By seven o'clock the next morning, four hours after he was supposed to have been on the road, only 46 trucks had arrived. Sharon decided that further delay would endanger the link-up of the brigade with the battalion near the pass. He mounted his troops in the available trucks, in halftracks, and in as many civilian vehicles as he could commandeer, and the brigade began to move.

It was nearly 100 kilometers from Ein Khussub to the Egyptian frontier near Kuntilla, and the trip was planned to take 13 hours. The attrition rate among the vehicles was very high, however. Most of the civilian trucks bogged down in the sand, and others had to be abandoned because of mechanical failures. Of thirteen tanks which started out with the brigade in the morning only seven reached Kuntilla. Nevertheless, most of the paratroopers covered the distance across the Negev in nine hours, and crossed the border at 4:00 p.m. on schedule.

The first Egyptian opposition was encountered at Kuntilla. The shallow entrenchments there were manned by one platoon of the Border Patrol, most of whose members were killed or captured by Sharon's reconnaissance company shortly after 5:00 p.m. The Israelis suffered the loss of one jeep and two halftracks to mines, and one man was wounded.

When Sharon arrived at Kuntilla at about 5:30, he sent his reconnaissance company south to secure the Ras en Nagb-Thamad track junction while he focussed his attention on concentrating the brigade, whose main body was now spread out for many kilometers between Kuntilla and the frontier, and east into the Negev. Those vehicles lacking front-wheel drive had been the first to become immobilized in the sand, but eventually all types of vehicles, including the new trucks, armored personnel carriers, and halftracks became stuck at one time or another. Some of them, however, were able to pull themselves out or to work together to do so, and a thin stream of vehicles trickled into Kuntilla. The location of the gasoline trucks in the rear of the column complicated the general predicament of the brigade, because these vehicles were unable to get around the miles of stuck vehicles to fuel those which had been freed in front.

Sharon was eager to move on toward Thamad before Egyptian reinforcements could reach it, and so he and his staff made frantic efforts to get the column moving. By 10:00 p.m. the fuel trucks began to get through, and Sharon had most of his 2nd Battalion in Kuntilla. He therefore ordered all available units to advance, following the reconnaissance company, with the brigade headquarters in the lead of the main body. Staff officers were left behind in Kuntilla, to order the remaining units to catch up as best they could.

EGYPTIAN REACTION

Meanwhile the first confirmed reports regarding the Israeli actions came in to Egyptian General Headquarters in Cairo at about 7:00 p.m. An observer near Kuntilla reported seeing a concentration of trucks on the road near the border, with Israeli aircraft overhead. Almost simultaneously came a radio report from the Border Patrol station at Nakhl, reporting that a number of planes had dropped paratroopers near the Mitla Pass. This report had been carried by the trucks that escaped the Israeli ambush.

Some time after 9:00 p.m. President Nasser received Israel's announcement that Israel Defense Forces had attacked guerrilla bases at Kuntilla and at Ras en Nagb and had taken up positions west of the Nakhl junction on the route to the Canal. Nasser soon joined his Commander in Chief, General Abdel Hakim Amer, at general headquarters where other messages were arriving, confirming the earlier reports.

Nasser learned that at 8:00 p.m. General Ali Amer's Eastern Command had ordered the 5th and 6th Battalions of the 2d Infantry Brigade at Fayid, just west of the Canal, to advance against the Israeli force at Mitla. Nasser had at once ordered that there should be no interruption of commercial traffic in the Canal; he seems to have feared that any stoppage of shipping would be seized upon by the British and French as grounds for intervention. At 9:00 p.m. the 5th Battalion began crossing the Canal by a drawbridge north of Suez. Because of Nasser's orders, it took the 5th Battalion eight hours to complete its crossing, while the 6th Battalion was twelve hours getting across the Canal.

By 11:00 p.m. Nasser and the Egyptian General Staff had completed their assessment of the situation. With Nasser's approval General Amer activated the prepared defense plan to deal with such an Israeli invasion. While the frontier forces were to delay and hold up the Israeli advance as much as they could, major Egyptian forces would mass in the rear in the vicinity of Bir Gifgafa and Bir el Thamada, preparing to carry out a simple envelopment, probably in the Abu Ageila area. This confrontation was expected to take place about November 2 or 3.

As part of the concentration, General Ali Amer ordered the 2d Light Reconnaissance Regiment, followed by the 1st and 2d Armored Groups (or brigades) of the 4th Armored Division to cross the Canal from the Deversoir area and assemble between Bir Gifgafa and Bir Rud Salim. Two National Guard brigades would follow these units into the same area. To deal with the immediate situation, the 2d Light Reconnaissance Regiment was to move south from the assembly area to cut off the paratroopers east of the Mitla Pass, while the 1st Armored Brigade blocked any Israeli movement from the north and central axes.

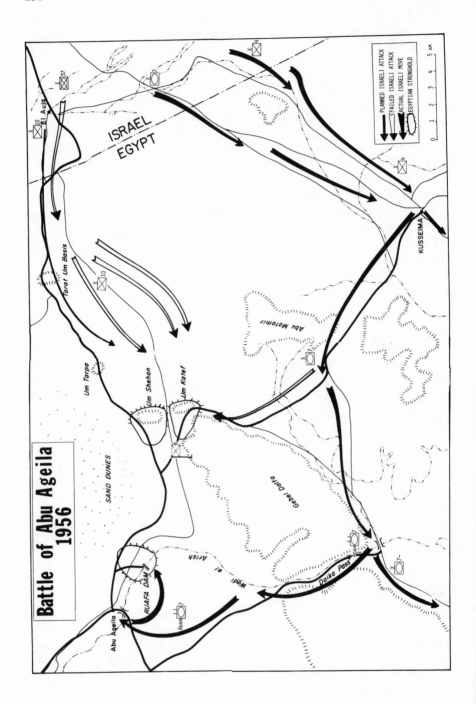

4

The Battle of Abu Ageila,
October 30-November 1

EGYPTIAN FORCES AND DISPOSITIONS

The second phase of the Israeli plan called for the Central Task Group to move from the vicinity of El Auja during the night of October 29-30, its first objective being the assault of the Egyptian positions in the Abu Ageila-Um Katef-Kusseima area the following day.

Abu Ageila is a desert road junction, then marked by a solitary police post, approximately 30 kilometers west of the border at El Auja. There the main east-west road to Ismailia is met by a road coming from Bir Lahfan and El Arish, to the northwest. Approximately twelve kilometers east of Abu Ageila—toward the Israeli frontier—there is another junction where a narrower road, but still paved, joins the main road from the southeast, in the direction of the Kusseima police post. Three kilometers to the east of this unnamed road junction the main road from Beersheba and El Auja to Ismailia crosses the edge of the Um Katef Ridge. Most of the ridge stretches south about six kilometers from the El Auja-Ismailia road. North of the Ismailia road at this point is an area of sand dunes which stretch unbroken for 40 kilometers to Rafah on the coast.

Just south of the main road the ridge rises to a low peak, known as Um Shehan. About three kilometers south is a higher eminence, Um Katef itself. Crossing the ridge between these hills, and parallel to the main road, is a secondary dirt track from El Auja, which joins the main road near Abu Ageila. To the west and south of Um Katef is a much larger, low-lying hill mass known as Jebel Dalfa. The road from Kusseima skirts the northern and eastern flanks of Jebel Dalfa, running between it and Um Katef.

Since an attacker from the east would be expected to make use of all three of these roads in advancing toward the strategic Abu Ageila road junction, and since the area north of the main road consisted of presumably impassable shifting sand dunes, the Egyptians quite naturally located their main defense on Um Shehan and Um Katef and a number of small hills between the sand dunes and Jebel Dalfa. Artillery positions

157

were located about four kilometers west of Um Katef and between low-lying spurs of Jebel Dalfa.

The Um Katef and Um Shehan positions consisted of networks of sandbagged trenches and bunkers in which were emplaced antitank guns, and eleven dug-in Archers (self-propelled 17-pounder, 76mm, high velocity antitank guns of British manufacture). Around the position was a concertina barbed wire barrier which on the north of Um Shehan extended beyond the main road into the dunes. Minefields blocked all of the likely avenues of approach, and a continuous barbed wire fence extended beyond the minefields, encompassing substantial stretches of the roads going through the area.

Another important feature of this area is the Wadi el Arish, dry most of the year, but a respectable stream in the springtime. The sources of this stream are in central Sinai; it flows in a northwesterly direction, west of Jebel Dalfa, crossing the main road just south and west of the Abu Ageila road junction. About three and a half kilometers southeast of Abu Ageila the Egyptians had built a large stone and earthen dam across the course of the Wadi el Arish. In the spring and early summer this impounds a shallow body of water known as the Ruafa Reservoir. High hills on both sides of the stream and of the dam lent themselves to defense, and provided a convenient place for fortifications protecting the rear of the main defensive positions at Um Shehan and Um Katef, and the supporting artillery positions.

South of the Ruafa Dam, the bed of the Wadi el Arish runs northward through a narrow defile between the Jebel Dalfa and Jebel Halal to the west. This defile, known as the Daika Pass, was covered by a patrol. Field fortifications blocked the road from Kusseima where it runs through the Abu Matamir defile, three kilometers south of Um Katef.

The Abu Ageila fortified area was part of a larger defensive area held by the Egyptian 3d Infantry Division, commanded by Brigadier Anwar el Qadi, with headquarters at El Arish. The Abu Ageila-Um Katef fortifications were held by the 6th Brigade, commanded by Colonel Sami Yassa, consisting of the 17th and 18th Battalions. Attached to Colonel Yassa's Abu Ageila command were the 3d Field Artillery Regiment of sixteen 25-pounders, and the 94th and 78th Antitank Batteries (both equipped with eleven Archers). In addition, Yassa had a jeep-mounted reconnaissance company and two companies of reservists. The 18th Infantry Battalion and the 78th Antitank Battery were on the Um Katef position; the 17th Battalion and the 94th Antitank Battery were at the Um Shehan position, with two companies in reserve in the Ruafa Dam area. The artillery regiment was stationed just west of the northern tip of Jebel Dalfa, where it could give 360° support. At the Abu Ageila road junction were assembled most of the brigade's support units, including vehicles, trains, and kitchens, protected by a strong security detachment. Thus the Abu Ageila position consisted of five separate well-defended, well-protected perimeters—Um Katef, Um Shehan, Ruafa Dam, Abu Ageila crossroads, and the artillery perimeter—any three of which were mutually supporting, with artillery, small arms, and antitank fire. Colonel Yassa had his own command post just behind the Um Katef position, and just in front of the artillery. The total strength of Colonel Yassa's command was about 3,000 men.

There were four principal outposts, each manned by a squad or platoon with automatic weapons and mortars. Two of these were on the main road, one near the border and another at Tarat Um Basis. The other two were to the south and southeast: Daika Pass and Abu Matamir defile.

About 20 kilometers to the southeast of Um Katef was the Kusseima police post, about 10 kilometers west of the border, and about 25 kilometers southwest of El Auja, with which it was connected by a good dirt road. Three other reasonably good dirt roads radiated southward from Kusseima. Just west of south was a road to Bir Hassna; southwest lay the road to Nakhl; the course of the road to Thamad was almost due south. Kusseima was thus an important communications center, but it lacked the readily defensible terrain to be found east of Abu Ageila.

Kusseima was also within the zone of responsibility of Brigadier Qadi's 3d Infantry Division. The principal unit there was an understrength, unreliable National Guard battalion of the 26th Brigade. One company held earthwords at the road junction itself; another company covered the roads to the south and southwest. A regular army independent jeep company covered the approaches to Kusseima from the north and northeast; another regular army company, from the 6th Infantry Brigade, reinforced with a bazooka antitank unit, blocked the easily-defensible defiles in the road between Kusseima and Um Katef. The total strength of these units was less than 500 men.

OPENING ISRAELI MOVES

Colonel Wallach's Central Task Group had three brigades assigned, and another—the 37th Mechanized Brigade—was available to him if he needed it to take Abu Ageila. In that case, however, his authority over the brigade would be limited, since it might at any time be called away by Southern Command or GHQ to support one of the other task groups. His control over the 7th Armored Brigade was also limited, but in another way. No Israeli armored units were to cross the frontier before late on October 31st, until it was certain that the British-French intervention was proceeding as agreed at Sèvres. Thus, for the first day and a half Wallach could count on employing only his two infantry brigades, the 4th and the 10th. He assigned to the 4th the task of taking Kusseima early on the 30th, as a preliminary to a full-scale attack by the 10th Brigade on the Um Katef position early the following day.

During the night of October 29-30, the 4th Infantry Brigade, under the command of Colonel Joseph Harpaz, advanced according to plan from its jumpoff point at Beit Hapir, south of Nitzana. The 4th Brigade had three missions. It was to open a route to Bir Hassna through Kusseima. It was to be prepared also to open a route to Nakhl to support the paratroopers if necessary. At the same time it was to unhinge the south flank of the Abu Ageila-Um Katef fortifications, to permit envelopment of that vital defensive position if the subsequent frontal assault by the 10th Infantry Brigade was not successful.

Although Harpaz's Brigade reached its jumpoff point on time, late in the afternoon of the 29th, it was in a state of some confusion. In its rapid mobilization the brigade had departed from its home areas without its full allocation of vehicles, and with only about one-third of its required ammunition load. More vehicles had been lost on the march, due to the same kind of difficulties with sand which were causing so many problems for the 202d Paratroop Brigade.

Nevertheless, shortly after midnight the brigade moved out across the frontier, the 2d Battalion on the right, advancing towards Kusseima, the 3d Battalion on the left, moving toward the height of Jebel Sabha, just across the frontier.

Shortly before dawn Harpaz's 3d Battalion climbed to the top of Jebel Sabha and found it unoccupied. The brigade continued westward, catching the National Guard Battalion at Kusseima by surprise at about 6:00 a.m., just as the 2d Battalion attacked from the northeast. By 7:00 a.m. the two battalions had overcome weak and ineffective resistance and secured Kusseima. The defenders withdrew either southwestward toward Bir Hassna, or northwestward toward Abu Ageila.

Harpaz immediately sent out two reconnaissance patrols to clear any outposts of continuing resistance on the roads to the south and west: to Thamad and Kuntilla, to Nakhl, and to Bir Hassna. Another patrol was to probe north toward Um Katef. By 10:30 the first two patrols had returned and reported the tracks were clear toward Kuntilla, Nakhl, and Bir Hassna. Shortly after this, however, the other patrol returned to report that Egyptians were holding the Abu Matamir defile, on the road to Abu Ageila and Um Katef.

With the 4th Brigade at Kusseima by this time were elements of the 7th Armored Brigade, commanded by Colonel Uri Ben-Ari. The presence of Ben-Ari's tanks in Kusseima was not according to the original plan. In fact, General Dayan's orders had been very specific: the armored brigade was not to cross the frontier into the Sinai until after daylight on the 31st, by which time it would have been decided whether to announce that a full-scale offensive was underway, or that the 202d Paratroop Brigade had merely been making a raid toward the Mitla Pass.

Late on the 29th, however, General Simhoni had become extremely worried about the 4th Infantry Brigade and its great difficulties in reaching its assembly point. He became doubtful whether the brigade would reach Kusseima in time to capture the place by dawn. If the Egyptians were alert, they might well reinforce the defense of Kusseima, then use it as a base for cutting off the paratroopers further south.

Because of the secrecy with which the plans had been prepared, Simhoni did not realize that the limitation on the commitment of the 7th Armored Brigade had been linked, by the direct orders of Prime Minister Ben Gurion, to the proven participation of France and England in the war. He did know, however, that the capture of Kusseima was important because of its potential use against Sharon's brigade. Thus he could see no sense in keeping a powerful and highly mobile military force idle when there was any doubt whether Kusseima could be captured on time. Shortly after midnight, therefore, he sent orders to Ben-Ari to send part of his brigade to cross the frontier at dawn and to reach Kusseima as soon as possible. Ben-Ari sent a task force of one tank company and one halftrack company.

As it turned out, the tanks were not needed at Kusseima. When the battalion arrived at 7 o'clock the 4th Brigade was already there, the Egyptians were withdrawing, and the tankers merely fired a few shots to hasten their retreat.

However, once those shots had been fired the presence of the Israeli armor across the frontier in the Sinai was known to the Egyptians. Since Simhoni could now see no sense in trying to maintain secrecy about the commitment of his armor, he decided to send the rest of the brigade to Kusseima, from which point they were to assist the attack of the 10th Brigade against Abu Ageila.

Having made the commitment of the 7th Armored Brigade, Simhoni could see no further reason for delaying the planned assault against Abu Ageila, initially intended for October 31. Accordingly he directed Wallach to send the 10th Infantry Brigade across the frontier immediately in order to attack Um Katef shortly after dark. The timetable for the attacks by the 7th Armored Brigade and the 4th Infantry Brigade from the south was also advanced.

As soon as Colonel Ben-Ari received instructions to advance to Kusseima and to be prepared to operate against Abu Ageila, he immediately ordered the remainder of his brigade to get on the road. He hastened to Kusseima himself and en route sent radio instructions to his combat team already at Kusseima to reconnoiter the Abu Matamir defile, and if this was open, to advance to within three kilometers of the Um Katef fortifications, and wait there for further orders.

As a result of either a misunderstanding or faulty communications, the advance guard of Ben-Ari's detachment combat team pushed through the Abu Matamir defile—which the Egyptians seemed to have abandoned too readily—until it came within 600 meters of the Um Katef position, at about 12:30. At this point the Israeli tanks were taken under fire by Egyptian field and antitank guns. Extremely accurate fire by the Egyptian Archers knocked out or damaged two or three Israeli tanks and about the same number of halftracks. After firing a few rounds, the surviving Israeli tanks and halftracks pulled back out of sight. Shifting the direction of their approach, the Israeli tankers moved forward again, more cautiously, through the hills to the west. But the Egyptians were alert and opened fire as soon as the Israeli tanks appeared. Again there was an inconclusive exchange of fire, and again the Israelis fell back, having suffered some damage.

Ben-Ari arrived a few minutes later and ordered the combat team to remain where it was, while maintaining contact with the Egyptians. He then returned to Kusseima, where he was directed to attend a meeting with General Dayan, General Simhoni, and Colonel Wallach.

Ben-Ari had also sent a reconnaissance unit to scout the Daika Pass, in order to see if it would be possible to attack the Abu Ageila position from the rear. This defile, some 12 miles long, links the Ismailia-Abu Ageila-El Auja-Beersheba road with the parallel road to the south from Kusseima through Bir Hassna to Suez. As the Israeli tanks approached the entrance to the pass, an Egyptian detachment blew up the bridge over the Wadi el Arish and withdrew. This did not seriously interfere with the movement of the tanks, however; they continued through the pass, which they found deserted, and advanced to a point about two kilometers south of the Ruafa Dam position.

About 11:00 a.m. the Chief of Staff, General Moshe Dayan, arrived by helicopter at Kusseima. He was furious to find tanks of the 7th Brigade in Kusseima in direct violation of his orders. Before dealing with this however, he first ordered Harpaz to send a task force to Nakhl, to effect a junction there with the paratroop brigade. Harpaz selected the brigade reconnaissance company, and two infantry companies, one in half tracks, the other in busses. This force moved out to the southwest before dark. Three hours later the rifle company on busses turned back because its vehicles could not negotiate the sand on the road to Nakhl. The remainder of the task force continued on its way, however, and effected the junction with Sharon's brigade shortly after midnight. The rest of the 4th Brigade remained in the vicinity of Kusseima, prepared to envelop the south flank of the Um Katef-Abu Ageila position, as soon as the 10th Brigade moved against the fortifications early the following morning.

Dayan then devoted his attention to the premature commitment of the 7th Armored Brigade. However, after an outbreak of temper, in which he let General Simhoni know exactly how he felt, Dayan philosophically proceeded to see what could or what should be done under the changed circumstances. When Ben-Ari reported shortly after noon that his tanks had taken substantial casualties in their two probes toward the Um Katef defenses, Dayan decided that the fortifications would better be taken by infantry, as was originally planned.

Since the armor was committed, Dayan decided to exploit its mobility. He ordered the 7th Brigade to bypass Abu Ageila, and to continue westward across the Sinai, by way either of Jebel Libni, on the north-central axis to Ismailia, or of Bir Hassna on the south-central axis to Suez. In accordance with his doctrinal beliefs he gave no firm instructions, merely telling the commanders concerned—General Simhoni of the Southern Command, Colonel Wallach, the task group commander, and Colonel Ben-Ari, the armored commander—to employ their forces in the most effective manner possible. He then returned to his helicopter and flew off to visit Sharon.

INITIAL EGYPTIAN REACTION

When the armored combat team of the Israeli 7th Armored Brigade made its first move against Um Katef at about 12:30 p.m., Colonel Yassa, recognizing that this was only a small force, began to prepare a counterattack. While he was getting this organized, with his subordinates gathered around him receiving his orders, the Israeli tanks made their second probe. In the exchange of fire, Colonel Yassa was hit in the chest by a shell splinter. At first he seemed unhurt, but then his officers saw a red stain spreading over his field tunic, and Yassa suddenly collapsed, unconscious. As his subordinates rushed to give him first aid they soon realized that he had not really been wounded. The shell fragment had pierced a red fountain pen in his pocket, and the stain that all of them thought was blood proved to be only ink. The shock of the experience, however, combined with the sharp blow on his heart, was too great for Colonel Yassa, who apparently suffered either a heart attack or a nervous breakdown. That afternoon he was evacuated to El Arish, and then flown to Cairo.

The sudden outbreak of hostilities with Israel had found Colonel Yassa's second in command on leave in Cairo. Brigadier al Qadi therefore ordered Brigadier Saad ed-Din Mutawally, commander of the 4th Infantry Brigade, in division reserve in El Arish, to take command at Abu Ageila. Mutawally reached the position and assumed command at 5:00 p.m. that afternoon.

Meanwhile al Qadi had come to the conclusion that this was a full-scale Israeli offensive. He ordered the two attached companies of the

17th Battalion at the Ruafa Dam to reinforce Um Shehan and Um Katef as soon as they were relieved by reinforcements he was rushing from El Arish. These were the 12th Infantry Battalion of the 4th Brigade, plus a field artillery battery, and three Archer self-propelled antitank guns. The Egyptian reinforcements arrived at the Abu Ageila defensive complex shortly after midnight, and the two companies of the 17th Battalion promptly moved to Um Shehan. This gave a total of 14 Archer SP antitank guns under Captain M.D. Zohdy's 78th Antitank Battery in the Um Katef-Um Shehan position, a respectable force to oppose the expected Israeli armored attacks.

THE FIRST ATTACKS

Early in the afternoon, soon after Dayan left Kusseima, Ben-Ari received word that his reconnaissance group had penetrated the Daika Pass. This suggested the possibility of striking the Abu Ageila fortifications from the rear. Since this was a situation that had been unknown to the Chief of Staff when he issued his earlier instructions, Colonal Wallach approved Ben-Ari's request to leave part of his tank brigade to attack Abu Ageila and the Ruafa Dam positions from the rear, but directed that this be done in coordination with the planned assault against Um Katef from the east by the 10th Infantry Brigade.

Complying with the instructions of General Dayan, as thus modified by his conversation with Colonel Wallach, Ben-Ari ordered his AMX battalion to move westward toward Bir Hassna, to arrive there as early as possible after dark. As soon as a battalion from the 4th Infantry Brigade arrived from Kusseima to relieve the armored task force south of Um Katef, its two companies would rejoin their respective battalions, the Sherman tank battalion, and the halftrack battalion. These battalions, under the command of Lieutenant Colonel Avrahan Adan of the Sherman battalion, would then move through the Daika Pass to assault the Ruafa Dam position in coordination with the attacks of the 10th and 4th Brigades on Um Katef.

In accordance with Simhoni's accelerated plans, the 10th Infantry Brigade, under the command of Colonel Shmuel Gudir, was to arrive in front of the Um Katef-Um Shehan positions shortly after dark of the 30th. The 10th Brigade would then attack frontally; simultaneously the 4th Brigade's battalion would attack from the south, while Adan's force hit the Ruafa Dam position from the west.

About 5:00 p.m. the 10th Brigade passed El Auja, and at 7:00 p.m. took the outpost of Tarat Um Basis, about five kilometers east of Um Katef. By this time the brigade was a little behind schedule, but Gudir pressed ahead, and shortly before 8:00 p.m. his leading battalion hit the

Count Bernadotte (saluting) meets General Glubb (extreme left) and Arab Legion Colonel Abdullah Tell (between Bernadotte and Glubb) in Jerusalem, 1948— *Tahboub*

just north of the main Tel
rusalem Road—*Israeli*
ment

gadier Yaakov Dori, Chief of
Haganah General Staff, and
el Yigael Yadin, Chief of the
tions Branch of the Haganah
General Staff—*Israel*

Brigadier General Yitzhak Sadeh, the trainer of the Haganah—*Israel Government*

Colonel Moshe Dayan, Israel Defense Force, and staff officers, near Jerusalem, November, 1948—*Israel Government*

Colonel Yitzhak Rabin and General Yigal Allon, Israel Defense Force, in the Negev, December, 1948—*Israel Government*

King Abdullah of Transjordan
—*Keystone*

Maj. Gen. Ahmad, Fouad
Sadek, second commander of
the Egyptian Expeditionary
Force, in Palestine, 1948—
Tahboub

Gen. Ahmed Ali Muwawi,
t commander of the Egyp-
ian Expeditionary Force in
Palestine, 1948—*Tahboub*

Col. Ahmed Abdul Azziz, Commander of Egyptian "Volunteers" in Palestine (on left), 1948—*Tahboub*

General John Glubb, commander of the Arab Legion of Transjordan—*Jordan Army*

Brigadier Mohommed Naguib, of the Egyptian Expeditionary Force (picture taken after the 1948 war)—*Keystone*

1. Habis el Majali, defender of Latrun, 1948 (picture
en later, when he was a major general)—*Jordan Army*

Abd el Kader Husseini, commander of the Army of Salvation
—*Tahboub*

Col. Sayyed Taha, Egyptian
Army, commander of Faluja
Pocket in late 1948, early 1949
—*Tahboub*

Ieneral Fawzi Kaukji, com-
nander of the Arab Liberation Army—*Tahboub*

Israeli armored car approaching Beersheba, October 1948—*Israel Government*

Israeli column at Bir Lahfan, Sinai, en route to El Arish from Abu Ageila December, 1948— *Israel Government*

Israeli armored cars at El Auja, on the border of Palestine and Egyptian Sinai, December, 1948—*Israel Government*

Haj Amin el Husseini, Mufti of Jerusalem, and Major General Mohommed Naguib, meeting after the 1948 war—*Keystone*

Lt. Col. Gamel Abd el Nasser, Egyptian Army, deputy to Colonel Taha in the Faluja Pocket—*Keystone*

Secretary of State John Foster Dulles, entertained in Cairo by General Naguib (right) and Lt. Col. Nasser (left) in May, 1955, before Nasser ousted Naguib from power—*Keystone*

Prime Minister Nasser of Egypt hoists Egyptian Flag over Navy House (administrative office of the Suez Canal) at Port Said, June 22, *1956—Keystone*

Lt. Col. Rafael Eitan, Israeli Army, commander of the paratroop battalion at the Mitla Pass Oct. 29, 1956—*Israel*

Lt. Col. Meir Pilavski, (Meir Pa'il), Israeli Army, commander of the battalion that broke through the Egyptian defenses south of Rafah Nov. 1, 1956 (picture taken after retirement from the army) —*Dupuy*

Gen. Haim Laskov, Israeli Army, commander of the mechanized forces that broke through Egyptian defenses north of Rafah, November 1, 1956 (picture taken as Major General)—*Israel Government*

Colonel Yitzhak Hoffi, Israeli Army, commander of the task force that captured Sharm el Sheikh November, 1956—*Israel*

Capt. M.D. Zohdy, Egyptian A[...] commander of the antitank contin[...] of the defense of Abu Ageila Octo[...] 1956 (picture taken as brigad[...]
E[...]

General Abd el Hakim Amer, Commander-in-Chief, Egyptian Army—*Keystone*

Maintenance and replenishment of Israeli 7th Brigade tanks after the battle at Jebel Libni Oct. 30, 1956—*Gonen*

Maj. Gen. Dan Tolkowski, Israeli Air Force Commander, 1956 War (picture taken as colonel)—*Israel*

Command conference near Rafah, June 5, 1967; Israeli Brigadier General Tal, hand on map; Col. Shmuel Gonen, 7th Brigade commander, wearing glasses; Col. Meir Pa'il (Meir Pilavsky), behind Tal and Gonen—*Gutman*

Israeli 7th Brigade column on the road, J 1967, waiting for Gonen to take Rafah—*G*

President Nasser of Egypt and Field Marshal Abd el Hakim Amer at a military review in Cairo before the 1967 War—*Keystone*

Israeli tanks near Bir Gifgafa, June 7, 1967; Patton M48 tanks with 90mm guns—*Gutman*

Gen. Yeshayahu Gavish, Israeli commanding general, Southern Command, June, 1967—*Israel*

Abandoned Egyptian vehicles on the road from Bir Gifgafa to Ismailia, June, 1967—*Gutman*

The Battle for Jerusalem; Israeli Super Mystere over the tower of Augusta Victoria—*Gutman*

Brigadier General Uzi Narkiss, Israeli Army commanding general, Central Command, June, 1967—*Israel*

Colonel Avraham Mendler, Israeli Army tank mander at Kuntilla and on the Golan He (picture taken as brigadier general)—*Israel*

June 7, 1967; Israeli paratroopers entering the Lion Gate in the Old City of Jerusalem wall—*Gutman*

Brigadier Sherif Ben Shaker, commander of the 40th Armored Brigade, Jordan Army in 1967 (picture taken as major general)—*Jordan*

Brigadier Ata Ali, Jordan Army, deder of Jerusalem, 67 (picture taken r retirement from Army)—*Dupuy*

Maj. General Amer Khammash, Chief of Staff, Jordan Army, 1967—*Jordan*

Egyptian *Osa* Class missile boat, carrying four Styx missiles—
Tahboub

Israeli Saar Mis
Boats; Gabriel r
siles in cove
launchers beside d
purpose gu
Gutr

first Um Shehan defense line from the road. In accordance with the plan the other two forces were to initiate their attacks at the same time.

The initial results of this hastily planned, and not very effectively coordinated, attack were disappointing. The 7th Armored Brigade tank and halftrack battalions ran unexpectedly into demolitions in the Daika Pass, and were far away from the Ruafa Dam when the 10th Infantry Brigade began its attack. The battalion of 4th Infantry Brigade south of the Um Katef position inexplicably had not been alerted, and by the time it was ready to support the 10th Brigade attack, that action had ended.

Taking little time to deploy from march column, the leading battalion from the 10th Infantry Brigade went straight up the road to the Um Shehan position. It was met by a hail of well-directed and intensive fire from an assortment of weapons. Egyptian Archers knocked out several Israeli halftracks. The attack was over almost before it began. Colonel Gudir spent the rest of the night trying to assemble his brigade at Um Tarpa, half way between Tarat Um Basis and Um Katef. At dawn several straggling units were still on the road, and the 10th Brigade was not ready to renew the attack.

Meanwhile, after having taken ten hours to negotiate the Daika Pass, at 5:00 a.m. on October 31st Adan's Sherman battalion, with an attached halftrack company, advanced on Abu Ageila. (The remainder of the halftrack battalion had been hastily pulled away by Colonel Ben-Ari for another mission.) The Egyptians in the Ruafa Dam and Abu Ageila positions had of course heard the Israeli armored movement during the night, and by the time the Israelis came within three kilometers of the Egyptian positions, they were taken under artillery fire which, despite the darkness, was extremely accurate.

As a result of an earlier reconnaissance, Adan decided to hit the Abu Ageila road junction first, then turn back to attack the Ruafa Dam. At 5:30 a.m. Adan's tanks were within 200 meters of the road junction defenses, at which point they encountered heavy antitank and machine gun fire. Pulling back, the tanks endeavored to envelop the position from the west, but found that the banks of the Wadi el Arish were too deep and too steep to cross at that point. However, the position at the edge of the wadi gave the tanks a clear field of fire into the Egyptian defenses, and under cover of the tank fire the halftrack company stormed across the wadi at an easier crossing point, and broke into the Egyptian road junction position. This was held only by the rear echelon and kitchens of the 6th Brigade, and was quickly subdued. At the same time a flank attack from the Ruafa Dam position was repulsed. By 6:30 the Abu Ageila crossroads was in Israeli hands. When the Egyptians attempted to surrender, Adan, following orders from Ben-Ari, refused to take them prisoners, and sent them north toward El Arish. He did not want to be encumbered with prisoners.

At El Arish, Brigadier al Qadi soon learned of the Israeli seizure of the Abu Ageila crossroads. He sent the 4th Brigade's 10th Infantry Battalion, reinforced by a tank company, to counterattack from the north, and sent a message by radio to Brigadier Mutawally, the new brigade commander at Abu Ageila-Um Katef, to mount a simultaneous coordinated attack from Um Katef against the Israelis at Abu Ageila.

Adan was alerted to the Egyptian movement from El Arish by Israeli air reconnaissance, and he redeployed his Shermans and halftracks north of the road junction. In the meantime, he found himself coming under increasing fire from the Ruafa Dam position, and from the artillery near Jebel Dalfa.

The Egyptian counterattacking force was formidable, and came close to being successful. The 10th Motorized Infantry Battalion, with its tanks and Archers, approached from the north shortly after noon. However, as they were deploying to attack, they were struck by several Israeli fighter bombers. The Egyptians stood their ground, but gave up on their attack plan. Their tanks kept up a desultory fire on Abu Ageila from a distance of several thousand meters. About this time a composite battalion from Um Katef, supported by Archers and a number of Bren carriers, advanced from the east, under the cover of effective artillery and antitank fire from the Ruafa Dam. Adan's Shermans, in a heavy exchange of fire, finally drove the attacking units back to Um Katef. Had the two Egyptian forces coordinated their attacks and converged on Adan, it is doubtful if he could have held Abu Ageila.

At 4 p.m., after only a brief rest, Adan continued with his mission of attacking the Ruafa Dam position. Leaving one tank company to protect his rear at the crossroad, Adan mounted a vigorous coordinated attack with his halftracks and remaining tanks, enveloping the position from the north, and succeeded in occupying the northwestern earthworks just as night fell. However, all of his tanks and most of his halftracks had been hit during the fierce fighting, and finding it difficult to coordinate the activities of his scattered elements in the darkness, Adan called them back from the captured position and regrouped near the crossroads. He immediately deployed for defense, while making repairs. A resupply convoy arrived at 2:00 a.m., permitting his troops to refuel their vehicles, and rearm their weapons.

At about 9:00 p.m. a company of Egyptian infantry, which had reoccupied the Ruafa Dam position, counterattacked against the Israeli tanks, covered by heavy supporting fire from artillery at Jebel Dalfa. Israeli battle reports call this a fierce and vigorous counterattack; the official Egyptian historian dismisses it as routine patrol activity. In any event, the exchange of fire was heavy and there were numerous casualties on both sides.

Meanwhile, General Dayan and the commanding general of the Southern Command, Brigadier General Simhoni, had become increasingly impatient with the performance of most of the Central Task Group. While Ben-Ari and his three armored and halftrack battalions had been marching and fighting, seemingly without rest day and night, the 4th Brigade was doing relatively little in the Kusseima area, and the 10th Brigade, while full of activity, was accomplishing nothing east of Um Katef.

Under direct pressure from General Dayan, Colonel Gudir had finally been able to get the 10th Brigade organized for a new attack on Um Katef at 8:30 a.m. on the 31st (shortly after Adan had taken the crossroads). But he seems to have been unable to coordinate the activity of his tank company or his artillery with this attack. The brigade's reconnaissance company and about half of the lead battalion of the brigade, mounted on halftracks and in trucks, advanced on a broad front across about 3,000 meters of open terrain toward Um Katef without either armor or artillery support. The inept attempt was beaten back by accurate Egyptian fire. Meanwhile, an effort just to the south was held up by an entrenched platoon outpost.

It was early afternoon before this fiasco was finally sorted out, and it was not until mid-afternoon that Gudir was able to get two infantry battalions ready again for coordinated attacks against Um Katef from north and south, to take place immediately after darkness. As far as Dayan was concerned, it was the final straw when he learned early in the evening that both of the battalions were lost in the darkness, and Um Katef was still unattacked. He ordered Colonel Gudir relieved from command and replaced him with Colonel Israel Tal. The 37th Mechanized Brigade, still in its concentration area near Rehovoth, was ordered to move at once to join Wallach's Central Command to spearhead a renewed attack on Um Katef.

After completing its long march, the halftrack battalion of the 37th Brigade was ready to assault by 2:00 a.m. of November 1. By 3:00 a.m., much to the annoyance of the brigade commander, Colonel Shmuel Golinda, his tank battalion still had not arrived. Golinda decided to carry out the attack with his infantry only: the halftrack battalion and a motorized infantry battalion. At 3:30 the column moved forward with its headlights on. The Egyptians greeted the Israeli advance with heavy antitank and artillery fire, causing severe losses. Pushing rapidly ahead, however, the remaining halftracks entered the minefield which surrounded the Egyptian position, and most of them were quickly damaged and put out of action, either by mines, or by the Egyptian fire. Colonel

Golinda was killed; most of his officers were wounded; and it was obviously impossible to continue the attack. Under covering fire from the artillery of the 10th and 37th Brigades, the survivors of the ill-fated attack withdrew, bringing with them their 80 wounded. Just after dawn, the 37th Brigade made one more tank assault, trying to push between the two main Egyptian positions. Again they were thrown back as a result of accurate Egyptian antitank fire. Meanwhile, at Tel Aviv, at almost the same time this attack was launched, General Headquarters decided to suspend further assaults on Um Katef. The Battle of Abu Ageila was over, although the victorious Egyptians were not yet aware of the fact.

5

Battle of the Mitla Pass,
October 30-November 1

FIRST ENGAGEMENT, OCTOBER 30

Shortly after 9:00 a.m. on Tuesday, October 30, four Egyptian MiG aircraft attacked the paratroop position near the Mitla Pass. They hit the battalion's Piper Cub aircraft, parked on the ground nearby, and wounded four men. At the same time, the blocking force outpost on the road to the west of the battalion's position reported that a small motorized column of Egyptian troops was emerging eastward from the pass. (This was the leading company of the Egyptian 5th Infantry Battalion.) Colonel Eitan ordered his heavy mortars to open fire on this column and radioed a request for air support. He prepared for battle.

As soon as the Egyptians came under fire, about four kilometers west of the Monument, they jumped from their trucks, deployed into a skirmish line and returned the Israeli fire. As additional Egyptian units moved up, they attempted to turn the Israeli flanks. Eitan blocked this, and tried to maneuver against both Egyptian flanks. For more than an hour the two forces were engaged in an action of small unit fire and movement, with no conclusive result. The Egyptians still held the entrance to the pass. At noon, when Israeli Air Force jets arrived, Eitan pulled back his maneuvering units to leave the situation to the Air Force.

The Israeli aircraft swept down to attack Egyptian mortar and infantry positions with rockets and bombs, and then turned their attention to a larger Egyptian convoy which was at that time moving eastward into the pass. This was the remainder of the Egyptian 2nd Brigade's 5th Battalion, which had been held up in crossing the Canal, closely followed by the 6th Battalion. The Egyptians returned the fire of the Israeli aircraft with their own light antiaircraft guns, but did not succeed in driving off the attackers. All afternoon successive waves of Israeli planes struck the stalled column in the western section of the pass, leaving many of the vehicles in flames. When the one-sided battle ended at sunset, the Israeli Air Force was satisfied that the Egyptian troops in the stalled column had been effectively destroyed as a cohesive fighting force.

SHARON'S MARCH, OCTOBER 30-31

Meanwhile, the paratroop brigade continued to advance westward across the peninsula. At 3:00 a.m. on October 30 the advance guard reached Bir el Thamad,[1] which was quickly taken by the brigade's reconnaissance unit. The fortified position of Thamad, five miles west of the *bir* (or well), was situated on cliffs on both sides of the track—which followed the dry stream bed of the Wadi el Aqaba. Barbed wire and minefields at the base of the cliffs protected the position. Thamad was held by two companies of the Egyptian 2d Motorized Border Regiment (a 5-company unit) and some National Guard troops. The only possible route of attack was from the track.

At 6:00 a.m. the reconnaissance unit, part of the 2d Battalion, and a troop of four tanks advanced toward the Egyptian strongholds, but one tank overturned almost immediately in the rough terrain. The Egyptians, with the sun in their eyes, opened ineffective long-range small arms fire; essentially a constabulary unit, they had no antitank guns. The Israelis pounded the position briefly with intensive mortar fire, then behind a mortar smoke screen they attacked. The outnumbered defenders fought bravely, but were soon overwhelmed. Resistance ceased by 7:30 a.m. as the surviving defenders withdrew to Nakhl leaving 50 killed—including all officers—and about as many wounded, who were captured. The Israelis had lost four killed and six wounded in the brief engagement.

Sharon spent the morning evacuating Israeli and Egyptian casualties, and concentrating the brigade for the push to Nakhl and on to the pass. At 8:00 fuel, spare parts and other supplies were air-dropped to the brigade. Shortly after 9:00 a.m. the four MiG aircraft which had attacked the 1st Battalion at the Monument appeared over Thamad and made two strafing passes, wounding three Israelis.

By 11:00 a.m. the 3d Battalion and the artillery had trickled in. By that time, also, Sharon had received radio reports of the air and ground attacks on the Monument position. He immediately issued orders for an advance on Nakhl, headquarters of the Egyptian 2d Motorized Border Battalion, and manned by two companies. At 1:00 p.m. the column again began to move, with the 2d Battalion in the lead.

At 5:00 p.m. the paratroopers approached Nakhl. Quickly deploying, they attacked, supported by an artillery preparation. After a brief exchange of fire, the defenders withdrew, and by 5:25 the position was secured. Sharon directed the 3d Battalion to remain in Nakhl with support weapons and continued with the remainder of the brigade toward the Monument. By 10:30 that night he had joined Eitan's battalion, less than 30 hours after he had crossed the frontier. Although opposition had

---

[1] Not the better known road junction of Bir el Thamada, 95 kilometers to the northwest.

been light, this fighting march of almost 250 kilometers in little more than one day was a significant achievement, for which the credit must go to its driving, aggressive, energetic commander, Colonel Ariel Sharon.

SHARON'S PATROL

Early on the morning of Wednesday, October 31, after a brief rest for himself and his fast-moving brigade, Colonel Sharon inspected the defensive deployment of Colonel Eitan's battalion. He had expected to find it farther west, between the Parker Monument and the entrance to the Mitla Pass, and was somewhat concerned that the location was so exposed, on the open desert. The nearest Israeli troops were 150 kilometers away, while he knew from reports of his reconnaissance plane pilots that there was an Egyptian armored brigade south of Bir Gifgafa, about 30 kilometers distant. Sharon had only three tanks operational, and had no antitank weapons. Just before departure he had received several new French recoilless rifles, but he had no men trained to use them, and they seemed to be short of some essential parts—in other words, useless. It seemed to him essential, therefore, to move to higher, more defensible terrain. He felt that he should either occupy the eastern entrance to the pass, or at the very least move to the high, rugged terrain just east of the pass, where he could block the Wadi Miliz, which was a likely avenue of approach for Egyptian armor at Bir Gifgafa.

Sharon had been told not to get into a major battle, and not to make any change in the original disposition established by the first battalion without approval from GHQ. Therefore, he submitted a routine request to GHQ to authorize the move to the eastern end of the pass. To his surprise, the request was promptly denied.

The Israeli General Staff had good reason for this apparently minor negative decision. Things had been relatively quiet on the southern axis in the vicinity of the pass since late the previous afternoon. The General Staff did not want to stir up the Egyptians in this area by a move to secure the eastern end of the pass. As Egyptian forces from Ismailia moved to Bir Gifgafa they were positioned to hit the paratroopers from the north with overwhelming strength (as of course Sharon was aware). But GHQ figured that Sharon would not be attacked from the north if he remained quiet. The effective strength of the Egyptian Air Force was not yet clear and the High Command did not want to get involved in a battle which might divert Israeli air support away from the heavily engaged 7th Armored Brigade and the 10th Infantry Brigade at Abu Ageila. Sharon's paratroopers were isolated from the bulk of the Israeli army by miles of sand, and could be supported only by air power. Since Israel's air space required protection, and since a major requirement for air support existed at Abu Ageila, the General Staff wanted to keep things quiet on the southern axis.

Sharon was frustrated by this decision, partly because it was contrary to standard Israeli doctrine which provided for local decisions to be made by local commanders. Furthermore, he was a man of driving energy, who found it difficult just to sit tight and await further orders and developments. Convinced that the bulk of the 5th and 6th Egyptian Battalions had been destroyed during the air attack the previous afternoon, and certain that the pass was largely unoccupied, Sharon radioed a request for permission to send a reconnaissance patrol westward into the defile. His request was promptly approved, but again he received a warning from Tel Aviv to avoid any large-scale involvement in battle.

The Mitla Pass is about 30 kilometers long and is divided into three distinct and uneven sections. In the east is the narrow Heitan Defile, about 6 kilometers long. Only 50 meters wide at its narrowest point, this defile is bounded on both sides by high steep walls. To the north is the height of Jebel Giddi, and to the south Jebel Heitan. Just west of the defile, the pass broadens into an area called the Saucer, where the mountains recede to the north and south. Finally, just west of the Saucer, which extends for nearly 20 kilometers, is the Mitla Defile, wider and shorter than the Heitan, flanked by towering cliffs.

Sharon faced the decision which has been posed to many aggressive and energetic commanders under similar conditions. How strong should his patrol be? In the light of his instructions from Tel Aviv it could not be a major unit; but given his conviction that opposition would be negligible, he wanted it to be strong enough to push aside any light resistance and to establish an outpost in the pass once this had been proven feasible. In fact, however, the situation in the pass was far different from what he expected.

The Egyptian 5th and 6th Battalions actually had suffered only light casualties during the afternoon of the 30th, even though practically all of their vehicles had been destroyed by the Israeli air attacks. The troops had dispersed, and then while Israeli aircraft were pounding their presumed positions east of the pass, had actually occupied previously prepared positions in the eastern half of the Heitan Defile, in rifle pits which had been dug along the tops of the ridges, and in a number of caves cut into the steep walls of the pass. These positions, most of them on the northern ridge, had been carefully selected and cut out, and were screened by rocks so as to be practically invisible to anyone moving along the track below.

THE ORDEAL OF MORDECHAI GUR

Sharon created a patrol consisting of two parachute companies from his 2d Battalion, mounted on halftracks, supported by the brigade reconnaissance company, three AMX tanks, and four 120mm mortars. Leading the patrol was Major Mordechai Gur, commander of the 2d Battalion. With Gur was a small air liaison unit, to keep contact with the brigade's reconnaissance plane, which would fly over the patrol.

Sharon had planned to accompany the patrol, but at the last minute he had learned that the Egyptian armor at Bir Gifgafa had started south. He decided to stay with the main body, and sent his second in command, Lieutenant Colonel Yitzhak Hoffi, to accompany the patrol, riding with the reconnaissance unit, just behind Gur's two infantry companies. Gur himself was in the third halftrack of this group, some 200 meters behind the first two. He was followed by the tanks, then the two infantry companies.

At about 12:30 p.m. the Israeli vehicles entered the Heitan Defile, and the first halftrack immediately came under fire. Gur ordered it to continue to advance, in the belief that the Egyptian force directing the fire could be no more than a small harassing unit. Immediately the fire intensified, and both of the first two halftracks were hit and disabled. As their crews dismounted, they were at once pinned down by Egyptian fire. Gur moved forward to rescue the trapped men, but his vehicle now became the focus of the intense Egyptian fire. He dashed on past the two halftracks until about 150 meters ahead he found an abandoned Egyptian vehicle, hit in the previous day's air attack, blocking the road. Trying to get around this vehicle, Gur's halftrack fell into a small wadi at the side of the track and was immobilized; Gur and his crew dismounted and took positions in rocks at the base of the southern ridge.

Meanwhile the remainder of the patrol column had been rolling into the pass. The fuel truck, an ammunition truck, and three other vehicles received hits and went up in flames. Most of the patrol was able to get by the abandoned Egyptian truck, however, and, not realizing what had happened to Gur, dashed on nearly to the Saucer, leaving another halftrack, one tank, a jeep and an ambulance destroyed or damaged in the defile. Gur sent the commander of the leading company, who had been in his halftrack, to try to stop these other units, but he was hit and killed before he could reach the road. Gur had radio communication only with the reconnaissance company and the heavy mortars still at the eastern entrance to the defile.

Lieutenant Colonel Hoffi sent a runner back to the brigade CP to inform Sharon of the situation in the pass. Sharon had heard the firing and was waiting impatiently for information.

Having received Hoffi's report, Sharon saw that he had two choices. He could call back the patrol, abandoning all who could not be quickly extracted, or he could rescue the entire force. As he said after the war, he really had no choice. The Israeli Army had for ten years been inspired by the slogan: "We don't leave wounded behind." There were wounded men in the pass, and others who were cut off. All had to be extracted.

Sharon at once sent two companies of reinforcements to the defile to relieve the ambushed patrol. He also ordered all his mortars and artillery to keep up harassing fire on the suspected Egyptian position on top of the cliffs on both sides of the road. Thus far no one realized that the Egyptian fire was originating from the cave positions in the walls of the cliffs. By this time Gur had concentrated part of his patrol, and under the cover of heavy mortar fire, the reconnaissance unit attacked Egyptian rifle positions on the north ridge of the pass. As the Israelis approached the top of the ridge, however, the Egyptians on the south ridge opened fire with light and medium weapons from their caves. The reconnaissance troops, now suddenly made aware of the caves, were unable to return the fire with their short-range submachine guns. Taking heavy losses, they quickly withdrew, seeking cover in the low hills just beside the road.

At this point the reinforcements sent by Sharon arrived, but they could do little more than evacuate the wounded. Meanwhile, Gur was able to get his damaged tank back into action, and he sent it to the western end of the defile to bring back the units there. At about this time four Egyptian Meteors appeared and attacked the Israeli heavy mortar positions and troops east of the pass.

At dusk, one of Gur's halftrack companies, still at the western end of the first defile, dismounted and attacked the north ridge and began to clear it. The other halftrack company simultaneously attacked the south ridge. Under Sharon's direction, the companies east of the defile also reached the eastern crests. By dark the ridge tops on both sides of the Heitan Defile were under Israeli control, but the Egyptians still held the caves below them. Under cover of darkness, which cut the effectiveness of the Egyptian fire, the Israelis cleared most of the caves on the northern side in two and a half hours of fierce hand-to-hand fighting. By 8:00 p.m. the area was quiet. The Israelis had lost 38 men killed and 120 wounded; Egyptian losses were between 100 and 150 men killed.

Just before midnight Sharon received information that Egyptian armored units, from the vicinity of Bir Gifgafa, were advancing toward his right rear. He therefore withdrew eastward about three kilometers, past the intersection with the road to Bir el Thamada, and organized a new defensive position. The pass thus remained under Egyptian control.

As it turned out, because of events elsewhere, the Egyptian armor never got past Bir el Thamada.

6

Maneuver—
Diplomatic and Military,
October 30-November 1

THE ANGLO-FRENCH ULTIMATUM

At 6:00 p.m., Tuesday, October 30, the British and French ambassadors at Cairo and at Jerusalem jointly presented notes to the Egyptian and Israeli governments. The notes were almost identical, and called for three main responses. First, both Egyptians and Israelis were immediately to cease all hostilities on land and on the sea and in the air. Second, all opposing forces on both sides were to withdraw, the Egyptians to the west bank of the Canal, and the Israelis to 10 miles east of the Canal. Third—part of the ultimatum to Egypt, but included only as information for the Israeli government—Egypt was to accept the temporary occupation of Port Said, Ismailia, and Suez by British and French forces in order to separate the belligerents and to guarantee freedom of transit through the Canal to ships of all nations, in accordance with existing international law.

As the British and French ambassadors pointed out to the Egyptian and Israeli foreign ministers, the notes required a reply from each country within 12 hours. If at the end of that period one or both governments had not complied with the Anglo-French commands, British and French forces would take whatever action was necessary to secure compliance. To the Egyptians the note was an ultimatum. To the Israelis it was a notification that the plan of the Sèvres Agreement was being implemented.

At this time, of course, the Israeli forces were not within ten miles of the Suez Canal. The Israeli government, after a brief delay, in which it pretended to consider the terms, responded that these were acceptable. At midnight, President Nasser rejected the ultimatum. At about the same time at an emergency United Nations Security Council meeting in New York, the British and French representatives vetoed two ceasefire resolutions.

THE EGYPTIAN RESPONSE

At 6:00 a.m. on October 31 Egyptian antiaircraft batteries in the Nile Delta and along the length of the Suez Canal were on the alert, anticipating an Anglo-French air attack either 12 hours after delivery of the ultimatum, or 12 hours after its rejection. If such an attack came, Nasser had issued orders to General Hakim Amer that all forces engaged in the Sinai were to be withdrawn to the Suez Canal to defend the waterway against the now increasingly expected Anglo-French attack.

When 6:00 a.m. on Wednesday morning came and went, and then the clock passed noon without any further evidence of British or French action to follow up on the ultimatum, the Egyptians relaxed somewhat, and refocussed their attention on operations east of the Canal.

The situation in the Sinai, to the extent it was known in Cairo, was serious, but far from disastrous. The Egyptian planners saw the central Sinai penetration by Sharon's paratroop brigade as a bold bluff which they could call by an encircling movement from the north. Abu Ageila had withstood the first assaults from the Israelis without difficulty. Although there were threatening concentrations of Israeli troops near the Gaza Strip, no attacks had been made, the Egyptian defensive positions there were alert, and there seemed no need for alarm.

The most serious problem in the minds of the Egyptian High Command, therefore, was the confused situation on the main Beersheba-Ismailia road, where Israeli armor was reported to be operating west of Abu Ageila and east of Bir Gifgafa. Israeli armor had also been reported near Bir Hassna. As long as Egyptian forces retained firm control of Rafah, El Arish and Abu Ageila, however, it did not seem likely that any major Israeli forces could operate in the north-central Sinai. There was, however, the danger of a linkup between that armor force near Bir Hassna, and the paratroop force moving along the Thamad-Nakhl-Mitla axis.

Thus the Egyptian staff believed that it was important for the 4th Armored Division to press forward as rapidly as possible to block any further Israeli armored advance from Bir Hassna, and also to send a force southward from Bir el Thamada to cut off the Israeli paratroop brigade east of the Mitla Pass.

Meanwhile the Egyptian Air Force had been busy. Caught totally by surprise by the Israeli attack of October 29-30, on the 30th the Egyptians had only been able to fly 40 combat sorties, less one flight each for the approximately 60 operational fighter-bombers. Most of these sorties were flown against the paratroop battalion east of the Mitla Pass. On the 31st, however, there had been 90 sorties, most of them by fighter bombers.

Thus the Egyptian ground crews had been able to maintain a respectable sortie rate of slightly more than one sortie per aircraft. They hoped to be able to do even better on November 1. That, however, was not to be.

ARMORED OPERATIONS IN THE CENTRAL SINAI

The 1st Brigade of the Egyptian 4th Armored Division had begun to cross the Suez Canal over the Firdan Bridge just after midnight on October 30. However, because of Nasser's order that commercial traffic on the Canal was not to be interrupted, the bridge was repeatedly opened to let ships and convoys pass by, holding up the crossing—interminably it seemed to the Egyptian soldiers. Thus the brigade's crossing took almost two hours, and the head of its column did not reach Bir Gifgafa until about 4 a.m. The 2d Brigade did not complete its crossing of the Canal until dawn. Each of these brigades had a battalion of T-34 tanks, a battalion of armored infantry, a company of eight Su-100 guns, and one battery of antiaircraft artillery.

During the morning Brigadier Ali Gamal Mahmoud, commanding the 4th Armored Division, ordered Colonel Talat Hassan Ali and his 1st Brigade to move eastward from Bir Gifgafa to Bir Hamma, about 40 kilometers west of Abu Ageila, to block any Israeli thrust down this central axis. The 2d Light Reconnaissance Regiment, commanded by Lieutenant Colonal Ahmed Ali Atiah, which had preceded the 4th Division and had been replaced under Gamal's command, was between Bir Gifgafa and Bir el Thamada. It was ordered to continue through Bir el Thamada, then head south and southwest to envelop and cut off the Israeli paratroop brigade near the Mitla Pass. Brigadier Gamal kept the 2d Armored Brigade, commanded by Colonel Ibrahim el Mogui, in reserve at Bir Gifgafa, to await developments to the east or south before committing it. Furthermore, he did not want to leave Bir Gifgafa, his base of maneuver, until two National Guard brigades, on the road to his rear, arrived to secure its defense.

The Egyptian units moved out before noon, but their progress was slow, due to incessant attacks from Israeli aircraft. Losses in men and tanks were severe, but the troops pushed on determinedly, reaching their preliminary objectives after dark.

Meanwhile, the Israeli High Command had learned from air reconnaissance of the move of the Egyptian 1st Armored Brigade from Bir Gifgafa toward Bir Hamma. Colonel Ben-Ari, commander of the 7th Armored Brigade, at that time moving from Kusseima toward Bir Hassna with his AMX battalion, was ordered to block the Egyptian movement, and to seize Bir Hamma.

Ben-Ari immediately radioed orders to Lieutenant Colonel Adan, then near the Daika Pass, to release the halftrack battalion, save for one company, which Adan could keep. The remainder of the halftrack battalion was to march north to the main east-west road, then advance westward to the vicinity of Jebel Libni. It was to set up an ambush for the advancing Egyptian armor near the Jebel Libni road junction, or further west toward Bir Hamma, if this seemed feasible. Ben-Ari then radioed his AMX battalion commander still advancing on Bir Hassna, on the parallel road to the south, to send a detachment north to link up with the halftrack battalion near the Jebel Libni road junction.

Meanwhile, under Egyptian air attack as it approached Bir Hassna, the AMX battalion was halted and dispersed off the road. Upon receipt of Ben-Ari's orders, however, the battalion commander sent one company north on a desert track to Jebel Libni, and with the remainder continued on to Bir Hassna, which he reached shortly after noon. An Egyptian jeep company evacuated the place after a brief exchange of fire.

Early in the afternoon, Ben-Ari's halftrack battalion reached the Jebel Libni crossroad, encountering there a platoon from an Egyptian jeep company—the one that had originally been at Kusseima, and that had just been driven from Bir Hassna by the AMX battalion. The exhausted Egyptians were soon ejected from their hasty positions, and after regrouping, the halftrack battalion continued westward on the road after them toward Bir Hamma. Shortly before dark the battalion was attacked by Egyptian fighter-bombers, which inflicted a number of Israeli casualties, and damaged two vehicles. After the Egyptian aircraft left, the halftrack battalion returned to the road, and continued to advance cautiously toward Bir Hamma. The battalion halted a few kilometers east of Bir Hamma before 10:00 p.m. There, less than an hour later, the armored infantry was joined by Ben-Ari and the AMX battalion, which had marched north from Bir Hassna.

Ben-Ari had planned to attack Bir Hamma at dawn, but while on the march he had received orders to assume a mobile defensive posture until further orders. So, after arranging for the replenishment of fuel and ammunition, Ben-Ari and his men prepared for an expected attack from the Egyptian 1st Armored Brigade next morning.

WAITING AND WONDERING

During Wednesday the 31st, tension had been high in both Cairo and Tel Aviv as they waited for the Anglo-French reaction to the Egyptian rejection of the allied ultimatum. During the afternoon hours the tension began to relax in Cairo. However, beyond the limited moves to be made by the 4th Armored Division, President Nasser and General Amer postponed major strategic decisions.

In Tel Aviv, to the contrary, tension mounted as the hours passed by without any British or French action. Prime Minister Ben Gurion became increasingly bitter and angry.

Ben Gurion had never trusted the British, and he had a particularly low opinion of Anthony Eden. It was this distrust which had led him to insist upon a signed protocol at the Sèvres Conference. Now, however, as the hours ticked away past the Allied ultimatum expiration time, the Israeli Prime Minister was convinced that the British had decided to back out. After a long argument with his Chief of Staff, about noon he ordered Dayan to withdraw his troops from the Sinai.

Dayan, however, was sure the allies would cooperate; so he dragged his feet in responding to Ben Gurion's order. Finally, under pressure from the Prime Minister, he sent out orders that all units except for the 9th Brigade were to go into mobile defensive posture. All offensive operations were to be suspended until further orders were issued. As we have seen, this order particularly affected the operation of Colonel Ben-Ari's 7th Armored Brigade.

Thus, by early evening of October 31, save for the furious fighting on the ridges at the eastern end of the Mitla Pass, a lull descended on the Sinai theater of the war. There were only two important movements. One was by the Egyptians' 4th Armored Division, completing its march from the canal to Bir Gifgafa, Bir Hamma, and Bir el Thamada. The other was the movement of the Israeli 9th Brigade, preparing to move down the western shores of the Gulf of Aqaba. The Israeli 10th Brigade was also engaged in its final fiasco in front of Um Katef.

7

The Egyptian Withdrawal

ANGLO-FRENCH AIR ATTACK

At 7:00 p.m. on Wednesday, October 31, twenty-five hours after the delivery of the British and French ultimatum, and thirteen hours after it expired, British and French aircraft began bombing Egyptian air bases. These attacks ushered in a new phase of this peculiar war.

Most of the allied aircraft taking part in the bombardment of the Egyptian bases were from the Royal Air Force, although some French bombers also participated. The attacking planes were based on Malta and Cyprus, and focussed their first attacks on the air bases at Almaza, Inchas, Abu Sueir, Kabrit, and Cairo International. By midnight three waves of bombers had come in over these bases, dropping contact and delayed action bombs.

After the first Allied assault the Egyptians claimed that they were able to get twenty Il-28 light bombers and twenty MiG-16 jet fighters airborne, to withdraw to previously arranged havens in Syria and Saudi Arabia. Twenty more Il-28s were withdrawn to Luxor, out of range of the Allied bombers.

During the morning of November 1 British carrier planes swept over the Delta and the Canal Zone to destroy any remaining Egyptian aircraft on the ground, and to prevent the Egyptians from repairing the damage of the night's raid. Similar carrier plane sweeps were made also on the 2nd and 3d, by which time the allies claimed that 260 Egyptian aircraft had been destroyed on the ground. This claim is believed to be exaggerated, however, since the Egyptian Air Force was estimated to consist of only 255 aircraft at the start of these raids, and at least 40 planes escaped.

During the early evening of October 31, and through November 2, Egyptian troops in the Sinai claimed that they were attacked by French fighter bombers based in Israel. These claims were denied by France, but since French aircraft had flown air cover over Israeli forces, and over Israel itself on the previous day, it seems very likely that the French did indeed support the Israelis by fighter bomber attacks against the withdrawing Egyptian columns and troop concentrations.

180

EGYPTIAN AND ISRAELI REACTION

When the first allied air attacks began, President Nasser at once called General Hakim Amer and issued orders that all movement of Egyptian troops into the Sinai be stopped, and that the forces already in the Sinai be withdrawn in order to avoid being cut off by the expected Anglo-French invasion of the Canal Zone. On the basis of estimates which had been submitted to him the day before by his staff, Nasser assumed that the allied landing would take place at either Alexandria or Port Said. In either case he was determined to resist.

Having issued his preliminary orders by telephone, President Nasser at once went to General Headquarters, where he arrived about 8:00 p.m. He stayed there during the night, listening to reports of the allied air attacks and supervising the transmission of orders to troops in the Sinai. By 10:30 the General Staff had forwarded directives for a general withdrawal to all major commanders east of the Canal. The troops most recently sent across the Canal were to fall back first; the units in defense positions on the northern and central axes were to carry out phased withdrawals, as was the garrison at Sharm el Sheikh. Nasser also ordered the staff to prepare plans to distribute weapons to civilians in the Canal Zone, to be used in guerrilla warfare against the British and French, in case the regular army was defeated.

The withdrawal from the Sinai was to begin at once and be carried out during the nights of October 31 and November 1, with the troops taking cover during the day of November 1. The troops in the Rafah area and the 2d Armored Brigade were to withdraw on the first night. Two companies of the 2d Infantry Brigade's 6th Battalion were to hold the western end of the Mitla Pass as the rear guard while the remainder of that battalion and the 5th Battalion withdrew. Remaining forces—including the garrison at Abu Ageila—would be evacuated the following evening, except for a small rear guard at Abu Ageila which was to delay the Israelis until early on November 2. By then it was hoped that the main forces, including all of the armor, would have recrossed to the west bank of the Canal.

Colonel Rauf Mahfouz Zaki, commanding the garrison at Sharm el Sheikh, reported by radio that he did not have enough transportation to withdraw his troops, to say nothing of his heavy equipment. He therefore requested permission to defend his post. After consulting President Nasser, General Amer approved Zaki's request. Zaki and his men courageously prepared themselves for their task. At first Zaki planned to use the guns of the frigate *Rashid,* attached to his command, to support the land defenses. But when he heard that British warships had sunk another Egyptian frigate, the *Damiatta,* in the northern waters of the Red Sea, he feared that the presence of the *Rashid* at Sharm el Sheikh might attract a British naval attack. So, during the night, the *Rashid* was sent to take refuge in a nearby Saudi Arabian port.

During the early evening of October 31, after confirming the Allied air attacks against Egypt, General Dayan sent an order to General Simhoni cancelling his earlier ban on offensive action. Simhoni was to have the Central Task Group press ahead with its operations against Abu Ageila, while the Northern Task Group was to initiate the attack against Rafah and the Gaza Strip as planned. The 9th Mechanized Brigade was directed to continue its movement toward Sharm el Sheikh. Only Sharon's 202d Paratroop Brigade was to avoid offensive operations. As we have seen, shortly after midnight this order was modified again when Dayan directed the cessation of operations against Abu Ageila, which was to be contained and bypassed by the Central Task Group.

POSTSCRIPT AT ABU AGEILA-UM KATEF

At the time when Brigadier Mutawally at Um Katef received withdrawal orders from Cairo and the 3d Division, he and his men were preoccupied with repulsing the last feeble attacks of the Israeli 4th, 10th, and 37th Brigades. Following that success, and unaware of the Israeli decision to abandon the attack, the defenders of Um Katef prepared to carry out the ordered withdrawal. They expected that this would be complicated by continuing Israeli attacks. The Egyptians destroyed or ruined as much equipment and materiel as they could late in the afternoon of November 1, without alerting the Israelis to what they were doing.

Mutawally then divided his forces into four groups for the withdrawal that night. Approximately one third left at 6:30 p.m., just at dusk. Since the Abu Ageila crossroads and the Kusseima road junction were both in the hands of the Israelis, the Egyptians had to abandon all of their heavy equipment and walk across the desert sand dunes to the northwest to reach the El Arish road near Bir Lahfan, where they hoped it was in Egyptian hands. Following the same route, the second group departed half an hour later, and the third group moved out at 7:30 p.m. Left in the almost deserted defenses were one company of infantry and one 25-pounder and its crew. While the infantry kept up sporadic fire from widely scattered positions, the artillery crew fired incessantly throughout the night, shifting from one position to another between rounds to mislead the Israelis. Just before dawn, this final rear guard pulled out, after burying the breechblock of their gun in the sand and destroying the rest of their heavy equipment.

About half of the gallant defenders of Abu Ageila reached El Arish in time to join the troops still withdrawing toward the Canal from there.

Most of the remainder were captured by the Israelis in the next few days, but a number died of starvation and thirst in the desert.

They had, however, done their job of deception very well. The Israelis had no idea that the evacuation was going on. Early in the morning the intelligence officer of Colonel Adan's battalion—the Shermans which had been holding the Abu Ageila crossroads for over a day—sent two prisoners into Um Katef with a demand for surrender. By coincidence the Central Task Group intelligence officer arrived in a Piper Cub while the preparations for this were going on. He agreed with the idea, read and approved Adan's surrender demand, then returned to his CP.

The two prisoners were given a captured Egyptian jeep and a large white flag. Not until that moment did the Israelis realize that neither of the Egyptians could drive, although one seemed to have some knowledge of driving. Adan personally gave him a quick driving lesson, then sent the pair off down the road with the surrender demand message.

About this same time patrols from the 37th Mechanized Brigade in Kusseima captured some Egyptian prisoners from Um Tarpa who informed them that Um Katef had been evacuated during the night. The 37th Brigade then asked permission from Colonel Wallach's headquarters to investigate this report. After some delay permission was granted, and late in the morning a company of 37th Brigade tanks was dispatched from Kusseima to Um Katef. Meanwhile the two Egyptians recently released by the 7th Brigade drove through the position without finding anyone to whom to give Adan's surrender demand. Suddenly they met the 37th Brigade tanks and found themselves recaptured.

After this brief delay, the 37th Brigade tanks continued westward through the abandoned position, planning to join the 7th Brigade at Abu Ageila. It was shortly before noon. As the tanks descended the Um Shehan ridge, they were observed by Adan and his troops, waiting for a reply to the surrender demand. Adan had prescribed that non-combat vehicles should come first, preceded by a flag of truce, followed by tanks and Archers. When Adan's men saw a column of tanks emerge from the Egyptian fortifications, without a flag of truce, they therefore assumed that this was a breakout attempt. The advancing tanks were immediately taken under fire at a range of about 1,100 meters. Eight of the 37th Brigade tanks were quickly knocked out; the other four, also assuming that they had encountered Egyptians, quickly withdrew, firing as they retreated to Um Shehan. Adan's tanks began to pursue.

Fortunately, an Israeli aircraft pilot had seen what happened and was finally able to get messages through by radio to the commanders on both sides, to bring the fight to a halt. The blame for this tragic encounter must go to Colonel Wallach's headquarters, for its failure to coordinate the 7th and 37th Brigades. The Task Group intelligence officer, who had approved Adan's actions, should have recognized the danger when the 37th Brigade requested permission to probe the Egyptian defenses. Soon after this Wallach ordered the 10th Infantry Brigade to move in and occupy the deserted positions at Um Katef and Um Shehan. The Battle of Abu Ageila was finally ended.

THE BATTLE FOR RAFAH

Meanwhile, shortly after midnight on the morning of November 1, General Haim Lascov's Northern Task Group finally got into action. Lascov's mission was to capture Rafah, seal off the Gaza Strip, and then advance westward through El Arish on the road toward Kantara and the Suez Canal.

The Egyptian Rafah fortifications occupied the northeast corner of the Sinai Peninsula, just south of the Gaza Strip. The complex of camps and installations was manned by the 5th Infantry Brigade of the Egyptian 3d Division, reinforced by the 87th Palestinian Battalion, two National Guard battalions, two motorized Border Patrol companies, one tank company of sixteen Shermans, one battery of eleven self-propelled Archer antitank guns, one regiment (24 guns) of towed 25-pounder field artillery, and one battery of twelve light antiaircraft artillery pieces. These units were deployed in a semicircular network of 26 mutually supporting company and platoon positions, mostly taking advantage of a series of barren, rocky ridges south and east of the Rafah crossroads. Each position was dug in and surrounded by barbed wire and minefields. South of the main fortified area, and running parallel to the Israeli-Egyptian border, were two minefields, about 300 meters apart, each about 50 meters deep and 5 kilometers long. A third and less extensive minefield was about 1,000 meters to the west, behind the first line of Egyptian defenses.

The force available to General Laskov consisted of the 1st Infantry Brigade and the 27th Armored Brigade. The armored, or mechanized, brigade, commanded by Colonel Haim Bar Lev, consisted of three armored task groups and a motorized infantry battalion. Each armored combat team consisted of a squadron of tanks (one AMX, two Shermans), one halftrack company of infantry, a troop of four 105mm self-propelled guns, a reconnaissance platoon, and a section of engineers. The 1st Infantry Brigade, better known as the Golani Brigade, commanded by Colonel Benjamin Givli, had three battalions of infantry, a battery of field artillery, a battery of heavy mortars, and an engineer battalion. Attached to the brigade was a company of 12 super-Sherman tanks (from Bar Lev's brigade), and a battalion of motorized infantry from the 12th Infantry Brigade.

Laskov's plan was for a double envelopment of the Egyptian fortified

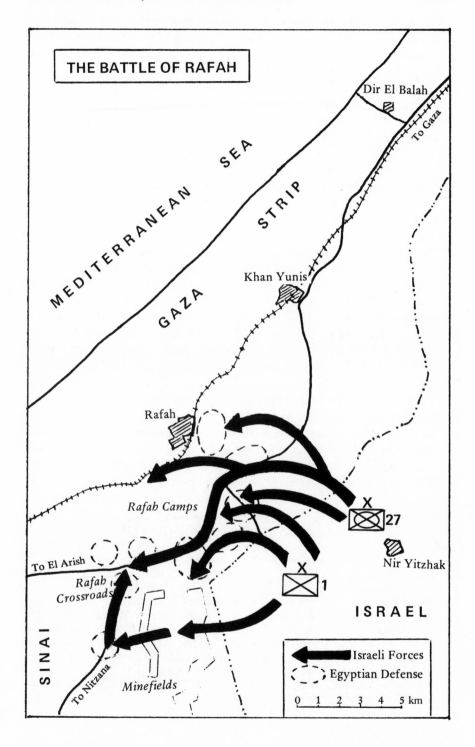

THE BATTLE OF RAFAH

Dir El Balah

To Gaza

MEDITERRANEAN SEA

STRIP

GAZA

Khan Yunis

Rafah

Rafah Camps

To El Arish

Rafah Crossroads

X 27

Nir Yitzhak

X 1

ISRAEL

SINAI

To Nitzana

Minefields

Israeli Forces
Egyptian Defense

0 1 2 3 4 5 km

complex. On the left a battalion of the Golani Brigade would clear a path through the Egyptian minefields, hit the extreme right wing of the defending Egyptians, and clear a path for the attached motorized infantry battalion from the 12th Brigade to reach the north-south road about five kilometers south of the Rafah Junction, or crossroads. The halftracks and trucks of this battalion, commanded by Lieutenant Colonel Meir Pilavski[1] and supported by the attached Sherman tank company, would then drive north to seize the crossroad. Simultaneously one other Golani battalion would be conducting a vigorous holding attack against the center of the Rafah fortifications.

The right hook of the double envelopment would be made by the remaining Golani battalion, in coordination with Colonel Bar Lev's 27th Brigade. This attack would not start until shortly before dawn, by which time it was expected that the Egyptians' attention would be focussed on the earlier Golani attacks and Pilavski's penetration further south. The right flank Golani attack would be directed against two strong Egyptian hill positions (known to the Israelis as Hills 29 and 31) south of the road and east of the encampments. On the extreme right, Bar Lev's tanks would strike for two fortified positions—known as Hills 34 and 36, just north of the road—which anchored the left rear of the Rafah defensive area. Bar Lev planned to use his two Sherman armored combat teams in this attack, one behind the Golanis, the other on the extreme right. He was holding out his AMXs for the exploitation phase.

During the night of October 30-31, 24 hours before the planned assault on Rafah, Israeli engineers quietly cleared three paths—9 meters wide and 150 meters apart—through the minefields southeast of the road junctions. Late the following day, however, the Israelis observed Egyptian soldiers moving through the minefields in the same general area where their engineers had been at work the previous night. Although the nature of the Egyptian activity was somewhat obscure, because of the sun in their eyes, the Israelis came to the conclusion that two of their paths through the minefield had been discovered and the mines replaced.

---

[1] Meir Pilavski, a veteran of the Palmach with a distinguished record in the 1948 War as a platoon and company commander, later changed his name to Meir Pa'il. He was the commander of the Israeli Officer School (roughly the equivalent of West Point) in 1967, and was assigned to the staff of General Tal's Division, where he served efficiently as the equivalent of a Deputy Chief of Staff; his 1956 experience at Rafah was thus useful in the opening battle of the 1967 War. Soon after that war, he retired from active duty, and obtained the degree of Doctor of Philosophy in History at Tel Aviv University. He has specialized in the history of the early years of the Israel Defense Force, and in the 1970s was possibly the leading military historian and military analyst in Israel. As an extreme left-wing socialist, and a strong advocate of a compromise peace with the Arabs, he is at the time of writing of this book one of the most controversial members of the Knesset.

Thus, on the night of October 31-November 1, only one of the three previously cleared paths was deemed safe for use by the assault force.

The signal for the attack was a French and Israeli naval bombardment of the Rafah defenses, which began at 2:00 a.m., and lasted until 2:30. This was followed by a brief but intensive air bombardment which lasted until 3:05. (According to General Dayan these two preparatory bombardments were very ineffective.[2])

Under cover of all this noise and activity, the Golani 3rd Battalion, which had crossed the border before midnight, advanced very slowly toward its objective; three Egyptian posts just beyond the first two minefields. (The Israelis didn't know that there was a third minefield.) In fact, the Egyptians, under orders from Cairo, had already begun their withdrawal several hours before the assault began. Their rear guard, however, carried out an effective delaying action with artillery and machine guns. Thus, without serious opposition, by 6:00 a.m. the Golani Battalion had occupied its assigned objectives on the rim of the Rafah defensive perimeter.

Things were not so easy, however, for the attached battalion of the 12th Infantry Brigade. In a column of 6x6 trucks and halftracks, followed by the attached squadron of super-Sherman tanks, Pilavski's battalion began to move across the border just after midnight, and by 2:00 a.m. had passed through the Golanis, and was moving toward Hill 5 and the road. Suddenly the leading vehicle entered the third minefield, struck a mine and exploded. The command halftrack, just behind, attempted to advance to the right of the burning vehicle, but it too hit a mine and started to burn. With these targets illuminated, the fire of the Egyptian rear guard increased in intensity and accuracy.

Israeli engineers hastily cleared a new path through the minefield to the left and south of the damaged vehicles. Pilavski, who had not been seriously hurt, then reassembled his column and started to advance again. Several halftracks and two tanks crossed through on the new path, but the third tank hit a mine and lost its tracks. The battalion was again immobilized, and the Egyptian artillery, mortar, and machine gun fire took advantage of this new aiming point.

It was now 4:00 a.m., only one hour until sunrise, and if the column remained stationary, the battalion commander realized that it might be destroyed in the daylight. He sent a radio to Colonel Givli, the brigade commander, to ask whether he should remove the remaining vehicles from the area while it was still dark, or whether he should continue.

Givli told Pilavski to press on. He was determined to have the battalion push through and complete its assignment. If the troops could not advance in their vehicles, then they should move on foot. It was obvious

[2] Dayan, *op. cit.*, pp. 127-128.

to Givli, however, that the battalion could not advance the seven and a half miles on foot, reach the crossroads on schedule, and capture the Egyptian position without tank support. The only alternative was to clear yet another path through the minefields. He sent his remaining engineers to help.

The Israeli engineers moved ahead on foot, working under fire with the assistance of headlights from the following halftracks. By 5:15 they had completed a new path north of the destroyed vehicles, and as dawn was breaking the remainder of Pilavski's battalion passed through without further incident; the battalion reconnaissance platoon in the lead, followed by the tank squadron and the halftracks.

Working in conjunction with the Golani 3rd Battalion, Pilavski's troops turned north and advanced toward the crossroads. With artillery support, the halftracks stormed the Egyptian positions dominating the crossroads, held by only a small Egyptian rear guard, which withdrew. By 9:00 a.m. the Rafah crossroads was in Israeli hands.

The right arm of the envelopment meanwhile had started from assembly areas west of the Israeli concentration area at Nir Yitzhak at about 3:40 a.m. The move was led by the right-flank Golani battalion, mounted in halftracks and trucks, followed by one of Bar Lev's Sherman combat teams. The advance was more difficult than expected because the defenders were alert. Accurate Egyptian artillery fire slowed the movement, and the Israelis didn't reach the vicinity of their objectives—Hills 29 and 30—until shortly after dawn. There was some tough fighting; then the Egyptians' resistance slackened as, following their orders, they began their withdrawal toward the Rafah crossroads and El Arish.

About this time, in accordance with the plan, Bar Lev's mechanized infantry battalion and the other Sherman combat team swung around to the east, then north, of the Golanis approaching Hills 29 and 30. Now Bar Lev's troops became the target for the Egyptian artillery. His infantry was particularly hard hit by this artillery fire, and Bar Lev decided that he would commit his reserve—the AMX combat team—to assure the accomplishment of his mission. By 8:00 a.m. his troops, infantry and armor, were securing Hills 34 and 36 just as the Golanis were consolidating positions on the hills to the south and west. The Egyptians were withdrawing completely from the Rafah defenses.

PURSUIT TO EL ARISH AND ROMANI

After an hour spent in reorganizing and evacuating the Israeli and Egyptian wounded, Bar Lev sent his AMX combat team down the road toward El Arish. The tanks passed the crossroads, cheered on by Pilavski's troops, shortly before 10:00 a.m. Close behind the AMXs came Bar

Lev with his Shermans and halftracks. The leading Israelis found that the Egyptian post at Sheikh Zuweid, ten kilometers west of the crossroads, was empty. Sixteen kilometers further on, the 27th Brigade encountered some fire near El Burj, but continued to advance.

Bar Lev's troops again met fire at El Jiradi, 16 kilometers east of El Arish. They had caught up with the Egyptian rearguard, an infantry company, a detachment of three Archers, and a supporting battery of six 120mm mortars. At 2:30 p.m. the Israeli armor advanced on the post. Following their instructions, the Egyptians withdrew after firing a few rounds.

Six kilometers east of El Arish, the 27th Brigade encountered still another Egyptian delaying position, manned by two infantry companies of the 11th Battalion of the 4th Infantry Brigade, supported by antitank weapons and a battery of eight 25-pounders. Since it was almost dark, and his troops had been moving and fighting all night and throughout the day, Bar Lev decided to postpone attack on this position until the morning. He had little choice; most of his tanks were out of fuel and ammunition. During the night the crews refueled and repaired their vehicles and snatched some rest.

Brigadier Gaafer el Abd, commander of the Rafah defenses, had received his orders to withdraw at 11:00 p.m. on the 31st. This, of course, was before the Israeli attack, and he had replied that he was under no pressure and that he would be able to hold his position, but the order to withdraw was repeated peremptorily. Accordingly el-Abd transmitted his instructions to his subordinate commanders, and prepared for a defiant withdrawal. When the attack did come, the orders were carried out faithfully; the rear guards destroyed much of the abandoned equipment, and, as the Israelis approached, they withdrew after a stubborn delaying action.

The evening of November 1 Brigadier el Abd was pleased with the way the withdrawal had gone. Most of his troops had been able to perform their delaying actions as planned. Some units had been so closely engaged by the Israelis, however, that they had been unable to carry out the planned, orderly delay. They had, nevertheless, fought stubbornly and had made things difficult for the Israelis. El Abd's losses had been higher than he had expected, but he believed (quite wrongly) that the Israelis had suffered equally.

While the Israelis rested, reorganized and refueled during the night, el Abd's troops continued their withdrawal down the road to the Canal. By dawn, when Bar Lev began his attack on El Arish, el Abd and most of his troops were back at the Canal, and many of them had already finished their crossing. Thus, as Bar Lev pushed into El Arish, he found the fortifications empty. He promptly sent his AMX battalion westward.

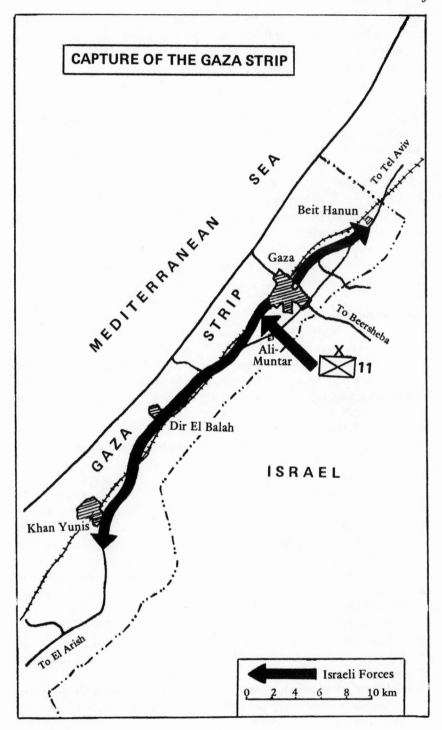

CAPTURE OF THE GAZA STRIP

MEDITERRANEAN   SEA

GAZA   STRIP

Beit Hanun

Gaza

To Tel Aviv

To Beersheba

Ali-Muntar

X
⊠ 11

Dir El Balah

ISRAEL

Khan Yunis

To El Arish

⬅ Israeli Forces

0   2   4   6   8   10 km

Another battalion cleared the road to Bir Lahfan, capturing many of the Egyptians withdrawing from Abu Ageila. The AMX battalion reached Romani at about 5:00 p.m. without encountering any opposition.

THE BATTLES FOR GAZA AND KHAN YUNIS

Meanwhile, the Israeli capture of Rafah had completely isolated the Gaza Strip. The northern half of the Strip, which includes the city of Gaza, was held by about 3,500 troops of the Egyptian 26th National Guard Brigade, scattered in some fourteen defense posts along the Israeli frontier. These outposts were supported by four sections of two 120mm mortars each, and two platoons of the motorized Border Patrol.

The defense of the southern half of the Gaza Strip was based on Khan Yunis, where the 86th Palestinian Brigade held three major positions around the city, with one battalion in each. These battalion positions were supported by centrally located artillery, mostly 120mm mortars. The 87th Palestinian Brigade, having been shifted earlier to Rafah, was now retreating to the Canal, with the other Egyptian units.

The task of capturing the Gaza Strip was assigned to the Israeli 11th Infantry Brigade under Colonel Aharon Doron. It consisted of two infantry battalions and one reconnaissance company, supported by a battalion of heavy mortars. Attached to the brigade was an armored combat team of tanks and halftracks from the 37th Mechanized Brigade.

Doron's plan was to make simultaneous attacks on the city of Gaza from three directions shortly after dawn on November 2. His 1st battalion, to which was attached a battery of heavy mortars, was to strike Gaza from the east; the 2nd Battalion, also with a battery of heavy mortars attached, was to attack from the north. The 37th Brigade's armored combat team, with the third battery of heavy mortars attached, was to cross the frontier near the Ali Muntar ridge,[3] three kilometers south of Gaza, to reach the Rafah-Gaza road, and then strike north to enter the city from the south.

The assault against Gaza began at 6:00 a.m. Resistance was sporadic, and although there were occasional bursts of heavy fighting, by noon much of the city was occupied. Egyptian Brigadier Mahmed Fuad el-Dugawi, the governor of Gaza, anxious to avoid unnecessary civilian losses, and knowing resistance was hopeless in light of the general Egyptian withdrawal, surrendered the city early in the afternoon. The Israeli 12th Infantry Brigade, less two battalions (one with the 1st Brigade and one following the 11th Brigade as Doron's reserve) took over responsi-

---

[3] Site of two disastrous British defeats at the hands of the Turks defending Gaza in 1917.

bility for securing Gaza and the northern part of the strip, while the 11th Brigade turned south toward Khan Yunis.

During the night the three task forces of the 11th Brigade positioned themselves north and west of Khan Yunis. They attacked at dawn on November 3. The armored combat team was held up briefly on the outskirts of the city by machine gun and antitank fire. Finally, however, with support from the infantry, this initial resistance was brushed aside, and Doron's 2nd Battalion poured into the city. By 1:30 the last defense post in the Gaza Strip had been taken. The 11th Brigade marched south to join the 1st Brigade at Rafah, having lost 11 killed and 65 wounded in the two days of fighting.

8

Conclusion of
the Sinai Campaign

CENTRAL SINAI

Late on October 31, Colonel Ben-Ari, with a battalion each of AMXs and halftracks, bivouacked far in front of the rest of the Israeli Army, on the road between Jebel Libni and Bir Gifgafa. About midnight he received orders directly from General Dayan to continue his advance westward the following morning. By 6:00 a.m. his two battalions, having passed through Bir Hamma, had reached Bir Rud Salim, the main Egyptian supply base in the central Sinai. As the Israeli advance guard tanks approached the base, they came under fire from an Egyptian armored unit, part of the 4th Armored Division, acting as rear guard for the troops still withdrawing from Bir Gifgafa. In the ensuing firefight, eight Egyptian tanks were knocked out, and several Israeli tanks were damaged. Having accomplished their delaying mission, the Egyptians then withdrew. At 6:30 a.m. the Israelis entered the base, and a company of nine tanks continued westward down the road toward Bir Gifgafa in pursuit of the Egyptians.

Eight kilometers west of Bir Rud Salim, however, the Israeli tanks again came under intense tank and artillery fire. After several hours of inconclusive long-range firing, and having lost two tanks, the Israelis returned to Bir Rud Salim to refuel and evacuate the wounded.

In the light of the strength of this opposition, Ben-Ari spent the remainder of the day and the night getting his tanks and halftracks repaired and ready for renewed combat the following morning. Before dawn on November 2, he left Bir Rud Salim and advanced toward Bir Gifgafa, which he thought was still being held by the 1st Egyptian Armored Brigade. However, by the time the Israelis reached Bir Gifgafa, in the middle of the morning, the Egyptians were all back at the Canal.

The 7th Armored Brigade pursued and at about 4:00 p.m., at Katib el Subha—almost midway between Bir Gifgafa and Ismailia—met the rear guard of the 1st Armored Brigade: one platoon of T-34 tanks, and one of Su-100s. In a short, intense engagement, four T-34 tanks and four

193

Su-100s were destroyed, and the remainder withdrew to the Canal. The Israelis had no losses. By sunset Ben-Ari and his troops reached their objective, a line 10 miles from the Canal, and there they stopped in accordance with the Anglo-French "ultimatum," which of course had been agreed on at Sèvres.

OBJECTIVE: SHARM EL SHEIKH

One of the main objectives of the Israeli war effort was to break the blockade of the Gulf of Aqaba, imposed by Egyptian troops based at Sharm el Sheikh, near the southern tip of the Sinai Peninsula. The mission of seizing this Egyptian fortification had been given to the 9th Mechanized Brigade, under the command of Colonel Avraham Yoffe. The brigade was to advance down the eastern coast of the peninsula, supported by a small naval task force on the Gulf, but its advance was not to begin until all of the other major operations were well under way. In particular Dayan did not want to expose it to air attack until he was sure that the Egyptian air force was destroyed or neutralized.

The 9th Brigade was composed of reservists from the northern part of Israel with concentration points near Haifa. After being mobilized, on October 28, Colonel Yoffe began moving his brigade southward on the various civilian vehicles he was able to commandeer. His assigned jumpoff point was Ras en Nagb, a junction in the eastern Sinai, just across the Egyptian border from Eilat. Yoffe's instructions were to reach Ras en Nagb in such a way as to avoid observation by the Jordanians. He decided, therefore, not to take the main road south from Beersheba to Eilat, but to follow behind Sharon's brigade to Kuntilla, and then take the desert track southeastward to Ras en Nagb on the Egyptian side of the frontier. Meanwhile, at sundown on October 29, a detachment of engineers and reconnaissance troops from Eilat seized the Ras en Nagb junction and cleared a path through the minefield laid by the Egyptians between Ras en Nagb and the border.

By 10:00 p.m. on October 31, Yoffe's brigade was concentrated at Kuntilla, and he immediately moved out for Ras en Nagb, which he reached during the afternoon of November 1. There he waited for orders to proceed down the coast.

Shortly before 5:00 a.m. on November 2, Yoffe received radio orders from General Dayan to proceed as planned. A few minutes later the 9th Brigade departed from Ras en Nagb along a desert track running about 15 kilometers inland from the coast. The first 140 kilometers were difficult terrain, the desert track often deep in sand, and the grade generally uphill.

The column consisted of three battalions, one artillery battery, one heavy mortar battery, a reconnaissance company, a troop of light antiaircraft guns, plus engineer and service detachments. Yoffe had left back all clerks and cooks, to bring his strength down to less than 1,800 men, in 104 6x6 trucks, 32 command cars, 14 halftracks, and 34 jeeps. The brigade carried with it sufficient food for five days, fuel for 600 kilometers, and enough water to provide each man five liters per day and each vehicle four liters per day for five days.

The brigade advance guard, consisting of one company of infantry in jeeps and halftracks, a troop of four 81mm mortars, and an engineer detachment, moved approximately 30 kilometers ahead of the main body. By 1:00 p.m. the head of the main body had reached Ein Furtaga, almost 100 kilometers south of Ras en Nagb. It took thirteen hours to go the next fifteen kilometers. This stretch of the route crossed deep sand above the Wadi Zala, where the track disappeared completely. Although the halftracks could move slowly through this difficult terrain, the artillery and antiaircraft weapons sank up to their axles and had to be pushed and towed. But this was only the beginning.

THE PARATROOPERS ENTER THE ACT

Chief of Staff Dayan was well aware of the difficulty of the route which he had assigned to the 9th Brigade, and, since operations elsewhere in the Sinai had moved so rapidly, with Israeli troops approaching their final assigned positions ten miles east of the canal, Dayan was afraid that a ceasefire might come into effect before Sharm el Sheikh could be captured. He therefore decided to expedite the operation against Sharm el Sheikh by sending part of Sharon's paratroop brigade in a southward advance down the Gulf of Suez. Sharon was ordered to release a battalion for this task, a battalion of the 4th Brigade was sent to Nakhl to relieve the battalion he had left there.

Shortly after dark on November 1 the 3d Battalion, from Nakhl, rejoined the main body of the brigade in its perimeter just east of the Mitla Pass. During the day, after having evacuated the wounded from the heavy fighting of the previous day and night, Sharon and his men had taken some time to rest, while reorganizing the defenses so hastily occupied the previous evening. During the night two companies of the 3d Battalion prepared for an air drop on the shores of the Gulf of Sinai, while Lt. Colonel Eitan and two companies of the 1st Battalion readied themselves for a move overland to link up with the 3rd Battalion airhead.

Shortly after noon on November 2, the two companies parachuted into the El Tor airfield with orders to capture the town, while the 1st Paratroop Battalion moved south from the Parker Monument toward Ras es Sudr by way of Ein Sudr. It is significant that Sharon sent this force around the Mitla Pass, instead of by the more direct route through the pass. This rather conclusively demonstrated his assessment of the outcome of the fighting on October 31.

Following the capture of the police station at El Tor, the airstrip there was repaired and an Israeli plane soon landed, the first of a series of 25 transport flights. They brought in an infantry battalion from the 12th Brigade and additional weapons and ammunition for the paratroopers, both those who had airdropped and those who were on the road further north.

At dawn on November 3 Eitan and his two 1st Battalion companies captured the oil fields at Ras es Sudr, then advanced south to El Tor, arriving in the afternoon. Before dark the combined task force—the 1st Battalion of the 202d Paratroop Brigade (including two companies of the 3rd Battalion), plus the battalion for the 12th Infantry Brigade—started moving southward toward Sharm el Sheikh. Lieutenant Colonel Eitan was in command.

That same day, after only a brief rest from the exertion at the Wadi Zala, the 9th Brigade continued southward. In mid-morning the advance guard captured the coastal village of Dahab, driving out an Egyptian outpost. The main body arrived before noon. The advance guard continued southward, but the main body of the brigade remained at Dahab until evening, when two landing craft arrived from Eilat with additional food, fuel, water and an AMX tank. At 6:00 p.m. the brigade was again on the road.

CEASEFIRE AND ALLIED CONFUSION

After the French and British vetoes of the Security Council ceasefire resolutions on October 30, next day upon the urging of the United States and Yugoslavia, an emergency meeting of the United Nations General Assembly was called by the Security Council for November 1. Britain and France opposed the resolution, but since it was an administrative matter they were precluded from using their vetos. At the meeting on the 1st the Assembly adopted an American resolution, calling for an immediate ceasefire, a withdrawal of the Israelis behind the 1949 Armistice lines, and the opening of the Suez Canal to navigation. It also enjoined other "members to refrain from introducing military goods into the area." Egypt, Israel, Britain and France were to respond promptly to the casefire demand.

Meanwhile, Egypt had blocked the Canal securely by sinking a number of ships in its narrow passages. The Syrian Army, while avoiding overt hostilities against Israel, had blocked the flow of all oil from Iraq to the Mediterranean, thus adding economic pressure to political and diplomatic weights which were beginning to crush Anthony Eden's government, under attack at home and abroad by outraged public opinion.

On November 2 the Israeli representative at the UN asked the Secretary General for "clarification" of the resolution of the 1st. The British and French, also stalling for time while their invasion flotilla labored slowly through the Mediterranean, replied evasively to that resolution. They suggested that a United Nations Emergency Force be established to enforce peace and to keep the Canal open; meanwhile they insisted that Egypt must accept the entry of French and British forces into the Canal Zone until the UNEF became effective.

On November 3 the United Nations General Assembly met again. Secretary General Hammerskjold reported that Egypt had accepted the ceasefire resolution of the 1st, but that Israel, Britain, and France had given negative responses. The Assembly approved a resolution by Canadian representative Lester Pearson, to set up the UNEF suggested by the British and French, while repeating the call for a ceasefire. Israel, Britain and France abstained, Egypt again agreed. On instructions from Ben Gurion, who expected that Sharm el Sheikh would be in the hands of Israeli troops by evening, Abba Eban, the Israeli envoy to the UN, also agreed.

The Israeli acceptance of the ceasefire shocked and dismayed the British and the French, who had large amphibious forces at sea converging toward the northern end of the Suez Canal from Cyprus, Malta, and Algeria. A ceasefire in the Sinai would negate the rationale for the Anglo-French invasion that was about to take place for the stated purpose of protecting the Suez Canal from the dangers of hostilities.

The allies urgently asked Prime Minister Ben Gurion to delay his acceptance of the ceasefire in order to give them additional time to carry out their operations. Ben Gurion neatly rescued his allies from their predicament by some quick and fancy diplomatic footwork. Early on November 4 Abba Eban "clarified" Israel's acceptance to the General Assembly's resolution by stating that it was conditional on the acceptance of "satisfactory positive replies" from Egypt to five questions:

1. Is there clear and unequivocal agreement on the part of the government of Egypt to a ceasefire? (A meaningless question, but good for at least a few hours of delay.)

2. Does Egypt still adhere to the position declared and maintained by her over the years that she is in a state of war with Israel? (A question so phrased that no possible likely answer by Egypt could be considered "satisfactory.")

3. Is Egypt prepared to enter into immediate negotiations with Israel with a view to establishment of peace between the two countries as indicated in the aide memoire of the government of Israel of November 4 to the Secretary General of the United Nations? (A sure delay-maker, since there was no possibility of an early "positive" answer from Egypt, whose government had not yet seen the aide memoire.)

4. Does Egypt agree to cease the economic boycott against Israel and lift the blockade of Israel's shipping in the Suez Canal? (A substantial

question, but one which was most unlikely to receive an immediate "positive" and satisfactory answer.)

5. Does Egypt undertake to recall the fedayeen gangs under her control and in other Arab countries? (A question most easily compared with "when did you stop beating your wife?")

Time for continuing Israeli and Anglo-French operations having thus been gained by these diplomatic maneuvers in the United Nations, hostilities continued. The British, however, were careful not to allow this embarrassing situation to arise again. When the Security Council again voted on a ceasefire, on November 5, the British representative vetoed the resolution.

THE BATTLE FOR SHARM EL SHEIKH

Meanwhile, on November 3, Israeli fighter bombers had destroyed two of the four 3-inch guns at Ras Nasrani, overlooking the Strait of Tiran. The planes also did considerable damage to the workshops, water filtration plant, and water tanks at Sharm el Sheikh. One of these Israeli planes was shot down, and Colonel Zaki learned from the wounded captured Israeli pilot that two columns were converging on his position from the northeast and northwest. He therefore decided to abandon the Ras Nasrani position and to collect all of his forces in Sharm el Sheikh, where there was an airstrip and a port. The remaining coastal guns at Ras Nasrani were then blown up, and the withdrawal was carried out after dark during the night of November 3-4. During the night, also, two small Egyptian sailing ships reached Sharm el Sheikh, where they picked up the wounded, including the captured Israeli pilot, and all civilian noncombatants, then returned with them to Suez.

Before midnight on the night of November 3-4, the advance guard of the 9th Brigade reached the defile of Wadi Kid, reporting by radio that the track there was only six feet wide and was covered by boulders. Yoffe decided to blast the rocks and widen the road in order to allow the passage of his tanks and halftracks; he sent his engineers ahead at once.

Meanwhile as the advance guard reached a point some one and one half kilometers from the end of the wadi, it was caught in an Egyptian ambush. The leading jeep was destroyed on a mine as the Egyptians opened fire with bazookas, machine guns and hand grenades. The advance group, after returning fire, withdrew, and joined the main body of the brigade at 2:00 a.m. just as it was entering the wadi from the north.

Yoffe decided to bivouac for the night at that position and at dawn sent the advance guard back to the ambush site, while the brigade's reconnaissance aircraft scouted the area from overhead. When the pilots reported that the area seemed deserted, the advance guard moved forward. But they soon found their way blocked by a large number of antivehicle mines planted along the track.

Once again the engineers were called upon. They removed some of the mines and marked a path through the field, and by 9 o'clock the entire brigade could continue the advance. By 11:45 the advance guard was in sight of Ras Nasrani. The brigade passed through that position without stopping, and advanced to a ridge some five kilometers north of Sharm el Sheikh. There, shortly after 2:00 p.m., the northernmost Egyptian outpost was overrun without difficulty. However, the brigade soon came under intense and accurate fire from posts on nearby ridges. Yoffe decided to break off action and give his men a brief rest.

At midnight, November 4-5, the 9th Brigade prepared to renew its assault. At about 2:00 a.m. the attack began, its specific objective to capture a defensive position held by two Egyptian companies on the northwestern flank of the Sharm el Sheikh defenses. The assault companies reached the barbed wire fence surrounding the Egyptian emplacement, but they were under heavy fire and unable to cross the minefield inside the fence. After the assault battalion took twenty casualties, Yoffe ordered a withdrawal. The wounded were evacuated by halftrack to the brigade base, three kilometers to the north.

At 5:30 a.m. Yoffe renewed his attack, with heavy mortar and air support. He committed all of his force except for the battalion that had made the previous attack, which was in reserve. After about an hour of fierce fighting along the northern perimeter of the Sharm el Sheikh defenses, the jeep detachment of the advance guard fought its way into the Egyptian emplacements. Despite fierce defense, one position after another was taken by the Israelis and at 9:30 the garrison at Sharm el Sheikh was surrendered by the second in command, Lieutenant Colonel Hanna Neguib, acting for Colonel Zaki, who had been wounded. The Egyptian losses were approximately 100 killed, 31 wounded, and 864 captured. In the entire campaign the 9th Brigade had lost 10 killed and 32 wounded.

Meanwhile Eitan's paratroopers and infantry, advancing on Sharm el Sheikh along the Gulf of Suez coastal road, had rounded the southern tip of the peninsula, and shortly after 5:00 a.m. were approaching Sharm el Sheikh from the southwest. At that time they established radio contact with the 9th Brigade. At 6:30 a 9th Brigade liaison plane brought a message to Eitan.

Yoffe, involved in the final preparations for his own climactic attack, asked the new arrivals to advance within 2,000 yards of the Egyptian post, to attract the attention of the Egyptians by fire, but to wait there for further instructions. However, before 8:30 Eitan recognized that the Egyptian defenses were beginning to collapse in the north and decided to take advantage of the situation by breaking through into the position from the south. Resistance was minimal, and at 9:30 the leading para-troop halftracks reached the entrance to the Egyptian command post, contributing to the Egyptian surrender decision.

Less than seven days after Eitan and his 1st Paratroop Battalion landed east of the Mitla Pass, they took part in the operation in which the Israeli Army completed its conquest of the Sinai Peninsula. All hostilities between Israelis and Egyptians had now ended, with all surviving Egyptian troops now west of the Canal, and the Israelis halted ten miles east of it. However, three hours before the fall of Sharm el Sheikh, the Egyptians had begun fighting another foe at the opposite extremity of the Sinai.

9
Operation "Musketeer"

At the allied command post at Malta the Allied Land Force Commander, General Sir Hugh Stockwell, and his deputy, General André Beaufre, received word of the initiation of Israeli hostilities late on the afternoon of October 29. During the afternoon British destroyers gathered off Malta and Cyprus in readiness to convoy the invasion fleets. At the same time three French destroyers, the *Kersaint,* the *Bouvet,* and the *Surcouf,* began patrolling the Mediterranean coast near Haifa and Tel Aviv.

General Stockwell had been ordered to make no overt moves, such as embarking his troops on their vessels, until the beginning of Allied air attacks on Egyptian bases. However, he had not been ordered to cancel any training or rehearsal schedules, and he had thoughtfully ordered a departure rehearsal to take place at 10 o'clock the following morning, Tuesday, October 30. Thus, by the time the British and French governments had issued their ultimata to the Egyptian and Israeli governments, most of the landing force were on their vessels. Stockwell ordered the rehearsal to continue through the night and neglected to order the troops back to their barracks the following day.

Thus when the Anglo-French air attacks struck Egypt at 7:00 p.m. on October 31, the loading of the Anglo-French amphibious fleet was complete. This saved one full day from the original plan, permitting Stockwell to advance the assault date from November 8 to 7. The main flotilla steamed out of Valetta Harbor during the night of October 31-November 1 and turned eastward. About the same time a contingent of French amphibious vessels left Constantine, Algeria, and fell in a few miles behind the main British-French convoy. The next day still another contingent was loaded at Cyprus and prepared to join the main body in the southeast corner of the Mediterranean on November 6.

While the thrust of the Anglo-French air assaults was redirected against Egyptian railroad yards, antiaircraft emplacements and barrack areas, the amphibious convoys steamed eastward, Stockwell and Beaufre fuming about the slowness of their vessels.

During these air attacks, the allies took great care to avoid inflicting civilian casualties. In the night of November 1-2, a squadron of French

F-84 Thunderstreaks from Cyprus struck south across the Sinai and the Arabian Desert to Luxor, where they destroyed the remaining Egyptian Il-28 bombers.

On November 3, after consultation with the naval convoy commander, Stockwell was able to gain still one more day in his timetable by having the slower ships in his convoy run above normal speeds, while the faster vessels forged ahead to take their places in a reorganized convoy formation. However, world domestic pressure on the allies, especially on Britain, was rapidly mounting.

The Anglo-French attack upon Egypt—thus far evident only in the air operations—had aroused a storm of international protest.[1] The reaction of the US Government was particularly strong, President Eisenhower and his assistants rightly believing that they had been deliberately misled by their two closest allies, Britain and France. But perhaps the most hostile reaction of all came from the British Parliament, where the Labor Opposition combined righteous wrath with recognition of a political opportunity on a silver platter.

On October 31, at an emergency session of the UN Security Council, the United States proposed a ceasefire between Egypt and Israel, the resolution also calling upon all UN member states "to refrain from the use of force or the threat of force in the area . . . [and] from giving any military, economic or financial assistance to Israel so long as it has not complied with the resolution." Seven of the eleven Security Council members approved, two abstained; Britain and France vetoed the resolution.

After this veto the Soviet Union (then involved in its sordid aggression against Hungary) for the record offered a similar resolution, but more clearly directed against Britain and France. Again the resolution was endorsed by seven of the eleven states represented on the Security Council, and again the British and French representatives applied the veto.

In the face of this massive tide of disapproval at home and abroad the British Government—which should have anticipated the criticism to which it was much more sensitive than the French—now tried desperately to hasten the amphibious operation so as to conclude the seizure of the Canal before international opposition could prevent action. Now Mr.

[1] Probably the best summary of the political aspects of the Anglo-French operations, their implications, and results, is to be found in Anthony Nutting, *No End of A Lesson; The Story of Suez* (New York, 1967). At the time the operation was planned, Nutting was Minister of State in the Foreign Office—in other words, the principal deputy to Foreign Minister Selwyn Lloyd. He resigned from the Government when the operation began because of his deep disapproval of the collusion between Britain, France, and Israel. Any lingering doubts that there was collusion is swept away by Nutting's narrative.

Eden and his ministers began to realize that the delays which they had imposed upon the departure of the amphibious flotillas had poliitcial consequences perhaps even more severe than the military ones.

After frantic consultations between the British and French Governments, and their military staffs, equally frantic messages were sent to Stockwell and to Durnford-Slater, to see what could be done about expediting the landings. The naval and land commanders, however, replied that for purely military reasons they had already done everything they could to accelerate the operation. The only remaining alternative that Stockwell could see was to advance the landing of the paratroopers by one day to November 5. Originally the paratroopers were scheduled to jump at key points inland at the same time that the amphibious troops hit the beaches. The decision to have the paratroopers land twenty-two hours before the assault over the beach was a grave risk, but Stockwell decided it was justified under the circumstances. Less worried about the military risk, the British and French Governments eagerly approved.[2]

Stockwell, Beaufre, and their planners then developed a modified airborne landing plan aboard their command ship, HMS *Tyne*. This hastily devised operation—given the code name "Telescope"—provided for British paratroopers to drop at Gamil Airfield, three miles west of Port Said, on November 5, and to advance on that city from the west while French paratroopers simultaneously captured Port Fuad on the east bank of the Canal. The waterworks providing fresh water to Port Said, and two bridges over the Raswa Canal at the southern end of the city, would also be taken by British paratroopers landed by helicopters. The revised plan was radioed to London, and late that evening, November 3, was approved by Prime Minister Anthony Eden.

Stockwell made one further change in the plan on November 4. Because there was some possibility of contact with Israeli forces on the eastern side of the Canal, he wanted all such contacts to be made by French troops, in the light of past Israeli condemnation of his even-handed role in the withdrawal of British troops in Haifa in 1948. Accordingly, he switched the assignment of capturing the waterworks and the Raswa bridges from the British helicopter force to French paratroopers. General Beaufre agreed with his decision, which was also approved by the British Government.

Port Said is a man-made city created on fill. It is connected to the Egyptian mainland on the west side of the Canal by a vulnerable,

---

[2] During this flurry of activity, the French offered to have their own paratroopers land one day earlier still, on November 4, if the Israelis would protect their flank by seizing Kantara. The Israelis agreed. This cooperative action, however, would have revealed the collusion to the world, and the British refused. (See Dayan, *op. cit.*, p. 153).

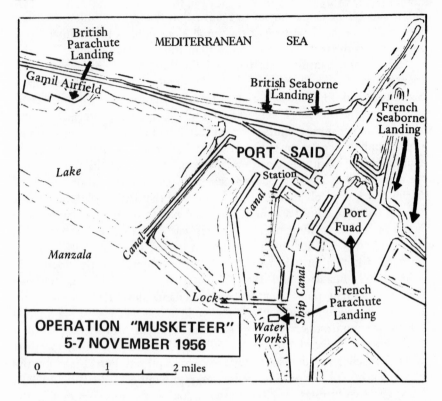

British Parachute Landing

Gamil Airfield

MEDITERRANEAN   SEA

British Seaborne Landing

French Seaborne Landing

PORT SAID

Lake

Station

Canal

Port Fuad

Manzala

Canal

Ship Canal

Lock

French Parachute Landing

**OPERATION "MUSKETEER"
5-7 NOVEMBER 1956**

Water Works

0   1   2 miles

narrow north-south embankment, carrying a road and a railroad. Beside these, to the west, runs the Sweetwater Canal, carrying fresh water from the Nile for the Canal Zone towns. This water is brought from the Nile Delta to the Raswa Canal by a causeway aqueduct across Lake Manzala, west and southwest of Port Said. On the south bank of the Raswa Canal, just after it reaches Port Said between the highway and the railroad bridges, are the waterworks that pump fresh water into Port Said and Port Fuad.

The Egyptian garrison at Port Said in October 1956 consisted of two battalions of infantry reservists, plus some regular antiaircraft and coastal defense batteries. When it became clear that an Anglo-French invasion was imminent, Nasser augmented these forces with three National Guard battalions, and a third battalion of reservists. During the evening of November 4, four Su-100 self-propelled guns arrived in Port Said from the Sinai. At dawn on November 5 small arms arrived by train for distribution to the citizenry in accordance with plans previously prepared by President Nasser and General Hakim Amer; Brigadier Salah ed-Din Moguy, Chief of Staff of the Eastern Command, volunteered to take direct command of the defense of Port Said; Nasser and Amer promptly approved.

Gamil Airfield, the site of the planned British paratroop drop, was defended by a company of reservists and a National Guard battalion. Sand-filled oil drums had been placed on the runways to prevent planes from landing, and four concrete emplacements with machine guns bordered the field.

Beginning at dawn on November 5, British carrier aircraft began attacks on defensive positions at Port Said and Port Fuad. At 8:20 a.m. the 3rd Battalion of the 16th Independent Paratroop Brigade Group landed at the airfield and at the outskirts of the city. Fifteen minutes later 500 paratroopers from the French 2nd Colonial Parachute Regiment jumped south of the Raswa bridges. By 9:00 o'clock the British had gained control of the airfield, and the French paratroopers had seized the waterworks and one bridge over the Raswa Canal. The Egyptians had succeeded in destroying the other bridge, with the result that the city was cut off from both fresh water and reinforcements. Fighting was fierce, as the Egyptians concentrated against the relatively small positions held by the British and French paratroopers.

At 1:45 in the afternoon, however, a second battalion of French paratroopers jumped to a position southeast of Port Fuad, while a company of British paratroopers dropped in to reinforce the battalion at Gamil Airfield. Continuing allied air attacks, plus the sight of the arrival of these reinforcements, did much to unnerve the Egyptian defenders.

By mid-afternoon there was no fresh water in Port Said, and fires which had been set by air attacks were burning out of control. Brigadier Moguy informed the civilian governor of the city, Mohammed Riad, that they should meet with the invading force commander to negotiate a temporary truce in order to reduce civilian suffering. He was not unaware of the fact, of course, that any such truce would also gain time for reorganization of his badly disorganized Egyptian troops, and provide time for the arrival of reinforcements promised by President Nasser.

At 4:00 p.m., under a flag of truce, Moguy contacted the French commander at the waterworks, appealing for permission to repair the pumping station for the sake of the civilian population. He then arranged for a meeting with the senior allied commander, British Brigadier M.A.H. Butler, to discuss a temporary truce.

Unable to reach Cairo by radio for instructions, Moguy nonetheless went ahead with his discussions with Brigadier Butler. After long and inconclusive negotiations, at 5:30 Butler (not realizing that Moguy had no intention of surrendering) stated his final terms for the surrender of Port Said and Port Fuad. He agreed to a brief truce—to end by 9:30 p.m. —to allow Moguy time to submit the terms to Cairo by radio.

Moguy kept his word about sending the terms to Cairo by radio, but he used the intervening time to repair the waterworks (with French permission) and to regroup his troops. At 9:00 he got Butler to agree to an hour's extension of the truce so that all wounded could be evacuated. At 10:30 fighting resumed in Port Said.

During the night, Stockwell, still at sea on the *Tyne,* received radio orders from London requiring still further changes in his plans for the amphibious assault. The British Government was extremely anxious to avoid civilian casualties, partly because of the pressure of world and domestic opinion and partly because of a desire to minimize inevitable Arab hostility against Britain. Therefore, the order stated that the caliber of guns to be used in the preliminary bombardment should be no greater than 4.5-inch. This eliminated the use of the main batteries of the cruisers of the Anglo-French fleet and the French battleship *Jean Bart.*

Soon after this another order was received, giving a revised target list, and eliminating some of the targets which Stockwell and Beaufre had considered key positions to be eliminated before the landing. Finally, about an hour later, there came still another jittery radio order from London, cancelling the preliminary bombardment entirely.

Stockwell had received messages from Butler warning that the assault force would meet with stiff resistance in Port Said. He was therefore reluctant to put his troops ashore without adequate fire support. He decided to draw a fine technical distinction between "naval bombardment" and "naval gunfire support." He accepted the London decision with respect to the naval bombardment, and cancelled it as ordered. He informed the admiral, however, that he expected normal naval gunfire support for the assault troops.

At 6:50 a.m. on Tuesday, November 6, the first wave of the 3d Royal Marine Commando Brigade hit the beaches at Port Said, while troops of the French Foreign Legion landed at Port Fuad. The Egyptians defending the waterfront had been driven back by 45 minutes of "support" fire and a ten minute air strike which preceded the landing. Air strikes were launched at the Governorate (local administration building) and the prison in order to weaken resistance at those strongpoints. (These places had been eliminated from the preliminary target list, but Stockwell considered them perfectly appropriate targets for support fire.) The assault waves were quickly followed ashore by British and French infantry in a landing that proceeded with textbook efficiency, quite different from the amateurish political bungling which had so delayed the operation.

At 10:00 a.m. Brigadier Moguy, gallantly in the forefront of the fight, was captured by the advancing British. By this time Egyptian resistance was collapsing, with Egyptian soldiers discarding their uniforms and merging with the heavily armed civilian population. At 11:00 a.m. Generals Stockwell and Beaufre and Air Marshal Barnett went ashore from their command ship to try to negotiate an unconditional surrender of the city with their captive, Brigadier Moguy. But that officer, stating that he no longer had a position of command authority, refused to order a surrender. Other efforts were made, through the Italian consul, to negotiate a surrender, but these also failed. Nevertheless, the allied troops were already consolidating their hold on the city, despite interference from sporadic sniper fire.

At 4:00 p.m. Stockwell issued orders to his commanders for the following day. Butler and the British paratroopers were to be flown ahead by helicopter to capture Abu Sueir airfield; French paratroopers under General Massu at the same time were to drop and capture Ismailia. The French commando brigade was to mop up guerrilla resistance in Port Said and Port Fuad, while British infantry pushed southward down the road and railroad.

At dusk Stockwell departed Port Said in a landing craft to return to his command ship, the *Tyne*. Outside the breakwater, however, his landing craft ran into a storm, and as a result—after nearly capsizing—did not reach the *Tyne* until 7:30 p.m. As Stockwell climbed to the deck, dripping wet, he received another message from London, ordering him to cease hostilities at midnight. The British Government had caved in under the pressures at home and abroad, and had agreed in the General Assembly to a Canadian proposal for a ceasefire. Reluctantly the French —who had no other course—also accepted the ceasefire.[3]

After hasty meetings with Beaufre and their joint staffs in the command cabin, Stockwell did what little he could in the time remaining. Since midnight in London was 2:00 a.m. in Egypt, Stockwell decided to assume that midnight meant London time, and to make the most of the two extra hours. He ordered Butler to advance as far down the Canal as possible. Butler received this order at 10:30 p.m. Within 20 minutes he was leading the second battalion of his paratroop brigade and a squadron of tanks in a dash south along the road and railroad corridor against sporadic resistance, reaching as far as El Kap by 2:00 a.m. Egyptian time, midnight London time. There he halted.

The last act of the 1956 Sinai-Suez War was over. It was a peculiar,

[3] Neither the British nor the French were influenced in this decision by the blustering threats of nuclear attack by Nikita Khrushchev's Soviet Government. Furthermore, had they been frightened, they received adequate reassurance by President Eisenhower's action in ordering a world-wide alert of American forces; otherwise the US did not relax its pressure upon its allies to agree to a ceasefire. The Soviets, deeply involved in Hungary, would never have done anything to back up their threats. However, these gained them much political kudos in the Arab world.

unnecessary, anticlimactic and essentially sordid act in political anger. Surprisingly, however, in purely military terms it reflected great credit on all participants. The Anglo-French operation, performed within exceptionally rigid limits, was superbly planned and executed.[4] The Egyptian resistance against the superior technological and numerical resources of the invaders was determined, resourceful, and essentially gallant.

---

[4] Extensive criticism of the operation (including that of General Dayan) is either uninformed or else ignores the political constraints placed on the British and French commanders, and simply overlooks their excellent performance within these constraints.

10

The War at Sea

GENERAL

The principal naval feature of the war was the Anglo-French naval participation in the amphibious operation against Port Said and Port Fuad. Next in significance was the British carrier air participation in the Anglo-French bombardment of Egyptian airfields and other strategic targets.

The Egyptian Navy endeavored to interfere with both of these Anglo-French naval actions, but without success. Egyptian torpedo boats made at least one ineffectual attack against the amphibious convoy, and engaged and apparently damaged a British destroyer. On two other occasions Egyptian destroyers vainly attempted to torpedo British aircraft carriers. On November 2 the Egyptians received unintended and unexpected help from the Israeli Air Force, which attacked the British HMS *Crane* near Sharm el Sheikh.

It has been difficult to obtain reliable, verifiable, information on operations. Accordingly, the two following sections present partial naval narratives from the separate standpoints of the two Middle East opponents.

ISRAELI OPERATIONS

Following its 1947-1949 War of Independence, Israel augmented its initial fleet with two surplus British Z-class destroyers, twelve torpedo boats, and several small frigates and patrol ships, including former U.S. Navy 173-foot subchasers and coastal escorts. In addition, a few landing craft were obtained to improve capabilities for commando incursions.

Early in the campaign, on October 30, 1956, an Egyptian destroyer of the British *Hunt* class, *Ibrahim Al Awwal*, bombarded Haifa with over 200 four-inch shells, starting at 3:30 a.m. Damage to military and industrial targets was slight. Shortly before 4:00 a.m. the French destroyer *Kersaint* opened fire on the *Ibrahim* at extreme range, scoring no hits. At 4:25 the *Kersaint* stopped firing, apparently because of the anticipated arrival of Israeli vessels. About the same time the *Ibrahim*, reporting her mission accomplished, steamed west.

209

Two Israeli Z-class destroyers, *Yaffo* and *Eilat* (the second Israeli ship so-named), were directed by Israeli Navy Headquarters to pursue and intercept the *Ibrahim*. At 5:25 they came within range and opened fire, inflicting minor damage on the Egyptian ship without sustaining any hits themselves. The *Ibrahim* reported this gun duel to Alexandria, which ordered the vessel to take refuge in a Syrian or Lebanese port; air cover was promised. At 6:30 a.m. two Israeli Ouragan fighters attacked the *Ibrahim* with rockets and cannon, damaging the steering and electrical systems, thus rendering her incapable of maneuver. The promised Egyptian aircraft never arrived.

At 7:00 the *Ibrahim* reported to Alexandria that she was out of ammunition, her engines were damaged, and she could not steer. The crew attempted to scuttle to avoid capture, and, after taking about 10 casualties, the Egyptian vessel and 151 men surrendered at 7:30. Israeli seamen boarded the vessel, closed the seacocks, and captured the log intact. (The crew had reported the log and code books destroyed at 7:25.) The vessel was towed into Haifa harbor, and was later commissioned in the Israeli Navy as the INS *Haifa*.

The other major Israeli naval activity of the war was the provision of "over the beach" logistical support for the column taking the difficult and barren overland route down the harsh eastern Red Sea coast of the Sinai Peninsula. At noon on October 28, five LCMs, designed to carry light tanks, left Haifa on modified railroad cars which took them to Beersheba. (This required removal of several structures bordering the tracks en route.) They arrived at Beersheba before dawn on the 29th and were hoisted onto large flatbed trucks (diverted from hauling phosphates from the potash works near the Dead Sea). Travelling only at night in order to avoid detection by the Jordanians, the craft arrived at Eilat at the northeastern apex of the Red Sea before dawn on the 31st. They were immediately launched on the waters of the Gulf of Aqaba.

The 9th Brigade, slowed down by the formidable terrain, was consuming much more fuel, water, and rations than had been estimated. Consequently, two LCMs were loaded with fuel and other supplies and proceeded to the coastal village of Dahab, about halfway down the peninsula. They arrived there on November 3, shortly after the 9th Brigade reached the village. The provisions' timely arrival enabled the brigade to continue its march, already far behind schedule, after only a brief pause. The LCMs next transported four light tanks to the 9th Brigade, and also brought more supplies soon after the brigade reached Sharm el Sheikh. A proposed amphibious assault on Tiran Island was cancelled, since it had been evacuated by the Egyptians.

Early on November 2 the Israeli Air Force attacked a warship a few miles south of Sharm el Sheikh, assuming that it was an Egyptian vessel.

Although the target ship fired back vigorously at the Israeli aircraft, it was hit by several bombs, but was not critically damaged. The Israelis later learned that they had attacked HMS *Crane,* a frigate which had been blockading Sharm el Sheikh and the Gulf of Suez.

EGYPTIAN OPERATIONS

At the outset of the war the Egyptian Navy was suffering from the handicap of a shortage of officers, since many had been assigned as Suez Canal pilots, and few of them were returned to the Navy until the Anglo-French air bombardment of October 31 caused the Egyptian Government to close the Canal.

From that time on the attention of the Egyptian Navy was focussed on interfering with Anglo-French naval operations, both carrier air and amphibious convoy. A number of clashes resulted from this effort.

During the night of November 1 the corvette *Damietta,* with one 4-inch gun, encountered the British cruiser HMS *Newfoundland,* with nine 6-inch guns and various smaller weapons, in the Gulf of Sinai, approaching Suez. After radioing information of the contact, the *Damietta* boldly engaged the *Newfoundland,* scoring two hits. The Egyptian vessel was soon sunk, but the radio information and the delay permitted Egyptian torpedo boats to arrive, and by repeated attacks to drive the *Newfoundland* away from Suez. The Egyptians believe that other British efforts against Suez were foiled by minefields laid in the Gulf of Suez.

One dramatic naval action took place within sight of the Alexandria waterfront. The Egyptian destroyers *El Nasr* and *Tarek* engaged a British aircraft carrier, just on the horizon. The carrier responded by gunfire, and then launched its aircraft for a dive-bombing attack. The two Egyptian ships were hit, both by gunfire and by bombs, but escaped serious damage by evasive action and intensive antiaircraft fire, then retired into Alexandria under the cover of a smoke screen.

On November 4 a squadron of Egyptian motor torpedo boats engaged a British destroyer off the northeastern Delta coast, near Bralous. Three of the attacking MTBs were sunk, but the surviving craft claimed to have made repeated hits on the destroyer, which they left in a sinking condition. The British do not admit any such loss, but the Egyptians claim that the vessel log book, several bodies, and warship debris washed up on the coast. The Egyptian claims must be considered very dubious.

That night—November 4-5—British warships bombarded the coastal town of Al Agony, just west of Alexandria, while carrier planes attacked two airfields near Alexandria. The purpose of this action, apparently, was to lead the Egyptians to believe that their amphibious flotilla, then approaching the Egyptian coast, was going to land near Alexandria.

There was no further action of significance before the ceasefire. Anglo-French naval and naval-air power had overwhelmed Egypt's small navy, but Egyptian sailors can be proud of their performance against great odds.

APPROXIMATE GROUND FORCE STRENGTHS
Suez-Sinai Campaign, 1956

	Egypt	Israel	Britain[1]	France[1]
Field Forces	150,000[2]	100,000[6]	13,500	8,500
Tanks	530[3]	400[7]	?	?
APCs	200	450[8]	?	?
Artillery Pieces	500	150	?	?
Self-Propelled AT guns	50[4]	0	?	?
Combat Aircraft	255[5]	155[9]	70	45

[1] Counting fleet and base and follow-up units in Malta, Cyprus, UK and Algeria, more than 100,000 Anglo-French uniformed personnel were committed against Egypt.
[2] Approximately 50,000 committed against Israel.
[3] Includes 100 Su-100 assault guns.
[4] Archer, 17-pounder, 3" high velocity gun.
[5] Includes 45 MiG-15s, 40 Vampires, 38 Meteors, 8 Furies, 49 Il-28s, 20 Commandos, 20 Dakotas, 35 miscellaneous transports; however, only about 60 fighters, 10 bombers, and 60 transports operational.
[6] Approximately 45,000 committed against Egypt.
[7] Includes 100 AMX-13 light tanks, 300 M-4 medium tanks.
[8] Halftracks.
[9] Includes 19 Mystères, 25 Ouragans, 25 Meteors, 29 Mustangs, 16 Mosquitos, 20 Harvards, 16 Dakotas, 3 Nords, 2 B-17s.

ESTIMATED LOSSES
Suez-Sinai Campaign, 1956

A. *Personnel Casualties*	Killed	Wounded	Captured/Missing	Total
Egypt vs. Israel	1,000	4,000	6,000	11,000
Egypt vs. Allies	650	900	185	1,735
TOTAL	1,650	4,900	6,185	12,735
Israel	189	899	4	1,092
Britain	16	96	0	112
France	10	33	0	43

B. *Aircraft Losses*

Israel	15
Egypt	215 (200 on the ground)
Britain	4*
France	1

* One of these was shot down over Syria by Syrian AA fire.

ORDER OF BATTLE
Israeli Armed Forces, 1956

Minister of Defense	David Ben Gurion
Chief of Staff	Maj. Gen. Moshe Dayan
Deputy Chief of Staff (Operations)	Brig. Gen. Meir Amit
Southern Command	Brig. Gen. Assaf Simhoni
Northern Task Group (Ugdah 77)	Brig. Gen. Haim Laskov
1st Inf Bde	Col. Benjamin Givli
11th Inf Bde	Col. Aharon Doron
27th Mczd Bde	Col. Haim Bar Lev
Central Task Group (Ugdah 38)	Col. Yehudah Wallach
4th Inf Bde	Col. Joseph Harpaz
10th Inf Bde	Col. Shmuel Gudir,
	Col. Israel Tal
7th Armd Bde	Col. Uri Ben-Ari
37th Mczd Bde	Col. Shmuel Golinda
Independent Brigades	
202d Para Bde (Mitla Pass)	Col. Ariel Sharon
9th Inf Bde (Sharm el Sheikh)	Col. Avraham Yoffe
12th Inf Bde (Gaza)	Col. David Elazar
Air Force	Brig. Gen. Dan Tolkowsky
Navy	Brig. Gen. Shmuel Tankus

ORDER OF BATTLE
Egyptian Armed Forces, 1956

Minister of Defense and Commander in Chief	General Abd el Hakim Amer
Eastern Military Zone (Sinai)	Maj. Gen. Ali Amer
3d Infantry Division	Brig. Anwar abd Wahab el Qadi
4th Inf Bde	Brig. Saad ed-Din Mutawally
5th Inf Bde	Brig. Gaafer el Abd
6th Inf Bde	Col. Sami Yassa;
	Brig. Saad ed-Din Mutawally
8th (Palestinian) Infantry Division	Maj. Gen. Yusef el Agroudi
86th Frontier Esct Bde	
87th Frontier Esct Bde	
26th Natl Gd Bde	Lt. Col. Ali Ali Gamal
4th Armored Division	Brig. Ali Gamal Mahmoud
1st Armd Group	Col. Talat Hassan Ali
2d Armd Group	Col. Ibrahim el Mogui
2d Inf Bde	Brig. Wagih Taher El Sherbieni
2d Lt. Reconnaissance Regiment	Lt. Col. Ahmed Ali Atiah
Sharm el Sheikh Region	Col. Rauf Mahfouz Zaki
21st Inf Bn Group	Lt. Col. Hanna Naguib
Gaza Command	Brig. Mahmed Fuad el-Dugawy
Port Said Region	Brig. Salah ed-Din Moguy*
Navy	Adm. Soliman Ezzat
Air Force	Air Ch. Marshal Mohomed Sidgi Mahmoud

---

* Chief of Staff of Eastern Military Zone.

ORDER OF BATTLE
Anglo-French Forces, 1956

Allied Commander in Chief	Gen. Sir Charles Keightley
Deputy Commander in Chief	Adm. Pierre Barjot
Allied Land Force Commander	Lt. Gen. Sir Hugh Stockwell
Deputy Allied Land Force Commander	Lt. Gen. André Beaufre
Allied Air Commander	Air Marshal Denis Barnett
Deputy Allied Air Commander	Gen. de Brigade R.G.A.A. Brohat
Allied Naval Commander	Adm. Robin Durnford-Slater
Deputy Allied Naval Commander	Adm. P.J.G.M. Lancelot
British Land Forces	
3d Inf Div (-)	Maj. Gen. J. Churcher
10th Armd Div (in readiness, not embarked)	Maj. Gen. R. Moore
16th Para Bde Gp	Brig. M.A.H. Butler
3d Royal Marine Commando Bde	Brig. R. Madoc
French Land Forces	
10th Para Div (-)	Maj. Gen. Jacques Massu
1st Para Bn, Foreign Legion	Col. Pierre Chateau-Jabert
7th Lt Mczd Rgt	
Marine commando bns (3)	
British Naval Forces—Royal Navy	
Carrier Group	Vice Adm. M.L. Power
Support Group	Vice Admiral Deric Holland-Martin
3 aircraft carriers (200 fighters)	
4 cruisers (1 in Red Sea)	
13 destroyers (1 in Red Sea)	
6 frigates (2 in Red Sea)	
5 submarines	
Assault Force	Commo. R. de L. Brooke
French Naval Forces	Adm. Y. Caron
1 battleship	
2 aircraft carriers (50 fighters)	
2 cruisers	
4 destroyers	
8 frigates	
2 submarines	
British Red Sea Force	Capt. J.G. Hamilton
British Air Forces	
9 bomber squadrons (120 bombers)	
4 fighter-bomber squadrons (100 fighters)	
1 reconnaissance squadron	
French Air Forces	
4 fighter-bomber wings (75 F-84, 25 Mystère IV)	
3 transport wings	

	Losses British		*French*	
Aircraft	3		1	
	k	w	k	w
Personnel	16	96	10	33

11

Envoie

The military outcome of the Sinai War between Egypt and Israel would probably have been the same whether or not Britain and France had intervened in the struggle. Yet this cannot be asserted categorically, because it is not even certain that the war would have taken place had the British and French not sought to use Israeli involvement as their own figleaf of respectability.

It should be remembered that at the time General Amer gave the order for withdrawal from the Sinai, as a result of the Anglo-British bombardment of Egyptian airfields, Abu Ageila-Um Katef was still holding out, and Israeli General Dayan had halted further attacks on that formidable position. The Israelis did not have control of the air, and it is not certain that their unquestioned qualitative superiority over the Egyptian Air Force would have been enough to overcome the Egyptian advantage in numbers of modern combat aircraft. It must also be noted that, if there had not been the threat of Anglo-French intervention from the outset of the campaign, Egyptian deployments would have been different, and there was a real possibility of Syrian, and possibly Jordanian, participation.

Nevertheless, despite the setbacks at Abu Ageila and the Mitla Pass, Israeli ground forces had demonstrated a distinct qualitative superiority over the Egyptians, and there is little doubt that the IAF could at least have kept the Egyptian Air Force off the backs of Israeli ground troops. Without the participation of Syria and Jordan, an Israeli ground force victory over the Egyptians, including the capture of Sharm el Sheikh, was almost inevitable. And had the Syrians and Jordanians entered, the result would probably not have been dissimilar to that in 1967.

Nevertheless, the fact remains that Britain and France did intervene, and the speed and ease of the Israeli conquest of the Sinai were undoubtedly facilitated by the Anglo-French operations. The principal Egyptian forces were withdrawn from the Sinai to meet the Anglo-French threat before they became seriously engaged with the Israelis. In fact, in the only two fully-contested battles of the war—at Abu Ageila and the Mitla Pass—the Egyptians defended successfully against brief but intensive Israeli attacks.

The Egyptians and their Arab Allies make much of the fact that the war was begun with a surprise Israeli attack, which they therefore characterize as "aggression," or "unprovoked aggression." However, this places them in the position of basing their case upon two inconsistent arguments. Either they were not at war with Israel—in which case their blockade of the Suez Canal, and even more of the Strait of Tiran, was an illegal violation of international law, and a clear *casus belli*—or they were at war with Israel (thus justifying their positions on the closure of the waterways), in which case the Israeli attack was merely a normal incident in such hostilities. Whatever one may think of the collusion between Israel, Britain, and France, there is no justification for accusing Israel of aggression. Egypt wanted the rights of belligerency without the consequences.

Early in the war Nasser warned his two major allies—Syria and Jordan —against entering the conflict, in the light of the Anglo-French involvement. Whether or not they received or heeded this warning from Egypt, on their own account they decided to avoid possible military entanglement with the two major western powers, and stayed out of the war.

As for the Anglo-French operation, it was a tragic mistake for both nations. Having decided upon it, however, the two governments should have encouraged their military subordinates to do their best, instead of following a wishy-washy policy of trying to retain as many friends as possible while carrying out an operation that was bound to alienate all friends and perpetuate and exacerbate old enmities.

The British Government was probably right in ruling out a proposed operation against Alexandria, even though on purely military grounds this was the safest and most efficient way of seizing the Suez Canal Zone. Such an operation was so clearly incompatible with the avowed "police action" aim, focussed on the Suez Canal, that ultimate anti-British and anti-French repercussions would probably have been worse than they actually were, and might even have led to some kind of retaliatory action by the Soviet bloc. Certainly the operation should not even have been considered if the two governments did not have confidence that their military forces could perform the difficult operation of landing at Port Said and Port Fuad. In fact those landings were extremely efficiently performed, against formidable local odds.

Those odds would have been substantially less, and the operation would have proceeded much more rapidly, if Eden had listened to Keightley and Stockwell, and let them schedule their landings for November 1, in accordance with the original approved "Musketeer" plan. The British and French would have been at Ismailia by the 2d, and Suez by the 3d, trapping much of the Egyptian Army east of the Canal. In that event the British and French might even have been able to salvage some diplomatic crumbs from the debacle, and their military would have been spared the embarrassment of ridicule by people who did not realize that the ineptitude was political, rather than military.

Under the circumstances, Khrushchev's bombastic threats of rocket attacks were rightly ignored by the British and the French, although they understandably flinched a bit. But Khrushchev, still engaged in one of the most immoral aggressive military actions of modern times—the brutal reconquest of Hungary—had no moral position from which to undertake any such retaliation against British and French aggression. And while the United States was foremost in denouncing the British actions, this country was well aware of the greater culpability of the Soviet Union at the same time, and would unquestionably have moved promptly and decisively in support of the British and French if they had been attacked by Russia. Khrushchev clearly recognized this situation, and thus the Soviet leader's threats were not credible.

It is not easy to assess who won the Suez-Sinai War of 1956 because of the very different perceptions of the war by the participants. To the Israelis there were two wars: their war against Egypt, and the Anglo-French invasion of the Suez Canal; so far as the Israelis were concerned these wars were only indirectly related militarily, although of course they were closely related politically. The British perceived their operations against the Canal Zone as being totally independent of those of the Israelis, although they recognized that the Israeli invasion of the Sinai was an indispensable preliminary to their invasion of the Canal Zone. The French perception of two separate wars was similar to that of the British, although they were involved in some aspects of the Israeli campaign, such as their provision of materiel to the Israelis, their agreement to defend Israel's skies, and the naval bombardment of Rafah.

To the Egyptians, however, this was one war, in which the distinct operations of their allied enemies were designed to place Egypt at the greatest possible military disadvantage. They point out that their initial deployment of forces was made in recognition of two interrelated threats, and that their withdrawal from the Sinai was caused not by the Israelis, but rather by the Anglo-French threat to northern Egypt.

From the Israeli point of view the war was an unqualified Israeli military victory. Politically the results were less clearcut, since Israel was later forced to give in to American and UN pressure and to evacuate the conquered areas of the Sinai. However, Israel gained her major political objectives. The blockade of the Strait of Tiran was broken; Eilat could become a major seaport, contributing greatly to Israel's economy. And the establishment of the United Nations Emergency Force along the Sinai-Israel frontier greatly reduced the "terrorist" guerrilla attacks against Israel. The demonstration of Israel's exceptional military prowess gained the nation greater respect in world affairs. These political gains, therefore, clearly justified Ben Gurion's initial gamble in risking war. It was a political as well as a military success for Israel.

For Britain and France, however, their operations were military and political failures. Despite a very high degree of professional competence displayed by the participating Anglo-French land, naval, and air forces, a combination of circumstances prevented them from capitalizing on their clearcut combat superiority over the Egyptians, and they failed to achieve their military objectives. Politically this last gasp of colonialism was an unqualified disaster, for reasons that have been amply discussed earlier.

For Egypt the war was not a military success; on the other hand, it was not a military failure. Egyptian troops performed both well and poorly against the Israelis, but they could claim—sincerely and with some justification—that their withdrawal was forced by the Anglo-French threat, and that they had not been defeated by the Israelis. And while they had been driven out of Port Said and Port Fuad by the Anglo-French, they were proud that their resistance against superior numbers and superior technology so slowed down the European invaders that they were unable to achieve their military objectives.

Politically, of course, Egypt won a spectacular victory over the Anglo-French allies. President Nasser's personal prestige was unquestionably enhanced by his acceptance of a showdown. And the fact that Israel was later forced to withdraw from the Sinai was deemed by the Egyptians a politically successful outcome of that aspect of the war, far outweighing the slight embarrassment of having to accept the presence of a United Nations Force on Egyptian territory at Sharm el Sheikh and along the frontier with Israel.

Thus Israel and Egypt each won its war. This paradox was possible, of course, only because of the abject defeat of Britain and France.

BOOK THREE

The Six Day War,
June 1967

1

Background of the War

TURMOIL IN THE MIDDLE EAST

Following Israel's occupation of the Sinai Peninsula in October 1956, the United States and the Soviet Union, in unlikely collaboration and for totally different reasons, put tremendous political pressure on Israel to withdraw from the conquered territory. Finally, and reluctantly, Israel agreed to the withdrawal, in return for the establishment of a United Nations Emergency Force (UNEF) which would have as its mission the prevention of the two critical situations which had triggered the Israeli decision to go to war: fedayeen raids into Israel from bases in the Sinai and the Gaza Strip; and Egyptian blockade of the Israeli port of Eilat at the Strait of Tiran from the fortifications at Sharm el Sheikh, at the southern tip of the Sinai Peninsula. With the UNEF taking up positions handed over by Israeli forces at Sharm el Sheikh and along Israel's borders with the Gaza Strip and the Sinai, and having received great-power assurances of continued freedom of passage of shipping to and from Israel through the Strait of Tiran, in early 1957 the Israelis withdrew to their prewar frontiers.

Again the results of an Arab war with Israel figured directly or indirectly in a number of upheavals in the Arab world. On July 14, 1958, King Faisal of Iraq was deposed; he and his prime minister, General Nuri es-Said, were both brutally murdered, and a new military regime, headed by rebel General Abdul Karim Kassem established an unstable government, strongly influenced by the USSR. Iraq withdrew from the Bagdad Pact and from its military assistance agreements with the United States. In following years the country was wracked by a number of coups and coup attempts, while its military forces were engaged in a costly war against Kurdish insurgents in northern Iraq.

Lebanon and Jordan suffered considerable unrest, essentially from internal, local problems, but also because these problems were used by Arab radicals, usually pro-Nasser and in some instances undoubtedly supported by Egypt, to stir up troubles. In the late spring and early summer of 1958 riots and insurrections spread through Lebanon, erupting into virtual civil war the day the Iraq coup took place. The President of Lebanon appealed to the United States for assistance, and the next day

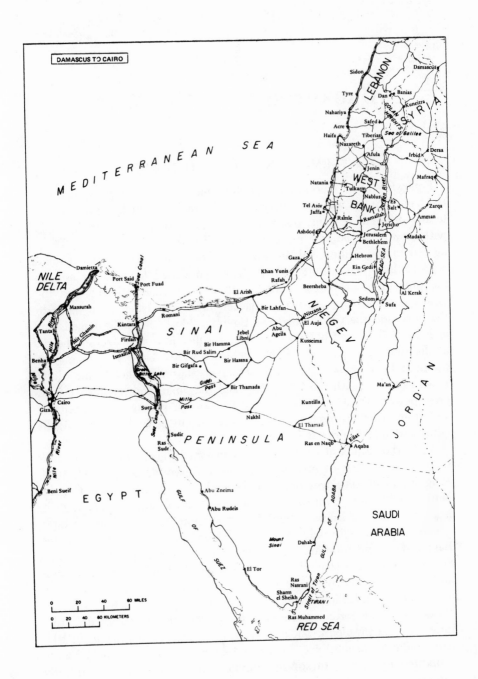

US Marines landed on the beaches of Beirut, spearheading a brief American military presence. On July 17, following a similar appeal to Britain from King Hussein, British troops flew into Jordan to help local forces restore order. By the end of October both American and British troops had withdrawn from the Middle East, having restored stability in Lebanon and Jordan, but not having ended the causes of unrest.

Meanwhile, in February 1958, Egypt and Syria had joined to create the United Arab Republic with President Nasser as its head. While this was to a great extent a natural consequence of pan-Arabism, Israelis were convinced that Nasser's principal purpose was to bypass the hampering presence of UN troops along his frontier with Israel, and to use Syria as a new base for anti-Israeli operations short of war. The move also undoubtedly contributed to the unrest in Jordan which erupted four months later.

Egyptian-Syrian efforts to neutralize, weaken, and if possible depose King Hussein continued after the British withdrawal from Jordan in October 1958. In September 1960 the Prime Minister of Jordan, Hazza Majali, was assassinated in a bomb explosion in Amman, probably at the hands of United Arab Republic agents. King Hussein concentrated his forces along the Syrian frontier, and may even have seriously contemplated a thrust to Damascus. If so, he was dissuaded by American and British pressure.

However, this particular aspect of Middle East unrest was lessened to some extent on September 28, 1961, when another coup d'etat in Syria overthrew the local government and disrupted the union with Egypt.

Since the end of the First Arab-Israeli War in early 1949, there had been sporadic outbreaks of firing along the ceasefire line between Israel and Syria. While most of the firing was done by the Syrians, the UN records and the published reports of three commanders of the United Nations Truce Supervising Organization (UNTSO) suggest that in most cases Syrian firing was in response to illegal Israeli actions in the three small demilitarized zones along the line.[1]

The people who suffered primarily from these disputes, however, were the farmers and villagers in the Israeli settlements in the Huleh Valley and along the shores of Lake Tiberias. Every kibbutz in upper and eastern Galilee had a number of bombardment shelters, where the inhabitants frequently had to take refuge, particularly during the semi-annual plowing periods, which UNTSO Commander von Horn wryly called the "Shooting Season."

In 1962 Egypt became involved in a civil war in Yemen, providing assistance to republican forces attempting to overthrow the decadent

[1] See for instance: Odd Bull, *op. cit.,* pp. 49-50; Carl von Horn, *op. cit.,* pp. 69, 115-116; E.L.M. Burns *op. cit., passim;* UN Documents S/2157, 1951; S/3128, 1953; S/3538, 1956; S/5111, 1962.

monarch. When Saudi Arabia supported the royalists, Nasser increased the scale of his aid to the rebels, and began to send troops to Yemen. By 1964 a quarter of the Egyptian regular army was fighting in Yemen.

By this time most of the other internal Arab differences had been patched up, and at a Summit Conference of the Arab League in Cairo, the heads of state of Syria, Jordan, and Lebanon—with the support of the rest of the Arab League—agreed upon a plan to divert the headwaters of the Jordan River. Such action would have seriously affected Israeli agriculture in the Huleh and Jordan Valleys. As the work began, Israeli artillery frequently harassed the workers, and in November 1964, Israeli aircraft began to attack those parts of the project out of artillery range. By the end of the year the project was abandoned, because it had become evident to the Arabs that its continuation would mean all-out war with Israel, and none of them felt ready for such a confrontation.

However, the Arab League at its summit conference had also endorsed the establishment of a "Palestinian entity," and it provided both material and moral support to intensified guerrilla activity along Israel's frontiers with Lebanon, Syria, and Jordan. As the raids increased in numbers and in cost—as measured by Israeli lives—Israel responded with increasingly strong retaliatory blows. To many Israelis it seemed as though the circumstances which had led to the 1956 war were being recreated.

BLUNDERING INTO WAR

There is little doubt that neither side wanted the war that broke out in the Middle East on June 6, 1967. Many Israelis believe that the Arabs were fully intent upon launching a war within a matter of hours, or, at most, days, from the time when the Israelis precipitated the situation by a preemptive strike. This is not so; neither President Nasser nor any other responsible Arab leader wanted war to break out at that time, nor indeed expected war to break out.

Nor is there any basis for the assumption by some Arabs that the war was merely the implementation of a deliberate Israeli plan for a war of aggression. Equally baseless is the suggestion by more sophisticated Arab analysts that Israel deliberately created a political crisis that would inevitably force President Nasser to take steps that would give Israel the opportunity to claim that the Arabs precipitated a crisis resulting in war.

But if Egypt had not intended to go to war, and if Israel did not want a war and did not precipitate the crisis which led to war, then how did it occur?

The answer is that both sides blundered into it. It would be difficult to say that either was more responsible than the other for the tragic series of escalations which led to the outbreak of hostilities, although in the final analysis President Nasser took the actions and made the decisions that made the war inevitable. It was a case of tragic, and classic, escalation and can be considered to have had its beginning in February 1966 when Syria had the seventeenth coup d'etat in its 21 years as a nation.[2]

The new government of Syria, militantly anti-Zionist, soon established close relations with the Soviet Union, and began to receive impressive quantities of military equipment. Meanwhile the Syrians encouraged the newly organized El Fatah Palestine Liberation Organization to establish bases on Syrian soil for terrorist-guerrilla incursions into Israel. While there were some fedayeen raids made from Jordanian and some from Lebanese territory after early 1966, most originated directly or indirectly in Syria.

The new government of Syria also began a rapprochement with Egypt. Relations between those two nations had been somewhat cool since the collapse of the short-lived United Arab Republic union of Egypt and Syria between 1958 and 1961. The extent to which the Soviet Union, which was supplying arms and advice to both countries, contributed to that rapprochement is not clear, but it is likely that it played some part. By early November a defense agreement had been made between Syria and Egypt, establishing a joint military command, under an Egyptian general, and providing for various other measures of military coordination and integration between the two countries.

The tempo of the fedayeen raids into Israel increased in the latter part of 1966, and in October two particularly serious incidents, in which several Israelis were killed, led to an Israeli appeal to the UN Security Council. But when that body passed a mild resolution suggesting only that Syria should take stronger measures to prevent such incidents, the Soviet Union vetoed the resolution. This was a pattern that had by now become familiar.

Israel decided, as it had done in the past, that, since it could get no satisfaction from the United Nations, it would undertake the punishment of the fedayeen and their Arab hosts. But for reasons that are not clear, and that in retrospect seem extremely shortsighted, the Israelis did not directly punish either the Syrians or the fedayeen based on Syrian soil. Instead, on November 13, 1966, an Israeli raid was mounted against Es Samu in Jordan. Eighteen Jordanians, mostly soldiers, were killed, and 54 were wounded.

Soon after this incident the Jordanian Prime Minister, Wasfi al Tal,

[2] One of the best analyses of the origins of the 1967 War was written by Charles W. Yost: "How it Began," in the January 1968 issue of *Foreign Affairs*, p. 304. The account on these pages is generally in agreement with Ambassador Yost's factual summary and assessment. It is also consistent with the version presented in Jordanian King Hussein's personal and official account (*My "War" with Israel*, New York, 1969), pp. 32-50.

somewhat bitterly accused both Egypt and Syria of failing to bear their share of the confrontation with Israel. He chided Egypt for having failed to provide air support, as had been promised in such circumstances, and suggested that it was about time that Egypt ended its involvement in Yemen and brought its troops back where they could help in the joint confrontation with Israel.

In subsequent months a number of incidents—involving exchanges of small arms fire, artillery fire, and small raids in both directions—took place along the Israeli-Syrian border. On April 7, 1967, particularly intensive Syrian artillery fire escalated into a tank battle, which in turn brought intervention by the Israeli and Syrian air forces. An aerial dogfight followed, which ended with six Syrian planes being shot down, without any Israeli losses, and the victorious Israeli aircraft sweeping threateningly over the outskirts of Damascus.

The Syrians joined the Jordanians in denouncing President Nasser for failing to punish Israel for this incident, which the Syrians described as aerial aggression. The press in other Arab countries joined in criticizing Nasser, suggesting that he was more interested in creating an overseas Egyptian colonial empire in Yemen than he was in supporting the joint Arab cause against Zionism in Palestine. Thin skinned and emotional, and ambitious to be recognized as the leader of a "United Arab Nation," Nasser found these criticisms and jibes almost unendurable.

The fedayeen raids continued, and in May escalated into violence against Israel such as a self-respecting nation could not ignore. On May 11, Israeli Prime Minister Levi Eshkol denounced this "wave of sabotage and infiltration."[3] He went on to say: "In view of the fourteen incidents of the past month alone, we may have to adopt measures no less drastic than those of April 7." Reference to the April 7 date jabbed sore spots in both Damascus and Cairo. Two days later, in a radio interview, Eshkol made this declaration: "It is quite clear to the Israeli Government that the focal point of the terrorists is in Syria, but we have laid down the principle that we shall choose the time, the place, and the means to counter the aggressor." If this sort of thing continued, he said, inevitably Israel would have to strike a decisive blow within enemy territory.

Eshkol was not the only one issuing warnings from Tel Aviv and Jerusalem. On May 12 a *New York Times* report stated: "Some Israeli leaders have decided that the use of force against Syria may be the only way to curtail increasing terrorism. Any such Israeli action against continued infiltration would be of considerable strength but of short duration and limited in area. This has become apparent in talks with highly qualified and informed Israelis who have spoken in recent days against a background of mounting border violence."

[3] Eshkol succeeded Ben Gurion, who retired in 1963.

MEDDLING BY THE USSR

Shortly after this there became evident a joint radio and press campaign from Moscow, as well as from Cairo and Damascus, asserting that the Israelis were massing troops in northern Israel for the purpose of invading Syria.

In response to these reports from Moscow, the Israeli government on at least three occasions, on May 12, May 19, and May 29, invited the Soviet ambassador to Israel to visit northern Israel and the Syrian border to observe the situation for himself; Ambassador Chuvakhin refused. On May 19, in a report to the Security Council, Secretary General U Thant referred to these allegations of Israeli troop movements and concentrations, and said: "Reports from UNTSO [United Nations Truce Supervision Organization] observers have confirmed the absence of troop concentrations and troop movements on both sides of the line."

Nevertheless, there seems to be no question that Moscow, Damascus and Cairo were all genuinely alarmed by the Israeli threats against Syria. As one knowledgeable diplomat later observed, "Israeli public statements between May 11 and 13, therefore, regardless of how they may have been intended, may well have been the spark that ignited the long accumulating tinder."

In any event these statements seemed to give credence to the reports Nasser apparently was receiving from Moscow about Israeli intentions. He decided that the time had come for him to restore his crumbling prestige, so sadly damaged by his inactivity following the Es Samu and April 7 incidents.

WITHDRAWAL OF UNEF

On May 16 Major General Indar Jit Rikhye, the Indian officer commanding the UN Emergency Force in the Sinai, received a letter from General Mohommed Fawzi, Chief of Staff of the Egyptian forces, demanding the withdrawal of all UN forces from the border with Israel. Rikhye quite properly transmitted this demand to Secretary General U Thant, who summoned the Egyptian ambassador to the UN to an urgent meeting. U Thant told the ambassador that Rikhye could take orders only from the Secretary General, and that if Egypt wanted a withdrawal of UN troops it should submit its request to him, U Thant. In that case, however, U Thant warned, he would also order the withdrawal of all UNEF troops from Gaza and from all of the Sinai, including the post at Sharm el Sheikh.

In retrospect it seems that President Nasser had not intended to precipitate this crisis, but, having done so, he probably expected U Thant to call a meeting of the Security Council, at which the only possible result would be a Security Council mandate for the forces to stay in position. In that case, considerably more Egyptian bluster would have been possible, and threats to overrun the UN posts might have been expected, but nothing more. The Secretary General's response, however, suggested that U Thant would withdraw the troops without consulting the Security Council if a direct demand were received from the Egyptian Government. This was not quite what Nasser had counted on, but he apparently thought that he had gone too far to back down, and after a two-day delay, on May 18, the Egyptian Government officially submitted to the Secretary General a demand for withdrawal of UN troops. Since U Thant had just that morning received a reiteration from Israel of its position that UNEF troops could not be stationed on the Israeli side of the line, the Secretary General issued an order for the withdrawal.

BLOCKADE OF THE STRAIT OF TIRAN

Meanwhile, on May 15, Egyptian reinforcements had begun moving into the Sinai area, most of them concentrating in the northeast corner, the Rafah-El Arish area. By May 22 there were close to 100,000 Egyptian troops in the Sinai, more than double the normal garrison.

On that day President Nasser announced his intention to reestablish the blockade of the Strait of Tiran.

In response, on May 23, Prime Minister Eshkol declared in Parliament: "The Knesset knows that any interference with freedom of shipping in the Gulf and in the Straits constitutes a flagrant violation of international law. . . . It constitutes an act of aggression against Israel."

There is some evidence that President Nasser gave thought to sending a private and secret message to Israel that he did not intend to use force to carry out the blockade, and that he was merely reaffirming the continuing state of war between Egypt and Israel, rather than initiating a physical blockade.[4] He never sent such a message, however, presumably because he feared that it would be made public by the Israelis, and further hurt his already damaged prestige. He seems to have expected that the Israelis would test his blockade announcement by sending some ships through the straits, at which time his non-belligerent intentions would become obvious.

The Israelis, however, had no intention of risking a merchant ship to test Egyptian intentions. They were convinced that Nasser was deadly serious, and they took his announced blockade at face value. They prepared to strike before they were struck, and set the date for June 5.

[4] Reported by a senior Egyptian official in a private conversation with the author.

Those Egyptians who believe that Israel did not have adequate provocation to launch the attack on June 5 insist that the non-belligerent intentions of their president were obvious. Despite the concentration of troops in northeastern Sinai, and despite the announced blockade of the Strait of Tiran, there was no hostile Egyptian action against Israel in the period of more than two weeks between the withdrawal of UN forces and the Israeli attack. In response to this, Israelis point to mounting belligerence in published statements by Arab leaders and reports of serious threats of imminent destruction of Israel from leading political authorities in Cairo, Damascus, and Bagdad. For instance, on May 26 Nasser told the Arab Trade Unions Congress that the Arab states were now determined to destroy Israel.

RECONCILIATION OF NASSER AND HUSSEIN

On top of this, and even more ominous than the mounting crescendo of verbal attacks, was the reconciliation between President Nasser and King Hussein of Jordan, at the personal initiative of the king.[5] On May 30 Hussein, accompanied by Saad Jamaa, his new Prime Minister, General Amer Khammash, the Jordanian Chief of Staff, and General Saleh Kurdi, Commander of the Jordanian Air Force, appeared in Cairo. He and Nasser concluded a mutual defense pact, bringing Jordan into the joint military command with Egypt and Syria, under the nominal overall command of Egyptian General Ali Amer. When Hussein flew back to Jordan later that day, accompanying the king was a recent bitter critic, Ahmed Shukairy, bombastic chief of the Palestine Liberation Organization—the PLO. Also that day Nasser and General Ali Amer appointed Egyptian General Abdul Moneim Riadh, one of the most respected senior officers in the Egyptian Army, as the joint commander of Arab forces on the Jordanian front. Riadh was sent to Damascus and Bagdad to explain this new development to Syria and Iraq, recently vociferous critics of Hussein's Jordan. On June 2, Riadh and a small staff arrived in Amman to take over his new command.

Next day, June 3, three battalions of Egyptian commandos were flown to Amman to assure a truly international Arab force on that front. It would be difficult to interpret these actions as other than serious preparations for war; to the Israelis these moves explained the temporary cessation of Egyptian activity in the Sinai; Egypt was waiting a few days until Jordan should be ready to assume a full-scale role in the impending conflict.

Yet despite these actions, it is very clear in retrospect that President

[5] Hussein, *op. cit.*, p. 43.

Nasser did not in fact have any intention of precipitating war against Israel at that time.[6] He apparently was aware of the fact that his army was woefully unprepared for such a war. He recalled that in 1960, under somewhat similar circumstances, he had increased the garrison in the Sinai and threatened a war against Israel and nothing had come of it; he seemed to believe that this would happen again. He was delighted by the results of his political and verbal activity. He had largely restored his prestige in the Arab world; he had brought about the reunification of a military coalition against Israel, which could take action in a year or two when times were more propitious, and he had gained a political victory over Israel, which now seemed to be backing down without serious protest in the face of all that Nasser had done.

It seems incredible that Nasser should not have recognized that the situation was far different from that in 1960; that Levi Eshkol, a weaker man than Ben Gurion, could not ignore the Arab threats and posturing so easily as Ben Gurion had.

It seems incredible, also, that Nasser and other Arabs expected Israel to sit complacently in the face of the situation they had created. Even if they somehow discounted the earnest statements of Prime Minister Eshkol, they should not have ignored the implicit—even though coincidental—warning contained in General Moshe Dayan's recently published and revealing book about the 1956 War. In that book Dayan pointed out that Israel had had three war objectives in 1956:

"Freedom of shipping for Israeli vessels in the Gulf of Aqaba; end to the Fedayeen; and a neutralization of the threat of attack on Israel by the joint Egypt-Syria-Jordan military command.[7]

Nasser had created a situation to which these war objectives were just as applicable in 1967 as they had been eleven years earlier.

Another comparison must be made to the 1956 situation, one that is generally ignored by the Arabs, and often overlooked by neutral observers. The blockade of the Strait of Tiran, like the continuing denial of Israeli passage through the Suez, was justifiable under international law only on the basis of Egyptian insistence that there was a continuing state of war with Israel. Thus, if a war already existed, Egypt could not logically accuse Israel of starting a war by its attack on June 5. As in 1956, Egypt was claiming the rights of belligerency but did not want to incur the risks or liabilities of that belligerency.

---

[6] *Ibid.*, p. 49.
[7] Moshe Dayan, *Diary of the Sinai Campaign, 1956* (London, 1967), p. 190.

2

On the Brink

ISRAELI PLANS AND PREPARATIONS

The mobilized Israel Defense Forces, on June 4, 1967, consisted of approximately 250,000 men, of whom 225,000 were in the Army. About 50,000 of these men were career professionals or conscripts in the standing army; the remainder, nearly 200,000, were reservists called up from their civilian pursuits.

Even at this late date[1] the security-conscious Zahal—Israel Defense Forces—has given no official information either on the number of troops in the armed forces in the 1967 War, or on the organization of fighting forces for combat. However, the army seems to have been organized in approximately 25 brigades, of which nine were armored, two were mechanized, ten were infantry (some partly mechanized), and four were paratroop. In addition to these field forces, there were about fifteen brigade equivalents (some 70,000 men) in local and frontier defense units. Twenty-two of the field force brigades, most of them components of some six *ugdahs* (division-size task forces), actually participated in the combat operations. The other three brigades presumably remained somewhere within Israel, performing various undefined reserve or security missions.

Israeli military and political leaders were well aware of the qualitative superiority of their forces over the neighboring Arab military forces, and also recognized something that went unnoticed by most of the rest of the world, and was not given sufficient attention even by the Arabs: they had nearly as many first-line troops as the combined Arab forces. (See table, p. 337). Although the Arabs had an advantage in major weapons, there was no doubt in the minds of Israeli military leaders that their own troops were technologically more sophisticated, or that they would be victorious in the event of another conflict. In fact, they expected to be as successful as in the 1956 War.

Egypt was recognized as the principal and most dangerous enemy. On the other hand Jordan posed the most immediate threat to the heart of Israel, with frontiers on the coastal plain averaging about 20 kilometers

[1] Written in mid-1977.

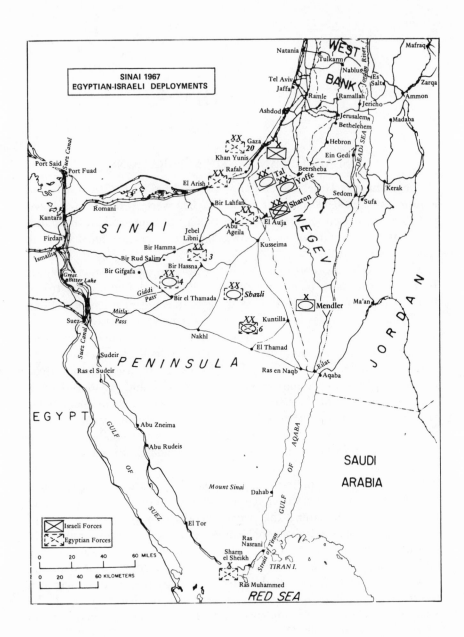

SINAI 1967
EGYPTIAN-ISRAELI DEPLOYMENTS

from the sea and at one point only 15 kilometers. Jordan also threatened Israeli Jerusalem, and occupied the Old City of Jerusalem, so important to Judaism. These were reasons for concentrating first against Jordan, while fighting delaying actions elsewhere, if the war should be on two or three fronts. However, there appeared to be a possibility of some eventual accommodation with King Hussein of Jordan; there was no such possibility with Nasser of Egypt. While Jordan might be able to resist pressure from other Arab states, and remain aloof from an Arab-Israeli war—as it had in 1956—Egypt would inevitably be an active participant in any future war.

Thus the Israeli General Staff decided to concentrate the bulk of its military power against Egypt in overwhelming strength at the outset of a new war. This meant trying to avoid active operations on the other fronts—or at least remaining on the defensive with the smallest forces security would permit—until the Egyptian Army was destroyed, or until the Israelis had seized a secure defense line in the Sinai Peninsula. Some Israeli planners even allowed themselves to think of the possibility that such a defensive line could be placed on the Suez Canal.

Recognizing that in the event of a serious threat of war the Egyptians would concentrate in the eastern Sinai, the Israeli plans for operations on the Egyptian front were designed to exploit their superior mobility and to envelop and destroy major portions of the Egyptian army. How the maneuver would be executed would depend on how the Egyptian forces were deployed; the Israelis were prepared to react flexibly in response to the Egyptian dispositions. However, the geographical features of the area would inevitably affect the Egyptian deployment pattern.

There were two major strategic routes into the Sinai, both of which would be important to both sides. The first of these was the axis along the coast, running westward from Rafah to El Arish to Kantara. The other was the central axis toward Ismailia, through the vital crossroad at Abu Ageila. Remembering how they had become bogged down in front of Abu Ageila in 1956, the Israelis had devoted careful study to the terrain in the vicinity of that crossroad, and had analyzed the 1956 record of that battle. By 1967, Israeli planners were confident that they had the answer to the Abu Ageila problem.

In the extreme north, there was considerable Israeli incentive for taking the initiative against the hated Syrians. However, the strict need for economy of force was recognized, and the Egypt-first concept was adhered to faithfully. Despite the near certainty of Syrian artillery fire deep into Galilee, and even the risk of some Syrian penetration into the Huleh Valley, the Israelis planned to leave only small forces, in clearly defensive postures, opposite the Syrian frontier. The Israelis realistically discounted any Lebanese involvement, or any serious Lebanese threat even if Lebanon were to become involved.

There was a major change at the very top level of the Israel Defense Force on the eve of war. While this did not change any fundamental operational concepts or doctrinal thinking in the Israeli Army, it had a significant effect upon attitudes.

Prime Minister Eshkol was also the Minister of Defense, following the custom of his great predecessor, Ben Gurion. Eshkol, however, was elderly, slow, and, in the eyes of many Israeli citizens and most military men, indecisive. He was widely criticized for his cautious responses to Nasser's provocations, and as he and his government were pushed slowly toward war, there were many doubts as to his ability to give adequate wartime direction to the armed forces. Recognizing this lack of confidence in his leadership, on May 30, 1967, Eshkol resigned as Defense Minister (although he remained Prime Minister), and appointed General Moshe Dayan, hero of the 1956 War, as the new Defense Minister. Dayan took over forcefully, and infused the IDF headquarters with his own brand of confident aggressiveness. He was strongly opposed to a multi-front war, and thus to any involvement against Syria, and hoped that conflict with Jordan could also be avoided. But he made clear his belief that the existing war plans against Egypt should be carried out with the utmost aggressiveness. He worked well with Major General Yitzhak Rabin, Chief of the General Staff.

ARAB PLANS AND PREPARATIONS

There had been no coordinated plans for allied Arab operations against Israel in 1948. Some general territorial objectives had been set; King Abdullah was the nominal commander in chief of the Arab armies; and liaison officers were exchanged between the armies. In fact, however, the jealousy among the Arab leaders prevented coordination, except rarely, between neighboring units at the boundary lines between two Arab armies. The liaison officers did not even have means of communicating with their home headquarters or governments and were completely useless from a military standpoint. Coordinated planning and operational cooperation were virtually unknown.

Such plans as existed in 1956—plans hardly more sophisticated than those of 1948—had not been set into operation because of the Anglo-French attack on Egypt.

The planning situation had not really improved by 1967, despite the fiction of a united Arab command. Nothing was done to assure any operational coordination between Syria and her two southern allies. Coordination between Egypt and Jordan was decreed on May 30 by the two heads of state, President Nasser and King Hussein, but no truly effective steps were taken to bring about such coordination.

Egyptian General Riadh arrived in Jordan two days before the outbreak of war to command an army which he didn't know (and which didn't know or trust him), in a theater with which he was unacquainted, in a situation foreign to his own past experiences. General Riadh was a competent man. It is doubtful, however, that he influenced the outcome on the Jordanian front in any way; when the fighting began the Jordanian chain of command seems to have operated through its chief of staff to the king, with only occasional perfunctory consultation with the Egyptian general.

The three commando battalions sent to Jordan from Egypt crossed to the West Bank and (the day before the war began) deployed in the area north of Latrun. Apparently it was intended that they would operate against Israeli rear areas in the coastal lowlands, but they were totally unready when the war unexpectedly broke out, and they accomplished little.

As a result of the 1956 experience, the Egyptians recognized the danger of having large forces trapped in the eastern Sinai, and (prior to May 1967) Nasser had generally avoided major concentrations east of the Suez Canal, in order not to attract an Israeli preemptive strike. This had been particularly important since the Egyptian involvement in Yemen, because many of the best trained units and most experienced officers were committed to that peculiar adventure, which so seriously divided the Arab world.

In late May 1967, however, Nasser found himself being drawn into the commitment of major forces in the Sinai somewhat against his better judgment. As has been discussed above, however, he seems to have expected that the threatening postures of Jordan and Syria would deter the Israelis from attempting to repeat the 1956 campaign. He may even have thought that the rebuilding of the Egyptian army with Soviet assistance, combined with the recent combat experience of many of his officers and men, provided a real chance of success in a new war, particularly with both Syria and Jordan committed, since this would prevent a complete Israeli concentration against Egypt. In the light of the prevalent Arab rationalization that the 1956 defeat was a successful delaying action, as the Egyptians withdrew to the Suez Canal area to face the Anglo-French threat, such an unreal assessment is at least understandable.

Less understandable is Nasser's willingness to risk, much less to plan for, another war while so many of his best officers and men were in Yemen. His most serious mistake was his willingness to entrust the field command and the responsibility for coordinating allied Arab operations to a political general whose lack of military talent had been painfully evident in the 1956 War: Field Marshal Abdel Hakim Amer.

It appears that relations between Nasser and Amer had sadly deteriorated by 1967, and that Nasser had failed to dismiss the dissolute field marshal mainly because he did not wish to admit to the world that he had chosen a poor man to be his commander in chief and first deputy. If Nasser believed—as did some of the people around him—that Amer was plotting to overthrow the president, he may have been waiting for some proof of Amer's disloyalty before moving against him. In any event, under these circumstances, the fact that Nasser allowed Amer to retain his command seems ample evidence that he did not expect a war to eventuate in 1967.

There are no accurate statistics available to the public about the strength of the Egyptian army in 1967. Apparently there was a force of at least 50,000 men in Yemen. Most of the remainder of the mobile Egyptian field combat units were in the 100,000-man force which Nasser committed to the Sinai Desert in late May of 1967. There may have been as many as 70,000 more in the scattered units west of the Canal, most of which were around Cairo. Actually the total mobilized strength of the Egyptian armed forces at the outbreak of war was probably close to 500,000 men. Most of these troops, however, were ill-trained, and were committed to local security tasks, such as guarding bridges over the Nile River, public buildings in the principal Egyptian cities, and the old Aswan Dam.

In the last week in May, the Egyptian Military Academy in Cairo graduated 750 cadets of the Class of 1967. Instead of receiving a month's leave, as was traditional after graduation, the new second lieutenants were given two days leave, and then ordered to report to their units, most of which were in the Sinai. A few days later a large proportion of these inexperienced but brave young officers were dead, wounded, or captured.

THE SPECIAL ROLE OF SYRIA

Since Syria's independence in 1946, the nation had been wracked by one military coup after another. The average tenure of the successive military dictatorships, more often than not socialistic but anti-communist in political orientation, was about fifteen months.

The last military coup had occurred in February 1966; the resulting government was an alliance between the group of left-wing officers who had seized control and the Baath political party, which provided the military leaders with a political power base. The regime, under the presidency of Dr. Nur al Din al Atassi, survived a coup attempt in September 1966 and then decided to seek to give some reality to the unified Arab command which had nominally been created in January 1965 at an Arab League summit meeting in Cairo. As a result of a visit to Cairo by a Syrian delegation, a five-year defense agreement was concluded in which the Syrians agreed again to accept the Egyptian commander in chief as the overall allied commander in chief in the event of war. The result was the so-called United Arab Command (UAC), with General Ali Amer of Egypt as its nominal commander. However, it had no substance, in the light of the intense mutual distrust existing among its four nominal members: The UAR of Egypt, Lebanon, Syria, and Jordan.

The extent to which Syrian support of Palestinian guerrillas had precipitated the crisis in 1967 has already been noted. Although the Israelis were well aware of the fact that the major guerrilla bases were in Syria, and that their financial, political, and psychological support came primarily from Syria, they aimed most of their retaliation at more vulnerable Jordan. Ironically, Damascus radio was giving open support to Al Fatah as a rival to Jordanian authority in Palestine, and at the same time calling for the overthrow of Syria's ally, King Hussein of Jordan, since he was not giving enough support to the Palestine liberation movement in those areas of Palestine under his control. During 1966 and 1967 there were a few armed clashes along the Syrian-Jordan frontier, and the enmity of Syria seemed to be directed almost as much against its nominal ally, Jordan, as against its avowed enemy, Israel.

THE ROLE OF SOVIET RUSSIA

It is beyond the scope of this book to analyze the multifarious interests and objectives of the Soviet Union in the Middle East in the decades following the emergence of an independent Israel. In essence the Kremlin believed that by supporting the Arabs against Israel there was an opportunity to increase Soviet influence and prestige, and to weaken the influence in the Middle East of oil-hungry Western nations.

An incidental, but nonetheless important, Soviet objective was to test the operational capabilities of Soviet weapons, when and if another war broke out in the Middle East. Russian-built weapons and communications and transportation equipment had been supplied in considerable abundance to three of Israel's most implacable foes: Egypt, Syria, and Iraq. These included major items of equipment for all three services in each of the Arab countries.

For the ground forces there were the latest Soviet T-54 and T-55 tanks, BTR-150 armored personnel carriers, Su-100 tank-destroyer assault guns, and substantial numbers of older, but still useful T-34 medium tanks and JS-3 heavy tanks. For their navies there were missile-firing *Osa* and *Komar* motor torpedo boats, plus older destroyers and submarines for Egypt. The new aircraft provided the Arabs were particularly impressive. In addition to substantial numbers of aging MiG-15 and MiG-17 planes there were MiG-19s, MiG-21s, and ground support Su-7s. To help the Arabs employ and maintain these sophisticated weapons there were in each of these countries several thousand Soviet officers and men as operational and technical advisers, staff consultants and instructors.

It is not known how the Soviets assessed the military capabilities of their Arab clients in comparison with the Israelis. Apparently by 1967 they assumed that the quantity and quality of Arab troops and Soviet weapons was adequate to overwhelm Israel. Otherwise it is doubtful if they would have so directly contributed to Middle East unrest as they did in May 1967. It is hard to avoid the suspicion that the Soviets were looking forward with considerable eagerness to an opportunity to see their weapons and doctrine employed in combat.

Israel had been observing this influx of Soviet weapons into the Arab countries with mounting concern. Israeli intelligence was active and seems to have been well informed on the quantity, characteristics, and quality of the new Arab weapons. The Israelis were particularly well prepared to deal with what many people considered to be the most formidable of the new Soviet weapons in the Middle East—the supersonic MiG-21 fighter. In August 1966, an Israeli intelligence agent in Bagdad was able—by an offer of a very large sum of money—to persuade an Iraqi Air Force pilot to defect to Israel with one of these planes. As a result the Israelis had been able to learn first hand all of its considerable capabilities, and not insignificant weaknesses, in practice dog-fights with their Mirages, Mystères, and Super-Mystères.

A comparison of the forces and weapons available to the potential opponents is shown in the table on p. 337. It is easily seen why the Soviets were so confident, and why so many Western sympathizers with Israel were so concerned, as the Middle East crisis intensified in late May 1967.

3

Sinai Mobilization

EGYPTIAN DEPLOYMENT

The Headquarters of the Egyptian Army and of the United Arab Command were in Cairo. The Sinai front commander, General Abd el Mohsen Mortagui, had his headquarters at Ismailia on the Suez Canal. The command post of the field army commander, Lieutenant General Sallah el Din Mohsen, was at Bir el Thamada. Committed to the Sinai at the beginning of June 1967 were six Egyptian divisions and an armored task force of somewhat less than divisional size, in varying states of readiness and effectiveness.

In the north, in the Gaza Strip, was the 20th Palestine Liberation Army Division, with a number of supporting Egyptian units, mainly artillery, and a brigade of about 50 Sherman tanks. The state of training, discipline and efficiency of this division—commanded by Egyptian Major General Mohomad Abd el Moneim Hasni (also Governor General of the Gaza Strip) with headquarters in Gaza—varied from mediocre to poor.

Just to the south of the Gaza Strip was the 7th Infantry Division, which had been hastily assembled during the crisis from two independent infantry brigades and placed under the command of the Commandant of the Infantry School, Major General Abd el Aziz Soliman. General Soliman's staff consisted of a handful of officers he had brought with him from the infantry school; while technically proficient they had had no recent experience in their staff positions, had not worked together, and had had little opportunity to develop teamwork.

Further to the southeast, in the Abu Ageila-Kusseima area, was the 2nd Infantry Division, with a tank brigade attached. This was considered to be one of the better divisions of the Egyptian army, but its commander, Major General Sadi Naguib, a political appointee, had only recently been assigned to the division. His only apparent qualification for the command was his experience as a drinking companion of Field Marshal Amer.

The 6th Mechanized Division covered the area of Kuntilla-Nakhl. This was a good division, at full strength, and its commander, Major General Abd el Kader Hassan, was respected and competent. The division was reinforced by the 1st Armored Brigade under Brigadier Hussein abd al Nataf. In its subsequent operations this division and its commander were to prove themselves worthy of the respect which they had in the Egyptian Army.

In Army reserve was the 3rd Infantry Division, in the Jebel Libni-Bir Hassna region. This division was also commanded by a political appointee, one of Field Marshal Amer's favorites, Major General Osman Nasser. He was destined to be court-martialed for incompetence and cowardice as a result of his performance in the coming operations; he would be found guilty and sentenced to five years in prison.

Also in Army reserve was an armored task force—consisting of a tank brigade, a commando brigade, and an artillery brigade—east of Bir Hassna and west of Lussan, generally backing up the 6th Mechanized Division. Commander of this task force was Major General Saad el Shazli.

In strategic reserve, under control of Marshal Amer's GHQ, was the 4th Armored Division, deployed in the Bir Gifgafa area, at full strength and equipped with modern Soviet tanks. Its commander was Major General Sidki el Ghoul, a competent, respected professional.

There was also an independent infantry brigade garrisoning the recently occupied positions at Sharm el Sheikh. During late May three hastily mobilized reserve infantry battalions, many of the soldiers still without uniforms, had been rushed to garrison the strategic Giddi and Mitla Passes.

The total Egyptian force in the Sinai was about 100,000 men with about 930 tanks.

In 1966 the Egyptian General Staff had evolved a defensive and offensive plan for the defense of the Sinai, with the code-name "Kahir." The basic concept was of a mobile defense in depth, the mass of the army to be concentrated in the center of the peninsula, with only a covering screen in the border area. Save for the retention of a few key defensive positions, such as El Arish and Abu Ageila, the Israeli enemy was to be allowed, indeed encouraged, to penetrate deeply into the Sinai to a previously designated "killing area," a triangle roughly defined by Jebel Libni, Suweitma (east of Bir el Thamada), and Bir Gifgafa. It was anticipated that by the time the enemy had marched and fought his way across the desert to this region he would have fully committed himself, and his deployment would be clearly known to the waiting Egyptians. If, as seemed likely, one portion of the Israeli army was in advance of the others, it was to be engaged frontally from the firm base and smashed by a close-in envelopment, from either the south or the north, as the events dictated. If, on the other hand, the bulk of the Israeli forces were committed in the center of the peninsula, a bolder and more sweeping envelopment was envisaged, with the objective of destroying the entire invading army.

In recognition of the danger that such a bold plan might be incompletely accomplished, and the possibility that some Israeli units might be able to evade the proposed envelopment, there was to be a second, last-ditch defensive line back at the three defiles. This line was to be well established and manned in advance to provide a base for the main army, should it be forced to withdraw that far.

Although the plan was committed to paper, little had been done to implement it. The bulk of the Egyptian military budget was committed to the expedition in Yemen, and almost no funds were available to prepare the installations in the Sinai for the planned strategy. Furthermore, during the undercover power struggle between the adherents of Amer and those of President Nasser, Amer had shifted out of the General Staff most of the planners who had developed Operation Kahir.

CONFUSION CONFOUNDED

When President Nasser ordered the massing of forces east of the Suez Canal in May 1967, he refused to permit redeployment in accordance with the plan. This would have meant the virtual abandonment of Gaza, Rafah, and Kuntilla, and even the possible loss of El Arish and Abu Ageila. He decreed that even the temporary abandonment of these places was unacceptable to him, and that the deployment would therefore have to be considerably further east. Thus the troops had no sooner reached their preplanned positions than they were ordered to move east. Then came a series of orders shifting units around from place to place. For instance, the 14th Armored Brigade—which was to have been the spearhead of the northern strike force in the envelopment plan of Operation Kahir—was moved east to the vicinity of Abu Ageila, then to El Arish, then to Rafah. This brigade's T54 and T-55 Russian tanks traveled some 1,200 kilometers across the desert in the three weeks before the war.

The experience of the 4th Infantry Brigade was not very different. The original plan had called for this brigade to go to Sharm el Sheikh after the withdrawal of UN troops. It started out to the south in mid-May, then was ordered to return to Suez since Sharm el Sheikh had already been occupied by paratroops. From Suez the brigade was ordered to the northern axis in the vicinity of Rafah. It had gotten halfway to Rafah when the war broke out, and it was ordered back to Cairo. Then while lead elements were crossing the Canal on June 6, Field Marshal Amer personally directed the dispersal of the brigade north and south in defensive positions west of the Canal. The rear elements of the brigade, on the march, were overrun by Israeli tanks before they could reach the Canal. A regular brigade, well trained and under competent command, was thus unable to contribute in any way to the battle.

On May 28 the field army commander, General Mohsen, frustrated by conflicting and confusing orders from Cairo, sent his chief of staff, Brigadier Hassan, back to higher headquarters to ask for clarification and guidance. In essence Hassan was to seek a definition of the objective of his field army in the Sinai, and guidance as to whether its role was to be offensive (as seemed to be indicated by its current deployment) or defensive, as had been originally planned in Operation Kahir. Unable to receive any illumination on the questions at Ismailia, either from General Mortagui, the front commander, or from his Chief of Staff, Major General Ahmed Ismail Ali (destined to be commander in chief in the 1973 War), Brigadier Hassan went back to Cairo to consult with Lieutenant General Anwhar al Khadi,[1] the Chief of Staff of the Armed Forces.

After a brief consultation with General Khadi, Brigadier Hassan returned to Bir el Thamada, General Mohsen's command post, with a simple response. The Armed Forces Chief of Staff, not in the confidence of Field Marshal Amer, could not answer any of the specific qusetions, nor could he give any clarification or guidance as requested by the field army commander.

A few days later, on June 4, one Lieutenant Hamid, a newly graduated Egyptian second lieutenant, assigned to a transportation company near Suez, was ordered to take a convoy of antitank ammunition to Kuntilla, near the Egypt-Israel frontier. He left that afternoon, bivouacked with his convoy east of Nakhl that night, and early the following morning reported to the commander at Kuntilla. The older officer looked at him in surprise. "We don't need any ammunition. There isn't going to be a war. Take it back." The lieutenant saluted, turned his trucks around, and started back toward the Canal. A half hour later his convoy was being strafed by Israeli aircraft.

ISRAELI DEPLOYMENT AND OPERATIONAL PLANS

There were three key elements to the Israeli plan for a Sinai offensive: surprise; early achievement of air superiority; and early and decisive engagement with the main Egyptian forces as far east in the Sinai as possible.

Surprise was to be achieved by attacking before the Arabs were ready to launch their own anticipated attack. Assurance of air superiority was to be combined with surprise by initiating the attack with a massive series of air blows designed to knock out the Egyptian Air Force, and (if necessary) the other neighboring Arab air forces as well. Engaging the main Egyptian forces in the eastern Sinai would depend, of course, upon the actual Egyptian deployment. But in the light of the circumstances

---

[1] By an interesting coincidence the name of the Egyptian Chief of Staff when translated into English means *judge*, and the name of the Israeli Chief of Staff, Rabin, when translated into English also means *judge*.

under which the Israelis expected to launch their attack, they anticipated that the Egyptians would already have committed themselves for their own attack and thus would be in the eastern Sinai with the bulk of their forces.

This general operational concept had been established by the Israeli Chief of Staff, Major General Yitzhak Rabin, soon after he became the chief of staff in 1963. One key contribution to the planned surprise initiation of hostilities had been started early in 1965. About that time the Israeli Air Force began the practice of frequent early morning massed flights westward into the Mediterranean. By mid-1967 the Egyptians paid little more attention to such early flights than they did to the sun's rising. It was a normal procedure for the Egyptian Air Force to have several fighter squadrons alert at each base at dawn, and for about an hour thereafter. But by about mid-1967 the alerts were no longer keyed in any way to the peculiar Israeli early morning practice of flying out over the Mediterranean.

The commander of the Israeli Southern Command was Brigadier General Yeshayahu Yehu Gavish, who had been in this position since 1965. General Gavish's plan had four phases:[2] (1) a breakthrough of the Egyptian front lines in two sectors: along the Rafah-El Arish coastal axis by an *ugdah*, or division, commanded by Brigadier General Israel Tal, and at Abu Ageila-Um Katef by another *ugdah* under Brigadier General Ariel (Arik) Sharon; (2) the introduction of a third division under General Avraham Yoffe—either between the Tal and Sharon divisions, or south of the Sharon division, depending upon the deployment of the Egyptians—which was to carry out a deep penetration into the Sinai and smash what was anticipated to be the second Egyptian defensive line in the vicinity of Jebel Libni; (3) concentration of the armored units of the Tal, Sharon, and Yoffe divisions in the general triangle Nakhl, Mitla Pass, and Bir Gifgafa; and (4) an advance to the Canal and the capture of Sharm el Sheikh.

The average strength of these three divisions was approximately 15,000 men, although their compositions differed considerably. General Tal's division included two standard armored brigades—one armed with Patton and Centurion tanks, the other with Sherman and AMX-13 tanks—a paratroop brigade, and a reconnaissance unit, roughly the equivalent of a light armored regiment. This division had a total of about 250 tanks.

General Yoffe's division consisted of two armored brigades, each with

[2] Edward Luttwak and Dan Horowitz in *The Israeli Army* (New York, 1975) assert (pp. 231-233) that this was one of two alternative plans prepared by Gavish. The other, more cautious, plan is said to have originally been favored by General Rabin, until he was prodded into a bolder approach by the new Defense Minister, General Dayan.

about 100 Centurion tanks. Yoffe was an infantry officer, but his chief of staff was an armor specialist, Colonel Avraham Adan, who had commanded the Sherman tank battalion at Abu Ageila in 1956.

General Sharon's combined arms division consisted of an armored brigade with Sherman and Centurion tanks, an infantry brigade, and a paratroop brigade. Sharon, with the formidable defenses of Abu Ageila and Um Katef in front of him, had several extra battalions of artillery attached to his division as well as a force of combat engineers. He had about 150 tanks.

There was an independent armored brigade at Kuntilla under the command of Colonel Albert Mendler, which was to cooperate with General Sharon in destroying Egyptian forces in the vicinity of Nakhl. A reinforced mechanized brigade under Colonel Yehuda Reshef was deployed along the Gaza Strip. A paratroop task force in central Israel was prepared to operate in support of General Tal and against Sharm el Sheikh.

The total combat strength of General Gavish's command was more than 70,000 men and 750-800 tanks.

Contributing to the general operational concept, as well as to the objective of trapping Egyptian forces deep in the Sinai, an elaborate deception plan was carried out while the Israeli Army was mobilizing in the last week of May. The three divisions in the northwestern Negev concentrated as quietly and secretly as possible, while the battalions and brigade further south made every effort to draw attention to their activities as they moved toward the border. Some units that had marched to the border in late May were pulled back some distance from the border on subsequent nights, and then marched back in early June. Light planes and helicopters were particularly active along this section of the border, contributing to the deception. The activity was designed to make the Egyptians believe that, as in 1956, the Israelis would wheel into the Sinai from the south around a pivot near the Gaza Strip. In fact, the Israeli plan was just the opposite, a wheel from the north, pivoting around Eilat.

4

The Israeli Air Offensive

THE ATTACK ON EGYPT

Shortly after dawn on the morning of Monday, June 5—about 7:00 a.m. Israeli time, 8:00 a.m. Egyptian time—approximately 40 Israeli Mirage and Mystère fighter bombers took off from their bases in Israel, and, as they had done so many times before, flew west over the Mediterranean. A few minutes later 40 more followed; and then still another 40. Presumably they were being tracked by Egyptian radar—of which there were several dozen, 16 in the Sinai area alone—and by those of the American and Soviet naval vessels in the eastern Mediterranean, including the American electronic intelligence ship USS *Liberty*. The Israelis were undoubtedly also picked up on the screens of American and British airborne radar patrols; those of the Americans from their aircraft carriers, those of the British from bases in Cyprus.

Then also, in conformity to routine practice, the Israeli planes dipped down low to the "deck." As they headed back to shore, flying low over the waves of the Mediterranean, they disappeared off the radar screens. This time, however, there was a difference in the manner in which they returned to shore. Instead of eastward, they turned south toward the Egyptian airfields. At 7:45 a.m. Israeli time, 8:45 a.m. Egyptian time, after the morning Nile mist had cleared, after the dawn alerts had closed down at Egyptian airfields, and while most Egyptian Air Force officers were en route to their offices or squadrons, nine of the airfields were struck simultaneously, and the tenth a few seconds later: El Arish, Bir Gifgafa, Cairo West, Jebel Libni, Bir el Thamada, Abu Sueir, Kabrit, Beni Sueif, Inchas, and Fayid.

Flying at altitudes between 30 and 500 feet, unseen by Egyptian radar, the first ten flights of four Israeli aircraft spent seven minutes over their targets—time enough for one bombing run and three or four strafing passes. Three minutes after these aircraft had left, a second wave, maintaining a ten-minute interval, struck the same bases for seven minutes. Three minutes later the third wave struck. The turnaround time for Israeli aircraft striking the Canal area was less than an hour. The Israelis attacked for 80 minutes, eight waves in all. There was a ten-minute lull and then another 80 minutes of bombing runs.

At the conclusion of approximately three hours some 300 Egyptian aircraft had been destroyed on the ground, including all 30 of Egypt's Tu-16 long-range bombers. Twenty-three radar installations and many antiaircraft sites were also destroyed. Twenty Egyptian aircraft—twelve MiG-21s and eight MiG-19s—had flown north from Hurghada following the initial strike, and these were either destroyed in the air or forced to crash land because of damage to the runways in the north. Approximately eight MiG-21s managed to take off from the attacked bases during this period and were able to engage some of the attacking Israelis. They were all shot down, but they did succeed in shooting down two of the Israeli attackers. Israel reported a total of 19 planes lost in the initial three-hour period.

Possibly the most serious loss suffered by the Egyptians was some 100 pilots killed—and an unknown number injured—during the attacks, most of them the victims of strafing by the first wave as they were in the open and unprepared for the attack. Since Egypt had only 350 qualified air pilots, this was a high percentage of casualties.

Egyptian antiaircraft fire had been lighter than expected, and caused only slight damage to the Israeli planes. The Egyptians fired some SA-2 missiles, but these were ineffective below 4,000 feet, and the attackers were well below that.

Two major elements contributed to this Israeli air success: surprise and precision. To ensure accuracy in their bombing, Israeli aircraft approached slowly, some even with their landing gear down to reduce air speed. They used three types of bombs. Conventional 500- and 1,000-pound bombs were employed generally to destroy installations and ruin the runways. Also used for runway demolition was a new bomb specifically designed for this purpose. As soon as this bomb was dropped, a retro-rocket stopped its forward impetus, while a booster rocket impelled it down into the runway, where it was detonated by a delayed fuse after it had penetrated the concrete. The advantage of this bomb was that it permitted higher speeds in the approach run; a conventional bomb dropped at low level, even at moderate speed, would have a tendency to skip and do only superficial damage; if dropped at low speed there was the danger that a conventional bomb blast would destroy the plane that dropped it.

Another guided bomb, apparently similar to the American "Bullpup," evidently was used for the precision destruction of parked aircraft, without damage to surrounding installations.[1] This was particularly useful at El Arish, the only base whose runways were not destroyed, since Israeli plans called for early use of this field as a forward supply and casualty evacuation center.

[1] Luttwak and Horowitz, *op. cit.*, assert (p. 228) no such rocket was used, and that the damage was caused by precise 30mm cannon fire; this is doubtful.

The task of the attacking Israeli pilots, whose average age was 23, was made easier by the Egyptian practice of concentrating one type of aircraft at one single base. While this is not an unusual practice in many air forces, it enabled the Israelis to assign priority to fighter bombers and interceptors, while leaving transports, for example, until later in the day.

ATTACKING OTHER ARAB AIR FORCES

Just before noon, aircraft from the Syrian Air Force dropped bombs near the Haifa oil refinery and attacked the Israeli air base at Megiddo as well as positions near Lake Tiberias. In retaliation the Israelis promptly launched mass attacks against the Syrian airfields, including a military air base on the outskirts of Damascus. Most of the Syrian Air Force was destroyed.

At noon aircraft from the Jordanian Air Force bombed near Natania and struck the Israeli base at Kfar Sirkin, destroying a Noratlas transport on the ground. Again the Israeli Air Force retaliated, attacking airfields at Amman and Mafraq, and destroying a radar station at Ajlun. The Jordanian Air Force was wiped out.

Around 2:00 p.m. Iraqi planes raided near the Israeli air base of Ramat David. Once more IAF planes retaliated. Flying 500 miles across Jordan to Iraq, three Israeli aircraft struck the military base, H-3, at Habbaniyah on the Kirkuk oil pipeline, and destroyed ten Iraqi planes on the ground.

All in all, during this brief but devastating aerial blitz, the Israeli pilots hit the following bases:

In Egypt: El Arish (7:45 a.m.); Bir Gifgafa (7:45); Cairo West (7:45); Luxor (12:30 p.m.); Jebel Libni (7:45 a.m.); Bir el Thamada (7:45); Mansura (10:00); Abu Sueir (7:45); Inchas (7:45); Fayid (7:45); Kabrit (7:45); Hurghada (12:15 p.m.); Ras Banas (6:00 p.m.); Minya (10:15 a.m.); Beni Sueif (8:15); Helwan (10:00); Cairo International (5:15 p.m.); and Bilbeis (12:00 mid.). In Jordan: Amman (12:45 p.m.); and Mafraq (1:00). In Syria: Damascus (1:00 p.m.); Marq Rial (1:15); Dmeir (1:15); Seikal (1:15); and T-4 (3:45). In Iraq: H-3 (3:00 p.m.). A total of twenty-five or twenty-six bases were hit at least once during the day.[2]

[2] From Israel Defense Force sources. While the list of bases hit and their times varies slightly in different sources, most agree that a total of twenty-five were attacked.

5

Battles for Rafah,
Gaza, and El Arish

While the Israeli Air Force was thus gaining complete air supremacy, at 8:15 a.m., Israeli time, the Israeli ground forces began their move across the Sinai Peninsula.

The first task of General Tal's division was to break through in the Rafah-El Arish sector, held by some six brigades of the 20th Palestinian Liberation Army (PLA) and Egyptian 7th Division, with the support of about 70 tanks. Rafah lies on the railway line that ran from Kantara on the Suez Canal eastward through El Arish on the coast and then on up to Gaza. The semi-arid coastal plain of Palestine merges into the Sinai desert near Rafah. The scant vegetation to be found in and around the towns in the vicinity of the road and railroad is intermixed with sand dunes. Further south this terrain changes to arid hills and wadis, traversed by unpaved tracks. Rafah's principal importance was as a junction between the main road and the dirt road which traversed the Egyptian side of the frontier down to El Auja. It also comprised an essential link in the Egyptian defensive system linking Gaza and Khan Yunis in the north, and Abu Ageila to the southeast, with the main Egyptian base at El Arish to the west.

Rafah was defended by a brigade of the 20th PLA Division supported by miscellaneous Egyptian units, including armor, artillery, antitank units, and antiaircraft units. The approaches to the Palestinian-Egyptian positions from the east and northeast were covered by scattered minefields. Running south-southwest from the town, for a distance of more than ten kilometers, was a strong defensive line, consisting of barbed wire, antitank guns, and extensive minefields. Just to the west of this defensive line two infantry brigades of the Egyptian 7th Infantry Division were deployed, supported by a 122mm howitzer brigade and a battalion of 100mm guns, capable both of firing long-range and of being used in the antitank role. This defensive zone to the south and southwest of Rafah was the principal Egyptian concentration in the area and would

248

have to be neutralized or destroyed before there was any possibility of further advance toward the El Arish base.

To avoid a frontal attack against this formidable defensive position, General Tal decided upon an envelopment. Since its southern end was bordered by sand dunes that could be traversed only with great difficulty, he decided to envelop the left flank by penetrating the Palestinian-Egyptian coastal defenses in the vicinity of Khan Yunis, which was also defended by elements of the 20th PLA Division. Once the Israelis had reached the main road and railroad in the vicinity of Khan Yunis, Tal intended to drive west, where he expected to have relatively little difficulty in overwhelming the PLA defenders of the town of Rafah itself, which would expose the left flank of the 7th Division's position south of the town.

THE BATTLE OF RAFAH, JUNE 5

At 8:15 a.m. on the 5th, Tal received the expected order from General Gavish to attack. In accordance with his plan the 7th Armored Brigade, under Colonel Shmuel Gonen, struck westward across the frontier into the Gaza Strip toward Khan Yunis. The other armored brigade, under Colonel Menachem Aviram, was to make a secondary effort south through the sand dunes and outflank the Egyptian defenses running south from Rafah. Tal rightly believed that the Egyptians, with their right flank secure in the sand dunes, would consider that this terrain was impassable by Israeli tanks and would not be expecting such a bold envelopment. To serve as a link between these widely divergent prongs of a double envelopment, the paratroop brigade of Colonel Rafael Eitan, supported by a company of 7th Brigade Pattons, would carry out a holding attack against the Egyptian-Palestinian force in Rafah itself. Colonel Uri Barom's armored reconnaissance regiment was in reserve.

Gonen thrust at Khan Yunis in column formation, his battalion of Patton M-48 tanks followed by his Centurion battalion. His mechanized infantry battalion was in brigade reserve. Also with Gonen's brigade was a mixed battalion of AMX-13 and Patton tanks from Colonel Barom's regiment. Ignoring the heavy fire from artillery, antitank guns, and machine guns, the Pattons and AMX tanks broke through into Khan Yunis. Under the circumstances, the loss of six tanks and a number of jeeps and half-tracks was relatively insignificant.

Without stopping, and in accordance with the previously prepared plan, Gonen's brigade thrust southwest from Khan Yunis toward Rafah in two columns. On the right Gonen himself directed the Patton battalion, which drove directly toward the town of Rafah along the railroad line. Following the road, which makes a detour inland in the vicinity of Rafah, Barom led his Pattons and AMXs, followed by the Centurions, directly toward the Rafah junction south of the town. Gonen's second-in-command, Colonel Baruch Harel, was with the Centurion battalion. The antitank positions just north of the intersection, supported by several dug-in tanks, were hit by a pincer movement, Gonen's Pattons striking them from the rear while Barom's Pattons and AMXs, and Harel's Centurions, hit them from the front. Surprised by the unexpected attack from the north, the Egyptian defenders put up little resistance, and were rapidly overwhelmed by the converging tank columns.

Gonen and his tankers did not tarry on the position they had overrun. They advanced quickly to Sheikh Zuweid, a strongly fortified position held by the northern of the two 7th Division brigades south of Rafah. Gonen sent Uri and Harel in column straight south toward Sheikh Zuweid, to strike the front of the hastily shifting Egyptian defense, while

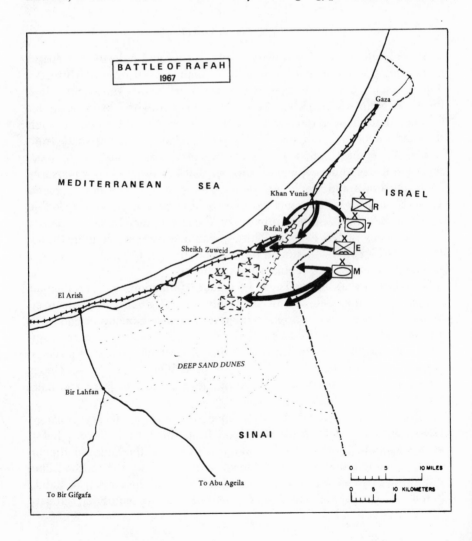

he and his Pattons first swung to the north and then turned and drove westward to envelop the Egyptian brigades. Once again the combined shock, surprise, and confusion created by the two-pronged tank attack enabled the tankers to overrun the infantry position with relatively few losses.

Gonen was about to continue his drive westward toward El Arish, when he received radio instructions from General Tal to return to Rafah with one of his battalions. He ordered Harel to continue the westward drive with the objective of seizing the fortified area of Jiradi, five miles east of El Arish. Preceding Harel's column was the reconnaissance company of Barom's regiment.

Meanwhile, following closely behind Gonen's two successive assaults at the Rafah crossroads and Sheikh Zuweid, came Eitan's paratroop brigade and its attached armor. The paratroopers captured and consolidated the Rafah strongpoints, after some hand-to-hand fighting in the trenches, and then continued west behind Gonen to Sheikh Zuweid. There, too, they encountered considerable resistance from the Egyptians, who were recovering from the shock of the armored blow. But the recovery was not sufficient for them to offer really effective opposition. Many of the Egyptians were captured, and the remainder withdrew in considerable confusion westward into the desert.

While this activity had been going on in the vicinity of Rafah, Aviram's armored brigade had moved slowly across the sand dunes to the south in a wide envelopment of the 7th Division entrenchments in the Rafah-Sheikh Zuweid area. As a diversion, and to entice the Egyptians to open fire and reveal their positions, Aviram sent his mechanized infantry battalion to make a holding attack against the Egyptian lines south of Sheikh Zuweid. With his two tank battalions he continued southward, seeking the southern flank of the Egyptian position in order to complete his envelopment.

For reasons that are not clear, Aviram's leading tank battalion turned short and passed between two of the Egyptian strongpoints, and then turned to strike the flank and rear of the one to the north, which the Israelis mistakenly believed to be the southern limit of the Egyptian position. The right flank Egyptian battalion, well concealed behind sand dunes, held its fire for a while, in order to permit the Israelis to commit themselves. Not until the second of Aviram's tank battalions had continued on through, heading toward the artillery positions, did this right flank Egyptian battalion open fire, hitting the rear of Aviram's leading battalion. In the confused fighting that followed, Aviram and this battalion were surrounded by the Egyptians and subjected to heavy artillery, antitank, and small-arms fire.

Unaware of the desperate situation of their brigade commander, the Israelis in Aviram's second tank battalion reached the 7th Division artillery positions shortly after these had been hit by an Israeli airstrike. The Israelis took advantage of the confusion, completely silencing the guns and killing and wounding many of the cannoneers. Then ranging up and down the 7th Division rear area, this battalion surprised and destroyed two Egyptian tank companies with about 20 Stalin and 20 T-34 tanks. It was while engaged with the T-34s that the battalion commander received a radio message from Aviram, informing him of the precarious situation of the surrounded battalion back in the frontline area. Immediately the battalion commander broke off the action and returned to help his brigade commander. But with the Egyptian infantry recovered from their surprise and shock, this battalion found it a more difficult job to return east than it had been to make the original rush to the west.

It was because of the confused and potentially dangerous situation in Aviram's brigade that Tal had ordered Gonen to return to Rafah with one of his tank battalions. But just as Tal was about to order Gonen to go to Aviram's rescue, Aviram's wandering battalion fought its way through the surrounding Egyptians and rejoined the brigade commander. Now, with considerable support from the mechanized infantry battalion to their north, the two tank battalions quickly reversed the situation, overrunning the Egyptian infantry positions, which were quickly seized by the Israeli infantrymen. In this vicious, confused fighting several hundred Egyptians were killed or wounded; survivors of the brigade withdrew to the west, into the desert, to join the fugitives already streaming west from Rafah. Aviram had suffered about 250 casualties.

While Aviram was regrouping his command after this confused engagement, Tal sent in helicopters to start bringing out the wounded. The first helicopter, however, was met by intense groundfire from the south, and only then, late in the afternoon, did the Israelis realize that there was still one Egyptian battalion intact in the positions to the south. Late in the afternoon Aviram took a tank battalion and an infantry company to assault the isolated Egyptians. They attacked shortly after dark; by midnight the battle was over, the Egyptian battalion retreating westward in confusion.

The main positions of the Egyptian 7th Infantry Division were completely in the hands of the Israelis. That division suffered more than 2,000 casualties; Israeli losses were less than 500 killed and wounded.

A combined airborne and amphibious assault on El Arish had been planned for late on June 5, or early on the 6th. By midafternoon, however, Tal's success made it clear to the Israeli General Staff that such an operation would be unnecessary. It was cancelled, thus permitting the transfer to Jerusalem of all of Colonel Mordechai Gur's paratroop brigade.

THE BATTLE OF EL ARISH, JUNE 5-6

Meanwhile, when it had become evident to Tal that the situation in Aviram's sector was under control, he ordered Gonen to return west toward the main Egyptian stronghold of El Arish, and sent with him the remainder of Barom's regiment, which had been in division reserve. Gonen had learned by radio from Harel that he had overrun the strongly fortified Jiradi position—where he left a reconnaissance company—and was advancing toward El Arish. Gonen radioed Harel to await his arrival, before attacking the defenses of El Arish and its nearby airfield.

As Gonen and his M48 battalion arrived at Jiradi, they unexpectedly found themselves under fire. This was the first inkling they had that Uri's reconnaissance company, which had been holding that position, had been overrun and practically wiped out by Egyptians retreating from Rafah.

Gonen's mechanized infantry had little trouble in clearing the Jiradi stronghold for the second time. While this was going on, Gonen learned by radio that Harel and his battalion were already fighting on the outskirts of El Arish. Despite the fact that his fuel tanks were almost empty, Gonen also pushed on ahead and reached the outskirts of El Arish at 3:00 in the morning, while sending back urgent radio requests for fuel to General Tal.

The fuel arrived at 5:00 a.m., and by dawn the tanks were refueled and ready for action. After a few hours of fighting, which centered mostly around the El Arish area, the town and its surrounding positions were secured.

Shortly after dawn, as Gonen's troops were mopping up in and around El Arish, they were joined by Aviram's brigade, followed closely by most of the remainder of the division, except for the paratroop brigade, which was left to participate in planned operations against the Gaza Strip.

Having accomplished the first phase of his assigned mission, Tal issued orders for carrying out the second phase. He sent one column, consisting of one of Aviram's armored battalions, most of the division engineers, and most of the division artillery in a thrust toward the Canal down the coastal road, under the command of Colonel Granit Yisrael. It was planned that this column would be joined by Eitan's paratroop brigade, to which was attached some armor from Barom's regiment, as soon as they had completed their mission in and near Gaza.

The remainder of the division, spearheaded by Gonen's brigade, was to strike south toward Bir Lahfan and then westward toward Jebel Libni, in accordance with the original plan.

BATTLE OF THE GAZA STRIP, JUNE 5-7

Meanwhile, another fiercely contested battle was taking place to the northeast, in the Gaza Strip.

The Gaza Strip, extending northeastward from the vicinity of Rafah to just north of Gaza, is 43 kilometers long and varies in width from 6 to 12 kilometers. The Egyptians had retained this small region of Palestine at the end of the 1948 War. Apart from the strip of sand along the coast, the land is traversable by all types of vehicles, and despite its aridity it supports a wide variety of semi-tropical agricultural crops. There are several good roads linking the towns. In 1967 the area was heavily fortified and was defended by the 20th PLA Division and several thousand armed civilians. One brigade held Dir el Balah, and another brigade garrisoned a series of strongholds around the city of Gaza itself. The third brigade, at Khan Yunis, had been badly cut up by Gonen's original assault through that town, but most of it had been able to withdraw to join the outpost positions along the main highway. Additional detached units held fortifications at Ali Muntar, El Kuba, Beit Hanun, and Beit Lahia.

Responsibility for seizing and occupying the Gaza Strip was assigned to an independent task force under the command of Colonel Yehuda Reshef. This was a standard Israeli infantry brigade which had been reinforced with a battalion of AMX-13 tanks and a paratroop battalion with some halftracks. To assist him in his task, Colonel Eitan's paratroop brigade from General Tal's division was to be attached to Reshef's command as soon as Rafah was secure.

On the morning of June 5 two infantry battalions and the armor and paratroops of Reshef's command followed Tal's armor to the outskirts of Khan Yunis. Passing through that city while it was still being mopped up by Eitan's paratroopers, Reshef's troops turned north, clearing a number of minefields, and overrunning several small outposts covering the road. They then attacked and captured the positions of El Kuba and Ali Muntar in a hard fight which lasted until dark. While this was going on, Reshef's third battalion attacked westward from Israeli territory, assaulted, and finally captured. the Egyptian position at Deir el Balah.

During the night Eitan's brigade (supported by a company of Patton tanks) moved up from Rafah through Khan Yunis to join Reshef's main body south of Gaza. At dawn on Tuesday morning an all-out assault on positions in and around Gaza was heralded by a strike by Israeli aircraft. Following this, an assault was launched from the south, spearheaded by the AMX-13 battalion, closely followed by the paratroopers and an infantry battalion. At the same time the remainder of the Israeli infantry closed in from the east and the north. During the fierce fighting, the

UNEF headquarters in Gaza was hit by Israeli artillery; fifteen Indian soldiers were killed and another 25 were wounded. By noon, after severe street fighting, most of the town was in Israeli hands. The Egyptian military governor of Gaza, General Abdul Monam Husseini, now recognized that his situation was hopeless. To prevent further loss of life in the civilian population, at 12:45 he surrendered.

Although the Israelis had been streaming up and down the road past Khan Yunis, to the west of the road the city itself was still held by Egyptian and Palestinian troops. While Reshef's brigade mopped up scattered pockets of resistance throughout the remainder of the Gaza Strip, Eitan's paratroopers turned back to clear out Khan Yunis. However, resistance was much more intense than they had expected, and by nightfall, Eitan's troops had failed to make any serious penetration. Therefore, he withdrew to the beach area north of the city, where he allowed his men to rest while their vehicles were being refueled.

Rested, and with some artillery support arranged from Reshef, at dawn on the 7th Eitan's paratroopers attacked again. The combination of rested troops and additional fire support gave added punch to the Israeli attack. At the same time, the Egyptian troops were by now aware that they were cut off and that, in the light of the general withdrawal of Egyptian forces from the Sinai, they had no chance of being rescued. After brief resistance, Khan Yunis surrendered. While a unit of Reshef's brigade occupied the town, Eitan's paratroopers got into their vehicles and raced westward along the coastal road to join Colonel Yisrael's force near Romani. The Patton company rumbled south, to rejoin Gonen near Bir Gifgafa.

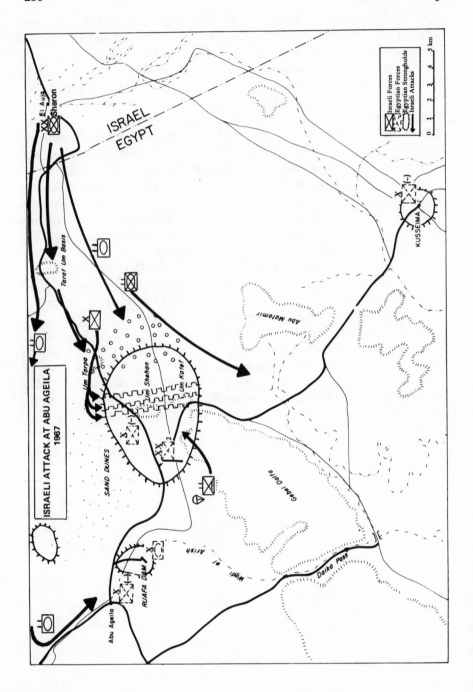

6

The Battles of Abu Ageila
and Bir Lahfan

OPPOSING PLANS AND DISPOSITIONS

About 30 kilometers west of the Israeli-Egyptian border, on the central road from Beersheba through Nitzana to Ismailia, lies the crossroad of Abu Ageila. The fortifications covering this crossroad had been attacked by the Israelis in both of the previous Arab-Israeli wars. In '48 it had been easily overrun by Yigael Allon. In the 1956 campaign the position had not been captured but was held by the Egyptians until they abandoned it in their general withdrawal. Since that war it had been further developed by the Egyptians into a major fortified area, including the position of Um Katef, about ten kilometers to the east on the Nitzana road, and the road junction of Kusseima, about 30 kilometers southeast of Abu Ageila. The Abu Ageila crossroad was important because, even though armor could maneuver in much of the desert area of the Sinai, control of the main central road across the peninsula was absolutely essential to the advance of Israeli infantry and for movement of logistical support units in any major campaign.

The Egyptian fortifications in 1967 were much more formidable than they had been in 1956, when they had defied repeated Israeli assaults. Making use of their experience in that and a number of other successful defenses, and utilizing engineering concepts suggested by their Russian advisors as well, the Egyptians had tied four powerful strongpoints together by barbed wire and minefields. As before, the main defensive position was at Um Katef, a hill about 20 kilometers from the Israeli border. There three lines of concrete entrenchments extended about five kilometers in length and one kilometer deep. The approaches were covered by a number of small outposts; between them and the main position there were extensive barbed wire entanglements and minefields. In the position were a number of antitank strongpoints, consisting of antitank and self-propelled artillery guns, as well as a number of dug-in T-34 and T-54 tanks.

Somewhat smaller, but equally carefully prepared and fortified were the positions at the Abu Ageila and Kusseima road junctions. Kusseima had been added to the fortified complex of Abu Ageila because the Israelis had used it to bypass Um Katef and Abu Ageila in 1956. Centrally located, and to the rear of the Um Katef position, was still a fourth fortification near the Ruafa Dam. This provided a central base, protecting some six battalions of 122mm guns which provided artillery support. Two brigades of the 2nd Infantry Division occupied the defenses. One brigade was in the Um Katef position, the other was divided among the three remaining strongpoints. A tank brigade of about 90 tanks was in reserve in the Ruafa Dam position.

General Sharon's division consisted of an armored brigade, commanded by Lieutenant Colonel Mordechai Zippori; an infantry brigade, commanded by Colonel Kutty Adam; a paratroop brigade, commanded by Lieutenant Colonel Dani Matt; and six artillery battalions of 105mm and 155mm howitzers.

Following the failure to take Abu Ageila in 1956, the Israeli General Staff had made intensive studies of the battle. Before abandoning the area in the withdrawal of late 1956, a team of officers carefully examined the position, and it was thoroughly surveyed, mapped, and photographed. In addition to detailed staff analyses, a major map problem in the Israeli Command and Staff College each year was an attack on the Abu Ageila position. This problem was updated each year to reflect everything that was known about any Egyptian improvements. Thus by 1967 most of the commanders and staff officers in the Israeli army were extremely familiar with the stronghold, with the causes of the 1956 setback, and with the current official General Staff concepts of how to avoid a similar setback in a future struggle. General Sharon, who had been the Director of Training in the Israeli Army shortly before the outbreak of the 1967 War, was probably as familiar with these matters as any man in the Israeli Defense Forces.

THE BATTLE OF ABU AGEILA-UM KATEF

Sharon's division crossed the frontier in the vicinity of El Auja and Nitzana at 8:15 a.m. on June 5. The former UN outpost at El Auja was deserted. The first contact with the Egyptians was made at Tarat Um Basis, a hilltop outpost surrounded by a minefield and supported by a company of T-34 tanks. The Egyptians withdrew after a brief defense, having accomplished their mission of delaying the advancing Israelis for about two hours. Similar delay was encountered at the outpost of Um Tarpa, but by 3:00 p.m. Sharon's reconnaissance battalion and armored brigade had reached the El Arish-Abu Ageila highway at several places north of the fortified complex. They established a block northwest of Abu Ageila to prevent any possibility of reinforcements arriving from El

Arish or Bir Lahfan. The reconnaissance battalion of AMX tanks and jeeps also overran the small position of Darb el Turki, connecting the Um Katef position with Kusseima.

Sharon's plan for dealing with the main Um Katef-Abu Ageila positions was now put into effect. The Centurion battalion of his armored brigade —crossing a supposedly impassable area of sand dunes—was to envelop the Abu Ageila-Um Katef complex from the north, while the Super Sherman battalion and mechanized infantry battalion from that brigade conducted a holding attack against the front of the Um Katef strongpoint. While the Centurions were occupying the attention of the defenders of the Abu Ageila crossroads, and the Super Shermans and mechanized infantry were attracting the attention of the Egyptians to the front of the Um Katef position, the main effort would be made by Adam's infantry brigade, attacking over sand dunes from north of Um Katef, parallel to the lines of entrenchments, one battalion assigned to each of the three lines. As the infantry advanced, the Super Sherman battalion would swing around to the right from the front of the Um Katef position into the sandy area to follow behind Adam's infantry, to strengthen the envelopment.

This assault was to take place after dark, when the Egyptian artillery would not be able to fire with precision against the attackers, and when the less disciplined Egyptian soldiers were likely to become disorganized. Sharon had equipped each of the battalions of Adam's brigade with flashlights—red, green, and blue—in order to signal the tanks, one company assigned to each infantry battalion, so that they could closely follow the infantry advance through the trenches. Close behind the infantry would be the engineers to clear the minefields, to facilitate the advance of the tanks into the position. While the Israeli artillery concentrated on the Egyptian infantry in front of the attacking units, one battalion of Colonel Dani Matt's paratroopers was to carry out a helicopter assault to neutralize the Egyptian artillery in the rear. The remaining battalion of the paratroop brigade was in division reserve.

The assault was made from the north because this was the area which had been deemed impassable by both the Israelis and the Egyptians in 1956, and thus—if it could be traversed—it provided a flank vulnerable to penetration. The Israeli terrain studies of 1956 had demonstrated that both infantry and tanks could move in the dunes; and this was a key element of Sharon's plan.

The operation began at dusk, with two pathfinder helicopters landing just north of the Egyptian artillery; they placed flares which guided the paratroop battalion into the artillery area in three waves. The Israeli artillery, which had been displaced well forward during the late afternoon and had registered on a number of important checkpoints before dusk, now began to hammer the Egyptian trenches. Egyptian artillery, confused by the paratroop attack, could not reply. The assaulting brigades got themselves into starting positions.

The tempo of Israeli artillery fire increased at 10:30 p.m. as the pre-assault preparation began. Half an hour later the fire lifted, and while diversionary actions were carried out by Zippori's brigade, Adam's infantry advanced on the Um Katef positions from the north. The first battalion, commanded by Lieutenant Colonel Dov, struck the first trench, the next trench was hit by the battalion of Lieutenant Colonel Ofer David, and the third by the battalion of Lieutenant Colonel Kastel. As the battalions moved forward, the Super Shermans swung in behind them, providing suppressive overhead fire down the trenches in front of the assaulting infantry.

Meanwhile, to the rear of the Egyptian position the paratroop battalion had performed its mission well. The Egyptian artillery was completely neutralized, much of its ammunition was blown up, a number of vehicles were demolished, and the gun crews were driven away from their guns. Having created as much confusion as they could, the paratroopers withdrew, since they expected the Centurions soon to advance from the north and did not want to be in the line of fire.

As to the Centurions, they had reached the El Arish-Abu Ageila road at dusk, then waited for H-Hour. As the fighting broke out to the south, they advanced and effectively neutralized the defenders of the Abu Ageila strongpoint. They then bypassed the crossroads and continued southward toward the center of the Egyptian position. There they were to be joined by the remainder of the Super Sherman battalion, ready to deal with an anticipated Egyptian counterattack. There were careful prearranged plans for nighttime coordination. The Israelis clearly remembered that in 1956 one aspect of their failure at Abu Ageila had been an encounter between two Israeli tank units, which had fired on each other with disastrous effect, each thinking the other was the enemy.

Although the Shermans were delayed by a number of Egyptian minefields and road demolitions, by 3:30 in the morning they were finally able to break through the Um Katef position and approach the area where they expected to meet the Centurions. This difficult crossing of the minefields had been facilitated by a superb mine clearing effort by Sharon's engineer battalion.

At about 3:30 Zippori recognized from the radio reports that he was receiving from the two battalion commanders that the Centurion and Super Sherman battalions were close to each other. Both reported that they were receiving intensive fire. Zippori ordered the Sherman battalion to cease fire, in case the two battalions were firing upon each other by mistake. When the Centurions continued to receive fire, both battalions

King Hussein and his uncle, retired General Sherif Nasr ben Jamil, inspect captured Israeli tank after the Battle of Kerama—*Jordan*

The village of Kerama, after destruction by the Israelis—*Jordan*

Maj. Gen. Mashrour Haditha, Jordan Army, commander of the 1st Division in the Battle of Kerama —*Jordan*

Brigadier General Gonen commander of Israeli troops at Battle of Kerama, talking to General Elazar—*Israel*

General Bar Lev, Israeli Chief of Staff, and Defense Minister Dayan (center) visit the Bar Lev Line after the 1970 Cease Fire; back to camera, Major General Ariel Sharon, commanding General, Southern Command; extreme left, Major General David Elazar, Bar Lev's deputy and successor—*Israel*

Arab reconciliation; Haj Amin el Husseini, Mufti of Jerusalem, and Premier Bahjat Talhouni of Jordan meet in Amman, in late 1968—*Keystone*

Israeli paratroopers raid into Lebanon in 1970 against
Palestinian commandos who had recently raided Israel; note
the hand grenade held by the paratrooper—*Israel*

General Bar Lev addresses Israeli
troops in a Bar Lev Line bunker—
Israel

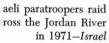

aeli paratroopers raid
ross the Jordan River
in 1971—*Israel*

Israeli T-55 tanks
(captured in 1967)
going into action in
the Sinai Desert,
1973—*Gutman*

Israeli-built 155mm self-
propelled howitzers (on
M4 chassis)—*Gutman*

The Israeli command con-
ference at Um Kusheiba,
Sunday, October 7th, 1973;
from left: General Mendler,
unidentified staff officer,
General Gonen, General
Elazar, General Adan,
General Ben Ari (seated
on desk), General Rabin
(extreme right)—*Israel*

Captured Sagger missile, held by Israeli captain, October, 1973—*Gutman*

Captured Egyptian (or Moroccan) self-propelled 85mm antitank gun, crudely mounted on
T-34 tank chassis—*Gutman*

Israeli ponton-ferry being towed toward Canal by tank; note over-watching tank, extreme upper left, and ring of self-propelled AA guns—*Gutman*

Israeli tank, towing ponton-ferry, stuck in sand; note in foreground a self-propelled 155mm howitzer, an M3 halftrack, and an armored personnel carrier; in background (partially obscured) more bridging equipment, an armored engineer vehicle, and a self-propelled 20mm AA gun—*Gutman*

Israeli tank driving off ferry on west bank at Deversoir—*Gutman*

Israeli tanks and APC getting on newly-constructed ponton bridge—*Gutman*

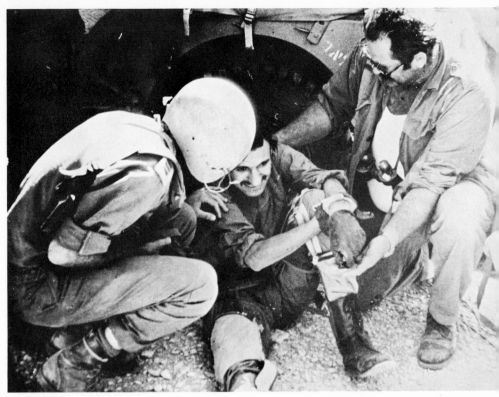

Egyptian MiG-17 pilot shot down over Israeli br[...]head near Deversoir, comforted by two I[...] officers—*Gu*[...]

Israeli tanks crossing the ponton bridge to Deversoir—*Israel*

Egyptian helicopter attacking Israeli bridges [...] Sweetwater Canal, October 17th; this helicopter [...] shot down a few seconds later—*Gu*[...]

Egyptian SA-2 captured by Israelis west of Suez Canal—*Gutman*

efense Minister Dayan and General Adan at captured SA-2 missile site west of Suez Canal—*Gutman*

Foreign Minister (former General) Yigal Allon (center) and General Bar Lev visit General Adan at his field division command post—*Gutman*

Israeli tanks of Adan's division at bay outside Suez City, October 24, 1973—*Gutman*

General Gonen, commander of
Israel's Southern Command,
October, 1973—*Dupuy*

The Chief of Staff, General Elazar, visits General Sharon
at his division field command post west of the Suez
Canal—*Israel*

Captured Syrian makeshift 100mm AA gun, crudely mounted on T-3 4 tank chassis—*Mayes*

Brigadier General Kalman Magen, commander of the Israeli division that captured Adabiya and cut off the Egyptian Third Army—*Israel*

Major General Dan Laner encourages one of his officers—*Israel*

Syrian T-62 tank captured by Israelis—*Mayes*

Syrian T-55 tank captured near Kuneitra; Israeli tank retrievers have replaced the turret that had been blown off—*Mayes*

Syrian T-55 tank, apparently knocked out by premature detonation of the projectile in the tube of the gun—*Mayes*

Israeli soldier on the Golan tests Syrian marksmanship—*Gutman*

Israeli soldiers re-occupy the Mount Hermon OP, October 23—*Gutman*

Major General Moshe Peled, commander of an Israeli division on the Golan Front—*Israel*

Israeli soldier, above the Mount Hermon OP observa tower, looks out over the Golan and the Damascus P October 23—*Gut*

After the war: recently-promoted Israeli Major General Rafael Eytan escorts distinguished sightseers to the Golan front: Prime Minister Rabin; Defense Minister Shimon Peres, General Eytan; Lieutenant General Mordechai Gur, IDF Chief of Staff.

were confident that they were shooting at Egyptians, rather than engaging each other.

What had happened was that, as anticipated, the Egyptian armor had moved up from reserve to help restore the battle in the contested position. A fierce and confused armor battle now took place, with the Sherman and Centurion battalions coordinating their actions with each other, and having considerably the better of the battle in the darkness. In a bizarre contradiction to this confused fighting, suddenly a column of tanks, headlights blazing, appeared to the northeast, marched past just north of the Abu Ageila crossroads, and continued southwest into the desert. It was the brigade of Colonel Elhanen Sela, of Yoffe's division, moving in accordance with plan, ignoring and ignored by the desperately fighting Israelis and Egyptians just to the south.

After losing about forty tanks—nearly half its strength—about dawn the Egyptian armored brigade began to withdraw, its commander recognizing that it would be hurt even more seriously if the Israelis were able to operate in daylight with air support. By this time the Israelis had lost 19 tanks. The infantry was starting its mopping up of the Um Katef position, which had been completely evacuated by the Egyptians. The Egyptians in the Ruafa Dam strongpoint, also, had withdrawn during the night. An eleven-year study of the 1956 Battle of Abu Ageila had paid off in a magnificent dividend to the Israeli Army in one of its greatest tactical successes, the overwhelming of Abu Ageila in less than 12 hours.

Sharon's division spent the morning and early afternoon resting, evacuating the wounded, and preparing for the next mission: an advance on Nakhl and the Mitla Pass. First, however, the Egyptian positions at Kusseima had to be captured. During the afternoon, also, Sharon received still another assignment from Southern Command headquarters: his infantry brigade would have to be sent north to mop up in El Arish. A number of units bypassed by Tal's division were still holding out there, threatening the security of the line of communications of "Task Force Granit," Colonel Yisrael's group, already en route from El Arish toward Romani. Infantry was needed, and Sharon's division at that time had the only unoccupied infantry in the vicinity.

By late afternoon Sharon's division was moving from the captured Abu Ageila-Um Katef position in three directions. The reconnaissance battalion, reinforced, was advancing southeastward from Darb el Turki, on the road between Um Katef and Kusseima. Following was part of Colonel Matt's paratroop brigade. Colonel Adam's brigade was beginning to move northwestward toward El Arish. Colonel Zippori's tanks were heading southwest toward Nakhl. Sharon hoped to follow the tanks the next day with most of his remaining troops.

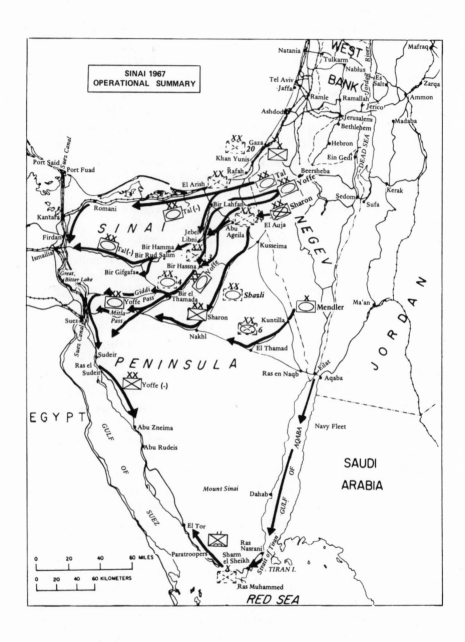

SINAI 1967
OPERATIONAL SUMMARY

During the night of June 6-7 the Egyptians withdrew from Kusseima. The Israeli reconnaissance battalion occupied the position early Wednesday morning, capturing much abandoned heavy equipment. By this time a battalion left by Colonel Adam had finished mopping up the entrenchments in and around Abu Ageila and Um Katef, and was on its way to join the other battalions en route to El Arish. All parts of the Abu Ageila fortifications were now securely in Israeli hands.

THE BATTLE OF BIR LAHFAN

While the divisions of Generals Tal and Sharon were fighting their fierce battles on the approaches to the northern and central corridors across the Sinai, General Avraham Yoffe's division was advancing across the trackless desert between them. The Egyptians, confident that these sand dunes were not traversable by military forces, either on foot or in tracked vehicles, had not bothered to put any defenses in this region. However, the careful Israeli reconnaissance of the Sinai desert during the weeks after the 1956 War showed that this desert was traversable by tracked vehicles, even though with difficulty.

One of Yoffe's brigades, commanded by Colonel Isska Shadni, considered by many Israelis as the best brigade in the army, headed across country, due west through the sand dunes, toward the road junction of Bir Lahfan. The other brigade, that of Colonel Sela, at the same time moved southwestward across a desert track just north of Sharon's division, as already noted. It was expected to reach the vicinity of Jebel Libni late on the 6th. There it was anticipated that the two brigades, Shadni's and Sela's, would combine, probably with some elements from both Tal's and Sharon's divisions, in what was expected to be a major battle for the central Sinai.

Shadni's brigade soon discovered that even though the Egyptians had not put any outposts in the sand dune wastes east of Bir Lahfan, they had emplaced minefields along those unmarked routes which were traditionally used by the local Bedouin. The advance was held up not only by the difficulty of the terrain but by the necessity for clearing out the mines. Thus it was almost dark when Shadni's brigade reached the vicinity of Bir Lahfan, after an advance of about eight kilometers. He did not bother with the small Egyptian force entrenched around the road junction, but waited till dark, when he moved around that position. Before midnight the brigade was in blocking positions across the three roads to the junction, from El Arish in the north, from Jebel Libni to the southwest, and from Abu Ageila to the southeast.

Meanwhile, as the Israelis expected, the Egyptians tried to reinforce Abu Ageila from the division at Jebel Libni. Two brigades—one armored and one mechanized—were sent northeast from Jebel Libni along the road through Bir Lahfan, planning to envelop Sharon from the north. At about 9:00 p.m. this force struck Shadni's roadblock southwest of Bir Lahfan, precipitating an all-night engagement. During the fight the Egyptians lost 28 tanks and the Israelis about half that number. The fight continued on into the morning.

Soon after dawn, Gonen's brigade, spearheading Tal's advance toward Jebel Libni, overran an Egyptian outpost midway between El Arish and Bir Lahfan. His reconnaissance units about this time informed him of the major battle taking place southwest of Bir Lahfan. Gonen, after establishing radio contact with Shadni, sent his mechanized infantry down the road—smashing through the Bir Lahfan position—to support Shadni. With his two available tank battalions, Gonen turned right into the desert, to envelop the Egyptian west flank.

At about 10:00 a.m. an Israeli air strike hit the Egyptians southwest of Bir Lahfan, in preparation for a combined attack by Shadni and Gonen. Then, as the assault was pressed home, the Israelis discovered to their surprise that the Egyptians were already withdrawing. This withdrawal—although the Israelis did not know it—was in response to orders from Jebel Libni. Gonen and Shadni immediately took up the pursuit.

DIVERSION AT KUNTILLA

There was one other major Israeli move in the Sinai area on the first day of the war. This was a thrust just across the border at Kuntilla by an armored brigade under the command of Colonel Albert Mendler. This was the brigade that had been so ostentatious in its movement to the border in the days just preceding the war, so as to attract Egyptian attention to the southern border region.

Continuing its role of diversion, Mendler's brigade swept across the border early on the morning of June 5, and by early afternoon had overwhelmed the defenses of Kuntilla. Patrols were sent down the road toward Thamad and Nakhl, but the overall Israeli plan called for the brigade to stay in Kuntilla for the next two days. It was to pose a continuing threat to Egyptian General Shazli's armored task force in the Thamad area, in order to hold it there as long as possible.

7

The Egyptian Collapse

Despite the escalation and tension of the last week in May and the first few days of June, the Egyptians had not anticipated the Israeli attack. Thus the air blows against the Egyptian air bases in the Delta, Sinai, and Cairo areas were a paralyzing shock, not only to President Nasser, but also to Field Marshal Amer and his staff at the Egyptian GHQ in Cairo. The numbing effect of this shock, strengthened by each of the succeeding waves of Israeli attacks, seems to have prevented any coherent reaction from the Egyptian GHQ, in terms of field orders to the combat forces in the Sinai, during that long, disastrous day. The forces in the Sinai, who had never received any comprehensive instructions for either offense or defense, sat motionless in their positions until attacked, as the Israelis picked them off one by one.

Perhaps the only significant conclusion reached in Cairo that day was that the Israelis could not have achieved their initial air success without the connivance, and probably the active participation, of the United States. It was, for instance, inconceivable to the Egyptians that the Israelis' turnaround rate for their aircraft was three or more times as fast as theirs. Since their intelligence had given them accurate figures on Israeli aircraft, the number of sorties that hit them during the morning of the 5th seemed to have come from more aircraft then the Israelis possessed. Furthermore, it seemed to the Egyptians that the air strikes were too well coordinated and too effective to have been carried out by the Israelis alone. Thus the Egyptians concluded that some of the aircraft which streaked into the Nile Valley from the Mediterranean must have been American planes, launched from carriers of the US Sixth Fleet. They remembered vividly and bitterly the manner in which the British and French had helped the Israelis in 1956.

When a report came from Amman that Jordanian radar in the Judean Hills had observed mass flights coming from the direction of Crete, where the carriers of the American Sixth Fleet were believed to be concentrated, the Egyptian conclusion seemed to be corroborated. In fact, however, the Jordanian radar sightings were merely "blips" from the intensive Israeli aerial activity over the southern Mediterranean.

There were other reasons for the Egyptians to think (as some still do) that there was American collusion and active support in the Israeli assault. One of these was the presence of a US electronic surveillance ship, the USS *Liberty*, only a few miles outside Egyptian territorial waters, north of El Arish and Port Said. The Egyptians believed that the *Liberty* was not only monitoring Egyptian radio and radar transmissions (as she probably was, and Israeli as well as Egyptian) but also was jamming those transmissions, and jamming the guidance radar for Egyptian SAM-2 missiles (which she most certainly was not).

Still one more reason for suspecting collusion was the possession of excellent high-level air photos by the handful of Israeli pilots shot down and captured by the Egyptians. For technical reasons, Egyptian specialists believed that the photos could have been taken only by American or Soviet high altitude "spy" planes. Since there could be no possible suspicion of Soviet assistance to Israel, this automatically meant American connivance by contributing the photographs to the Israelis. In fact, however, in this as in so many other respects, the Egyptians simply underrated the Israelis.

Finally, looking back on the events of the past few days, Nasser thought he saw further evidence of collusion. About May 28 he had received strong pressure from the US Government urging him not to attack Israel. Although he had had no intention of making such an attack, he now interpreted the American diplomatic pressure as having been designed to give the Israelis time to get ready. (He seems to have forgotten that Soviet pressure upon him at about that same time was just as great as that from the Americans.) And then, on June 4, the Egyptians had been asked by the United States to send a senior diplomat to New York to enter next day into United Nations negotiations for prevention of war. This too seemed to follow the 1956 pattern when, on the day of the surprise Israeli attack, the Canal Users Association had also asked for negotiations in Geneva, to mislead Egypt. Under the circumstances, the Egyptians could not accept the fact that these American actions were logical elements of an intensive and sincere effort by the United States Government to prevent the outbreak of war.

Meanwhile, radio reports from the front brought tidings of disaster to Field Marshal Amer's GHQ, even though only a relatively small portion of the Egyptian forces in the Sinai were as yet involved. As word came in of the fall of Rafah, and then of the approach of the Israelis to El Arish and Abu Ageila, the Egyptian staff was paralyzed.

To a number of the individual Egyptian staff officers, however, these events appeared to be not inconsistent with their previous scenarios of a renewed outbreak of war in the Sinai. After all, their original plan—Kahir—was based on an assumption that this was exactly what the Israelis would do. Thus they urged that these unpleasant events should be considered in the broader context of the planned defensive-offensive campaign. Marshal Amer seems to have paid no attention to these suggestions, and through much of the day remained in a funk without transmitting the messages to the Sinai that were urged upon him by his subordinates.[1]

By late afternoon, however, Amer turned from inaction to feverish activity. He began to send messages directly to division commanders, bypassing both General Mortagui, the front commander-in-chief, and General Mohsen, the field army commander. He was also on the phone frequently to General Mortagui, demanding that he send reinforcements to Abu Ageila and to El Arish. He seems to have ignored completely the fact that there was a plan designed to deal with exactly the kind of attack which was being received, and that it still could have been implemented, despite the manner in which he had confused the deployments in the days before the war. Israeli intelligence, monitoring all of the Egyptian channels, heard Amer's well-recognized voice throughout the night, as he kept coming on the radio-telephone to Mortagui, and to the various division commanders, continuing to urge the dispatch of reinforcements to Abu Ageila, and exhorting all to fight vigorously.

By the morning of the 6th, messages from the frontline units made it evident to Egyptian GHQ that Abu Ageila either had fallen or was about to fall, and that El Arish was already in Israeli hands. There is some evidence, also, that during the night Amer and President Nasser, in convincing themselves of the similarities of the presumed American support for the Israelis in this war and that of the English and French in 1956, began to fear the possibility of an American amphibious attack upon the Suez Canal and the Nile Delta. While there does not seem to be any evidence that this possibility was taken seriously by anyone else on the Egyptian General Staff, it possibly affected Amer's personal assessment of the situation.

In any event, early on the morning on June 6, Amer seems to have made the same decision that was made in 1956, after the first overt Anglo-French involvement. He decided to withdraw his army from the Sinai, behind the protection of the Suez Canal. It is not known whether he consulted President Nasser on this; apparently he did not. He most certainly did not consult any member of his staff. He sent telegraph messages directly to Generals Mortagui and Mohsen, and to each of the division and independent unit commanders. There was no mention in this message of a plan or procedure for carrying out the withdrawal; the order was simply to withdraw.

Like Amer, most of the division commanders in the Sinai were political officers. Aware of the spectacular Israeli victories in the opening

---

[1] Amer is reliably reported to have been both a drug addict and an alcoholic; many Egyptians believe that he was either "stoned" or intoxicated when the Israeli offensive began, or that he quickly got himself that way to enable himself better to bear the shock of the Israeli air attacks.

battles, these officers seem to have thought more of their own skins than they did of their troops. Pausing only long enough to pass on the withdrawal order to their subordinates, many of the senior commanders jumped in their cars, and ordered their chauffeurs to drive west toward Kantara and Ismailia.

The Egyptian General Staff, which was beginning to recover from the first shock of the Israeli attack, was almost as greatly shocked when it learned of Amer's withdrawal orders to the units in the Sinai. The staff officers had still been counting on implementation of the original Egyptian plan. Thus they were assuming that the Israelis would be allowed to continue their offensive into the central Sinai, where they would be overwhelmed in an Egyptian counteroffensive somewhere in the region between Jebel Libni and Bir el Thamada. At the very least, such a counteroffensive should stop the Israeli offensive well east of Bir Gifgafa, and the Giddi and Mitla Passes. At best, the counteroffensive could be successful, overwhelming the Israelis, and possibly permitting an invasion of southern Palestine.

The Egyptian staff was therefore completely unprepared for Amer's withdrawal orders. With the Israeli momentum built up during the first day and a half of the war, this retreat order would probably make it impossible to coordinate defensive efforts east of the Canal. Thus not only would it probably result in the loss of all of the Sinai, it could also well mean the destruction of much of the Egyptian Army by the pursuing Israelis.

Three senior staff officers demanded an immediate interview with Amer, who during the previous night had cut himself off from all direct contact with the staff. After a brief delay, these officers were able to persuade Amer's aides that they must see the field marshal on urgent business. Finally they were ushered in to Amer's office. The three were Major General Mustafa el Gamal, Chief of Research; Major General Bahein el Din Naffa, Deputy Chief of Operations; and Major General Refaat Husseinin. They soon convinced the shaken Amer that his order could only result in disaster. He then authorized them to send out messages stopping the withdrawal.

But, as Kipling once wrote: ". . . there ain't no 'Stop, conductor!' when [an army's] changin' ground."[2] Save for units already cut off, all of the elements of the four front line divisions (20th PLA, 7th, 2nd, and 6th), the 3rd Division, and Shazli's armored task force were already rapidly retreating westward. Some of those units whose retreat was cut off by the Israelis were disintegrating. The disaster feared by Generals Gamal, Naffa, and Husseinin was already becoming a fact.

[2] In the text of his poem "Snarleyow," Kipling was referring to movement by a battery of horse artillery; the simile is apt.

Meanwhile, the Egyptian Government's assertions that American (and British) planes were supporting the Israelis were being broadcast to the world, arousing great indignation throughout all Arab countries. Late on June 5th, representatives of the Arab League, meeting at Bagdad, ordered an oil embargo against the United States and Great Britain. Nasser closed the Suez Canal, and despite denials from the British and American Governments, broke relations with both nations. This diplomatic action was soon followed by many of the other Arab states.

The Israelis apparently monitored a radio-telephone conversation between President Nasser and King Hussein at 4:00 in the morning on June 6th. As evidence, there was a tape, later released by the Israeli Government. In the taped conversation, Nasser and Hussein apparently agreed to fabricate charges that the United States—and probably Britain—had participated in the original air attacks on Egypt. The text of the conversation released two days later by the Israelis suggests that by this time both of the Arab leaders knew that this was not so. However, in his book, Hussein asserts, with apparent sincerity, that at the time of the conversation—which he admits is authentic—he was still convinced that the size and scope of the Israeli air assault was explicable only if they had received assistance from American carrier planes and British aircraft in Cyprus.[3]

As the magnitude of the Egyptian defeat grew ever larger, the charges of American and British involvement were repeated more frequently by Cairo, and then taken up by Damascus radio. After release of the Israeli tape on June 8th, however, Jordan stopped all further reference to the charge of American intervention. By this time Hussein was not only aware of the fact that Egyptian reports of their own air attacks against Israel were not accurate, but recognized that neither the United States nor Britain had taken any part in the operation.

[3] Hussein, *op. cit.*, pp. 82-85.

8

Israeli Conquest

of the Sinai

THE BATTLE OF JEBEL LIBNI

Late in the afternoon of June 6, the reconnaissance unit of Colonel Shadni's brigade, approaching Jebel Libni from Bir Lahfan, reached the minefields in front of the Jebel Libni defensive position, and came under long-range tank fire. Quickly Shadni and Gonen—immediately behind him on the road—deployed their brigades for action and attacked the Egyptian fortified camp. About the same time they were joined on their left flank by Yoffe's other brigade—Colonel Sela's—just arriving by way of the Abu Ageila Road. It had bivouacked most of the day just west of Abu Ageila.

The battle for the Jebel Libni camp began at dusk and continued on into the night. Actually the Israelis were engaged by only the Egyptian rear guard, since—as a result of the orders from Cairo—the main body of the division was already moving down the road toward Bir Gifgafa and Ismailia. In its desperate defense the Egyptian rear guard lost 32 tanks.

This is one of those interesting anomalies of military history, a battle in which both sides accomplished their assigned missions. That of the Israelis had been to defeat the Egyptians at Jebel Libni, and capture the fortified camps and airfield there; the mission of the Egyptian rear guard had been to delay the Israelis for several hours, in order to permit the main body of the division to escape. Both sides could, and did, claim success.

Under cover of darkness the Egyptian rear guard withdrew westward toward Bir Hamma. The three Israeli brigade commanders decided to let their units, exhausted from two days of marching and fighting, rest and regroup until dawn.

GENERAL GAVISH'S PURSUIT PLAN

Meanwhile, late on June 6, General Gavish called his three division commanders—Tal, Yoffe, and Sharon—to his command post for a conference. It was now clear to the Israeli commanders that a full-scale

Egyptian withdrawal was taking place. The Egyptians had changed from stubborn defense to delaying tactics. Furthermore, air reconnaissance was reporting massive Egyptian movements to the west. It was evident to the Israelis, therefore, that if they did not move fast, all or most of the Egyptians might escape and withdraw across the Canal. On the other hand, a routine pursuit, no matter how aggressive, would merely serve to hasten the Egyptian withdrawal; while a number of individual stragglers might be cut off, it would be extremely difficult to accomplish the command mission of destroying the Egyptian army.

Gavish therefore came up with an original and unorthodox pursuit concept. Each of the two northern divisions (Tal and Yoffe) was to send armored spearheads driving westward along the three central Sinai roads, thrusting through the retreating Egyptians to set up defensive roadblocks in the vicinity of Bir Gifgafa, the Giddi Pass and the Mitla Pass. The remainder of these two divisions and Sharon's division would continue a rapid broad front advance, driving the retreating Egyptians westward in front of them toward the waiting spearhead roadblocks. In this way, although Gavish probably did not think of it in these terms, the Israelis would be following the Moltkean concept of achieving the maximum possible military advantages from a combination of strategic offense and tactical defense.

After the conference, the three division commanders flew by helicopter back to their command posts. Sharon's was on the road east of Nakhl; Tal and Yoffe's were together near Jebel Libni. At Jebel Libni, late on June 6, and continuing over to the early morning hours of June 7, Tal and Yoffe had a joint conference with their brigade commanders, issuing orders for the next day's operation. It was agreed that Tal's forces would take the northern route through Bir Gifgafa and block the road to Ismailia, while Yoffe's division would take the southern route and block both the Giddi and Mitla Passes. In Tal's division, Gonen's brigade was, as usual, to be the spearhead; in Yoffe's division it would be Colonel Shadni's. The remainder of both divisions would then follow in a rapid but deliberate advance, in accordance with General Gavish's overall plan.

The two generals then sent off a joint message to General Gavish, informing him of their plans. Shortly thereafter they received confirmation and approval by radio.

BIR HAMMA AND BIR GIFGAFA

At dawn on June 7, Gonen's brigade struck westward toward Bir Hamma. There the Israeli tanks hit the rear guard of the 3d Infantry Division, an infantry brigade with some supporting tanks. After a brief fight, the position was taken; the Egyptians, having accomplished their delaying mission, withdrew westward.

Meanwhile, however, Colonel Aviram's brigade had been continuing westward along the road past Gonen's engagement at Bir Hamma, thus becoming Tal's spearhead. As Gavish had foreseen, Aviram's tank units soon became involved in a running battle with the retreating Egyptian units from Bir Hamma. Pushing these Egyptian aside, the Israeli tankers continued their headlong drive westward on the road toward Bir Gifgafa. They encountered a number of other Egyptian units as they went, all going the same way. The Israelis either went around the Egyptians or drove them off the road or pushed through them in a series of running battles. By early afternoon, Aviram's brigade had reached the road junction north of Bir Gifgafa. He sent his AMX battalion to the west to take a defensive position in the hills just beyond Bir Gifgafa, blocking the road from Ismailia. His Sherman battalion and motorized infantry battalion moved just south of the road junction to block the road to Bir el Thamada.

Meanwhile, Gonen's brigade, quickly regrouping after its engagement at Bir Hamma, was close behind Aviram. Approaching the Bir Gifgafa road junction, Gonen swung southward, hoping to encircle part or all of the Egyptian 4th Armored Division, which had been concentrated in the Bir Gifgafa area. It was a classic envelopment, but the results were disappointing. One Egyptian armored brigade, which was already trying to fight its way through Aviram's Sherman battalion, was caught and quickly destroyed by Israeli tanks. Otherwise, except for a number of stragglers, the trap was empty. Most of the 4th Armored Division was already west of the encirclements and some of its elements were crossing the Suez Canal.

BIR HASSNA, BIR EL THAMADA, GIDDI PASS

Further south, Yoffe's division had had similar experiences but encountered much more serious resistance. At 4:00 in the morning, Shadni's brigade had moved out toward Bir Hassna, running into the Egyptian rear guard in that fortified area shortly after dawn. While one battalion attacked the fortifications, Shadni's other two battalions bypassed the engagement, to reach the Bir el Thamada road southwest of Bir Hassna. By 9 o'clock that position had been overrun, and Shadni's third battalion continued down the road after the other two, leaving Sela's brigade to mop up the various outposts around Bir Hassna.

At Bir el Thamada—now completely evacuated—Shadni divided his forces. He sent one battalion northwest to block the Giddi Pass; and with the other battalion he went southwest toward the Mitla Pass.

The battalion which went to the Giddi Pass had a relatively uneventful time. Some Egyptian stragglers were pushed aside or overrun, but the battalion had little trouble in reaching the pass. There it established a roadblock, as ordered, and held off a number of scattered Egyptian units that tried to get through during the late afternoon and evening.

STRUGGLE FOR THE MITLA PASS

The combination of geography, the Egyptian deployment at the outset of the campaign, and the course of operations in the central and eastern Sinai meant that most of the withdrawing units of the 3rd Infantry Division, the 6th Infantry Division, Shazli's armored task force, and some elements of the 4th Armored Division, were all converging on the road between Bir el Thamada and the Mitla Pass. Coordinating this confused withdrawal as best he could was General Ghoul, commander of the 6th Division. His task was not made easier by the fact that General Nasser, of the 3rd Division, and General Shazli had long since crossed the Canal in their private cars, leaving their units still on the road in the Central Sinai.[1]

Shadni's Israeli tankers had great difficulty in fighting their way through and around the mass of retreating Egyptians. Most of Shadni's supply vehicles—including fuel trucks—had either broken down or were shot up in encounters with Egyptians on the road. About 30 kilometers east of the Pass, Shadni's tanks began to run out of fuel. Using steel cables, the Israelis attached the broken-down tanks to those that still had fuel and towed them on to the Pass. However, half of Shadni's tanks were out of fuel when he was still 20 kilometers from the Pass, and most of them had to be abandoned.

At 6:00 p.m., Shadni arrived at the eastern end of the pass with nine tanks, four of these having been towed for the last few kilometers. Accompanying them, or following a short distance behind, were a few halftrack carriers with infantry and mortars. With this handful of troops and tanks, Shadni set up an ambush position just east of the pass, catching the first Egyptian units that followed him completely by surprise.

The tide of Egyptian vehicles continued to flow to the Pass. As they converged at the entrance to the defile, just east of Shadni's ambush position, the Israeli Air Force strafed and bombed them with high explosives, rockets, and napalm. Hundreds, then thousands, of vehicles were soon piled up in the area, leaving little room for maneuver. Now doubly blocked by the jam of burnt-out vehicles, which they could not get through, and by Shadni's still aggressive handful of ambushers, and finding it impossible to get around the Pass, the desperate Egyptians

[1] General Shazli's flight from the Sinai has been reported to the author by one Egyptian general who should know. It has been emphatically denied by another Egyptian general who should know.

endeavored to overrun Shadni's tiny unit. At 8:00 p.m. Shadni reported to General Yoffe by radio that he was completely immobilized and was surrounded. Yoffe immediately ordered Sela's brigade—back near Bir el Thamada—to refuel and dash to the assistance of Shadni; he was told that he must arrive at the Pass by 3:00 a.m.

As Sela's brigade marched in blacked-out column down the road to relieve Shadni's forces at Mitla Pass, one company became intermingled with a column of Egyptian tanks. In the dark it was impossible to determine who was Egyptian and who was Israeli. Although the Israelis recognized that they were in the midst of an Egyptian column, the Egyptians apparently did not realize that they had been joined by Israeli tanks. The Israeli commander radioed to his tanks that all should continue on in the darkness for a few minutes. Suddenly he sent out a radio order for all of his tanks to move sharply to the right, to get off the road, turn on their searchlights, and to shoot up anything that remained on the road. The result was the destruction of an Egyptian tank battalion.

Shadni and his little force held on throughout the night, despite numerous Egyptian attacks, but before dawn they had exhausted all of their ammunition. They had scavenged a number of Egyptian guns, but by early morning they also had used up most of the Egyptian ammunition that they had been able to pick up on the battlefield. However, as Sela's column approached the Mitla Pass before dawn, the Egyptians, aware that they were being caught in a trap, began to abandon their vehicles and set off on foot through the hills and across the desert. It was late morning, however, before Sela's leading units finally reached the Pass and relieved Shadni.

BIR GIFGAFA REVISITED

Meanwhile, north and west of Bir Gifgafa, another desperate night engagement was taking place. An Egyptian armored brigade from Ismailia had been ordered to reinforce the 4th Armored Division in the vicinity of Bir Gifgafa. In the confusion of the withdrawal orders, none of the intermediate Egyptian commanders seem to have realized that by the time this brigade could arrive at Bir Gifgafa the 4th Armored Division would already have returned to the Canal. Nevertheless, following orders, this brigade pushed along the road toward Bir Gifgafa and shortly after midnight unexpectedly ran into the AMX-13 tank battalion of Colonel Aviram's brigade, blocking the road northwest of Bir Gifgafa.

The Israelis had positioned themselves with the AMX tanks on the outer rim of a semicircle facing west; their fuel, ammunition and supplies were on halftracks in the center rear. They had the advantage of a prepared defensive position, but numbered only about 30 light tanks. The attacking force numbered between 50 and 60 T-54 and T-55 tanks, with 100mm high velocity guns. The puny 75mm guns of the AMX-13s could penetrate the T-54/55s only at very short range.

Early in the battle the Egyptians scored a direct hit on an Israeli half-track loaded with ammunition, and 20 Israeli soldiers were killed instantly when the vehicle exploded. In the resulting chain reaction seven other halftracks and one tank were destroyed. Shortly afterward two additional AMXs were destroyed by direct hits. The Israeli 75mm shells merely ricocheted off the heavily armored T-54s and T-55s. After a desperate defense of over two hours, the Israeli battalion began to withdraw. But at this moment, a battalion of Gonen's Centurions arrived to support the hard-pressed AMXs. The Egyptians, believing themselves to be victorious, were now suddenly surprised to find themselves enveloped by a force of medium tanks. In a few minutes ten T-54s and T-55s had been destroyed, and the remainder withdrew in confusion back toward the Canal.

SHARM EL SHEIKH

Meanwhile, in the extreme south of the Sinai Peninsula, final preparations for a combined naval and land attack on Sharm el Sheikh were completed. While a small paratroop force prepared to fly from Eilat, on June 7, a naval task force of three torpedo boats carefully worked its way through the Strait of Tiran (which it reported was unmined) and headed toward the Egyptian coastal base. As the Israeli vessels approached they could see no signs of life, and a landing party was sent ashore.

Sharm el Sheikh was deserted. Early that morning, in accordance with the orders from Field Marshal Amer, evacuation had been completed by the Egyptian garrison. The sailors, therefore, ran an Israeli flag up the flagpole. When the paratroops came over, about an hour later, seeing no activity on the ground, they did not jump, but landed on the airstrip. They soon discovered that the Navy had already arrived.

The paratroopers then moved northwest along the coast. By nightfall they had reached El Tor, where they dug in and waited for further orders.

NAKHL

Slowed by very difficult terrain, and a number of Egyptian minefields, Sharon's division (less his infantry brigade at El Arish) did not approach Nakhl until mid-morning on June 8. Shortly after dawn, however, his leading elements came across an entire brigade of abandoned JS-3 self-propelled guns. Investigation soon revealed that this was the 125th Egyptian Armored Brigade, using the JS-3s as tanks.

The mystery of the abandoned tanks was cleared up the next day when the commanding officer, Brigadier Ahmed abd el Naby, was taken prisoner with a number of his men not far from Nakhl. He informed his captors that on the night of June 6-7 he had become alarmed after hearing a body of tanks approaching him, although as it turned out they were Egyptian. That night he received orders to withdraw, and did so during the day, although he spent most of the time in the shadows of sand dunes to avoid being detected by Israeli aircraft. During the night of the 7-8th, after he had learned of the Israeli advance through Abu Ageila and Bir Hassna, he again heard tanks. This presumably was the advance guard of Sharon's division.

Since he had been ordered to withdraw, and since under the circumstances he did not feel that he could resist an Israeli attack, Naby abandoned his tanks and withdrew with his men in halftracks toward Bir el Thamada. After finding that this, too, was held by the Israelis, he abandoned his men, who were by that time in total disorder, and with two other officers headed southwest on foot. It was soon after this that he was captured by a patrol from Yoffe's division. When asked why he had not destroyed his tanks, Naby replied that he had been given orders to withdraw, that these orders said nothing about destroying his tanks, and furthermore that he was worried that if he destroyed the guns in the proper way by exploding a round in the tubes, the noise would give his position away to the approaching tanks of Sharon's division.

Unaware, of course, of the answer to the mystery of the tanks they had found, Sharon's troops continued to advance toward Nakhl.

Sharon soon thereafter received word by radio from Colonel Mendler, whose brigade had captured Kuntilla on June 5, that he had just taken Thamad, and that the Egyptian force, apparently an infantry brigade and an attached tank brigade from the 6th Division, was withdrawing toward Nakhl. Close behind the Egyptians, harassing their rear guard, was one tank battalion of Mendler's brigade.

Sharon pressed on, and his tank brigade reached Nakhl a few minutes before his patrols sighted the head of the Egyptian column retreating westward from Thamad. Quickly Sharon put his two tank battalions into ambush positions just east of Nakhl, and soon a furious battle was raging. Sharon himself took a mechanized infantry battalion and swung south to hit the middle of the Egyptian column about 15 kilometers east of Nakhl.

This Battle of Nakhl began at about ten in the morning, and was ended at about two-thirty in the afternoon. During those four and a half hours of fighting, Sharon's force and Mendler's battalion destroyed approximately 60 Egyptian tanks, about 100 guns, and more than 300 vehicles. Several hundred Egyptians were killed or wounded, and the remainder, at least 5,000 disorganized soldiers, were dispersed in the hills and wadis south of the road.

Quickly regrouping, Sharon continued west to link up with Yoffe's division near Bir el Thamada.

GRANIT FORCE

On the morning of the 7th, Colonel Yisrael's task force, having completed its march along the coastal road, reached the edge of the Suez Canal, near Kantara. He reported this by radio to General Tal, who in turn informed the Israeli General Staff in Tel Aviv. The Minister of Defense, General Moshe Dayan, immediately issued an order for Yisrael to withdraw 20 miles from the Canal. It has been suggested that Dayan was afraid of provoking an international controversy over the Canal. It is doubtful, however, if Dayan was worried about international controversy. Otherwise he never would have agreed to the preemptive attack on the 5th. What worried him, however, was the fact that if it were reported that Israeli troops were on the banks of the Suez Canal, international pressure for a cease-fire would increase, at a time when the Israeli forces were far from having secured their major objectives. Until there was enough Israeli strength in the area to take and hold the east bank of the waterway despite any opposition, political or military, Dayan wanted to avoid any Israeli presence there.

Early the next day—the 8th—Colonel Yisrael received authorization to move westward again from Romani toward the Suez Canal. About ten kilometers east of Kantara, Yisrael's troops met a mixed Egyptian task force of tanks and commandos. The resulting engagement lasted most of the morning, until Yisrael committed a reconnaissance company of jeeps with recoilless rifles against the right flank of the Egyptian tanks, while his tank battalion struck them on the other flank. Several Egyptian tanks were knocked out, and the Egyptian defending force slowly withdrew back through Kantara to the Canal. Early next morning Yisrael and his troops moved south, bypassing central Kantara to take up positions opposite Ismailia and Firdan by 7:30 a.m. Five hours later they were joined by elements of Colonel Gonen's 7th Armored Brigade, spearheading Tal's main body on the north-south road east of the Canal and northeast of Ismailia.

ON TO THE CANAL

Tal's division, with Gonen's brigade in the lead, had begun moving west from Bir Gifgafa before dawn. There were armored battles all along the route. In some instances, the Egyptian tanks, mostly T-55s, used the crests of the dunes for hull defilade, so that the approaching Israeli tanks were fully exposed, while only the guns and turret tops of the Egyptians were visible. Expecting Israeli attempts to envelop positions near roads, the Egyptians had also pulled back some distance from the roads and laid ambushes in likely avenues of movement. In the early morning several Israeli Centurion tanks took direct hits and were destroyed.

Gonen then deployed his brigade on a broad front. One battalion of tanks moved in three columns, with the center company advancing on both sides of the road, while two companies were placed on each flank, moving across the dunes several kilometers from the road. Approaching each crest carefully, taking advantage of the longer range of their guns, the Israelis were able to destroy several T-55s at long range. Every time an Egyptian tank fired, several tanks in Gonen's central column opened fire at the muzzle flash. By the time the Israelis had reached the Canal opposite Ismailia shortly after noon, they had destroyed about 50 Egyptian tanks. The Israelis had lost no more than five tanks. Gonen now joined up with Yisrael's command.

Further south, by early afternoon Sela's brigade had pushed its way through the mass of wrecked vehicles in the Mitla Pass—victims of Israeli air attacks. Sela now found further advance blocked by several Egyptian strongpoints between the Pass and the Canal. These were supported by considerable Egyptian armor. Yoffe pulled Sela's division back to the edge of the Pass, and had them rest until dark. Then Sela's tanks rushed eastward from the Pass toward the strongpoints with lights on and guns blazing. This tactic unnerved the Egyptians, although desperate resistance continued in several of the strongpoints. By 2:00 a.m. on the 9th, however, the spearheads of Sela's brigade had reached the Suez Canal opposite Shallufa, having overrun and captured intact a missile base complete with nine Russian-made SA-2 missiles.

By nightfall, also, Shadni's brigade had been assembled, and had recovered from its exhausting and unnerving experiences of the previous days. It also moved west through the Mitla and Giddi Passes. Before dawn one of Shadni's battalions arrived at the southern end of the Little Bitter Lake, and the others were soon beside the Canal to the south.

One company from Sela's brigade moved southwest from the Mitla Pass, and shortly after midnight it reached Ras Sudr on the Gulf of Suez. A paratroop unit was dropped at Ras Sudri shortly after that town had been entered by Sela's tanks. The combined force then proceeded southward along the road east of the Gulf of Suez, while the paratroop force which had moved to El Tor from Sharm el Sheikh moved north. The two forces joined at about midday on the 9th at Abu Zneima. Except for the marshlands east of Port Fuad, the entire Sinai Peninsula was now under Israeli control.

At 9:35 p.m. Thursday night in New York—4:35 a.m. Friday, November 9, Egyptian time—Egypt's representative at the UN informed Secretary General U Thant that Egypt unconditionally accepted the ceasefire which the Security Council had resolved upon almost 24 hours earlier. The Second Sinai Campaign was ended.

Total Egyptian combat losses in a little more than four days of intensive fighting are not known, although Egyptian casualties were officially reported as 10,000 soldiers and 1,500 officers. Perhaps half of these were killed or wounded in battle; many of the remainder probably died of thirst and exhaustion in the desert. The Israelis captured 5,000 soldiers and 500 officers, and of these about half were wounded. The Egyptians left some 700 tanks in the Sinai, 600 having been destroyed and 100 captured intact and undamaged. In addition, either destroyed or captured intact were about 400 Russian-made field guns, 50 self-propelled guns, 30 155mm guns, and about 10,000 trucks and other vehicles. On November 23, when announcing Egyptian casualties, President Nasser confirmed that 80% of Egypt's military equipment that had been committed in the Sinai battle had been lost.

Israeli losses on this front were about 300 men killed, more than 1,000 wounded, and 61 tanks destroyed.

9

The Confrontation
of Israel and Jordan

THE WEST BANK

At the close of the 1947-1949 War more than one-third of Palestine was securely occupied by the Arab Legion of Transjordan. Thus, alone among the Arab participants in that conflict, King Abdullah of Transjordan had substantially achieved his war objectives. The addition of territory, population, resources, and prestige enabled him to change the name of his country; it became the Hashemite Kingdom of Jordan. And the region Abdullah had acquired soon became known as "the West Bank" of Jordan, reflecting its location west of the Jordan River.

This West Bank region comprised most of two ancient provinces of Palestine: Samaria and Judea. The entire ridge line of eastern Palestine, from north of Jenin in Samaria to south of Hebron in Judea, was under Jordan's control. Thrusting eastward into this Jordanian salient was the Israeli-held Jerusalem Corridor, linking the new city of Jerusalem, with its population of approximately 100,000 Israeli Jews, to the coastal lowlands of central Israel. Overlooking the Jerusalem Corridor from the north, and securing the southern shoulder of the northern Jordanian salient of Samaria, was the village of Latrun, successfully and gallantly defended by the Arab Legion in the '48 War against a number of equally gallant but unsuccessful Israeli assaults. Northward from Latrun the Samarian salient extended into the eastern edge of the lowland coastal plain, never more than 20 kilometers from the sea; the distance between the Jordan-held city of Tulkarm and the Israeli coastal city of Natania was less than 15 kilometers. The most important towns in this salient were Nablus in the center, Jenin to the north, Tulkarm to the west, and Ramallah to the south.

The southern, or Judean, salient of Jordan's West Bank was considerably smaller and less populated than the northern region. Perched in the highest hills of the Judean range is its principal city of Hebron. The other important town of this region is Bethlehem, really a suburb of Jerusalem.

Linking these two salients was Jordan's eastern part of the divided city of Jerusalem, perched on a shallow saddle in the Judean hills at an elevation of about 2,000 feet above sea level, and more than 3,000 feet above the Jordan and Dead Sea Valleys to the east. Surrounding Jerusalem are some of the highest peaks of the Judean hills, and the ridge running north of the city, between Jerusalem and Ramallah, was the key to the control of the entire Judean plateau. This ridge dominated all of the roads leading up to Jerusalem from Jericho in the Jordan Valley to the east, and from the coastal plain to the west, including the Israelis' main Tel Aviv-Jerusalem highway.

JORDANIAN DISPOSITIONS

In 1967 most of the Jordan Army was stationed in the West Bank area, disposed in two defensive sectors: a northern defensive region in Samaria, based on the cities of Jenin and Nablus; and a Judean region on the spine of the Judean hills, extending south from Ramallah through Jerusalem to Hebron. In both sectors units were deployed forward along the eastern edge of the coastal lowlands, bordering the narrow waist of Israel.

Two Jordanian brigades were east of the Jordan. One was an infantry brigade in the Amman area; the other was in the north opposite Beit Shean. Five of the remaining six infantry brigades were strung in an essentially linear defense of the West Bank region. Three of them held a perimeter around Jordanian Samaria. Another garrisoned the Judean ridge line southward from Bethlehem, with its principal strength centered in Hebron. The equivalent of two brigades was concentrated in and around Jerusalem. The 27th (King Talal) Brigade, under the command of Brigadier Ata Ali, was responsible for the Old City and its immedate vicinity. Just to the north were elements of the El Hashim Infantry Brigade with headquarters in Ramallah. To the south was a battalion of the Hittin Infantry Brigade (headquarters in Hebron), extending northward from Bethlehem to the Adumin Hill just east of Old Jerusalem. A tank battalion was in reserve near the ridge line east of the city. The sixth brigade, the Qadisiyeh Infantry Brigade, was deployed in the valley, just west of the Jordan, near Jericho.

Jordan's only mobile striking forces, the 40th and 60th Armored Brigades, were also based in the Jordan Valley, east of the Judean hills. The 40th Brigade, with a battalion near Nablus, was concentrated west of the Damiya Bridge. The 60th Brigade, with detachments just east of Jerusalem, was located in and around Jericho. Its commander was Brigadier Sherif Ben Shaker, a cousin of the King and a graduate of the U.S. Army Command and General Staff College. Also in northeastern Jordan, located near Mafraq at the outset of the war, was an Iraqi armored division.

Attached to each of the Jordanian brigades was approximately one battalion of light field artillery, either British 25 pounders, or American 105mm howitzers. There were also two batteries of 155mm "Long Tom" guns stationed in Samaria. One of these, in position due east of Tel Aviv, could reach the Israeli metropolis. The other, north of Jenin, was within range of the principal Israeli airfield in northern Israel, Ramat David.

Overall supreme command of the Jordanian armed forces was vested in young King Hussein, the dashing grandson of King Abdullah. The nominal commander in chief of the Jordan Army was Field Marshal Habis el Majali (hero of Latrun in 1948), but real authority was exercised by his deputy, Major General Sherif Nasir Ben Jamil, uncle of the king. Chief of Staff, and responsible for plans, readiness and operational direction of the Army, was youthful Lieutenant General Amer Khammash, an Arab Legion veteran and another graduate of the Command and General Staff College at Fort Leavenworth.[1] Operations on the West Bank were under the command of Major General Mohammed Ahmed Salim.

To this reasonably efficient chain of command, however, a new element had been added. This was Egyptian General Riadh, allied commander of the Jordan front under the terms of the recently negotiated Egyptian-Jordanian mutual defense pact, who had arrived in Amman only a few days before the outbreak of the war. He knew little about the Jordan Army, was totally unfamiliar with the terrain of the sector he was to command, and had had little time to learn anything about the details of the military situation on that front. Both before and after this war General Riadh demonstrated considerable military competence. He never had a chance to exercise it on this front in 1967.

* * *

The Jordan Army was the lineal descendent of the old Arab Legion of Transjordan, created between the World Wars by British General Sir John Glubb as the military instrument of Emir, later King, Abdullah of Transjordan. The Legion, under Glubb's command, had performed creditably in the 1948 War—it was the only Arab force to fight really effectively against the Israelis.

In 1956 King Hussein came under considerable pressure from his allies to get rid of General Glubb, who was seen by many Arabs as both a symbol and an instrument of hated colonialism.[2] But although Glubb was dismissed from the Jordan Army, his influence and that of British military tradition remained. The Army retained British military customs and uniforms, and a substantial element of British efficiency. But economically weak Jordan, despite some assistance from Britain and more recently from the United States, had not been able to keep up with the weapons modernization of Israel and its Arab neighbors. It remained to be seen whether tradition and discipline were enough to enable Jordan

---

[1] After the war, General Nasir and General Khammash were severely criticized as being responsible for the Army's unreadiness. King Hussein seems to have shared the general displeasure in the Army about General Nasir; he relieved his uncle from command, and assigned overall command responsibility to General Khammash, who, however, retained the title of Chief of Staff. The King thus made clear his belief that Khammash had not been personally responsible for the disaster. This is also made explicit throughout King Hussein's own approved account of the war (*My "War" with Israel*, New York, 1969).

[2] Considerable insight on this incident is provided by Anthony Nutting, *No End of a Lesson*, pp. 28 ff.

—with an overexpanded, underequipped army—to fight the Israelis on equal terms.

By 1967 the Jordan Army had approximately 55,000 men under arms, with combat elements consisting of eight infantry brigades, two armored brigades and four or five separate infantry and armored battalions. Aside from the few "Long Tom" cannon, the armored force, equipped with American-made M48 Patton tanks and British Centurions, was the only element of the Jordan Army which was truly modern.

ISRAELI DISPOSITIONS AND PLANS

Brigadier General Uzi Narkiss, commanding Israel's Central Command, had a mobilized force of six brigades to carry out a mission which was intended to be completely defensive. The largest of these brigades, consisting of eight infantry battalions, was the Etzioni Brigade commanded by Colonel Eliezer Amitai, its soldiers mainly reservists drawn from the New City of Jerusalem. Near Lod (Lydda) was the reserve infantry brigade of Colonel Moshe Yotvat. Further north, in the vicinity of Natania, was another reserve infantry brigade, commanded by Colonel Ze'ev Shehem. Two infantry brigades, each with an armored attachment, were in northeastern Samaria, in the Jezreel Valley and in the vicinity of Beit Shean.

Facing the northern frontier of Jordan's West Bank were elements of Brigadier General David Elazar's Northern Command. Elazar's command, when fully mobilized, had seven brigades with which to face three hostile frontiers: Lebanon to the north, Syria to the east, and Jordan to the southeast. Of these brigades, one—near Nazareth—was deployed opposite Jordan. To the north and west, generally between Safad and Nazareth, and ready for deployment against either Jordan or Syria as the situation required, was an armored *ugdah*, or division, of two armored brigades, under the command of Brigadier General Elad Peled.

The Israeli war plan was to hold the line opposite the Jordanian and Syrian fronts in a completely defensive posture, since the mass of their forces would be engaged in the decisive battle against the Egyptians in the Sinai Peninsula. When General Dayan became Minister of Defense, shortly before the outbreak of the war, he reaffirmed the necessity for maintaining this defensive posture, to avoid a multifront war.

When final orders for the preemptive blow against Egypt were issued on June 4th, General Narkiss was instructed by the Israeli General Staff to retain essentially a defensive posture. The Israelis hoped that, as in 1956, King Hussein of Jordan would be able to keep his country neutral. Narkiss was told to expect some firing on his front, since it was believed that Hussein could not avoid some gesture of hostility, and the Israeli forces of Central Command were to refrain from responding to intermittent artillery or small arms fire, unless the nature and intensity of the fire indicated a full-scale commitment of Jordan to the war. At 8:30 a.m. in the morning of June 5 the Israeli Government sent a note to King Hussein through General Odd Bull, the Norwegian officer commanding the UN Truce Supervision Organization (UNTSO) with headquarters in Jerusalem, informing the Jordanian monarch that Israel would not attack on the West Bank unless the Jordanians attacked first. General Bull says that King Hussein received the message before 10:30 a.m.; the king asserts that he did not receive it until after 11:00, when full-scale operations were already under way.[3]

The Israeli General Staff recognized, however, that Jordan *might* enter the war on the side of Egypt and Syria. This possibility was increased somewhat when King Hussein joined the Arab Alliance in his dramatic trip to Cairo on May 30. But even the arrival of Egyptian General Raidh, and the commitment of three Egyptian commando battalions to the Jordanian front, did not lead the Israelis to conclude that Jordan would surely attack.

Nevertheless, if an attack came, Narkiss was to be prepared to seize the tactical offensive in the Jerusalem area as rapidly as possible. He was promised two additional brigades: the Harel Mechanized Brigade, from GHQ Reserve, commanded by Colonel Uri Ben-Ari; and part of the paratroop brigade of Colonel Mordechai Gur, which was otherwise earmarked for an air drop against El Arish and/or Sharm el Sheikh. Elsewhere on his long front Narkiss was to remain strictly on the defensive. He could count on Northern Command to keep the Jordanians occupied in northern Samaria.

THE TENSION RISES

At 8:50 a.m. on Monday, June 5, 1967, King Hussein received a radio message from Cairo informing him that Israel had attacked Egypt. Ten minutes later Egyptian General Riadh received a coded message from Field Marshal Amer in Cairo, informing him that Egypt had put out of action 75% of the attacking Israeli planes, and that the Israeli ground attack in the Sinai was being successfully contained. Amer ordered Riadh to open up a second front against Israel on the Jordanian frontier in Samaria and Judea.

Riadh at once conferred with General Sherif Nasir, Deputy Commander in Chief of the Jordan Army, and Lieutenant General Amer Khammash, the Jordanian Chief of Staff; then all three generals reported to the king shortly after 9:00. Details of the conference are unknown, but from available evidence it seems that King Hussein ordered limited artil-

[3] Odd Bull, *op. cit.*, p. 113; Hussein, *op. cit.*, p. 64.

lery fire against Israeli positions, to demonstrate the solidarity of Jordan with Egypt. Evidently, however, while he seems to have approved plans for an air offensive against Israel, he seems to have directed that no air or ground operations be undertaken without further orders.[4]

During the next two hours the two Jordanian batteries of American-made "Long Tom" 155mm long-range guns sporadically shelled Israeli military installations near Tel Aviv and in the Jezreel Valley northwest of Jenin. Apparently, under orders from General Riadh, and with or without the connivance and agreement of Jordanian military authorities, elements of the recently-arrived Egyptian commando battalions began to infiltrate into Israeli territory west of Ramallah and in the direction of Lod Airport. There was also sporadic small arms and mortar fire along the Jerusalem ceasefire line, most of this by armed Arab civilians and apparently not by the Arab Legion troops.

The Israelis had expected some Jordanian artillery fire, since King Hussein could thus demonstrate his solidarity with the Arab cause without taking the risk of an all-out war. But if Hussein had not yet made up his mind whether to go to war, he made a serious mistake in not issuing strict orders to limit the targets against which his long-range guns were to fire within Israel. By 10:00 a.m. several rounds from the accurately directed 155mm guns had landed on the Ramat David Airfield in the Jezreel Valley, doing some damage to installations and, more serious, putting a number of craters in the runways.

Ramat David, as the largest Israeli Air Force base north of Tel Aviv, was essential to Israeli defense plans for the Syrian front. The possibility that it might be put out of action for several hours by Jordanian artillery fire posed a very severe threat to Israel's military capability in the north, where the strategy of defense by small bodies of troops in upper Galilee was dependent upon the availability of air support.

THE DECISION FOR WAR

There has been no official public announcement of what it was that prompted Israel to go to war against Jordan that morning. Newspaper reports at the time, and published accounts later, have implied that the Israeli decision for an offensive into Jordan was taken only after the beginning of a Jordanian offensive in Jerusalem and Samaria. There seems little doubt, however, that the only Jordanian offensive action up until this time—which certainly provided the Israelis with an adequate

---

[4] King Hussein's own version of these events is ambiguous (*op. cit.*, pp. 60-75). His book stresses his firm determination to honor his new alliance with Egypt. But the long delay in air operations, and in any ground operations other than artillery fire, suggests that Hussein had not yet in fact decided on all-out participation in the war.

casus belli if they were seeking one—had been the long-range artillery fire in the Tel Aviv and Ramat David areas. The initiation of large-scale ground operations seems to have been an Israeli decision, prompted apparently by the threat which artillery fire from Jordanian guns posed to their ability to maintain effective air operations on the Syrian front.

On the other hand, King Hussein makes it amply clear in his book[5] that Jordan was already totally committed to the war, and says unequivocally that orders for Jordanian offensive operations on the West Bank had already been issued by General Riadh with his (the King's) full approval as early as 9:00 or 9:30. He implies that the artillery fire already hitting the outskirts of Tel Aviv and other parts of Israel was the preliminary manifestation of these orders. But Jordanian air and ground operations—obviously fully prepared—did not actually begin until after 11:00 a.m. This delay is surprising, to say the least. However, Hussein's post-war statements must be assessed within the Middle East political context of 1968 and 1969—when the book was written and published. It was to his interest to maximize and emphasize the extent of his total commitment to the Arab cause. Nevertheless, despite possibly inconclusive evidence of Jordanian hesitation in the early hours of June 5, the King's personal commitment to his pledged word to his Arab allies seems sincere.

Although the Israeli General Staff had not anticipated making the decision for war against Jordan as early as it did—before 11:00 a.m., with hostilities to begin at 11:15—its careful planning had envisaged this possibility. General Narkiss was directed to carry out the planned offensive operations in the Jerusalem area and western Samaria. Assignment of the Harel Brigade to his command was confirmed; a decision on Colonel Gur's paratroop brigade would be made shortly. Narkiss was relieved of responsibility for operations against northern Samaria, which were entrusted to General Elazar's Northern Command.

[5] Hussein, *op. cit.*, p. 60 *et seq.*

10

The Battle of Jerusalem:
The First Day

THE BATTLEGROUND

For more than eighteen years the ancient city of Jerusalem had been cleaved by the front-line field fortifications of two warring armies. During most of that time a ceasefire had been in effect, with both sides eyeing each other warily over parapets, through embrasures, and across barbed wire entanglements; but there had been no peace treaty, and there had been no real relaxation of tensions or hatreds.

The division of the city centered at the western face of the thick, frowning medieval walls of the Old City of Jerusalem. Jordan's Arab Legion held the historic Old City, with its revered shrines of three religions, and the eastern, predominantly Arab, suburbs of the city. To the west lay New Jerusalem, a modern, bustling city built in and around what had been the western suburbs of Old Jerusalem. The population of the urban area held by Jordan was about 80,000, mostly Arabs; New Jerusalem had a population of well over 100,000, predominantly Jews. The people on both sides of the barrier had learned to live with constant tension, even those dwelling in houses or apartments abutting on the front lines went about their daily business with only occasional thought to the nearby machine guns, bazookas and cannons which held them in their sights.

Jewish New Jerusalem was the tip of a narrow Israeli salient defined by the ceasefire and armistice lines of 1948 and 1949. Thus the city itself was surrounded on three sides by Jordanian military positions, which took advantage of the heights of the Judean Hills to the north, east, and south of the divided city.

The Jerusalem Corridor, connecting this exposed salient with the coastal lowlands of Israel, was also overlooked on both sides by fortified mountain and hill positions. The principal threat to the corridor, however, was to the north. During the 1948 War the Jordan Arab Legion had been able to hold the heights on that side, overlooking the road which geography decreed as the main access route to Jerusalem from the west. This line of Jordanian positions was anchored on the west by the fortified village of Latrun, which thus became the southwestern shoulder of the Samarian Salient of the West Bank.

Complicating the military problems of Israeli and Arab commanders in the Jerusalem area were two enclaves created by the "freezing" of the 1948 ceasefire lines. One of these was the Israeli enclave of Mount Scopus, the site of the original Hebrew University and of Hadassah Hospital. This area was completely surrounded in late 1947, but had been successfully defended against Arab attacks in 1948. Geographically Mount Scopus was a commanding height on the spine of the Judean Hills, running north and south just east of the Old City. Under the terms of

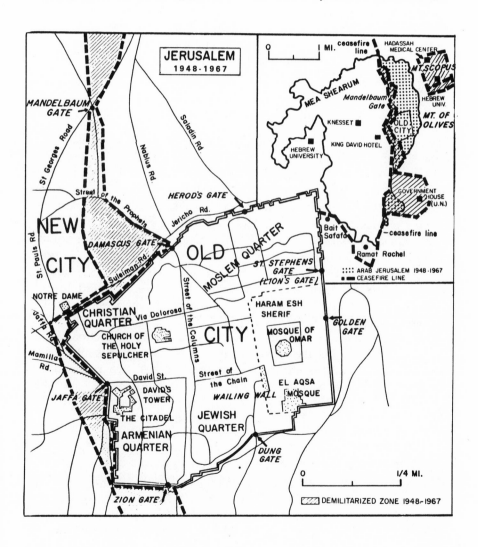

the Armistice Agreement, this technically demilitarized zone was held by 120 Israeli policemen, who were rotated every two weeks. To carry out this rotation, and to carry supplies to the small number of Israeli settlers remaining in the area, one Israeli convoy was allowed to pass each way every two weeks, under UN supervision. The arms and ammunition that the Israelis could provide to this small paramilitary force of policemen-soldiers were theoretically limited to an amount considered reasonable for local security.

The other enclave was that surrounding Government House, the former residence and office of the British High Commissioner of Palestine, which had been taken over by Prince Bernadotte when he became the United Nations mediator, and had continued as the headquarters of the United Nations Truce Supervision Organization following the war and the Armistice Agreement. It was in a large demilitarized zone south of the Old City, on a spur jutting out eastward into the Jordan Valley from the ridge linking Jerusalem and Bethlehem.

ISRAELI DISPOSITIONS

General Narkiss had two brigades already under his command and immediately available to him for operations in and around Jerusalem and the Jerusalem Corridor. One of these, the Etzioni Brigade, commanded by Colonel Eliezer Amitai, was really a small division, with seven infantry battalions and one tank battalion, plus artillery and other supporting elements. Its reservists, however, were not considered to be as well trained as some other reserve units. Opposite the Latrun shoulder, and responsible for holding open the entrance to the Jerusalem Corridor, Colonel Moshe Yotvat commanded another infantry brigade, made up partly of Regular Army units and partly of reservists. A third brigade under Colonel Ze'ev Shehem, observing the dangerous western frontier of Jordan's Samarian Salient, southward from Tulkarm to Lod,, would initially also have an essentially defensive mission: the protection of Lod Airport, Tel Aviv, and the coastal road and settlements; it would not be available for operations affecting Jerusalem. Narkiss' two northernmost brigades, facing the Samarian Salient from the north, were now taken over by Northern Command, so that Narkiss could focus his attention on the defense of Jerusalem and the protection of Tel Aviv.

By noon, the Regular Army Harel Mechanized Brigade, stationed southeast of Tel Aviv, and just west of the Jerusalem Corridor, was on the road heading for Jerusalem. Colonel Gur's paratroop brigade, at its base south of Rehovoth, was preparing for an airborne assault on El Arish, in cooperation with Tal's division, but Gur received orders that at least part of his unit would be reassigned to Central Command.

Narkiss had three major defensive concerns to consider before he could contemplate any offensive operations. First was the vulnerability of the Mt. Scopus enclave, completely surrounded as it was by Jordanian territory. Second was the possibility of a Jordanian move, without prior warning, to encircle and cut off Israeli New Jerusalem, using the two infantry brigades and elements of an armored brigade which were stationed in the immediate vicinity. Third, but easier to anticipate because of the necessity for prior Jordanian troop movements, was a possible attempt to cut Israel in two by pushing through to the coast in the area of Natania, where Israel was only about 15 kilometers wide.

JORDANIAN DISPOSITIONS

In and around the Old City of Jerusalem, and primarily responsible for its defense, was the 27th (King Talal) Infantry Brigade of the Arab Legion under the command of Brigadier Ata Ali. Supporting the King Talal Brigade, but not under Ata Ali's command, were elements of three other brigades. To the north was a battalion of the El Hashim Brigade (stationed in and around Ramallah). Across the Kedron Valley from the Old City was one battalion of the 60th Armored Brigade. (The remainder of the 60th Armored Brigade was in and around Jericho.) Another infantry battalion was located on high ground between Jerusalem and Bethlehem, in the village of Sur Baher, just south of the Government House enclave, overlooking the main ridge road linking the northern and southern salients of the West Bank. This battalion was part of the Hittin Brigade (with headquarters in Hebron). After the outbreak of hostilities—but not before—it was placed under the direct command of Brigadier Ata Ali. Jordanian failure to provide for integrated command of these several forces in the Jerusalem area was a serious error.

The King Talal Brigade consisted of three infantry battalions, an artillery regiment, and a field engineer company. The northern half of the Jerusalem perimeter, from the Old City's Damascus Gate north to Ammunition Hill, was the most strongly fortified Jordanian position in the Jerusalem area. It was held by Ata Ali's most reliable unit, the 2nd King Hussein Battalion. The Old City itself was held by a battalion of reservists recruited from the West Bank, with forward positions on the west walls from Damascus Gate south to Zion Gate. One company held the village of Abu Tur between the Old City and Government House; another occupied the villages of Neve Yaakov and Nebi Samuel, north of New Jerusalem. A reserve of approximately two companies was held in the vicinity of Ata Ali's command post at Karm el-Alami. A battalion of eighteen 25-pounder guns was in position northeast of the Mount of Olives. In addition there were two 120mm mortars within the Old City, and a number of jeep-mounted 106mm antitank recoilless rifles were attached to the infantry battalions. He also had a battery of light 40mm

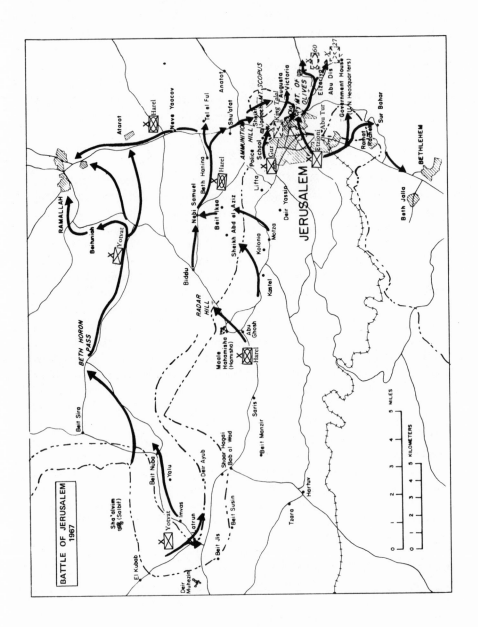

BATTLE OF JERUSALEM
1967

antiaircraft guns. Ata Ali had no tanks under his command, nor any antitank weapons heavier than the 106mm recoilless guns.

The total strength of Ata Ali's force was about 5,000 men. In addition, he had the assistance of the small Palestine militia force of East Jerusalem, less than 1,000 men, under the command of Colonel Fouad Tahboub, a Palestinian who had served as a company commander in Kaukji's ALA; and who had been an officer in the Syrian Army until the union of that country with Egypt.

In support of the Jerusalem garrison, to the north, to the east, and to the south, were forces totalling perhaps another 5,000 men, including about 40 tanks. There were no provisions, however, for the coordination of these forces with those of Ata Ali.

THE OPENING OF HOSTILITIES

At about 8:30 a.m. on June 5, sporadic small arms firing broke out along the Jerusalem perimeter, but there was no sustained fighting, and before 11:15 a.m. the Jordanians insist that no large weapons were fired in the Jerusalem area itself. Israelis, however, assert that there were frequent machinegun bursts from Jordanian positions, as well as occasional rounds of mortar and artillery fire from the Old City and the Mount of Olives.[1] All agree that in the distance could be heard the occasional sound of artillery fire, presumably the Jordanian 155mm "Long Toms" north of Latrun, which were firing sporadically toward Tel Aviv.

The first sustained firing in the Jerusalem district came at 11:15, when Israeli artillery and small-arms fire suddenly erupted against the Jordanian positions. The Jordanians, who had been on the alert in anticipation of the outbreak of hostilities, immediately responded. Brigadier Ata Ali informed higher headquarters of this opening of hostilities, and at 11:30 he received orders to put into effect his carefully-prepared contingency plans for the defense of the city.

Shortly after noon General Salim's West Bank Headquarters issued orders to Ata Ali to occupy the UN Headquarters at Government House, using troops from the nearby battalion of the Hittin Brigade, placed

---

[1] There is a clear and irreconcilable difference in the descriptions of what went on in Jerusalem before 11:15 a.m. on June 5th, as told by Abraham Rabinovich in *The Battle for Jerusalem* (New York, 1972), and as recounted to the author by Brigadier Ata Ali in several meetings in 1975. After further conversations and correspondence with Mr. Rabinovich, I have concluded that Brigadier Ata Ali's memory is faulty in some respects, but that there were no major Jordanian provocations in Jerusalem before 11:15. General Odd Bull, who was in Jerusalem, is surprisingly reticent in dealing with this question. He dismissed the whole question of the outbreak of hostilities in one sentence: "Our chief hope was that nothing would start in Jerusalem, but at 11:25 the Jordanians opened fire." (*op. cit.*, p. 113).

under his command for this purpose. Ata Ali, who recognized that Israeli occupation of the commanding location of Government House would put the Israelis in a position to threaten his left rear and his communications with Jericho, had already made plans to carry out this operation, and was merely awaiting authority to move. He immediately ordered the Hittin battalion to seize the building, and to organize the demilitarized zone for defense. The troops moved into the compound at about 1:30.[2] General Bull and his international UNTSO staff of truce observers protested, but they offered no opposition to the Jordanians. The UN officers moved to the upper floors of the building, while the Jordanians occupied the lower floors.

ISRAELI PLANS

When General Narkiss received orders to initiate hostilities in the Jerusalem area shortly before 11:00 a.m., he at once put into motion long and carefully prepared plans for an operation against the Old City of Jerusalem, adapting the plans to the forces now available to him. While half of Colonel Amitai's Etzioni Brigade held the northern and eastern perimeters of New Jerusalem, the other half of the brigade was to seize the Abu Tur area south of the Old City, to cut communications between Bethlehem and Jerusalem, and to threaten the Jordanian line of communications from Jerusalem back to Jericho. Colonel Ben-Ari's mechanized Harel Brigade was to seize the main ridge line north of Jerusalem, between that city and Ramallah, then to take the high ground to the north and east, to prevent the arrival of reinforcements from either Ramallah or Jericho. The main effort of the Israeli offensive against Jordanian Jerusalem would be made by Colonel Gur's paratroop brigade, which was to envelop the city from the north.

ACTION AT GOVERNMENT HOUSE

Narkiss made his first modification of his plan when he received word, shortly after 1:30 p.m., that the Jordanians had seized Government House. Amitai was ordered to oust the Jordanians from that position and also to attack Sur Baher. In fact, if this counterattack was successful, the Israeli positions south of the city would be improved since the dominating ridge on which Government House stood projected eastward to overlook the Jericho Road.

Shortly before 3:00 p.m. Amitai's attack on Government House and Sur Baher began, with approximately four battalions deployed against the two understrength—and uncoordinated—Jordanian battalions defending those positions. The Etzioni Brigade's tank battalion spearheaded

[2] Odd Bull, *op. cit.*, p. 114.

the attack, with twelve tanks driving toward the Sur Baher position, and twelve against Government House. After brief resistance, the Hittin company at Sur Baher found itself being enveloped by Israeli infantry, and fell back to the south toward Bethlehem.

The Israelis had more trouble, however, against the remainder of the Hittin battalion at Government House. A first assault was driven back, two tanks destroyed, and six others badly hit. But in the exchange of fire, all three of the Jordanian recoilless rifles were knocked out. Within half an hour the tanks from the Sur Baher assault moved north to threaten the east side of Government House. With the four remaining tanks to the west renewing their attack, this threatened the Jordanian position with a pincer movement. Under heavy fire, the outpost troops fell back into the main buildings of the Government House compound, taking their wounded with them.

The battalion commander, seeing that he was being surrounded by the combined Israeli infantry and tank force, at about 4:30 decided to evacuate the position, despite radio orders from Ata Ali to hold at all costs. Carrying their wounded with them, the Jordanians slowly fell back to the northeast, in a well conducted withdrawal. It had been a costly battle, however, with approximately 100 Jordanians killed, wounded or missing, out of the total battalion strength of approximately 500 men.

THE ORDEAL OF ATA ALI

Meanwhile, Colonel Ben-Ari's Harel Brigade had moved into the Corridor near Abu Ghosh and Motza, and was deploying to assault the lightly defended mountain ridges north of the Corridor and northwest of the city. At 5:00 p.m. the Harel tanks moved out northward in four columns toward Biddu and Nebi Samuel. Their immediate objectives were the positions at Sheikh Abdul Azziz, Radar Hill, and Beit Iksa. They found these positions either abandoned or lightly manned. Assisted by a mine clearing operation which had been begun by Narkiss' engineers earlier in the afternoon, in growing darkness Ben-Ari's columns advanced steadily north and then eastward.

During the afternoon, after the Jordanian Air Force had been wiped out, Israeli planes made repeated attacks against Jordanian positions in the Jerusalem area. They focussed their attention primarily on the main elements of Ata Ali's brigade, which consequently was able to give little support to the troops fighting at Government House and Sur Baher. By 6:00 p.m. all telephone lines from Jerusalem back to Jordan had been knocked out by the Israeli bombardment. At 7:30 the Ramallah radio transmitter became silent, and soon after that Ata Ali's Jerusalem radio was knocked out. Ata Ali was able to maintain field radio communications with the 60th Armored Brigade near Jericho, but his efforts to gain radio contact with the West Bank Command Post were unsuccessful. Later in the evening, however, those communications were restored, and Ata Ali learned that the West Bank Headquarters, having been bombed out of its command post near Jericho, had withdrawn after sunset across the Jordan.

During the afternoon, before communications were disrupted, General Salim had promised Ata Ali that he would be reinforced by four brigades, including the 60th Armored Brigade. At 8:00 p.m., after unsuccessfully trying to reach the West Bank headquarters, Ata Ali was informed by the 60th Brigade radio that a relief column, consisting of one tank battalion of the 60th Armored Brigade and an infantry battalion from the Qadisiyeh Brigade, was on its way up from Jericho.

At about 9:00 p.m. the Jordanian defenders in Jerusalem could see flares falling in the distance, far to the east, and this was followed by the sound of bombs in back of and beyond the Mount of Olives. What was happening, as Ata Ali was able to guess, was that the Israeli Air Force was smashing the relief column from Jericho.

By 11:00 p.m. all had become quiet again to the east. Soon after this time 60th Brigade Headquarters at Eizeriya radioed Ata Ali that the relief column had been wiped out. The brigadier, aware of the arrival of Israeli reinforcements—Gur's brigade—in the New City, then asked for support from the Hittin Infantry Brigade in the Hebron area. He also requested that all or part of the brigade in Ramallah be moved down to join him rather than allowing both units to be defeated in detail. After a brief pause, the 60th Brigade replied by radio that the brigades in Ramallah and Hebron were braced for attack, and could not be moved.

About this time the West Bank Command Headquarters came back on the air, and General Salim informed Ata Ali that the Qadisiyeh Infantry Brigade, now concentrating at Jericho, was being prepared to come to his relief. This force would be rushed part way up the mountain road by truck in the next few hours. The men would unload below the crest, then force-march through the hills to evade Israeli air interception. Ata Ali could expect them to reach the city by early morning. In Amman, General Khammash approved this plan.

11

The Battle of Jerusalem: The Climax

THE ISRAELI OFFENSIVE

Colonel Gur's paratroop brigade, in its garrison near Rehovoth, had been alerted about possible commitment to Jerusalem at 11:00 a.m. on Monday, June 5. Gur first received orders to send one battalion to Jerusalem at about 2:00 p.m. Then he was told to send two battalions, and finally the whole brigade was assigned to the task. Colonel Gur, aware of the difficulty of his assignment—breaking through fortifications into a built-up area—had studied the terrain, fortifications and deployments of the enemy forces as part of prewar preparations for contingency plans. However, his unit commanders were not completely familiar with the situation in Jerusalem and he therefore immediately took them with him by jeep to make a reconnaissance; their battalions were to follow by truck. By twilight the battalions had reached Beit Hakerem, where they were issued brief instruction sheets before proceeding to the city.

Gur had hoped to attack around midnight, but was held up by problems resulting from unfamiliarity with the area. In addition, due to the nature of the assigned axes of advance, Gur realized that there would be many casualties, thus creating the need for a more extensive evacuation system than his own scant medical resources would provide. To take care of these things, he changed his H-Hour to 2:00 Tuesday morning. The General Staff wanted to postpone the attack until 8:00 a.m., coupling it with an artillery bombardment and air strikes, but the paratroopers were ready, and Narkiss told the staff that the objectives were too close to Jerusalem for air strikes; the 2:00 a.m. timing was approved.

A little after 11:00 p.m. on June 5th, Israeli artillery and mortars began to hammer Jordanian positions north of New Jerusalem, and between Jerusalem and the Mount Scopus enclave. Particular attention was paid to the vicinity of the Police School and Ammunition Hill. To facilitate these mortar and artillery concentrations, searchlights from the New City and the Mount Scopus enclave focussed their beams on target after target.

It was well past midnight when a Jordanian observer noticed that the

Israeli searchlights were meeting on empty spots of terrain and fixing there for minutes at a time. It was soon realized that they were marking hovering points for helicopters to land troops. Within fifteen minutes, people from Wadi Juz were reporting that a small force of paratroopers was landing on the slope above their village in an attempt to outflank the frontier positions along the Nablus Road, the UNRWA building and Ammunition Hill. At least 40 paratroopers were landed behind the Jordanian lines in four separate drops.

Ata Ali ordered a platoon off Ammunition Hill and into the wooded area northwest of the British Military Cemetery on Mount Scopus to cut off the advancing paratroopers. A band of armed civilians operating in loose coordination with the 2d Battalion (holding the threatened northern perimeter), was sent to Wadi Juz to open fire on the paratroopers' flank. The paratroopers were soon pinned down not far from St. Joseph's Hospital.

At 2:20 in the morning, the main body of Colonel Gur's paratroopers moved out across the demilitarized zone into the area generally between the Mandelbaum Gate and the Police School, and leading into the so-called American Colony. Two of Gur's battalions were in columns of companies following a powerful artillery preparation; one headed toward the Police School and Ammunition Hill, and the other through Sheikh Jarrach and the American Colony to the Rockefeller Museum. Fighting was intensive in entrenchments, concrete bunkers, and fortified houses. Casualties were severe on both sides, and a number of Israeli tanks in the tank battalion attached to Gur's brigade were knocked out.

Shortly before dawn on June 6, Israeli planes finished off the remaining Jordanian artillery positions north of the city. The last center of Jordanian resistance on the Nablus Road, a gas station, was wiped out by a column of seven Israeli tanks, which then pushed down the road to the Damascus Gate and opened fire against Jordanian positions along the Old City wall. The return fire from Arab soldiers manning the positions was intense and the tanks withdrew to rejoin the main paratrooper thrust past the Rockefeller Museum. Between 7 and 8 o'clock, however, most of the American Colony area had been cleared, communications had been reopened with the enclave on Mount Scopus, and the paratroopers were at the bottom of the valley below the Augusta Victoria heights.

Meanwhile, Ben-Ari's armor was fighting elements of the El Hashimi Brigade in the ridges to the north of the city. Following the seizure of Sheikh Abdul Azziz and Radar Hill, the armored column encountered stiff resistance at the fortified position at Biddu, but by 4:00 a.m. that had been overwhelmed, and the spearhead of the Harel Brigade pressed on to take Nebi Samuel with little difficulty. By about 6:00 a.m. the brigade was gathering on the ridge, along the Jerusalem-Ramallah road.

Soon after this, Ben-Ari's patrols encountered a force of approximately 30 Patton tanks, just east of the road and north of Tel el Ful—a hill north of Jerusalem, dominating the nearby heights. This was apparently the 60th Armored Brigade battalion which had been originally assigned to the Jerusalem area. As dawn broke, a fierce tank battle broke out near the Beit Hanna road junction, from which the Jordanians withdrew after about half an hour, having lost six tanks.

Ben-Ari's tanks then advanced on Tel el Ful. There, too, Jordanian defenses were sparse, and the hill was taken against only moderate resistance. The Harel Brigade then turned south to advance through the valley, but was halted by the defenders of Shu'fat Hill, part of Ata Ali's brigade.

Soon after dawn, Ata Ali called the civilian Governor of Jerusalem to report the breakthrough on the city's northern perimeter. The Israelis were opposite the Damascus Gate, had pushed through the center of the Zahera commercial district and were threatening Salah ed-Din, the last street leading to the Old City remaining in Jordanian hands. By this time the Israeli flag was flying over Sheikh Jarrach, and the suburbs were lost. Major Mansour Kraishan, commander of the 2d Battalion, reported that aside from a detached company now dug in on Shu'fat Hill, there were only 69 men left under his command. The brigadier thereupon withdrew his CP into the Old City to avoid being cut off.

Ata Ali established his new CP in the basement of the Armenian Convent on the Via Dolorosa. He was able to reopen radio contact with 60th Brigade Headquarters at Eizeriya, which reported that there was no word from the force-marched relief column.

A DESPERATE SITUATION

Ata Ali's situation was critical: all of his gun emplacements had been destroyed with the exception of two heavy mortars within the Old City; he had 500 soldiers left from the brigade within the walled city; and the only positions outside the wall still in Jordanian hands were Shu'fat Hill (cut off from Jerusalem by Israeli troops), the August Victoria position between Mount Scopus and the Mount of Olives, Abu Tur and Ras al-Amoud (a reinforced police station on the southern slope of the Mount of Olives). Ata Ali still believed that the Old City, with ample ammunition supplies, could hold out, but the advance of Ben-Ari's tanks from Beit Hanna threatened to envelop the Old City and block the Jericho Road. He had also learned that a separate column of Israeli armored infantry (Yotvat's brigade) had taken Latrun.

At 12:00, following a series of unopposed air attacks, Ben-Ari's tanks again moved against the Jordanian company on Shu'fat Hill (reinforced early in the morning by survivors of the Wadi Juz and Ammunition Hill battles). The first Israeli assault swept into the lower trenches, only to be thrown back by the Jordanians. The Israelis withdrew, but shortly after noon their second assault carried the hill, and the position fell. At this point, Ben-Ari was given permission to rest his tired men, to regroup, to refuel, and to replenish ammunition.

It was about this time, beginning in the early hours of the afternoon, that Amitai's Etzioni Brigade attacked Arab positions in Abu Tur, a fortified area on high ground just south of the Old City's walls, overlooking the Jerusalem railway station. After heavy house-to-house fighting, the Israelis took the position and descended into the Kedron Valley. Encountering intense fire from Jordanians to the north and east, the brigade halted. It was decided not to move further until after dark, when the advance would continue, in coordination with Gur's planned encircling movement north of the city.

By mid afternoon of the 6th, the situation in Jerusalem had become even more critical. Ata Ali still had two battalions relatively intact, one in the Old City, and one on the high ground to its immediate east on the Augusta Victoria hill and the Mount of Olives. The road to Jericho was still open to Jordanian transit, although under constant Israeli fire and useless for any substantial movement of troops or supplies. Gur's paratroopers had partially penetrated between Ata Ali's two battalions, and Ben-Ari's mechanized units north of the Augusta Victoria height posed a threat to the Jericho Road.

Ata Ali reported his situation back to West Bank Headquarters and in the middle of the afternoon received a personal message from King Hussein assuring him that additional efforts to relieve Jerusalem would be launched that night. In response, Ata Ali said that he would hold on. He also reported, however, that despite the fact that he had plenty of ammunition, medical supplies of all types were exhausted, and the situation in the city's hospital was critical.

LATRUN AND RAMALLAH

Further west, the brigade of Colonel Moshe Yotvat was fighting in Latrun. Yotvat's troops, spearheaded by tanks, had pushed from the vicinity of Rehovoth toward Latrun during the afternoon of the 5th. The Jordanians—from the El Hashimi Brigade—had allowed the tank company to penetrate their outpost line, then had blocked the advance of the remainder of the brigade, isolating the tanks all night. The Israelis attacked early in the morning, and a desperate struggle ensued. By 11:15 the Trappist monastery at Latrun was in Israeli hands. While a convoy of trucks set out to use the Tel Aviv-Jerusalem highway for the first time in 19 years, the infantry units proceeded north, and toward evening the armor and infantry were on the way to Beit Horon and Ramallah, where they expected to join the Harel Brigade.

That brigade, after capturing Shu'fat Hill, had taken a few hours to rest, regroup, refuel, and replenish ammunition. Then, following directives from Central Command, at about 5:15 p.m. Ben-Ari took two of his battalions north toward Ramallah, leaving one battalion to secure the ridgeline northeast of Jerusalem.

Ramallah, a city of about 50,000, is located on and around a peak of 870 meters, about 16 kilometers north of Jerusalem. The main Jerusalem-Nablus road, following the crest of the ridge, passes through the city.

Ben-Ari and his tankers arrived at the outskirts of the city at about 6:00 p.m., just before dark. Having met little opposition, Ben-Ari decided to take his tanks into Ramallah, employing the standard Israeli urban warfare doctrine inspired by Moshe Dayan's successful drive through Lydda in 1948. Guns blazing, and firing in all directions, the Israeli tanks dashed into and through the city, crossing and recrossing it several times while dusk became darkness. Although the tankers had met scattered pockets of resistance, including some bazooka fire, by about 6:45 the town fell silent, except for the rumble of Israeli tanks, and occasional bursts from Israeli machine guns.

Ben-Ari, however, feared that his tanks would be at a disadvantage if they spent the night in the city; so he pulled his troops out, and they formed laagers, bivouacking north and south of the city. He sent his reconnaissance unit probing to the southeast, on the road to Jericho.

THE JORDANIANS HANG ON

At sunset on the 6th, while Ben-Ari was shooting up Ramallah, Gur's brigade renewed its offensive north of the Old City. The paratroop brigade and its attached tanks moved out from their concentration points near the Rockefeller Museum, and began an assault up the hill toward Augusta Victoria. While one tank company shelled the hillsides, another tank company and the reconnaissance company spearheaded the advance of two paratroop battalions attempting to force their way up the heights. In the darkness and under heavy fire from Jordanian positions scattered across the hillside, some of the Israelis became confused, and lost their direction. Two tanks and several jeeps were destroyed, and the attack bogged down. Before midnight Gur called his troops back to regroup and prepare for a new assault. This was the first and only clearcut Jordanian success of the entire battle for Jerusalem.

Meanwhile, as promised by King Hussein, another relief infantry brigade was attempting to reach Jerusalem from Jericho. As before, the plan was to go only half way by road, then to advance across country to the Mount of Olives. Israeli air attacks had delayed the planned departure of the brigade from Jericho, and so the commander—in his eagerness to relieve the desperately hard-pressed troops in Jerusalem—decided not to follow his cautious instructions, but instead planned to dash up the hill in trucks until he reached the roadblock created by the vehicles left after the destruction of the Jordanian column the previous night. At this point he planned to dismount his troops and continue on foot past the Mount of Olives. Shortly before midnight, the brigade's advance guard reached this point and began to dismount, just as the movement was discovered by the Israeli Air Force. Israeli artillery and air strikes thereupon struck the entire column on the road, bringing the column to a halt and inflicting severe casualties.

This development, however, had not been unexpected by the Jordanians. Despite their losses the Jordanian infantry quickly assembled in march columns about a hundred meters from the road, and continued the advance on foot toward Jerusalem. They were still more than eight kilometers away when the break of dawn forced them to take cover to avoid observation by Israeli aircraft.

ATA ALI ADMITS DEFEAT

It was already too late for the relief column to be of any assistance to the Jordanian forces in the Old City. Shortly after midnight, in fact, when Ata Ali learned by radio that the relief column had been blocked on the road, he knew that it could not possibly arrive before evening of the following day. By that time he knew that he and his few remaining troops in Jerusalem would have been overwhelmed. Furthermore, he had learned by radio that most of the Jordan Army units to the north and south had already withdrawn from the West Bank. Thus, unless he was able to get out of the city before dawn on the 7th, he and his few remaining troops would be trapped.

Ata Ali had been charged with the defense of one of the most important places in his nation, and one of the holiest shrines in Islam. He had to make the difficult choice of attempting to continue a defense which he knew was hopeless, and could not last another 24 hours, or of abandoning an almost sacred mission in hopes that he and his few remaining troops would survive to fight another day. Reluctantly he decided that only the latter course made sense militarily. So he went to see Governor Khattib of Jerusalem to tell him of his decision. He urged Khattib to withdraw with him to Jericho, but the governor refused. The brigadier then sent staff officers to the commanders of the units manning the wall and holding the fortifications on Augusta Victoria Hill, ordering them to withdraw at once. Shortly before dawn the evacuation was skillfully and efficiently completed, undetected by the Israelis.

THE FINAL ISRAELI ASSAULT

Colonel Gur and his staff had spent the night making plans for a new assault, which Gur decided to postpone until daylight on the 7th in order to avoid another failure in the confusing lanes and fortifications of Augusta Victoria hill. Meanwhile his paratroopers, after regrouping and replenishing their ammunition supplies, caught some much needed rest.

Early in the morning General Narkiss called Gur to tell him that time was running out. It was essential that the attack be pushed as quickly as possible, in order to seize the Old City before the United Nations imposed a ceasefire. Gur assured Narkiss that he was about to move and told Narkiss his plan. One battalion was to advance eastward and then southeastward by way of Mount Scopus, to envelop the Augusta Victoria position. A second battalion was to drive through the valley between Augusta Victoria and the Mount of Olives on the east, and the Old City wall on the west. These two battalions, from positions blocking and overlooking the Old Jericho Road, would prevent any possible Jordanian interference from the valley, while Gur's third battalion pushed along the city wall from Herod's Gate to St. Stephen's Gate, where it would break through to the Temple Mount.

In Jerusalem there remained over 100 armed Arabs, mostly civilian volunteers, plus a few soldier stragglers who had lost their way in the darkness. By dawn these men were mainly clustered around the Damascus Gate and Herod's Gate. The mayor of the city and the city council met with the governor about 7:00 a.m., just as a squadron of Israeli planes dropped high explosives and napalm on the now empty Augusta Victoria positions. At the same time the Israeli paratroopers, still unaware that most of their opposition had disappeared, were moving out from their positions. The Israeli planes swept on to bomb and strafe the Jordanian gun emplacements behind the Mount of Olives, which had again become active, under the personal direction of Ata Ali.

Following this air strike there was a heavy Israeli artillery preparation. Then suddenly, shortly before 7:00 a.m., the Israeli tanks and recoilless guns dashed forward, guns blazing in every direction. Advancing almost without opposition in a two-pronged assault, the tanks and paratroopers swept across the Augusta Victoria Hill and the Mount of Olives and into the northern end of the Kedron Valley, below the city walls. While the two battalions took blocking positions overlooking and along the Jericho Road, Gur drove in his halftrack to join the third battalion and tank battalion, which were advancing into the valley from the Rockefeller Museum, beside the wall. The advance continued to the bridge below St. Stephen's Gate, which Gur saw was half open. At 9:50 Gur led an advance party of foot soldiers and pushed cautiously through the gate, soon followed by the main body of his brigade. Just inside the city wall Gur was met by the Governor, the Mayor, and city officials, who informed him of their decision not to defend the city.

By 10:15 General Narkiss, accompanied by the Chief Rabbi and General Bar Lev, joined Gur at the Wailing Wall. The ceremony at this liberated shrine of Israel was brief but moving. Gur and his men continued to occupy the city, with only occasional interference from snipers, who were quickly routed out.

SECURING JERUSALEM, HEBRON, AND RAMALLAH

While Colonel Gur's paratroopers were carrying out their final assault on the heights east of the Old City, and on the Old City itself, Colonel Amitai's Etzioni Brigade had continued its advance from Mount Zion along the southern edge of the Old City walls, to Silwan and the Dung Gate. This was completed, without opposition, at about the same time the paratroopers were entering the eastern part of Jerusalem. Amitai then concentrated his command in the Ramat Rachel area and awaited orders for an attack southward toward Bethlehem and Hebron. He did not have to wait long.

At 2:00 p.m., with the advance spearheaded by a small armored group, the Etzioni Brigade moved southward to overrun the Arab positions at Mar Elias, and to continue on toward Bethlehem. The Hittin Brigade had already evacuated Bethlehem, and withdrew from Hebron at about noon. So the Israeli advance southward along the Judean Ridge encountered only occasional sniper fire. Advancing quickly from Bethlehem, the Etzioni Brigade occupied the Etzion Bloc and Hebron before dark.

North of Jerusalem, on the morning of June 7th, Colonel Ben-Ari's two battalions in the Ramallah area reentered the city. They were soon joined by Colonel Yotvat's battalion from Latrun, which completed the mopping up. Ben-Ari's tank battalions by noon were advancing eastward behind their reconnaissance company toward Jericho. Moving in two columns, on either side of the road, they encountered little resistance along the way. When they reached Jericho in the late afternoon they found that the city had been evacuated, all Jordanian forces having withdrawn eastward across the Allenby and King Abdullah bridges. One battalion took the police station, while the other secured the town by crossing and recrossing the city, eliminating scattered resistance. Sniping continued throughout the night, however.

Meanwhile, a Jordanian tank battalion withdrawing from the Hebron hills through Jericho discovered that the retreat route was blocked by

Ben-Ari. When they realized that they would not be able to get their tanks through to Jericho on the mountain tracks leading from the Judean hills down toward the Dead Sea and the Jordan Valley, the Jordanians abandoned their tanks, and proceeded by foot to the Abdullah Bridge. Ben-Ari pursued, and pushed units to the east bank of the Jordan. These were quickly called back by General Dayan, who ordered both bridges near Jericho to be destroyed.

Total Jordanian casualties in the fighting in the Jerusalem-Ramallah-Hebron area were probably nearly 1,000 killed and wounded. Total Israeli casualties in the fierce fighting in and around Jerusalem were more than 800, of which nearly 200 were dead.

12

Samaria: The Battles
of Jenin and Nablus

JORDAN'S SAMARIAN SECTOR AND DEPLOYMENTS

Like most of Jordan's West Bank, the Samarian Salient was mostly mountainous, except for a narrow stretch of coastal lowlands on the west, and the Jordan Valley on the east. However, the region is less arid than Judea, to the south, and there were and are many Arab villages scattered throughout. The three principal towns were Nablus, Ramallah, and Jenin. Ramallah, however, was included in the Judean defensive sector of the Jordan Army. The defense of the Samarian sector, therefore, was related mainly to Jenin and Nablus.

Jenin is located at the foot of the Shomron Hills, controlling the approaches to the Jezreel Valley in Israeli territory just to the north. Southwest of the town is the Dotan Valley, which opens west to the coastal plain.

Nablus, about 30 kilometers directly south of Jenin, lies in a valley between Mount Gerazin and Mount Ebal. Two roads run between Nablus and Jenin; the eastern road passes through Tubas and Wadi Farra, while the western one runs through Silat ed Dhahr and Dir Sharah.

Jordanian forces in the Samarian sector consisted of three infantry brigades, one reinforced armored brigade, two independent battalions of infantry (one of which, mechanized, was attached to the 40th Armored Brigade), and two independent armored battalions—one of these also attached to the 40th Armored Brigade. The 25th Infantry Brigade, under Lieutenant Colonel M. A. Khalidi, held Jenin with two battalions, with a reserve battalion near Tubas. A tank battalion, reinforcing the 25th Infantry Brigade, was also in Jenin, with a detachment attached to the reserve battalion. The Princess Alia Brigade, with headquarters in Nablus, had two battalions deployed on the coastal plain in the Tulkarm-Azzon area. The Hashimi Brigade, with headquarters in Ramallah, had one battalion deployed opposite Tel Aviv and another holding Latrun and the northern flank of the Jerusalem Corridor; the third was between

Ramallah and Jerusalem, as noted in the previous chapter. The main body
of the 40th Armored Brigade was back near the Damiya Bridge, providing a powerful general reserve for the Samarian sector. This brigade,
commanded by Brigadier Rakan Enad el Jazi, was also available for the
reinforcement of Jericho and Jerusalem should this be needed.

The Jordanian deployment was essentially defensive. Apparently the
Jordanians did not expect a major attack from Israeli forces in northern
Samaria or Galilee, but were more concerned about the security of their
troops on the coastal plain in the extreme western portion of the West
Bank sector. This region, while posing a potential threat to the narrow
waist of Israel, was itself extremely exposed to attack from Israeli forces
deployed in that waist. The concentration of troops in the Jenin-Nablus
area, therefore, seems to have been considered by the Jordanians more
as a northern anchor to their troops deployed on the coastal plain than
as a seriously threatened defensive zone.

ISRAELI DISPOSITIONS AND PLANS

On the Israeli side responsibility for the northern frontier with Jordan lay with the Northern Command under Brigadier General David Elazar. Responsible for surveillance and protection of frontiers with three hostile countries—Lebanon, Syria, and Jordan—Elazar had four of his seven brigades deployed forward close to the frontiers. One was in the north of Galilee overlooking the Lebanese border, from which no hostile threat was really expected; two were deployed in eastern Galilee, along the upper Jordan opposite Syria, and one was in northern Samaria south of Nazareth. In reserve in central Galilee, Elazar had an armored division under the command of Brigadier General Elad Peled, comprising two armored brigades. A third armored brigade was further east, as a local reserve for the Syrian front.

When General Elazar received orders to attack Jordan's Samarian sector, with a view to securing the entire West Bank area as far as the Damiya Bridge, his forces were deployed in anticipation of operations against Syria, not against Jordan. However, there were long standing plans for the Jordanian operation, and he immediately ordered these into effect. His reserve units, the two armored brigades of General Peled's division, were to move out at once from their assembly areas, regrouping into combat deployments while on the road. The brigade of Lieutenant Colonel Moshe Bar Kochva was to move into the Dotan Valley through Yamun, thus approaching Jenin from the southwest. The other armored brigade, under Colonel Uri Ram, was to advance southward, passing east of Mount Gilboa, then turn west to reach the Jenin-Nablus road just south of Jenin, near the Kabatiya road junction. From here he would again advance south along the road to Nablus. The infantry brigade near Nazareth and the Jezreel Valley, commanded by Colonel Aharon Avnon, was to be part of Peled's division, with its objective to support the thrusts of the two armored brigades against Jenin.

Also placed under Elazar's command was an infantry brigade in the Beit Shean and eastern Jezreel Valley area, part of Central Command. Initially this brigade would remain in defensive deployment. Coordination was also to be maintained with Colonel Shehem's brigade of Central Command deployed in the lowlands near the Tulkarm area; that brigade would also remain in essentially defensive deployment until Peled's division had secured Jenin.

While Peled's brigades were marching to their assembly areas, Israeli aircraft were hammering Jordanian positions in Samaria. Their principal attention was devoted to the battery of 155mm guns located in the upper Dotan Valley west of Jenin, which had been responsible for stimulating the Israeli offensive against Jordan.

THE BATTLE OF JENIN

At 3:00 p.m. on June 5, Israeli forces began to cross the frontier north and west of Jenin. While Colonel Avnon's infantry pushed southward in two columns along the Afula and Givat'oz roads, Colonel Bar Kochva's tanks, also in two columns, converged on the Dotan Valley. One of Bar Kochva's columns moved southward from Umm el Fahm toward Ya'abad. The other advanced eastward on a converging course up the Dotan Valley. Shortly after dark the columns of Bar Kochva's brigade met southeast of Ya'abad and continued eastward, an armored battalion in the lead. They encountered their first resistance west of Jenin from several batteries of antitank guns, protecting the long-range 155mm guns. After a brief exchange of fire, the leading battalion bypassed the antitank positions, while the second battalion, armored infantry, deployed against the antitank guns and the long-range artillery.

Although surprised by the Israeli offensive, and having up until this time been mostly concerned with protecting themselves from Israeli air attacks, Colonel Khalidi's troops put up fierce resistance. It was nearly midnight before the Israeli armored infantry had secured the positions. At about the same time, the tank column reached the road southwest of Jenin, where it halted. At 3:00 a.m., after the armored infantry caught up, the brigade began an assault on the city from the southwest, through the Kabatiya junction.

Bar Kochva's main attack was made by his armored infantry battalion; he kept his three tank battalions, totalling about 100 tanks, concentrated behind the infantry, ready to deal with either of two possible Jordanian armored threats. He knew an armored battalion was located southeast of Kabatiya; he also recognized the possibility that the entire 40th Jordanian Armored Brigade might move against him.

The Jordanians had anticipated the possibility of an Israeli attack against Jenin from the south. Three coordinated defensive lines, well equipped with antitank guns, barred the approach. In the first of these lines, rough and varied terrain was held by infantry, reinforced with antitank guns; the second line, consisting primarily of entrenched antitank guns, dominated all access roads traversable by tanks; the third, consisting also of infantry and antitank emplacements, was supported by about 30 Patton tanks.

The Jordanian defense was tenacious and skillful. The antitank guns were well concealed and could be located only by muzzle flash. Since the antitank fire was accurate, it was impossible for the Israeli tanks or halftracks to attack the Jordanian infantry that held the hills dominating Jenin until these antitank positions had been eliminated. While the Israeli infantry was attempting to overrun them with little success, the Jordanian tank companies moved in against the Israeli flanks in a well-conceived classic double envelopment.

Bar Kochva, however, had been prepared for this eventuality, and immediately threw two of his own battalions into the fight, blocking the Jordanian envelopments. The Israelis had older, Sherman tanks, but as they had expected, they found that at a range of 1200 meters the improved Super Sherman, with its 105mm gun, could fight the Pattons on equal terms. Although the Israeli counterattack relieved the pressure on the flanks of Bar Kochva's infantry, the Jordanian tanks fought fiercely, in a confused night armored battle. Sensing that he had regained the initiative from the Jordanians, Bar Kochva put in one more battalion of tanks, enveloping the original Jordanian envelopment. This ended the fight, and the surviving Jordanian tanks withdrew in considerable confusion.

Meanwhile, with their flanks protected, Bar Kochva's infantry had been able to overrun all three of the Jordanian antitank positions. The Israeli armored infantry halftracks then moved against the main Jordanian infantry positions on the hills east and west of Jenin.

By this time, shortly before dawn, Avnon's infantry brigade arrived from the north, closing in on the city in conjunction with Bar Kochva's attack from the south. In coordination with Avnon's attack, Bar Kochva sent two of his tank battalions northward along the main road into Jenin. Covering the rear, guarding against a possible attack by the Jordanian 40th Armored Brigade, was Bar Kochva's reconnaissance battalion, consisting of a company of tanks and two companies of motorized infantry in jeeps.

As Bar Kochva's tanks approached Jenin, they were taken under fire by Jordanian tanks hidden behind buildings. There was another brief armored battle, but the Jordanians were outnumbered, and unable to operate in effective coordination. Those defending tanks that were not destroyed slipped out of the town to the east, and endeavored to work their way southward to rejoin their main body on the Tubas road.

The two attacking brigades now converged on the town, following standard Israeli street-fighting doctrine, firing in all directions against snipers, machine guns and antitank guns. Determined resistance persisted, even after the Jordanian tanks had left, but the two Israeli brigades slowly converged on the police station in the northern portion of the city.

THE BATTLE OF KABATIYA

Just as the police station surrendered, Bar Kochva was informed by radio from his reconnaissance battalion that a force of 60 Patton tanks was advancing from the direction of Tubas. Leaving Avnon's infantry to mop up the scattered but fierce resistance still continuing in Jenin, Bar Kochva withdrew to the southern outskirts of the city and regrouped his tank and armored infantry battalions. He then moved along the road to the southwest, toward the Kabatiya Junction, where the first pre-dawn tank battle had taken place.

Meanwhile, the reconnaissance battalion had been attacked by Jordanian Patton tanks southwest of the road junction. While one Jordanian tank battalion carried out a holding attack on the road, another battalion enveloped the reconnaissance battalion, moving around it to the east, arriving at the Kabatiya Junction just before Bar Kochva's tanks appeared down the road from Jenin. Thus, the reconnaissance battalion was completely surrounded. Bar Kochva, arriving from the north with the equivalent of about one exhausted tank battalion, and a badly depleted and exhausted battalion of armored infantry, found himself facing a rested and ready Jordanian tank battalion at the junction.

Bar Kochva's situation was critical. Although he probably had a slight superiority of force over the Jordanian tanks, his supplies of fuel and ammunition were very low, and his men were exhausted from a march of 24 hours and very tough fighting. He reported his situation by radio to General Peled, who called in air support. Under the cover of continuous waves of fighter attacks against the Jordanian tanks, Bar Kochva had breathing time to regroup and refuel his main body, and to make plans to rescue the isolated unit to the south.

By this time it was midmorning; Colonel Khalidi had been able to rally much of his 25th Infantry Brigade and with the tanks had formed a firm defensive position in and around Kabatiya. Repeated efforts by Bar Kochva's brigade to smash through the Jordanian defenses were thrown back. Fierce fighting continued along this new battle line for approximately twelve hours. Shortly after dark Bar Kochva sent one of his tank companies around the flank of the Jordanian position, to smash a hole through the lines surrounding the isolated reconnaissance battalion. By radio he told the reconnaissance battalion to be ready. Thus while the attacking tank company held open the gap, the surrounded troops quickly streamed out, and fell back to join Bar Kochva's main body north of Kabatiya.

ACTION AT TILFIT-ZABABIDA

Meanwhile, to the east and south Colonel Ram's armored brigade was encountering comparably fierce Jordanian resistance. Ram's brigade did not cross the border until early on Tuesday morning. Advancing south from the eastern and southern slopes of Mount Gilboa, Ram passed through Tilfit (Salpit) in the valley east of Zababida. His objective was to reach the eastern Jenin-Nablus road at Zababida, and then turn south through Tubas toward Nablus. While going through Tilfit with his advance party, Ram could hear the sound of battle not far to the west at Kabatiya. The Israelis did not have long to wait before they themselves came under fire. At 10:15 Ram's reconnaissance company in the valley below Tilfit encountered heavy fire from the high ground near Zababida to the west. The company commander reported that there were about 30 Jordanian Patton tanks between Zababida and Aqqada. Jordanian armor was established in well concealed positions on the far heights on the western side of the valley, covering the road and entire valley below.

Ram deployed his tanks on the heights on the eastern side of the valley, sending several halftracks down into the valley to draw fire so that the Jordanians would reveal their locations by their tank gun muzzle flashes. This was the beginning of a long range, static armor battle, which lasted from about 10:30 in the morning until dusk. Little damage was done to either side in this long range exchange. Just before dusk, however, Ram observed a Jordanian tank company shifting its position on the far ridge, and called in an Israeli air strike, which destroyed a number of these tanks. Then, as darkness fell, he was able to use the burning tanks as reference points to direct his guns on other Jordanian tank positions that had been located during the day, as well as on the defenses in the village of Zababida itself on the heights above. He then radioed to General Peled, asking permission to make a night attack on the Jordanian tanks in Zababida.

Peled having approved, Ram's artillery opened fire on the known Jordanian positions on the hills opposite his position at 12:40 a.m. Wednesday morning, June 7. Under the cover of a 20 minute artillery preparation, Ram advanced in two columns, with four tank companies in each. One of these columns, with medium tanks in the lead, advanced along the Tilfit-Zababida road. The other column moved downhill along some dirt tracks that Ram's reconnaissance unit had discovered during the day, only to find that the track was blocked by concrete antitank obstacles as it came into the valley. However, the advancing Israelis quickly used their tank guns to blast these obstacles, and the column continued its advance down into the valley and up the far side, still undetected by the Jordanians.

As the column on the main road entered the valley, it encountered Jordanians in and around Tilfit. For the next hour a short range armor battle raged in the valley until the other Israeli column revealed its presence by attacking Jordanian positions on the hills near Zababida. The Jordanian tanks in the valley immediately broke contact, scrambling back up the hill to avoid being cut off. They were closely pursued by the Israelis. By 3:00 a.m., Zababida was in Israeli hands, and the Jordanians were retreating southward down the main road toward Tubas.

While resting his main body, Colonel Ram sent a reconnaissance company to secure the Tubas-Damiya-Nablus junction. At 9:30 a.m. on the 7th, as he was on the march again toward Nablus, Ram received a report from the reconnaissance company that it was within eight kilometers of Nablus and that the town seemed quiet. Ram was now faced with a difficult decision. He knew that the Jordanian 25th Infantry Brigade and at least two battalions of tanks were behind him in the Katbatiya area. He knew that there was another battalion of tanks somewhere east of Tubas in the Jordan Valley. And he knew that there was at least one, and possibly two more tank battalions—the main body of the 40th Armored Brigade—in the Jordan Valley to the southeast, near the Damiya Bridge. Thus he was in serious danger of being isolated and attacked from two or three different directions. He decided to leave the bulk of his brigade near the road junction, and with one tank company he advanced to join the reconnaissance company outside Nablus. He sent orders ahead for the reconnaissance company to continue to reconnoiter to the outskirts of Nablus.

THE BATTLE FOR NABLUS

As the Israelis advanced down the road approaching Nablus from the east, they were astonished to find a crowd of Arab residents waiting outside the city to greet them. The people of Nablus had been informed that Iraqi reinforcements could be expected from Damiya, and, when the Israelis arrived from the east, they were at first assumed to be the Iraqis. The error was soon recognized when an Israeli soldier tried to disarm a nearby Arab; scattered firing immediately broke out.

Ram, arriving at this moment, quickly occupied the center of Nablus, sending the reconnaissance company to the western edge of the city. The company commander soon reported back that a large force of Jordanian tanks, probably about a battalion, was just west of town. Ram at once sent for two tank battalions to join him in Nablus, leaving one to hold the road junction to the northeast.

When the two battalions arrived, Ram sent one tank company to the north of Nablus, to protect his right flank, and then moved out to the western edge of the town with his main body to engage the Jordanian tanks. At the same time the Arab inhabitants in the city, who had remained quiet during all of this activity, opened fire on the rear of the Israeli units. For the next six hours a confused battle took place in and around the western edge of Nablus. Ram ordered his troops to keep maneuver to the minimum, and to fire only at nearby targets, in order to retain reserves of both fuel and ammunition.

Meanwhile, southwest of Jenin, shortly after dawn, Bar Kochva renewed his attack on the Kabatiya junction. At about the same time a battalion of Avnon's brigade, which had swung to the west through Ya'abad, then southeast through Arraba, reached the western Jenin-Nablus road, threatening the rear of Jordanian positions at Kabatiya. The Jordanians at once withdrew to the southeast, toward Damiya.

Bar Kochva did not pursue, but in accordance with his orders he advanced down the western axis toward Nablus, joined on the march by Avnon's infantry battalion. They cleared the road through Silat ed Dhahr, Sebastiya, and Dir Sharah, approaching Nablus from the west. At Dir Sharah they encountered heavy Jordanian armored and infantry resistance. This was the rear of the unit which was engaging Ram's brigade on the outskirts of Nablus. By this time it was late afternoon.

Finding themselves caught between two converging Israeli forces, the Jordanians withdrew in considerable confusion, some going to the south, and some to the north of Nablus. Those to the north were soon joined by another tank battalion of the 40th Armored Brigade, which had been investigating a diversion by the Israeli brigade in the Beit Shean region. Once these Israelis had been contained by the arrival of Jordanian infantry from the El Yarmouk Brigade, this tank battalion responded to an urgent call from the 40th Armored Brigade commander to reinforce the units engaged at Nablus.

Thus, hardly had the armored battle to the west of Nablus died down, when a new engagement broke out north of the city, its combatants including the fresh battalion, some of the defeated tanks, and portions of Ram's brigade from Nablus and from the Nablus-Tubas Road.

By this time, however, the Jordanians' morale had plummeted. It was evident that they had suffered severe defeats throughout the West Bank, and more than half of the tanks of the 40th Armored Brigade had already been destroyed in and around Nablus. Furthermore, they had reports of another Israeli infantry brigade approaching Nablus from Kalkilya to the west. (This was the brigade of Colonel Ze'ev Shehem, of Central Command.) The surviving Jordanians fought their way across the road, to reach the Damiya Bridge road, and by dusk were well on their way to the Jordan Valley and Damiya.

Firing in and around Nablus stopped at about 6:30 in the evening, and the Israelis put a curfew into effect at 7:00. While Nablus was still being cleared, just after dusk, Bar Kochva's brigade headed south on the road to Ramallah and linked up with a battalion which Colonel Ben-Ari had sent north from that city. At the same time Ram sent his reconnaissance battalion of tanks down the road to Damiya, where it seized the bridge in midevening. Thus, the Israelis now held all three bridges over the Jordan, assuring their control of the West Bank.

Meanwhile, at 7:30 p.m. King Hussein made a radio speech to the people of Jordan, calling upon them to fight "to the last breath, and the last drop of blood." However, he had already authorized his senior commanders to negotiate with the United Nations Truce Supervision Organization, in response to a UN call for a ceasefire. At 8:00 p.m., both Jordan and Israel accepted the ceasefire call.

On July 7 Premier Sadd Jumas announced that Jordanian casualties had included 6,094 killed and missing, but actual losses were lower. Precise, although probably incomplete, figures were later calculated by the Jordan Army, and are believed to be reliable: 580 killed, 351 wounded and 530 prisoners of war. At least another 2,000 were missing; these were mostly West Bank inhabitants who simply went home after the defeat. Presumably, some of these were wounded, and some of those unaccounted for were dead; thus figures for dead and wounded have been arbitrarily increased by 20%, and total dead are estimated at 696, total wounded at 421, or overall casualties at 3,117. Total Israeli casualties against Jordan were 550 killed and 2,400 wounded.

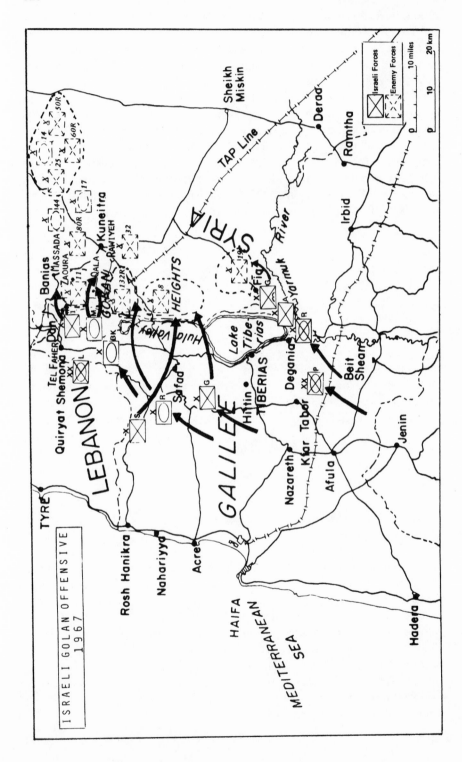

13

Battle for
the Golan Heights

THE TERRAIN AND FORTIFICATIONS

Between 1948 and 1967 the Syrians had built a defense zone of bunkers and tank and gun emplacements along the heights overlooking the entire ceasefire frontier with Israel. This escarpment, marking the western edge of the Golan Plateau, runs 70 kilometers from Mt. Hermon in the north to the Yarmouk Valley in the south. The western slope of the escarpment dominates the Huleh Valley and Sea of Galilee in Israeli territory 1500 feet and more below the crest. After the war, Israeli General Elad Peled (with some exaggeration) described the defense as being more than ten miles in depth with no established first, second, or third line, just row after row of emplacements and guns. At the same time, General Elazar stated (without exaggeration) that the Syrians could launch more than ten tons of shells per minute from the 265 guns that they had placed along and just behind the ridge. This figure did not include several Russian-made Katyusha multiple-barrel rocket launchers, each carrying twelve rockets with a ten mile range and a ten to twelve pound warhead. The Syrian defenses were extremely formidable.

East of the escarpment the rocky volcanic Golan Plateau—also called the Golan Heights—extends eastward some 30 kilometers to the Damascus Plain. Rising abruptly from the rough, boulder-strewn rock surface of the plateau are a number of volcanic hills, called tels, mostly cone-shaped. Vegetation is sparse, particularly in the north, and the terrain becomes progressively more rocky as it rises from an elevation of about 120 meters above sea level in the south to about 1000 meters as it merges into Mt. Hermon's foothills. In winter and summer a cool breeze, sometimes rising to gale force, sweeps constantly across the plateau from northwest to southeast. Completely dominating the plateau, and the flat plain which extends away to the east and northeast toward Damascus, is the 3000-meter towering height of Mt. Hermon, where the frontiers of Israel, Lebanon and Syria meet.

THE OPPOSING DEPLOYMENTS

On May 16, 1967, Syria followed Egypt's lead in declaring a state of emergency, and in mobilizing its army. This mobilization was essentially minor in its impact, since Syria had a standing army and did not depend upon reserve mobilization. The forces under the command of General Ahmad Soueidany totalled about 70,000 troops, with combat elements organized into thirteen brigades: six infantry, two armored, one mechanized, and four reserve infantry. Eight of these brigades were massed on the Golan Heights west of Kuneitra, in two echelons of three brigades each, plus a local reserve. Four brigades were deployed between Kuneitra and Damascus; one (the 23d Infantry Brigade) was stationed near Latakia.

The Syrian forces on the Golan Heights were organized in three division-sized task forces, which the Syrians called group brigades. These task forces were primarily administrative, and provisions for coordination and control of the operations of the component brigades were rudimentary. North of the road from the Bridge of Jacob's Daughters to Kuneitra was the 12th Group Brigade, commanded by Colonel Ahmed Amir. The 11th Infantry Brigade was concentrated just south of Mount Hermon in the Banias-Masa'ada-Qala area, covering the road from Qiryat Shimona in northern Israel thorugh Dan to Kuneitra. To the south of the 11th Brigade, and just north of the main road, was the 132d Reserve Infantry Brigade. The second echelon of the 12th Group Brigade consisted of the 80th Reserve Infantry Brigade, northwest of Kuneitra, and the 44th Armored Brigade just northeast of the city.

South of the main road through Kuneitra was the 35th Group Brigade, commanded by Brigadier General Said Tayan. The 8th Infantry Brigade was deployed along the escarpment south of the road, overlooking the Huleh Valley and the northern portion of Lake Tiberias. To its south the 19th Infantry Brigade covered the road through Fiq, El Al, and Rashid. The second echelon of the group brigade included the 32d Infantry Brigade, just southwest of Kuneitra, and the 17th Mechanized Infantry Brigade, just south of the Damascus Road, east of Kuneitra.

In general reserve was the second echelon of the field army, comprising the 42d Group Brigade, commanded by Brigadier General Abdul Razzak Dardari. This group brigade occupied a second defense line, between Kuneitra and Damascus. It consisted of the 14th Armored Brigade, the 25th Infantry Brigade, and the 50th and 60th Reserve Infantry Brigades.

Each of the infantry brigades included three infantry battalions and an armored battalion of T-34 or T-54 tanks, plus several SU-100 self-propelled assault guns and a number of antitank weapons. The mechanized infantry brigade consisted of two infantry and two armored battalions. The reserve infantry brigades consisted of three under-strength infantry battalions.

Israeli Brigadier General David Elazar's Northern Command (including attached units from Central Command) consisted of eight brigades, three armored, and five infantry. Most of the infantry brigades had a company or battalion of tanks, and at least one of the battalions in each brigade was mounted in halftracked armored cars. Of these brigades, two were deployed opposite the Syrian frontier, one was nearby, opposite Lebanon, and an armored brigade was in reserve not far from the Syrian frontier. Elazar's other units—beginning June 5 —were deployed against the northern regions of Jordan's West Bank.

THE FIRST FOUR DAYS

The Syrian-Israeli border was the least active of the three combat fronts during the initial four days of the war. However, although there was little ground activity, Syrian artillery units kept up constant heavy shelling of the Israeli forces in the valley beneath them.[1] This artillery fire was answered by Israeli counterbattery fire, and frequent IDF air strikes on Syrian positions. The only ground action during these days occurred on Tuesday, June 6th, when Syrian troops near Mount Hermon made three separate company-size reconnaissances in force to develop the Israeli position. One of these was against Tel Dan, the mound marking the ancient city of Dan, at the extreme northeastern point of modern Israel; another was against nearby Kibbutz Dan, just to the south of the tel; the third was against the village of She'ar Yashuv, about 2 kilometers inside the frontier. In each of these attacks approximately one infantry company crossed the frontier, accompanied by 3 to 5 tanks. The Israelis claimed that these probes were easily repulsed with the aid of air support, but the Syrians insist their actions had not been intended to hold ground.

The Syrians had briefly contemplated the possibility of an offensive into northern Galilee, and this indeed had been the principal reason for the reconnaissances in force on the 6th. Plans were made to bring bridging material up from Damascus for a crossing of the Jordan. However, by evening of the 6th all possibility of a successful Syrian offensive had faded, with the destruction of the Syrian Air Force. Israeli planes, dominating the skies over southwestern Syria, were preventing the movement of bridging materials, and were attacking all daylight moves by the Syrian Army. In subsequent days, as the magnitude of the Jordanian and Egyptian defeats became apparent,

[1] Since Israeli troops were deployed in or near some settlements, the Israelis could claim with some justification that nonmilitary targets were attacked.

Syria became convinced that successful combat operations against the Israelis were impossible, even from the strong defensive positions on the Golan Heights. Consequently, they contented themselves with shelling Israeli Army concentrations and fortified kibbutzim near the frontier, and waiting for a ceasefire, to which they intended to adhere.

However, there was great pressure for an offensive against Syria from the Israeli inhabitants of eastern Galilee. They wanted to have the Syrians punished for the years of harassment which Syrian guns (with considerable Israeli provocation) had inflicted on the Huleh Valley farms and settlements. A delegation from the region visited the Israeli Government in Jerusalem shortly after the outbreak of war, requesting the government to launch an offensive against the Syrians, in order to drive them from the heights overlooking the valley.[2]

After the ceasefire on the Jordan front began, late on June 7th, Elazar received permission from the General Staff to attack the Syrians on June 8th. Shortly after midnight, however, he was ordered to wait until the 9th.

Dayan was no longer worried about fighting on three fronts, since the Egyptians had been driven across the Suez Canal, and a ceasefire on the Jordanian front ratified the expulsion of the Jordan Army from the West Bank. But Dayan wanted to give the Air Force—now able to turn its full attention to the north front—more time to soften up the formidable Syrian positions on the Golan escarpment. He also wanted to give some rest to the troops coming up from Jordan, who had been fighting continuously since June 5th.

There was possibly a third consideration in Dayan's mind, although this has never been confirmed. On June 8 the Syrians would either have to accept or reject the United Nations ceasefire call, since the ceasefire was already in force on the Egyptian and Jordanian fronts. If Syria was under heavy attack, and losing ground, the Syrian Government would be more likely to accept and observe a ceasefire while they still held all or most of the western Golan Plateau. This could prove embarrassing to the Israelis, who were anxious to gain control of the entire Golan Heights, in order to end the Syrian artillery dominance of the valley to the west. If, however, the Syrians rejected the ceasefire, or accepted it and then broke it (as Dayan seems to have expected) the Israelis would have time for two or three days of intensive operations before a new ceasefire could be arranged. There is some reason to believe, therefore, that Dayan was being Machiavellian in postponing the assault for twenty-four hours.

---

[2] Syrian officials believe this peculiar lobbying activity was suggested by General Elazar.

At 5:20 p.m. on June 8, the possibility of such a Machiavellian denouement was seriously lessened when the Syrian Government accepted the ceasefire. A lull followed, and lasted through the night and into early morning on the 9th. In what was a clear violation of the ceasefire, which Dayan reports straightforwardly in his memoirs, without apology or explanation, he ordered Elazar to attack as soon as his units were in place. He then innocently adds that "The ceasefire went into effect a day and a half later."[3]

THE ISRAELI PLAN

On the basis of long prepared plans General Elazar decided that the main breakthrough would take place in the Tel Azaziyat-Qala-Zaoura area of the northern Golan Heights. The Israeli advance would begin with an infantry-armor thrust up the ridge south of Tel Azaziyat, through territory that was so difficult and steep that it had been only lightly fortified by the Syrians. Such a drive, if successful, would open the old road through Banias, at the foot of Mount Hermon, permitting an armored advance through Masa'ada toward Kuneitra from the north.

At the same time, secondary attacks would be made along the heights farther south, near the Jordanian strongholds of Darbashiya, Dardara, and Jalabina. Armor would be brought up to support all of these attacks, and during the night these Syrian defensive positions would be attacked and captured. In the southern sector paratroopers and armor would attack Tawafik, Kfar Hareb, Fiq, El Al, and Boutmiya, to open up the southern access into the Golan Heights. Concentrated air support would be available to the attacker throughout the operation.

The Israeli main effort in the north was to be made by a division-size task force commanded by Brigadier General Dan Laner, Elazar's deputy. The assaulting forces were to be an armored brigade under Colonel Albert Mendler (who had been rushed north for this assignment after successfully commanding the diversionary force in the Kuntilla-Nakhl area in the Sinai) and the Golani Infantry Brigade, under the command of Colonel Yona Efrat. While Mendler's brigade, assisted by bulldozers, was driving its way up the mountainside north and east of Kfar Szold, the Golani Brigade, just to the north, would follow the old main road from Dan toward Banias, first striking the Syrian fortifications at Tel Azaziyat, then driving eastward against Syrian positions on the heights of Tel Fahar. In reserve was the

[3] Moshe Dayan, *Story of My Life* (Tel Aviv, 1976), p. 300; see also p. 306.

armored brigade of Colonel Bar Kochva, which arrived from the Jordanian front soon after the offensive began.

This Israeli plan took advantage of years of study of the terrain and of the Syrian fortifications. By carefully checking with field glasses, and by aerial photographs, where the local Syrian farmers tilled their fields, the Israelis knew where there were possibilities of maneuver, and this information was passed to commanders at all levels, even down to platoons.

THE ISRAELI OFFENSIVE

At 11:30 a.m. Mendler's brigade—to which several Golani companies, in halftracks, were attached—jumped off from the vicinity of Kfar Szold and crossed the border. This unit immediately ran into several severe problems. The route lay over extremely difficult terrain, which had to be negotiated during daylight, while the entire column moved along a single axis. The ascent to the top of the ridge had to be carried out smoothly, despite heavy Syrian fire, because any stoppage of vehicles en route would block the entire column, and would leave it completely vulnerable to devastating fire from Syrian guns on top of the ridge.

Mendler's advance headed generally east and northeast up the steep, rocky slope, led by an engineer detachment with eight unprotected bulldozers, followed closely by Centurion tanks and halftracks. The bulldozers almost immediately came under withering fire from dug-in Syrian tanks, which had only the guns and turrets exposed. These tanks were later destroyed by Israeli infantry, but all of the bulldozers were hit, three of them were destroyed, and each of them lost several crews during this terribly costly advance.

Surprisingly, the advance never faltered. The position of Naamush was easily overrun by the advancing tank force. From there it was to follow a rough road that led in the general direction of Zaoura. Unknown to the leading Israeli battalion commander, however, there were two of these mountain tracks, and his battalion took the wrong one, leading east through Sir Adiv to Qala, instead of northeast to Zaoura. This mistake was due to the fact that Mendler and his officers, having been suddenly shifted from the Sinai front to the Golan, were not so familiar with the Golan roadnet as officers of the Northern Command.

It was not until the leading tank battalion was engaged against the defenses of Sir Adiv and Qala—which included antitank obstacles, Su-100 guns, and a variety of antitank weapons—that Mendler realized the mistake. This was not serious, however, since the crest had been reached. Mendler therefore split his brigade, allowing the lead column to continue the attack on Qala, while his second battalion advanced on Zaoura, which was quickly captured at about 4:00 p.m.

The formidable defenses of Qala, however, continued to frustrate Mendler's leading battalion, which was repulsed several times. By this time the attacking battalion had only two tanks still in operation. Shortly after dark, however, Mendler's battalion from Zaoura moved south to envelop the Qala position, which the Syrians then promptly evacuated. Thus the initial mistake in direction resulted in Mendler's brigade being in positions the Israelis had not expected to take until the next day.

Simultaneously, the Golani Brigade had jumped off from the vicinity of Dan, advancing in two columns, each preceded by tanks of the attached armored battalion. One of these columns took the old road toward Banias; the other went across country, between the Syrian positions of Tel Azaziyat and Tel Fahar. Tel Azaziyat was bypassed, and the two principal columns of the brigade converged on Tel Fahar. This Syrian position was surrounded by three double-apron barbed wire fences, was protected by several minefields, and consisted of a number of trenches, machine gun and antitank positions, and dugouts. It was not until after three hours of fierce hand-to-hand fighting in and around the trenches that Colonel Efrat's troops finally cleared this key fortification. This intense, but relatively brief, fight was the most serious of the entire short campaign on this front.

The defenders of Tel Azaziyat, exposed to fire from their right rear, withdrew about dark, and the Golani Brigade soon occupied this height as well. Patrols were pushed further up the height, and by midnight the Golanis had secured positions at the top of the first crest, having achieved their first day's objective.

While the efforts of the main Israeli attack force were thus crowned with success, the infantry brigades of Colonel Emanuel Shehed and Colonel Yehuda Gavish, deployed further south as far as the old Syrian bridgehead across the Jordan at Mishmar Hayarden (at that time a demilitarized zone), carried out their assigned secondary attacks. Shehed's brigade had been in Northern Command reserve; Gavish's brigade had been at Beit Shean. Three key Syrian positions were taken at Darbashiya, Jalabina and Dardara, just northeast of the Sea of Galilee. Soon after nightfall Colonel Uri Ram's armored brigade, which had moved up from Jordan, jumped off from the vicinity of Gonen, north of Darbashiya, and pushed its way up the winding mountain road to seize the village of Rawiya, on the Trans-Arabian Pipeline (known as the TAP line). There was little firing between midnight and dawn, as the Israeli units regrouped, rested, and prepared for continuing the advance the following day, and as Syrian troops continued their withdrawal.

In Damascus the Syrian Government and high command were both surprised and embittered by the Israeli violation of the ceasefire. Since both Egypt and Jordan had been knocked out of the war, the Syrians had no hope of success. They sent an immediate protest to the United Nations Security Council, and issued orders for a withdrawal from the front line defensive zone to a deployment defending Damascus.

It is obvious from the results of the fighting at Qala and Tel Fahar that the Israeli offensive would have been successful even had the Syrians decided to stand and fight all along the line. It is equally obvious from that fighting, however, that a serious Syrian resistance effort would have greatly impeded the Israeli advance. As it was, by late afternoon on the 9th, the Syrians were withdrawing all along the line.

THE SECOND DAY

Shortly after dawn on the 10th of June, General Laner committed Lieutenant Colonel Moshe Bar Kochva's armored brigade, which had followed behind the Golani Brigade up the road from Dan, to attack toward Tel Harma, and the village of Banias. These attacks, virtually unopposed, were successful, and the two brigades, now securely on the Golan Plateau, sent detachments northwest to take the villages of Nukheila and Abassia on the Lebanese border. At the same time the main bodies of the two brigades moved eastward from Banias, north of Zaoura, to clear Ein Fite and Masa'ada on the southern slopes of Mount Hermon.

Also shortly after dawn General Laner sent Mendler's brigade eastward from Zaoura and Qala in the general direction of Kuneitra. At the same time Ram's brigade, after advancing southeast along the TAP line to Kfar Naffakh, also turned northeast toward Kuneitra. Thus by late morning four Israeli brigades were advancing toward Kuneitra on a broad front, in an arc extending from Masa'ada in the north to Kfar Naffakh in the south. The Golani brigade and Bar Kochva's tanks were moving down the road through Mansura; Mendler's brigade, having reached the road junction at Qassett, was driving due east; Ram's brigade was advancing in a northeasterly direction. An expected Syrian counterattack did not materialize, since the Syrians, as has been noted, had decided not to oppose the offensive. By 1:00 p.m. the Israelis had the city of Kuneitra completely surrounded. Mendler's brigade then advanced into the center of the city, encountering no opposition except for an occasional sniper, and after crossing and recrossing the city several times, in standard Israeli urban warfare tactics, reported by 2:30 that it was secure.

Meanwhile, an equally successful but very different kind of operation was taking place on the southern Golan Heights between the Sea of Galilee and the Yarmouk River.

Early on the 10th, General Peled, with a substantially reconstituted division, followed a winding, treacherous road up the almost sheer slope against little opposition. In addition to Colonel Avnon's infantry brigade, Peled's division included Colonel Gur's paratroop brigade and a mixed armored and infantry brigade from Central Command (presumably under Colonel Uri Ram). Avnon's brigade led the advance, climbing the cliffs to Tawafik and capturing the abandoned village at about 3:00 p.m. The armor then followed, along the winding Yarmouk Valley road to the heights. Simultaneously a helicopter-borne paratroop battalion took the towns of Fiq and El Al, cutting the lines of communication of the few Syrian troops remaining in the southwestern Golan area. This battalion then proceeded to dash northward toward Boutmiya and the Rafid junction.

Colonel Shehed sent his armored battalion eastward and southeastward from Darbashiya, sweeping through the central section of the Golan to join Peled and his paratroopers at Boutmiya. At the same time Shehed's infantry and paratroop battalions drove south into the demilitarized zone at Mishmar Hayarden, and captured the Bridge of Jacob's Daughters. From there they turned eastward to follow their armored battalion toward Al Kushniya and Boutmiya. At the same time the brigade of Colonel Gavish moved southward from Dardara to clear the eastern shore of the Sea of Galilee.

Meanwhile, in New York, the United Nations Security Council had met again in emergency session on June 9, after the outbreak of fighting on the Golan front. By late evening of the 9th—early morning of the 10th in the Middle East—a final vote on a generally acceptable resolution seemed to be approaching. Tel Aviv was informed by Israeli Foreign Minister Abba Eban, who was conducting the debate for Israel. By this time General Rabin knew that a complete breakthrough had been achieved on the Golan front, but (as he later told this author) was reluctant to call off the exploitation until his troops had captured Kuneitra, and had established a reasonable defensible perimeter on the eastern Golan Heights, overlooking the Damascus Plain. At his request, therefore, Mr. Eban was able to stall for time, on the logical basis of need "to consult his government." When, shortly before noon in Tel Aviv, Rabin was certain that Kuneitra would soon be taken, the word was flashed to Mr. Eban in New York. It was just after dawn, New York time, when the Security Council approved the resolution, calling for a ceasefire to be effective in six hours.

Meanwhile the Israeli troops had taken all of their objectives, and

so were ready to comply when the ceasefire became effective at
6:30 p.m.

Israeli losses in this two-day battle of the Golan Heights are estimated
at 127 killed and 625 wounded; 160 Israeli tanks were knocked out, but
most of them were soon repaired. Syrian losses have never been officially reported, but were estimated at about 600 killed, 700 wounded,
and about 570 captured or missing. The Syrians lost 73 tanks and 13
Su-100s; of these about 40 were captured intact. The Syrians also lost
about 130 artillery pieces, half of these destroyed by Israeli artillery or
air strikes, the rest captured.

There were a number of reports that Soviet officers were present
with the Syrian troops during the battle, that they had been heard
conversing in Russian on the radio, and that five Soviet officers had
been captured. It was also reported that Russian radio transmissions
were intercepted by the Israelis and that some had been heard by
Russian-speaking news correspondents who were privately monitoring the
airwaves. After the war General Elazar implied that Russian radio signals had been heard. The Israeli military spokesman categorically denied,
however, that any Soviet officers or other Russian advisers had been
captured.

The Syrians vigorously deny that there was any participation either
in planning or in operational direction by any Russian officer. They
say that absolutely no Russian transmissions were made on their radio
nets. If there was any Russian transmission, they suggest it was by
Russian-speaking Israelis. There is no reason not to accept at face
value both the Syrian statements and that of the IDF spokesman.

14

The War at Sea

EGYPTIAN NAVAL PREPARATIONS

In the years following the 1956 War the Egyptian Navy had been substantially reorganized, largely along Soviet lines. The major changes had been increased emphasis on submarine warfare and the use of small guided missile boats. Numbers of Russian-built submarines, and *Komar* and *Osa* guided missile boats armed with Styx missiles, were received, as well as destroyers, patrol boats, minesweepers, and minelayers. The crews were well trained in the operation of their new craft, equipment, and weapons. While the reorganization was not complete, by mid-1957 the Egyptian Navy was probably better prepared for combat than any of the other three armed services: Army, Air Force, and Air Defense Force.

The Egyptian Navy, however, was not really alerted to the possibility—let alone the likelihood—of war in late May and early June. President Nasser, so clear in his own mind that he would not allow the crisis to get out of hand and degenerate into war, and so strangely oblivious to the effects of his actions on the Israelis, had not thought to provide the Navy with any warnings for more-than-usual alertness. Thus when the war suddenly broke out on June 5, the Navy had a number of long-prepared contingency plans, but was quite unready for any immediate action other than general coastal defense and local security.

ISRAELI NAVAL PREPARATIONS

Between 1956 and 1967 the Israeli Navy, unable to find funds or resources to purchase new warships abroad, dwindled with the retirement of most of its original destroyers. The only acquisitions, two British S-class submarines (World War II veterans) and several landing craft, did not offset the contraction. Meanwhile, Israeli naval planners watched Egypt expand and modernize its fleet.

Israeli naval technicians responded to this by developing a new ship-to-ship cruise missile and then, in conjunction with a West German shipbuilder, designing a cheap, efficient, and versatile fast patrol boat as a delivery platform. Thus, Israel was planning to base its entire naval capability on a flotilla made up of a single` type of fast patrol vessel, each with missiles that would theoretically give it the explosive firepower of a fleet of eight-inch cruisers without the vulnerability, expense, and complexity of an all-gun armament.

The design evolved into the 250-ton *Saar* class, specially adapted to "Gabriel" surface-to-surface missile (SSM) system. Two variants were planned: (1) six boats with differing combinations of Israeli-developed Gabriel missiles, 40mm AA guns, and ASW torpedoes; (2) six gunboat versions armed with a 76mm dual-purpose gun replacing the 40mm guns and one or two of the missile launcher tubes.

Because of political developments in West Germany, which was under economic and political pressure from the Arab League, the Israelis had to transfer the building contract to a shipyard in Cherbourg, France. Considerable time was consequently lost, and construction did not begin until late spring 1965. Originally it was planned that six boats would be built in the foreign yard while Israel observed and garnered the technology for domestic construction of the next six craft. Because of the delay, however, all twelve boats were assigned to the French builders. The Israelis planned to build an improved *Saar* class at home after the first twelve had been delivered.

The Gabriel missile was designed to follow a wave-skimming flight path which evaded all known acquisition and tracking sensors. The combined storage/launcher rack was weatherproofed, carrying all projectiles in instant readiness.

All this, however, was in the future. By May, 1967, not one of the new missile craft had been delivered.

The line-up of the principal combat elements of the opposing fleets at that time was as follows:

Type	Israel	Egypt
Destroyers	3	7
Submarines	3	12
Missile-carriers	—	18
Antisubmarine craft	1	12
Motor torpedo boats	8	32

Only one of the Israelis' three destroyers was in service, and of their three World War II-vintage submarines, one, the *Rahaf*, was not fit to submerge, and another was in mothballs. On May 19, Israel embarked on a crash program to bring its navy to peak readiness, notwithstanding the limited number and the age of its vessels.

At this point, the Israeli Navy had twice as many seamen as could be accommodated by the existing ships and craft. A new naval base was set up at Ashdod from which MTBs and light naval craft could operate; new radar and new guns were installed in a number of vessels. Several fishing trawlers were armed for patrol work. The submarine which could not submerge, *Rahaf*, was fitted with sonar and armed with depth charges to serve as an antisubmarine patrol vessel. Toward the end of May, the ex-Egyptian destroyer *Ibrahim-Al-Awwal*, re-christened *Haifa*, was refitted, repainted and put to sea within the amazingly short period of 48 hours. Several landing craft being built in Israeli yards, and not due for completion until August, were readied for sea within five days of the alert; one of them had but two of its three engines and an improvised rudder, but it was nonetheless pressed into service.

The Israelis, due to their overall numerical inferiority, relied extensively on deception and surprise to "multiply" combat power. This was particularly applicable to their navy, by far the weakest of the three Israeli services. The major goal of the Israeli Navy was to weaken Egyptian naval presence in the Mediterranean as much as possible in order to diminish the threat to the Israeli population centers on the Mediterranean coast. One move to this end was accomplished by moving four landing craft overland to Eilat conspicuously by daylight, then removing them 15 kilometers inland by night to move them back into Eilat the following day. The maneuver was repeated several times during the first days of November to give the illusion of a major surface threat to Sharm el Sheikh. It was reinforced by dispatching the only three MTB's based at Eilat on patrols toward the Red Sea. Actually, the Israeli vessels had very limited cruising radius and could make the round trip only if they had favorable winds both ways.

The ruse was successful. On the outbreak of hostilities 30% of the Egyptian fleet was in the Red Sea, where its activities contributed little to the war effort. When Nasser blocked the Suez Canal with old ships, the vessels of the Red Sea flotilla could no longer return to the Mediterranean, and they finally docked at the Yemeni port of Hodeida, near the southern end of the Red Sea.

OPERATIONS

It had been an Egyptian naval action which precipitated the war. In mid-May, as has been noted earlier, President Nasser proclaimed a blockade against Israeli and Israel-bound shipping in the Strait of Tiran. Actually, the blockade was never enforced—but it was never tested, either.

The evening of D-Day, Monday, June 5, Israeli frogmen tried to attack Egyptian warships in both of Egypt's main Mediterranean harbors,

Port Said and Alexandria. The principal objective was to damage as many Egyptian warships as possible.

At Port Said, as the attacking torpedo boats approached, two *Osa* missile craft came out from behind the breakwater and challenged. However, the range was too short for use of their missiles and, after a brief exchange of fire, they withdrew into the harbor.

Israeli frogmen swam into the harbor to search for three MTBs and three antisubmarine corvettes believed sheltered there, in addition to the two *Osa* craft just repulsed. These vessels could not be found, and two oil tankers discovered instead were not attacked, due (say the Israelis) to fear of harming the port's civilian population. The frogmen returned, their misssion unaccomplished.

All through the night of the 5th, the Israeli vessels patrolled the mouth of the harbor to block any attempt to bring naval reinforcements from Alexandria. The Israelis were particularly concerned about the fast *Osa* and *Komar* patrol boats with their capability of a fast approach to within 35 miles of Tel Aviv (the Styx missile's extreme range), from which they could send 1,000-pound warheads against the city.

The movement from Alexandria did not, in fact, take place, since a handful of other Israeli vessels had tied up the Egyptian Navy at that port as well. The next morning, June 6, the Egyptian naval detachment pulled out from Port Said and withdrew to Alexandria, where the feared *Osa* and *Komar* launchers posed no threat to the Israeli coast.

In the Israeli attempt to disable vessels at Alexandria, the single operational Israeli submarine disembarked frogmen bearing explosive charges, who penetrated the harbor without incident. The Israelis believe that two Egyptian *Osa* boats and two submarines were either damaged or destroyed, but this was not confirmed. The Egyptians insist that the frogmen at Alexandria, like those at Port Said, completely failed in their mission. In accordance with standard security precautions, the Egyptians had shifted the locations of all warships. They report that the frogmen damaged only one dredge, which was not sunk. The Israeli submarine patrolled at the rendezvous point all that night, and again at an appointed hour the following night. However the frogmen did not return. The Egyptians captured all six Israeli frogmen.

An Israeli amphibious assault against El Arish, the Egyptian logistics center in Sinai, had been planned for Monday night, June 5, in conjunction with a para-drop, but this was cancelled a few hours before H-hour, due to the excellent progress of Tal's armored forces through Khan Yunis and Rafah.

After dark on June 6, carrying out a previously-prepared plan, an

Egyptian flotilla in the Red Sea entered the Gulf of Aqaba, for the purpose of carrying out a night attack on Eilat. The flotilla, consisting of two destroyers and six missile and torpedo boats, intended to hit the Israeli port shortly after midnight, and then be out of the confined waters of the Gulf before sunrise. The original plan, however, had contemplated support from the Egyptian Air Force, which of course was unable to provide such support after its devastating losses the previous day. When the naval commander, Admiral Sheikh, realized that he could have no air support, he decided that the risk to his ships would be too great. Thirty miles from Eilat the flotilla reversed course, and it returned to the Red Sea through the Gulf of Tiran early in the morning. The Egyptian admiral's decision was probably justified; 20 miles south of Eilat the three Israeli MTBs were lying in ambush position, and the Israeli Air Force had also been alerted to move in to their support.

There was only one other Egyptian naval offensive action of any significance. On the evening of June 6, three Egyptian submarines approached the Israeli coast, two at points immediately north and south of Haifa and the third near Ashdod. It is not known whether they came to attack shipping or to land saboteurs. Although they had only four sonar sets in their fleet, the Israelis detected and depth-charged all three of the submarines. All were driven off, and one was believed damaged. The commander of the Israeli Navy, Rear Admiral (then Brigadier General) Shlomo Erell, was pleased that, despite all the sophisticated equipment aboard the Egyptian submarines, they were not able to "fox" the Israeli sonar completely. However, the conspicuous and excessive use of their periscopes by the Egyptians was a major factor in the Israeli success.

Due to its lack of pre-war preparation, the Egyptian Navy had only just begun to move to its planned blockading stations when the end of the war halted further deployment. During the final hours of the conflict the Egyptian Navy did become involved in the land operations. On June 8 a squadron of missile boats, patrolling off the Sinai coast between Port Said and El Arish, scored some long-range hits on an Israeli armored convoy on the coastal road. That same day Egyptian warships added their defensive firepower to the ground forces, as Israeli tanks approached the Suez Canal near Suez, Port Tewfik, and Port Said.

THE *LIBERTY* INCIDENT

The USS *Liberty*, an Elint (Electronics Intelligence) vessel, was operating in the southeast corner of the Mediterranean when the war broke out. On the afternoon of June 8 she was steaming west-northwest at five knots, some 14 nautical miles north of El Arish, when she was unexpectedly attacked by Israeli MTBs and fighter planes. Thirty-four members of her crew were killed and 164 wounded. By excellent seamanship and good luck the vessel was saved, and was able to reach Malta on June 14.

An official U.S. release issued June 8 noted that the *Liberty* had departed Rota, Spain, on June 2 and had been sent to the Sinai coast to assure communications between U.S. Government posts in the Middle East, since there would be heavy message traffic caused by evacuation of U.S. citizens from the various combatant countries. This explanation seems odd in view of the extensive communications installations available in U.S. consulates and embassies.

The extent of the U.S. casualties sustained, the Israeli failure to identify the ship as American despite prominent display of flag and signals, and the persistence of the attack after identification should have been obvious, all contribute to the suspicion that Israel knew the ship to be American from the start, and attacked because of fear that the vessel's intelligence-gathering efforts could harm Israel. Although Israel expressed regret, it has never apologized or admitted culpability, and offered to make restitution to the injured and families of the dead—nearly $7 million—only to retain U.S. goodwill.

The incident has never been satisfactorily explained by either the U.S. or the Israeli governments.[1]

---

[1] See "A Conspiracy of Silence," by Anthony Pearson, *Penthouse,* May and June 1976, for a sensational, but well documented, review of the incident and its aftermath.

15

Envoie

LOSSES

All participants have published (or have provided to the author) official reports of casualties and equipment losses, in varying degrees of completeness. For a variety of reasons even the official reports of the participants are not fully reliable. For instance, the reported Israeli figure for killed in action apparently does not include casualties who later died from wounds, and the wounded statistics do not include lightly wounded who were not evacuated to general hospitals.

The figures listed below, however, come from a variety of sources and are a composite estimate as close to accurate as is possible from available unclassified data.

	Killed	Wounded	Captured /Missing	Total Casualties	Tanks Lost	Aircraft Lost
Israel	983	4,517	15	5,515	394[1]	40
(vs. Egypt)	303	1,450	11	1,764	122	—
(vs. Jordan)	553	2,442	0	2,995	112	—
(vs. Syria)	127	625	4	756	160	—
Arabs	4,296	6,121	7,550	17,967	965[2]	444
(Egypt)	3,000	5,000	4,980	12,980	700	356[3]
(Jordan)[4]	696	421	2,000[5]	3,117	179	18
(Syria)	600	700	570	1,870	86	55
(Iraq)	—	—	—	—	—	15

[1] At least half of these were repaired and returned to full operational status.

[2] About 150 captured T-54/55s were modified by the Israelis and put into their postwar inventory, thus largely offsetting unrepairable losses during the war.

[3] Of these, 322 were lost the first day.

[4] Recent figures, official except for estimate of missing; 20% factor added to killed and wounded to allow for these losses among missing.

[5] Of these, 530 were prisoners of war.

333

QUALITATIVE ASSESSMENT

Comparing the military performance of the Arabs and the Israelis in this war is difficult, since it was in effect three wars, with three very different Arab armies—united in ideology and to some extent in culture, but almost entirely independent of each other in their military traditions and customs—and of course three entirely different kinds of combat situations. The Arab armies were full-time, regular forces, but the bulk of the Israeli combat trooops were part-time soldiers, hastily mobilized for combat.

Because the Israelis clearly won the war, it must be agreed that their overall combat performance was better; and this superiority is evident in assessing *how* they won. They were more effective in combat, that is to say, their overall losses as well as unit losses in relation to their strength were consistently lower than those of any of the Arab armies, and the losses they inflicted on their opponents were consistently greater. Israeli combat units were more aggressive, more effective in the integrated employment of their weapons, more responsive to leadership.

Among the Arabs the Jordanians performed best. It is difficult to assess the Syrian performance, since on the basis of a political decision they did not make a determined defense; in the one serious engagement that took place the Syrians were not very effective in use of strong fortifications and very defensible terrain. The poor Syrian performance reflects the lack of continuity in leadership, training, and doctrine that resulted from the frequent changes in the Syrian government in previous years. The Egyptians individually and as units for the most part performed as well as the Jordanians, in a more difficult strategic situation, but the top Egyptian leadership was a fatal handicap.

The failure at the top of the Egyptian command cannot be overemphasized. Because of the demonstrated difference in Israeli and Egyptian combat effectiveness not even a firm and competent senior commander could have changed the final outcome of the war, but he certainly could have altered its course. Although some of the commanders below Field Marshal Amer proved their incompetence, and in some instances their cowardice, others gave highly creditable performances, and like the Jordanians, both commanders and staff officers reacted promptly and effectively to difficult combat situations. If there was one common weakness among higher and intermediate commanders of all of the Arab armies, it was inadequate coordination between brigades and divisions. The Israeli top-level leadership was consistently superior to that of all of the Arabs. This was reflected not only in the preparation of plans, but also in rapid adjustment and accommodation of plans to unexpected circumstances.

What was the reason for this Israeli superiority both in unit combat effectiveness and in top-level leadership? There appear to be three elements to the answer. In the first place, from company to top command, the Israeli leaders were more flexible, aggressive, and dynamic. Second, their doctrine, and its execution, were more suitable to the conditions in which they fought. Third, the more Western-oriented and more cosmopolitan Israelis seem to have adapted better to the weapons and technologically sophisticated equipment with which they had been provided. Because of the differences in the two cultures and societies they were clearly more self-reliant, while at the same time they were better able to cooperate with each other in team tasks and were more receptive than the Arab soldiers to military discipline and training. They were more flexible, more alert, more aggressive than their opponents, although individually they do not seem to have been braver, more intelligent, or more highly motivated. In combat as a group they were more effective. Research into the records of German troops in World War II shows a similar superiority in combat effectiveness over the forces of all opposing Allied nations. The extent to which national forces consistently perform at a certain degree of effectiveness is a subject that calls for serious analysis.

There were three other extremely significant factors in the Israeli 1967 victories. First, and most important, was the successful achievement of surprise. The unexpected attacks from the air and on the ground seriously disrupted the Egyptian command, and the Jordanians to a lesser extent. The Egyptians made no adequate response, giving the Israelis an initial advantage in the Sinai which would have been very difficult to overcome even had the top command been competent.

The second factor, of almost comparable importance in the continuing battle, was the Israeli superiority in the air, achieved by the carefully planned and superbly executed attacks which started the war in the early morning of June 5. With almost complete control of the air the Israelis were able to capitalize on the ground on their initial advantage of surprise and their superior combat effectiveness without having to defend against attacks from their enemies' air weapons. The full significance of this air superiority, and the devastating effect of the air attacks upon the Arab ground troops, seems not to have been fully appreciated even by the Israelis, who after all have never been under truly effective hostile air attack themselves.

Third—and, while less important than the other two, in itself probably a decisively significant factor—was the Israelis' superior use of armor. They had a substantial number of good tanks and other armored vehicles, and they used them well. Their armored doctrine emphasized shock action and mobility, and their performance was characterized by boldness, flexibility, and aggressiveness. These combined to make armor the principal ground-force element in the Israeli victory. In analyzing the battles of this war, however, the Israelis may have over-emphasized the extent to which their armored forces were responsible for their overwhelming victory, and failed to give due weight to the contribution of surprise and their devastating airpower. Consequently, in the years that followed they seem to have neglected infantry and artillery as they built up their strength in tanks.

Other considerations, here mentioned only briefly, were:

While the two previous Arab-Israeli Wars had been fought largely with weapons and equipment of World War II vintage (with some facelifting in the 1956 War), some completely new weapons appeared on the 1967 battlefields and in the air encounters overhead. The most important of these were antiaircraft and antitank missiles. However, these new weapons did not seem to have much effect upon the tactics of either side, or upon the outcomes of any major engagements.

A new generation of tanks was also employed; on the Arab side the Soviet-made T-54/55 had largely replaced the T-34, and on the Israeli side the British-made Centurion and the American-made Patton (M48) were replacing the World War II-type Sherman. On the other hand, Israeli modifications of the Sherman (a new and bigger gun and a new engine) enabled it to compete on virtually equal terms with the Jordanians' M48 Pattons.

American military men, their eyes glued on Southeast Asia, and seeing future conflict largely in terms of "counterinsurgency," gave less attention to these developments in the Middle East than they should have. European soldiers, sailors, and airmen, however, were not so distracted, and probably better evaluated the military significance of the three Israeli lightning campaigns. None were more interested, or paid greater attention, than the Soviets, whose advisors and observers on the ground had an opportunity to see some of their best materiel in action against modern weapons and equipment the Israelis had procured from the West. Despite the generally poor performance of the troops equipped with their weapons, the Soviets apparently saw no major technical or conceptual shortcomings, while noting possible ways to improve their equipment's performance and to degrade that of the West. On the other hand, at least comparable and offsetting ob-servations and deductions were being made by the Israelis.

APPROXIMATE LAND AND AIR FORCE STRENGTHS
1967 War

	Israel	Arabs	Egypt	Jordan	Syria	Iraq
Mobilized Operational Manpower[1] ...	250,000	328,000	210,000	55,000	63,000	—
Brigades	25	42	22	10	12	—
Artillery Pieces	200	960	575	263	315	—
Tanks	1,000[2]	2,330	1,300[5]	288[7]	750	—
APCs	1,500[3]	1,845	1,050	210	585	—
SAMs	50	160	160	0	0	0
AA Guns	550	2,000+	950	143	1,000	—
Combat Aircraft	286[4]	682	431[6]	18	127[8]	106[9]

[1] On the Arab side includes only forces available for commitment.

[2] 200 M48s, 250 Centurions, 150 AMX-13s, 400 Shermans and Super-Shermans.

[3] M3 Halftracks.

[4] Includes 92 Mirages, 24 Super-Mystères, 82 Mystères, 55 Ouragans, 24 light bombers.

[5] Includes 400+ T-34s, 450+ T-54/55s, 100+ Su-100s, 100+ JS-3s.

[6] Includes 55 Su-6s, 163 MiG-21s, 40 MiG-19s, 100 MiG-15/17s, 30 Tu-16s, 43 Il-28s; only 350 pilots.

[7] Includes about 200 M48s, about 90 Centurions.

[8] Includes 40 MiG-21/19s, 68 MiG-15/17s, 15 Tu-16s, 4 Il-28s.

[9] About 45 committed.

ESTIMATED NAVAL STRENGTHS
1967 War

	Israel	Egypt	Syria
Manpower	4,000	13,000	1,000
Patrol and Torpedo Boats	9	44	17
Guided Missile Boats	0	18[1]	4[2]
Destroyers and Frigates	3	7	0
Submarines	3	12	0
Amphibious Craft	0	5	0
Small Craft	?	?	?
Vessel Totals	15+	86+	21+

[1] Includes 8 *Komar* class and 10 *Osa* class.

[2] *Komar* class, just received; not ready for combat.

ISRAELI ORDER OF BATTLE
1967 War

Minister of Defense	(Gen) Moshe Dayan
Chief of Staff	Lt Gen Yitzhak Rabin
Southern Command	BG Yeshayahu Gavish
Armored Division	BG Israel Tal
Armored Brigade (7th)	Col Shmuel Gonen
Armored Brigade	Col Menachem Aviram
Paratroop Brigade	Col Rafael Eitan
Recon Task Force (Armored Regt)	Col Uri Baron
("Granit" Task Force)	Col Granit Yisrael
Armored Division	BG Avraham Yoffe
Armored Brigade	Col Isska Shadni
Armored Brigade	Col Elhanan Sela
Armored Division	BG Ariel Sharon
Armored Brigade	Col Mordechai Zippori
Infantry Brigade	Col Kutty Adam
Paratroop Brigade°	Col Danny Matt
Ind. Armored Brigade	Col Albert Mendler°°
Ind. Infantry Brigade (+)	Col Yehuda Reshef (Gaza area)
Ind. Paratroop Task Force	Col Aharon Davidi (Sharm el Sheikh area)
Central Command	BG Uzi Narkiss
Infantry Brigade (Jerusalem, Etzioni)	Col Eliezer Amitai
Paratroop Brigade°	Col Mordechai Gur
Mechanized Brigade (Harel)	Col Uri Ben-Ari
Infantry Brigade	Col Ze'ev Shehem (Kalkyllia)
Infantry Brigade	Col Moshe Yotvat (Latrun)
Northern Command	BG David Elazar
Jordan—	
Armored Division	BG Elad Peled°°
Infantry Brigade°	Col Aharon Avnon
Armored Brigade°	LTC Moshe Bar Kochva
Armored Brigade°	Col Uri Rom
Ind. Infantry Brigade (+)°	Col Yehuda Gavish (Beit Shean)
Syria—	
Composite Division	BG Dan Laner
Armored Brigade	Col Albert Mendler
Infantry Brigade (Golani)	Col Yona Efrat
Infantry Brigade	Col Emmanuel Shehed

° Unit diverted north to Syria.
°° Commander and hqs transferred north to Syria.

EGYPTIAN ORDER OF BATTLE
June 1967

Commander in Chief and 1st Deputy President	F.M. Mohammed Abd el Hakim Amer
Chief of Staff Armed Forces	Lt. Gen. Anwhar al Khadi
Front Commander in Chief	Gen. Abd el Mohsen Mortagui
Front Chief of Staff	Maj. Gen. Ahmed Ismail Ali
Field Army Commander	Lt. Gen. Salah el din Mohsen
2nd Infantry Division	Maj. Gen. Sadi Naguib
3rd Infantry Division	Maj. Gen. Osman Nasser
4th Armored Division	Maj. Gen. Sidki el Ghoul
Armored Task Force	Maj. Gen. Saad el Shazli
6th Mechanized Division	Maj. Gen. Abd el Kader Hassan
1st Armored Brigade	Brig. Hussein abd el Nataf
125th Armored Brigade	Brig. Ahmed El-Naby
7th Infantry Division	Maj. Gen. Abd el Aziz Soliman
20th PLA Division (Gaza)	Maj. Gen. Mohommed Abd el Moneim Hasni
Independent Infantry Brigade (Sharm el Sheikh)	Brig. Mohommed Abd el Moneim Khalil
Air Force	Gen. Mohammed Sidki Mahmoud
Navy	Admiral Soliman Ezzat
Commander in Chief, United Arab Command	Gen. Ali Amer

JORDANIAN ORDER OF BATTLE
June 1967

Allied Commander of the Jordanian Front	Gen. Abdul Moneim Riadh (Egyptian)
Commander in Chief	Field Marshal Habis el Majali
Deputy Commander in Chief	Gen. Sherif Nasir ben Jamil
Chief of Staff	Maj. Gen. Amer Khammash
Commanding General, West Front	Maj. Gen. Mohommed Ahmed Salim
Immam Ali Infantry Brigade	Brig. Ahmed Shihadeh
Hittin Infantry Brigade (Hebron)	Brig. Bahjet Muhaisin
25th (Khalid Ben El Walid) Infantry Brigade (Jenin)	Lt. Col. Awad Mohommed El Khalidi
60th Armored Brigade (Jericho)	Brig. Sherif Zeid ben Shaker
40th Armored Brigade (Damiya)	Brig. Rakan Inad El Jazi
27th (King Talal) Infantry Brigade (Jerusalem)	Brig. Ata Ali
Qadisiyeh Infantry Brigade (Valley Sector)	Brig. Qasim El Maayteh
Princess Alia Infantry Brigade (Nablus)	Brig. Turki Baarah
El Hashimi Infantry Brigade (Ramallah)	Col. Kamal El Taher
El Yarmouk Infantry Brigade (Northern Sector)	Col. Mufadi Abdul Musleh
Air Force	Gen. Saleh Kurdi

SYRIAN ORDER OF BATTLE
June 1967

Minister of Defense	Lt. Gen. Hafiz al Assad
Chief of Staff, Commanding	
General, Field Army	Maj. Gen. Ahmed Souedani
12th Group Brigade	Col. Ahmed Amir
11th Infantry Brigade	
132d Reserve Infantry Brigade	
89th Reserve Infantry Brigade	
44th Armored Brigade	
35th Group Brigade	Brig. Gen. Said Tayan
8th Infantry Brigade	
19th Infantry Brigade	
32d Infantry Brigade	
17th Mechanized Infantry Brigade	
42d Group Brigade	Brig. Gen. Abdul Razzak Dardari
14th Armored Brigade	
25th Infantry Brigade	
50th Reserve Infantry Brigade	
60th Reserve Infantry Brigade	
23d Infantry Brigade (Latakia)	
Air Force	Lt. Gen. Hafiz al Assad
Navy	Brig. Gen. Mustafa Shuman

BOOK FOUR

The War of Attrition, 1967-1970

1

From Disaster to Defiance

REACTIONS TO THE "THIRD ROUND"

Israel's stunning military victory in the Six Day War of June 1967 left in its wake a profound feeling of humiliation and bitterness among the defeated Arabs. Driven by a desire to regain their conquered territory and restore their battered sense of self-respect, but all too aware of their inability to do either by military means—at least in the immediate future—the Arabs turned their attention to possible political and diplomatic solutions. At the same time, to place some pressure on Israel, as well as to seek a means of restoring some of their badly damaged military capability, they followed a policy of harassment against the Israeli troops in the occupied territories, attacking readily available targets for the purpose of inflicting limited, but painful, casualties on the Israeli forces. Palestinian guerrillas undertook increasingly intensive operations along and within the borders of Israel itself.

Egypt, where the shock and cost of defeat had been greatest, took the lead in this grim effort to recover. In immediate reaction to the defeat, for which he assumed full responsibility, on June 9 President Nasser resigned the presidency of Egypt. To the surprise of some Western observers, however, there was a spontaneous popular reaction in Egypt (and other Arab countries as well), demanding that Nasser retain his governmental posts, and provide the leadership so badly needed. Some foreigners have suggested that this reaction was orchestrated by Nasser and his associates; it may have been, but the popular and emotional response was obviously sincere and overwhelming. The vast majority of the Egyptian people—with the support of much of the Arab world—made clear its collective will; Nasser, obviously moved by a popular and democratic vote of confidence, withdrew his resignation and again took up the reins of government. On June 19 he made a sweeping reorganization of his government, including the dismissal of inept Field Marshal Amer, who was replaced by General Mohammed Fawzi. General Abdul Moneim Riadh became Chief of Staff.

On June 21 President Nikolai Podgorny of the Soviet Union led a Russian delegation to Egypt, to dramatize the willingness and determination of the Soviet Union to support the military recovery of

Egypt under the leadership of Nasser. In early July Podgorny made similar visits to both Syria and Iraq. In all three countries joint communiques were issued in which the USSR pledged itself to assist the Arabs against "Israeli aggression" and to support the "practical measures that should be taken to wipe out the results of this aggression." As evidence of this determination, Marshal Matvei Zakharov remained in Egypt for a month to supervise the initiation of Soviet military assistance.

In Israel the outcome of the war gave rise to feelings of jubilation, increased security, and some complacency. The IDF had seized control of the Old City of Jerusalem, which—although a Holy City to Jews, Christians, and Moslems—had been closed to Israelis since the 1948 War. On June 28 Israel officially annexed the Old City—in defiance of Security Council resolutions—but otherwise, the occupied territories remained under military government. The occupation of Syria's Golan Heights meant that the Israeli settlements in the Huleh Valley, which had suffered frequent artillery bombardment from Syria for nineteen years, were now beyond the range of Syrian guns.[1] The seizure of the West Bank of the Jordan River provided Israel with a new, defensible eastern frontier—however temporary it might be as a ceasefire line. Finally, the IDF had occupied Egypt's Sinai Peninsula, which, with its 23,200 square miles of desert and its crucial water obstacle—the Suez Canal—served as an enormous and effective buffer zone between the Israel Defense Forces and the Egyptian Army, the most dangerous potential antagonist.

In their euphoria the Israelis had at first expected that the regime of Egyptian President Nasser, discredited in the eyes of the Arab world by his devastating losses in the recent war, would soon be replaced by a new administration which would be willing to negotiate a lasting peace setttlement.[2] Disappointed in this hope, the Israelis nonetheless were satisfied that even if a peace settlement were not immediately forthcoming it would be many years—some said many generations—before the Arab armies would again be able to pose a credible threat to Israeli security. For this reason, and because of political uncertainty over the future of the occupied territories, the Israelis did not believe it necessary to take expensive measures for the defense of the Sinai Peninsula; there was even some discussion in Israel of reducing the strength of the IDF to minimum levels.[3]

Most foreign opinion—at least in the West—assessed the results of

[1] However, the Israelis promptly built settlements in the newly occupied Golan territory, which were then, of course, within Syrian artillery range.

[2] Luttwak and Horowitz, *op. cit.*, p. 314.

[3] Zeev Schiff, *A History of the Israeli Army (1870-1974)* (San Francisco, 1975), p. 241.

the war much as did the Israelis. Most people in the United States and Britain, where before the war generally pro-Israel public opinion had been fearful for Israel's chances of survival in a three-front conflict, were pleased by the scope and decisiveness of the Israeli victory. French President Charles de Gaulle, on the other hand, had warned during the pre-war crisis that, if Israel started a war, he would stop all sales of military equipment to Israelis. Accordingly, he denounced Israel for having started the war, and put an embargo on military sales to Israel and her neighboring "confrontation" Arab states. Since France was not at that time supplying weapons to the Arab states, this affected only Israel immediately. At the same time, however, as de Gaulle of course recognized, this action opened up far wider markets for French military sales to other Arab states. However, neither de Gaulle nor other responsible French leaders were under any illusions as to the extent of the Arab defeat. Retired French General André Beaufre, for instance, predicted that it would take a generation for the Arabs to recover.

The Israelis quite rightly attributed their resounding success to more effective military manpower, which, understandably, they called a "better quality" of manpower. In this qualitative comparison, however, they seem to have underrated some of the factors which contributed to the outcome. For instance, they apparently did not fully recognize the extent to which their task in the Sinai was made substantially easier by Field Marshal Amer's withdrawal order of June 6. This order had had two adverse effects on Egyptian performance, effects which the Israelis recognized, but did not properly evaluate. In the first place, after June 6 the Egyptians were delaying rather than defending; second, the uncoordinated and unsystematic withdrawal had a psychological effect which substantially reduced the effectiveness even of the delaying actions.

The Israelis' experience in the 1967 War seemed to confirm their 1956 War assessment of the apparent inability of the Egyptians to offer sustained resistance. The Israelis paid little attention to the coincidence of early withdrawal in both wars, or else they tended to assume that Egyptian mention of the coincidence was merely a face-saving excuse. In fact, however, the Israeli victory in both wars was certain before the withdrawal orders, and, save for the determined Egyptian defense of the Mitla Pass and Abu Ageila in 1956, the Israelis encountered little really determined and effective defense in either of these wars. And the success of the carefully-planned 1967 Israeli response to the 1956 setback at Abu Ageila seems to have contributed to their general underestimation of the Egyptians' military capabilities.

While clearly realizing the importance of what their Air Force had accomplished in June 1967, the Israelis also do not seem to have fully recognized the devastating physical and psychological effects of their airpower on the Arabs' combat capability. In other words, they failed to understand that without the full effect of that airpower, their margin of combat effectiveness superiority over the Arabs woud have been lessened to a substantial degree.

These two misinterpretations of the operational developments of the 1967 War apparently contributed to some questionable conclusions about the importance and use of armored forces. Evidence of this is found in a serious and scholarly history of the Israeli Army, which suggests that Israeli military planners interpreted the tactical operations of Israeli armored formations, and particularly those of General Tal's division, as "a basic innovation over the grand tactics developed during the Second World War [that] represented a new stage in the integration of armour and infantry," and were convinced of "the diminished role of the infantry" in the 1967 War.[4] Subsequent events offer further evidence that the Israelis overestimated the capabilities of their armored units as self-contained, all purpose forces.

These critical comments are not intended to imply that Israeli military men shared the tendency toward complacency which was undoubtedly present in their civilian society. They recognized that the Arabs were bent on revenge, and they had considerable and proper respect for Arab numbers. So the years after the 1967 War were not frittered away by the IDF. On the contrary, Israeli military leaders at all levels continued unceasing efforts to improve themselves and the army, to make their mobilization more efficient, and to avoid any tendency toward complacency.

Although plunged to the depths of gloom and frustration, the Arabs —particularly Egyptians and Jordanians—seem to have read the lessons of the 1967 War somewhat better than did the Israelis. Perhaps the most important thing was their recognition of their own cultural tendency toward self-delusion, and their efforts to control this characteristic in the future. The outcome of the war was so stark, of course, that there was litttle basis for any self-delusion. And so for the first time, and with little or no coordination across national boundaries in the Arab world, Arabs in general began to take a more objective view of the struggle with Israel.

First and foremost, they faced up to the fact that Israel "was here to stay." It was obviously ridiculous to think of "annihilating" a state that had so clearly demonstrated its military superiority over all of its neighbors, individually and in combination. Sights which had previously been set on the "destruction" of Israel, or a return to the 1947 UN Partition plan boundaries—which the Israelis considered

---

[4] Luttwak and Horowitz, *op. cit.*, pp. 291-292.

tantamount to destruction—were now lowered to regaining the territories occupied by Israel during the Six Day War. Connected with this was a somewhat nebulous demand for "restoration of the rights of the Palestinian Arabs," but within the neighboring countries that battle cry was at the time largely pro forma.

This shift by the Arabs toward reality and objectivity also required a begrudging acknowledgement that Israel had won because of battlefield superiority, not because the Americans or the British or the French had won their battles for them. This, in turn, required two kinds of actions. First was to try to learn why the Jews were so good. In other words, instead of trying to ignore the existence of Israel, as they had in the past, they turned to more detailed and objective study of Israel, as exemplified in a politico-military study group established in Cairo—at the suggestion of a senior Egyptian officer—by Mohamed Heikal, editor of the influential Cairo newspaper *El Ahram*, with the support and approval of Nasser; the group was called "Center of Palestinian and Zionism Studies." (Later the title was changed, and the objective possibly broadened, to "Center for Political and Strategic Studies.") Second was to try to analyze how the Arabs could offset the Israeli superiority, until (through training, equipment, alliances, or otherwise) this superiority could be matched by the Arabs.

In this effort General Ahmed Ismail Ali, who had on July 1 been appointed by President Nasser to command the remnants of the Egyptian field army on the Suez Canal, took a very pragmatic approach. The Israelis excelled the Arabs in two principal aspects of modern war, and Ismail did not see an early opportunity for the Arabs to catch up. The Israelis were superior in the air, and would probably remain so for the foreseeable future. They were also superior in mobile, armored warfare, and there, too, Ismail saw no quick change likely. Ismail believed, however, that the qualitative difference was less than the Israelis assumed, and he also believed that Egyptian soldiers were as good as or better than the Israelis on the defensive. And the Arab numerical manpower superiority—even the manpower of Egypt alone—was so great that ways should be found to trade manpower losses with the Israelis in situations of static combat where the Israelis could not employ their superior capabilities against the Arabs.

The new Chief of Staff of the Armed Forces, General Abdul Moneim Riadh, as well as other forward-looking Egyptian officers, held views similar to those of Ismail. As a result, with surprising resilience, the defeated Egyptian Army began to seek ways and means of fighting the Israelis under circumstances in which the Israelis could not bring their superiority to bear.

The Arabs, however, had not changed so much that they could get rid of the lingering suspicion that there must have been some kind of covert American support of the Israelis, although some objective Arabs began to question the specious logic behind such suspicions. In the process they began to understand themselves, as Arabs, as well as understanding the Israelis as Jews and Zionists.

BEGINNING OF "DEFIANCE"

The Egyptian city of Port Fuad lies just east of the northern end of the Suez Canal and the 1967 ceasefire line which ran down the middle of the waterway. However, save for a narrow causeway on the east bank of the Canal, the city was separated from the remainder of the Israeli-held Sinai Peninsula by a vast area of almost impassable mud flats and marsh, and was never occupied by Israeli troops. The area south and east of Port Fuad was initially regarded as a no man's land by both Israelis and Egyptians. Approximately three weeks after the UN-imposed ceasefire ending the Six Day War, fighting broke out between Egyptian and Israeli forces for control of Port Fuad and the surrounding area. In late June, despite heavy fire from Egyptian artillery on the west bank and warships off Port Said and Port Fuad, Israeli forces began probing toward Port Fuad from the south while their artillery returned the Egyptian fire. On July 1 General Ismail sent an Egyptian unit, probably less than 100 men, across the Canal on barges, to take up positions at the village of Ras el Ush, on the causeway, about twelve kilometers south of Port Fuad. An Israeli force with armor support advanced almost immediately from Kantara against the Egyptians. After a three hour battle which resulted in casualties on both sides, the Israelis called off the engagement after negligible gains. The Egyptians strengthened their positions at Ras el Ush, and the Israelis never attacked again during the following six years.

More exchanges of artillery fire across the Canal took place on July 2-3, causing substantial casualties to both sides. In an effort to ease the pressure on the ground forces, on July 8 two Israeli jet fighters attacked Egyptian artillery emplacements and tanks on the west bank of the Canal opposite Kantara and Ras el Ush. However, only three hours after the assault the Egyptians reopened fire on Israeli-held Kantara, thereby demonstrating the inadequacy of air attack as a deterrent. And, on July 14, to the astonishment of the Israelis, the Egyptian Air Force, with most of its few remaining planes, made a quick hit-and-run raid against Israeli positions near Kantara.

Meanwhile, a political conflict was developing over the use of the Suez Canal. On July 14 Israeli Defense Minister Moshe Dayan told the UNTSO Chief of Staff, General Odd Bull, that in the current situation either both sides or neither should be able to use the Canal, and to profit from its use by others. Egypt wanted to reopen the Canal, but refused the Israeli demand for sharing royalties. Three days later Radio Cairo announced that Egypt would view the presence of any Israeli vessel in the Canal as a violation of the ceasefire to be met with appropriate force.[5] As a result, the Canal remained closed to all shipping until June 1975.

Between July and October 1967 there were a number of artillery duels between the Israeli and Egyptian troops stationed along the Canal. Still, the Israelis saw no need to construct any permanent fortifications to secure their occupation of the Sinai and the eastern bank of the Suez Canal.

THE *EILAT* INCIDENT

Although no major incidents occurred along the Canal during this period, on October 21, 1967, the flagship of the Israeli Navy, the destroyer *Eilat*, was sunk in the Mediterranean Sea off Port Said. The Israeli Navy had traditionally been the weakest of the services, being chronically underarmed and undermanned as Israeli's defense spending had flowed into the Army and Air Force. In the aftermath of the Six Day War the Navy suddenly found itself with the job of patrolling some 660 kilometers of new coastline (for a total of 900 kilometers) with a fleet containing only two destroyers. When the *Eilat* left port on October 21 to conduct her daily patrol of the Sinai coast, she was without the benefit of air or naval support. As she passed close by Port Said—well inside Egyptian territorial waters—she was struck and sunk by three missiles fired from Soviet-made *Osa*-class missile boats inside the harbor. A total of 47 men were killed and 91 wounded from the *Eilat's* crew of 200. On October 24 Israel retaliated for the sinking of the *Eilat* by shelling the oil refineries near the city of Suez and igniting the fuel storage tanks.

At the request of UNTSO observers, the Egyptians had refrained from firing at Israeli search and rescue activities near the site of the sunken *Eilat*. Thus, with dubious logic, they felt that the Israeli retaliation against civilian installations was an improper and inhumane act. The retaliatory Israeli action may have had some deterrent effect upon the Egyptians; during the next eleven months both the frequency and the intensity of the combat along the Suez front diminished markedly. However, a more likely reason is that, having expressed their defiance, and having secured a triumph by the sinking of the *Eilat*, the Egyptians were devoting themselves to rebuilding their sadly depleted armed forces.

[5] At least one Israeli test of that announcement was made; a small Israeli boat launched on the Canal was promptly destroyed by Egyptian artillery.

2

The Battle of Kerama°

ISRAELI RESPONSE TO FEDAYEEN

It is hardly surprising that the occupation by Israel of the territory on the west bank of the Jordan River that had formerly been part of Jordan was not accepted without protest and that the protest was repeatedly manifested in clashes of small units along the river. Fedayeen incursions on the west bank usually stimulated Israeli patrol activities, involving firefights across the river and occasionally Israeli patrols on the east bank and Jordanian patrols on the west. In a few instances, these minor engagements escalated to involve tanks, infantry, heavy weapons, and sometimes artillery. In early 1968 several official statements were made by Israelis that if such fedayeen activities continued, Israel would undertake appropriate reprisals.

From March 15 to 18, 1968, Israeli patrol activity along the west bank of the river increased in the area between the King Abdullah and Damiya bridges. There were also a number of Israeli air reconnaissance flights over the river valley in that area, and Jordanian intelligence, gained largely from observation posts on the hills east of the river, reported an increase of Israeli forces around Jiftlekh and Jericho. Intelligence also reported two conferences of high-ranking Israeli officers in this area during the period.

Late on March 20 the Jordanians estimated that the Israelis had assembled an armored division in the Jericho-Jiftlekh area. Jordanian intelligence identified elements of the 7th Armored Brigade, the 60th Armored Brigade, the 35th Paratroop Brigade, the 80th Infantry Brigade, an engineer regiment, and five battalions of artillery, both 105mm and 155mm.

JORDANIAN PREPARATIONS

On March 18 the Jordanian 1st Infantry Division—stationed east of the Jordan between Damiya and the Dead Sea—was alerted. All training was stopped, and the division was deployed for combat. Antitank

° This account is based upon extensive discussions with Israeli and Jordanian participants. There has been no opportunity to obtain fedayeen comments.

350

weapons were emplaced to cover likely tank crossing points and routes. Recognizing that a fedayeen unit (perhaps the equivalent of a battalion) was located in the vicinity of Kerama, the Jordanians realized that this might be the main Israeli objective, and an infantry company, supported by a tank platoon, was deployed in and around the town. One infantry brigade was deployed in the Damiya-Arda area, another to cover the King Hussein (or Allenby) Bridge, in the Kerama-Wadi Shuweib area, and the third was based on Nauer to cover the King Abdullah Bridge. Each of the brigades was reinforced by a tank company. Small garrisons (probably about a platoon each) were placed in other villages in the Kerama-Hussein Bridge area, with the mission of establishing roadblocks, to be covered by small arms and light automatic weapons fire. Included in each of these garrisons were small groups of antitank suicide troops, who had volunteered to go into battle with TNT strapped to them. A reserve consisting of one tank battalion (less a platoon), seems to have been concentrated in the foothills east of Shumrat Nimreen and below Es Salt. The division artillery was deployed forward to cover the river, with maximum concentration for the Kerama area; artillery observation posts were already established on the hills overlooking the valley, and forward observers were with the infantry and tank battalions.

On March 19, Major General Mashur Haditha, commanding the Jordanian 1st Infantry Division, called his subordinate commanders to the division command post near Es Salt for a conference, where he issued his final orders. When they returned to their units, the commanders, as directed by General Haditha, asked all of their men to swear on the Holy Koran that they would fight to hold their land, and that the Israelis would advance only over their dead bodies.

It is not clear to what extent the fedayeen unit near Kerama played a part in the overall Jordanian defense plan, or even whether there was any pre-battle coordination between the fedayeen and the Jordan Army units in and around Kerama. In later descriptions of the engagement the Jordanians hardly mention the fedayeen, yet there were at least 500 of them there, and the Israelis say that they fought hard when trappped against the river bank. They also suffered more casualties than the engaged units of Israeli and Jordanian armies combined.

ISRAELI PLANS AND PREPARATIONS

There is no doubt that the Israelis were indeed assembling a sizable force on the other side of the river. In overall command was Brigadier General Shmuel Gonen. Although the reports are conflicting, his force seems to have consisted of the equivalent of an armored brigade (consisting of elements from two brigades), an infantry brigade commanded by Brigadier General Rafael Eitan, a parachute battalion, an engineer battalion, and the five battalions of supporting artillery reported by the Jordanians.

An additional force, probably no larger than an armored battalion in size, was in the vicinity of Sedom (ancient Sodom). It was to create a diversion by crossing the salt flats south of the Dead Sea, threatening Safi.

What the Israelis planned to do with these forces is not clear. They have stated that their sole objective was to punish the fedayeen in the Kerama area, and that they had no intention of getting involved with regular units of the Jordan Army, but it is difficult to see how they could have expected to avoid the Jordanians. They certainly knew the 1st Division was there. The Jordanians claim that during the battle they captured a staff officer's map showing clearly that the Israelis planned to occupy the right bank of the Jordan River between the Damiya and King Abdullah bridges, and to extend a bridgehead into the hills to the east.

The primary Israeli objective was unquestionably to punish the fedayeen in and around Kerama. But, in the light of the size of the attacking force, and its deployment, they may well have planned temporary occupation of a bridgehead east of the river. Probably the instructions to General Gonen were permissive, and a tank drive as far as Es Salt may have been envisaged, if the situation seemed propitious. It should be recalled that on October 29, 1956, the Israelis were prepared to describe the paratroop operation against Mitla Pass as a raid if circumstances were not propitious for a larger offensive.

Available evidence indicates that the attack force (not including the unit south of the Dead Sea) was organized in three task groups, one each for the Damiya, Hussein, and Abdullah bridges. The largest of these was the Hussein force, directly under the command of General Gonen. This group had as its objective the seizure and destruction of Kerama, and an armored thrust eastward to protect operations against Kerama, possibly as far as Es Salt. The much smaller Abdullah force, also under Gonen's command, apparently had the missions of making a demonstration, and of covering the right flank of the main effort by blocking the arrival of reinforcements from Nauer and Amman. The Damiya force, commanded by General Eitan, was to perform a similar blocking mission to the north, while making a drive toward Kerama from that direction.

THE ASSAULT

The operation began at 5:30 a.m. March 21, with simultaneous Israeli attacks on the three bridges, without any prior artillery preparation.

The Jordanians, alert and expecting the attack, disputed all of these crossing attempts.

Israeli spearheads had pushed across the Hussein Bridge and were advancing toward Shumrat Nimreen at 6:30, when 15 helicopters landed the bulk of a battalion of paratroopers just northeast of Kerama. The paratroopers were immediately engaged by the local garrison, with some assistance from the fedayeen. Both Israelis and Jordanians report that Yasser Arafat was at Kerama, but that he escaped on a motorcycle just before the paratroopers isolated the town.

Just west of Shuna, Gonen's force fanned out in three directions from the Hussein Bridge. One or more companies drove north toward Kerama, to seek a linkup with the paratroopers. Some infantry and tanks (probably an infantry battalion and a tank battalion) advanced eastward through Shuna to block the Es Salt road. Another small force (probably a reinforced infantry battalion) turned south, possibly to try to assist the Abdullah force, which had been unable to secure a crossing. General Gonen has stated, however, that the action at the Abdullah Bridge was merely a diversion, and not a serious crossing effort; thus the battalion moving south from the Hussein Bridge may merely have been securing the south flank of the bridgehead.

Meanwhile, the Damiya force, avoiding the bridge, had been able to ford the Jordan and establish itself on the east bank south of the bridge. While engineers began the construction of a new bridge, Israeli tanks and infantry advanced east to the T-junction at Musri, and then turned south toward Kerama.

While these operations were going on, Israeli jets were vigorously attacking Jordanian artillery positions, command posts, and front-line defensive positions. Despite this, Jordanian artillery fire provided excellent support to all elements of General Haditha's division. By about 8:00 a.m. the Israelis seem to have made their maximum advance. The situation from north to south was as follows:

The Damiya force held Musri, but its further advance to the south was blocked by the northern brigade of the Jordanian 1st Division.

After the paratroopers at Kerama had suffered severe losses, they were joined by the northern column of Gonen's Hussein Bridge task group. The combined force was intensively engaged in and around Kerama by the original garrison of the town, plus a number of fedayeen, and the bulk of the central brigade of the 1st Division.

The remainder of Gonen's Hussein Bridge task group was being blocked to the east and south of Shuna by elements of the central and southern brigades of the Jordan 1st Division, and by the tank battalion from Es Salt.

The Israeli force at the Abdullah Bridge, despite repeated efforts or demonstrations, had failed to obtain a foothold east of the Jordan, and was engaged in an intensive firefight with the Jordanian screening force, consisting of an infantry company supported by a tank platoon.

East of Sedom, and south of the Dead Sea, the diversionary force was also held up by defensive Jordanian fire in a network of canals, streams, and salt pans.

In the next two hours Israeli artillery concentrations and a series of air strikes attempted to break open the Jordanian defense positions on the Musri-Kerama Road, on the Es Salt Road, and east of the Abdullah Bridge. Also with the assistance of air and artillery, the Israeli hold on Kerama was consolidated, and the town and nearby fedayeen camp were systematically destroyed.

By early afternoon the Israelis, recognizing that any further advance could be accomplished only at the expense of substantial casualties, and having accomplished at least a portion of their mission, began to pull back from their most advanced positions. Under the cover of continuing air strikes, and with strong artillery support, an orderly evacuation was begun. All Israelis were back on the west bank of the Jordan before 9:00 p.m., which was the time of a final Israeli air strike near Kerama.

ASSESSMENT

Israeli losses were initially reported in the press as 20 killed, three missing and 90 wounded, with four tanks, two armored cars, one 90mm gun, one truck, one jeep, and one plane also lost. A more likely estimate is 30-40 killled, more than 100 wounded, 20 tanks destroyed or damaged, 15 other armored vehicles and several trucks destroyed or damaged, and one aircraft shot down and several damaged by Jordanian antiaircraft fire. (This is about half the Jordanian estimate of Israeli losses.) The Israelis abandoned four tanks on the east bank, as well as three armored personnel carriers, two armored cars, one 90mm SP gun, one truck, and one jeep.

Jordanian losses are reported as 61 dead (including six officers), 108 wounded (including 12 officers), 13 tanks destroyed, 20 tanks damaged, and 39 additional vehicles damaged or destroyed. About 100 fedayeen were killed, more than 100 wounded, and the Israelis reported capturing 128.

Beginning at about 11:00 a.m. the UN Observer Force made a series of efforts to bring about a ceasefire. The Jordanians are convinced that this effort was initiated by the Israelis, but the IDF spokesman has insisted that Israel made no request for a ceasefire, and such a request would have been inconsistent with Israeli practice. Whatever the truth may be, the Jordanians, satisfied that their defenses were holding, refused to agree to a ceasefire until about 9:00 p.m., by which time the Israelis had completed their withdrawal.

The Jordanians offer a number of reasons to support their belief that the Israeli objective was more than an anti-fedayeen raid against Kerama. Partly on the basis of the captured map, they believe the objective was to occupy a bridgehead about 15 kilometers deep, extending from the Damiya Bridge south to the Dead Sea, with armored raiding forces striking as far east as Amman. They think the Israelis intended to hold this bridgehead for bargaining purposes, to force Jordan to drive out the fedayeen.

The Jordanians assert that the Israelis employed more force than was necessary if their objective was only to raid fedayeen installations near Kerama. Also they believe that the Israeli operations were extended over too wide an area for such a limited objective. They report that leaflets were dropped in Es Salt, enjoining the people to be calm and passive when the Israelis occupied the town.

A major Jordanian argument in support of their assessment of Israeli intentions is based upon the activities of Israeli Defense Minister Moshe Dayan that day. They claim that at 6:00 a.m., shortly after the attack was launched, Dayan held a press conference near Jericho, on a hill overlooking the Jordan, and informed the assembled correspondents that an anti-fedayeen operation was going on. He then told them, or at least hinted strongly, that he would give a further press conference that evening on Jordanian territory, possibly in Amman. At 10:00 a.m., however, the correspondents were all driven back to Jerusalem, without any satisfactory explanation, and Dayan gave no further press conference that day.

For several reasons, the Israeli objectives appear considerably more limited than the Jordanian assessment, although possibly more extensive than they themselves have admitted. In the first place, the actual results demonstrate that the Israeli force was not excessive for punishing the fedayeen under the existing circumstances, since it was obvious that at the least they would have to neutralize a Jordanian division. Even with the force employed, the full Israeli mission was not accomplished. While the Israelis may have underrated the Jordanians, it is doubtful that they were as unreastic as the Jordanian assessment would suggest.

As to the Dayan press conference, newspaper reports show that he had the day before—March 20—suffered a serious accident in one of his archaeological explorations, and on the day of the Kerama battle he was in bed in the Tel Hashomer Hospital, near Tel Aviv, unable either to move or speak.[1] There *was* a press conference, and some public relations official may have hinted at a renewal later in the day on

[1] See also Dayan, *Story of My Life*, pp. 337-339.

Jordanian territory. But the Defense Minister himself was certainly not there and did not make any public promise of an Israeli advance to Amman. On the other hand, Prime Minister Eshkol visited the scene, and crossed the King Hussein Bridge into Jordanian territory at about 10:00 a.m. This information may have reached Jordanian intelligence in garbled form.

There is little doubt that the Israelis ran into much more effective opposition than they had expected and suffered much heavier casualties than anticipated. For this reason there was considerable popular criticism of the raid in Israel. However, General Gonen and his troops did accomplish the objective publicly proclaimed for the operation, so that Kerama cannot be classified as an Israeli defeat, even if it was not a great success.

On the other hand, the Jordanians have substantial basis for considering that, from their standpoint, Kerama was a victory. Despite considerable casualties, and the temporary occupation of Kerama, the Jordanians fought an aggressive defensive action, and they are convinced that they repulsed the Israelis and prevented them from accomplishing what they had expected to do.

The Kerama battle had some significant long-term effects on the fedayeen movement. Fedayeen leaders were stimulated to increase their recruiting efforts, using a somewhat fanciful exaggeration of the role they had played in the battle. This recruiting drive was so successful that the guerrilla movement in Jordan became virtually a private army rivalling the Jordan Army.

On the other hand, their losses at Kerama led the fedayeen to withdraw all of their units from the river valley to safer inland locations. Since this made their operations more difficult, it supports the Israeli claim that the raid was successful.

In the Egyptian underground command post near Cairo, early in the war; left to right: General Ismail; President Sadat; Dr. Abdullah (assistant to the President); General Shazli, Chief of Staff—*Egypt*

In the Egyptian underground command post late in the war, left to right: Major General Taha el Magdoub; Maj. Gen. Mohammed el Gamasy, Director of Plans and Acting Chief of Staff; President Sadat; General Ismail—*Egypt*

In the Egyptian underground command post: Maj. Gen Nafal, General Ismail, Major General Nassar, Chief of Intelligence, and President Sadat—*Egypt*

Egyptian assault boats approaching the east shore of the Little Bitter Lake—*Egypt*

Egyptian infantry climbing the sand embankment east of the Suez Canal—*Egypt*

ptian infantry heavy weap-
being ferried to the east
k of the Suez Canal; note
ers left on embankment by
wave—*Egypt*

Egyptian soldiers landing on east bank of the Suez Canal—*Egypt*

Egyptian infantrymen clamber to the top of the sand embankment at the eastern edge of the Suez Canal, October 6th—*Egypt*

Egyptian soldiers raise an Egyptian flag over a captured Bar Lev Line bunker, October 6, 1973—*Egypt*

Egyptian troops in a captured Bar Lev Line stronghold—*Egypt*

Egyptian helicopters carrying commandos into the Sinai, over advancing Egyptian infantry,
late Ocober 6, 1973—*Egypt*

Breach in Israeli
sand rampart
made by Egyptian
engineers—*Egypt*

Israeli M48 tank destroyed and abandoned beside
Bar Lev Line stronghold—*Egypt*

October 7th;
Egyptian armor
and infantry a
vancing eastw
from the Cana
Egypt

Israeli 155mm gun in Bar Lev Line emplacement opposite Suez, captured by Egyptians,
October 7, 1973—*Egypt*

The defenders of the "Quay" stronghold surrender after a week seige; Port Tewfik, on the
opposite side of the Suez Canal in the background—*Egypt*

Captured Israeli Centurion tank on display in Ismailia—*Egypt*

Captured Israelis after the surrender of their Bar Lev Line stronghold—*Egypt*

Israeli M107 175mm self-propelled gun, destroyed and overrun by the Egyptians—*Egypt*

Israeli helicopter shot down behind the Egyptian lines—*Egypt*

Looking westward across the Suez Canal from a captured Bar Lev Line stronghold—*Egypt*

Egyptian MiG-17 in attack run against Israeli Suez Canal bridge—*Gutman*

Egyptian MiG-19 over the Sinai Desert—*Gutman*

Egyptian-ZSU 23-4, self-propelled four-barrelled anti-aircraft gun—*Egypt*

Sagger in flight from a Soviet-built
BRDM-2, armored reconnaissance
vehicle; note three more Saggers
ready for launch—*Egypt*

Soviet-built SA-6 (Gai
surface to air missile (SA
E

General Ahmed Ismail Ali, Commander in Chief of the Arab armies—*Egypt*

Maj. Gen. Mustafa Tlass, Syrian Minister of Defense—*Syria*

President Hafaz al Assad of Syria, former Minister of Defense and former Commander in Chief of the Syrian Air Force

Syrian T-62 tank—*Mayes*

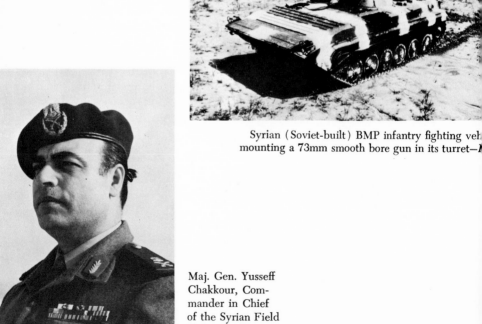

Syrian (Soviet-built) BMP infantry fighting veh
mounting a 73mm smooth bore gun in its turret—*M*

Maj. Gen. Yusseff
Chakkour, Com-
mander in Chief
of the Syrian Field
Forces in the Oc-
tober War—*Syria*

Tanks of the Jordanian 40th Armored Brigade in position near Naba, Syria, October, 1973—*Jordan*

Brigadier Khaled Hajhouj Majali, commanding the Jordanian 40th Armored Brigade, October, 1973 —*Jordan*

Brigadier Majali, Jordan Army, and his battalion commanders, near Naba, Syria—*Jordan*

Jordanian tanks in actions, October, 1973—*Jordan*

3

War Short of War—
Active Defense to Attrition

BOMBARDMENTS AND RAIDS

During 1968 Egyptian Generals Fawzi and Riadh made considerable progress in rebuilding the Egyptian Army. At the same time Riadh and his staff were preparing to resume limited operations along the Suez Canal. The Israeli Army, concerned about the slow but steady buildup of Egyptian artillery on the west bank, also began to concentrate more of its own artillery on the east bank. Among the weapons so deployed by the Israelis were some experimental super-heavy short-range rocket launchers which could fire warheads up to half a ton in weight for a range of about two kilometers. These formidable, but so far untested, weapons were emplaced opposite Suez and Ismailia.

Instead of serving as deterrents to a resumption of Egyptian activity, however, these large weapons seem to have triggered just the opposite reaction. On September 8 a massive artillery bombardment was launched by Egyptian artillery along the entire length of the Canal. Particular attention was given to the Israeli experimental heavy rocket launchers. In a period of several hours more than 10,000 shells from 150 Egyptian artillery batteries rained down on the Israeli forces. Surprisingly, according to Israeli announcements, only ten Israeli soldiers were killed and 18 wounded as the men sought protection in makeshift field fortifications which had not been designed to provide cover against heavy bombardment.

Once again Israel retaliated by shelling the Suez refineries as well as the cities of Ismailia and Suez. These bombardments of civilian targets were bitterly denounced by the Egyptians. To demonstrate their determination not to allow the Israeli counterbombardments to deter them, the Egyptians made no attempt to repair the refineries and began to evacuate some 400,000 people from the Canal Zone area. It was evident that Egypt was willing to pay a substantial price in order to continue artillery harassment of the Israeli-held east bank.

On October 26 the Egyptians repeated their artillery bombardment, this time killing 13 Israelis. In retaliation for the bombardment and

357

in lieu of an appropriate target along the Canal, on October 31 the Israelis launched a commando strike against strategic targets deep inside Egypt.[1] A helicopter-borne detachment under the command of Colonel Dani Matt attacked two Nile River bridges, blew up a power transformer on the high voltage line between Cairo and the Aswan Dam, and slightly damaged the Naj Hammadi Dam (or Barrage) in Upper Egypt. Beyond demonstrating Egypt's vulnerability to Israeli attack, it was hoped that the raid would force the Egyptian General Staff to redeploy the bulk of its forces to the interior of Egypt and away from the Canal Zone. Although no major Egyptian redeployment was carried out, there were no further artillery bombardments of similar intensity during the next five months; nonetheless, artillery harassment continued.

THE BAR LEV LINE

Because of Israel's small geographic size and limited manpower, it was a fundamental tenet of Israeli military doctrine that any war between Israel and the Arab states would have to be short and decisive, with major battles quickly carried into and fought on enemy terrain.[2] This doctrine required not only a strategy based on a rapid offensive, but also a high degree of mobility to sustain continuous forward movement. Little or no attention had been paid by the IDF to the development of a purely defensive strategy.

Now, however, the expanding, but undeclared, "war of attrition" was forcing the IDF to engage the Egyptians along the static defensive line of the Suez Canal. It was essential, therefore, to develop quickly an appropriate Israeli doctrine to deal with this situation. Consequently, the Israeli Chief of Staff, Lieutenant General Haim Bar Lev, appointed a board, with Major General Avraham ("Bren") Adan as president, to develop the concept for a defense system in the Sinai.[3]

Adan's plan, as presented to the Israeli General Staff, called for the construction of about fifteen small, fortified observation posts at eleven kilometer intervals along the length of the Suez Canal. These positions would be sited to provide a maximum degree of observation and a minimum degree of exposure to the troops stationed in them. Each fortification would be manned by a contingent of about fifteen soldiers. Mobile armored forces would patrol the areas between the fortified posts,

[1] The Egyptians assert that many of these were civilian targets, even though some had strategic significance.

[2] Yigal Allon, *The Making of Israel's Army* (London: Sphere Books Limited, 1970), p. 73.

[3] This discussion of the planning, construction, and manning of the Bar Lev Line is based largely on Chaim Herzog, *The War of Atonement* (Tel Aviv: Steimatzky's Agency, Ltd., 1975), pp. 5-7, and on personal interviews with General Adan.

while larger armored and artillery forces would be held in reserve
to the rear of the line. These local reserve units could be brought
quickly forward to meet any attempted Egyptian crossing of the Canal.

Major General Yeshayahu Gavish, the General Officer Commanding
Southern Command, approved the Adan plan. He and Adan (an
armored force officer) were aware that a series of fortifications adjacent
to the Canal would provide the Egyptians with convenient artillery
targets, and that a defense based on a static defense line was contrary
to previous IDF doctrine and experience. They concluded, however,
that these liabilities were more than offset by the defensive and surveillance value of the fortifications as visual and electronic observation
and listening posts. Furthermore, they believed that such a line of
fortifications, providing a base for counterattacks by local armored
forces, could effectively delay any Egyptian crossing until larger armor
and infantry forces could be mobilized and deployed either along the
Canal or along the line of the passes in the central Sinai. Otherwise,
they feared, intense Egyptian artillery fire could hold purely mobile
forces back from the Canal while Egyptian infantry units crossed the
waterway and established a bridgehead on the east bank. The Egyptians
could then be expected to attempt immediately to obtain a new United
Nations-sponsored ceasefire which would establish a new and unfavorable *status quo* with Arab troops in the Sinai, once again poised for a
future advance against Israel.[4]

The views of Adan and Gavish were opposed by Major General Ariel
Sharon, Director of Training, and Major General Israel Tal, Chief of the
Planning Staff in the Defense Ministry. (Sharon was a paratrooper by
training; Tal a tanker.) These men favored a defense based on mobile
armored forces kept concentrated beyond artillery range east of the
Canal, while the bank of the waterway was patrolled constantly by
small, mobile armored units. Sharon and Tal doubted that a line of
fortifications would restrain a concerted crossing effort by Egyptian
forces, and they felt that a mobile system based in the rear of the
Canal zone would be more consistent with past IDF doctrine and experience and would at least keep the bulk of the IDF forces beyond
the range of the Egyptians' artillery.

In early 1969 General Bar Lev decided in favor of Adan's proposal.
Construction of the Bar Lev Line, as it came to be called, was largely
completed by the end of January 1969, but with 30 fortified positions
(counting two south of the Canal on the Gulf of Suez, and one to the
east on the Mediterraneant coast) at average intervals of about five
kilometers. A major feature of the line was a sand rampart, 20 to 30 feet
in height, along the entire east bank of the Canal. A 45° slope on the

---

[4] Luttwak and Horowitz, *op. cit.*, p. 319.

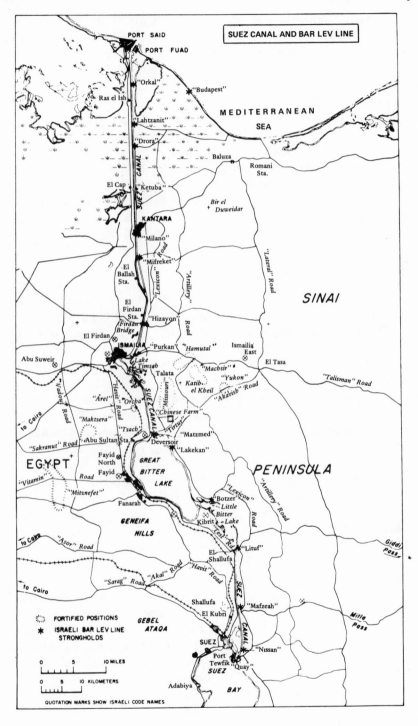

SUEZ CANAL AND BAR LEV LINE

PORT SAID
PORT FUAD
"Orkal"
Ras el Ish
"Budapest"
MEDITERRANEAN
SEA
"Lahtzanit"
"Drora"
Baluza
Romani Sta.
El Cap
"Ketuba"
Bir el Duweidar
KANTARA
"Milano"
"Mifreket"
El Ballah Sta.
SINAI
El Firdan Sta.
"Hizayon"
Firdan Bridge
El Firdan
ISMAILIA
"Purkan"
"Hamutal"
Ismailia East
El Tasa
Abu Suweir
Lake Timsah
Talata
"Macbsir"
"Yukon"
"Talisman" Road
"Arel"
Orcha
Katib el Kheil
"Akavish" Road
"Chinese Farm"
"Maktsera"
"Tsach"
"Missouri"
"Matzmed"
Abu Sultan Sta.
Deversoir
"Lakekan"
EGYPT
Fayid North
Fayid
GREAT BITTER LAKE
PENINSULA
"Vitamin"
"Lexicon" Road
"Mitznefet"
Fanarah
"Botzer"
Little Bitter Lake
"Artillery" Road
GENEIFA HILLS
Kibrit
"Asor" Road
El Shallufa
"Lituf"
Giddi Pass
to Cairo
"Akal" Road
"Havit" Road
"Sarag" Road
Shallufa
"Mafzeah"
El Kubri
Mitla Pass
FORTIFIED POSITIONS
GEBEL ATAQA
SUEZ
"Nissan"
ISRAELI BAR LEV LINE STRONGHOLDS
Port Tewfik
Quay
0   5   10 MILES
SUEZ
0   5   10 KILOMETERS
Adabiya
BAY
QUOTATION MARKS SHOW ISRAELI CODE NAMES

water face of this massive rampart precluded an ascent by any known amphibious vehicle. Each fortification, built into the top of the rampart, dominated about one kilometer on each of its flanks, while the approximately three remaining kilometers between the fortifications could be observed from observation towers and covered by patrols. Platoons of tanks were stationed within the area controlled by each of the fortifications, and ramps were sited on the rampart, between fortifications, to provide hull-defilade positions for enfilade fire along the Canal. To the rear of the first line, mobile firepower was to be provided by concentrations of armor. A second sand rampart was constructed about 500 meters behind the main fortifications, also with firing ramps, allowing a second line of tanks to provide covering fire for the fortifications and the approaches to the Canal. Portions of a third line, one to two kilometers further back, were built along the main east-west axes. In addition, a network of roads, underground headquarters, water and communication systems, repair facilities, and stores was constructed behind the second defense line.

During the period of feverish Israeli fortification construction activity the Egyptians, despite some artillery harassment, were relatively quiet. Apparently this was because of a high-level staff debate in Cairo, with one faction arguing that nothing should be done until new Russian equipment had completely replaced the losses of the Six Day War, while others argued that the Israelis' work should be interrupted in order to prevent the fortifications from becoming too strong. By the time the second point of view finally won out—in early March 1969— most of the Russian equipment had been received, and it was almost too late to damage the Bar Lev Line seriously. Most of the planned work had been completed by the Israelis, although improvements were still being made.

THE "PERIOD OF ATTRITION" BEGINS

On March 8, 1969, a massive Egyptian bombardment signalled the opening of a War of Attrition, which President Nasser formally announced that same day. By this time the Egyptian General Staff had formulated its operational concept for the coming operations. The period from June of 1967 through August of 1968 was formally declared to have been "the Period of Defiance," the period from September 1968 through February 1969 was called "the Period of Active Defense," and the new activity, inaugurated on March 8, was to be called "the Period of Attrition." The objectives of this attrition campaign[5] were stated as follows by General Riadh, Chief of the General Staff:

[5] Based on personal interviews with Egyptian General Staff officers.

- To destroy the Bar Lev Line fortifications;
- To prevent the Israelis from reconstructing fortifications after they were destroyed;
- To make life intolerable for Israeli forces on the east bank of the Canal;
- To inspire offensive spirit in Egyptian troops;
- To carry out practice Canal crossing operations.

The rationale behind this campaign was that the static defensive posture of the two armies largely negated Israel's qualitative superiority in mobile warfare. Egypt, by means of its numerical superiority in manpower and firepower, hoped to weaken Israeli resolve by inflicting unacceptable casualties on IDF forces along the Canal. The attrition of Israeli troops through bombardment, and the simultaneous destruction of the Bar Lev Line, would be combined with a series of Egyptian commando attacks across the Canal. This was expected eventually to create a situation favorable to a massive crossing of the Canal by Egyptian forces and, ultimately, reoccupation of the Sinai.

The artillery fire of March 8 was the beginning of an 80-day period of almost incessant bombardment. Although extensive damage was done to the fortifications,[6] Israeli artillery conducted a spirited response with counterbattery fire and repeated concentrations against known Egyptian troop positions. On March 9, one day after the initiation of the attrition campaign, General Riadh, standing with a group of officers on the west bank of the Canal near Ismailia, observing the effects of fire on the Bar Lev Line, was hit and instantly killed by Israeli retaliatory artillery fire. But this tragedy did nothing to lessen the intensity of the campaign he had initiated. Riadh was replaced as Chief of Staff by Lieutenant General Ahmed Ismail Ali.

Throughout March and April 1969 the Egyptians carried out frequent artillery barrages along the length of the Bar Lev Line. Although much damage was inflicted, most of the Israeli positions survived the shelling. In mid-April, raising the level of tension, Egyptian commando units made several raids across the Canal and began to attack Bar Lev fortifications, Israeli patrols, supply convoys, and rear installations. Despite the fact that Israeli commandos undertook reprisal raids in other areas, and Israeli artillery bombarded the west bank of the Canal, the Egyptians maintained their substantial firepower superiority, and, as the fighting escalated, Israeli casualties rose once again.

Throughout the War of Attrition, Israeli standard operating procedures during an emergency called for all reservists on the Bar Lev Line to be replaced by troops of the standing army, or by reserve parachute forces (whose level of training was maintained more intensively). During

---

[6] The Egyptians claim 80% destruction; this is doubtful.

those periods, some of the garrisons were increased to as many as 90 men per position. In emergencies each position was commanded by an officer, with field officers, usually majors, commanding the more important posts. General Bar Lev normally maintained two armored brigades along the Canal, with a third in reserve in the central Sinai. A fourth armored brigade, usually composed of reservists training in the Sinai area, was added during emergency periods.

On July 10 an Egyptian commando unit of company size surprised and successfully attacked an Israeli armored unit opposite Port Tewfik by daylight, inflicting heavy casualties on the Israeli force. As a result, the Israeli Government approved a General Staff recommendation to commit the Air Force to this escalating war of attrition.[7]

During the night of July 19-20, a large Israeli commando unit, transported in landing craft, assaulted Green Island in the Gulf of Suez, where the southernmost radar installation in the Egyptian antiaircraft defense network was located. The installation's 60 defenders were taken completely by surprise when Israeli frogmen came over the wall surrounding the radar station. Once inside, the Israelis broke up into seven groups and were quickly able to demolish both the radar and the island's antiaircraft guns before returning to Israeli-held territory, having lost six killed. During the battle the Egyptian battery commander called for artillery fire on his own position, which caused the Israelis to hurry their departure. Egyptian losses were about 25 killed in the hour-long assault.

Beginning July 20 the Israeli Air Force conducted a ten-day series of intense retaliatory raids against Egyptian artillery positions and SAM sites on the west bank. This was the first time the Israeli Air Force had been employed in mass since the Six Day War. Following these raids there was a lull along the Canal.

Two months later, as Egyptian artillery bombardments again intensified, the Israelis launched a second major commando operation. On the night of September 8, Israeli frogmen sank two Egyptian torpedo boats at Ras Sadat, thereby clearing the northern shores of the Gulf of Suez of all Egyptian naval attack craft.

On the morning of September 9 an Israeli force several hundred strong, equipped with Russian tanks and troop carriers captured in the 1967 War, was transported by landing craft to a position just south of El Hafayr on the western shore of the Gulf of Suez. Meeting practically no opposition, the Israeli force, commanded by General "Bren" Adan, moved down the coastal road, destroying a number of prepared (but unoccupied) radar sites and missile emplacements, as well as all vehicles in its path. At the same time, Israeli aircraft attacked El Hafayr

[7] Schiff, *op. cit.*, p. 247.

and positions in and near Ras Zafrana, as well as convoys in the area travelling to and from Suez. In nine hours the Israeli raiders travelled approximately 45 kilometers without encountering any serious opposition. (There were no Egyptian Army forces in the region.) The only casualties were two wounded pilots, while the Egyptian losses were estimated at over 150 men, most of them civilian workers. The Israelis then embarked in their landing craft and returned home from what the Israeli press described as an "invasion of Egypt."

That same day, September 9, the new Egyptian Chief of Staff, Lieutenant General Ismail, was removed from office after a tenure of only six months. Israelis and other foreign observers suggested that his removal was a result of the failure of the Egyptians to oppose the Israeli raid. This contention was hotly denied by Egypt, which announced that the already scheduled change reflected an unexplained ideological difference of opinion within the Egyptian High Command.

THE AIR VERSUS AIR DEFENSE STRUGGLE

On September 11 the Egyptians launched a major air strike at Israeli positions in the Sinai in retaliation for the Gulf of Suez raid. Despite Israeli fighters' attempts to drive off the attackers, the Egyptian aircraft inflicted substantial damage. But the Egyptians lost seven MiG-21s, one MiG-17, and three Su-7s. There were no Israeli air losses. This was the largest commitment of Egyptian air forces during the War of Attrition.

When Israel introduced its Air Force into the War of Attrition, the Israeli aircraft found that they were being tracked by an advanced low-level radar, the P-12, with a range of 188 miles, which Russia had provided to Egypt. Anxious to learn more about the new Egyptian device, on the night of December 25-26 an Israeli heliborne reconnaissance unit seized a highly secret P-12 station at Ras Gharib. A team of engineers worked for one hour to dismantle the seven-ton radar station, which was then transported to Israel by two heavy-lift helicopters.[8]

In addition to the new radar, the Egyptians had begun experimenting in August with an integrated air defense system, based upon the collaboration of air defense aircraft and a Russian-made surface-to-air missile (SAM) system which extended along the length of the Egyptian front. The initial results were disappointing to the Egyptians, but they persevered, despite the loss of a number of their MiG-17s and new Mig-21s to Israeli Mystères and F-4 Phantoms. On December 9 an

[8] This radar may subsequently have been turned over to the United States for study.

Egyptian MiG-21 finally shot down an Israeli Phantom, but the SAMs remained generally unsuccessful.

Between July and December 1969 the Israeli Air Force attacked Egyptian antiaircraft guns, convoys, and artillery batteries, but the focus of the assaults rested on the Soviet-built SA-2 high-altitude missile system. By October the Israeli Air Force had succeeded in destroying a major part of the missile system in the Canal area, and Israeli aircraft were able to roam at will over the Canal Zone, although they stayed at high altitudes to avoid antiaircraft gun fire.

By the end of the year the Israelis were satisfied that the Egyptians had failed to accomplish their War of Attrition objectives. The Bar Lev fortifications, although severely battered, had withstood the most intensive Egyptian artillery bombardments, Israeli casualties were decreasing steadily while Egyptian losses were increasing, and the Israelis were under no serious pressure to relinquish any captured Arab territory. Between June 1967 and January 1970, Israel lost only 15 aircraft on all fronts while Egypt had lost 60 on the Sinai-Suez front.[9]

ISRAELI DEEP PENETRATION RAIDS

In January 1970 a major turning point in the war was reached when Israel decided to expand the war and bring pressure on Egypt. The Israeli Air Force instituted a series of deep penetration air raids against targets of military significance in Egypt. On January 7 Israeli aircraft, in the first of these raids, attacked Army and Air Force supply depots near Inchas and Helwan. Considerable damage was done, but the Israelis missed their main target, the principal Air Force ammunition depot.

On February 12, as part of the campaign against the Egyptian SAM sites, the Israelis apparently further escalated the war by a raid against a steel and ferroconcrete factory at Abu Zabaal, which produced much of the construction material used in building the SAM sites. The attack came at 8:00 a.m., just as a change of shift was taking place in the plant. As a result, 70 workers were killed, and many more were injured. The Egyptians accused the Israelis of having selected this time for the raid in order to increase its terror effect. The Israelis, not very convincingly, attributed the attack "on a pipe factory" to faulty target identification, since the plant was located near an army base.

Not long after this another Israeli air raid caused an even more tragic loss of civilian life. The bombs hit a primary school at Bahr

[9] Neither side reports its own losses, but unofficial estimates are usually obtainable from Israeli sources, rarely from Arab sources.

El Baqar, 120 kilometers north of Cairo, and at least 50 schoolchildren were killed and wounded. This time, however, the Israeli explanation of pilot error was probably correct; the school was adjacent to an army installation.

For the most part, however, the Israeli targets were unquestionably military, and focussed on the Egyptian SAM sites. The effectiveness of these deep penetration raids and the destruction of the SA-2 missile defenses, seem to have influenced President Nasser to journey secretly to Moscow on January 22 to request further Soviet aid. After some initial hesitation,[10] the Soviet response was positive, and beginning in February, Russian advisors and vast amounts of Soviet equipment, including SA-3 missiles and MiG-21J aircraft, began to arrive in Egypt.

GROWING SOVIET INVOLVEMENT

In March Israeli reconnaissance showed that new missile sites equipped with SA-3 missiles and manned by Soviet personnel had been constructed in depth in Egypt. By the end of June 1970 a total of 55 SA-3 sites were in operation. Gradually, the Soviet forces, which at the height of their involvement in the spring of 1972 totalled approximately 16,000 men, assumed considerable responsibility for the defense of Egyptian air space. On April 18 Israeli aircraft encountered several MiG-21J interceptors while on a mission over Egypt's Red Sea coast. Although the planes carried Egyptian markings, Israeli radio monitors overheard the pilots of the MiG aircraft conversing with the control tower in Russian. In view of Israel's long-standing policy of avoiding confrontation with a superpower, in mid-April the General Staff suspended deep penetration raids, while making it known that it would resist any efforts on the part of the Russians or Egyptians to extend the missile system into the Canal Zone, an area understood to be some 30 kilometers deep along the west bank of the Canal.[11]

During the next two months a new *status quo* developed along the Egyptian front, for the Russians apparently did not wish a direct confrontation with the Israelis. But on June 30 two Israeli Phantom F-4 fighter aircraft were shot down by new missile batteries which had been installed within 25 kilometers of the Canal.

The growing effectiveness of the revitalized air defense system was demonstrated in July, when nearly 20 Israeli aircraft were shot down. At the same time, incidentally, the effectiveness of the Israeli American-made "Hawk" SAMs was also demonstrated, since five intruding

[10] Mohamed Heikal, *The Road to Ramadan* (London, 1975), pp. 83 ff. This book is particularly valuable for political events in Egypt from 1967 to 1973.
[11] Luttwak and Horowitz, *op. cit.*, p. 324.

Egyptian aircraft were shot down by these missiles east of the Canal.

The Egyptian-Russian air defense system was composed of batteries of SA-2 high-altitude missiles (mostly manned by Egyptians) combined with batteries of SA-3 low-altitude missiles (mostly manned by Russians). Both types of missiles were protected by an integrated network of ground-based radar, more than 1,000 antiaircraft guns, and some 600 SA-7 shoulder-fired missile launchers. The system was further reinforced by more than 100 MiG-21J aircraft. Those aircraft with Russian pilots initially patrolled only the immediate Cairo and Aswan areas. But on July 25 Russian fighters attempted to intercept Israeli aircraft near the Canal.

The Israeli General Staff, with approval of the government, decided that a confrontation with Russian aircraft could no longer be avoided. On July 30, 1970, one squadron each of Israeli Mirage and Phantom aircraft, manned by the best pilots in the Israeli Air Force, went out to attack a radar station in Egypt near the Gulf of Suez, anticipating Russian interception. While the Phantoms went in to attack the station, the Mirages provided top cover. Suddenly a force of sixteen MiG-21s appeared and engaged the Israeli Phantoms. In a classic Israeli air ambush, within a matter of minutes four MiGs had been shot down and a fifth damaged by the waiting Mirages. The remaining Russian aircraft quickly withdrew, and the Israeli planes returned to their base with no losses.[12]

THE WAR AT SEA

The long shoreline the Israeli Navy had to protect after the 1967 War provided an opportunity for Arab commando raids, limited hit-and-run naval bombardments, arms smuggling and intelligence gathering forays. There was also the danger of a major Egyptian landing to bypass the Bar Lev Line. Previously, the Israeli Navy had defended two coastal perimeters with a light force of fast motor torpedo boats and lightly armed motor patrol boats skirting the shore, and a screen of torpedo boats, destroyers and antisubmarine patrol ships further offshore. The new situation called for a deeper defensive belt and a strategy of seeking and engaging Arab (mostly Egyptian) units in their home waters and keeping hostile naval forces off balance.[13]

As a result of the '67 War, President de Gaulle of France had put an embargo on all arms deliveries to the warring nations in the Middle East, which prevented the delivery of the *Saar* vessels completed shortly after the war. However, seven of the boats, in a celebrated incident,

[12] Schiff, *op. cit.*, p. 246.

[13] See p. 328 for the planning, designing, and production of the "Gabriel" missile and the *Saar* boats to meet these requirements.

were smuggled from France by Israeli agents on Christmas Day, 1969, from under the noses of the French, and made a five-day Mediterranean passage to Haifa, with the assistance of a refueling tanker. The other five were sold by the French to a Scandinavian corporation, which turned out to be an Israeli "front," and these boats also soon showed up in Israel.

The first generation *Saar* craft measured 147 feet in length, and displaced 220 to 250 tons. Their three diesels propelled them at more than 40 knots. The Gabriel missile, which the new vessels carried, was the first non-Soviet ship-to-ship missile to become operational. Its container was also the launcher, designed to allow the full battery of missiles to be stored in a ready-to-launch state with no prelaunch manual "mixing" required. The original version had a range of 22 kilometers.[14] Guidance at launch was inertial, with a lock-in to automatic homing in the terminal phase. Advanced ECM "foxers" built into the guidance unit, combined with the wave-skimming trajectory, rendered the missile virtually immune to all known ECM systems. The ECM system installed aboard the *Saar* vessels themselves was probably the most sophisticated in use aboard small combat craft, while intricate target detection electronics—surface, submerged and air—was available for either attack or evasion.

After the *Saars* had been in operation for a number of months, Israeli naval engineers designed and commenced construction on an improved and enlarged version to be known as the *Reshef* class, after its prototype. The *Reshefs* were to measure 190 by 25 feet and displace 415 tons. Each vessel would carry eight ready-to-launch Gabriels in addition to two fully-automatic 76mm and two automatic 20mm AA cannon. The *Reshefs'* key advance over the *Saars* was to be in their much longer range and better seakeeping characteristics.

During the War of Attrition, aside from its mission of coastal protection, the Israeli Navy's principal role was to perform a number of frogman commando attacks, which resulted—the Israelis claim—in the destruction of nine Egyptian vessels of varying sizes at unprotected anchorages.

Egyptian naval activities were comparable. On November 8, 1969, two Egyptian destroyers successfully bombarded Romani and Baluza on the Sinai Mediterranean coast, but after that the Egyptians also concentrated most of their efforts on clandestine frogman activities. On November 16 Egyptian frogmen sank three Israeli LCTs in Eilat harbor. This success was announced by the Egyptians as their answer to the Israelis' major commando raid in September 9, which had been called the "invasion of Egypt."

---

[14] A later version had a range of 41 kilometers.

On February 6 the Egyptians made another frogman attack on Eilat harbor, this time destroying two LCTs, which they claimed were loaded with personnel and ammunition, apparently in anticipation of a raid of their own. As in the November 8 raid, the Egyptians claimed that they had suffered no losses.

CEASEFIRE

On August 8, 1970, a US-sponsored and Soviet-supported ceasefire ended the fighting between the Israeli and Egyptian forces. The ceasefire agreement provided for a total military standstill within a zone fifty kilometers wide on either side of the Canal. However, two days after the ceasefire came into effect this provision was violated by the Egyptians, who moved missile batteries up to the Canal. Israel protested, but the then-current political climate in the world precluded any major Israeli reaction, and thus, for a time, the front fell quiet.

To demonstrate its support for Israel, however, the US agreed to supply additional aircraft to Israel to restore the local balance.

There was an indirect Israeli response; this was an intensive effort to improve the Bar Lev Line fortifications. The Egyptians claim, in fact, that this Israeli violation of the ceasefire was initiated before they moved their new SAMs into the Canal zone. In any event, the Israelis heightened and strengthened the sand rampart on the bank of the Canal, and repaired or rebuilt the damaged strongpoints along the waterway. By the time this improvement effort was completed, one foreign observer remarked that the overhead cover of rock, railroad tracks, and reinforced concrete could stand anything except a direct hit by a nuclear weapon.

Between June 1967 and August 1970 Israel admitted the loss of more than 500 soldiers killed and 2,000 wounded on all fronts. In addition there had been 127 civilian deaths and 700 wounded. The Egyptian front alone accounted for about 400 troops killed and 1,100 wounded. Precise figures for Egyptian losses are not available, but the Israelis' estimates of 15,000 killed are at least three times too high.

4

No Peace, No War

THE "ROGERS PLAN"

The diplomatic effort of US Secretary of State William Rogers, which brought about the ceasefire on August 8, 1970, had been initiated by him in a speech on December 9, 1969, in which he endeavored to clarify the United States Government's interpretation of UN resolution 242 of November 22, 1967. The provisions of that British-sponsored document were so skillfully worded that it had been interpreted by the Israelis as justifying their demands for "secure and defensible frontiers" which would include some undefined—and presumably substantial—portions of the Arab territories conquered in June of that year, while simultaneously it had been interpreted by the three Arab countries whose territory was involved—Egypt, Syria, and Jordan—as endorsing their demands for the return of *all* of the territory occupied by Israel in the Six Day War, and for a just resolution of the Palestinian refugee problem.

The relevant provisions of this short, controversial resolution are as follows:

The Security Council, . . .
Emphasizing the inadmissibility of the acquisition of territory by war and the need to work for a just and lasting peace in which every State in the area can live in security, . . .
1. *Affirms* that the fulfillment of Charter principles requires the establishment of a just and lasting peace in the Middle East which should include the application of both the following principles:
(i) Withdrawal of Israeli armed forces from territories occupied in the recent conflict;[1]
(ii) Termination of all claims or state of belligerency and respect for and acknowledgement of the sovereignty, territorial integrity and political inde-

[1] The peculiarities of the three official languages permit some uncertainty as to the precise intent of this provision. Omission of the article before "territories" in the English version implies that Israel might retain some of the occupied land. In the French version the limiting article appears but is ambiguous. The Russian version, since the language has no definite article, can also be interpreted as referring to all or to only part of the conquered territories.

pendence of every State in the area and their right to live in peace within secure and recognized boundaries free from threats or acts of force;

2. *Affirms further* the necessity

(a) For guaranteeing freedom of navigation through international waterways in the area;

(b) For achieving a just settlement of the refugee problem;

(c) For guaranteeing the territorial inviolability and political independence of every State in the area, through measures including the establishment of demilitarized zones;

3. *Requests* the Secretary-General to designate a Special Representative to proceed to the Middle East to establish and maintain contacts with the States concerned in order to promote agreement and assist efforts to achieve a peaceful and accepted settlement in accordance with the provisions and principles in this resolution; . . .

On November 22, the council appointed Dr. Gunnar Jarring of Sweden as the Secretary General's Special Representative under the resolution.

The United States had voted for the resolution, but during the two succeeding years had carefully avoided an interpretation that would almost automatically conflict with the interpretation of either Arabs—focussing on Sections 1-i and 2-b—or Israelis, equally intent upon Sections 1-ii, 2-a, and 2-c. Lack of a definite statement from Washington was generally interpreted by both sides, however, as implicit support for the Israeli interpretation, which considered the words "secure and recognized boundaries" as the crucial phrase of the resolution.

Thus Mr. Rogers created a sensation in Middle East capitals when he announced, on December 9, 1969, that it was American policy "to encourage the Arabs to accept a permanent peace based on a binding agreement, and to urge Israel to withdraw from occupied territory when her integrity is ensured." He suggested that "detailed provisions of peace relating to security safeguards on the ground should be worked out between the parties" with the assistance of Dr. Jarring (by that time Swedish Ambassador to Moscow).

Rogers suggested that the negotiations could follow the pattern set at Rhodes in 1948 and 1949.[2] He added that "in the context of peace and agreement on specific security safeguards, withdrawal of Israel from Egyptian territory would be required." Such security safeguards were specifically related to Sharm el Sheikh, demilitarized zones in the Sinai, and "final arrangements in the Gaza Strip." Perhaps most significant to Arabs and Israelis alike were Mr. Rogers' statements to the effect that the United States interpreted the resolution as meaning that "any changes in the pre-existing lines should not reflect the weight of conquest and should be confined to insubstantial alterations required for mutual security," and that "we do not support expansion."

[2] See page 114.

While there was no rejoicing in Cairo, Damascus, or Amman, there was at least quiet satisfaction. There was outrage in Jerusalem. At the same time in Washington, Mr. Rogers was subjected to tremendous pressure from the so-called "Jewish Lobby" to disavow the statement. However, although he never repeated his strong words on Israeli withdrawal, Mr. Rogers did not retract the statement, and implicitly it remained United States policy on the territorial issue.

This, then, was the "Rogers Plan," which through skillful diplomacy on the part of Ambassador Jarring and of American diplomats, brought about the ceasefire of August 8, 1970. As Mohamed Heikal has recently confirmed, a major consideration in President Nasser's agreement to this was the powerful and effective Israeli air response to the Egyptian "War of Attrition." Nasser, who had no illusions that this ceasefire was a preliminary to peace, had come to the conclusion that by continuing the War of Attrition "we are bleeding ourselves to death" as long as the Israelis had complete air superiority. In the lull provided by the ceasefire he was determined to build up an effective missile air defense, and, once this was accomplished, he planned to send his army across the Canal to strike for the Sinai passes. In late August or early September of 1970 he ordered General Fawzi to initiate plans for such an operation.[3]

DEATH OF NASSER; RISE OF SADAT

Less than two months after the ceasefire, on September 28, 1970, President Nasser died of a heart attack, and was succeeded by the Vice President, Anwar el-Sadat, one of the original group of Army officers associated with Nasser in the coup against King Farouk. In the following months Sadat maintained a low profile nationally and internationally. In part this was probably a reflection of innate caution, and recognition of the tremendous responsibility he had inherited from the man who had dominated Egypt and the Arab world for nearly two decades. On the other hand, it may have been that he recognized that —despite apparent solidarity in the support he had received from Nasser's former colleagues—there was strong opposition to his succession to power from a substantial clique within the oligarchy.

The leader of this opposition was Ali Sabri, a former Vice President, and before that an Air Force intelligence officer. Next to Sadat he had been the most powerful of Nasser's subordinates. Sabri had therefore expected that Sadat would appoint him Premier, and when in November 1970 Sadat appointed Dr. Mahmoud Fawzi to that post, Sabri

---

[3] Heikal, *op. cit.*, p. 97.

probably initiated the conspiracy that Sadat seems to have very promptly discovered. There is considerable evidence that Sabri and possibly
other conspirators were given some covert support and encouragement
by the Soviet ambassador. In any event, as has happened in other
countries, the downfall of the conspirators came from their own taped
recordings of conspiratorial conversations, which were discovered by
loyal Egyptian police officers.

On May 14, 1971, President Sadat dismissed the conspirators from
their various governmental positions; a few days later they were jailed;
subsequently they were publicly tried, convicted, and given long jail
terms. Although not directly implicated as a conspirator, the Minister
of War, General Fawzi, had been a close associate and obvious sym-
pathizer of Sabri's; he also was dismissed and replaced by the Chief of
Staff, General Mohommed Ahmed Sadiq. General Ahmed Ismail was
called from retirement and appointed Chief of National Intelligence
in place of one of the conspirators.

Sadat then moved firmly and decisively to consolidate his control of
the government and of the armed forces. Observers—in Egypt and
abroad—who had assumed that he would be a weak president began to
recognize that they had misjudged him. In subsequent months, the
pendulum of opinion began to swing back. Sadat had made strong
statements about 1971 being "the year of decision" on the Arab-Israeli
issue, but the year ended without any progress toward a diplomatic
settlement of the confrontation, and without any action by Sadat's
Egypt.

Meanwhile, by May 1971 it had become evident that Ambassador
Jarring was making no more progress toward a peace settlement than
he had three years earlier. So American Secretary of State Rogers made
another effort to get negotiations moving again. He tried to get both
Egypt and Israel to agree to a first step in a step-by-step approach to
peace. The first step he proposed was an "interim Suez settlement"
whereby both sides would agree to the reopening of the Suez Canal.
At first Israel and Egypt both showed some interest, but President Sadat
refused to proceed when Israel would not make a partial withdrawal
to permit reopening of the Canal under Egyptian control.

EGYPT AND THE SOVIET UNION

By early 1972 President Sadat had evidently come to the conclusion
that Israel was quite satisfied with the *status quo*, and was in no hurry
to explore seriously any potentially realistic formula for trading the
occupied territories for a definitive peace settlement, under the Resolution 242 concept. Nor did he detect any really serious effort by either

of the superpowers, or by the United Nations, to put any pressure on Israel to withdraw. Particularly annoying to Sadat was the slowness of Soviet weapons deliveries, which had fallen seriously behind agreed schedules. The American and Russian governments were making much of their moves toward *detente,* and Sadat came to the conclusion that the Soviet Government would be happy to keep things quiet in the Middle East, and was slowing down arms deliveries for that reason.

There were other problems with the Soviet Union and the Russian advisors. The advisors tended to be arrogant, and to treat the Egyptians—officers and soldiers—with condescension. And also, after Egyptian crews had been trained to handle the more advanced SAMs, the Russians were reluctant to turn control of these weapons over to them. The Egyptians were frustrated when the Russians would not give them the most up-to-date Soviet weapons; for instance, only MiG-21s instead of MiG-23s and 25s. And then there was the question of payment. While long-term credits (on stiff terms) were generally provided the Egyptians by the Russians, for some of the more modern weapons they demanded cash payment, despite the weakness of Egyptian finances.

In the late spring of 1972 Mohamed Heikal began writing a series of articles in *Al Ahram* entitled, "No Peace; No War," in which he made the point that the Soviets seemed to be quite content with this anomalous situation, and were doing nothing either directly or indirectly to end it.

On July 8, 1972, after a discouraging exchange of communications with Marshal Grechko and Secretary Brezhnev regarding the continued failure of Soviet arms deliveries to meet agreed schedules, President Sadat demanded that Russian military advisors and operational personnel be withdrawn from Egypt by July 17. In a conciliatory gesture, however, he suggested that following this withdrawal he would be willing to discuss future cooperation under the terms of the Soviet-Egyptian Treaty of Friendship. He also allowed a limited number of Russian technical specialists and technical school instructors to stay in Egypt.

The Soviets accepted this rebuff with considerable dignity and forebearance; they were pleased that Sadat had at least agreed to retain the Treaty of Friendship, and they hoped to be able to rebuild the alliance through the provisions of that treaty. Meanwhile, without fuss, most of the 21,000 Soviet military advisors and technicians left Egypt within the time prescribed by Sadat.

Sadat had hoped—but not seriously expected—that his strong action might shock the Soviet Union into speeding up arms deliveries. This was what in fact occurred. After renewed negotiations, by late 1972 the Soviets began to pour equipment into Egypt. According to Mohamed Heikal, "between December 1972 and June 1973 we received more arms from them than in the whole of the two preceding years." And he reports that President Sadat said to him at one time early in 1973, "They are drowning me in new arms."[4]

EGYPT AND LIBYA

Another of President Sadat's problems during his early years as President was the naive and fanatic exuberance of President Muammar Qadaffi of Libya. When Qadaffi—an army captain in his late twenties—led the coup which overthrew the monarchy in Libya in September of 1969, he had almost immediately sought to unify Libya with Egypt, under the leadership of President Nasser. While the idea was not displeasing to Nasser, who had a dream of creating a union of all the Arab states, he felt that a union of Libya and Egypt at that time would be premature, would be more likely to alienate other Arab states than to attract them to join such a union, and would create severe internal political problems in both nations. The recent failure of the similar union with Syria was still fresh in his memory.

Soon after Sadat succeeded Nasser, Qadaffi also endeavored to get his agreement to such a union. Initially Sadat did agree, in cautious principle. But, as had been the case with Nasser before him, he did not want to rush into a union that would have difficult international implications, and which could create some serious internal political, economic, and social problems. Furthermore, Sadat was beginning to think that Qadaffi was at best immature, and at worst mentally unbalanced.

On February 24, 1973, the peculiar diplomatic dance between the youthful, eager Qadaffi and the reluctant, wiser Sadat was complicated by a tragic, and still slightly mysterious, incident. A Libyan Airlines plane lost its way, strayed over the Sinai, failed to respond when Israeli planes signalled it to land at an Israeli air base, and was shot down by the Israelis with the loss of 108 lives. Adding unpleasantness to the tragedy was a suspicion that the Egyptian Air Force had seen all of this on radar and had failed to take advantage of an opportunity to guide the airliner to safety. The Egyptian Air Force seems to have offered the lame excuse that the weather was unsuitable to scramble planes for such a rescue. Qadaffi, somewhat logically, noted that the weather did not seem to have prevented Israeli planes from scrambling.[5]

After several weeks of brooding, Qadaffi saw an opportunity for revenge against the Israelis. A group of wealthy American Jews had chartered the British liner *Queen Elizabeth II* to take them to Israel

[4] *Ibid.*, p. 181.
[5] *Ibid.*, p. 192.

from England, to arrive in time for the 25th anniversary of the independence of Israel. The vessel sailed from Southampton on April 15.

Under a military reciprocity agreement between Egypt and Libya, an Egyptian submarine, based in Tripoli, was nominally under Libyan military command. As Commander in Chief of the Libyan Armed Forces, Qadaffi ordered the commander of the submarine out to sea to sink the *Queen Elizabeth II*. The young officer took his vessel secretly out in the Mediterranean, as ordered, but that night sent a radio to the Egyptian Navy headquarters in Alexandria, reporting his mission. The information was immediately transmitted through the Minister of War to President Sadat who, horror struck, ordered the submarine to return at once to Alexandria.[6] Qadaffi was bitter about this thwarting of his planned revenge.

Nevertheless, despite these problems with the mercurial Qadaffi, Sadat was grateful for the financial assistance Egypt received from Libya during the period 1971-1973. More than one billion dollars of Libyan oil wealth was contributed toward the rearmament of Egypt, and was particularly useful to pay for those items of equipment for which the Soviets demanded cash.

REORGANIZATION OF THE EGYPTIAN WAR MINISTRY

Although President Sadat was grateful to General Sadiq for his loyalty during the Ali Sabri conspiracy, the two men did not get along very well. As a professional soldier, Sadiq was understandably unhappy about President Sadat's growing determination to end the "No War, No Peace" situation by force of arms. He kept reminding the President that Soviet failure to meet the arms delivery schedule meant that Egypt lacked the weapons and equipment required for major military operations.

On October 24, 1972, after it became evident that the Soviets were about to step up their long-delayed program of arms deliveries, President Sadat called a meeting of the Supreme Council of the Armed Forces at his residence in Giza (a residential district in Cairo). Present at the meeting, in addition to President Sadat and General Sadiq, were Lieutenant General Saad el-Shazli, Chief of Staff; Major General Abd el Kader Hassan, a deputy to the Minister of War; Admiral Abdul Rahman Fahmy, Commander in Chief of the Navy; and twelve other senior Army generals. Sadat expressed his desire that plans be initiated for starting a limited war, as soon as Soviet deliveries had built up Egyptian strength to acceptable levels. Generals Sadiq and Hassan argued vehemently against such a war without much more preparation. They were supported by Ad-

[6] *Ibid.*, pp. 192-194.

miral Fahmy and several of the generals. Agreeing with the President were Generals Shazli and Ahmed Ismail, now the Director of Intelligence and a former Chief of Staff. After a bitter, inconclusive argument, Sadat adjourned the meeting.

Two days later President Sadat dismissed General Sadiq, General Hassan, and Admiral Fahmy. He appointed Ahmed Ismail as the new Commander in Chief and Minister of War; he left Shazli as Chief of Staff, and accepted Ismail's recommendation for recalling Admiral Fouad Abu Zekri from retirement, to become the new Commander in Chief of the Navy.

Sadat had decided on war.

5

The Palestinians,
Jordan, and Syria

PALESTINIAN GUERRILLAS AND THE JORDAN ARMY

King Hussein and the Jordan Army leaders had mixed feelings about the Battle of Kerama. They were pleased with their performance against the Israelis, but they were resentful that the fight had been forced upon them by the Palestinian guerrillas, who, although they had taken heavy casualties, had nevertheless played a relatively minor role in the fighting. The Jordanians had noted with some contempt Yasser Arafat's flight from Kerama during the early minutes of the battle.

Hussein demanded that the guerrillas, who by that time (1968) had more than 2,000 armed men based in Jordan, accept the military orders of the Jordan Army Headquarters. The Palestinians assumed, probably correctly, that under Jordanian military control they would be prohibited from operating across the Jordan River against Israel, and they refused. By November 1968, the mounting tension led to violence, with exchange of fire between PLO guerrillas and Jordan Army troops.

King Hussein was in an extremely awkward political and military situation. More than half of Jordan's population of 2,000,000 were either former Palestinians, or one generation removed from Palestinian forebears, or recent refugees from the Israeli occupation of the West Bank in 1967. A large proportion of these people were admirers of the Palestinian guerrillas, and were ideological supporters of Nasser's pan-Arabism. And their sentiments were shared by some of the other Jordanians, who did not have a long tradition of Hashemite rule. The only element of the population on which Hussein could rely was the 60,000-man Jordan Army, a large proportion of which had been recruited from desert Bedouin tribes, and whose officers were largely members of the Bedouin aristocracy.

Even before the 1967 War Hussein had been under considerable pressure from the other Arab states to allow the Palestinian guerrillas to use his country as a base. Because the UNEF was patrolling the

Israel-Egypt ceasefire line in the Sinai, Jordan then provided the longest, most easily accessible frontier over which the guerrillas could penetrate into Israeli-held territory. This situation, of course, was still true after the 1967 War. Yet Hussein could see the possibility, if he allowed the guerrillas to build up their armed strength without control, that they might join with a substantial element of his subjects to overthrow him and his government. At the very least they would invite more Israeli reprisals. On the other hand, if he opposed the guerrillas, or tried to eject them, he could see the possibility that, with the assistance of the other Arab states and support from the substantial dissident element in his country, they could also overthrow him. At best, therefore, his options were limited.

For the next two and a half years Hussein operated within the narrow limits of those options with great courage and considerable skill. His army, which would have been much happier fighting Israelis, nonetheless resented the guerrillas, and their presence as a rival military force in Jordan. Hussein allowed that resentment to erupt into occasional outbreaks of violence between his troops and the guerrillas, but without ever letting either his troops or the situation get out of his control. Had the Army been truly unleashed, there is little doubt that they could have destroyed or driven out the guerrillas in a few days. But the consequences of this could have been disastrous, both in stimulating rebellion among his people, and in attracting against himself and his impoverished nation the combined wrath and financial and military might of the other Arab states.

Between November 1968 and July 1970 there were frequent incidents, as many precipitated by the guerrillas as by the Jordan Army. Seven different times Hussein and the PLO leaders—usually Arafat—arranged a ceasefire and signed solemn agreements to work together in peace and harmony against the common foe.

On July 8, 1970, there was a new outbreak of fighting between guerrillas and the Jordan Army. It was the result of orders from the Jordan Army that no weapons could be carried in Amman save by army troops in uniform. For five days sporadic fighting took place around the country, with fighting particularly intense in and around Amman. King Hussein narrowly escaped an assassination attempt during this strife. Finally, on July 12, after the Syrian government of President Nureddin al-Attassi announced its full support of the Palestinian guerrillas, Hussein made his eighth agreement with them. In return for their acceptance of the decree forbidding weapons in and around Amman, he agreed to dismiss the commander in chief, Major General Nasir Ben-Jamil, and to relieve his cousin, Major General Sherif Ben Shaker, from his position as commander of the 3rd Armored Division in the Amman region. Both generals were known to oppose the guerrillas.

BLACK SEPTEMBER

The uneasy peace did not last long. On September 2 Hussein again escaped an assassination attempt. Fighting broke out a few days later; then there was a brief truce. On September 15 Hussein dismissed his civilian government, and established a new military government. The Premier was Brigadier Mohommed Daoud, a soldier of Palestinian background, but the King called from retirement the Army's hero of Bab al Wad and Latrun in the 1947-1949 War, Field Marshal Habis el Majali, a fiercely loyal Bedouin, to be Commander in Chief of the Army. As Chief of Staff the king appointed General Ben Shaker, hated and feared by the Palestinian guerrillas.

The guerrilla response was quick and violent—as the Army apparently expected. The most serious fighting yet to take place between the guerrillas and the Army broke out the next day, and continued for eleven days. The Army very quickly cleared the guerrillas out of Amman, from nearby Zarqa, and from most of the other major towns. Army task forces destroyed a number of guerrilla camps around the countryside.

On September 20, however, a new element was introduced into the conflict. A Syrian armored brigade attacked across the border near Ramtha, and forced the Jordan Army units in the north to turn their attention from the guerrillas to this more formidable threat. By the 21st the Syrians had been driven back into Syria, but late on the 22nd, or early on the 23rd, the Syrian Army began a full-scale invasion of northern Jordan. The Syrian forces consisted of elements of the 5th Infantry Division, the 9th and 88th Armored Brigades and the 67th Mechanized Brigade, with T-54/55 tanks, and a Ranger battalion—about the equivalent of two divisions, with substantial supporting artillery. By the 24th the Syrians had occupied Irbid and, in active collaboration with the Palestinian guerrillas, controlled much of northern Jordan.

On September 22 an emergency meeting of Arab heads of state convened in Cairo. The next day, with news of the larger Syrian involvement, the meeting was temporarily adjourned, while a delegation visited Amman and Damascus. On the 25th the delegation returned to Cairo to announce that an agreement had been reached between King Hussein and a number of captured guerrilla leaders. But Arafat and other Palestinian leaders denounced this so-called agreement, and insisted that the fight should continue. That day Jordanian Prime Minister Daoud resigned and mysteriously disappeared. (It later turned out that Libyan President Qadaffi—and Daoud's daughter—had persuaded Palestinian Daoud to put loyalty to the Palestinian cause ahead of loyalty to the Jordanian king.)

On September 25 and 26 the Jordanians won a substantial military victory over the invading Syrians, with the 40th Armored Brigade particularly distinguishing itself. A major element in the victory was the use of close support aircraft, Hunters, as tank-killers. The Syrian Air Force, fearful of provoking Israeli intervention, provided no air cover for the Syrian tanks, which were like sitting ducks for the Jordanian fighter planes, working in close coordination with skillfully employed Jordanian armor. By evening of the 26th the Syrians had been driven back across the border. President Attassi seems to have considered escalating the battle, but he was dissuaded by clear threats from Jerusalem of Israeli intervention.

NEW GOVERNMENT IN SYRIA

On October 18, 1970, Syria's Defense Minister, Air Force General Hafez al Assad, seized virtual control of the government, although President Attassi retained his nominal position as President. Less than a month later, however, Assad completed his coup—the 21st to be successful since Syrian independence 24 years earlier—and ousted Attassi.

The ignominious Syrian defeat in Jordan the previous month had played a part in this latest Syrian coup, but internal political and social causes were primarily responsible. As in each of the previous coups, there was a purge of senior officers of doubtful loyalty to the new regime. While this did not directly affect officers of intermediate and junior rank, the practical and psychological effects of the high level changes created turmoil. However, this time the military reforms were apparently more efficient than they had been after previous coups. Assad, after all, was a military man, and he selected as Chief of Staff and Minister of Defense Major General Mustafa Tlass, who, like Assad, was a dedicated soldier as well as an astute politician.

General Tlass had an opportunity to demonstrate his political skills early the next year, after another eruption of violence between guerrillas and Jordan Army troops in Jordan. On April 9 in Amman, Tlass, as mediator, got the opponents to sign yet another agreement for future cooperation—the tenth since November 1968.

President Assad dealt skillfully with the issue of Palestinian refugees and guerrillas in Syria—the issue that was at that time apparently tearing Jordan apart. The new Syrian President took every possible opportunity to announce his solidarity with, and support for, the guerrillas in their campaigns against both Israel and the government of Jordan. At the same time the military situation on the Golan Heights was such that there was no opportunity for the guerrillas to operate against Israel without involving the Syrian Army; and this Assad naturally could not permit. He also refused to allow any political activities by Palestinians in Syria. When members of Al-Fatah seemed to be violating this decree, he arrested them.

Assad also very quickly established cordial relations with the Soviet Union. In January 1971, shortly after he had consolidated his authority in Damascus, he visited Moscow, seeking both financial and direct military assistance. He got both, and by June substantial numbers of MiG-21s, Sukhoi-7s, and other types of aircraft and weaponry arrived in Syria from the USSR. Also arriving were substantial numbers of military and technical advisors, to help rebuild the Syrian Army from the depths into which it had been plunged by defeat and internal political turmoil.

JORDAN SOLVES THE GUERRILLA PROBLEM

Early in 1971 Palestinian extremists—probably led by Dr. George Habash, radical leader of the Popular Front for the Liberation of Palestine (PFLP)—established in Jordan an organization called the Free Jordan Movement, with the twin objectives of attracting members from Jordanians of Palestinian origin, and overthrowing King Hussein. This was followed by renewed clashes between the guerrillas and the Jordan Army in March, and again in April. The guerrillas accused King Hussein of breaking the agreement reached the previous September. Jordanian spokesmen responded, however, by pointing out that, although under the terms of that agreement armed fedayeen were supposed to keep out of towns, all of the disturbances had taken place in towns.

Meanwhile, strong internal differences among the Palestinians came to the surface. Yasser Arafat, chief of Al-Fatah, the largest of the Palestinian groups, denounced the aims of the Free Jordan Movement. Also, in response to Habash's call for the overthrow of the Jordanian Government, Arafat said that his group would oppose with force any Palestinian efforts to overthrow Hussein. Nevertheless, soon after this, on March 31, 1971, Arafat warned that Hussein's government was "preparing a new massacre."

This dispute among the Palestinians, and the continuing guerrilla warfare being carried on by Palestinian extremists, made it evident to King Hussein and his advisors that—despite the temporary accord which Syria's General Tlass negotiated in early April—no real agreement could be reached with the guerrillas. (It is possible, of course, that Hussein never intended to abide by the agreement, but there is no clear evidence that he did not.) Furthermore, the disunity among the Palestinians seemed to offer an opportunity to destroy their already-weakened strength. The death of Nasser and internal turmoil in Egypt made the opportunity more attractive.

By mid-July King Hussein, Field Marshal Majali, and General Ben Shaker seem to have decided that the time was propitious for a final solution of the guerrilla problem. On July 13 another outbreak of fighting occurred, seemingly little different from the tens of incidents that had preceded it. However, this time Hussein was not holding a leash on the Army, and its plans were as good as Ben Shaker, a graduate of the US Army Command and General Staff College, could make them.

Systematically, a task force of two armored brigades and one infantry brigade overran the guerrilla camps one by one. In each of these the guerrillas who were not killed either surrendered or fled. Of nearly 4,000 armed guerrillas in Jordan, by July 19 the Jordan Army had captured 2,300, killed about 600, and dispersed another 600.[1] Interestingly, over a period of six days, about 80 crossed the Jordan River to surrender to the Israeli Army rather than to the Jordan Army. The remainder took refuge in Lebanon. The Jordanian government announced that only about 200 guerrillas were still at liberty, as fugitives. Two days later, in a wise gesture of magnaminity, Hussein released all of the prisoners, and most of them also immediately went to Lebanon.

The strain on the loyalties of the population of Jordan had been great. However, the demonstration of Army efficiency discouraged any popular uprising in support of the guerrillas, and Hussein's internal political situation was better than it had been since the Six Day War.

Externally, however, things were different. On July 19 Iraq closed its frontiers with Jordan, and withdrew from Jordan a force of about 12,000 men that had been stationed in northeastern Jordan against the possible outbreak of another war with Israel.

On July 20 Syrian artillery shelled Ramtha and other towns in northern Jordan, and Jordanian artillery immediately responded. President Assad, however, had no intention of repeating Attassi's short-sighted invasion of Jordan. Instead, he closed the frontiers, then on August 12 formally broke diplomatic relations with Jordan.

Charges of ruthlessness and atrocities inflicted upon the guerrillas and upon unarmed Palestinians were flung by other Arabs against Hussein and his army. Jordan became virtually a pariah among the Arab League states. When Prime Minister Wasfi Tel of Jordan, attending an Arab League meeting in Cairo, was assassinated on November 28, the press in other Arab countries expressed little sympathy for the murdered diplomat or his isolated country, but were full of praise for the daring and skill of the Palestinian assassins. These were apparently members of a small offshoot of the PLO and the Popular Liberation Front of Palestine (the Habash Group, or PLFP) who called themselves the Black September Group, in grim remembrance of the bitter struggle in Jordan in September 1970. There is reason to believe that, despite official PLO disclaimers, this group was mainly composed of anti-Arafat elements of the PLO.

[1] Some Arab sources insist that as many as 10,000 Palestinian noncombatant refugees were killed during these operations.

BOOK FIVE

The October War, 1973–
The War of Ramadan;
The Yom Kippur War

1
Egyptian Plans and Preparations

In his memoirs,* President Anwar Sadat implies that his firm decision to go to war in 1973 was taken on November 30, 1972. The considerations on which the decision was made are now clear. On the basis of the assessments of the state of readiness of the Egyptian armed forces, supplied to him by the new Minister of War and Commander in Chief of the Armed Forces, General Ahmed Ismail Ali, neither Sadat nor Ismail could have been under any illusion that Egypt had reached—or in the foreseeable future would reach—tactical military parity with Israel. Sadat had obviously come to the conclusion, however, that Israel was satisfied with the status quo as it had existed since the 1967 War, and with its de facto annexation of the territories occupied in that war. Thus no Israeli moves toward reasonable negotiations on the issues of UN Resolution 242 of 1967 could be expected without pressure from one or both of the great powers. Sadat obviously believed, therefore, that the only possibility of moving toward a Middle East settlement was to precipitate action that would force the major powers and the United Nations to pay attention to the "No Peace, No War" situation in the Middle East.

Sadat has given no reason to believe that he was thinking of peace or a Middle East settlement for reasons other than national and self-interest. The economy of Egypt, precarious at best, had been badly hurt by the closure of the Suez Canal. The country could not afford the tremendous burden of armaments costs that it had assumed, and while for the most part these armaments had been received from the Soviet Union on long repayment terms, the economic future of Egypt was mortgaged.

As the leader of Egypt, Sadat had to answer two strong, and not necessarily consistent, desires of his people. He had to give them hope for, and some evidence of progress toward, eventual satisfaction of their rising expectations, stimulated by what they could read, see, and hear in the press, on television, and on the radio. One obvious way of moving

* Anwar el-Sadat, *In Search of Identity*, New York, 1978, p. 237.

387

in this direction was to achieve an international situation which would permit the opening of the Suez Canal, and be sufficiently stable to relax some tensions in the Middle East, and somewhat reduce the heavy burden of Egyptian armament expenditures.

At the same time Sadat had to cater to the fierce Moslem, Arabic, and nationalistic chauvinism of a volatile people who demanded that Egypt must recover the lands lost in 1967, and that Egypt play its part in rectifying the wrong that they so fervently believed had been done to their fellow Arabs, the Palestinians. A peace that came from surrender or appeasement would not be satisfactory to either the Egyptians or Sadat. At the same time, a heavy armaments burden, without employing the arms to right the wrongs against the occupier of Egyptian territory, would not do either. Thus Sadat came to the conclusion that it would be better and more satisfactory for the Egyptian people to fight a war and lose, than not to fight at all simply because defeat was likely. This, in fact, was the rationale which had caused him to dismiss military leaders like Sadiq, Hassan, and Fawzi, who failed to recognize that likely honorable defeat was a preferable alternative to an inglorious peace. And furthermore, the disruption of war was certain to force the superpowers to turn their attention back to the Middle East. Whether at the time he was thinking farther ahead to the post-war possibility of reestablishing relations with the United States, with ultimate economic and political benefits from such a rapprochement, can only be surmised. It is doubtful, but possible.

In any event, it was because of his intent to use the war to kindle new initiatives in the Middle East that Sadat selected the code name "Sharara"—meaning "spark"—for the war.

In essence, then, Sadat's decision to go to war was a political gamble designed to end a political stalemate, since for Egypt and for Sadat any change was likely to be better than the stalemate. Furthermore, Sadat, who after all had started his adult life as a soldier, did not believe defeat was inevitable, and General Ismail agreed that there was a possibility of limited military success. Since 1967, when he had assumed command of the shattered remnants of Egypt's field army on the banks of the Suez Canal, Ismail had been thinking of ways to limit or offset the known and undeniable elements of Israeli military superiority, and to enhance the fewer, but nonetheless substantial, Egyptian advantages.

GENERAL ISMAIL'S STRATEGIC CONCEPT

General Ismail, a burly, erect, impressive-looking six-footer, had learned the military trade from the British, and had studied the higher direction of war at Russia's Frunze Academy and at Egypt's Nasser

Higher Military Academy—roughly equivalent to the National War College in the United States. Whether from the British, or from the Russians, or from study of the writings of Clausewitz, or simply from his own intelligent perceptions, General Ismail well understood the relationship of war and politics. When, soon after he became Commander in Chief in November 1972, he received President Sadat's directive to initiate war planning, he formulated a strategic concept which he then expressed quite explicitly to his staff.

A complete military victory would be impossible for either side, since the two superpowers would not permit it. Whether or not President Sadat or General Ismail received any confirmation from the Kremlin about this in 1972 or 1973, this was a primary consideration in their planning.

Two major Israeli military advantages had to be clearly recognized, and offset insofar as possible by Egyptian strategic or tactical countermeasures. The first of these advantages was Israeli preeminence in the air, and the ability of the Israeli Air Force to provide effective support to ground operations. Second, Israel possessed a general tactical-technological superiority over the Egyptians in mobile ground combat, epitomized by Israeli excellence in tank warfare.

Ismail, however, interpreted the record of the three previous wars as demonstrating that in defensive combat the Egyptians could more than hold their own with the Israelis; all that was necessary was to assure the confidence of every soldier in this capability. Ismail was convinced that the Egyptian soldier could be inspired with such confidence in himself and in the new weapons being received from the Soviet Union; then he would be steadfast in combat. This inspiration would come through training, through discipline, and through indoctrination.

The new Egyptian commander in chief was determined to exploit the Israeli inferiority in manpower, and the known extreme sensitivity of Israel to human casualties. Ismail repeatedly said to his staff, "Loss of personnel is more painful to Israel than loss of territory or combat material."

Israel was also known to fear the possibility of a major two-front war, which would cause division of limited Israeli resources. Preliminary explorations had revealed Syrian willingness to join with Egypt in such a war, and with greater and more effective coordination of effort than had yet been achieved by the Arabs against Israel.

With these considerations in mind, the basic operational concept which General Ismail provided to his planners was for a joint strategic offensive in cooperation with Syria, in order to force Israel to divide its forces in a two-front war. The specific Egyptian tasks were: to defeat Israeli forces in the western Sinai by a deliberate assault crossing of the Suez Canal; to seize five or more bridgeheads 10 to 15 kilometers deep on the eastern bank of the Canal; to repel Israeli counterattacks; to inflict maximum losses on the enemy; and to be prepared for further missions, depending on the success of this initial assault and concurrent Syrian operations. They hoped the bridgeheads would include the Mitla Pass, and if possible the Giddi Pass, but a ceasefire with firm Egyptian military control of a substantial strip of territory on the east bank of the Canal would be deemed a success.

The Egyptians insist that from concept to implementation their operational plans were developed without any outside assistance, other than for essentially strategic coordination with the Syrians. Specifically, the Egyptians deny all suggestions that they received any assistance from Russian advisors, either in developing or in carrying out the plan. They assert, in fact, that they went out of their way to keep their intentions and plans secret from the Russians lest the US-Soviet detente impel Moscow to try to prevent the attack. Some Egyptians have even gone so far as to suggest that one of the reasons President Sadat ordered all of the Russian military advisors out of the country in July of 1972[1] was so that they would not know about or interfere with the planning for his proposed war.

There is no reason to doubt Egyptian assertions that they received no Russian assistance in their war planning. There is, however, considerable evidence that in the years between 1967 and 1972, Soviet and Egyptian staffs had jointly considered the problems of crossing the Suez Canal and had developed hypothetical plans for doing so. Certainly the buildup of the Egyptian Army with Soviet equipment during that period, with its heavy emphasis on the most advanced bridging equipment and techniques, was clearly done with the concept of such an assault crossing in mind. Thus there can be no question that Soviet military men had made some contributions, even if only indirectly, to the planning process.

On the other hand, there is no doubt that the man essentially responsible for the plan which was actually employed was General Ismail himself, and that the formulation of the plan was done most skillfully and professionally by the Egyptian staff under the leadership of its Chief of Staff, Lieutenant General Saad el Shazli, and the Director of Operations, Major General Mohommed el Gamasy.

General Ismail and his staff sought three conceptual goals for Egyptian performance in the proposed operation: surprise, thoroughness, and tactical-technical efficiency. Their efforts to achieve these operational goals are worth elaboration.

---

[1] About 200 technicians remained, as well as a few instructors at the Nasser Higher Academy.

THE EFFORT TO ACHIEVE SURPRISE

Among the many measures taken to secure both strategic and tactical surprise, the following are significant.

Regardless of what President Sadat's motives for the expulsion of the Soviet experts from Egypt in mid-1972 had been, the Egyptian planners rightly assumed that this would lead the Israelis to conclude that war was unlikely, since they believed that the Egyptians would not dare to undertake a major, complex, offensive operation without Russian technical advice.

Beginning in late November 1972, every month the Egyptians carried out large- or small-scale maneuvers or command post exercises near the Suez Canal, always in such a manner that some evidence of this activity was observed by the Israelis.

Quite early in the planning the Egyptians decided to attack on a Saturday (the Jewish Sabbath) or on a Jewish holiday, when—they had observed—the alertness of the Israeli forces was notably reduced. General Ismail was therefore particularly pleased when his planners calculated that on Saturday, October 6, 1973, the moon and Canal tides would be favorable. Not only was October 6 a Sabbath, it was also the Yom Kippur holy day, the most solemn fast day of the Jewish religion. It was also during the Moslem holy month of Ramadan, when the Israelis would not expect Arab activity. One additional consideration was that elections were scheduled in Israel on October 28; and the attention of Israeli citizens would be focussed on that event.

Strict security measures assured absolute secrecy. The October 6 date was agreed upon between Presidents Hafez al Assad and Sadat, and General Ismail (and possibly General Mustafa Tlass, the Syrian Defense Minister), at a secret meeting during an Arab summit conference in Cairo on September 12. There is every reason to believe, however, that for three weeks they did not inform even their closest advisors of the specific date—although, of course, the imminence of war was obvious to all senior Egyptian and Syrian officers.

But, as Dr. Avi Shlaim has written, "The Arabs went far beyond mere secrecy and resorted to active deception designed to create a misleading impression concerning their capabilities, plans and intentions."[2] Sadat was even able to convert personal embarrassment to the cause; the world was subtly reminded of how he had said that 1971 was "the year of decision," and now almost three years had passed by without anything more than sound and bombast. When Secretary of State Kissinger proposed peace initiatives in September,

[2] Avi Shlaim, "Failures in National Intelligence Estimates; The Case of the Yom Kippur War." *World Politics*, April, 1976, p. 348.

these were welcomed eagerly—but not too eagerly—by the Arabs. The kidnapping that month of the Soviet Jews in Austria by Palestinian Arabs may or may not have been part of the deception plan; in any event it was seized upon by the Arabs to draw world attention from the Suez Canal and the Golan Heights. As to the Canal, a news item was planted in a Lebanese newspaper commenting on the neglect and deterioration of Soviet equipment in the Canal Zone. As to the Golan, the digging in of Syrian tanks was ostentatious—but not too ostentatious—to encourage Israeli agents to report that the Syrian buildup was intended to stop an anticipated Israeli retaliatory assault, rather than for an offensive. Again quoting Dr. Shlaim: "These efforts were part of an imaginative, intensive, and well-orchestrated strategy of deception which brought rich rewards. Particularly effective was the exploitation of Israeli weaknesses by deliberately acting in such a way as to confirm the Israeli leaders' known belief that the Arabs were not ready and not willing to go to war."[3]

On September 26, in separate, routine press releases, both Syria and Egypt announced the concentration of troops for annual maneuvers. Thus an even larger concentration of troops than was usual for monthly exercises was to be expected. Israeli and American intelligence duly noted this fact, but were unaware of what the Egyptians had been doing for several months to make this concentration still larger. As troop units had been brought in to the Canal zone for exercises, or had been rotated through training areas in the desert region between Cairo and the Canal, each time a smaller number returned to their garrisons than had left. The others, usually about a quarter to a third of the command, had been left in the area, their presence undetectable among the substantial troop concentrations that were already based west of the Canal.

The actual H-Hour, 1405 hours (2:05 p.m.) on the 6th, was apparently not agreed upon until General Ismail visited Damascus on October 3. The two Egyptian field army commanders and selected planners were informed of the decision the same day, but apparently the exact hour of the attack was not given to the division commanders until 8:00 a.m. on the 6th. Brigade and regimental commanders were not informed until 10:00 a.m., and the assault battalion commanders did not receive their orders until noon, two hours before H-Hour.

Meanwhile, on October 4, 1973, President Sadat called in the Soviet Ambassador, Vladimir Vinogradov, and informed him of the planned Arab offensive. Evidently by preagreement, President Assad was at the same time giving this information to the Soviet Ambassador to Syria.

[3] *Ibid.*

Later that day the chief of the reduced Soviet technical mission in Egypt asked to see General Ismail, who at once received the Russian officer. The mission chief told Ismail that he had been informed by the ambassador of the pending attack. He said that he and his technicians had already assumed that the operation would begin soon, but had not been certain of the date. The Soviet government had, of course, been informed and requested permission to send aircraft to Cairo to fly out all civilians, including the families of the handful of Russian technicians remaining in Egypt. Ismail at once approved this request, without comment. The Russian wished the Egyptian general good luck, then departed. The airlift began late that night, and continued through the 5th.

A similar Russian air evacuation was taking place from Damascus airport. A Danish UNTSO officer and his wife, returning home from a party near midnight, October 4-5, passed two busloads of Russians heading toward the airport. They were puzzled by this, but thought little about it for the next 38 hours.

THE PLANNING PROCESS

The professional competence of the Egyptian planning for Operation "Badr"—named after the place where the Prophet Mohammed won his first victory in 624—could probably not have been excelled by any other army in the world.[4] The Egyptian planners had weighed the various considerations and selected a D-Day late enough to permit maximum familiarization of the troops with their new equipment (some of which was only received from Russia, Britain, Italy and Germany as late as September), yet before there was any possibility of snow on the Golan Heights, which would complicate any Syrian offensive.

Another consideration was meteorological conditions. The deception planning had suggested the suitability of October 6 (Yom Kippur in the month of Ramadan). Happily, on that day the ebb and flow of Canal tides would give maximum levels of the water through most of that night, and the nights immediately thereafter.[5] The moon phase was equally favorable, with good moonlight before midnight, and darkness thereafter. A month later, not only would there be the possibility of bad weather on the Golan, but meteorological conditions on the Canal would be unfavorable.

An unusual H-Hour was selected: 1405 hours, instead of the more

[4] The Egyptian code name for the war was "Sharara," spark; the code name for the crossing operation was "Badr."

[5] The reason for wanting maximum rather than minimum tides was so that there would be periods of several hours each day when assault boats would not run aground on the gradually shelving banks of the Canal between the deep channel and the embankment.

normal dawn or dusk timing of major assaults. The Syrians would have preferred a dawn H-Hour with the sun in the eyes of the Israeli defenders on the Golan Heights. However, after long discussions, they finally deferred to the Egyptians, who wanted a few hours of daylight to start the Canal crossing, but did not want to give the Israelis time to mount a counterattack before dark.

Assigned to work in close coordination with the assault elements were some 15,000 well trained engineer troops, organized in about 80 company and battalion sized units. These soldiers were highly motivated and had been trained interminably in practice crossings over branches of the Nile, or dry ditches constructed to the dimensions of the Suez Canal, or across the El Balah Channel, a short stretch of the Canal west of Balah Island, retained by Egypt.

There were two major obstacles facing the Egyptians on the Sinai front. The first of these was the Canal itself, more than 170 kilometers long, a continuous water-filled channel some 180 meters in minimum width. Prior to 1967 the central channel had been dredged to a minimum depth of more than 18 meters to accommodate the largest vesssels; even after disuse for some six years the greatest accumulation of silt was less than a meter; in no place was it fordable. Being at sea level along its full length, the Canal has no significant current, but it has minor eddies and substantial tides (particularly in the south), creating currents which change directions four times a day and which could affect swimmers or very light watercraft. In the north, the tidal current reaches 18 meters per minute; in the south, 90 meters per minute. In periods of minimum tide the change of the Canal level is about 60 centimeters every six hours; at time of maximum change, as on October 6, there are 180 centimeters between flood and ebb levels in the south. The shoulders of the Canal cannot be climbed by amphibious vehicles except along the shores of the Bitter Lakes.

THE BAR LEV LINE

The second obstacle was the Israeli system of fortifications and mobile defensive reserves in depth, known as the Bar Lev Line. This was an expensive fortification and observation system stretching some 160 kilometers along the east bank of the Suez Canal from ten kilometers south of Port Fuad in the north to the outlet at the Gulf of Suez. (The area northeast of Kantara is swampland totally unsuited for operations, but it was traversed by several Israeli-built hard-surface roads.) This fortification system had been constructed by the Israelis at an estimated cost of 300 million dollars. Working eastward from the Canal itself, the Bar Lev Line comprised six major elements.

Under the water, beside the east bank, were installations of under-

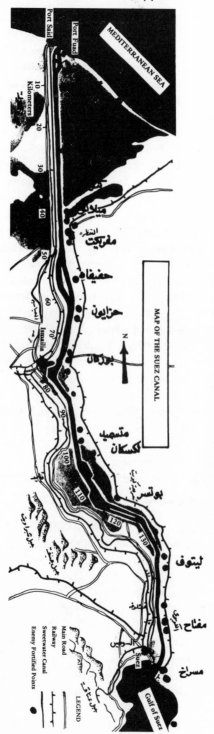

(The Bar Lev Line Consisted of 22 Fortified Positions Containing 31 Strongpoints)

ground and underwater pipelines containing inflammable crude oil, which—when valves were opened—would float on the surface where it could be ignited, so as to cover the Canal with a sheet of flame. There is considerable controversy as to whether there really was a comprehensive flame barrier system—as opposed to the unquestionable existence of one or two experimental installations—and whether either the system or the installations were operating on October 6. The Israelis had certainly tested the system and—as intended—the Egyptians had naturally observed the tests. Some Israeli sources have claimed that the tests showed that the concept was unreliable, and that it had been abandoned. Other Israelis admit, however, that sometime prior to October 6 the new commander of the Israeli Southern Command, Major General Shmuel Gonen, had ordered the reactivation of at least part of this system. They insist, however, that by October 6 not more than one or two of the taps were operational. In any event, the Egyptians assert that on the night before the attack they sent frogmen to block the working taps with concrete, and that this operation was successful. They also assert that on October 6 they captured two engineers working on the system; the Israelis tacitly admit this.

Rising abruptly from the east edge of the Canal was a high embankment along the entire east bank, southward from Kantara. This was based upon nearly a century of Canal dredging residue, which had been made higher and wider by the Israelis. In most places it was 20 or more meters high and at least 10 meters thick. This had a dual purpose. In the first place, it was to conceal Israeli movements just east of the Canal. Second, its 45 degree slope from the water ensured that no amphibious vehicle could possibly climb it.

Scattered along the Canal were some 33 strongpoints and observation posts with thick overhead cover, made of railroad rails and an Israeli adaptation of the old engineer's gabion, bundles of heavy rocks held together by wire net. These strongpoints, each with a watchtower observation post as well as pillbox OPs, were located on and in the embankment overlooking the Canal itself. However, before early 1972, while General Sharon was commanding the Southern Command, he had closed all except 16 of the posts. All of these were well supplied with food, ammunition, and water. Gonen had issued orders to have some of the others reopened, but this had not yet been done. Between the strongpoints, at intervals of 50 to 75 meters, were hard-surface ramps, providing hull-defilade positions from which tanks could fire on the Canal or the west bank.

Behind the embankment was an extensive, but not completely continuous, minefield system, running from Kantara south to the shores of the Gulf of Suez. These minefields were concentrated around the strongpoints, and could be covered with fire from the tank ramps on the main embankment to the west, and also from comparable ramps on a second embankment, a few hundred meters to the east. This second embankment line was not continuous, and not so high as the first line; it was designed to provide both cover and fields of fire for defenders against any possible attackers who had penetrated the first line. In some places there was a third embankment line, covering major access routes.

Further back were mobile reserves in depth, mostly tank units. These reserves, as well as the artillery deployed near the Canal, could use an extensive roadnet that facilitated lateral and transverse communications and movement. The first lateral road, just east of the embankment, providing lateral communications between the Bar Lev strongpoints—and rarely more than 1,000 meters from the Canal—was called "Lexicon" by the Israelis. Further east, running continuously from the Mediterranean coast to the Gulf of Suez, about 6,000 to 10,000 meters east of the embankment, was the Artillery Road, so called because its main purpose was to facilitate lateral artillery displacement. The next road, about 30 kilometers east of the Canal, running south from Baluza, was called the Lateral Road. These three roads were linked to each other and with the area further east by numerous transverse roads.

Just east of the Artillery Road was a line of command posts, six in all, from the northern swamps to the Gulf of Suez. These concrete structures were built into the east or defiladed sides of hills or ridges, and (like the strongpoints) provided with heavy overhead cover of railroad rails and rock and wire netting gabions. These command posts were linked with the Canal-side strongpoints, with each other, and with four larger rear-area command posts, by radio and by telephone wires laid underground.

The rear area command posts were at Tasa, Romani, Bir Gifgafa (called Refidim by the Israelis) and Um Kusheiba. Tasa was a small military installation at the intersection of the main Beersheba-Ismailia road (called Talisman by the Israelis) and the Lateral Road. It included the underground command post of General Mendler's Sinai Division, most of the divisional support units, a small airstrip, and also an advanced depot of a wide variety of weapons, equipment, spare parts, ammunition, and—particularly—engineer supplies. There was a similar installation at Romaru, on the northern road.

Refidim or Bir Gifgafa was about 50 kilometers east of Tasa, on the Talisman Road, and thus about 90 kilometers east of the Canal. It was in the broad depression at the northern end of the Khatmia Ridge, sometimes known as the Khatmia Pass. Refidim was a sizable administrative-logistical installation, with a large airfield, and also with an underground command post, which could be used as an alternate command post by either the Sinai Division or by Southern Command.

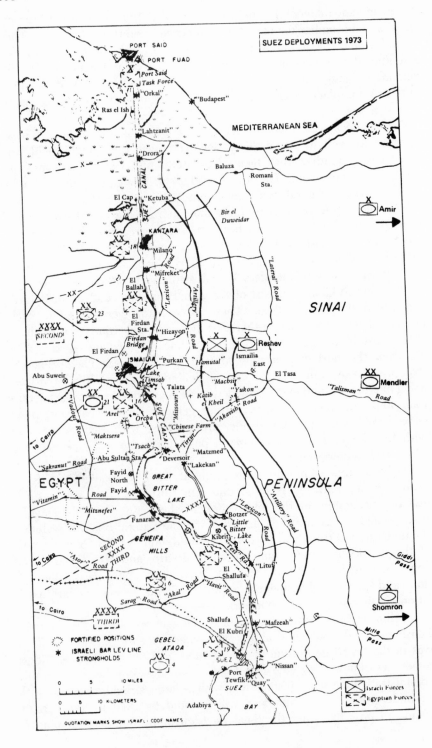

SUEZ DEPLOYMENTS 1973

The peacetime headquarters of Southern Command was at Beersheba, but its wartime command post was at Um Kusheiba, on a high bluff, just north of the Giddi Pass, and overlooking the West Sinai Plain, the desert extending from Khatmia Ridge westward 40 kilometers to the Suez Canal. The installation included not only an observation post with the best possible visual equipment, but also a large and complex electronic facility for monitoring hostile and friendly electronic transmissions.

In addition to the fifteen strongpoints on the Canal, and the sixteenth just east of Port Fuad on the Mediterranean Coast, there was one more comparable strongpoint on the Gulf of Suez, about 25 kilometers south of Port Tewfik on a promontory called Ras Missalah. This was not usually considered to be a part of the Bar Lev Line, and was not seriously attacked by the Egyptians during the war, although they occasionally took it under artillery fire.

ISRAELI DEPLOYMENTS IN THE SINAI

When it was built, the Bar Lev Line had not been intended as a fortified position, but rather as a line of strongly defended observation posts to protect observers who could direct artillery fire and mobile armored counterattacking forces to deal with any possible Egyptian crossing of the Canal. Obviously the fortified observation posts were also strongpoints, providing useful ground bases for armored maneuver. But it was never thought of as, and could not be remotely compared to, such well-known fortifications as the Maginot Line, the Siegfried Line, or the Mannerheim Line.

Although Israeli deterrent propaganda stressed the fortified aspects of the Bar Lev Line, Israeli military men were well aware that the strength of the defensive position lay primarily in the availability of armored forces, supported by artillery and aircraft, and only incidentally and locally in the formidable protection of each strongpoint.

There were two frontline units in the Bar Lev Line defensive concept. First there was a brigade of infantry, with about half of its combat elements—some 500 officers and men—deployed in the 16 strongpoints. In early October 1973, this was a reserve brigade made up of units from the Etzioni Brigade in Jerusalem. These reservists were serving their active duty at this time so that the regulars who normally manned the posts could go home for the holy days. Behind them, in battalion concentrations distributed along the Artillery Road, was a Regular Army armored brigade. Approximately twelve batteries of artillery were located in frequently-changed positions in front of or behind the Artillery Road. These included about one battery each of 175mm and 155mm self-propelled long-range guns, probably six bat-

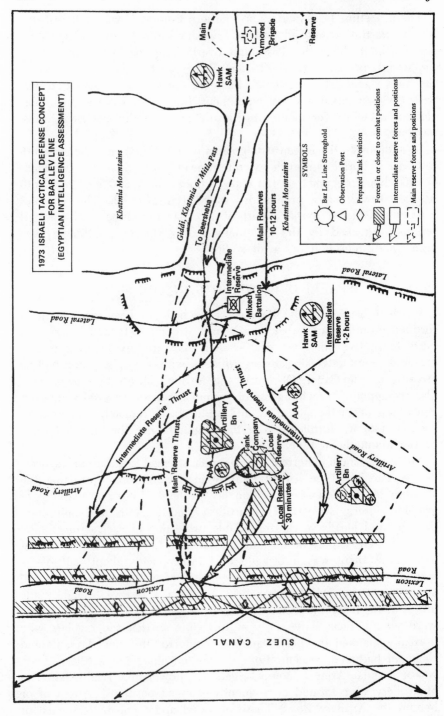

1973 ISRAELI TACTICAL DEFENSE CONCEPT FOR BAR LEV LINE (EGYPTIAN INTELLIGENCE ASSESSMENT)

teries of self-propelled 155mm howitzers, and about two batteries each of 160mm and 120mm mortars, mounted in half-tracks. These infantry, armor, and artillery units, with their command, communications, and support personnel, totalled nearly 8,000 troops.

One additional armored brigade was normally stationed in reserve, between Refidim and the Sinai-Israel frontier. The third armored brigade of the division was normally stationed in garrison further east, inside the Israeli Negev, southwest of Beersheba, but because of the state of alert which Defense Minister Dayan had ordered, this brigade had also moved into the Sinai. It was evidently located southwest of Refidim, along the southern lateral road. There were also four Nahal battalions in the Sinai, available for combat as infantry.

In addition to the twelve batteries of field artillery available in the mobile support element of the Bar Lev Line, there were two artillery emplacements in fortifications in or just behind the so-called line. The first of these, containing six French-built 155mm guns, was about ten kilometers east of Port Tewfik. The guns, with overhead cover of railroad irons and wire-mesh rock gabions like the other Bar Lev Line installations, fired through large embrasures, permitting coverage of the entire Suez-Port Tewfik area. This emplacement had been built during the War of Attrition, and had been used to destroy the Suez oil refinery. The other was a battery of four American-made 175mm guns in the "Budapest" strongpoint, which anchored the Bar Lev Line on the Mediterranean, about fifteen kilometers east of Port Fuad. These guns were capable of hitting any installation in the Port Said-Port Fuad area.

The total force in the Sinai available to Major General Albert Mendler, commanding the division-sized Sinai Defense Force, consisted of about two brigades of infantry and three of armor, a total combat force of nearly 18,000 men, including normal divisional support elements.

The Egyptians were well aware of these Israeli dispositions. They also knew that, under the Israeli mobilization system, this small force could, in three to five days, be built up to 20 brigades and over 100,000 men. But, if they could achieve surprise, an Egyptian force crossing the Canal would, for several hours, be faced by only 8,000 troops, with another 8-10,000 available for commitment soon afterward. It would be more than 24 hours before any additional Israeli forces, in significant numbers, could be deployed to the Sinai.

THE EGYPTIAN FORCE DISPOSITIONS

The total strength of the Egyptian Armed Forces, when fully mobilized, as they were on October 6, was 1.1 million men. More than half of these were in the Army, but in turn almost half of the Army consisted of National Guard units with little training, generally with obsolescent or obsolete equipment, who were used for a variety of rear area and home defense tasks; preeminent among these tasks was protection of the many Nile River bridges. Egypt's mobile field forces consisted of about 310,000 men, of which the major combat units were five infantry divisions, two armored divisions, and three mechanized divisions, plus seven independent armored brigades (one for each of the infantry divisions plus two additional), two independent infantry brigades, two independent airborne brigades, and two commando brigades.

These combat units were allocated among two field armies (each equivalent to a US army corps) and a central military district in and around Cairo. Since the two frontline armies were numbered respectively, Second and Third, Western press correspondents[6] erroneously assumed that the forces of the central military district were organized as the First Army. There was, however, no such army organization, and the central military district was directly under the Armed Forces GHQ as reserve units to be held on the western side of the Suez Canal, at least during the initial phase of the planned operations.[7]

The Second Army, commanded by General Saad el Din Mamoun, consisted of three infantry divisions and one armored division. Attached to the army from the central military district, but not to be committed east of the Canal without GHQ permission, was a mechanized infantry division. The zone of the Second Army was the region between the Mediterranean Sea and the southern edge of the Great Bitter Lake; for all practical operational purposes it was between Kantara in the north and Deversoir in the south.

The Third Army, commanded by General Abd el Moneim Wassel, had two infantry divisions and one armored division, and also had a mechanized infantry division attached from the central military district, with the same limitations on its employment. This army was responsible for the front from the southern end of the Great Bitter Lake down to the head of the Gulf of Suez.

Each infantry division was composed of two infantry brigades, a

[6] As well as Mohamed Heikal, whose otherwise splendid book, *The Road to Rámadan* (London, 1975), reveals a surprising ignorance of military affairs and of the military aspects of the 1973 War.

[7] These numerical army designations had their origin in the shortlived United Arab Republic union of Egypt and Syria. At that time the army in the north, Syria, was designated the First Army, and the other two designated field armies were in Egypt. This is also the origin of the similar insignia of the Syrian and Egyptian armies, which differ only by one star on the shield in the Syrian insignia, two stars in the Egyptian insignia.

mechanized infantry brigade, and an artillery brigade of 72 guns. For this operation an armored brigade was also attached to each infantry division. Thus the normal tank complement of the crossing infantry division had been increased from about 95 to about 200, and personnel strength from less than 12,000 to more than 14,000.

The armored divisions consisted of two armored brigades of about 100 tanks each, a mechanized brigade with an additional 50 tanks, and an artillery brigade. The normal personnel strength of these divisions was also nearly 12,000, but in both armies the armored divisions were kept in reserve, and each had detached an armored brigade to be attached to one of the frontline assaulting infantry divisions.

The mechanized divisions consisted of two mechanized infantry brigades, an armored brigade, and an artillery brigade. At standard strength these divisions included about 200 tanks and nearly 12,000 men.

The combined strength of the Second and Third Armies, with attachments, was about 200,000 men, about 110,000 in the Second Army and about 90,000 in the Third Army. This was considerably more manpower concentrated just west of the Canal than had been stationed there a few months earlier.

A small force, about one reinforced brigade in strength, was in the Port Said-Port Fuad area.

The Egyptian forces west of the Canal were protected and concealed by a system of earthworks, the principal component being a massive sand embankment about 20 meters high in most places and about 15 meters wide, extending for most of the 120 kilometer length of the Canal southward from a point opposite Kantara. A masonry trench ran along the top of this sand embankment, which was set back from the Canal several meters just behind a road parallel to and adjacent to the Canal bank. Scattered along the embankment were a number of broad truncated pyramidal mounds, or towers, each about 30 meters high (i.e., rising six to eight meters above the bank) and each averaging about 180,000 cubic meters of sand. Each of these towers was large enough to accommodate a platoon of tanks in prepared hull-down position to provide direct fire against Israeli strongpoints and tank hardstands on the opposite bank. Also scattered along the embankment, but concentrated particularly on or near these towers, were a number of antitank missile and antitank gun batteries. Hard surfaced ramps sloped up from the old British military road on the western side to the top of the embankment at each of the towers, to make it easy for tanks and guns to get to the top.

Extending 40 to 55 kilometers behind the earthworks ran a belt of fortifications which included artillery compounds, fortified hospitals, airfields, and some 130 SAM missile sites. Most of these missile sites

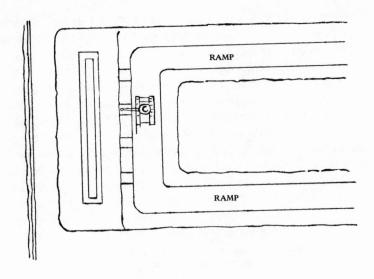

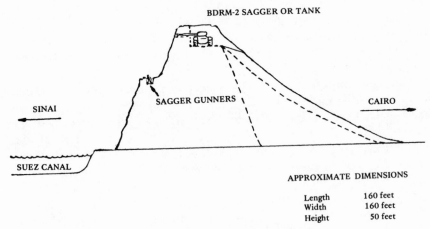

RAMP

RAMP

BDRM-2 SAGGER OR TANK

SINAI

SAGGER GUNNERS

CAIRO

SUEZ CANAL

APPROXIMATE DIMENSIONS

Length	160 feet
Width	160 feet
Height	50 feet

EGYPTIAN FORTIFICATION (RAMP) ON CANAL
(From Israeli Sketch)

were occupied by batteries of six SA-2 or SA-3 Soviet launchers. At perhaps 30 of these SAM sites there were also three SA-6 mobile launchers. In addition to the operational SAM sites, there were perhaps half as many additional dummy sites to mislead Israeli aerial reconnaissance.

There had been many changes in the Egyptian airfields in the Suez Canal and Nile Delta areas since the 1967 War. The combat aircraft were dispersed in camouflaged concrete bunkers, vented so as to relieve blast effects. To permit more rapid takeoff, and also to reduce the possibility of becoming inoperational through bomb craters, there were multiple runways on most of these airfields. In some Nile Delta bases the main roads that ran beside the bases had been widened and resurfaced so that they, too, could be used as runways.

2

Israeli Preparations

THERE WILL NOT BE WAR

On August 10, 1973, Defense Minister Moshe Dayan spoke to the Israeli Staff College. "The balance of forces is so much in our favor," he said, "that it neutralizes the Arab considerations and motives for the immediate renewal of hostilities."[1]

The concentration of Egyptian troops west of the Canal in the last days of September did not escape the notice of the efficient Israeli intelligence. It was clear, however, that these units were, as usual, engaged in the monthly exercises which had been occurring regularly in the Egyptian Canal zone for the previous ten months. On several past occasions these exercises had alarmed the IDF, and in late May and early June a partial Israeli mobilization had been ordered. But when the Egyptian exercises ended in early June, some people had criticized the government and the army for incurring the expense and economic disruption of mobilization. This was the third time since 1971 that such a false mobilization alarm had taken place.

This time, in late September, Israeli intelligence was concerned by the added factor of heavy concentrations of Syrian troops in the area between Damascus and Kuneitra. But this, too, was normal Syrian practice. Every year since 1968 the Syrians had moved from the end of the summer training period into the occupation of operational positions near the Golan Heights during fall maneuvers. Thus, when this was repeated again in late August 1973 and continued into September, the concentrations were recognized as routine practice, and did not create any undue alarm in Israel. Also, when school opened in early September, the Israelis were not alarmed by practice mobilizations of school training units (comparable to ROTC units in the United States), since this also had been done in previous years.

The extent to which Israeli and American military intelligence kept each other informed, and exchanged information, is not clear. Certainly it was not as close a coordination or collaboration as some postwar journalistic comments have suggested. On the other hand, that there

[1] Avi Shlaim, *op. cit.*

406

was some coordination is undeniable and has virtually been officially admitted in the United States. It appears that in late September US intelligence agencies became sufficiently alarmed by these concentrations in Egypt and Syria to discuss this with the Israelis. The Americans were reassured, however, when Israeli intelligence officials informed them that they were aware of what was going on, and were not alarmed. Not unreasonably, the American intelligence agencies assumed that the Israelis would be more sensitive to the nuances of danger from possible Arab attack than they would be.

Nevertheless, by September 26, Defense Minister Moshe Dayan and the Chief of Staff, Lt. General David Elazar, were concerned about the Arab concentrations in the north and in the south, despite assurances that they were receiving from the Director of Intelligence, Major General Eliahu Zeira. While they did not think an attack was likely, Dayan and Elazar feared that lack of alertness on the part of local Israeli commanders might afford the Arabs an irresistable opportunity for a successful surprise attack. In the light of the intelligence reports, neither Dayan nor Elazar had any intention of ordering another expensive mobilization. They did, however, order a partial alert in order to assure maximum readiness in case of a surprise attack, or in the event mobilization should become necessary.

After a staff meeting on September 26, Defense Minister Dayan decided to visit the Northern Command front on the Golan. He found that Major General Yitzhak Hoffi, commanding the Northern Command, was worried about his very small garrison manning that 65-kilometer front. This force consisted of about one infantry brigade, spread out in a number of strongholds scattered along the front line, and one understrength armored brigade with approximately 75 tanks. These were good troops. The infantry mostly came from the elite "Golani" Brigade; the armored brigade was the 188th or "Barak" Brigade, whose regulars could quickly be reinforced by mobilized reservists. But, as Hoffi pointed out to Dayan, the Syrians could go out on maneuvers one morning and simply turn their five divisions and 1,500 tanks westward. He did not see how the Barak Armored Brigade, with its tanks spread out about one per kilometer, could stop them.

Dayan agreed with Hoffi, and, when he went back to Jerusalem, he ordered the immediate transfer from central Israel of one battalion of the Regular Army 7th Armored Brigade, which vied with the Golani Brigade in considering itself the elite of the Israeli Army. (The 7th Brigade, part of Southern Command, was garrisoned near Beersheba.) This battalion would move to the Huleh Valley, to be available to General Hoffi as a mobile reserve. At the same time, the reserves of the Barak Brigade were mobilized, to give it a strength of nearly 100 tanks.

Meanwhile, the indications of possible Arab offensive action continued to be noted, and also continued to be discounted, by Israeli intelligence. Despite this, on about October 3 Dayan and Elazar decided to send the rest of the 7th Brigade to the Northern Command. Either late on October 4 or early on October 5, the Israelis learned that all Soviet dependents were being sent by plane from Cairo and Damascus back to Russia, and with them were a number of civilian advisors. When this information reached him, General Elazar expressed concern, but General Zeira soon reassured him. Nonetheless, Dayan and Elazar ordered the Army and Air Force on full alert. However, at a cabinet meeting on the afternoon of October 5, just before the ministers dispersed for the holiday, General Zeira's deputy (Zeira was ill) assured Prime Minister Meir and her colleagues that war was very unlikely.

THERE WILL BE WAR

At 4:00 o'clock in the morning of October 6, General Elazar received a telephone call from General Zeira, who informed him that the previous evidence against an Arab attack had been misleading. It was now clear, unmistakable, and undeniable, that the two Arab armies, Egyptian and Syrian, would start a war that day, with the time of attack apparently planned for 6:00 p.m.

Immediately after receiving this information from Zeira, Elazar called Prime Minister Golda Meir and Defense Minister Dayan. Elazar urged an immediate preemptive air attack against Syria and also the immediate mobilization of the entire Israeli Defense Force. Neither Dayan nor Meir would approve such drastic action without Cabinet agreement, and a Cabinet meeting was scheduled for 8:00 o'clock.[2] It was difficult to reassemble the Cabinet, whose members had scattered to their homes for the religious holiday.

At the Cabinet meeting Elazar again urged an immediate preemptive air strike, and full mobilization. Meir said that a preemptive strike was politically impossible; if a war came there must be no doubt in the eyes of the world that it had been started by the Arabs and not by the Israelis. Dayan apparently not only supported the Prime Minister in this assessment (which was politically and strategically wise and sound),[3] but felt that, in the light of previous intelligence doubts about Arab intentions and the earlier problems of unnecessary mobilizations, only a partial mobilization should be ordered. This decision for partial mobilization was taken at about 10:00 a.m.

[2] Meir, *op. cit.*, p. 358; Dayan, *op. cit.*, p. 375.

[3] It is understood that Secretary of State Henry Kissinger and US Ambassador to Israel Kenneth Keating had more than once told Israeli diplomats that there could be no US aid to Israel in a future war if the Israelis fired the first shots.

In the next few hours the Israeli mobilization machinery began to move, in some ways aided by the circumstances of the holiday, since it was quite easy to locate every individual to be mobilized, either at home or at the synagogue. It was also easy to send messengers, since there was no other traffic on the roads. On the other hand (as the Egyptian planners had anticipated), radio and television were not functioning on Yom Kippur, and thus it was impossible to broadcast messages with mobilization codewords.

The information that an Arab attack was expected at 6:00 p.m. was transmitted early in the morning to both the Northern and Southern Commands. In the Northern Command apparently the information was promptly disseminated to the three brigade commanders, and by them to their front line unit commanders. In the Southern Command, however, dissemination of the information seems to have been slower. By 2:00 p.m. the information appears to have reached some of the Bar Lev strongpoints, but not all. At that hour alert Egyptian observers could see Israeli soldiers bathing and washing their clothes in the Canal near some of the strongpoints.[4]

FAREWELL PARTY FOR GENERAL MENDLER

On October 6 the disposition of Israeli troops in and behind the Bar Lev Line was no different from what it had been for several months. These troops, perhaps 8,000 officers and men in all, were part of General Mendler's division, a Regular Army formation except for the reservists temporarily in the strongpoints. Mendler, who was scheduled to be reassigned on October 8, had for several days been concerned about the Egyptian buildup which his intelligence officers reported to him and to higher authority. At a pre-holiday farewell party given for him on October 4 by the division officers at his Tasa command post, in the central Sinai, he confided to one of them his belief that he would probably not be leaving after all, since he expected an Egyptian attack before the 8th.

Mendler had also confided this concern by telephone to General Gonen, Southern Command commander, whose headquarters was at Beersheba. Gonen assured Mendler that all of this information had gone back to Tel Aviv, but that Zeira and his people were convinced that there would not be war. Mendler had then asked permission to bring forward, at least to the central Sinai, his two reserve armored brigades that were stationed further east, between Refidim and the Sinai-Israel frontier. Gonen—after consulting either with General Elazar

---

[4] General Gonen insists that all installations were warned before noon. Some, misled by apparent lack of activity on the far bank, either ignored the warning, or took too literally the anticipated attack time of 6:00 p.m.

or General Israel Tal, the Chief of the Operations Staff—had not permitted this because it might be considered provocative by the Egyptians.

On the morning of the 6th, after receiving word that the war would break out at 6:00 p.m., Mendler again asked permission to move his two reserve brigades forward. Again Gonen refused permission, for two not fully consistent reasons. One was that there was still a possibility that war would not break out, since intensive diplomatic efforts were in progress to try to cause the Arabs to halt the planned attack. The other reason was that such a move would reveal to the Egyptians that Israeli intelligence was aware of their plans. In the early afternoon, however, presumably with approval from Tel Aviv, Gonen called Mendler to tell him that the two armored brigades could begin to displace forward at 4:00 p.m.

By this time Gonen was receiving intelligence reports suggesting that the Egyptians were about to move. Shortly before 2:00 p.m. he again called Mendler on the telephone to discuss this situation. Finally he said, "Albert, I think you had better start those two brigades moving forward."[5]

"Yes, I think so," Mendler replied calmly. "We are under air and missile attack."

It was 2:05 p.m.

Simultaneously air raid sirens began to wail in the cities of Israel itself. In some instances people on the home front knew that Israel was at war a few seconds before soldiers on the front line. This was because long-range Israeli radar had picked up the flights of Arab aircraft coming from the general direction of Damascus (the Egyptian planes all flew too low to be picked up by radar) and automatically flashed out the air raid alarm.

In retrospect it seems incredible that the Israelis ignored evidence and signals that should clearly have warned them to expect war. But in retrospect any surprise seems incredible. In brief it seems that the Israelis' overconfidence made them so certain that the Arabs would not dare to attack, that they simply could not believe the abundant evidence that was inconsistent with their preconceptions.

---

[5] Unless otherwise indicated, remarks or thinking attributed here or later to General Gonen are based upon interviews with him by the author.

3

"We Imposed Our Will on Them" *
October 6-7

BREACHING THE BAR LEV LINE

At precisely five minutes past two o'clock, October 6, approximately 4,000 Egyptian weapons on the west bank of the Canal simultaneously opened fire on the strongpoints and front area command posts of the Bar Lev Line. At the same instant 250 Egyptian aircraft flew across the Canal, headed for rear area artillery positions, ten Hawk air defense missiles sites, command posts, radar sites, electronic jamming and monitoring stations, commmunication facilities, and particularly airfields at El Meliez (Refidim), Bir el Thamada, and El Sur. With meticulous timing, FROG[1] long-range missiles were streaking toward the Israeli bases at Bir Gifgafa and Tasa.

The ground barrage was controlled by Major General Mohommed el Mahy, Chief of Artillery. It was conducted by approximately 1,850 indirect fire artillery pieces and heavy mortars, between 100 and 180 millimeters in caliber, and about 1,000 tanks and approximately 1,000 antitank guns in direct fire positions on the embankment. During the first minute, 10,500 artillery shells fell on Israeli positions. The firing continued for 53 minutes, battering and shaking—but not destroying—all of the Bar Lev Line strongpoints, known artillery positions, tank concentration areas, and local command posts. While this was going on, Egyptian engineers were hastily knocking down previously thinned-out sections in the west bank embankment, which had been held in place by sandbags. These were pulled down by hand or knocked away by bulldozers, to make openings through which thousands of waiting soldiers carried motor assault boats and pontons. Further west amphibious vehicles and ponderous tank ferries lumbered into position to come through the hastily made gaps.

At the same time Egyptian officers escorted amazed foreign officers of UNTSO from their 17 observation posts along the Canal. So

---

* Words of an Egyptian staff planner to the author, 1974.
[1] NATO code name: an acronym for Free Rocket Over Ground.

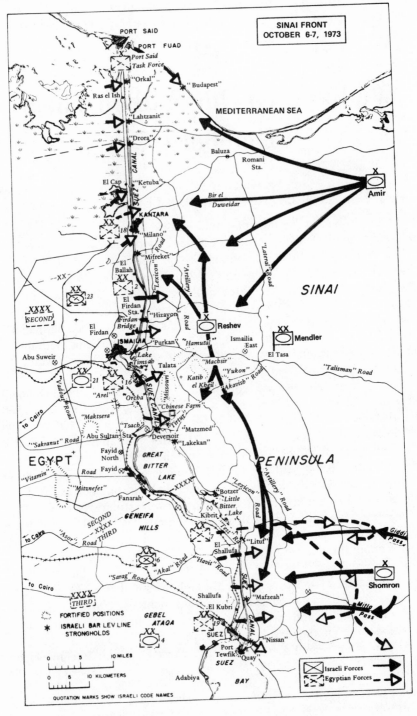

successful had been the Arab measures to achieve surprise that the UNTSO Chief of Staff had gone on leave one day before the offensive began.

When the thunderous barrage began, a number of Ranger groups began to cross the Canal in collapsible assault boats, some with outboard motors, some being rowed. Fifteen minutes later some 8,000 specially selected and trained commando and infantry troops followed, also using collapsible assault boats. These highly motivated men had been selected for their agility; they carried as few rations as possible so that they could handle their personal weapons plus their primary assault weapons. These included manned portable "Sagger" antitank wire-guided missiles, light infantry RPG-7 bazooka-like antitank rocket launchers, and SA-7 "Strella" shoulder-launched, heat-seeking antiaircraft missiles. Each soldier's supply of rations, weapons, and pack weighed about 25 to 35 kilograms and was placed in a towing cart or trolley, specially devised for this operation. Each man had a specific, assigned place in his boat, and despite the tremendous noise and excitement each went calmly about his business, as though he had done this many times before; in fact he had, in practice.

Some of these soldiers carried light combat ladders of bamboo and rope. These flexible ladders were carried up the face of the Israeli embankment by the leading men, as the boats arrived at their prearranged disembarkation points, carefully located between the widely spaced Israeli strongpoints. Spikes anchored the ladders at the top of the embankments, and other soldiers quickly climbed them.

It took the first wave seven minutes to cross the 180-220 meter width of the Canal. As the boats almost simultaneously reached the embankment, at twenty or more points from Kantara south to Suez, the barrage was lifted from the forward positions, and concentrated further east on the Israeli roads and forward command posts. The men scrambled up their ladders, towing the trolleys behind them. Soon Egyptian flags were waving over the Israeli rampart, from Kantara to Port Tewfik.

The men in this first wave did not stop to attack the Bar Lev bunkers, but rapidly deployed to preassigned blocking positions approximately 1,000 meters past the embankment, taking positions just below the crest and on the west side of the second or third line of Israeli ramparts. Men armed with single Sagger missiles or RPG-7 launchers placed themselves along likely armor approach routes, while those carrying Strellas took positions behind them to provide air defense.

In general, to the extent that the terrain and the location of the Israeli ramparts permitted, the men in these groups fanned out in broad arcs, guarding all approaches to the initial crossing points. Their mission was to hold the bridgeheads against the first expected attacks of the Israeli tanks in the local reserve; these were known to be very close behind the front lines. The Egyptians were to hold these hasty positions until more complete defenses were organized by subsequent waves and until sufficient Egyptian armor could be gotten across to repel attacking Israeli tanks. In fact, all of these groups arrived on time—but with little to spare. They were soon engaged in desperate battle with tank companies of the forward Israeli armored brigade.

Approximately 15 minutes after the first wave started, a second wave of boats was in the water, passing the returning assault boats from the first wave. The troops of this wave quickly moved out to join their predecessors and to strengthen the hasty defense created by the first wave. And so it continued for the next four hours, a total of twelve waves, until by 8:00 p.m. there were nearly 80,000 Egyptian soldiers on the east bank. Meanwhile, some units had encircled and begun to attack the Israeli strongpoints. In every instance, however, as the Egyptians approached they found themselves assailed by fierce defensive fire. Only at "Orkal," the strongpoint just south of Port Fuad, were the Egyptians able to overpower the defenders in their first rush, at 4:00 p.m.

All this time, of course, repeated waves of Egyptian aircraft had struck the forward Israeli base at Tasa, the base and the airfield at Bir Gifgafa, the suspected Israeli Southern Command forward command post and communications center at Um Kusheiba, and communication centers along the Kantara-Abu Ageila axis. During this period some Tu-16 medium bombers launched standoff guided bombs (Kelts) toward various command, communications, and radar centers in the central and eastern Sinai. The Israelis claim, however, that this violent air assault inflicted only nine casualties on Israeli forces east of the Canal. The Egyptians assert that this claim is totally irreconcilable with frantic radio messages they were monitoring from various bases and command posts in the Sinai.

THE ENGINEER EFFORT

Meanwhile, by the time the fourth wave was crawling up over the embankment, the Egyptian engineers were beginning their carefully planned tasks on the east bank. They, too, crossed in rubber boats, and fired special demolition rockets at preselected points where gaps were to be created in the Israeli embankment. At these points powerful water pumps operated by portable gasoline engines were put into operation. The high-velocity water jets of these pumps—called water cannon by some Egyptians—quickly sliced gaps in the sand bank. The purpose was to cut down the banks as rapidly as possible to make them traversable initially for amphibious vehicles, and eventually to be the terminals for ferries and ponton bridges. Some 82 of these gaps were created, each of them seven meters wide, by removing on the average about 1,555 cubic meters of sand and earth. Depending on the nature of the soil, flooring material was placed in accordance with plan —wood, sand bags, metal netting, and steel plates. The surface enabled bulldozers, brought on ferries, to start work to complete solid, dry roadbeds.

Before the war, the Israelis had calculated that it would take the Egyptians a day and a half to two days to make a few of these gaps by the combined use of demolitions and bulldozers. But with their water jets Egyptian engineers had some of the gaps open as soon as two hours from beginning their work, or before 6:30 in the evening. (Israeli intelligence knew of Egyptian practice with these water jets, but had apparently discounted their effectiveness.) Amphibious tanks and armored cars and vehicles now began to cross, and a few tank ferries were put into the water on the west bank and began to move tanks across. Then came more infantry, borne by boat ferry or by amphibious APCs (Soviet BTR-50 and 60), heading toward the gaps. These joined the infantrymen already encircling the Bar Lev primary positions, providing additional support with flame throwers and anti-tank missile launchers.

As the gaps began to be opened, other engineers began to work at their next task: throwing ponton bridges across the Canal. They used both Soviet-made bridging equipment, and equipment made locally by Egyptians, most of it at workshops at the High Dam near Aswan, and brought down the Nile River by boat. Two general types of bridge were laid that night. The light infantry bridges formed of interlocking sections of three-meter length two by fours, supported by plastic floats, were laid down rapidly by amphibious vehicles. The technique for these light, quickly installed infantry bridges had been learned from the Soviets. Beside them, heavier ponton bridges, most of them also of Soviet design and suitable for tanks, were under construction. There were ten bridges of each type, thus providing four bridges for each of the five assaulting divisions.

Before midnight some 50 tank ferries were in operation all along the Canal. Some of these were Soviet-made GSP self-propelled barges built in two sections, each driven by its own transporter to a predesignated crossing point, where it was unloaded and joined to the other half. A waiting tank lumbered up a hollow-tubed steel ramp onto each barge. The ramp was then pulled up on the barge, and used for off-loading at one of the gaps on the other side. Even after the ponton bridges were completed, these tank ferries continued to operate, to speed the buildup of armor and heavy vehicles on the east bank.

Among the first tanks ferried were T-54s with "mine harrows" mounted in front. These were inverted-V rakes designed to shift the AT mine from one tooth to the next until it was dropped off to the side of the tank's path.

On the Second Army front the twelve bridges were in operation from six to nine hours from the beginning of the bridging effort; in other words, all were in place shortly after midnight. However, difficulties were experienced in the Third Army sector south of the lakes. The Israeli ramparts in that area were hard packed earth walls and not easily susceptible to the water erosion process. The greater tide also interfered with bridging. Thus none of the Third Army's bridges were in before 9:00 a.m. on the 7th, and it was not until dark that day that all were completed. It was while supervising this effort, under heavy artillery fire from 175mm long-range guns, that Brigadier Hawdi, the Third Army Engineer Officer, was killed by an Israeli shell.

ARMORED THRUST TOWARD THE PASSES

During the afternoon of October 6 the 130th Brigade of the 3d Mechanized Infantry Division—a specially organized amphibious armored brigade, equipped entirely with PT-76 light tanks—"swam" across the Great Bitter Lake to begin a thrust toward the Giddi and Mitla Passes. By late afternoon the tanks were within sight of the passes, creating great alarm among Israel rear-area units along the Lateral Road and near the passes. Some of the Egyptian tanks were actually within range of the Southern Command advanced headquarters at Um Kusheiba, to which General Gonen was then en route.

However, at this very moment one of General Mendler's reserve brigades, advancing from Bir el Thamada, was rushing westward through the passes, on its way to support the Bar Lev Line. The two forces met just west of the passes. There was a short, sharp fight, with the principal engagement near the Giddi Pass. The Egyptians' light and thin-skinned PT-76s were no match for the Israelis' M60s and Centurions. The Egyptian commander, realizing that it would be impossible to take either pass by coup de main, ordered a withdrawal, after suffering severe losses. The Egyptians withdrew before the Israelis could firmly engage them in one-sided battle.

Two platoons, however, apparently did not receive the order. Bypassing the Mitla Pass, one platoon commander thrust eastward to reach and shell the Bir el Thamada air base at 10:10 on the 7th. During the next night, the two platoons worked their way back to the west to join the 7th Infantry Division in its bridgehead opposite Kabrit.

THE EGYPTIAN BUILDUP

To assist the tanks and APCs in joining their respective infantry units already in the bridgeheads, the infantry had hammered into the sands previously prepared signs in different distinctive colors. Colored lamps were attached to them for guidance to drivers in the darkness. These led the tanks from the bank to various preselected positions, so that the tank commanders of the second echelon, arriving in the predawn hours of October 7, merely had to follow the designated colored signs and lamps to join the troop units to which they were attached.

By 3:30 p.m. on October 6 the initial Sagger and RPG-7 antitank teams on the east bank had been reinforced with infantry recoilless, smoothbore guns, 82mm and 107mm. By 4:30 the artillery had 85mm and 100mm high-velocity antitank rifled guns also in action on the east bank. Not until the bridges were in position, however, did the ZSU-23-4—quadruple-mounted, 23mm, automatic, self-propelled AA cannon—get into position on the east bank.

Among the first vehicles to be ferried across during the night were Sagger-equipped antitank scout cars—the BRDM-2. Each of these carried fourteen Saggers, six mounted for launching, with eight more in storage. Also among the early vehicles on the east bank were a number of antitank armored personnel carriers—the redoubtable BMP, which some armored specialists believe was the most sophisticated armored vehicle in the world in 1973—carrying, in addition to the weapons of an infantry squad, a Sagger and a coaxially-mounted 73mm smooth-bore antitank gun. Three of these vehicles, and a fourth, in which the commander rode, and which mounted a 14.5mm heavy and a 7.62mm medium machine gun coaxially in the commander's turret, were combined in four vehicle platoons.

During the night, the troops of Brigadier Fuad Aziz Ghaly's 18th Division spread through Kantara East. By early morning Ghaly—a Christian—was able to set up his command post in the almost abandoned town, the first major Arab city to be reconquered from the Israelis.

The combination of thorough and efficient planning, careful security, the achievement of complete surprise, and the highly efficient execution of carefully prepared plans, resulted in one of the most memorable water crossings in the annals of warfare. As with the planning, no other army could have done better. During this first day, moreover, the Egyptians report that they had less than 200 men killed. The results of the first day were better than the Egyptians had expected; only the thrust against the passes had failed. It was clear, however, that despite surprise the Israelis were not collapsing.

THE RANGER AMBUSHES

Just at dusk some 30 large Egyptian Mi-8 troop-carrying helicopters lumbered over the Canal, fanning out to the northeast, east, and southeast. Each helicopter deposited about 25 Rangers at carefully-chosen points, in the Sinai, ten to twenty kilometers east of the Canal. The general mission of the Rangers—armed with mines, demolitions, Saggers, and RPG-7 rocket-launchers—was to disrupt Israeli lines of communications and installations. Some of them set up roadblocks and ambushes on the four main roads leading toward the Canal from the east. Others attacked Israeli command posts and radar and communications units. In the south, near the shores of the Gulf of Suez, one group was to attack the oil fields near Abu Rudeis and Ras Sudr. Inland from Ras Sudr another group set up a roadblock in the Sudr Pass.

The results of this major Ranger effort were not concretely significant. The Rangers created considerable alarm in the Israeli rear areas; they knocked out a few tanks of an armored brigade passing Baluza on its way to the Canal; some Israeli radar installations were damaged; fires were set in the oil fields and installations at Abu Rudeis early on the 7th, but were quickly extinguished; the Ranger group in the Sudr Pass held out for 16 days, and successfully blocked the pass. But except for the group in the pass, most of the Rangers were killed or captured by the Israelis by evening of the 7th.

Nevertheless, the rate of movement of Israeli reserves toward the Canal was significantly slowed down by the cautious approach which became necessary when the presence of the Rangers was realized by the Israelis. Considerable Israeli effort, particularly in helicopter-borne patrols, had to be diverted to dealing with these Rangers. Communications and rear area activities were disrupted. The Rangers did not accomplish as much as the Egyptians had hoped for; they did far more damage than the Israelis had ever anticipated.

ISRAELI AIRCRAFT MEET THE SAMs

Isolated sporadic Israeli air attacks began 26 minutes after the opening of the Egyptian offensive. However, Israeli air strikes in force did not really begin until shortly after 4:00 p.m. All of these air attacks were effectively countered by a dense air defense barrage from the west bank consisting of the older and known SA-2s and SA-3s, as well as the relatively unknown SA-6s. In front of this high level and intermediate level shield thrown up by the long-range missiles, was a low level shield of Strella SA-7s and lethal ZSU-23-4s.

At least half of the first attacking Israeli planes were shot down by the unexpectedly accurate and devastating Egyptian antiaircraft fire. And in one massed raid in the late afternoon, a United Nations observer reported that four out of every five of the attacking aircraft were hit. Not all of these were shot down because it soon became evident that the Strella, while highly accurate, was not so deadly as the larger Soviet missiles. The Strella missiles, optically guided and infrared homed, performed as they were supposed to, going straight for the tailpipes of the attacking aircraft, but their puny warhead more often than not failed to bring down the rugged American-built A-4s (Skyhawk) and F-4s (Phantom), which were usually able to limp back to their bases.

ISRAELI REACTION ON THE GROUND

Israeli artillery units suffered little damage or loss in the opening Egyptian barrage and air strikes. Outnumbered more than ten to one, however, the prompt return fire from the Israeli guns could do little in response to the massive Egyptian concentrations of high-explosives.

Shortly after 2:30 the tank companies of Mendler's advanced armored brigade moved quickly to the counterattack, in accordance with their doctrine. These tank companies had bivouacked near the Artillery Road during the night in accordance with their standard procedure, and were in their assembly areas when the Egyptian barrage began. Mostly in company strength, eight to ten tanks, the Israeli armor rushed forward to meet the attackers in piecemeal charges with little or no reconnaissance. This kind of tank "charge" had been successful in 1967. Now, however, Egyptian infantry, moving into the positions to which they had been assigned, stood fast in the face of the approaching tanks.

The RPG-7 men, who had to hold their fire until the range was down to less than 200 meters, inflicted heavy losses on the Israelis, as did the Saggers. In a number of instances, the Israeli tanks were able to push through the thin infantry screen of the Egyptian first wave, and approached or even reached the bank of the Canal. There they were immediately brought under fire by guns, tanks, antitank guns and Saggers on the Egyptian towers on the west bank, and they suffered severely. Recoiling from the unexpectedly heavy and accurate fire, the surviving Israeli tankers regrouped a few thousand meters to the east, then moved back to repeat the attacks and to incur the same kind of casualties. By evening the brigade had lost almost all of its 100 tanks.

Soon after 8:00 p.m. the leading elements of General Mendler's two reserve brigades arrived at the front. They repeated the same tactics which had almost wiped out the first armored brigade—and suffered the same kind of casualties. Nevertheless, some of the tanks were able to fight their way to the Bar Lev strongholds, and they helped the garrisons to evacuate the positions. During the wild and confused fighting that took place that night just east of the Suez Canal, one of the strongholds was overrun, two surrendered, five were evacuated with the assistance of the tanks, and eight remained isolated and under blockade. The Egyptians were not yet ready to undertake a major effort against the strongholds.

Soon after his 2:00 p.m. phone conversation with Mendler, General Gonen and key members of his staff flew in several helicopters to the Sinai. Discovering that Um Kusheiba was under heavy attack by Egyptian planes and FROG missiles, Gonen initially went to the northernmost of the Bar Lev Line command posts south of Baluza, then to the larger installation near Romani. Shortly after dark he flew to Um Kusheiba, which had not been seriously damaged by the Egyptian bombardment. During all this time he had kept in close radio contact with Mendler, as well as with GHQ at Tel Aviv, but was unable to get a clear picture of the battle.

By morning of the 7th, Mendler's division still had in action fewer than 150 of about 300 tanks that were on hand the previous noon. And during the fighting that continued on the 7th, that strength further dwindled to a little more than 100 operational tanks.

In Israel itself, by this time, full mobilization was being rushed with maximum intensity. Little was known about what was actually occurring on the two combat fronts, but the confident announcements over Cairo and Damascus Radios—with no explicit denials from the official Israeli radio reports—provided stimulus for the utmost exertion in getting the mobilizing units ready for combat. There were failures; some equipment was found not to be ready; there was confusion. But on balance, the mobilization moved with incredible speed and efficiency. Before midnight elements of two reserve divisions were on the roads to the Sinai.

During October 7, the bulk of the armor of the five Egyptian assault infantry divisions crossed to the east bank with a total of about 500 tanks, 300 in the Second Army sector, 200 for the Third Army. Helicopter activity continued. More Rangers were ferried by helicopter to blocking positions near the three passes, as well as near Israeli command and communication centers in north Sinai. Israel claimed that ten of these troop-carrying helicopters were knocked down, resulting in 250 to 300 Egyptian casualties.

AIR VERSUS AIR

The Egyptian planes, continuing their deep strikes into the Sinai until dark, encountered both accurate antiaircraft fire and Israeli interceptors.

The Egyptians admitted to the loss of eight aircraft that day, while claiming that they destroyed 27 Israeli planes. Israel, on the other hand, claimed that 30 Egyptian planes were destroyed on the first day, in exchange for a loss of four Israeli planes. Front line Israeli soldiers, who had seen a number of Israeli planes crash, heard these claims as they listened to their radios for the evening news broadcast. According to an Israeli newsman, one soldier commented with grim humor about these reports. "We have taught the Egyptians how to fight, and they have taught our radio announcers how to lie."[2]

Early the next morning, about 6:30 a.m., the Israeli air force attempted to hit Egyptian air bases, striking at ten airfields. But the dispersed, hardened hangars, and the heavy SAM defenses, made this difficult. At least five Israeli planes were lost in that particular effort, and it was not repeated. The principal Israeli air effort was made against the Egyptian bridges and ferries, but these attacks were not very effective, because the Israeli planes, cautious after the serious losses they had been incurring, stayed at high level and dropped their bombs and rockets from maximum range.

Israeli communiques claimed that during the first two days nine of twenty Egyptian bridges across the Canal were destroyed. No doubt the claim was sincere, but at high altitude and high speed the attacking pilots could not distinguish between hits and near misses. The Egyptians insist that not a single Israeli air attack knocked out any of their bridges during the war; they attribute the few temporary interruptions during the campaign to hits by long range artillery fire. In any event, the bridge sections were easily replaced, the whole operation taking less than half an hour.

---

[2] Israeli authorities insist, however, that no deliberately false announcements were made, although some may have been in error, some may have been vague, and some overconfident.

4

"They Defeated Us Again,"°
October 7-8

ARRIVAL OF ISRAELI RESERVES

During the morning of October 7, in a most impressive demonstration of efficient mobilization, the leading elements of an Israeli reserve division, which had begun its mobilization after 2:00 p.m. of the previous day, moved westward along the road from El Arish toward Baluza and Kantara. This division moving down the northern axis toward the Canal included two tank brigades and a mechanized infantry brigade, commanded by Major General Avrahan ("Bren") Adan, a hard-fighting diminutive soldier who had served in the Palmach in the 1948 war as a young man. Adan, the commander of the Israeli Armored Forces, had taken over his mobilization assignment as a division commander and moved immediately to the front.

On the road Adan's column was ambushed near Romani at 7:00 a.m. by some of the heliborne Egyptian Rangers and slowed down. (Adan himself, at the head of the column, had passed by the ambush position at 6:00 a.m.) The Egyptians sat tight in the sand dunes, near the road, letting the tank columns pass, then hit them from flank and rear with multiple launched Saggers at ranges up to a kilometer, and with RPG-7 fire at 150 meters. Two or three of the tanks were knocked out, several were damaged, and a number of lighter vehicles destroyed. It was not a severe loss, most of the columns bypassed or dashed through the roadblocks, and in counterattack Israeli detachments wiped out most of the commandos. The action delayed the Israeli movement westward by an hour at most, but by causing the columns to move more cautiously for the rest of the day added still another two or three hours to the delay.

Coming simultaneously down the central axis was another Israeli division only a few hours behind Adan. This was a mixed paratroop-armored division commanded by Major General Ariel ("Arik") Sharon. He was the man who had conducted the spectacular march across the

° Words of an Israeli combat commander to the author, 1975.

central Sinai to the Mitla Pass in 1956 and who had directed the prompt capture of Abu Ageila in 1967.

General Gonen, from his command post at Um Kusheiba, issued orders to Adan by radio to take over the northern sector from the remnants of General Mendler's division. Sharon was ordered to take over the central sector; Mendler was told to take what remained of his division and move to establish a southern sector opposite Suez.

Adan reached his assigned area late in the morning and found that Mendler's units in his sector were in bad shape. He deployed his troops, and reorganized the withdrawing Israeli soldiers. These could give him little information about the location and disposition of the Egyptians. Then in response to a radio order from Gonen, he took his helicopter and flew to Um Kusheiba for a command conference.

COMMAND CONFERENCE AT UM KUSHEIBA

At the outset, the principal participants in this conference were General Gonen, the hard-driving tank hero of the 7th Armored Brigade's many successes in the 1967 war and now commander of the Southern Command; General Mendler, whose division had been so badly hurt the previous day and that morning; General Adan; General Uri Ben-Ari, Gonen's Chief of Staff; and various members of Gonen's staff. During the conference they were joined by Lt. General David Elazar, the Israeli Chief of Staff, who was accompanied by Lt. General Yitzhak Rabin, the former Chief of Staff. Sharon was delayed by a helicopter breakdown.[1]

The conference concerned itself with three principal topics. The first was the question of what to do about the isolated strongpoints from which repeated radio appeals for help were being received. Second was the question of what the Egyptians were doing and where they were. There was very little hard information, because most of the Israelis who had been able to discover where the Egyptians were by this time were either dead or Egyptian prisoners. The third question was when and how the Israelis should seize the initiative back from the Egyptians. There seems to have been little or no panic or alarm among the four generals, who matter of factly accepted a situation which they probably never expected to eventuate, but for which they had often planned. None of them had any doubt that they would assume the offensive, or that they would be successful; it was merely a question of when. There was even brief discussion of possible sites for the eventual Israeli assault crossing to the west bank of the Canal.

[1] A Southern Command helicopter was supposed to pick Sharon up. Sharon, in an interview with the author, has stated his suspicion that its late arrival was because "someone didn't want me there."

Since they knew so little of the Egyptian dispositions, and since they were desperately short of both infantry and artillery—and would not receive more of these from their mobilized reserves until the 8th or 9th—the conferees quickly agreed that they could not relieve the strongholds in the near future. When Elazar joined them, he immediately agreed. The strongpoints would have to hold out as best they could, and it was hoped that Southern Command would have enough strength to relieve them by the 9th or 10th.[2]

The conferees also agreed that they urgently needed more information about Egyptian strength and dispositions in order to plan effectively for a counteroffensive. The most pressing problem, however, was to stop the Egyptians to throw them off balance. They therefore agreed that on the 8th they would make limited attacks which would enable them to regain the initiative and to obtain information about Egyptian dispositions, while at the same time avoiding major commitments. All were agreed that they should avoid further direct attacks toward the Canal, where the Israeli tanks would again come under the deadly fire of antitank guns and missiles on the Egyptian west bank towers. There seems to have been litttle or no argument about this course of action, and Gonen at the time issued verbal orders confirming the general consensus. At the initiative of either Elazar or Gonen, however, Gonen's orders did provide for the possibility that the Egyptians might collapse under the limited attacks. If so, the opportunity should be seized to advance and to capture one or more of their bridges, and even to put an Israeli armored brigade across the Canal. None of the four principal conferees, however, seemed to consider this a very likely possibility.

Since Adan's division was already arriving, and Sharon's division was still on the road, Gonen ordered Adan to begin the limited counter-offensive, early on the morning of the 8th. He was to attack by echelon from the north with probes generally parallel to the Canal to minimize the danger of getting within range of the Egyptian west bank towers. Sharon would continue these probes further south as he moved into position in the central sector opposite Ismailia.

---

[2] This version of this meeting is based upon interviews by the author with Generals Elazar, Gonen, and Adan. It is not inconsistent with relevant passages in Golda Meir's *My Life* (pp. 360-361, which have, however, some peculiar chronological inconsistencies) and of Moshe Dayan's *The Story of My Life* (pp. 406-409), both of which suggest that Elazar's visit to Um Kusheiba was in large part a result of Dayan's negative reports to Meir on what he had seen in visits to the front that day, and that Elazar was anxious to regain the initiative. Dayan's version of Elazar's report to Dayan and the General Staff at midnight, however, is not fully consistent with the recollections of all participants in the Um Kusheiba conference, as here reported. Dayan is careful to say, however, that there had been "no written summary of the consultations" at Gonen's command post (p. 408).

The conference ended in the late afternoon or early evening. Elazar, Rabin, Adan, and Mendler went out to their helicopters, the Chief of Staff and Rabin to go back to Tel Aviv, the division commanders to return to their command posts. As they were walking out of the command post General Sharon arrived. Beside the command post he earnestly expressed to General Elazar his belief that urgent measures were needed to relieve the beleaguered strongpoints along the Canal. It was also important, he said, to hold the waterline so a crossing could be made. Sharon emphasized that his opinions were based on his recent experience as Southern Command commander. Elazar gave a noncommittal answer, telling Sharon to discuss this matter with Gonen; he then went on to his helicopter. Mendler and Adan, concerned about a possible change in plans, walked back into the command post with Sharon for a new meeting with Gonen.[3]

Sharon repeated to Gonen his appeal for an immediate assault to relieve the strongholds. Gonen calmly replied that this was what had been happening for the past 14 to 16 hours, that few of the strongpoints had been relieved, and the uncoordinated, piecemeal attacks had resulted in the loss of more than 100 Israeli tanks. (Actually, by that time the toll was closer to 200). He categorically refused to consider Sharon's suggestion, but did go so far as to say that if the situation changed an attack might be possible. He told Sharon, therefore, to make preparations for such an attack, but generally repeated the orders he had given less than an hour earlier. On the following day Sharon was to conform to the original plan, continuing the limited attacks begun by Adan, and staying well away from the Canal. The previous order for a series of limited attacks having been reaffirmed, the three division commanders left to return to their divisions. By this time it was probably between 9:00 and 10:00 p.m.

Later that night Sharon called Gonen and told him that he had completed plans to relieve the three strongholds still holding out in his division sector. He planned to send a tank battalion and a battery of artillery to each stronghold, while the remainder of his division kept the Egyptians occupied all along the line. He would be ready to attack at 6:00 a.m. Gonen neither approved nor disapproved; he said his decision would depend upon developments during the night, and that he would inform Sharon before 6:00 a.m.

During the night of October 7-8 the remnants of the garrisons of two of the isolated strongpoints were able to infiltrate through the surrounding Egyptians and reach the Israeli lines. Two others surrendered during the night. Since eight strongpoints had either been

---

[3] Mendler may not have taken part in this second conference; memories are not clear.

abandoned, overrun, or surrendered on the 6th and 7th, by morning of October 8 only three isolated Israeli garrisons were still holding out on the banks of the Suez Canal, and one on the Mediterranean shore east of Port Fuad.

This development, combined with information that more Egyptian troops had crossed the Canal during the night, caused Gonen to decide not to approve Sharon's plan for relieving the one remaining stronghold still holding out in his sector. At 5:45 he called Sharon, told him about the changed situation, and directed him not to make the attack at 6:00. Sharon, who had been moving forward in preparation for the attack, was disappointed. He kept his troops alert to support Adan's attack, scheduled for 8:00 a.m.

Meanwhile, that same night, troops of the Egyptian 18th Infantry Division completed their occupation of Kantara and two nearby strongholds. The division commander, Brigadier Ghaly, inspected the captured areas as his troops dug in for defense.

ADAN'S OCTOBER 8 BATTLE

Shortly after 8:00 a.m., Adan's division began the series of limited attacks which he had been directed to initiate during the conferences of the previous afternoon and evening. He had two brigades on line, Colonel Natke Baram's on his right flank, opposite Kantara, and Colonel Gabi Amir's on his left, opposite Firdan. (Amir's brigade, which had been part of Mendler's division, had lost about half its strength in the bitter fighting of the previous hours, and had been reorganized in two understrength battalions.) Adan's reserve brigade, under Colonel Arieh Karen, was behind, approximately midway between Tasa and Baluza. His armored infantry brigade had arrived during the night, but he had been directed to leave it in the Baluza area, to prevent any possible Egyptian infiltration through the swamps or drive along the coastal road to El Arish. This brigade had been placed under the command of Brigadier General Kalman Magen, who, under Adan, was responsible for securing the exits from the swampy region north of Kantara. Available for operations on the morning of the 8th Adan had about 170 tanks in three understrength brigades.

Around 9:00 a.m., while Baram's brigade was beginning its limited probes into the Egyptian lines north of Kantara, Adan discovered that Gonen had issued revised instructions during the night.[4] Sometime

---

[4] This interpretation of the Gonen-Adan controversy is based upon interviews with both generals. Adan insists the instructions were new—a deviation from the agreed plan. Gonen asserts that he was merely confirming and elaborating on some aspects of the original plan.

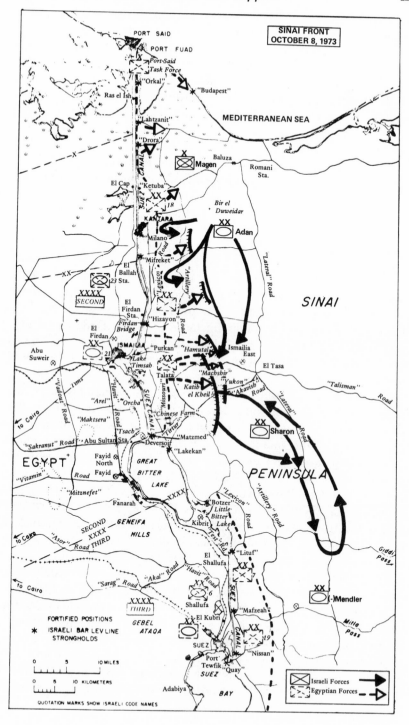

SINAI FRONT
OCTOBER 8, 1973

PORT SAID
PORT FUAD
Port-Said
Task Force
"Orkal"
"Budapest"
Ras el Ish
MEDITERRANEAN SEA
"Lahtzanit"
"Drora"
Magen
Baluza
Romani
Sta.
El Cap
"Ketuba"
Bir el
Duweidar
18
KANTARA
Milano
Adan
"Mifreket"
El Ballah
23 Sta.
SECOND
SINAI
El Firdan
Sta.
"Hizayon"
El Firdan
Firdan
Bridge
Abu Suweir
ISMAILIA
21
"Purkan"
"Hamutal"
Ismailia
East
Lake
Timsah
El Tasa
"Talata"
"Machshir"
"Yukon"
"Talisman"
Katib
el Kheil
"Akavish"
Road
"Arel"
Orcha
Chinese Farm
Sharon
"Maktsera"
"Tsach"
"Matzmed"
EGYPT
Deversoir
"Lakekan"
Fayid
North
Fayid
GREAT
BITTER
LAKE
PENINSULA
"Vitamin"
Road
"Mitznefet"
Fanarah
"Botzer"
Little
Bitter
Lake
Kibrit
SECOND
GENEIFA
HILLS
THIRD
Giddi
Pass
El
Shallufa
"Lituf"
6
Shallufa
(-)Mendler
THIRD
GEBEL
ATAQA
El Kubri
"Mafzeah"
Mitla
Pass
FORTIFIED POSITIONS
ISRAELI BAR LEV LINE
STRONGHOLDS
SUEZ
19
Port
Tewfik
"Nissan"
"Quay"
SUEZ
0   5   10 MILES
Adabiya
BAY

Israeli Forces
Egyptian Forces

QUOTATION MARKS SHOW ISRAELI CODE NAMES

after midnight Gonen had tried to reach Adan on the radio, and un-accountably got no response. He therefore called Magen and asked him to pass on the instructions to Adan. According to Adan, this new order required him to seize an Egyptian bridge near Firdan; in other words, he was no longer expected to make a limited attack, but rather was to drive right up to and across the Canal. According to Gonen, this was not a deviation from the limited attack plan; he was merely making certain that Adan did not miss a chance to cross the Canal if the opportunity appeared.

When Adan finally realized what was expected of him—or what seemed to be expected of him—he called Gonen on the radio for confirmation. Gonen told him that he should be prepared to drive to the Canal, link up with one of the beleaguered strongpoints ("Hizayon") still holding out near the Firdan bridge, and to seize one or more of the Egyptian bridges and push one brigade to the west bank. As had been agreed the previous evening, Adan's attack was to be conducted by echelon from north to south (for reasons which have never been satisfactorily explained) and this sequential attack by echelon would be continued on his south flank by Sharon, opposite Ismailia and Deversoir. If the opportunities for crossing in the Firdan area did not appear to be promising, as an alternative Adan was told that he could try to put his brigade across near Deversoir, although this was in Sharon's sector.

Adan reminded Gonen of the previous night's decisions for a limited offensive. Baram's first limited probes toward Kantara had indicated that the Egyptians were full of fight, and that he did not have either the artillery or the infantry to undertake the kind of major offensive action that Gonen now seem to expect. Gonen, however, insisted that this was no change in the orders of the previous evening; it was merely to carry out the alternative plan, since he now had reliable information that the Egyptians were close to breaking. He said he felt certain that Adan would not have serious trouble in making the attack, and that a crossing would probably not be difficult under the changed circumstances. Adan then responded that he needed extensive air support, particularly in the light of the absence of his artillery. Gonen assured him that there would soon be substantial air support.

After a long delay—at least an hour—four Israeli planes appeared, made short bombing, strafing, and rocketing attacks from high level against Egyptian forces in the general area of the Canal, and then flew away. A few minutes later four more planes appeared, and followed the same procedure. Then there was nothing. Adan assumed that this was all the air support he would get, and so moved to carry out his orders.

Since Baram had already made one limited attack early in the morning, and had suffered some losses, Adan had Amir make the first serious probe toward the Canal. It soon became evident that Gonen's information about the Egyptians breaking was quite incorrect. As Amir's two battalions, in line abreast, pushed forward determinedly toward the Canal and Firdan, they were met with devastating fire from Egyptian Saggers and RPG-7s. The Israeli tanks pressed on, however, and one battalion got close to the embankment, within range of the Egyptian guns and missiles on the towers on the far bank, and got a taste of the same medicine which had wiped out half of Mendler's tanks the previous day. After losing more than 20 tanks in a few minutes—nearly half of his strength—Amir pulled back and reported the situation to Adan. Adan in turn reported to Gonen, and then ordered Baram to carry out his attack, further north near Kantara.

With one battalion in reserve, Baram pushed forward with two battalions abreast. The northern battalion, pushing past the area where it had made its limited probe in the morning, soon found itself under heavy fire from Saggers and RPG-7s in the swamps to its right. First it stopped, then it pulled back, leaving the left wing battalion—commanded by Lieutenant Colonel Asaf Yaguri—to push forward by itself.

The Egyptians, having recognized the signs of an impending Israeli tank charge, were ready for this move. General Hassan Abou Seeda, commanding the 2d Infantry Division just south of Kantara, rapidly set up a rather extensive ambush composed of all the various antitank weapons available in his left hand brigade. When Yaguri and his 190th Battalion[5] pushed aggressively into the area previously chosen by the Egyptians to be a killing ground, they found themselves under devastating antitank fire from three directions. Within ten minutes the 190th Battalion was practically annihilated. All except four or five of its tanks were knocked out, and most of the crew members were killed or captured. Among the captives was Colonel Yaguri. It was about 1:00 p.m.

For a few minutes Baram did not realize what had happened to his left battalion. Then, as Yaguri's calls for support and assistance faded into silence, he recognized that he had lost approximately one-third of his command. Rushing his reserve battalion into the gap, but not allowing it to advance beyond the original start line, he reported the situation to Adan.

---

[5] This is not the correct designation of the battalion. Apparently Yaguri, in accordance with standard instructions, gave this number when he was captured. The Egyptians, assuming that this was the 190th Brigade, also assumed Yaguri was a brigade commander; Yaguri did not correct them, or he may have deliberately misled them. In any event, the Egyptians announced that he was a brigade commander.

That harassed general, however, did not have time to give much consideration to the disaster to his right hand brigade at that moment. He had just learned from General Gonen that the day's attack plan had been changed once more. He, Adan, was to continue his efforts to put a brigade on the west bank, but Sharon's division was to be pulled out of the line opposite Ismailia, to move south, and in the late afternoon to attack toward Suez, and establish a similar bridgehead west of the Canal and just north of Suez. Adan was told that he must extend his front to cover the sector as far south as Deversoir and the northern end of the Great Bitter Lake. In carrying out these instructions, Gonen warned him, Adan must not leave Kantara uncovered. In vain did Adan protest that he had been given a mission exceeding the resources at his command—he only had about 120 tanks left—and that it would be impossible to carry out the mission. Gonen told him he must try.

Adan immediately got on the radio to Magen to ask if he could extend his brigade front down to cover Kantara. Magen, dealing with aggressive Egyptian probes from Port Fuad along the northern road and through the swamps, could not. Adan therefore ordered Baram to move south with one battalion and the remnants of the 190th, leaving one battalion to cover Kantara. Magen agreed to assume responsibility for this battalion. Adan pulled one battalion from Karen's reserve brigade and sent it to Baram to replace Yaguri's battalion. Thus his division now consisted of three brigades of two understrength battalions each. With this force he was to cover a front of about 40 kilometers, and was also expected to try to cross the Canal. However, he had his orders. He moved south.

Meanwhile, shortly after 10:20 a.m., Sharon received orders from Gonen to be prepared to pull his brigade out of line, and to move south on the Lateral Road until he was opposite Suez. He was then to attack in a northwesterly direction, to roll up the Egyptian Third Army bridgehead in the same manner that Adan (presumably) was rolling up the Second. He was told that Adan would take over responsibility for his sector, but that he should leave his reconnaissance regiment in the vicinity of a hill called Kishuv, just northeast of the Great Bitter Lake, to provide an anchor for Adan's extended front.[6] Gonen says that the reason for this order was that reports from Adan gave him the impression all was going well on the northern front.

---

[6] There is disagreement about the order affecting the reconnaissance regiment. Sharon says that he was told to take his entire division south, but left the reconnaissance unit there on his own responsibility. Gonen says that he specifically directed that the regiment should be left near Kishuv.

At 11:45 Gonen confirmed his earlier warning order, and told Sharon to pull out of line and start south. By this time Sharon's two armored brigades on line opposite Ismailia were extensively engaged by attacking units of the Egyptian 16th and 2d Divisions. Sharon says that when he tried to explain this to Gonen, he was abruptly, "even rudely," told to carry out his orders. When Sharon ordered the two brigade commanders to withdraw and move south, they protested. They recognized that the Egyptians in front of them were aggressive, and they feared that the front might collapse if they withdrew. Sharon, however, said that the order had to be obeyed. He assured the two colonels—as Gonen had assured him—that intelligence had reported that the Egyptians were about to break and that prompt action was necessary to seize the opportunity. Reluctantly the brigade commanders complied and got their brigades on the road shortly after 1:00 p.m.

By this time, Karen had reached the vicinity of Tasa. Adan radioed to him to move west with his two battalions to occupy the area being vacated by Sharon's two brigades. Concerned about the possibility that the Egyptians might try to envelop his open, southern flank, Karen advanced with two battalions in column—one behind the other —each battalion being extended in a long line. His objective was to reach the high ground between the Talata crossroads (east of Ismailia) and the Talia hill mass further south and east. From this high ground (called "Missouri" by the Israelis) the land slopes down to the south toward an abandoned experimental farm area near the Great Bitter Lake. This farm had been established before the 1967 war by a Japanese agricultural assistance mission to Egypt. The various inscriptions on the walls in the area had led the Israelis, who not surprisingly could not distinguish between Japanese and Chinese calligraphy, to call the area the "Chinese Farm."

As Karen moved forward toward the Chinese Farm, Talia, and Talata, he quickly discovered what Sharon's brigadiers had already reported: the Egyptians were alert and full of fight. Karen quickly became involved in a fierce fight against Egyptian infantry supported by a number of T-54 tanks. As he feared, the Egyptians attempted to envelop his left flank, forcing him to pull back his leading battalion. He reported to Adan that he would not reach his objective and that he was under great pressure.

Adan was in a desperate situation. The Egyptians opposite his center and right were following up their early successes and pushing hard. With pressure thus mounting all along his front, Adan was prepared to issue an order to withdraw. Before doing so, he reported his situation to Gonen. It was by this time nearly 3:30 p.m.

THE RETURN OF SHARON

Meanwhile Gonen—whose headquarters was monitoring the radio transmissions—had begun to realize that Adan was not going to be able even to reach the Canal, much less to cross it. Some time before 3:00 p.m., therefore, he had radioed to Sharon to stop his movement to the south, and to return to take the Talia-Missouri hill mass. Thus Sharon, who had been on the Lateral Road opposite the Little Bitter Lake, was already on his way back to the north when Adan radioed his desperate appeal for help to Gonen. But his division was stretched out for about 30 kilometers along the Lateral Road south of Tasa.

Gonen now asked Adan to hold on long enough to permit Sharon to make the planned attack on Missouri on his left flank. Adan—now under attack from the Egyptian 18th, 2d, and 16th Divisions—believed that he could hold his positions until Sharon arrived. He ordered his brigade commanders to do the best they could; he shifted one of Amir's two battalions down to support Karen, who was under the greatest pressure, and then held tight.

Gonen again called Sharon on the radio. He asked if Sharon could send one of his brigades to support Adan's threatened left flank, while he attacked Missouri with the other two. Sharon thought about this briefly, then told Gonen that he feared that such support to Adan would "attrit" one of his brigades without accomplishing any significant results. While Gonen and Sharon were debating this question, and the best place for Sharon to make his principal attack, Adan began to feel that he had the situation on his long front finally under control. He therefore broke into the conversation between the other two generals, and suggested that the best place for Sharon's division to be committed was in a coordinated, two-division attack toward Ismailia. He felt that the impact of an attack by Sharon's fresh division would have a devastating effect upon the tired Egyptians in front of him.

Sharon, however, did not like that suggestion, and said that he could not do it. Then, somewhat surprisingly, he suggested to Gonen that he be allowed to attack toward the Canal between the Chinese Farm and the Great Bitter Lake. He did not explain why he could mount such an attack to the west, while he could not attack in a northwesterly direction from the same general location to relieve the pressure on Adan. Gonen did not debate the question; he merely disapproved the proposal and repeated his earlier order to return to Tasa. He had decided that he did not want to commit Sharon at all. As Gonen said later, "At that time, if the Egyptians should break through Adan, Sharon was all that I had left between them and Tel Aviv."

In fact, one of Sharon's brigades, as well as his reconaissance regiment, was engaged on Adan's left, and this extension of the Israeli line, making it impossible for the Egyptians to envelop Karen's left flank, contributed to the success of Adan's defense that afternoon.

Some Israeli officers believe that, if Sharon had been committed in a counterattack toward Ismailia with Adan in the late afternoon of October 8, this would have more than offset the dismal Israeli events earlier in the day. These officers believe that the psychological effect of such an attack by Sharon's fresh troops might have shattered the Egyptian 16th and 2d Divisions. In any event, it would have seized the initiative from the Egyptians.

EGYPTIAN PRESSURE

The Egyptians had not been idle while all of this Israeli activity had been going on in Adan's and Sharon's sectors. In addition to the ambushes and counterattacks which had given Adan so much trouble, the Egyptians had been hastily consolidating the bridgeheads, and thrusting systematically eastward against spotty resistance.

The most spectacular advances were made by the 19th Infantry Division on the southern flank of the Third Army. One battalion pushed south to occupy an abandoned Israeli stronghold near Uyun Moses. Another force captured the fortified Israeli artillery position which had been constructed in the desert opposite Port Tewfik during the War of Attrition in 1968. Here they captured the six French 155mm guns that the Israelis had been unable to move before the position was captured. Since it would have been necessary to knock down some of the fortification walls to get the guns out, the Egyptians blew up the guns while fighting off Israeli counterattacks.

AN ASSESSMENT

October 8, 1973, on the Sinai front was in many ways the most critical day of the war, and beyond a doubt the most controversial. Equally without a doubt it was the worst defeat in the history of the Israeli Army.

Before exploring what had gone wrong, and why it had gone wrong, however, one fundamental point needs to be made. The single most important element in the Israeli defeat was the fighting quality of the Egyptian Army, and its performance in accordance with carefully prepared plans to deal with anticipated Israeli counterattacks. The integration of infantry; antitank missiles, rockets, and guns; and an effective air defense system had brilliantly achieved General Ismail's major prewar objective: the neutralization of Israeli superiority in the air and in mobile armored warfare.

However, the Egyptian victory on the 8th was greatly facilitated by a number of serious Israeli misconceptions, misunderstandings, and just plain blunders.

First, there is the question of the orders issued late on the 7th, and the various modifications during the night and the following morning. Here it would seem that General Gonen was primarily at fault. If the orders were not clear, or were (or appeared to be) contradictory, he was responsible. He had three divisions available that day, and two of them were fresh and ready, even though short of important components. He had an opportunity to use two of those divisions—commanded by two of the most experienced and respected commanders in the IDF—in coordination, and failed to use that opportunity.

General Gonen says that he did not want a coordinated attack that day. Adan was to attack the Second Army in the morning, and Sharon the Third Army in the afternoon, in each case leaving him a division in reserve. It is hard to see how a division committed to defense of a long line against an attacking, numerically superior enemy could be considered to be in reserve. But most seriously, this plan violated the classical military principles of Mass, Simplicity, and Economy of Force.

Gonen's principal error seems to have been in underestimating the enemy, and he was not the only Israeli commander who made that mistake. According to General Bar Lev, Gonen learned from his mistakes of that day, and Bar Lev believes that had it not been for his controversy with Sharon—which began that day—Gonen could have conducted the remainder of the campaign with distinction.

Another controversy based upon a clash of personalities also began that day: the dispute between Generals Gonen and Adan about the orders issued by Gonen. The issues in this dispute are not clear, and the statements of the generals directly contradict each other. Since Gonen was severely criticized for his conduct of the operations by Israel's high-level post-war investigating committee (the Agranat Commission), and since Adan was not so criticized, it could be assumed that Gonen was wrong and Adan right. But there have been no public findings of the Agranat Commission on that specific issue, and it is hard to avoid the conclusion that there was simply a misunderstanding—a grave one—between the two men. Since copies of all of Gonen's orders were available to General Elazar and the General Staff in Tel Aviv, and since they did not note any inconsistency in Gonen's orders, it was probably not all his fault.

As to Adan's performance, this was unquestionably the worst day in the life of possibly the best armored force commander that Israel has produced. How much his generally poor performance in the morning can be attributed to confusion over orders is hard to assess. But even if his orders were to attack by echelon, and even if these were contradictory, there was no excuse for his complete failure to coordinate the attacks of Baram's and Amir's brigades in the morning. In the afternoon he seems to have performed well in an almost impossible situation, trying to hold a line 40 kilometers long against the attacks of three infantry divisions with a force of nothing but about 120 tanks. But the credit for success in holding this line goes more to the tankers and the low-level commanders than to the division commander, who had lost all capability to influence the outcome further when he committed his last reserves.

Sharon has been blamed by many Israeli officers for his failure to get into any significant action on that day, save for some defensive fighting at its beginning and at its end. General Adan was undoubtedly upset at having to carry the burden of the fighting during the day, while Sharon—who had been the one most eager to attack—was either on the road, or concentrating behind Adan at Tasa. And Sharon's failure to come to the assistance of Adan's hard-pressed division in the late afternoon has been particularly criticized by a number of Israeli officers.

It is hard to avoid the suspicion that Sharon was as eager to move south, and attack the Third Army, as Gonen initially was to have him do it. He does not seem to have tried seriously to convince Gonen that he should not make this move, but this is also explicable in the light of Gonen's apparent brusqueness in ordering the shift. On balance, the responsibility for Sharon's failure to make a decisive contribution to the battle was Gonen's, including the final decision to hold Sharon back from support to Adan.

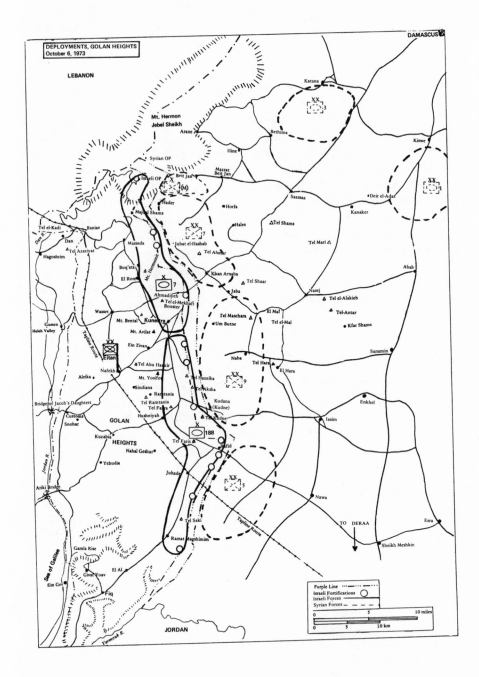

DEPLOYMENTS, GOLAN HEIGHTS
October 6, 1973

5

The Opponents on the Golan

THE GOLAN AND ISRAELI DEFENSES

The Golan Heights,[1] which had been occupied by Israel since the 1967 war, looks on a map roughly like an elongated parallelogram, 65 kilometers from north to south, with a maximum width of 30 kilometers. The western boundary is the abrupt escarpment which falls sharply into the Huleh Valley and the Sea of Galilee on the Israeli side. The northern boundary is the towering ridge of Mt. Hermon, extending in a generally northeasterly to southwesterly direction. The southern boundary is another escarpment, falling from the heights into the Yarmouk River valley, a tributary of the Jordan, which flows into that river just south of the Sea of Galilee. The eastern boundary is an irregular north-south line, the "Purple Line," so called since this was the color of the ceasefire line shown on the UNTSO maps.

Movement of wheels over much of the volcanic plateau is difficult, sometimes impossible, except on tracks or roads. Even tanks find it hard to traverse many areas, particularly in the north. The plateau is much flatter and less rocky in the south, where much of the surface is grassland and easily traversable. The numerous old volcanic cones scattered across the plateau also offer excellent observation and fields of fire.

During their period of occupation, the Israelis had constructed a system of obstacles and fortifications, most of them along the eastern edge of the plateau. Just west of the Purple Line was an antitank ditch, four to six meters wide and about four meters deep, along the entire length of the ceasefire line. The earth from the ditch had been thrown up to create a high embankment on the Israeli side. Behind it was a system of concrete observation posts and strongpoints with heavy overhead cover, assuring continuous observation over all of the approaches from the east. Including fortified posts immediately behind the ditch, as well as those somewhat farther back on volcanic cones, there were seventeen such fortified positions, with 112 separate fortified pillboxes or blockhouses; each of these seventeen positions had garrisons varying from ten to thirty men. In front of and behind the ditch was

[1] See description, p. 317.

437

an integrated minefield system on the important avenues of approach, and around each strongpoint. The latest electronic observation devices were used all along the line, many of these monitored from a heavily fortified observation post perched more than 2,000 meters above sea level on the Mt. Hermon ridge.

Only one major road enters the Golan from central Syria, that from Damascus to Kuneitra, which continues in a southwesterly direction, bisecting the parallelogram, to the famous Bridge of Jacob's Daughters over the Jordan River at the base of the escarpment. There are a number of other secondary roads in the region. One of these is a road to northern Israel, passing through Banias, just east of the old Syrian border, and Dan, on the Israeli side of the old frontier. Another leads southward through El Rom at Kuneitra. Another road extends east from Gonen, about midway between Dan and the Bridge of Jacob's Daughters, up the escarpment to Wasit and thence eastward to join the El Rom-Kuneitra road. There is a road from the Arik Bridge, just north of the Sea of Galilee, up the escarpment to Hushniyah, where it intersects with the main north-south Rafid-Kuneitra road. Finally, in the south, a road starting from the southern end of the Sea of Galilee winds up the Yarmouk River escarpment through El Al to the Rafid junction. In addition to the main road from Rafid through Kuneitra to Masa'ada, another road parallels the Trans-Arabian pipeline (TAP line)—an oil pipeline which runs from Bahrein and Saudi Arabia to a sea terminus in Lebanon, just south of Sayda (Sidon). Except for one brief interruption as a result of one Arab guerrilla raid, that pipeline had been pumping oil under and through Israeli occupied territory since the Six Day War.

On the Israeli side of the Purple Line in mid-September 1973 were elements of two infantry brigades, which totalled less than the equivalent of one brigade in strength, and one armored brigade. Most of the infantrymen were from the 1st (Golani) Brigade. The 188th, or Barak, Armored Brigade, commanded by Colonel Yitzhak Ben Shoham, had its three slightly understrength battalions—totalling about 90 tanks—extended in line west of the Purple Line, from north of Kuneitra to Rafid. In support were eleven field artillery batteries—44 pieces—some 105mm howitzers, some 155mm, all self-propelled. This force was commanded by Brigadier General Rafael Eitan, a distinguished Israeli paratroop commander, whose ability to command tank forces was regarded with considerable skepticism by members of the Israeli Armored Force. Eitan's district headquarters at Nafekh was on the main road, about midway between Kuneitra and the Bridge of Jacob's Daughters. Eitan operated under the overall direction of Major General Yitzhak Hoffi, whose Northern Command headquarters was west of the Jordan River near Rosh Pina and Safad.

The Syrian Director of Intelligence, Brigadier General Gabriel Bitar, was quite well informed about the Israeli defenses and deployments. He had directed an aggressive program of combat patrolling into and through the Israeli positions for several months prior to the war. Various expedients were used to avoid leaving footprints on the two continuous strips of raked white soil on either side of the hard-surface road which ran the entire length of the Israel side of the Purple Line, from Mt. Hermon to the Yarmouk Valley. Other expedients were able—usually—to "fox" the Israeli electronic warning and automatic firing systems. As a result of the aggressive patrolling the Syrians had detailed, large-scale maps of each section of the front, and had constructed a mock-up of the Israelis' Mt. Hermon observation post.

THE SYRIAN CONCENTRATION

In the six years since the Six Day War the Syrians had also built up an extensive system of fortifications just east of the Purple Line, running generally from the vicinity of Nawa in the south through Naba to the slopes of Mt. Hermon. Further to the east was a second line of defenses, about midway between Kuneitra and Damascus, running generally through Sanamin, Kfar Shams, and Saassaa.

The forward positions in the first defense line, just east of the cease-fire line, were manned almost continuously by two or three Syrian brigades, except in midwinter, when snow and mud made all movement virtually impossible. Then most of the units were pulled east to the arid Damascus region for training, leaving skeleton forces in the fortifications.

During September of 1973 a formidable Syrian buildup east of the Purple Line had become evident to the Israelis. However, since there had been similar late summer training exercises in previous years, this development was not considered too alarming by the Israelis, until about September 20. Then aerial photographs and other intelligence made it evident that there were three full infantry divisions, with attached tank brigades, occupying the first Syrian line, with additional tank, mechanized, and infantry units in the second line. Israeli intelligence estimated that in this area there were at least 670 tanks and 100 batteries of artillery, a formidable force concentrated just a few kilometers to the east of one Israeli armored brigade and part of one Israeli infantry brigade behind the Purple Line.

This concentration was particularly worrisome to General Hoffi because of an incident that had taken place on September 13. On that date an Israeli air patrol, flying over the eastern Mediterranean in the vicinity of the Syrian port of Latakia, had been attacked by a force of Syrian fighters. Such Israeli patrols into Syrian air space were frequent, and apparently the Syrians were attempting an ambush. The Israelis, however, had a counterambush ready, and in the ensuing fight 12 Syrian MiG-21 fighter planes were shot down, while only one Israeli plane was lost. Some sort of Syrian retaliation for this incident was expected.

At a meeting in Tel Aviv with the General Staff on September 24, at which both Defense Minister Dayan and Chief of Staff David Elazar were present, Hoffi expressed his concern. In the light of the short distance between the two opposing lines, with no natural barriers, the Syrians could mount an attack with overwhelming force without warning. Hoffi felt that he should be authorized to reinforce his infantry and armored units that were scattered along the length of the Golan.

On September 26, Dayan and Elazar visited Northern Command and inspected a number of frontline positions. Hoffi pointed out to them the great strength of the Syrians, clearly visible a few thousand yards away, with only modest effort at camouflage. Dayan thereupon made two decisions that proved to have considerable significance. In the first place he ordered that all or part of the 7th Armored Brigade be sent to the Golan to reinforce the Barak Brigade. The 7th Armored Brigade, a Regular Army unit garrisoned in southern Israel, had been created in 1948 as the first armored unit in the IDF and had been the spearhead of the Israeli drives across the Sinai Desert in both 1956 and 1967. Dayan also ordered the Israeli Army to go on a state of alert. Although this did not involve any step toward mobilization, it did require units on active duty to place themselves on a war footing.

By Tuesday, October 2, Israeli intelligence, with the assistance of the latest air photos, estimated that Syrian forces in and immediately behind the first Syrian line had grown to include 800 tanks and 108 batteries of artillery. By Friday this was more than 900 tanks and 140 batteries of artillery, by far the largest concentration of forces which Syria had ever assembled. Identified in position and ready to attack in the front line were, from north to south: a Moroccan brigade in the Mt. Hermon foothills; in the area just north of the Kuneitra-Damascus road, the 7th Syrian Infantry Division, with an attached armored brigade; just south of the road and generally opposite Kuneitra and extending down almost as far as Rafid was the 9th Infantry Division, also with an attached armored brigade; then, south and east of Rafid and just north of the Yarmouk Valley, the 5th Infantry Division, which had a larger component of tanks than either of the other two infantry divisions, and also had an armored brigade attached.

Behind these units, generally in the second Syrian defense zone, were the 3d Armored Division, deployed between Katana and Saassaa, and the 1st Armored Division south and west of Kiswe. One or more independent armored brigades, infantry brigades, and mechanized brigades were also believed to be in this area. Actually, rather than the 900 tanks conservatively estimated by the Israelis, there were probably closer to 1,260 tanks in this region by October 6.

The principal combat elements of a Syrian infantry division were one infantry brigade, one mechanized infantry brigade, and one armored brigade. The infantry and mechanized infantry brigades each had three infantry battalions, a battalion of 40 tanks, an AA artillery battalion, and a field artillery battalion. The armored brigade had three battalions of 40 tanks each. The division also included a regiment of division field artillery; a divisional AA artillery regiment; a reconnaissance battalion (with one company attached to each brigade); and a chemical company (with one section per brigade); giving a total of approximately 10,000 men, 200 tanks, 72 artillery pieces, and about the same number of antiaircraft guns and SAMs. However, only the 5th Division had its full complement of armored and mechanized vehicles. The 7th Division had about 80% of its tanks and APCs; the 9th Division about 50%.

The armored divisions—both at full strength—were made up of two armored brigades of 120 tanks each and one mechanized infantry brigade, giving each armored division more than 250 tanks, plus the same supporting units as the infantry division, with a total strength also of about 10,000 men. The independent armored brigades each had about 2,000 men and 120 tanks.

The total Syrian field army east of the Purple Line included approximately 60,000 men, nearly 1,300 tanks, close to 600 artillery pieces, at least 400 antiaircraft guns, and more than 100 batteries of SA-2, SA-3, and SA-6 surface-to-air missiles, with between 400 and 500 launchers. Overall field command was exercised by the Syrian Chief of Staff, Major General Youseff Chakkour, from GHQ in Damascus.

As has been noted, Israeli intelligence, keeping close track of this Syrian concentration, was convinced that it was solely for routine autumn maneuvers. General Zeira and his people were confident that their agents would have discovered any attack plans, if there were any.

The Syrian Air Force had more than 300 combat aircraft; these included 30 Su-7s and 80 MiG-17 ground attack fighters, 200 MiG-21 interceptors, and a few Il-28 light bombers. Its commander, however, Major General Maji Jamil, had recently been reminded of the substantial superiority of the Israeli Air Force in aerial combat. So, like the Egyptians, the Syrians entrusted the security of their air space mainly to SAM missiles and antiaircraft guns, but also, like the Egyptians, integrated their air force into the air defense system. Approximately 100 batteries of SAMs, including SA-2, SA-3, and SA-6 units, were deployed west of Damascus. With these—in addition to divisional AA weapons—were 27 antiaircraft companies, with 162 guns, many of them ZSU-23-4.

THE SYRIAN PLAN

Like the Egyptian plan, that of the Syrians was completely their own, yet it was greatly influenced by schooling which many Syrian officers had received at Russian military academies,[2] and by the operational advice they had received from Russian advisors over a period of more than 15 years of force buildup with Soviet equipment. It was a Syrian plan, but strongly influenced by Soviet doctrine.

In typical Soviet manner the offensive was to be initiated by a rather short but extremely intensive firepower shock, delivered by all available combat aircraft, artillery pieces, tank guns, and mortars. Also in typical Russian fashion, the offensive would be launched on a broad front, so that Syrian numerical superiority would force the widest possible dispersion of the Israeli defensive effort. Then, concentrating massive superiority of manpower and firepower at two critical points, the Syrians expected to make two penetrations through the overextended defenses before the Israeli mobilization system could get reserve forces to the battlefront.

Specifically the Syrian plan provided for a double breakthrough by the 7th Division near Ahmadiyeh in the north, and by the 5th Division near Rafid in the south. This would be followed by a double envelopment of the bulk of the Israeli forces on the Golan, with the 7th Division striking west toward the upper Jordan through El Rom and Wasit to the northern Jordan crossings, and the 5th moving on a parallel course toward the Arik Bridge just north of Lake Tiberias. Both divisions were prepared to advance in two echelons; hopefully the second echelon of each division would exploit the initial breakthrough created by the first echelon.

To keep the Israelis pinned down all along the line, the 9th Division, in the center, south of Kuneitra, would strike west, between the 5th and 7th Divisions. At the same time Brigadier General Safrawi's Moroccan Brigade, north of the 7th Division, would make a strong demonstration in the direction of Masa'ada and Banias, in the foothills of Mt. Hermon. The 9th Division—least experienced of all of the Syrian divisions—would seize a line of hills extending south of Kuneitra, cut the Israelis' lateral road, and then send its right-wing brigade northwestward to join a similar spearhead of the 7th Division to encircle the Israeli defenders of Kuneitra. Both the 9th Division and the Moroccan Brigade were given limited objectives, and were not to advance further without authority from GHQ Damascus.

The second echelon of the field army consisted of the 1st and 3d

---

[2] Soviet military academies are the equivalent of American service schools and staff colleges.

Armored Divisions. If the 5th Division made a breakthrough, or if both 5th and 7th Divisions broke through, the 1st Division would exploit this, and drive between the 5th and 9th Divisions for Nafekh, pulverizing the Israeli force already caught between the 5th and 7th Division pincers. If, however, the 5th Division should be held up, and the 7th Division made a breakthrough, alternative plans called for the commitment of the 3rd Armored Division between the 7th and 9th Divisions. In no case, however, were both the 1st and 3d Armored Divisions to be committed; one of them was to be held as a general reserve in the event of failure or unexpected developments.

As with the Egyptians, the Syrian plan provided vaguely for a second phase of the offensive, across the Jordan into eastern Galilee. But the Syrians realistically expected a UN ceasefire before such a further operation could take place. Furthermore, they doubted whether it would be feasible, in the light of probable Israeli control of the skies westward of the Syrian air defense umbrella. The Syrians hoped to recover all or most of the Golan. This would be success enough.

ISRAELI PREPARATIONS

From the high ground on the Golan, and particularly from the observation post on Mt. Hermon, General Hoffi's Northern Command had been able to observe the concentration of Syrian troops on the Damascus Plain in a manner that had been denied to the Israeli troops of the Southern Command. Thus, despite a general tendency to discount the seriousness of the threat, the potentiality of a major onslaught was more clearly understood by Hoffi and his subordinates. It was this concern and understanding that Hoffi had communicated to Dayan, and that resulted in the early October movement of part, and then all, of the 7th Armored Brigade from its training garrison location in southern Israel first to eastern Galilee, and then to the Golan Heights. However, there had been many previous alerts on the Golan front, and most Israeli officers assumed that this would not be more serious than the earlier crises.

To facilitate the transfer of the 7th Brigade, the General Staff ordered the brigade commander, Colonel Avigdor Ben Gal, to leave his own tanks at the garrison, and to take over tanks and heavy equipment held in reserve stock in Northern Command, earmarked for reserve units in the event of mobilization.[3] By October 5 the 7th Brigade tankers had most of these tanks—about 100 in all—ready for operations. That day Colonel Ben Gal was directed to send one of his tank battalions to the

---

[3] Herzog, *op. cit.*, p. 66. Although not officially confirmed, the same technique was apparently used in the south on October 6, to enable Baram's regular army brigade to get ready so rapidly for combat.

Heights, to be a reserve for Colonel Yitzhak Ben Shoham's four-battalion Barak Brigade. This consisted of two Regular Army armored battalions and two mobilized reserve battalions, one of tanks and one of mechanized infantry, nearly 90 tanks in all. One of his armored battalions was in readiness north of Kuneitra, and another armored battalion, reinforced with a company, between Kuneitra and Rafid. Brigadier General Rafael Eitan, the division commander of the forces on the Golan, to whom the 7th Armored Brigade had been assigned, believed that a larger armored reserve was necessary than the approximately 20 tanks still available to Ben Shoham; thus the order to Ben Gal to send a battalion to the plateau.

Later in the day, alarmed by the continuing Syrian buildup, Eitan received Hoffi's permission to move the entire 7th Brigade to the Heights, to be concentrated near Nafekh, and available for counterattack either north or south of Rafid. General Hoffi's staff believed that if the Syrians made an attack—and they were now divided in their assessment of this possibility—it would most likely be directed at Kuneitra, and seek to envelop that city from the north. Eitan, however, was more concerned about the danger of a Syrian main effort across the better tank country south of Kuneitra. In any event, the Israelis were carefully avoiding committing any of their forces in the city of Kuneitra.

In response to Eitan's order, Colonel Ben Gal, his reconnaissance unit, and one of his two remaining armored battalions moved up on the Heights at Nafekh on the 5th. The other battalion, after completing the reconditioning of its new tanks during the night, joined the rest of the brigade at Nafekh on the morning of the 6th. At that time Ben Gal was at Northern Command Headquarters, learning of the confirmed intelligence report of the planned Syrian attack. As on the Egyptian front, the anticipated time of the attack was set at 6:00 p.m.

When the attack came—just after 2:00 p.m. instead of 6:00—Eitan's troops on the Heights were at least alert to the possibility of attack, and he had a respectable force under command. Counting the detachment holding the Mt. Hermon Observation Post, there was roughly the equivalent of a full brigade of infantry; one slightly understrength armored brigade deployed behind the frontline fortifications, and a full-strength armored brigade in reserve. There were also eleven batteries of artillery in position, as many as Mendler had for the entire Sinai front. Counting combat and support troops, Eitan had almost 12,000 men on the Heights, and about 200 tanks: some 105 with the 7th Brigade and nearly 90 with the Barak Brigade.

6

The Syrian Offensive

THE ASSAULT

The Syrian attack was launched at five minutes past 2:00 p.m. on the afternoon of October 6, coordinated with the Egyptian assault on the Suez Canal to assure complete surprise. The Syrian offensive began with an intensive artillery and air bombardment along the entire 65-kilometer front. Under the cover of this fire, which lasted for one hour, the three Syrian frontline divisions moved to attack.

In the north the 7th Division struck generally westward or southwestward through Ahmadiyeh, south of Tel el Shiha (called Mt. Hermonit by the Israelis), along the road to El Rom. In the south, the 5th Division focussed its effort through Juhader, generally northwestward along the TAP line. Between these main efforts the 9th Division attacked westward midway between Kudna and Kuneitra, with one thrust just south of Kuneitra and another near Kudna.

Less than half an hour after the Syrian artillery barrage and air strikes began, and while they continued, the three divisions began to move to their jump-off positions. Both of the main assaults by the 7th and 5th Divisions initially comprised two parallel columns as spearheads, striking directly into the Israeli lines. Eyewitnesses[1] report that in each of these thrusts the two parallel columns of armored vehicles (tanks and APCs) moved slowly, almost bumper to bumper, intermixed with various command and support vehicles as well as a number of towed and self-propelled antitank and antiaircraft guns. Close to the front in both columns were armored engineer units.

The 5th Infantry Division, moving up the TAP line, appears to have been in good order and maintained good march discipline, except for the lack of intervals between vehicles. The columns of the 7th and 9th Divisions, moving through Ahmadiyeh and south of Kuneitra, on the other hand, gave evidence of some confusion from the outset, with little unit integrity. For instance, the bridging tanks needed for crossing the

[1] The author has interviewed four UNTSO (United Nations Truce Supervision Organization) observers who were in observation posts between the two armies.

445

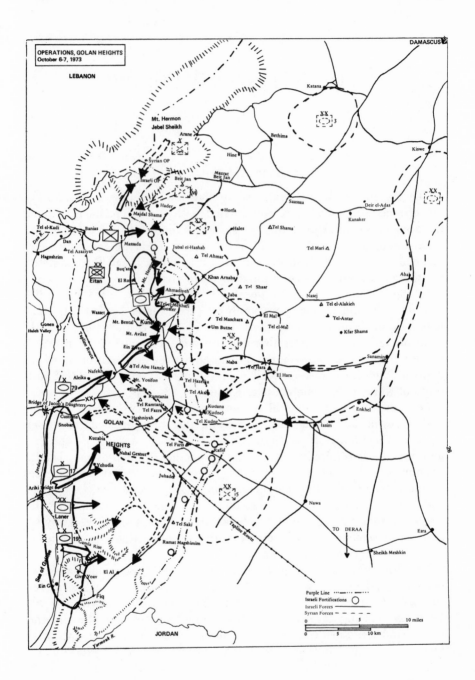

OPERATIONS, GOLAN HEIGHTS
October 6-7, 1973

Israeli antitank ditch were well back in these columns. This confusion seems to have been the result of the eagerness of all units to get into action, with inadequate measures for control and road discipline. (One observer has described the sight as something like a race of Damascus taxicabs.) Strangely, there was at this time no Israeli air action against any of these vulnerable columns.

By midafternoon, despite early success in throwing back initial Syrian assaults, General Eitan had come to the conclusion that the Barak Brigade had inadequate force to hold the entire Golan front. He was particularly concerned about the weight of the Syrian attack south of Kuneitra, and wanted Colonel Ben Shoham to be able to focus his attention and increased strength there. Accordingly, he ordered Ben Gal's 7th Brigade to transfer one battalion to Ben Shoham, and at the same time to take over responsibility for the defense north of Kuneitra, assuming command of the Barak Brigade battalion already in action there. While it was not yet detached from his command, one of Ben Gal's battalions was to be held out of action as a possible division reserve. Anticipating that he would probably soon lose control over that battalion, Ben Gal collected a few tanks from each of his battalions to build up his reconnaissance unit to a small brigade reserve task force of about 20 tanks.

Thus, by midafternoon the Barak Brigade, which still had about 90 tanks in action, was responsible for the front south of Kuneitra, which it was holding but under increasing pressure. The 7th Brigade was in action north of Kuneitra, with two battalions (including the one transferred from the Barak Brigade) on line—still almost 60 tanks—and about 20 in local reserve, while an additional battalion, 30 tanks, was virtually in division reserve.

NORTH OF KUNEITRA

A result of the confusion in the Syrian columns north of Kuneitra was that when the antitank ditch was reached infantrymen and tankers had to get off their vehicles and use shovels under severe Israeli fire, to fill in the ditch. Some bulldozers were finally able to work their way forward to help. Meanwhile the columns behind this unexpected activity were halted, stretching back for miles behind the front.

Because of this initial confusion, the assault of the 7th Infantry Division in the Ahmadiyeh area became bogged down in a small, dish-shaped valley just west of the Purple Line. This valley, about 2,000 meters north to south by about 1,200 meters in width, was overlooked to the north by Mt. Hermonit, and to the south by a hill called "Booster" by the Israelis and Tel el Mekhafi by the Arabs. Over the long saddle stretching between these heights ran the road to El Rom, apparently an initial objective of the 7th Division.

Engineers equipped with antimine devices succeeded finally in clearing approaches and in laying bridges over the ditch. Bulldozers were able to clear away the embankment on the Israeli side. But as the Syrian tanks advanced through these defiles in the embankment they were taken under fire by Israeli tanks, hull down in prepared ramps just behind the saddle. Looking down the slopes toward the Syrians, they picked off Syrian tanks as they came through. Syrian infantry dug in on the embankment, but except for occasional patrols could get no farther.

During the night Syrian tanks were able to work their way through the embankment, which was largely leveled by engineers and infantry during the darkness. Despite the fact that the Syrians were better equipped with night vision devices than the Israelis, they were unable to push their way through the valley to the saddle, even though intensive artillery support seriously interfered with the Israelis' defense. Fighting was bitter and intense, often at extremely short range, through the night, but Syrian efforts to fight through the valley were unavailing. By morning of the 7th more than 100 tanks, over half of those with the 7th Infantry Division, were scattered—damaged and abandoned—throughout the valley, which by now the Israelis were calling the Valley of Tears.

At about the same time that the three Syrian divisions began their thrusts across the Purple Line, a bold and well-prepared Syrian commando assault struck at the Israeli fortified observation post on Mt. Hermon. A Syrian helicopter-borne force approached the OP from the rear, or north, while a ground unit attacked directly up the slope from the northeast, moving from the Syrian OP. These forces surprised and annihilated the Israeli garrison. Later that afternoon elements of the Israeli Golani Brigade undertook the first of several attempts to retake the position, but were repulsed by the Syrians, now well dug in on all approaches to the captured Israeli OP.

Elsewhere, however, the Syrians had been unable to seize any of the other Israeli strongpoints by surprise. Bypassing and containing these, they drove westward; the strongpoints would be mopped up later after the principal division objectives had been seized.

SOUTH OF KUNEITRA

The 9th Division in the center of the Syrian line crossed the ditch just south of Kuneitra, taking heavy losses. By morning of October 7 the division had advanced about eight kilometers and, except for its right-wing brigade, had reached its assigned objectives. On the right, efforts to advance toward Kuneitra had been stopped completely by the right-flank companies of the 7th Brigade.

The 5th Division, meanwhile, was moving with good discipline on terrain less favorable for defense and more favorable for armor, which the Syrians possessed in overwhelmingly superior numbers. Nevertheless, during the afternoon of the 6th the 5th Division made little progress, held up by vigorous and repeated Israeli armored counterattacks. After nightfall, however, the 5th Division made a clean breakthrough in the south, and immediately fanned out in three columns. The northern column moved northwest along the TAP line, then turned west toward Yehudia (known to the Arabs as Yarubia) and the Arik Bridge. The southern column struck south down the road from Rafid toward El Al; the third column, branching off from the southern one, drove westward from Ramat Magshimim. By morning of the 7th, the northern or right-most column had advanced approximately 10 kilometers and was engaged in a running firefight of tanks and APCs between Nahal Geshur and Yehudia. The southern column was between Ramat Magshimim and El Al, and the central column was west of Juhader.

In opposing the thrust the Barak Brigade had a nearly impossible task. With only 90 tanks to cover a front of 40 kilometers, over terrain that was much more favorable for maneuver than that in the north, Colonel Ben Shoham soon had to cope with multiple breakthroughs along his entire front. His performance in dealing with these was at first remarkably successful. After dark, however, the Israelis lost the observation advantage that had helped them in the afternoon, and were unable to match the night-fighting effectiveness of superior Syrian materiel. Ben Shoham's left battalion was holding its own against the limited 9th Division thrusts. However, his center and right had been smashed by the massive breakthrough of the 5th Division south of Rafid and Tel Faris.

When the weight of the onslaughts was recognized, Ben Shoham permitted the defenders of four of the eight frontline strongholds to evacuate their positions. The others, however, had been quickly enveloped and were soon isolated. Ben Shoham's regular and reserve battalions fought staunchly, but the Syrian infantry made very effective use of their man-portable Sagger missiles and their RPG-7 bazookas, and the Israeli tankers were hopelessly outnumbered by the Syrian armor. The defenders were forced to give ground and by midnight had lost close to half their tanks.

The Syrians, well supplied with night-vision equipment, continued the attacks during the night. Ben Shoham, having lost contact with several of his frontline units, left his command post at Nafekh, adjacent to the command post of the District Commander, General Eitan, and went southeastward down the TAP line in his personal tank, accompanied by his mobile command post in an APC. By dawn he was involved in the desperate fighting west of Hushniyah.

THE AIR BATTLE

The Syrian Air Force flew a number of close support missions. The normal Syrian flight pattern consisted of MiG-17s and Su-7s, flying ground attack missions at extremely low altitudes, with MiG-21s providing top cover. On the 6th Israeli air opposition to these attacks was spotty, since at that time the major preoccupation of the IAF was the Egyptian crossing of the Suez Canal. However, a number of attacking Syrian planes were destroyed by Israeli Hawk SAMs. But even more Israeli planes were victims of the Syrian air defense system.

On the 7th, as the seriousness of the Syrian threat began to be appreciated by both Israel's Northern Command and the High Command in Tel Aviv, the bulk of the IAF was committed to the northern theater. The Israeli aircraft dominated the skies over the Golan, denying the area effectively to Syrian planes. The Israelis repeatedly attacked the Syrian armored spearheads on the ground, and had some effectiveness against their lines of communication back to the Purple Line. But when the Israelis tried to cross over into Syrian territory they ran into the same kind of impenetrable barrier of SAMs and AA guns that was frustrating Israeli pilots near the Suez Canal.

On October 7, 8, and 9, Israeli pilots flew an average of about 500 sorties per day over the Syrian front, the maximum effort coming on the 9th, when the level of effort probably approached 600 sorties. The Syrians counted more than 1,000 Israeli sorties on the 9th, but careful postwar comparison of the Syrian and Egyptian reports of 20,000 Israeli sorties during the war shows that these were almost double the maximum Israeli capability of about 11,000 sorties. Israeli sortie figures are classified, but it is possible to calculate from Israeli reports on losses per sortie that they actually flew more than 10,500, quite close to the theoretical maximum capability. The higher Arab estimate, of course, is due to multiple sighting reports.

BAR LEV'S MISSION TO NORTHERN COMMAND

Early on October 7 Defense Minister Moshe Dayan made flying visits to both fronts. Apparently he was only partially reassured by General Gonen's calm claims—later proved to be overly optimistic—that the southern front was becoming stabilized. But he was shocked by the situation in the north, where he discovered that the Barak Brigade was collapsing, that the Syrians were rampaging on the TAP line road, and that there was no solid force to stop them from reaching the Jordan and the Sea of Galilee.

Dayan rushed back to Tel Aviv to report to Prime Minister Golda Meir, and is said to have spoken to her as follows:

"Golda, I was wrong in everything. We are headed toward a catastrophe. We shall have to withdraw on the Golan Heights to the edge of the escarpment overlooking the valley and in the south in Sinai to the passes and hold on to the last bullet."[1]

It was not for nothing that former Prime Minister Ben Gurion had spoken of Golda Meir as the "strongest 'man' in my Cabinet." She pondered the pessimistic report of Dayan, then called in for consultation one of his successors as Chief of Staff, retired Lieutenant General Haim Bar Lev, now Minister of Trade and Industry, a man she respected for both calmness and intellect. The situation in the north was obviously much more critical than that in the south, and a disaster there could have a directly catastrophic effect upon the citizens of Galilee. She asked Bar Lev to put on a uniform, and go to the Northern Command headquarters as her representative, to find out what was happening, and then to advise her as to what she and the Israeli Government should do.

Bar Lev at once agreed, but pointed out that such an appointment could not be made without at least informing—preferably consulting— both Defense Minister Dayan and Chief of Staff Elazar. Both were enthusiastic, and even went to the extent of authorizing Bar Lev to issue emergency orders in the name of the IDF Headquarters, if this should appear necessary.

By 8:00 p.m. on the evening of October 7 Bar Lev had reached Northern Command Headquarters in Galilee. He immediately spoke to General Hoffi and quietly observed the calm, but depressed, performance of his tired, gloomy staff. He approved the plans that Hoffi had made for the early deployment of the mobilizing reserve divisions of Major Generals Dan Laner and Moshe Peled, and for the interim piecemeal commitment of mobilized reserves as they arrived. Following that, Bar Lev then drove to Laner's headquarters—three tanks and three APCs—at the

[1] Chaim Herzog, *War of Atonement* (Tel Aviv, 1975), p. 116. Herzog's comments about Dayan in this and other instances must be accepted with some caution. This author has been informed by apparently reliable authority that Herzog did not interview Dayan, and that his quotes about Dayan are second- or third-hand. The reader should at least check what Dayan has to say in his *Story of My Life* (Tel Aviv, 1976). Dayan does not mention seeing the Prime Minister after his early morning visit to the northern front (see pp. 394-396) but does mention a conversation with her later that day after visiting the southern front (see p. 406), and also frankly discusses a cabinet meeting in which the Prime Minister and other ministers appear to have assumed that he (Dayan) had lost his nerve. Dayan's version is also consistent with that in Golda Meir's *My Life* (London, 1975), pp. 360-361.

northern end of Lake Tiberias, where he spoke briefly to staff officers
and senior commanders.

By his presence, his few useful suggestions, and his general confirmation and approval of what the Northern Command was doing, Bar Lev
did much to reestablish the crumbling morale of the commanders and
staffs in the north. And he also was able to come to the conclusion that—
despite the extreme gravity of the situation—the Syrians could be, and
would be, stopped.

After midnight Bar Lev flew back to Tel Aviv to report to Mrs. Meir
on what he had seen, and the conclusions he had drawn. The Prime
Minister was extremely relieved to get this word from a proven competent soldier in whom she had full confidence.

7

So Near—And Yet So Far, October 7-9

DESPERATE DEFENSE

By mid-morning of October 7 the confused situation on the Golan front was obscure to the frontline commanders on both sides, although General Eitan, in his command post at Nafekh, probably had a slightly clearer picture than did his Syrian counterparts.

In the north the Syrians held the Israeli Mt. Hermon observation post, and had repulsed several counterattacks by the Golani Brigade. Along the ridge line from Mt. Hermon toward Kuneitra, the Israeli 7th Armored Brigade was having little difficulty in repulsing continuing efforts of the Syrian 7th and 9th Infantry Divisions to penetrate north and south of Kuneitra.

Further south, however, the remnants of the Barak Brigade, fighting a number of scattered and uncoordinated defensive actions, were being encircled or pushed back westward toward the escarpment, and northwestward into the central Golan past Hushniyah and toward Nafekh. The only reason that Colonel Ben Shoham's tanks and men had not completely collapsed under the pressure was the piecemeal arrival of reinforcements. Aware of the desperate situation on the Heights, General Hoffi had ordered mobilizing reserve units to move to the front as soon as they were ready, without waiting to concentrate in battalion or brigade formations. As individual tank companies and platoons arrived, Eitan rushed them to the southern sector, to bolster Ben Shoham.

On the Syrian side, General Chakkour was committing the 1st Armored Division between the left wing of the 9th Division and the right of the 5th Division. The 1st Division was to exploit the success so far achieved, and continue the drive to the Jordan and Huleh Valleys through Hushniyah, Nafekh, and the Bridge of Jacob's Daughters.

Shortly after noon on that grim Sunday, Colonel Ben Shoham's tank was destroyed, and he was killed, just west of Hushniyah. By this time components of the Syrian 5th Division had almost reached the edge of the escarpment overlooking the Sea of Galilee and the Jordan River. Also at about this time, approximately 1:15 p.m., tanks of the 1st Armored Division reached the Israeli command post at Nefekh. General Eitan, who had been coolly directing the northern battle, left his command post to observe the nearby action. After he hit an approaching Syrian tank with a bazooka round, he decided this was not where a division commander should be. With his advance headquarters group and APCs, he withdrew northward up the TAP line. About five kilometers away he halted and reestablished his command post in the open.

By this time, however, larger elements of a hastily organized Israeli reserve division under the command of Major General Dan Laner were beginning to arrive at the Arik Bridge and the Bridge of Jacob's Daughters. At 10:00 a.m. Laner had been assigned responsibility for the southern portion of the Golan. Laner sent the 79th Armored Brigade, under the command of Colonel Uri Or, to support Eitan and relieve beleaguered Nafekh. Some tanks from this brigade arrived on the southwest side of the Nafekh position a few minutes after Eitan had pulled out, and while the Syrians were still being held up by a small mixed force which had stayed behind at Nafekh. A fierce armored battle then took place between the leading elements of Or's brigade and the 51st Armored Brigade of the Syrian 1st Armored Division. The bitter battle swirled around the Nafekh area during the remaining hours of daylight, but by dark the Nafekh position had been secured by the Israelis, and Or was able to send newly arriving elements of his brigade north toward Kuneitra, to take position on the right flank of the 7th Armored Brigade.

Meanwhile Laner was concentrating his attention on the threatening advance of the Syrian 5th Division toward the Sea of Galilee and the lower Huleh Valley. From his command post just northwest of the lake he could see occasional Syrian tanks on the distant heights, less than five kilometers from the escarpment. He had earlier given orders to the mobilizing brigades of his division that they were to send units forward by platoon, as they were ready, and not to wait to assemble companies or battalions. As units of two or three tanks approached the Arik Bridge just north of Lake Tiberias, where Laner had placed his forward command post of three halftracks, he assigned them to one of the three brigade areas into which he had divided his divisional sector, and sent them up the escarpment by one of the three winding roads that led eastward from the bridge: the road to Yehudia in the north, the road to Juhader in the center, and the road up the Gamla Rise to Givat Yoav and El Al.

By noon Laner had between 50 and 60 tanks committed on his front, including fewer than twenty that remained from the Barak Brigade. These were now operating as three brigades, even though each was hardly larger than a company in strength. Holding the last high ground just east of the escarpment, these tanks were engaged in desperate battle with the tanks of the 5th Syrian Division, and its attached armored brigade. During the afternoon the Syrians gallantly pushed forward, only to be halted by the equally gallant and determined defenders, who by dusk had about 90 tanks deployed: 40 on the left, 30 in the center, and 20 on the right.

In this bitter struggle the greatest strengths and greatest weaknesses of the Syrians combined to work against them. Mindful of their defeat in 1967, Syrians from top leadership to private soldiers were determined not to retreat under any circumstances except upon orders of higher commanders. This meant that when the attackers ran into obstinate Israeli resistance they were afraid to withdraw even a few hundred meters for maneuvering purposes. They simply regrouped, and survivors then smashed forward again in renewed—and usually fruitless—efforts to drive their way through the Israeli defenses. This demonstration of Syrian persistence and courage was of course noted by the Israelis, whose former contempt for the Syrians was now turned to grudging respect.

The Israelis, however, benefitted enormously from this inflexible Syrian demonstration of courage. And they also benefitted from the apparent inability of the Syrian higher commanders—from battalion to division level—to coordinate these suicidal attacks. As a result, before the end of the day the southern Golan, from Nafekh to the Yarmouk Valley, was littered with about 250 destroyed and damaged Syrian tanks, 150 of which were in front of Laner's makeshift division.

The first echelon of the 7th Armored Brigade was still heavily engaged north of Kuneitra, with the principal action continuing in the valley between Mt. Hermonit and Tel el Mekhafi. By midafternoon of October 7, close to 200 destroyed or damaged Syrian tanks and APCs were scattered across the valley. Colonel Ben Gal had only two tank battalions and his mechanized infantry; his other battalion had been sent south from Kuneitra to help the remnants of the Barak Brigade slow down the drive of the 5th and 9th Syrian Divisions. Ben Gal's troops were becoming exhausted, but, more serious, they were running low on both ammunition and fuel. Under constant artillery fire, and under equally constant pressure from the Syrian tanks and from infiltrating infantry units, the rapidly moving and rapidly firing tanks of the 7th Armored Brigade had little opportunity to replenish either fuel or ammunition. Even darkness gave little respite, as the Syrians continued their pressure throughout the night.

While recognizing the increasingly dangerous situation of the 7th Armored Brigade north of Kuneitra, General Hoffi was much more concerned about the south, where the Barak Brigade had been virtually wiped out, although the piecemeal arrivals of reinforcements were apparently keeping the Syrians from seizing the victory almost in their grasp. Thus Hoffi—as well as Eitan and Laner—concentrated most of his attention on directing the arriving reserve units to the places where the Syrian threat was greatest.

THE "LOST" OPPORTUNITY

As to the Syrians, both General Ali Aslan of the 5th Infantry Division and Colonel Tewfiq Juhni, commanding the 1st Armored Division, seem to have realized their opportunity, and continued their efforts to reach the Jordan bridges and the eastern shores of the Sea of Galilee. They believed that it would not take much more pressure to smash through Laner's division or Or's 79th Brigade to reach the Bridge of Jacob's Daughters, and they tried to exert that pressure. But the Israeli defense was desperate. And every time a Syrian breakthrough became imminent, Laner or Eitan rushed another recently arrived reserve platoon or company to plug the gap.

After the war there was speculation among foreign observers, and even within the IDF, as to the reasons for the inability of the Syrians to break through. The Syrian failure has been variously attributed to the self-sacrificing efforts of the Israeli Air Force, to the breakdown of the Syrian logistical system, and to general Syrian ineptness and failure to realize how close they were to victory.

The contribution of the Israeli Air Force to the Syrian slowdown cannot be ignored. However, after the war a close inspection of abandoned Syrian tanks found on the Golan revealed no clearcut evidence that any had been destroyed by air weapons. Nevertheless it was air strikes that prevented ammunition and fuel resupply convoys from reaching them, and the constant air harassment contributed to Syrian caution and confusion. But basically, the Syrian attack was stopped by the skillful and determined fighting of Israeli tank units.

By midafternoon of October 7, with some units actually in sight of the Jordan and the Sea of Galilee, the Syrian attack ground to a halt. But the Israeli mobilized reserves continued to arrive, and by midevening there was a thin, continuous line of Israeli forces stopping further advance of the Syrian spearheads. Israeli troops now blocked the TAP line, they were near the old French customhouse above Jacob's Daughters Bridge, and they securely held Yehudia on the escarpment above the Sea of Galilee, and El Al further to the south and east.

By morning of the 8th the Israelis had seized the initiative in the central and southern Golan. Or's brigade, now constituting the right wing of Eitan's division, was driving generally east toward Ein Zivan, Sindiana, and Ramtania. This advance was being closely coordinated with a nearly parallel movement by Colonel Ran Sarig's 17th Armored Brigade, on the left of Laner's division, through Kuzabia, and across the

TAP line toward Hushniyeh. Joining in this offensive, beginning about 2:00 p.m., was the division of Major General Moshe Peled with three armored brigades, which concentrated during the night and the early morning south of the Sea of Galilee. On Peled's left, climbing eastward from Ein Gev through the winding defile of the Gamla Rise through Givat Yoav, were the 14th and 19th Brigades; further east, on the main northward road through El Al, was the 20th Brigade.

The advance of Laner's left and Peled's right now threatened the Syrian 5th Division with a double envelopment. With more than one brigade committed to blocking the Israeli infantry strongholds along the Purple Line, and with all of his remaining forces committed to the attacks which had come so close to success the previous afternoon, Brigadier General Ali Aslan, the 5th Division commander, had no reserves to commit against either of the envelopment threats. He informed General Chakkour of his situation, and was authorized to withdraw to form a new line across the southern Golan, from Hushniyah, through Nahal Geshur, to Tel Saki. Having completed this movement by early afternoon, and having replenished his remaining tanks with fuel and ammunition, General Aslan committed them in another effort to regain the initiative.

At about this same time Colonel Tewfiq Juhni, commanding the 1st Armored Division, committed his last tanks in another effort to get to Nafekh. Once more intense fighting swirled around and along the roads in the central and southern Golan. But the Israelis would not relinquish the initiative. By evening, after a seesaw battle, Or's 79th Brigade securely held Sindiana, Sarig's brigade had reached the TAP line west of Hushniyah, and the leading brigades of Peled's division had captured Ramat Magshimim and were attacking a hastily but strongly prepared Syrian antitank defense area, extending generally north from Tel Saki to Juhader.

THE ORDEAL OF THE SEVENTH BRIGADE

The assault of the Syrian 7th Infantry Division against the Israeli 7th Brigade continued unabated. By the end of October 8 that brigade, for all the success it had achieved on the heights north of Kuneitra, and the terrible toll of casualties it had inflicted upon the Syrians, was close to complete exhaustion. Syrian Brigadier General Omar Abrash, commanding the 7th Division, pulled back the depleted units of his first echelon and committed his second echelon to the fight, planning to take advantage of the superior Syrian night vision equipment. At dusk, however, just as he was getting his tanks ready to renew the attack, Abrash's command tank was hit, burst into flames, and he was killed.

The death of Abrash—a courageous leader, and a graduate of the US

Army Command and General Staff College at Fort Leavenworth, Kansas—was a disaster to the Syrian Army. The planned attack was postponed until morning, giving some respite to Ben Gal's exhausted troops.

When the attack of the 7th Division's second echelon came, shortly after dawn on the 9th, it may or may not have had the force which Abrash's presence would have assured. Even so, supported by perhaps the most accurate artillery concentration which they had yet employed north of Kuneitra, at about 9:00 a.m. 7th Division units once more worked their way through the Valley of Tears toward the high saddle between Mt. Hermonit and Tel el Mekhafi. The artillery fire was so devastating that at about 9:00 a.m. Ben Gal ordered the tanks of Lieutenant Colonel Augidor Khalny's 77th Battalion to fall back, hoping to be able to recapture the commanding ground of the saddle after the artillery fire had lifted, and before it could be really secured by the Syrians. But the Syrians were too fast. They seized the crest, continued on rapidly over it, and enveloped the remnants of Khalny's battalion. For a while the 7th Brigade, or what was left of it, found itself fighting enemies in all directions.

At about 10:00 a.m. Ben Gal, who had had no sleep since the morning of October 6, radioed to Eitan to inform him that it was doubtful that he could hold on. When Eitan tried to encourage him Ben Gal calmly but dully described the condition of his brigade. "Hold on, Avigdor, hold on!" Eitan entreated his brigade commander over the radio. (Interestingly, Eitan did not use Ben Gal's nickname, "Yanush.") "Give me another half hour. You will soon be receiving reinforcements."

But the Israeli situation north of Kuneitra was to grow even darker in the next few minutes. Suddenly ten or more Syrian Mi-8 helicopters flew over the Hermonit-Tel el Mekhafi saddle, and the raging tank battle there, headed west toward El Rom. At the same time Eitan's command post received word that Syrian infantry was approaching Buq'ata, just north of El Rom. Thus, if the 7th Division tanks broke through the remnants of the 7th Brigade, as now seemed likely, they would be able to join a substantial force of infantry in the Buq'ata-El Rom area, and there was nothing available to stop them short of Dan and Qiryat Shimona. Eitan called for air attacks on the threatening infantry, and sent for a battalion of the Golani Brigade, further north on the slopes of Mt. Hermon, to try to pin the Syrians down.

At this moment, the remnants of the Barak Brigade, a force now totalling eleven tanks which Lieutenant Colonel Yossi Ben Chanen had reorganized just below the escarpment, was moving back into Eitan's divisional area, north of Kuneitra. Eitan hastily put Ben Chanen under Ben Gal's command, letting him move eastward into the midst of the confused tank battle now taking place just to the west of the saddle between Tel el Mekhafi and Mt. Hermonit. Ben Chanen and his eleven tanks came over the rise of Tel el Mekhafi and hit the left flank of a Syrian tank brigade as it was closing in on the seven remaining operational tanks of Ben Gal's brigade. The Syrians recoiled, but Ben Gal was sure they would be back. Again he radioed back to Eitan and said it was doubtful that he, even with this reinforcement by the Barak Brigade, could hold any longer.

At almost exactly this moment Eitan's headquarters received a radio message from surrounded Israeli stronghold A-3, at Ahmadiyeh, where the Syrian 7th Division had made its initial breakthrough. The stronghold reported that the Syrian supply trains were withdrawing, and that their tanks were pulling back down from the saddle and from the flanks of Mt. Hermonit. Not long after this the Syrian infantry near Buq'ata began to pull back. The battle was over.

Forgetting their exhaustion, the 7th Brigade, led by Ben Gal and Khalny, swept back up to the top of the saddle, and pursued the retreating Syrians, as Israeli artillery also hammered at the withdrawing column. Eitan spoke over the radio to Ben Gal and his men: "You have saved the people of Israel." In turn Ben Gal said over the radio to Khalny, "You are the true saviour of the people of Israel."

What had happened, of course, was that the magnificent defense that the 7th Brigade had put up on the 6th, 7th, and 8th had led Eitan and Hoffi to assume that Ben Gal and his men could continue indefinitely. The generals focussed their attention on areas that seemed to be more seriously in danger. Hoffi was mainly concerned with getting Laner's and Peled's divisions to regain the ground lost on the 6th and 7th by the Barak Brigade. Eitan's concern was to hold Nafekh, with the 79th Brigade, while getting the remnants of the Barak Brigade reorganized and refitted and as many of its tanks repaired as quickly as possible and back in action with the 7th Brigade. On the 8th, also, Eitan had been distracted by an unsuccessful attempt of the Golani Brigade to retake the Mt. Hermon observation post. As a result, the situation in the south was restored, but the situation in the north almost became another disaster.

The Syrians and the Israelis fought each other to a standstill on the slopes of Mt. Hermonit and Tel el Mekhafi. In this situation the superior training and combat skill of the regular army Israeli soldiers, and the death of a Syrian general, provided the margin between victory and defeat.

At the end of the battle, the little valley between Ahmadiyeh and the saddle was filled with nearly 300 Syrian tanks, and more than 200 other varieties of armored vehicles.

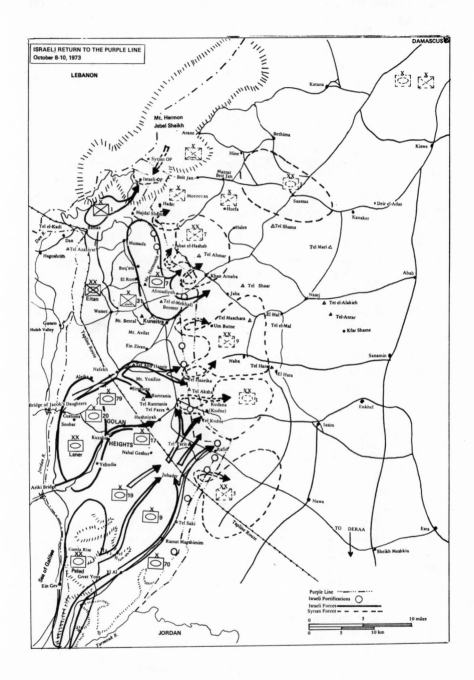

ISRAELI RETURN TO THE PURPLE LINE
October 8-10, 1973

BACK TO THE PURPLE LINE

Elsewhere on the front, by evening of the 9th, Laner's division had reached the old ceasefire line in the vicinity of Tel Hazeika, had captured Ramtania and had reached Hushniyah. Peled's division had relieved most of the beleaguered strongpoints in the southern Golan, including the fortifications on Tel Faris, and reached the Purple Line and slightly beyond in several places. Progress was not easy, and Syrian counterattacks were frequent and fierce.

On Wednesday, October 10, all three of the Israeli divisions on the Golan continued to press slowly forward, toward the Purple Line. The 7th Brigade, having had a good night's sleep, and with a number of its lightly-damaged tanks repaired and returned with some of their original crews and with replacements, was again a fighting force. Ben Chanen's contingent from the Barak Brigade was now near battalion strength, and was part of Ben Gal's brigade. During the day, these amazingly recuperated units pushed beyond the Purple Line in several places.

One of Peled's brigades cooperated with Laner's division in encircling and then destroying the remnants of two Syrian brigades in the vicinity of Hushniyah. Both divisions then completed the move up to the Purple Line.

8

The Damascus Plain—
October 10-13

ISRAELI DECISION

During October 10 there were other developments affecting the northern front. Iraq officially entered the war, declaring that it was fully committing its air force to the war effort. Approximately 100 Iraqi aircraft had been moved to advanced bases in western Iraq, most of them to T-3, on the old Haifa oil line, east of Mafraq. Upwards of 18,000 men and several hundred tanks were heading for the Golan Front. That same day Jordan also announced that it was calling up reserves and mobilizing its resources for the "war effort," and Palestinian guerrillas in southern Lebanon began to take advantage of the concentration of Israel's forces on the Syrian front. There were several raids along the Lebanese border, and approximately 25 Soviet-made Katyusha rockets and bazookas were fired at civilian settlements by Palestinian guerrillas in Lebanon. Qiryat Shimona was the principal target. Also that day another Golani Brigade effort to retake the Mt. Hermon observation post failed.

In Tel Aviv that night the senior officers of the Israeli General Staff conferred on the question of whether they should consolidate positions along the Purple Line, or continue the attack into Syria. Defense Minister Dayan sat in on the conference, and expressed some reservations about an advance, since Soviet reaction to an Israeli penetration of Syria was unpredictable. Elazar insisted, however, that a continuation of the offensive was essential in order to neutralize Syria, to discourage the participation of Jordan, and to gain sufficient breathing space to allow Israel to focus its full efforts against Egypt. Dayan did not disagree, but felt that this was a decision that should be made by Prime Minister Meir. After listening to the arguments, Mrs. Meir approved Elazar's plan for continuing the push into Syria, and the Chief of Staff issued the orders accordingly. The offensive was to begin as early as possible on the following day.

The Israelis had to choose among three principal alternative possibilities. An advance from the northern part of the Golan directly toward Damascus would have the benefit of posing the most immediate threat to the Syrian capital. The left flank of the attacking force would be protected by Mt. Hermon, and thus could not be threatened by any Syrian armored operation against that flank.

A second alternative was to drive eastward south of Damascus, to cut the Damascus-Deraa road, in order to threaten the Syrian capital from the south and east. Such a move would have the advantage of avoiding the heaviest concentrations of Syrian defenses southwest of Damascus, but would create a long and vulnerable line of communications. This had to be balanced against the advantages to be gained by cutting off Syrian ground communications with Jordan and Iraq. An attractive variant to this alternative would have been an envelopment from the north of the Syrian 9th and 5th Divisions along the central and southern Purple Line.

The third alternative was an advance all along the front to gain additional territory and increase the depth of the Israeli salient in Syria. This would make it even more difficult for a future Syrian offensive to reach the Jordan Valley, but it might require an excessive postwar occupation force.

General Hoffi, with the approval of the General Staff, chose the first of the three alternatives. On Thursday morning, October 11, Eitan's and Laner's divisions were to drive abreast to the northeast, while on their right Peled consolidated along the Purple Line. Eitan's division, on the left, would initially make the main effort, but once a breakthrough was made Laner would exploit, either by passing through Eitan, or by pushing for a separate breakthrough along the road.

ACROSS THE PURPLE LINE

On the morning of Thursday the 11th, four separate Israeli armored spearheads pushed across the Purple Line into the main Syrian defensive line. Built with Soviet guidance after the 1967 war, this was a zone seven to fifteen kilometers in depth, with closely integrated concrete emplacements, linked by trenches and screened by mines and barbed wire. The forward positions of this zone—protected by minefields and antitank ditches—were located between a few hundred meters to three kilometers east of the ceasefire line. The line was anchored on the right to Mt. Hermon, and on the left to the equally impassable Roked-Yarmouk Canyon.

The northern Israeli spearhead was the 77th Battalion of the rejuvenated 7th Armored Brigade, moving generally northeastward along the foothills of Mt. Hermon toward Hader and Mazrat Beit Jan. A few kilometers to the south was the remnant of the Barak Brigade, now a

battalion of the 7th Armored Brigade, still under the command of Lieutenant Colonel Ben Chanen. His task was to drive due eastward through
Jubat and Hales to seize the commanding hill of Tel Shams. The advance
of these two battalions began at 11:00 in the morning of October 11.

Facing Lieutenant Colonel Khalny's 77th Battalion in front of Hader
was the Moroccan Brigade, supported by about 40 Syrian tanks. Just to
the south of the Moroccans were the scattered remnants of the two
brigades of the Syrian 7th Infantry Division, only partially reorganized.
The third brigade of that division, the 68th Infantry Brigade under the
command of Colonel Rafiq Halaweh, a Druze officer, was in reserve,
deployed just south of Hader.

By late afternoon both of Ben Gal's spearheads had broken through
the resistance to their immediate front. As the left column of the 7th
Brigade seized the Hader crossroads, Colonel Halaweh, with his right
flank threatened, and the Barak Battalion moving up and threatening
to envelop his left, attempted a counterattack, and was killed leading
it. In confusion, the 68th Brigade fell back. Halaweh was posthumously
promoted to brigadier general in recognition of his gallantry.[1]

Two hours after the 7th Armored Brigade began its offensive, Laner's
division drove eastward from Kuneitra along the main Damascus road.
Laner, who was prepared to shift north to follow Eitan, decided to try
a thrust down the road, using Sarig's 17th Brigade as his spearhead,
with covering fire provided by Or's 79th Brigade (now returned to Laner's
command). Sarig was almost immediately held up by determined Syrian
resistance in the carefully prepared defensive works, and quickly lost 20
tanks. While Laner was debating how he could best withdraw the brigade from its precarious position, Sarig committed his reserve and broke
through to the crossroads of Khan Arnaba. Laner immediately exploited,
sending Or's brigade through Khan Arnaba followed by the 19th Brigade,
which had been transferred to him from Peled's division. While the 79th
Brigade drove northeastward, the 19th Brigade moved to the southeast
to Jaba to seize the high ground at Tel Shaar.

Remembering 1967, the Israelis half expected the Syrians to collapse
and run as a result of these breakthroughs. They were soon disappointed.
Despite the confusion of Israeli tanks rumbling through and around
their positions, the battle-weary Syrian 7th, 9th, and 1st Armored Divisions stuck stolidly to their defenses, withdrawing in orderly fashion
when they received orders to do so, exacting every possible toll with

---

[1] The story of Halaweh's death later reached Israel, apparently through the Druze
community. According to that story, Halaweh was not killed, but his brigade withdrew. The Syrian high command was then supposed to have had him court-martialed
for withdrawing without orders; he was stripped of his rank and executed by a firing
squad. The Syrians suggest that this story was fabricated by Israeli propaganda
specialists in a crude effort to alienate Syria's Druze community.

their Saggers and RPG-7s. Covered by this stubborn withdrawal, the 3rd Armored Division moved back into the Saassaa defensive line, southwest of Damascus.

The Syrian High Command, however, was gravely disturbed by the turn of events. Even more disturbing were the losses; nearly 1,000 tanks had been lost in five days of battle. During the afternoon of October 11 a senior officer was sent by plane to Cairo to request the Egyptians to mount an offensive to draw Israeli pressure from the Syrian front. It was particularly important to reduce the punishment Syria was receiving from the Israeli Air Force.

THE ISRAELI AIR OFFENSIVE

During the three previous days there had been a dramatic change in the air situation on the northern front. On the 6th and 7th the Israelis suffered severe losses from the Syrian air defense. The SAMs knocked down high-flying Israeli aircraft, and the ZSU-23-4s knocked down planes at low level. On October 8, however, the Israelis had begun a systematic effort to knock out the Syrian SAM system. This meant that they reduced their efforts to provide close support to the Israeli ground troops, which in any case had not been very effective, and had resulted in serious losses. Beginning on October 8 they focused their efforts almost entirely upon the missile sites, using a variety of evasive techniques. Slowly they began to whittle away at the strength of the SAM umbrella over the Syrian front. By the 11th a number of Syrian SAMs had been destroyed, more had been forced to displace, and the integrated effectiveness of the SAM system had been seriously damaged. As a result, Israeli aircraft were able to return to more effective close support missions as well as continuing their suppressive efforts against the remainder of the SAMs.

On October 9 the Israeli Air Force had begun another kind of aerial activity against Syria. On the 7th and 8th Syrian long-range FROG surface-to-surface missiles had struck throughout central Galilee, seemingly indiscriminately, leading the Israelis to believe that this was an effort to terrorize the civilian population of Galilee. In fact, the Syrians had been trying to hit such air bases as Ramat David, but their fire was very inaccurate. Apparently in severe retaliation, the Israeli Air Force began an intensive long-range strategic air bombardment campaign against Syria. Syrian ports, storage depots, electric power plants, and industrial facilities were all attacked in wide-ranging sweeps of Israeli aircraft over much of the country. On the 10th, Israeli planes attacked and hit the Syrian Defense Ministry in Damascus with rockets, causing a few casualties. This attack also destroyed a number of nearby civilian dwellings. Among the dead were several Russians and a Norwegian UNTSO observer and his family. The Syrians, noting that the normally accurate

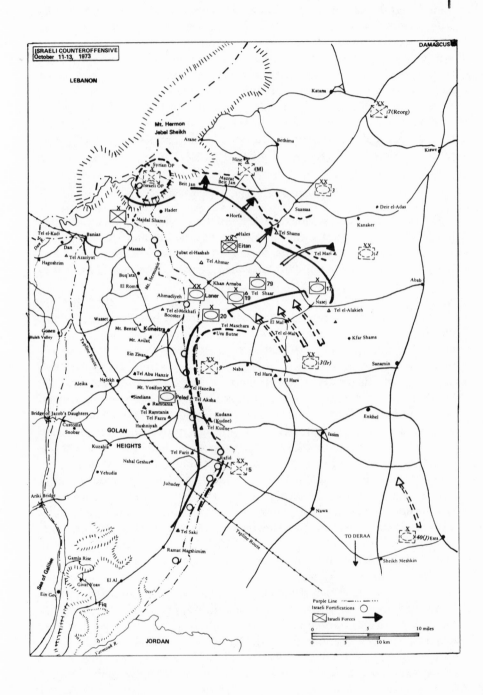

Israelis did little damage to their prominent target—the Defense Ministry —believe that this was essentially a terror raid.

The strategic air campaign continued on the 11th with a number of attacks against economic centers and Syrian air bases. Hoping to draw the Israeli planes away and put an end to these persisting air strikes, the Syrians asked the Egyptians to make a major effort on the Sinai front.

ENTER THE IRAQIS

The Israeli air and ground offensive against Syria continued unabated. By the morning of Friday, October 12, Laner's division swept eastward past Jaba and Tel Shaar through Nasej, and thence northward toward Deir el Adas, east of Kanaker, to envelop the strong Syrian defenses in front of Saassaa, where the Syrian 3d Armored Division was holding up the advance of Eitan's division. But, while observing his troops' advance from the dominating height of Tel Shaar, Laner suddenly noticed clouds of dust and intense activity to his south. More than 100 tanks were advancing against his exposed right flank from the area just east of El Hara.

At first Laner thought that this might be part of Peled's division. Then he recognized that these were hostile forces, although he did not yet realize that these tanks were from two units of the Iraqi 3d Armored Division: an armored brigade and a mechanized brigade. Laner pulled back the 17th and 19th Brigades from Kanaker. He ordered the 79th Brigade, which had been behind them refueling near Nasej, to deploy to the south. The 20th Brigade, just assigned to Laner from Peled's division, was deployed between Tel Maschara and Tel el Mal.

It has been suggested by some commentators that the arrival of the Iraqi division at this critical moment, forcing Laner to abandon his effort to envelop the Saassaa position, and seriously threatening his flank and rear, was a demonstration of the greatly improved planning and operational capabilities of the Arabs in this war. There is, however, no evidence to back up this assessment of the Iraqi arrival as a well-planned maneuver. It was pure coincidence that the Iraqis arrived when they did, and their approach to Tel Shaar from the southeast was merely a logical result of the direction from which they had come: up from Deraa, after marching through northern Jordan. There was no attempt at maneuver; there was no evidence of an attempt to achieve optimum tactical timing. On the contrary, the Iraqi arrival was entirely fortuitous, and their failure to press forward vigorously, under such fortuitous conditions, is ample evidence that this was not part of a tactical plan.

Laner expected an attack about dusk, but surprisingly the Iraqis halted. During the night, however, the Iraqi division was reinforced by its remaining armored brigade. Early in the morning of October 13, with a full complement of 310 tanks, the Iraqis advanced northward into the area between Maschara and Nasej.

Laner, meanwhile, had deployed his four brigades in such a fashion as to create a box in which he hoped to ambush the entire Iraqi division. The northern side of the box was formed by the 19th and 79th Brigades deployed east of Jaba at the foot of Tel Shaar, with the 79th deployed just east of the 19th. The east side of the box was made up of Sarig's 17th Brigade, in a line running generally north and south through Nasej. The west side of the box was the 20th Brigade, along the Maschara-Jaba road. When the Iraqis had ceased their forward movement earlier the previous night, Laner feared that their reconnaissance or air intelligence had revealed his plan. But apparently they had merely stopped to await the arrival of the additional brigade.[2]

Dawn was just breaking as the Iraqis approached the foot of Tel Shaar, all unaware that 200 tank guns and at least 50 artillery pieces were zeroed in on them. The signal to open fire was given by the Super Sherman tanks of the 19th Brigade as the Iraqis came within 200 yards of them. In a few minutes 80 Iraqi tanks had been knocked out, and the remainder were in great disorder. Not one Israeli tank was hit. About half of the casualties were suffered in the 8th Iraqi Mechanized Brigade, which was almost completely destroyed. Personnel casualties, however, were relatively light. Israelis, Syrians, and Jordanians have remarked that the Iraqis abandoned their tanks whenever they were hit, even if not seriously damaged.

The arrival of the Iraqis, the steadiness of the Syrian 3d Division, the exhaustion of the Israeli troops (who had been fighting steadily in defense and offense without letup for a full week), and concern of the Israeli General Staff about exceptionally high consumption of tank and artillery ammunition (and the consequent depletion of Israeli stockpiles), caused Elazar to order Hoffi to stop his offensive on the Syrian front. The Israelis began to dig in.

It should be noted that the defense of Tel Shams, and the Israeli inability to exploit beyond the hill without a greater effort than they were prepared to make, was indirectly due to the arrival of the Iraqis. This had permitted the Syrians to shift a brigade northwestward to block that approach to Damascus. While the Iraqis' performance in battle has been criticized by both their enemies and their allies, they performed a major service to Syria simply by occupying a major sector of the front, and permitting the Syrians to concentrate their troops for the defense of Damascus.

---

[2] One Syrian general contemptuously commented to this author that the Iraqis had probably only stopped for afternoon tea, and then decided that it was too close to supper to start up again.

The principal role in that defense was played by the Syrian 3d Armored Division, which had not been committed in the first five days of the battle, and which was fresh and battleworthy when given the mission of holding the Syrian second defense zone, centered around Saassaa, about midway between Kuneitra and Damascus. On the 12th and 13th they halted the advance of Laner's and Eitan's divisions toward Damascus.

Meanwhile, just a few miles to the north of Laner's division ambush, the Barak battalion of the 7th Armored Brigade was attempting to seize Tel Shams, one of the most commanding heights in the plain southwest of Damascus. The Syrians, despite the fact that they were shaken from the beating they had been taking the previous three days, held their position and repulsed the attack, severely wounding Lieutenant Colonel Chanen. The next night (October 13-14), however, a determined Israeli attack took the hill.

9

Sinai Standoff, October 9-13

TURBULENT STALEMATE ON THE GROUND

On the Sinai front, by October 9 the bridgeheads of the Egyptian Second and Third Armies had coalesced into two continuous fronts, one north of the Great Bitter Lake, held by the Second Army, and that of the Third Army south of the Little Bitter Lake. No effort was made by either army to occupy the desolate sand region just east of the Bitter Lakes. The depth of these bridgeheads east of the Canal varied generally from about seven to ten kilometers, although in some places the Egyptians were dug in nearly 15 kilometers east of the Canal. Two or three kilometers east of the Egyptian front line, the Israelis were also organizing a mobile defense.

By this time the Egyptians had about 800 tanks and over 90,000 troops east of the Canal. About 900 more tanks of the armored and mechanized divisions of the Second and Third Armies remained on the west bank in reserve.

Early on the 9th General Gonen authorized the garrisons of the remaining strongholds not yet taken by the Egyptians either to surrender or to try to break out to reach the Israeli lines to the east. As a consequence the Egyptians captured three more strongholds that night; one surrendered, but two of the garrisons slipped out after dark. Only two strongholds remained in Israeli hands: the northernmost, "Budapest," on the Mediterranean, and the southernmost, "Pier" or "Quay," on a spit of land opposite Suez and Port Tewfik where the Suez Canal opens into the Gulf of Suez. General Magen's troops, advancing along the coastal road, tried to link up with Budapest on the 9th, but were repulsed by Egyptians surrounding the fort. There were no Israeli units near Quay.

The only important Egyptian offensive action on October 9 was a thrust south from the zone of the Egyptian 19th Division toward Ras Sudr. As soon as this force of mixed armor and infantry got beyond the protection of the SAM umbrella, however, it was attacked and slowed down by the Israeli air. Israeli paratroopers deployed in roadblocks on the road north of Ras Sudr brought the advance to a halt, and the Egyptians also soon found themselves harassed by an armored battalion detached from Mendler's Division near the Mitla Pass. Suffering particularly heavily from the air attacks, the Egyptians soon withdrew.

During the day, however, the Egyptian 19th Division captured the Israeli emplacement of six 155mm guns opposite Port Tewfik. Unable to evacuate the guns, the Israelis had destroyed them before withdrawing from the position. They also took the nearby Bar Lev Line command post—the fifth (out of six) to fall into their hands. Only the one south of Baluza was still held by the Israelis.

Although neither side attempted a major coordinated attack on the 9th or the days immediately following, the Egyptians remained aggressive and continued to improve their positions with numerous local actions. They expanded their control over parts of the Artillery Road, but the Israelis claim that the Egyptians lost 200 tanks during the period October 9-13. The Israelis for their part launched repeated counterattacks at company, battalion, and occasionally brigade level, generally containing the Egyptian drives. The Egyptians counted a total of 64 organized Israeli counterattacks between October 6 and 14.

General Adan was still responsible for the region from Kantara almost to the Ismailia-Bir Gifgafa road (called Talisman by the Israelis). Sharon was responsible for that road, and south to about opposite the junction of the Great and Little Bitter Lakes. Mendler was responsible for the approaches to the Giddi and Mitla Passes, and down to the Gulf of Suez below Suez and Port Tewfik. Magen, who now had a division of two brigades, still held the northern district, from Kantara north to the Mediterranean.

Gonen was no longer responsible for the southern Sinai, which had been made into a separate district. The paratroops defending Ras Sudr and the garrison of Sharm el Sheikh were included in this Southern Sinai District under the command of Major General Yeshayahu Gavish, who had been commander of Southern Command in the Six Day War.

TURBULENT STALEMATE IN THE AIR

The Egyptian Air Force continued sporadic hit-and-run attacks against Israeli command and logistic centers, but the pilots were careful to avoid bases protected by Hawks, such as Bir Gifgafa, and also to avoid combat with Israeli air patrols. Similarly, the Egyptian SAM umbrella discouraged Israeli air efforts at close support, although continuing attacks were made against the Egyptian bridges with little success.

Between October 7 and 16 the Israeli Air Force launched a number of strikes against Egyptian airfields, with major efforts against two: Mansura and Qatamia—but were severely hampered by the tight-knit Egyptian ground defenses. Many attacking planes dropped their bombs short, achieving nothing. Egypt claimed that on October 10 sixteen Phantoms and Skyhawks were brought down in these operations and in the continuing attacks against the bridges. They also claim that not a single Egyptian plane was destroyed on the ground during the war.

The Israelis were making intensive efforts to develop new air tactics to counter the highly effective SA-6. They first tried a modification of a tactic which had been effective against the SA-3, what the airmen called a high-G, split-S evasive dive to "the deck." However, success was limited, and those pilots that survived reported that the Israeli planes were being chewed up by the ZSU-23-4s when they flattened out close to the ground.

Although SA-2 and SA-3 missiles could be countered by electronic counter measures (ECM) which were installed on most Phantoms, the Phantoms were taking heavy casualties from the SA-6s. So another tactic was tried. Since the missiles traveled at a rate of Mach 2.8, the puff of white smoke at the launcher had to be detected instantaneously by the pilot in order to start effective evasive tactics. Experiments were made with helicopter spotters to detect smoke puffs and warn attack planes to evade them. The helicopters also attempted to pinpoint launchers for immediate counterstrikes. Helicopter losses to Egyptian SAMs (and one to Egyptian aircraft) soon caused abandonment of this experiment.

Another tactical innovation was based on the observed flat initial launch trajectory of the SA-6s. To exploit this, Israeli planes made a very high altitude approach and a near vertical dive when directly over the launcher. The Israelis were also improvising "chaff" dispensers, which were not standard equipment on the Israeli F-4Es. They filled air brake wing slots with chaff, and then opened the air brakes near the missile sites. Also, observation of the Egyptian Air Force's safe corridors through the screen assisted the Israelis in mapping routes for target approach. But results were only marginally satisfactory.

THE LAST STRONGHOLDS

The Egyptians continued their efforts to take the two remaining Bar Lev Line strongholds. Budapest was under almost continuous attack for the first three days of the war. It was isolated by an Egyptian commando unit, which blocked the one road leading to the fort along the seacoast from the east; there was no approach from the south, which was impassable swampland. In addition to numerous air attacks, the fort was bombarded frequently by heavy coast defense guns from Port Said and Port Fuad. On Wednesday, October 10, however, General Magen personally led a relief column which broke through the Egyptian commando encirclement, and brought food, ammunition, and other supplies to Budapest, and took out the wounded. Next day the garrison was relieved by fresh troops.

Two days later the Egyptians again succeeded in isolating Budapest, and mounted another intensive effort to capture the fort. By the 15th, Israeli troops of General Sassoon's division broke this new blockade, and, although Budapest was frequently under hostile fire, it was never again seriously threatened. It was the only Bar Lev Line stronghold which the Egyptians were unable to capture.

Meanwhile, at the southern end of the Canal, the Quay position was also under vigorous attack. Egyptian efforts to capture the position were frequent and powerful, but the position was difficult to reach, and easy to defend, and despite tremendous odds and the most intensive bombardment of the war, the Israeli defenders took the maximum advantage of the position's potentialities. Finally, after having run out of medicine and anesthetics for the wounded, and almost out of ammunition, the commander and 36 other survivors, out of a garrison of 42, surrendered on Saturday, October 13, after one week of resistance.

THE CEASEFIRE ISSUE

As early as the evening of October 6 the Soviet Union began diplomatic efforts to obtain Egyptian and Syrian agreement to a ceasefire. Soviet motives are obscure, but apparently the two most important were a fear that the Middle East eruption would endanger detente, and a belief on the part of Soviet military men that, once the effects of surprise had worn off, the Israelis would defeat both Syria and Egypt.

President Sadat was both surprised and annoyed by this Soviet effort, which on the 7th seems to have included a mysterious endeavor to misrepresent communications between Moscow, on the one hand, and Cairo and Damascus on the other. Both Presidents Sadat and Assad seem to have been informed by their respective Soviet ambassadors that the other would agree to a ceasefire if his partner would.[1] Surprised by these reports, Sadat and Assad by direct communication soon clarified their mutual opposition to a ceasefire.

By October 8, when it became evident that the Egyptian success east of the Canal was no flash-in-the-pan, and before the Syrian situation had noticeably deteriorated, the Russians seem to have lost their eagerness for a ceasefire. In the UN Security Council the Soviet delegate sup-

---

[1] Herzog, *op. cit.*, p. 77, believes that the Soviet story as told to Sadat was correct, and that Assad was seriously considering a ceasefire to take advantage of the gains of the first 12 hours. This does not, however, seem to be consistent with Assad's position before and after the 6th.

ported the strong Egyptian position that any ceasefire agreement would have to include an Israeli commitment to withdraw to the pre-1967 frontiers. Since Israel—supported by the United States—refused to consider such a thing, nothing came of the early Security Council efforts to achieve a ceasefire.

On October 10, however, the gravity of the Syrian situation became evident. Relations between the Arab allies cooled somewhat during the day as the Egyptian government reluctantly refused to escalate the war by air attacks on Israeli cities, which the Syrians demanded in retaliation for the Israeli bombardments of Damascus and Homs.

Once again Soviet Ambassador Vladimir Vinogradov suggested a ceasefire to President Sadat. The ambassador told the president that the USSR fully understood Egypt's lack of interest in a ceasefire, but the Syrians had lost 600 tanks and apparently were ready to stop. Since the Americans had called for another Security Council meeting to discuss a ceasefire, the Soviet Union wanted to be able to have Egypt's advice as to the course of action it should take in the UN debate and vote.[2]

Sadat was annoyed by this continuing pressure, since he did not believe the Syrian position had changed. He made clear to the Russian that he and President Assad were in full agreement that they did not want a ceasefire. The issue was again dropped for a few days.

SHARON VERSUS GONEN

By October 9 most of the activity in the Egyptian Second Army area was concentrated against the zone which had been assigned to General Adan's division. His force was down to 123 tanks, in three very much reduced brigades. Following traditional tactics he spread out two of his brigades so that each covered about half of his 50 kilometer front, with his third brigade in reserve behind. He discovered, however, that he could stop the Egyptian attacks only by frequent movements, in which he shifted companies and battalions and even brigades to meet the greatest danger at any given time. Once his third brigade was committed it was hard to withdraw it, and he found that his units were getting badly mixed up. In the following days he developed a new defensive technique; he put all three of his brigades in line, each in depth with a large reserve. He found that even though he sometimes had to shift units across brigade fronts it was easier to get them back where they belonged under this deployment plan.

Sharon's zone, being largely opposite the Great Bitter Lake, where there were few Egyptians, was far less busy than that of either Adan or Mendler. Thus on the 9th he was able to send his reconnaissance battal-

[2] Heikal, *op. cit.,* pp. 216-217.

ion on a maneuver which brought it to the northeastern shore of the Great Bitter Lake without encountering any serious resistance. He ordered the battalion to stay where it was, and immediately appealed to General Gonen to permit him to make a crossing of the Canal near Deversoir, just north of the Great Bitter Lake. Gonen, annoyed that Sharon had attacked against his orders, peremptorily refused, and ordered Sharon to withdraw at once. He flew by helicopter to Sharon's headquarters to repeat the order, then returned to Um Kusheiba.

Thereupon Sharon simply radioed directly to Tel Aviv, where an old friend and former subordinate of his, Brigadier General Dov Sion, was Deputy Chief of the Operations Division, under Major General Avraham Tamir. Sharon told Sion, "I have my feet dipping in the waters of the Great Bitter Lake," and asked him to get Major General Israel Tal, the Deputy Chief of Staff, to persuade either General Elazar or Defense Minister Dayan to authorize the crossing that Gonen had refused to approve. The matter was given very serious consideration in the General Staff, but naturally General Gonen's views were sought as well.[3]

Meanwhile as a diversion, to keep Egyptian attention focussed elsewhere, Sharon had ordered the brigade of Colonel Haim Erez to make a limited attack in the general direction of Talata—called Missouri by the Israelis. The Egyptians, using the same tactics that had been so successful against Adan the previous day, used their antitank weapons —Saggers, RPG-7s, and antitank guns—to knock out between 23 and 36 of Erez's tanks.[4]

When Gonen realized what had happened he was furious at Sharon. First, it seemed to him to be unpardonable that a subordinate would bypass him and seek to have his orders countermanded by higher authority. Even worse was the fact that Sharon had deliberately disobeyed his order, and in the process incurred serious, unnecessary casualties. Bitterly he told GHQ in Tel Aviv that he was as anxious as Sharon to cross the Canal as soon as possible, but that the strength of his command was nowhere near adequate to permit any thought to be given yet to such a risk operation. Not until all reserves had been mobilized, and it was certain that the Egyptian offensive had been brought to a complete halt, would it be reasonable or logical to consider an Israeli assault crossing of the Canal. Meanwhile resources should be husbanded, and not frittered away as Sharon was doing. The General Staff agreed, and Sharon was informed that he would obey the order from Gonen to withdraw to his regular position. Reluctantly Sharon complied.

Gonen at once requested the Israeli high command to relieve Sharon

[3] Based on interviews with Generals Sion, Sharon and Gonen.

[4] In an interview with this author General Bar Lev said that he was told by Erez, on October 11, that he had lost 23 tanks. General Gonen insists that the loss was 36 tanks.

from command for insubordination. There were a number of reasons, however, that General Elazar could not approve Gonen's recommendation. In the first place Sharon was a proven, competent, and aggressive field commander who had had a remarkable record of combat successes in the two previous wars. Second, he was now a politician in uniform, who had, until the outbreak of the war, been busily engaged in conducting a political campaign to get himself elected to the Knesset in the elections scheduled for October 26. Since he was in opposition to the government, to relieve him without overwhelming justification would open the government to charges of a politically motivated vendetta, which would probably work to the political advantage of Sharon, and the disadvantage of the government. Furthermore, Sharon was a friend of Defense Minister Moshe Dayan, and even though they were now in different political parties the political and military thinking of the two men was remarkably similar.

At the same time General Elazar knew that he could not ignore the obviously severe friction which now existed between Gonen and Sharon. While it seemed to the Chief of Staff to be unfair to relieve Gonen from command simply because he could not get along well with a subordinate who had always been difficult for military superiors to control, there seemed to be no alternative.[5] He asked Lt. General Bar Lev if he would return to active duty as commander of the Southern Command. Bar Lev agreed to take on this task, if this was agreeable to Defense Minister Dayan and Prime Minister Golda Meir. Both approved eagerly.

When General Gonen was informed of this decision, however, he protested bitterly. He asked why he should be displaced from his command because one of his subordinates has been insubordinate. Elazar—who agreed with Gonen—then suggested a face-saving compromise. Gonen remained the commander of Southern Command, with Bar Lev at his side as the Special Representative of the Chief of Staff, and with full command authority to make decisions in the name of the Chief of Staff. As Gonen somewhat ruefully remarked to his staff the next morning, October 10, when he was introducing General Bar Lev to them at a staff meeting, "I have the honor of having my own special Chief of Staff."

Gonen thought seriously about resigning and then decided that in wartime every Israeli soldier had to do what he was told by higher authority. At first things were tense between Bar Lev and Gonen, but soon they developed a routine, with Gonen making the decisions and issuing the orders, but always checking them with Bar Lev. For all

[5] Apparently Dayan had already suggested to Elazar that Gonen should be relieved. See *Story of My Life,* pp. 410-411. Dayan's story of the decision to relieve Gonen, however, is not quite consistent with the recollections of Elazar (as reflected by Herzog, *op. cit.*) and Bar Lev.

practical purposes, Gonen was Bar Lev's deputy and chief of staff. At Bar Lev's insistence one of them was always at the command post until the end of the war. They took turns going to the front to visit subordinate commanders.

SHARON VERSUS BAR LEV

After the war, Gonen confided to his friends that he had been unable to control Sharon, and that Bar Lev had been sent down for the single purpose of exercising the control over that general that he, Gonen, was incapable of exercising. "But," Gonen added, "Bar Lev could not control Sharon either."

In fact, as Bar Lev commented during the controversy which swirled about these three men after the war, he was operating under some severe disadvantages in his relationship with Sharon that did not affect Gonen. After all Gonen was a regular soldier, with no political ambitions, and did not have to worry about the political implications of his decisions and orders. But Bar Lev, who just a few days earlier had been engaged in an acrimonious political campaign on the opposite side from Sharon, had to recognize that there would be political implications in anything that he said or did to, or with respect to, Sharon.

The principal tactical problem with which Generals Gonen and Bar Lev were concerned was when and how they could carry the war back to the Egyptians by crossing the Canal. From the beginning all Israeli commanders had been operating on the assumption that they would make such a crossing. But from the standpoint of Gonen and Bar Lev that tactical problem continued to be enmeshed in their principal administrative problem: the control of General Sharon.

From October 9 on, the questions of when and where—not whether—the Canal crossing should be made had been the principal topics for discussion in commanders' conferences at Southern Command headquarters, at Um Kusheiba. As a result of his discovery on the 9th that the Deversoir area was undefended, Sharon had urged a crossing there, since it was in his zone. About the same time, however, Adan's reconnaissance had ascertained that there was a gap between the Egyptian 2d and 18th Divisions just north of Firdan, near El Balah Island in the Canal. He urged crossing just south of the island and north of Firdan, since that was in his zone.

Bar Lev, Gonen, and Mendler favored the Deversoir site, and on the 10th, when Adan suggested a crossing at both places, Sharon agreed, but Gonen reaffirmed his preference for the Deversoir site, and Bar Lev supported this. From that time on, then, the Southern Command plan was for a Deversoir crossing, as soon as the situation permitted and Tel Aviv would approve.

General Sharon was upset by this decision, since he felt that in a static situation time was working against the Israelis, and that a cease-fire might be imposed by the United Nations before the initial Egyptian success could be offset by any Israeli successes. Therefore he proposed a new plan. His division would attack the northern flank of the Egyptian Third Army, then sweep south to disrupt the entire Third Army bridgehead.

Next day, October 11, Bar Lev called Sharon and his three brigade commanders back to the Um Kusheiba command post to discuss this plan. Present at the discussion were Bar Lev, Gonen, Gonen's chief of staff—Brigadier General Ben Ari—Sharon, and his three brigade commanders: Colonels Amnon Reshev, Tuvia Raviv, and Haim Erez. Sharon presented his plan, and his justification for it. After a general discussion, Bar Lev asked for the opinions of all present. Mainly on the basis that they believed that Sharon totally underestimated the defensive capabilities of the Egyptians, everyone—including Sharon's brigade commanders—disagreed with Sharon's proposal. Further—again with the notable exception of Sharon—they agreed that time would work against the Israelis in the UN only when they were defeating the Arabs, not while the Arabs were successful.

Sharon did not take this repudiation gracefully. In a somewhat heated discussion he made clear that his complete contempt for Gonen applied equally to Bar Lev. A remark about "slow talking and slow thinking" could only apply to Bar Lev's typically deliberate manner of speaking. Next day, to the wry amusement of Gonen, Bar Lev recommended to General Elazar that Sharon be relieved of his command. (He was to repeat this recommendation at least twice more in the next ten days.)

This, of course, was not what Elazar had expected when he sent Bar Lev to Southern Command. He consulted with Dayan, who said that the political implications of relieving Sharon were too great; Bar Lev, Gonen, and Sharon would simply have to get along somehow or other.

THE NATURE OF GENERAL SHARON

In his book, *The War of Atonement*, Major General Chaim Herzog provides a very interesting thumbnail sketch of General Sharon.[6] In it Herzog refers to Sharon's "natural instincts" and "healthy intuition" as substitutes for the "logical process of staff work." Herzog says that Sharon is "a genius in improvisation," and that Sharon can devote himself to a problem "one day to the exclusion of all other matters, while the next day he can without warning ignore it. He is utterly unpredictable. . . ."

Sharon resents Herzog's characterization, which he says totally misrepresents him as an "impulsive person." Sharon maintains that he is the

[6] *Op. cit.,* pp. 192-193.

antithesis of impulsive; rather he claims that his many military successes are the result of cool, careful, dispassionate planning. If, he says, he is a genius at improvisation it is because his careful planning has dealt with all possible alternatives. Certainly his victory at Abu Ageila in 1967 was a triumph of just such methodical, meticulous planning. But anyone listening to General Sharon deny his "impulsiveness" cannot but note the strong emotion which prompts the denial.

It is probable that General Sharon has never been intentionally or deliberately insubordinate. His military instincts and his respect for orderly military processes and discipline are unquestionable. He is a man who feels strongly, indeed passionately. And he believes that the first duty of a soldier is to do what is right. As a field soldier of considerable experience he is convinced that the commander on the spot has a far better understanding of what needs to be done then some commander or staff officer miles away from the scene of action. Being a man who is highly intelligent, with a very quick mind, and with a record of remarkable success in battle, it is evident that Sharon almost automatically assumes that what he thinks about a military situation is right, and therefore that anyone who holds a contrary opinion is automatically wrong.

Interestingly, a substantial number of responsible Israeli military men agree with Sharon's assessment of his military capabilities. There are senior Israeli officers who believe that Gonen was wrong to give orders to Sharon as though he were an ordinary subordinate. After all, Sharon had been Gonen's superior; three months before the war he had concluded two years as GOC Southern Command and had turned over the post to Gonen, who was young and inexperienced. Rather than giving orders to Sharon, these officers believe, Gonen should have sought Sharon's advice. "After all," one has commented, "he is our Patton, and should be treated accordingly."[7]

The important point is that however one may characterize his performance in military terms, Sharon does not seem to be a willful glory seeker, deliberately disobedient and insubordinate in order to further his own personal ambitions. I am convinced that General Sharon did what he did, and said what he said, during the war because he was honestly convinced that the actions he proposed or advocated were in the best interests of Israel.

That having been said, it seems incredible that General Sharon was not relieved of his command for repeated undisciplined insubordination.

---

[7] That officer might want to look up General Patton's record more thoroughly, including how he was relieved of command in Sicily by a much younger officer who had been, until quite recently, his junior, and how later, when Patton was returned to grace, he served loyally and obediently under two commanders who had been his juniors during most of their service.

He was not relieved, apparently, only because the Minister of Defense, Moshe Dayan, would not approve the recommendations of either General Gonen or General Bar Lev, partly because of his respect for Sharon's brilliant, charismatic military leadership, and partly for political reasons.

ISRAELI PLANNING FOR THE CANAL CROSSING

Meanwhile Gonen and the Southern Command staff had worked out the details of an offensive based upon a Deversoir crossing. Gonen presented this to Bar Lev and the three senior division commanders—Mendler, Adan, and Sharon—late on the 11th. Gonen said that the crossing—a two division operation—should take place at a previously-selected spot on the east bank of the Canal opposite Deversoir. There, as at several other places along the Canal, preliminary arrangements to facilitate a crossing had been prepared long before the outbreak of hostilities. (These places had been selected by General Sharon when he was GOC Southern Command.) The embankment was thinned out at these points, so that it could easily be knocked down by bulldozers to permit the emplacement of the abutments of a ponton bridge. Also, a large area behind each of these thinned out points had been surfaced with bricks, to provide a hardstand about 700 meters long by 150 meters wide where vehicles and engineer equipment could be efficiently concentrated. This hardstand was surrounded by a solid sand rampart for local security. Sharon's division would make the crossing, and Adan's division would cross behind, to exploit the breakthrough.

The Deversoir site was selected by Gonen for three principal reasons. In the first place the left flank of the crossing force would be protected by the Great Bitter Lake. Second, the far bank offered better opportunities for maneuver south of Ismailia than would be the case to the north. Third, the Deversoir crossing point would be near the boundary between the two Egyptian armies, and both ground and air reconnaissance had shown that the crossing site was not covered by troops on either bank of the Canal. These arguments were persuasive to Bar Lev, who approved Gonen's concept.[8] Two bridges, one a partially prefabricated ponton bridge in nine sections, the other a long prefabricated span which had been permanently stored at Tasa for just such an eventuality, were moved south from Tasa to a place code-named Yukon, about 15 kilometers east of the selected crossing site.

The only question remaining open was the timing of the crossing. Elazar had anticipated an Egyptian thrust from their bridgehead by the 11th or 12th, and when plans for crossing had been discussed with him earlier he had indicated that it should not take place until the Egyptians had

[8] This account of the process of deciding on the crossing concept is based upon interviews with Generals Bar Lev, Gonen, Sharon, and Adan.

committed more of their armor to the east bank, and had been given a "bloody nose" in trying to break out of the bridgehead. Then the Israeli crossing should be made while the Egyptians were still disrupted from such a failure.

But there was no evidence yet of an Egyptian attack. Accordingly, on October 12 General Bar Lev flew back to Tel Aviv and presented the Southern Command plan first to General Elazar, then to Defense Minister Dayan, and then to Prime Minister Meir and the Cabinet. During this last meeting, when it appeared that the decision would be to adhere to Elazar's original counterthrust idea, word was received that the Egyptians were clearly preparing for an offensive, and that their armor was pouring across the bridges to the east bank. So, the plan was approved in principle, but the timing was left open. That night the three division commanders—Sharon, Adan, and Mendler—presented their operational plans for Bar Lev's approval. Despite his annoyance with Sharon, Bar Lev was impressed by Sharon's plan, and his presentation.

When Elazar visited Southern Command the following day, he told Gonen and Bar Lev that, whether or not the Egyptians attacked on the 14th, as Israeli intelligence predicted, they should initiate their planned crossing operation that night. This decision was made at Sharon's command post, west of Tasa.

Later in the day General Adan's division was pulled out of the line north of Tasa, to be ready to exploit Sharon's expected crossing on the 14th. The whole northern sector was placed under the responsibility of a newly established armored-infantry division commanded by Brigadier General Sassoon. Magen had been slated for this command, but instead he was sent south to take over the command of Mendler's division after that general was killed by Egyptian artillery fire on October 13. Sharon's division, still deployed in the central area midway between Ismailia and Tasa, took over a small portion of the front from which Adan had been pulled back. Sharon was assigned Colonel Dani Matt's paratroop brigade; this and Colonel Haim Erez's armored brigade prepared themselves for the thrust to the Canal, now planned for early evening of the 14th.

ISMAIL VERSUS SHAZLI

While top-level Israeli generals were engaged in acrimonious debate, there was a somewhat similar—through less acrimonious—debate going on in the Egyptian command echelons. Encouraged by the successes of the first three days, Egyptian Chief of Staff General Shazli on October 9 recommended an armored strike into the Sinai along the northern coastal route toward El Arish. However, the Egyptian Commander in Chief, General Ismail, overruled him. Ismail was determined to make no major advance until an adequate SAM defense had been moved to the east bank to provide cover for such an attack, and he did not plan to move the SAMs across until he knew that the front line was completely stabilized. Later that day in an interview for the newspaper *al Akhbar*, Shazli hinted at his dissatisfaction with this "overcautious" attitude, but then added that the Egyptian Army would wear down the Israeli Air Force on its missile shield; this, he said, would be the rock on which Israel would break its sword.

This was the first indication of a deep-seated antipathy between these two generals which until that time both had endeavored to conceal. Mohamed Heikal, a good judge of people, describes the two men as follows:

Ismail was the classic officer, the soldier *par excellence*, an infantryman, professional, honest, wholly above politics. He compensated for any lack of intellectual brilliance by dogged hard work; in Moscow he was the most studious of all our generals—while many of his colleagues considered it beneath their dignity to take notes like students once more, Ismail was always writing, always sketching. He had not been part of the Free Officers' Movement: he was even then considered so unpolitical that the movement's leaders did not dare to tell him of the plot. But it was, apart from any considerations of expertise, largely because of Ismail's lack of politics that the President appointed him—that, plus the fact that he and the President came from the same class: they shared many attitudes. . . .

Shazli was quite a different character: his stocky, handsome figure contrasted with Ismail's bulk. Shazli was dashing; he could socialize, talk well, impress people—after tours as a military attache in London and then at the United Nations, Shazli was *mondain* in a way that few Arab generals are. He was a paratrooper—one of the first generals from that branch in the Egyptian Army—and he jumped until very recently, which of course added to his allure.

In all prima donnas there must be something of the actor and Shazli was no exception. But he knew what he was doing in using his glamour to achieve his military ends, above all the raising of the army's morale for the task it faced. Beneath his charm and his daring, Shazli was a calculating and meticulous officer. He was not a military genius, but he did have that precise grasp of logistics and attention to detail which is essential to the paratroop officer. . . .[9]

Heikal suggests that Shazli's dislike for Ismail went back to 1960, a result of resentment when Ismail had been sent from Cairo to inspect an Egyptian United Nations contingent which Shazli had commanded in the Congo.[10] While this may account for Shazli's attitude, Ismail's lack of respect for his Chief of Staff more likely went back to friction between them during the 1967 war.

Heikal's comments on the Egyptian officer who was in some ways caught between the hostility of these two senior officers, and who had to

[9] Heikal, *op. cit.*, p. 181, quoted with permission of Mr. Heikal.

[10] The UN Commander in the Congo, Swedish General Carl von Horn, had no use for Shazli. See *Soldiering for Peace* (New York, 1967), pp. 213, 214, 236.

coordinate and make effective their sometimes differing directives, are also worth quoting:

> But the inevitable differences in attitude and sometimes opinion [between Ismail and Shazli] gave added importance to the work of the man who, in any recounting of the operation, should properly be named with the pair, the Director of Operations under Shazli, General Mohommed Abdul Ghani el-Gamasy.
> Intellectually, Gamasy was perhaps Egypt's best equipped general; he read a good deal and he pondered what he read. He would take articles of mine from *Al Ahram*, annotate them with a stream of comments and send them back to me. At meetings, however, he was very quiet, though his advice, when given, was listened to with respect because of its shrewdness. Gamasy, too, was nonpolitical—indeed, Arab politics shocked him to his bones. I once advised President Nasser to take some generals with him to the summit conference in Tripoli and he decided to take General Hassan el-Badri and Gamasy. As we sat round the negotiating table, they were in the usual advisers' seats behind; and as he surveyed the quarrelling factions, I heard Gamasy mutter to himself: 'My God, *this* is the united Arab front we are to fight with?' [11]

During the afternoon of October 9 there was an event which had some bearing on the Ismail-Shazli debate. After dark a brigade of the Egyptian 6th Mechanized Division struck south from the 19th Division bridgehead, toward Ras Sudr. The Egyptians got as far as Iyun-Mussa, about 15 kilometers south of Suez, where they were engaged and repulsed by an Israeli parachute battalion supported by a battalion of about 20 tanks. Air support was provided by about 10 close support sorties—the Israeli aircraft were able to operate freely, since they were beyond the range of Egyptian air defense weapons. The attacking Egyptians lost about half of their tanks and APCs, and a number of trucks—a total of more than 100 vehicles.

---

[11] Heikal, *op. cit.*, p. 182. Quoted with permission.

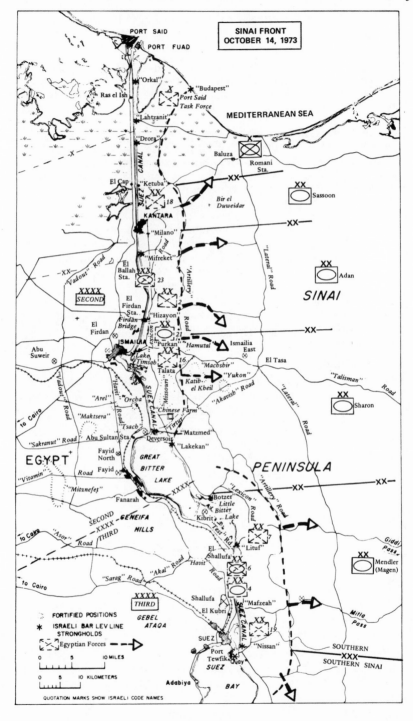

SINAI FRONT
OCTOBER 14, 1973

QUOTATION MARKS SHOW ISRAELI CODE NAMES

10

Opportunities Lost and Gained, October 14

SYRIAN APPEAL FOR HELP

On October 11 General Ismail received the urgent Syrian appeal for help to reduce Israeli pressure on the Golan front. As we have seen, Ismail had decided against a possibly premature offensive until the bridgehead had been consolidated and expanded eastward. He was reluctant to risk the SA-6s east of the Canal in the vulnerable bridgeheads. At the same time, he did not want to initiate a major offensive until these missiles were east of the Canal, so as to extend the SAM umbrella deep into the Sinai. Apparently he thought the expansion would be possible after the Israelis had suffered another week of attrition.

However, the Syrian appeal forced Ismail to modify his views. He keenly felt the need for mutual confidence and cooperation among Arab allies, something so lacking in the previous conflicts. Accordingly, with considerable reluctance, he ordered a limited tank offensive, to be launched on the 13th. Next day, after delays were encountered in preparing for the attack, the date was pushed back to the 14th.

On October 12th and 13th the 21st Armored Division and one Brigade of the 23d Mechanized Infantry Division crossed to the east bank of the Canal in the zone of the Egyptian Second Army, while two thirds of the 4th Armored Division and part of the 6th Mechanized Division crossed over in the Third Army zone, preparing to take part in the planned offensive on October 14. To support the assaulting forces a few SAM batteries also were sent to the east bank.

On October 13 the next to the last uncaptured Bar Lev position surrendered to the Egyptians. This was the Quay strongpoint opposite Port Tewfik. Thirty-seven Israelis, including five officers, surrendered. Fifteen of these were wounded and in need of medical assistance. Only Budapest was still holding out.

Also on this day the Egyptians reported sighting two aircraft, flying at very high altitude, which they were unable to reach either with missiles or with their fastest and highest flying aircraft. They assumed, and it was reported in the Egyptian press, that these were American SR-71 aircraft on a reconnaissance mission over the battle front.

THE ASSAULT

At 6:00 a.m. on the morning of October 14 an intensive artillery preparation all along the front heralded the anticipated Egyptian exploitation offensive. At 6:30 six armored columns, each about one brigade in strength, thrust out eastward from the Egyptian lines. In addition to the six major attacks, a number of minor holding attacks were launched all along the line. The Egyptian objective was to seize and block the three main passes—Khatmia, Giddi, and Mitla.

Three of the six Egyptian thrusts were directed by General Mamoun's Second Army from its headquarters near Ismailia. The northernmost of these struck northeastward from Kantara and the sector of the 18th Infantry Division toward Romani. Further south an armored brigade of the 21st Armored Division drove from the 2d Infantry Division front in an easterly direction north of, and parallel to, the road from Ismailia toward Tasa and the Khatmia Pass. From Talata, in the 16th Infantry Division sector, another 21st Division armored brigade was expected to converge with the first at Tasa.

In General Wassel's Third Army zone the northernmost thrust came from the sector of the 7th Infantry Division, and was directed due eastward toward the Giddi Pass and the Southern Command advance headquarters at Um Kusheiba. From the 19th Division sector there was a similar armored drive toward the Mitla Pass, a mere 15 kilometers away. From the southern portion of the 19th Division sector another armored brigade struck southeastward toward the Sudr Pass, south of Mitla.

When the northernmost of the Egyptian thrusts began to press against Sassoon's overextended line, General Gonen ordered Adan's division—not yet completely withdrawn—to move back in and assume responsibility for the area it had just vacated. Adan's troops quickly threw back the Egyptians, and inflicted heavy casualties upon them. By early afternoon the Egyptians had been pushed back to their starting point, having lost about 50 tanks.

The central Second Army thrust—directed toward Tasa and the Khatmia Pass—fared no better against Sharon's righthand brigade. Halted by the determined defenders, the Egyptians lost 30 tanks. Sharon's left brigade met the thrust from Talata and stopped that also with a loss of about 30 Egyptian tanks.

The twin thrusts from the Egyptian 7th and 19th Division areas toward the Giddi and Mitla Passes initially had greater success against the somewhat thinner defenses of Magen's division. Nonetheless neither of these attacks got as far as the main Lateral Road, although the effort toward the Mitla Pass did briefly threaten to break through. By the end of the afternoon Magen's troops had contained the attack, after giving up some ground, but had extracted a toll of about 60 Egyptian tanks.

Initially the greatest Egyptian success, and eventually its greatest loss, came in the sixth thrust toward Sudr. In that attempt the Egyptian tanks broke through and advanced more than 20 kilometers, almost reaching the pass. They were finally brought to a halt in a desperate defensive effort by combined paratroopers and armor, with strong air support. By the time this column finally turned back, late in the afternoon, it had lost more than half of its strength, nearly 90 tanks.

During the day the Egyptian High Command, in its deep dugout southeast of Cairo, kept receiving optimistic reports from the two field army headquarters, and a great success was anticipated. These optimistic reports were soon reflected. in claims of victory sent out to the world by Radio Cairo. By midevening, however, pessimism had replaced optimism in the reports received by General Ismail. As staff officers plotted the final positions of the columns on the operations map in the command post, Ismail could see that only three narrow fingers had been poked a few miles into the Israeli lines in front of the Giddi and Mitla Passes, and along the coast road toward Ras Sudr. He knew that in the morning these exposed salients, sticking out beyond the effective coverage of his SAM umbrella, would be the focus of intensive Israeli air attacks. He ordered all units back to their original starting positions.[1]

The magnitude of the losses was not yet clear to the Egyptians. By the next day they realized that they had suffered more than 1,000 casualties, and that about 260 tanks had been destroyed by the Israelis. They believed that they had destroyed 144 Israeli tanks, but in fact total Israeli tank losses had been no more than 40.[2] The Egyptians also lost about 200 other armored vehicles.

One Egyptian casualty was General Mamoun, who suffered a heart attack in his Second Army CP early in the morning, at about 8:30 a.m. Ismail ordered him evacuated to a Cairo hospital, and appointed Major General Abdul Moneim Khalil to take his place in command of the Second Army.

ISRAELI DEFENSIVE TACTICS

By this time the Israelis had devised very effective infantry-artillery-armor tactics for dealing with the Egyptian Saggers and RPG-7s. Work-

[1] Interview with Field Marshal Ismail.

[2] Unclassified Israeli sources are confusing. However, of a total of about 40 Israeli tanks lost that day, all but about six were soon back in action.

ing in cooperation with each tank or pair of tanks was an APC, usually located some distance to the flank or rear, whose mission was to protect the tank from the infantry antitank weapons. (Israeli armor formations on the average had only one APC for every three or four tanks, but for this operation they were teamed one-to-one or one-to-two.) The APC machine guns were especially effective against the infantry Saggers, since these wire-guided missiles had to be kept constantly in the sights of the controller for the 10 to 15 seconds of flight time. A few bursts of machine gun fire in the direction of the Sagger position would usually cause the firer to duck, and the missile would fly off harmlessly into the air or into the sand. Saggers mounted on BMP armored personnel carriers were immune to the Israeli machine gun fire. But these vehicles were taken under fire by artillery, and if they stopped long enough for the operator to guide his missile to the target, the BMP was usually knocked out before the missile could be effective.

While these tactics were useful in counterattacks against Egyptian infantry, they were particularly effective when the Israeli armor was on the defensive, in hull-down position, and sometimes in ambush, and when the attacking Sagger and RPG-7 operators had to expose themselves to get into firing position. On October 14, however, the Egyptians made things easier for the Israelis by failing to provide any supporting infantry with the attacking armored and mechanized columns. Thus the Israelis could devote the undivided attention of tanks, APCs, and artillery against the Egyptian tanks and APCs.

The Israelis had been prepared for the Egyptian attack. They had correctly estimated the time and place of the Egyptian thrusts, although they had expected more powerful combined arms attacks. Instead of charging headlong to meet the Egyptians, as they had been wont to do in the past, the Israelis had sited their tanks in open pincers—a kind of V open toward the west—along each anticipated route. The tanks were positioned hull-down in hollows, some natural and others dug by bulldozers. They fought by companies of eight to twelve tanks, each with its own fire controller. After firing a few rounds, the tanks moved to prepared positions further to the rear, to confuse the Egyptians' indirect artillery fire support. Then, after firing a few more rounds, the Israeli tanks returned to their original positions. Throughout, of course, the accompanying APCs and attached artillery forward observers had continued their defensive mission with their assigned tanks.

Where opportunity offered, the Israeli commanders used enveloping maneuvers to strike the flanks of exposed Egyptian columns. Such envelopments were particularly effective in General Sharon's sector, and to Magen's division in defending the Mitla Pass.

Without detailed, prearranged fire plans, such as they had employed on October 6, the Egyptian artillery concentrations fell largely on empty rock and sand dunes. The Israeli artillery, on the other hand, was well coordinated with the tank fire, and helped to break up Egyptian formations. Israeli tactical air support was effective throughout the entire zone and—as noted above—particularly effective north of Ras Sudr. The Israeli pilots were able to take full advantage of the fact that the Egyptian spearheads were operating beyond the effective range of their SAM shield. Although nominally the Egyptian air defenses had a "slant range" up to 30 kilometers, the SA-6 acquisition and tracking radar was not very effective beyond 15 kilometers, and SA-6s were not yet risked on the east bank.

Although the Israeli tanks opened fire upon the Egyptians at extreme ranges, the Egyptians persevered and were not deterred by this long-range fire. Most of the engagements that day were fought at ranges of 400 to 500 meters. Although this was the range at which the Soviet tank guns were most effective, Israeli tank gunnery and maneuvering skill were far superior to the Egyptian; in addition they had the inherent advantage of defensive posture, with tanks in hull-down positions, hard to spot before the attackers had become attractive targets.

As the Israelis maneuvered among various concealed positions to thwart Egyptian antitank teams mounted on BRDMs and BMPs, their tank guns picked off the Egyptian medium tanks (T-54s, T-55s, and some T-62s). They also hit accompanying Egyptian heavy AT guns before these came within effective range. The supporting artillery fire and the additional machinegun firepower of the attached APCs helped hold back the dismounted Egyptian mechanized infantrymen who attempted to maneuver their missiles in support of the tanks.

This Egyptian effort to break out of the bridgehead precipitated the largest tank battle since World War II. It involved perhaps 1,000 Egyptian tanks and not more than 5,000 mechanized infantrymen, and was opposed by at least 800 Israeli tanks. Interestingly, the Israelis did not pursue the battered Egyptian columns as they withdrew; this apparent failure was perhaps due to the inability of the IAF to carry its tactical air support into the SAM "box," and the unwillingness of the Israelis to expose themselves to Egyptian defensive AT firepower without such support.

The following day there were two relatively minor Egyptian attacks. One was a thrust along the Romani-El Arish road toward the Israeli base and airfield at Baluza. This was repulsed by Sassoon's troops after hard fighting. There was another smaller thrust east of Ismailia toward Bir Gifgafa, but this was not pushed strenuously, and was easily contained by Sharon's troops. Neither attack was considered significant by the Israelis.

ISRAEL'S PLANNED COUNTEROFFENSIVE

Because of the battle on October 14 neither Sharon's nor Adan's division had been able to complete the preparations necessary for the planned thrust that night to and across the Canal. So Gonen postponed the operation for 24 hours, with the approval of Tel Aviv. At the same time, the outcome of the battle confirmed the original judgments that had led Elazar, Bar Lev and Gonen to believe that the best chance for a successful counterblow would come after the Egyptians had shifted their armored reserves east of the Canal, and had suffered tank losses that would help to reestablish the prewar balance of forces. Most important of all, the Egyptian 21st Armored Division, which would have posed a counterattack threat had the crossing been made any time up to October 13, was now in no position to block the west bank exploitation of a crossing, and in no condition to move back quickly.

Early in the evening General Elazar confirmed the order for a cross-Canal counteroffensive to begin the next evening, October 15.

WHY THE EGYPTIANS FAILED

General Ismail had been right to adopt a broad-front approach in his initial Canal-crossing offensive of October 6. This apparent violation of the time-honored Principle of Mass was the best way in which he could bring to bear his enormous numerical superiority against the hard—but thin and brittle—overextended Israeli defense line. He was also right in later rejecting General Shazli's conventionally bold proposal for prompt and aggressive Egyptian exploitation of the successes of October 6, 7, and 8. As we have seen, such exploitation might have risked losing everything won on those days by providing the Israelis with an opportunity to make full use of their unquestioned superiority in airpower and in mobile, armored warfare.

When, however, Ismail received the Syrian appeal for help on October 11, as the overall Arab commander-in-chief he had no choice but to respond positively. His error, however, was in the manner of his response.

Clearly a substantial effort was necessary, if the offensive was to accomplish its major purpose of relieving the pressure on the Syrians. Equally clearly the offensive must be so handled as not to give the Israelis the opportunity he had so far denied them. Therefore Ismail decided to commit only six brigades to the offensive, while more than twenty other brigades securely held the hard-won bridgehead lines.

However, by October 14 that bridgehead had been so solidly consolidated that its security would not have been jeopardized by allocating four to six more brigades to an offensive effort, thus more effectively achieving the primary mission of putting such pressure on the Israelis that they would be forced to reduce their pressure on the Syrians. But, whether the offensive force consisted of six, ten, or twelve brigades, it had little chance of success when the effort was dispersed in a series of divergent, mutually unsupportable thrusts along a front of nearly 200 kilometers. At least equally serious was the decision that this would be essentially an armored or mechanized offensive, holding back the reliable Egyptian infantry to secure the bridgehead lines. In this instance the conventional military wisdom that suggested a combined arms effort was buttressed by the experience of the first three days of the war, when the Egyptian infantry so gallantly proved its worth against Israeli armor.

Thus, however large the force used for this offensive effort, it could have a chance of doing severe damage to the Israelis, and of gaining some important terrain objectives for the Egyptians, only if the offensive effort was concentrated, and included infantry to work with the armored and mechanized elements. There is little doubt that a powerful, coordinated thrust of six brigades, with a carefully planned and coordinated air defense umbrella concentrated overhead, could have reached Romani, or the Khatmia Pass, or the Mitla Pass. Had that force been increased to ten or twelve brigades, it is not likely that the Israelis could have rolled them back without a major effort which would clearly have forced redeployment of units from the Syrian front. Furthermore, under such circumstances, there could not have been an Israeli thrust across the Canal the following day. In retrospect, it is clear that the greatest chance of Egyptian success would have been in a concerted advance on a narrow front toward the Mitla and Sudr Passes. But any coordinated, concentrated, combined arms effort almost any place along the front was bound to be better than what was done.

General Ismail had lost an opportunity, and had provided an opportunity to the Israelis.

11

Operation "Strongheart" and the Chinese Farm, October 15-16

ISRAELI PREPARATIONS

General Gonen's plan for crossing to the west bank of the Suez Canal was based upon prewar plans—actually developed while Sharon was the commander of Southern Command—to which the code name "Strongheart"[1] had been given. Strongheart provided for a two-division crossing, to establish a bridgehead on the west bank from which a thrust would be made to the north or to the south, with the probable ultimate objective of isolating either Ismailia or Suez. Gonen had decided that in this case the breakout would be to the south, for reasons already noted.

The initial crossing operation was to be carried out by General Sharon's division of three armored brigades, with a fourth brigade of paratroopers attached. Sharon's armored strength was now about 280 tanks. The paratroopers, supported by part of a brigade of tanks, would make the crossing during the night of October 15-16. As soon as they had established a bridgehead on the west bank, Sharon would bring up both bridges and install them while the paratroopers and their attached tanks were expanding the bridgehead beyond the Sweetwater Canal to the west, and at least four kilometers north and south of the bridges, to prevent direct fire on the bridges from Egyptian antitank guns on either bank. It was expected that at least one of the bridges would be operational early on the morning of the 16th.

Meanwhile, the rest of Sharon's division (more than two brigades) was to hold open a corridor north of the Great Bitter Lake and simultaneously make diversionary attacks to the north to make the Egyptians believe that this was a threat to the right wing of the Second Army.

[1] Translation of the Hebrew words: *Abiray-lev*. A Western newsman seems to have understood that the code name was "Gazelle," and this mistake has been perpetuated by many other commentators and historians.

492

Adan's division was to begin crossing as soon as the bridges were installed. Now back to full strength, with three brigades of about 100 tanks each, Adan's division would make a breakout from the bridgehead to the west and south either late on the 16th or early on the 17th.

Once Adan had broken out, General Magen's division (formerly Mendler's) of one infantry and two armored brigades would relieve Sharon's division and assume responsibility both for the bridges and for holding open the corridor to the east. Sharon then would follow to Adan's right rear, to provide protection as well as to assure adequate power in the drive to the south.

Early on the 15th Adan's division was again pulled out of the line, and Sassoon's division once more took over responsibility for the entire northern sector. Adan's troops moved south on the Lateral Road to an assembly area south of Tasa.

THE TERRAIN

For the next two days the principal ground operations on the Sinai front were concentrated in a roughly triangular area with its base approximately 40 kilometers along the Suez Canal and Great Bitter Lake south of Ismailia; the vertex of the triangle was at Tasa, on the Lateral Road; one arm extended west about 30 kilometers from Tasa along the Talisman Road to the Canal just north of Lake Timsah; the other arm lay southwest from Tasa across almost impassable sand dunes to the former Israeli stronghold of "Botzer," at the junction of the Great and Little Bitter Lakes.

Within this triangular area there were five principal hardsurfaced roads. Just east of the Canal, at some places no more than 100 meters from the Israeli embankment at the water's edge, and at others as much as 1,000 meters to the east, was the road which the Israelis called Lexicon, which connected the strongholds of the Bar Lev Line. There were four such strongholds along the base of the triangle: Botzer was held by the Egyptian 7th Division; 15 kilometers north was Lakekan, on the northeast shore of the Great Bitter Lake, abandoned; 7 kilometers further north was Matzmed in the zone of the Egyptian 16th Infantry Division, overlooking the junction of the Canal and the Great Bitter Lake; 20 kilometers to the north was Purkan, at the junction of the Talisman and Lexicon Roads, and held by the Egyptian 2d Division. Both Lakekan and Matzmed were unoccupied.

To the east of Lexicon some 5,000 to 10,000 meters was the so-called Artillery Road, built to permit flexible artillery support of the Bar Lev defenses. Roughly bisecting the triangle, running southwest from the Tasa vertex to meet the Lexicon Road between Matzmed and Lakekan, was a road called Akavish. Just to the west of the Akavish-Artillery Road crossroad, another road—called Tirtur—forked to the right from Aka-vish, which at that point began to swing in a southerly direction toward Lakekan.

Tirtur was a specially constructed road, with minimum grades and ample clearance on each side, its principal purpose being to permit direct movement of bulky bridges and bridging material to the previously-prepared crossing point opposite Deversoir. The brick-surfaced hard-stand of the "yard"—terminus of the Tirtur Road—was located a few meters north of the point where the Canal joins the Great Bitter Lake, and just southwest of the Matzmed stronghold. The Tirtur Road crossed the Lexicon Road about one kilometer northeast of Matzmed, and continued directly past that stronghold to terminate in the yard. The fifth road, called Nahala by the Israelis, connected the strongholds of Lakekan and Matzmed, running west of and generally parallel to Lexicon, skirting the shore of the Great Bitter Lake.

There were five other terrain features between the Artillery and Lexi-con Roads that would figure prominently in the coming events. In the north, just southwest of the Talisman-Artillery crossroad, was a hill mass called Hamutal by the Israelis and Talia by the Egyptians. There had been hard fighting for this position in previous days, but it was now securely held by the left-flank brigade of the Egyptian 16th Division. About 12 kilometers to the south, just west of the Artillery Road, and overlooking the eastern end of the Tirtur Road, was a smaller hill, called Televisia. This was partly occupied by the frontline units in the center of the 16th Division. To the west of Televisia, filling most of the area between the Lexicon and Artillery Roads, was a large hill mass known by the Israelis as Missouri and by the Egyptians as Talata. South-west of the Akavish-Artillery crossroad was a small but prominent hill to which the Israelis gave the code name Kishuf.

The fifth important terrain feature, known by the Israelis as the Chinese Farm, was in the flat lowlands south of Missouri, and lying mostly to the northwest of the Tirtur Road.[2] What made this Chinese Farm militarily significant were the criss-crossed irrigation ditches and embankments separating the cultivated fields. These provided ready-made trenches and ramparts for infantrymen.

SHARON'S PLAN

On October 8, Sharon had assumed control of Mendler's central ar-mored brigade—commanded by Colonel Reshev—and had transferred his own armored infantry brigade to Mendler's command in the south. On the 14th, therefore, he had three organic armored brigades in his division—Reshev's and the brigades of Colonels Tuvia Raviv and Haim

2 See p. 431 *supra.*

Erez—and the attached paratroop brigade of Colonel Matt, which had previously been in reserve in the Mitla Pass area, under the control of General Magen.

Sharon's northernmost brigade—Raviv's—was to start the operation on the division's right in the late afternoon with an artillery-supported diversionary attack toward the Artillery Road and the Egyptian positions at Talata and Televisia. Approximately an hour later, just at dusk, Reshev's brigade was to advance cross-country south of the Akavish road to the Great Bitter Lake, near the abandoned Bar Lev Line stronghold of

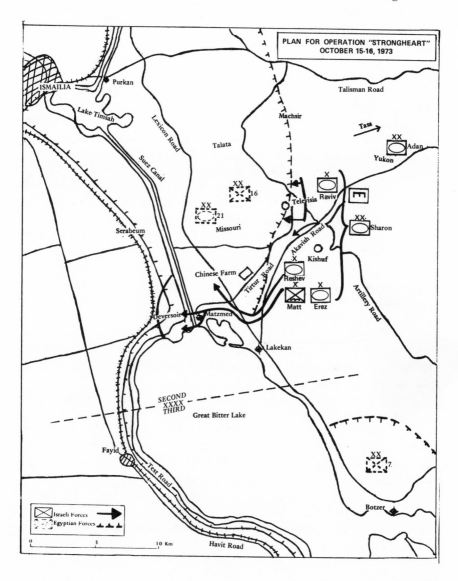

PLAN FOR OPERATION "STRONGHEART"
OCTOBER 15-16, 1973

Lakekan. Reshev would then turn northwest, along the shore of the lake, to seize the Bar Lev Line stronghold of Matzmed, and the nearby yard, from which the crossing was to be launched across the Canal to Deversoir.

For this operation Reshev's brigade was reinforced with an armored battalion from Raviv's brigade, with the armored infantry battalion from Erez's brigade, and with an independent armored infantry battalion which had been attached to Sharon's division. Thus Reshev's command included four armored battalions (five, counting his reconnaissance battalion) and three armored infantry battalions; it was a powerful force, almost half of Sharon's organic division.

Once he reached Matzmed and the crossing site, Reshev was to divide his command into three separate contingents. One tank battalion (that attached from Raviv) was to turn northeast along the Akavish Road, to clear that road of any Egyptians who might be on it, and to secure the road for Matt's paratroopers, who would be advancing southeast down that road to the crossing point. With his three remaining tank battalions, Reshev would continue north past the Lexicon-Tirtur crossroad, as though making an envelopment of the right wing of the Egyptian Second Army; it was upon this thrust that the Israelis wanted the Egyptians to focus their attention, so that they would not notice the Canal-crossing activities to the southwest. Reshev's reconnaissance battalion would stay at the yard, to secure this until Matt's paratroop brigade arrived. The three infantry battalions were to remain in brigade reserve, just east of Matzmed.

Matt's paratroop brigade, reinforced with a company of tanks, was to advance down the Akavish and Lexicon Roads to the crossing point, being met en route by Reshev's attached battalion (from Raviv's brigade). Meanwhile the division's engineers, who had been accompanying Reshev's brigade, would have opened up the exits from the yard to the Canal, and Matt's paratroopers would move right across in collapsible rubber boats. The crossing was expected to take place before 11:00 p.m.

Sharon's other armored brigade, commanded by Colonel Erez, was in division reserve, and was to follow behind Matt's paratroopers. Part of this brigade was responsible for towing the sections of the ponton bridge and the prefabricated bridge from Yukon, midway between Tasa and the Artillery-Akavish crossroad. The large ponton sections for which Erez was responsible could also be used separately as tank ferries, and before the bridges were put in one of Erez's armored battalions was to use these ferries to cross the Canal behind Matt.

Once on the west bank Matt, supported by Erez's tanks, was to push ahead to seize crossings over Sweetwater Canal, and to extend the bridgehead the required four kilometers north and south of the landing points.

"THE MOST TERRIBLE NIGHT"—SHARON

The plan was a good one, and it succeeded. But for two major reasons it came very close to failure. In the first place, the Israeli bridging equipment, even the sectionalized pontons, was very cumbersome and clumsy. The Israeli prewar planning for Operation Stronghart had assumed that the Bar Lev Line strongholds would provide a firm base for the operation, and that the bridging materials could be assembled and prefabricated on or just behind the Lexicon road. The Israelis had never envisaged the possibility of towing these unwieldy loads some 20 kilometers across the desert, under artillery and small-arms fire.

The second reason the crossing almost failed was that the Egyptians had much more strength concentrated in the vicinity of the Tirtur and Akavish Roads than the Israelis had expected, and their resistance was more stubborn than anticipated. In fact, had the Egyptians quickly recognized the nature of the Israeli operation, there is little doubt that they had the force, on both east and west banks, to smash the Israeli attempt.

As it was, Sharon's diversionary attacks were completely successful; for more than 24 hours the Egyptians were totally misled, assuming that the Israeli objective was merely to roll up the right flank of the Second Army. Otherwise, however, the Israeli operation ran into problems from the beginning.

Colonel Raviv's initial attack toward Talia and Televisia began at 5:00 p.m. on schedule. It was quickly halted by alert Egyptian defense but that had been expected. Elsewhere, however, the Israeli operation was already falling behind the planned schedule. Matt's brigade did not receive either its boats or its transport—some 60 half-tracks—when it was supposed to. In fact, to be able to move at all the paratroopers had to commandeer some vehicles at Tasa that were supposed to be delivered to another unit.

Reshev's brigade also was a little late in getting started, but then it found the movement toward the Great Bitter Lake and Lexicon deceptively easy. Only sporadic resistance was encountered, presumably by small Egyptian patrols covering the flank of the 16th Division, on the right wing of the Second Army. Reshev reported that the Akavish Road was clear, and he went on to seize the Matzmed stronghold and the crossing yard without any difficulty. While his reconnaissance battalion was securing this area, and helping the engineers open the two crossing exits from the yard, Reshev sent the attached battalion up Akavish to meet Matt, and took his three remaining armored battalions and two of his infantry battalions northward and eastward to threaten the right rear of the 16th Division. Two battalions, advancing abreast on either side of the Lexicon Road, crossed the Tirtur Road, easily dispersing slight resistance at the crossroad. Reshev's other armored battalion struck northeast to secure the Tirtur Road. One infantry battalion followed each of these armored thrusts; the third remained in reserve near the intersection at the Lexicon and Akavish Roads.

Suddenly Reshev and his units found themselves engaged in a desperate struggle, with the survival of the brigade in doubt most of the night. It seems that the only reason they had not encountered serious resistance earlier was that they had taken the Egyptians completely by surprise. The patrols they thought they had encountered south of the Akavish Road, and at the Tirtur-Lexicon crossroad, were elements of strong Egyptian infantry forces, which had gone for cover as the Israeli tanks unexpectedly appeared in the darkness, but which came out and formed for defense immediately thereafter. On top of this, the main forces of both the 21st Armored Division and the 16th Division and its attached armored brigade were concentrated generally in the area of Missouri, and between Missouri and the Chinese Farm. Although they had suffered severely in the previous day's fighting, these were still formidable forces, far outnumbering the seven battalions (including his reserve) Reshev had available.

Thus the two armored battalions advancing north along Lexicon soon were engaged by major Egyptian infantry and armor units. And the other armored battalions, attempting to clear the Akavish and Tirtur Roads, found both held in great strength. At least one Egyptian infantry brigade was deployed in and around the Chinese Farm, and the Lexicon-Tirtur crossroad was also held in great strength, thus isolating units from each other. Having recovered from their surprise, the Egyptians were making vigorous local counterattacks.

Meanwhile the paratroop brigade was encountering more delays. For reasons that are not clear, the roads into Tasa, and the Akavish Road southwest of Tasa, were clogged with traffic. Part of this was due to the fact that the problems of moving the brigades were far more serious than had been anticipated. And part was due to a failure on somebody's part—Gonen's or Sharon's or both—to assure adequate traffic control on these vital arteries at this crucial time. Another important contributor to the delay and confusion was considerable Egyptian artillery fire.

By 9:00 p.m., when Matt's brigade was still northeast of Yukon, reports were coming back to Southern Command headquarters about the unexpected difficulties encountered by Reshev's brigade west and south of the Chinese Farm. Defense Minister Moshe Dayan, who was waiting anxiously at Southern Command headquarters, became discouraged and suggested to General Gonen that he should call off the operation. Gonen replied to the effect that the problems seemed to be greater than he had expected, but that the operation should be pushed ahead until or unless it became evident that the crossing could not be made. Bar

Lev agreed with him. Dayan, ever meticulous in avoiding issuance of direct military orders, did not argue.

The paratroopers, preceded by Sharon's advanced command post in half-tracks, continued slowly down the Akavish Road. Soon they came under artillery and small-arms fire from Egyptians on the Tirtur Road and in the Chinese Farm. Following radio advice from Reshev they left the Akavish Road, and pushed slowly through the sandy hills just to the east, past the Lexicon Road to the Nahala Road and the edge of the lake. There they turned northwest, passing less than a kilometer from the bitter battle raging around the Lexicon-Tirtur crossroad, then passing Matzmed, with Sharon's vehicles reaching the yard well after midnight. Casualties had been slight during the march. However, as the column was approaching the yard Matt sent his attached tank company to cover his right flank near the Lexicon-Tirtur crossroad. The company commander, unaware of the nature of the battle that was taking place there, advanced between two of Reshev's battalions and attempted to seize the crossroad. Every tank in the company was destroyed; the company commander was killed and most of his men were killed or wounded.

THE CROSSING

Unaware of this disaster, Sharon and Matt supervised the crossing preparation, while the remainder of the paratrooper column closed into the yard after 1:00 a.m. It was discovered that the hardstand was incomplete at one of the two crossing points, and so just the southern one was used. Meanwhile, Sharon had called in all available artillery to plaster the opposite shore of the Canal. When the first wave of paratroopers was ready, about 1:30 a.m. on the 16th, the artillery fire was called off, and the first wave of paratroopers reached "Africa"—as the Israelis called the west bank region—at 1:35 a.m. There was no opposition—not because of the artillery fire, but because there were no Egyptians there. Before 2:00 a.m. Sharon crossed to take personal charge of operations on the west bank. By dawn Matt's entire brigade had crossed the Canal, and ferries were beginning to bring over one of Erez's tank companies.

On the east bank shortly after dawn Reshev made another attempt to take the Lexicon-Tirtur crossroads. With about a company of tanks, using alternate fire and movement, he advanced slowly against the Egyptian position from the west—in other words, from the direction of the Canal—while an infantry company pushed steadily toward the crossroad from the south. This was the last straw for the defending Egyptians, whose strength and endurance had been gradually whittled away during the night. They withdrew northward, and the Israelis occupied the positions.

Reshev then attempted to continue his advance northeastward up the Tirtur Road, but was soon forced to stop. Egyptian tanks, antitanks guns, and missiles opened up from the slopes of Missouri, and Reshev fell back to the crossroad.

Meanwhile Gonen had called Adan before dawn and warned him that he would probably have to help Sharon open the corridor before he could think about crossing. Adan had already sent his leading battalion, commanded by Lieutenant Colonel Amir, down the Akavish Road, expecting to be able to cross the bridge soon after dawn. The tanks broke through the Egyptian positions on Akavish, and soon after daybreak joined Reshev, who had by that time withdrawn southwest of the crossroad. Sharon, learning of the arrival of this fresh formation, and knowing that all of his tanks were almost out of fuel and ammunition, radioed Adan and requested that Amir's battalion be loaned to him while Reshev regrouped. Adan at once agreed, and so this battalion, supported by one of Sharon's infantry battalions, took up positions south and west of the crossroad, to prevent possible Egyptian interference with the crossing site. Reshev, with the remaining 27 tanks of his brigade—about two-thirds of his tanks had been destroyed or damaged during the night—pulled back to rest, regroup, and replenish near the Lakekan stronghold.

The first phase of Operation Strongheart, and the first phase of the Battle of the Chinese Farm, had ended. During that bitter night of fighting Sharon's division had suffered more than 300 men killed, and lost about 70 of its 280 tanks. As General Sharon has said, "Everyone was fighting like mad!" About 150 Egyptian tanks were knocked out.

THE EGYPTIAN GAP

In the light of the thoroughness of the planning which had preceded the Egyptians' attack of October 6, it is surprising that they left a gap in the soft dune area east of the Canal, and that they failed to have adequate security on the west bank. This seems to have been due less to a reliance on the "impassability" of the terrain than to the fact that this area coincided with the boundary between the two armies. Egyptian General Khalil later said that an Egyptian armored brigade from the 21st Armored Division had been in the general vicinity of the area where Sharon established his bridgehead. The brigade, however, had crossed the Canal on the 13th to take part in the attack on the 14th.

The Egyptians are convinced that an American satellite, or the two high level reconnaissance planes which they had seen flying over the area on the 13th, found the gap for the Israelis. The Israelis, on the other hand, claim that they found the soft spot themselves, and that they received no satellite or high level reconnaissance data from the Americans. They point out that this crossing had been planned many months earlier, that Sharon had discovered the gap between the Egyptian armies on the 9th, and that the actual decision for the operation had been made on October 11, two days before the American planes were over the area.

At first the Egyptians assumed that Sharon's thrust to the Canal was an effort to envelop the south or right flank of their own northern bridgehead, rather than an effort to make major penetrations across the Canal. Thus the Israeli diversion against the right flank of the 16th Infantry Division was completely successful. The Egyptians focussed their attention on this, and initially assumed that the Israeli forces on the west bank were merely scattered raiders. Israeli routine security measures contributed to this Egyptian assessment. Save for one armored raid by elements of Erez's brigade, the troops in Sharon's bridgehead kept themselves concealed from air observation in the undergrowth of the "Green Belt" between the Suez Canal and the Sweetwater Canal, and concealed most of their tanks in the hangars of the abandoned Deversoir airfield.

AMERICAN ASSISTANCE—AND THE MYSTERIOUS TOWS

As early as October 8 the Israelis informed American officials of their need for specialized items of American equipment, and also requested additional ammunition to replace the heavy expenditures of the first two days of war. On October 12, three days before the planned crossing, the Israeli Government officially informed the United States Government that expenditures of ammunition and losses of weapons and equipment—particularly tanks and armored personnel carriers—had been so heavy that the IDF had almost exhausted its war reserves. Without immediate resupply, Israel might be destroyed. After the war it became evident that although losses and expenditures had indeed been heavy, they had not yet come close to exhausting the Israeli stockpiles. However, the panic of the beginning of the war had not yet worn off in the offices in Tel Aviv, and the panic was soon transmitted westward some 7,000 miles.

As will be recounted later, a resupply air lift was quickly initiated with results that had a much greater effect on Israeli civilian morale than on the outcome of the war. The first American supply plane landed at Lod Airport on October 14, with much fanfare and publicity. Meanwhile a trickle of American supplies to Israel carried on Israeli planes had begun on October 9.

Among the weapons being carried across the Atlantic and Mediterranean by Israeli and American cargo aircraft were a number of the new wire-guided antitank missiles known as TOWs. These were a very sophisticated second generation improvement over the early French SS-10 and SS-11 wire-guided missiles, and were also much more accurate and reliable than the Soviet Saggers, which had been used so effectively by the Egyptians and Syrians in the previous week.[3] A number of Israeli students attending colleges and universities in the United States were mobilized late on October 6, and ordered to the US Army Infantry School at Fort Benning, Georgia, to take a crash course in the use and maintenance of the TOW. But by the time these eager young students were able to bring their new training and knowledge back to Israel, and to teach Israeli soldiers how to use the new weapons, it was October 24, and a ceasefire was finally settling over the fighting fronts.

It has been reported by Uri Dan, a journalist with Sharon's division, that on October 14—or possibly one or two days earlier—soldiers in Sharon's division had received TOWs, and were being trained in the use of these weapons.[4] Dan also mentions that there were TOWs in some of the half-tracks that advanced to the edge of the Suez Canal the evening of October 15. Before his untimely death General Elazar also confirmed to the author that TOWs were used by the IDF during the war: ". . . and they were very effective, too."

The Egyptians have stated that they have conclusive evidence that TOWs were used against them by the Israelis, probably as early as the great tank battle on October 14. The Jordanians say that on the Golan Heights their tanks were taking devastating TOW hits at least by October 19. There is no reason to doubt the sincerity of these Arab assertions, but the Israeli Military Spokesman has insisted officially that no TOWs were issued to IDF units before the ceasefire. General Adan has personally assured the author that his division received no TOWs before about October 24 or 25. He and other Israeli officers suggest unconvincingly that the Egyptians and their own journalists possibly confused the TOW with the much less powerful LAW and DRAGON missiles.

After careful consideration of the known facts and conflicting evidence, I have concluded that the Israelis had TOWs, and trained crews for these weapons, available for employment by October 14 and 15. A few may have been used on the 14th, although this is doubtful. But they were probably in use by the 16th, although in limited numbers.

If so, then from where did General Sharon's division receive its TOWs? Why didn't Adan's division get any? Who trained Sharon's operators? How many other Israeli units also received TOWs before October 24?

The answers to these questions are elusive.

[3] The Israelis had a number of SS-10s and SS-11s. However, they had become so dissatisfied with these weapons that they had ceased to use them, and reliable Israeli sources insist they were not employed in this war.

[4] Uri Dan, *Sharon's Bridgehead* (Tel Aviv, 1975), p. 215. This is a most unreliable book on issues involving General Sharon and his controversies. However, there is no possible reason that the assertions about the TOW would have been included if they were not believed by Dan to be factual.

12

Battle of the Chinese Farm, October 16-17

SHARON IN "AFRICA"

During the morning of October 16 parts of two battalions of Erez's brigade—approximately 30 tanks in all—joined Sharon and Matt's paratroopers on the west bank of the Suez Canal, the tanks crossing by heavy ponton ferry. Seeing how smoothly this operation was going, and having encountered almost no resistance along the bridgehead perimeter, Sharon called Gonen and urged that Adan's division also be ferried across the Canal, ignoring and bypassing the Egyptian resistance along the Akavish and Tirtur Roads.

Gonen at that very moment was trying to figure out how to cope with this unexpectedly strong resistance, and he rather curtly rejected Sharon's proposal, which he considered amazingly irresponsible. Sharon then called Bar Lev to see if he would overrule Gonen. Bar Lev once more agreed with Gonen, but took the time to explain to Sharon why his suggestion was impossible. In the first place, the logistical requirements of two divisions fighting west of the Canal would be enormous; it was not at all certain that adequate supplies could reach them by ferry, even if a supplementary airlift were to be put into effect. Second, with two Israeli divisions west of the Canal there would not be enough strength east of the Canal to force the corridor open, and keep it open. Unless the corridor could be opened wider than it now was, there was serious doubt if even Sharon's troops—less than half a division—could be maintained west of the Canal.

It was this consideration, in fact, which shortly after noon led Bar Lev to issue an order that no more Israeli troops or tanks would cross to the west bank of the Canal until further orders. Meanwhile, however, a battalion of 175mm guns had been ferried across, and was already firing its long-range cannon at Egyptian SAM sites. (The boldness of this move can be assessed by noting that such long-range guns are usually kept at least 5,000 meters behind the front lines.)

About noon Sharon sent Erez on a raid westward from the bridge-

503

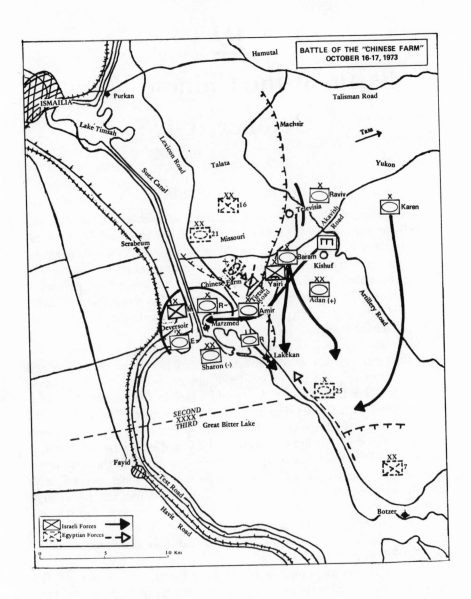

BATTLE OF THE "CHINESE FARM"
OCTOBER 16-17, 1973

head with the mission of overrunning any SAM sites he could find, and generally disrupting the Egyptian rear areas. The raid was quite successful. The Israeli tanks destroyed three SA-2 positions, and apparently forced the displacement of at least one SA-6. Resistance was negligible, except for one Ranger company in an abandoned supply depot at Sultan. Several supply and maintenance installations were overrun, and hoped-for disruption was achieved.

EGYPTIAN REACTION

From the Israeli standpoint, however, there was one unfortunate result of this otherwise successful operation. The inaccurate and contradictory reports that flowed in to the Second Army and GHQ command posts revealed to the Egyptian command for the first time that a substantial number of Israeli tanks were on the west bank of the Canal. The Second Army began to send reserve units to contain the penetration, and some units in the GHQ reserve were alerted for possible movement. However, by evening local commanders were reporting that there was only one company of Israeli tanks and one company of infantry west of the Canal, and declared their ability to deal with this minor threat. Egyptian artillery, which had been firing intermittent harassing rounds in the general direction of the Israeli bridgehead, now began concentrated fire against both the east and the west bank bridgeheads of Sharon's isolated division.

Late on the afternoon of the 16th there was a substantial attack on the bridgehead forces by aircraft of the Egyptian Air Force. This led to a short air battle above the Canal, in which the Israelis claim that they destroyed ten MiG-17s without any loss to themselves, while the Egyptians claim ten Israeli planes were destroyed—six in air-to-air combat, and four shot down by their SAM and ZSU-23-4 air defense. The Egyptian claim is inconsistent, however, because it is unlikely that Egyptian planes would have been operating in the air over terrain actively defended by their SAMs.

In a speech to the Egyptian parliament that day—October 16—Sadat declared the readiness of Egypt to make peace. He said, however, that peace could be made only on terms in which the Israelis withdrew from all of the occupied territories. He also warned that he had Zafir long-range surface-to-surface missiles ready for launching against any spot in Israel, should there be any deep-penetration Israeli air raids into Egypt. Israelis seem to have assumed that Sadat was aware of their bridgehead when he made the speech; in fact he did not learn about it until later that evening.

ADAN'S MISSIONS

General "Bren" Adan had been warned by General Gonen before dawn on October 16 that the operation had been delayed and that his division might have to do some fighting in the Akavish-Tirtur corridor before crossing the Canal behind Sharon. But even with this warning Adan was not prepared for the situation he found as he followed his leading battalion—commanded by Lieutenant Colonel Amir—down the Akavish Road toward the yard. Not only was there no bridge yet installed, but both roads to the crossing point were blocked. The Egyptians had cut off Sharon's division. Adan passed the damaged preconstructed bridge near the Akavish-Tirtur intersection, and then he saw—a few kilometers further to the south, stuck in a monumental traffic jam—the several ponton sections of the other bridge. After ordering Lieutenant Colonel Amir's battalion to bypass the resistance on Akavish, Adan set up a new command post southwest of Kishuf Hill, and just south of the road from this traffic jam. He was soon joined there by Gonen, who also had been out reconnoitering the road.

It was obvious to Gonen that Sharon, isolated with three fourths of his division in two unconnected bridgeheads east and west of the Canal, could no longer exercise command control over the forward movement of the two bridges. Gonen therefore ordered Adan to clear the Akavish and Tirtur Roads, and to move the bridges forward to the crossing site.

Immediate responsibility for moving the ponton bridge was assigned to Brigadier General Dovic Tamari, Adan's second in command. Similar responsibility for the preconstructed bridge movement was given to Brigadier General Jack Evans, who was Sharon's second in command, but under Adan's authority for this mission.

Shortly before noon Adan sent Colonel Amir's and Baram's brigades to open the two roads, by parallel drives from the northeast. However, both brigades were soon halted by concentrated fire from artillery, tank guns, antitank missiles, and antitank guns of the Egyptian 21st Armored Division and 16th Infantry Division. Adan then asked to have his third brigade—Karen's, in general Southern Command reserve—released to him, but Gonen refused to commit his last reserve. Instead, he told Adan that Colonel Uzi Ya'iri's brigade of paratroopers was being sent up from Ras Sudr, and would be assigned to him to help clear the Akavish-Tirtur-Chinese Farm area.

It was almost 10:00 p.m. before Colonel Ya'iri reported to Adan that he and his paratroop brigade had arrived, and were ready for action. Adan explained the situation to Ya'iri. After a brief discussion Ya'iri prepared a plan for a southwesterly drive to clear the two roads and the area between them. At 11:30 the paratroopers moved out.

They had moved less than two kilometers from the Akavish-Tirtur intersection before they ran into heavy fire from the front, and particularly the right flank, the direction of the Chinese Farm. Promptly the paratroopers endeavored to overwhelm and outmaneuver the opposition, but as they moved north of the Tirtur Road into the Chinese Farm itself, they were soon pinned down by intense fire. Adan thereupon attached one of Amir's tank battalions to the paratroop brigade and ordered Ya'iri to concentrate on clearing the Akavish road. It soon was evident, however, that the paratroopers had suffered severe losses and were too firmly pinned down to be able to maneuver.

It was nearly 3:00 a.m., and neither of the bridges had moved for more than 24 hours. Adan feared that if he were not able to get one of these forward to the Canal, not only might the whole operation fail, but most of Sharon's division might be cut off. He sent a reconnaissance company down the Akavish Road to test the strength of the opposition, in order to see if there was any way to push the ponton bridge through.

Shortly before 3:30 Adan got a radio message from the reconnaissance company commander on the Akavish Road; he had reached the yard without opposition. There were Egyptians a little north of the road, but their attention was occupied by the struggle against the paratroopers along the Tirtur Road and in the Chinese Farm.

Adan at once ordered General Tamari to move down the Akavish Road with the ponton sections. For the moment the preconstructed bridge would have to wait; it could move only down the Tirtur Road. At about 4:30, just as dawn was breaking, the ponton sections began to lumber slowly into the yard. Sharon's engineers at once began to move them to the water's edge to start building a bridge.

CLEARING THE CORRIDOR

While waiting most of the afternoon for the paratroopers, Adan noticed that Raviv's brigade, of Sharon's division, had been sitting quietly opposite Talata and Televisia while his two brigades were vainly struggling to open up the two roads. Late that night he asked Gonen to have Raviv's brigade put under his command. Gonen agreed.

Having at least partially accomplished one of his two missions, Adan now concentrated his attention on the other one: to open a corridor to the crossing point by clearing the Akavish and Tirtur Roads. This task had become even more urgent because of the plight of the paratroopers—pinned down along the Tirtur Road and in the southeastern corner of the Chinese Farm—whose casualties were steadily mounting.

Adan sent Amir's brigade after the pontons down the Akavish Road, to turn and be prepared to drive north to the Tirtur Road and the southwest corner of the Chinese Farm. Baram's brigade was to attack west across the Akavish Road, from the vicinity of Adan's CP near Kishuf. Raviv, now under Adan's command, was to move down just west of the Tirtur-Akavish intersection and to drive westward toward the Chinese Farm.

This Israeli attack, which began shortly after 6:00 a.m., ran head-on into a southeasterly attack toward the Akavish Road by elements of the Egyptian 16th Infantry and 21st Armored Divisions, which had been given the mission of closing the Israeli corridor. For more than five hours the battle raged between the two roads, and in and around the southern edge of the Chinese Farm. Twice the Egyptians—tanks as well as infantry —pushed across the Tirtur Road, and twice Adan's tankers drove them back.

All day on the 16th, two Egyptian tank brigades, one from 23rd Mechanized and one from 21st Armored, had attacked southward down the Lexicon Road against Lieutenant Colonel Amir's battalion at the Tirtur-Lexicon crossroad, but had failed to reach the crossroad. Early on the 17th, in coordination with the main attack further east, the 14th Armored Brigade made one more attempt. By midmorning this last attack had also failed, and the remnants of the Egyptian brigade withdrew northward toward Missouri, unable to continue the fight. By noon Baram had reached the Tirtur Road. In an area of about seven kilometers by three kilometers a total of about 250 tanks had been destroyed in about 36 hours of intensive fighting; about two thirds of these were Egyptian.

Meanwhile, by 11:00 a.m. Colonel Baram's brigade had advanced far enough to reach the isolated paratroopers, and to extract them from their awkward position. After all of the wounded had been evacuated, the Israeli tanks pulled back to the Tirtur Road, which they now held firmly. The Egyptians still held most of the Chinese Farm, and their guns could still sweep the road from the slopes of Missouri, but the narrow corridor along the Akavish Road was secure. The Egyptian 16th and 21st Divisions had, however, secured the right flank of the Second Army between the Chinese Farm and the Canal.

With the situation looking more favorable, Bar Lev authorized Sharon to send ten more tanks across the Canal by ferry.

KISHUF CONFERENCE

Soon after this an extraordinary conference took place on a low hill just southwest of Kishuf, at Adan's command post. At about 11:00 a.m.

Defense Minister Dayan, Chief of Staff Elazar, and Assistant Chief of Staff Bar Lev arrived by helicopter at Adan's command post. Somehow Adan was able to direct a battle while taking part in the conference. Soon after the visiting dignitaries arrived at Adan's CP, Sharon arrived from the yard by halftrack.

The previous afternoon Dayan had met at Um Kusheiba with Bar Lev and Gonen, and had come to the conclusion that Operation Strongheart had failed. And so, when he and Elazar arrived near Kishuf, having heard of the paratrooper disaster, they were prepared to order that the operation be abandoned. Bar Lev was hardly more optimistic when they arrived. Suddenly these senior generals found the situation entirely different from what they expected. One bridge was being installed, and would be ready for traffic in a few hours; the Akavish Road was open, and the Tirtur Road was being cleared. While they were conferring word was received that the paratroopers had been extricated, and the Egyptian counterattacks had been repulsed.

So, instead of calling off Operation Strongheart, the commanders found themselves discussing how it should be exploited. Sharon, who earlier in the morning had again urged that Adan's division be ferried across the Canal, now had a new scheme to suggest.

Sharon recommended that his units in the bridgeheads and at the crossing site be relieved by Adan's troops so that he (Sharon) could lead the exploitation drive from the bridgehead southward behind the Egyptian Third Army. Bar Lev, apparently relieved that there was at least one Sharon recommendation that he did not have to veto, was obviously prepared to agree. Adan, however, was incensed. As he saw it—perhaps less than completely objectively—he had been fighting steadily for 30 hours to perform tasks that Sharon had been supposed to do, but had not done, and he could see this recommendation only as an effort by Sharon to gain all of the honor and glory. Adan was still smarting from his defeat on the 8th; he thought his men had now demonstrated that they deserved to share a little of the glory Sharon had already won by his crossing. Furthermore, as an aggressive officer, he wanted to attack, not defend. Of course Sharon felt the same way.

Before the argument could become heated, however, Elazar spoke up. The plan had been drawn up as it was for good reason. Although the operation had been somewhat delayed, he saw no reason to make any changes in the basic concept of the plan. Sharon would continue to hold the bridgehead and corridor; Adan would pass through to exploit; later Sharon would join Adan, and Magen would hold the crossing. Meanwhile, Bar Lev told Sharon he could ferry the remainder of Erez's brigade across the Canal while the bridge was being constructed.

MODERN "BATTLE OF LAKE TRASIMENE"

During the latter part of this discussion, sometime after 1:00 p.m., the conferees had been devoting as much attention to the distant south as they were to the conversation. Early in the conference a message had been received from Magen, whose observation posts had sighted an Egyptian armored column moving north from Botzer not far from the east shore of the Great Bitter Lake. Soon after this another message was received from Reshev, still busy repairing damaged tanks near Lakekan, that a column of dust to the south indicated the approach of an Egyptian column from the Third Army front. Aerial reconnaissance soon confirmed that this was a column of about 100 Egyptian T-62 tanks. As it later turned out, this was the Egyptian 25th Armored Brigade.

The dust column was soon clearly visible to the conferees near Kishuf. Adan interrupted the discussion to ask Bar Lev to release his third brigade—Karen's—from reserve. Bar Lev promptly approved. Adan quickly issued orders to Karen and to the three brigade commanders engaged at the Chinese Farm, then returned to the discussion to renew his demand that he be allowed to exploit the crossing, as planned.

Once Elazar made his decision to have the plan continue as originally conceived, Adan excused himself and jumped into his command APC to direct this new battle personally.

The approach of the Egyptian armored brigade seemed to offer an opportunity, but it complicated Adan's already complex problem of tactical control by forcing him to fight simultaneously in two different directions. Fighting was still severe on the Chinese Farm front. Adan decided to pull out Baram's brigade, with two battalions, leaving one battalion to hold the center of the line at the Chinese Farm. Amir was to extend his front to the right and Raviv to the left to permit Baram to pull out his two flank battalions.

While Adan raced south down the Artillery Road, followed by Baram's brigade, he could hear Reshev—who had less than 30 operational tanks near Lakekan—calling on the radio for support against the approaching 25th Brigade. Adan put Baram in position due east of the head of the Egyptian column. Karen, meanwhile, had been marching rapidly westward from the Lateral Road to the Artillery Road to a position southeast of the Egyptians. One of his battalions was to continue southeastward, to get behind the Egyptians to ambush them from the rear if they tried to turn back to the edge of the Third Army front, near Botzer.

Although it did not cross his mind at the time, Adan had set up a plan for a modern counterpart of Hannibal's famous victory at the Battle of Lake Trasimene, in April, 217 B.C.

At about 2:30 p.m. Baram's and Reshev's tanks opened fire simultaneously at the head of the Egyptian column, which halted and began to deploy eastward, away from the lake. Baram's brigade opened fire on the deploying tanks and the column behind them. Some of the Egyptian tanks boldly and properly charged toward Baram's tanks. Others, confused by fire from two directions, tried to turn back. Suddenly all of the Egyptian tanks found themselves under fire from Karen's brigade, to their right rear.

Confusion now pervaded the entire column of the 25th Armored Brigade. Nevertheless many of the Egyptian tanks were fought boldly and skillfully. However, outnumbered and outmaneuvered, they did not have a chance. Of the 96 tanks in the column, 86 were destroyed in less than an hour of fighting.[1] Ten Egyptian tanks escaped, reaching the safety of the Botzer position, where Adan called off the pursuit, after some of his tanks ran into a former Israeli minefield. Four of them were lost to mines, the only Israeli losses in the battle.

By this time it was 4:00 p.m., and Adan led his tanks back to the vicinity of Kishuf, where they were refueled and their ammunition was replenished.

It was just about this time that the ponton bridge was completed. While returning to Kishuf in his tank Adan heard Sharon calling over the command radio net: "Where is Bren? Everything is ready. Where is Bren? Why is he holding things up?"

Coldly furious, Adan brusquely reported to Gonen where he was, what he had been doing, and his plans for resupply. He told Gonen that he would carry out his orders promptly, and that he would be able to cross the bridge soon after dark, as soon as Sharon's troops relieved his battalions still engaged south of Missouri and the Chinese Farm. He expected to have his entire division across the bridge by morning. Nevertheless, at intervals through the next hour and a half, until Adan's first tanks arrived at the yard, Sharon kept calling into the radio: "Where is Bren?"

On the 16th and 17th, as on the 8th, combat activity on the Sinai front was focussed on one Israeli division: Adan's. While this division was carrying the heaviest part of the fighting, other Israeli units were doing their part. But just as with the failure of Adan's division on October 8 Israel suffered the most crushing military defeat in its history, so with the division's success on the 17th came the most outstanding Israeli victory of the war.

---

[1]The Israelis did not have an opportunity to evacuate these tanks after the battle or later in the war. The Egyptians claim that their losses were fewer than 80, and that of those lost several had been knocked out by TOWs; this is doubtful; see p. 502.

13

The Gathering Storm, October 17-19

POLITICAL PRESSURES ON PRESIDENT SADAT

On October 15 President Sadat decided that the time had come to seek a political resolution of the war. This decision was based on both political and military considerations. He was under increasing pressure from the Soviet, American, and British governments to accept a cease-fire. Furthermore, the failure of the Egyptian offensive of October 14 made it clear that further military gains were unlikely on the Sinai front, and it seemed equally obvious that the Syrian military situation, now also in stalemate, would not improve. Accordingly he scheduled an address to the National Assembly for the next day, Tuesday, October 16. Obviously at the time he made this decision he knew nothing of the Israeli plans for a cross-Canal assault.

Sadat's midday address, on television and radio, was of course monitored by the whole world. Prime Minister Golda Meir, scheduled to speak to the Knesset at the same hour, postponed her speech until 4:00 p.m., apparently in order to be able to analyze whatever Sadat said.

The Egyptian President reiterated the basic Arab and Egyptian position. Egypt would continue fighting until it had regained its lost territory and until the legitimate rights of the Palestinian people had been restored to them. However, if Israel agreed to withdraw from all of the territories occupied in June 1967, then Egypt would accept a ceasefire, and in turn would attend a peace conference with Israel, and endeavor to get the rest of the Arab world also to take part in definitive peace negotiations. As evidence of peaceful Egyptian intentions, Egypt would start immediately to clear the Suez Canal and reopen it for international shipping—by implication this meant the passage of shipments to Israel and possibly of Israeli vessels also.

When Prime Minister Meir spoke a few hours later, she noted, but did not respond directly to, Sadat's proposals. She did, however, include with considerable emphasis the remark that Israeli forces were at that time fighting "east and west of the Suez Canal."

According to Heikal,[1] this seems to have been the first word that Sadat had received regarding the Israeli crossing. He evidently telephoned General Ismail, who is supposed to have responded that he had reports only of "three infiltrating Israeli tanks," and that Egyptian reserves would soon take care of these infiltrators. Both Sadat and Ismail were inclined to believe that both the raid and Mrs. Meir's reference to it were mainly psychological warfare.

Late that afternoon, Prime Minister Kosygin of the Soviet Union arrived in Cairo. During the evening Kosygin and Sadat met, and again the Russian emphasized the desirability for a ceasefire. It is doubtful if Kosygin knew anything about the Israeli crossing when he left Moscow; he seems to have been impelled mainly by concern about the terrible losses of Soviet equipment taking place on the two fronts, by fears that a likely Israeli counteroffensive would be successful, and by the belief that the setback of October 14 would influence Sadat to soften his position on a ceasefire. Obviously the Russian was pleased by the slight move in this direction which he could detect in Sadat's noontime address.

Kosygin's talks with Sadat continued for the next two days, with news of the Israeli crossing adding strength to the Russian's arguments. When Sadat said that this was merely a raid, late on October 18 Kosygin was able to give the Egyptian president photos taken by Soviet satellites, and flown urgently to Cairo, which clearly showed the Israeli bridgehead. He urged Sadat to soften his position on demanding an Israeli agreement to withdraw to pre-1967 lines before ceasefire talks could open. Sadat began to recognize the attractiveness of such a relaxation, but was concerned about the psychological effect upon his people, and the political effect on the other Arab states, particularly Syria.

BREAKOUT PRELIMINARIES

While Sadat and Kosygin were conferring in Cairo on the afternoon of the 17th, Adan was trying to get his division ready to cross the Canal. The problems of refueling and rearming his tanks south of Akavish were easily resolved, but coordination with Sharon was more difficult. In order to permit Adan to carry out his task Sharon had to relieve Amir's brigade on the Chinese Farm-Missouri front. (Baram's third battalion had been pulled out during the afternoon.) But for some reason Sharon delayed in shifting portions of Reshev's and Erez's brigades to relieve Amir. In fact it was after 9:00 before Amir's third battalion—the one that had been attached to Sharon the morning of the 16th and had been fighting west of Missouri—rejoined the division.

Thus it was evening when General Adan's blacked-out column ap-

[1] *Op. cit.*, pp. 230-231.

proached the ponton bridge between Matzmed and Deversoir. At that time he received a message from General Gonen's headquarters, informing him that Karen's brigade had again been withdrawn from his control to become the general reserve for Southern Command. Since Raviv's brigade automatically reverted to Sharon's control when Adan moved to the crossing, Adan's command had again been reduced to about 200 tanks, and a total manpower strength of perhaps 9,000 men.

At 9:30 p.m. Adan's APC, leading the division, rumbled onto the bridge. When he reached the west side of the Canal, Adan pulled his vehicle off to the side, to watch the column cross behind him. He had barely stopped when, to his horror, he realized that only two tanks had followed him. There was steady harassing Egyptian artillery fire falling around the bridge and its approaches, and at first he thought the bridge had been hit. It turned out that this was not the cause of the interruption; a link between two pontons had broken after the first two heavy tanks had crossed. While Israeli engineers rushed out from the shore along the bridge on foot and in boats to repair the damage, Adan ordered the ferries to start carrying tanks across the water. Then, as the engineers had trouble making repairs, he ordered a bridging tank to fill the gap.

The column of tanks again began to stream across. Egyptian artillery fire sank a ferry with two tanks aboard. There were more interruptions during the night, but by dawn the rest of Adan's tanks were securely in the bridgehead between the Suez Canal and the Sweetwater Canal.

During the early morning Adan's two armored brigades took position along the perimeter, preparatory to a breakout effort. It was at this time that Adan discovered that Sharon had taken very literally his instructions on the establishment of the bridgehead. Adan had expected that Sharon would have pushed his line across the Sweetwater Canal to the edge of the "green belt," which extends from about 100 meters to several kilometers on each side of the Sweetwater Canal. Sharon, however, had put his line along that canal, although he had established a few bridgeheads on the west bank.

The result was that when Adan's tanks tried to advance through the vegetation they found themselves opposed in short-range actions by a variety of antitank weapons, including dug-in tanks, Saggers, and RPG-7s. Adan pulled back these preliminary probes, ordered a heavy artillery preparation, and mounted a two-brigade attack across the Sweetwater Canal. On the right, Baram's brigade broke through quickly and by 8:00 a.m. reached the edge of the green belt north of the main east-west road from Deversoir. Repulsing an Egyptian armored counterattack, Baram pushed ahead about five kilometers to seize a fortified hill (called Arel by the Israelis) overlooking the main north-south Ismailia-Suez road. He consolidated the area in cooperation with a paratroop battalion from Sharon's division.

On the left, however, the Egyptian defense was much more effective. It was midafternoon before Amir's brigade was able to reach the edge of the green belt, and, as his tanks tried to poke their way out into the open, they found themselves under intense fire from Egyptian tanks hull-down behind a parallel north-south road just beyond. Amir's men were able to take the position which the Israelis called Uri, but he was stopped at Tsach.

Soon after Baram had reached the open desert, and while Amir was still entangled in the green belt, Adan received a radio message from Gonen, asking if he could raid against SAM sites farther inland. Adan at once sent Baram with two battalions ranging generally westward and northwestward for more than 20 kilometers. They bypassed all serious opposition, but shot up a number of undefended or lightly defended rear area installations, as well as convoys and individual trucks on the road. Three SAM sites were put out of action before Baram turned back to rejoin the division at the edge of the green belt that night.

During the day Adan was visited by Defense Minister Dayan, who came across the bridge in a halftrack. While Dayan was at Adan's headquarters the Egyptians initiated a major air attack against the bridgehead. Their principal targets seem to have been the ponton bridge across the Suez Canal and the several bridges which the Israelis had seized over the Sweetwater Canal. Following a strike by MiG-17s, which caused no serious damage, about five Egyptian cargo helicopters came over at low level, conducting a clumsy, makeshift attack. Not intended for the combat attack role, these helicopters had been loaded with fuzed barrels of napalm and high explosive, which were kicked out of the cargo doors as they passed over their targets. One barrel of napalm narrowly missed General Dayan. However, again no serious damage was done, and all of the helicopters were shot down. This was apparently the only time during the war that helicopters were used in a direct attack combat role by either side.

Meanwhile a major air battle had been going on over the Israeli bridgehead. By prearrangement the Egyptian SAMs remained quiet, while MiGs, Mirages, and F-4s cavorted overhead. About 20 planes shot down during this fight, and all of them were apparently MiGs.

That night Adan reported his situation to Gonen on the radio. He felt confident that he could make a clean breakout on the 19th, and urged Gonen to release his reserve brigade to him. Gonen agreed. By morning Karen's brigade had completed the crossing, and was inside the perimeter. This gave Adan a total of slightly more than 250 serviceable tanks just west of the Sweetwater Canal for the next day's attack.

NEW MISSION FOR SHARON

During the night of October 17-18, Sharon had succeeded in getting approval of a substantial change in the original breakout plan. Originally it had been intended that Sharon would follow to the right rear of Adan, to widen the sweep of the breakout, and to assure adequate protection to the flanks of Adan's spearheads. Magen's division was to have relieved Sharon in holding the bridges (the preconstructed bridge had been brought up and installed late on the 18th), the corridor, and the west bank bridgehead. Now Sharon received permission to continue guarding the bridges, and at the same time to mount a drive to the north to capture Ismailia. Magen was given the job of protecting the flank and rear of Adan's thrust.

Neither Gonen nor Bar Lev was in agreement with Sharon's idea, which appeared to them to be strategically unsound since it involved a dissipation of Israeli offensive effort. However, they were inclined to approve, simply in the hope that this would satisfy Sharon's prima donna complex, and that they would have no more trouble with him. Bar Lev was determined that there would be no diversion of resources from the main effort. Gonen was satisfied with this, because he had been unhappy about trying to control Sharon in a two division drive toward Suez with Adan. Possibly for similar reasons, both General Elazar and Defense Minister Dayan also approved. As it turned out, however, the higher commanders found that they continued to have undiminished problems with Sharon, even when he was "doing his thing."

14

Crisis in Cairo, October 17-20

CONFUSION AND UNCERTAINTY

Following Erez's raid on the afternoon of October 16, the Egyptian High Command had issued orders to the Second Army to contain the penetration near Deversoir and to close the corridor east of the crossing site. The Egyptians were still convinced, however, that this raid was largely intended as a diversion, to keep the Egyptians from recognizing the threat to the right flank of the Second Army. Lack of further reports from the Second Army about the Israeli penetration seemed to confirm this assessment. In fact, the Egyptian uncertainty about the location and strength of hostile attacking forces was very similar to Israeli uncertainty ten days earlier.

By afternoon of the 17th General Ismail had learned from aerial reconnaissance and other sources that the Israelis were installing a bridge over the Canal. It was also evident that the east bank corridor had not been closed, and that the bitter fight in the Chinese Farm area might have been waged by the Israelis more to protect that corridor than to threaten the south flank of the Second Army. Dissatisfied with reports he was receiving from Second and Third Army headquarters about the Israeli activities east and west of Deversoir, Ismail sent General Shazli, his Chief of Staff, to investigate at first hand. Ismail had apparently begun to lose some of his former animosity toward Shazli, having been pleased by a report his Chief of Staff had rendered after a visit to the east bank bridgeheads on October 15 and 16, when he had found the units recovering well from their setbacks of the 14th.

SHAZLI'S MISSION AND REPORT

From personal observation and from conversation with local commanders, Shazli soon began to recognize that a major Israeli effort was being made to establish a bridgehead on the west bank. He was in Ismailia, early in the evening of the 18th, when reports were received of

517

Baram's raid west of Deversoir. He apparently telephoned General Ismail, and the two agreed that all SAM sites in the vicinity of the bridgehead should be withdrawn.

Late next day, October 19, Shazli completed his survey and returned to the underground command post just east of Cairo, to give his report to General Ismail, and also to give him the benefit of the conclusions that he had drawn about the situation. Shazli, aware of the fact that most of the Egyptian Army's tanks and antitank weapons were on the east bank, feared the possibility of a major Israeli breakthrough, which might even be followed by an offensive toward Cario. Shazli was convinced that there were not enough first-class Egyptian troops available on the west bank of the Canal to be able to stop such an Israeli operation. He therefore recommended to Ismail that most of the Egyptian units east of the Canal be drawn back to the west bank, so as to be able to contain the Israeli offensive. He expected—quite rightly—that the attack would begin that morning; thus immediate withdrawal of troops from the east bank was essential.

Ismail had long ago recognized the mercurial nature of Shazli. This had last evidenced itself ten days earlier in the disagreement of the two generals over Ismail's cautious strategy. Everything that Shazli said might be correct, including his deductions about the Israeli plans. But Ismail was confident that the Israelis would not be able to break through to Cairo—he doubted if they would even try. But whatever they did on the west bank, he did not want to surrender a single inch of the recently conquered territory on the east bank, if this could be avoided. He remembered all too vividly the panic which had occurred in 1967 when Field Marshal Amer had ordered Egyptian troops in the Sinai to withdraw across the Canal.

ISMAIL-SHAZLI CONFRONTATION

Ismail therefore told Shazli to direct that all GHQ units in and around Cairo be alerted, and that the Second and Third Armies be given a peremptory order with two principal elements: they should concentrate all of the troops they had available on the west bank, to contain, and if possible eliminate, the Israeli bridgehead; they must not withdraw a single soldier from the east bank to deal with this west bank situation.

Shazli at once protested. An argument broke out between the two generals, unable any longer to control their mutual animosity. Shazli seems to have made some uncomplimentary remarks to Ismail, which caused the Commander in Chief to order the Chief of Staff to report to his quarters in the underground command post, and await further instructions.

Ismail then immediately called President Sadat on the telephone, and told him that he was needed urgently at the command post. When Sadat asked why, Ismail—concerned about the possibility of electronic eavesdropping—merely said he would prefer to discuss the matter in person with the president.

INTERVENTION OF SADAT

When Sadat arrived, shortly after midnight, October 19-20, Ismail called Shazli to his office, and the two generals—now in control of their tempers—presented their different views to the president.[1] Sadat at once agreed with Ismail, and then and there relieved Shazli of his position as Chief of Staff. General Gamasy was appointed temporary Chief of Staff. For several days no announcement was made of this important change in the Egyptian High Command. Later it was announced that General Shazli had suffered a nervous breakdown.

Following this historic meeting, Sadat and Ismail spoke alone. Apparently they agreed that Egypt should seek a ceasefire as soon as possible, in order to avoid the possibility of jeopardizing what had already been won on the east bank. Ismail pointed out, however, that he had one and a half armored divisions, one and a half mechanized divisions, two reserve infantry divisions and several independent brigades available to contain the Israelis on the west bank.

As soon as he returned to the presidential palace, Sadat had a meeting with Kosygin. As a result of the meeting urgent messages were sent by Kosygin to Washington and Moscow. In a few hours it was arranged that Secretary of State Kissinger would fly to Moscow to meet with Soviet leaders to see what the two superpowers could do to arrange a ceasefire. Kosygin then flew back to Moscow to confer with his Kremlin colleagues and await Kissinger's arrival.

SADAT AND ASSAD DISAGREE ON CEASEFIRE

Following Kosygin's departure, Sadat sent a telegram to President Assad of Syria:

We have fought Israel to the fifteenth day. In the first four days Israel was alone, so we were able to expose her position on both fronts. On their admission the enemy have lost 800 tanks and two hundred planes. But during the last ten days I have, on the Egyptian front, been fighting the United States as well, through the arms it is sending. To put it bluntly, I cannot fight the United States or accept the responsibility before history for the destruction of our armed forces for a second time. I have therefore informed the Soviet Union that I am prepared to accept a ceasefire on existing positions, subject to the following conditions:

---

[1] Heikal, *op. cit.*, p. 238, suggests that several other officers were present. This is doubtful, although Gamasy may have been in the room.

1. The Soviet Union and the United States to guarantee an Israeli withdrawal, as proposed by the Soviet Union.

2. The convening of a peace conference under United Nations auspices to achieve an overall settlement, as proposed by the Soviet Union.

My heart bleeds to tell you this, but I feel that my office compels me to take this decision. I am ready to face our nation at a suitable moment and am prepared to give a full account to it for the decision.[2]

Early the next morning—October 20—Sadat received a reply from Assad, the critical portion being as follows:

. . . I beg you to look again at the military situation on the northern front and on both sides of the canal. We see no cause for pessimism. We can continue the struggle against enemy forces, whether they have crossed the canal or are still fighting east of the canal. I am convinced that by continuing and intensifying the battle it will be possible to ensure the destruction of those enemy units that have crossed the canal. My brother Sadat, for the sake of the morale of the fighting troops it is necessary to emphasize that although the enemy have as a result of an accident been able to break our front this does not mean that they will be able to achieve victory. The enemy succeeded in penetrating the northern front several days ago, but the stand we then made and the subsequent heavy fighting have given us greater grounds for optimism. Most points of enemy penetration have been sealed off and I am confident that we shall be able to deal with those remaining in the course of the next few days. I consider it imperative that our armies should maintain their fighting spirit.[3]

To what extent Assad was deceiving himself, and to what extent he was making a case for the record, is not clear. Actually, as will be seen, the situation on the Syrian front was better than Sadat realized. In any event, Sadat considered this to be an emotional, unrealistic appeal, and it did not cause him to change his mind about seeking a ceasefire.

[2] *Ibid.*, pp. 238-239.
[3] *Ibid,* p. 239.

15

Israeli West Bank Breakout, October 19-22

WEST BANK TERRAIN

In the area between Ismailia and Suez there are three principal north-south roads, and six major east-west roads. Close to the Canal, and running generally parallel to, and east of, both the Sweetwater Canal and the railroad is the so-called Test Road. One to five kilometers farther west, and running through Fayid and Geneifa is the main road, known to the Israelis as Havit.[1] About ten kilometers farther west is the road called Vadaut by the Israelis, constructed primarily for lateral rear area communications by the Egyptians.

Running due west from Ismailia is a road, parallel to the main railroad and canal, which goes to Cairo by way of the Nile Delta. The main Ismailia-Cairo road extends in a southwesterly direction from Ismailia across the desert. Running due west from Deversoir is a road code-named Sakranut by the Israelis, intersecting the main Ismailia-Cairo road about 35 kilometers west of Deversoir. Twelve kilometers farther south is an east-west road from Fayid, called Vitamin. Another 20 kilometers to the south is a road called Asor, the northernmost of the two principal routes from Suez to Cairo; Asor intersects Havit about midway between Geneifa and Shallufa. Ten to twenty kilometers farther south is the road the Israelis called Sarag, the main Suez-Cairo road.

Among the numerous hills and hill masses in this generally bare, arid desert land, there are six of major importance, each valuable for purposes of observation and defense. Just west of Deversoir, the Havit and Sakranut roads cross each other on the Tsach Hill. Five kilometers to the north is Arel, seized by Baram on the 18th. In the northeast quadrant of the Sakranut-Vadaut crossroad is the hill of Maktsera. Miznefet Hill lies just west of the Vitamin-Vadaut crossroad. Much larger and more prominent is a rugged region known as the Geneifa Hills, extending due

---

[1] Whenever possible the original Arabic names are used to identify terrain features and roads. However, for descriptive convenience Israeli code-words are used when the Arab designations are not precise.

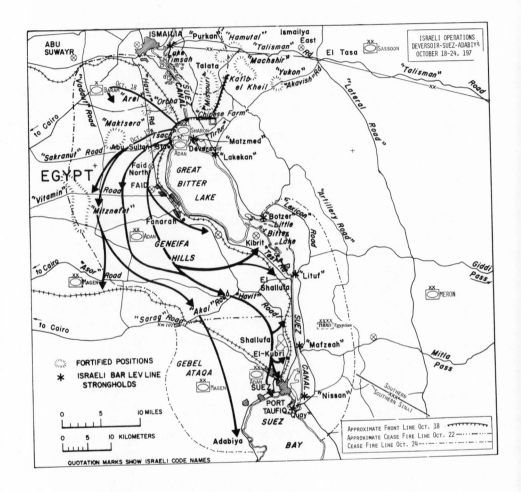

west of the Little Bitter Lake. These hills stretch from the Havit Road and the outskirts of Geneifa westward approximately twenty kilometers, and are bounded on the south by the Asor Road—which runs across some of the southern slopes of the hill mass. Still larger is a vast mountain mass west of Suez and south of the Sarag Road, called Jebel Ataka, or Mount Ataka. Its high bluffs frown over the desert and provide visibility for many miles. On these heights the Egyptians had a major communications complex, including one of two principal electronic monitoring stations, used to listen to Israeli radio transmissions.

ADAN STRIKES SOUTH

On the morning of October 19 Adan attacked west and then south with two brigades, and directly south with part of another. On the right Baram's brigade drove due west from its bridgehead perimeter, north of the Sakranut road, to reach Maktsera Hill and Vadaut road. South of Sakranut, Amir also attacked westward, bypassing the strongly fortified Tsach Hill. Karen's brigade had the responsibility of covering the rear and left rear of the division.

Baram, having turned south down the Vadaut road, ran into severe opposition north of Miznefet, where a reinforced Egyptian mechanized brigade was in position. Baram called for help, and received one of Karen's battalions, with which he blocked the Egyptian front. This permitted Baram to swing to the left, crossing the Vitamin Road about midway between Miznefet and Fayid, overrunning scattered Egyptian resistance en route. This easterly movement took him across the rear of Amir's brigade, and thus Baram was now in the center of Adan's division line.

Amir, meanwhile, after bypassing Tsach, had moved in a southwesterly direction from Tsach, toward the Vitamin-Vadaut crossroad. This brought his brigade under fire from the eastern slopes of Miznefet, west of Vadaut. While one battalion engaged in a firefight with Egyptian tanks on Miznefet, another of Amir's battalions pushed south across the Vitamin Road to reach the northern edge of the Geneifa Hills. Adan had considered it vitally important to seize this centrally-located hill mass as early as possible, before the Egyptians had a chance to organize it for defense. Amir's third battalion advanced southward along the Havit Road toward Fayid, but was soon held up by large Egyptian forces holding the airfield and the town of Fayid.

Further to the rear, Magen's division, with two armored brigades, and one mechanized infantry brigade, had crossed into the bridgehead during the night of October 18-19. He was beginning to clean up pockets of resistance bypassed by Adan, one of the first being Tsach. Two of Magen's battalions relieved Karen's and Amir's units that were blocking the area north and east of Miznefet. With the remainder of his division Magen continued west and south across the Vitamin Road. On the 20th Magen continued his thrust to the south, carrying out his mission of protecting Adan's flank and rear. By evening his right brigade was about 30 kilometers west of the Suez Canal, less than 100 kilometers from Cairo.

On the 20th, for the first time since the outbreak of the war, Adan's division was receiving effective close air support. The fabric of the Egyptian SAM umbrella had been ripped by the Israeli armored drives and artillery concentrations of the previous day, and Israeli aircraft could now begin to operate without serious interference from Egyptian air defense units in the area over and west of the bridgehead. Comparable air support was to be provided to the Israeli ground forces for the remainder of the war.

By this time Baram's and Karen's brigades were deep in the Geneifa Hills, and at about 10:30 Baram reached the Asor Road where it passes through the southern edge of the Geneifa Hills. There Baram set up a roadblock, taking a heavy toll of Egyptian traffic between Cairo and Suez. Following instructions from Adan, he sent a battalion further south to try to cut the Sarag road—the main Suez-Cairo road—but this unit could not break through, although it was able to harass traffic on the road with long range fire from its tank guns. Afraid that the battalion might be cut off, Baram pulled it back for the night into his main position at the southern edge of the Geneifa Hills.

Karen, in the meantime, had been pushing through the eastern portion of the Geneifa Hills, and by nightfall was close to the intersection of the Asor and Havit Roads. Amir—now behind the other two brigades—had been trying to open up the Havit Road north of Fayid, since Adan wanted to use this main artery as the supply route for his division. However, Egyptian resistance at Fayid was too strong; so Adan and his troops had to share the more roundabout Vadaut Road with Magen's division.

On October 21 Adan received two additional battalions, one of infantry and one of engineers. He assigned these new units to Amir. With this additional strength, Amir was able to clear all resistance in and south of Fayid, opening Adan's supply road. This also permitted Israeli aircraft to use the Fayid airstrip for evacuation of wounded, reconnaissance, and emergency supply.

At the same time Baram and Karen had driven south of Asor, with the objective of cutting the Sarag Road and isolating Suez from Cairo. Just south of Asor, however, they were slowed down by increasing Egyptian resistance. In the late morning they were halted by a counterattack from two brigades of the Egyptian 4th Armored Division. Regrouping, the two Israeli brigades attempted to resume their advance again in the afternoon, but once more they were halted by a counterattack of the Egyptian tanks. However, by long range fire, at about 10,000 meters the Israeli tank guns were able to interdict Egyptian traffic on the Sarag Road, the Egyptian Third Army's only remaining link with Cairo.

CHARGE TO THE CANAL

Before dawn on October 22 Adan received a radio call from Gonen, telling him that there would be a ceasefire soon after 6:00 p.m. Adan was to make all possible efforts to reach the Suez Canal south of the Bitter Lakes, and to push as far toward Suez as he could. Magen would at the same time be continuing his advance to the west, to cut the Sarag Road if possible. Adan decided to have Baram continue the advance southward, in coordination with Magen, to cut the Sarag Road in his sector, while Amir's and Karen's brigades drove due eastward toward Kabrit and Shallufa, and the Canal just beyond.

Baram's leading elements, supported by Magen's artillery, reached the Sarag Road by midmorning. Turning this sector over to Magen, Baram moved east to join the other two brigades, which were meeting strong Egyptian resistance along the Havit Road south of Geneifa.

By noon Adan became fearful that he would not reach the Canal before the ceasefire went into effect. He was arguing by radio with Bar Lev about the problem of trying to make divergent thrusts when he learned that Baram had been relieved by Magen. With all three of his brigades concentrated, Adan decided to try once more the "tank charge" tactics that had been so successful in the 1967 war, but so disastrous in the first three days of this war.[2] His three brigades, with Karen on the left, Amir on the right, and Baram moving in between them, were to attack on a broad front across the Havit Road between Geneifa and Shallufa.

Shortly after noon the Israeli tanks charged eastward, going as far and as fast as they could, bypassing major areas of resistance insofar as possible. The result was a wild and confused battle, because this was the rear area of the Egyptian Third Army, with substantial numbers of troops of all varieties. All three brigades reached the green belt and the Sweetwater Canal, and one of Karen's battalions reached the southern shore of the Great Bitter Lake north of Kabrit. That battalion, however, was terribly battered in the effort, and found itself the object of repeated Egyptian counterattacks; Adan ordered it to fall back to Karen's main line along the Sweetwater Canal.

By this time it was dark, and the ceasefire was supposedly in effect. And, although, as one of the Israeli commanders remarked after the war, "firing continued," there was indeed a lull in the operations.[3]

[2] Contributing to this decision was Adan's realization that the Egyptians had few Saggers and RPG-7s west of the Canal, and that he had substantial air support.

[3] Responsible Israeli and Egyptian descriptions of this situation are totally irreconcilable. Both Egyptians and Israelis complain (I believe with complete sincerity) that this "neutral" description is unfairly tilted to the other side. Thus, I believe these paragraphs are reasonably close to objective truth.

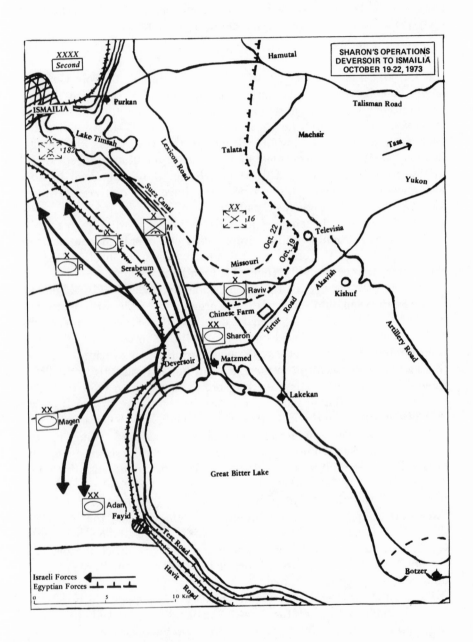

SHARON'S OPERATIONS
DEVERSOIR TO ISMAILIA
OCTOBER 19-22, 1973

When the ceasefire went into effect at 6:52 p.m. on October 22, Adan and Magen had occupied an area 20 to 30 kilometers deep west of the Canal and the Bitter Lakes, and extending from the Sakranut Road in the north to Shallufa and the northern Suez-Cairo Road (Asor) in the south, with some advanced elements actually blocking some sections of the main Suez-Cairo Road (Sarag). However, Adan controlled only part of the green belt between Geneifa and Shallufa. Within most of the region which his division and Magen's had overrun there were few Egyptians. In the area east of the Havit Road, and north of Shallufa, however, Adan's units were badly intermingled with Egyptian units.

This confused situation was to cause considerable trouble during later negotiations, since both sides could, with considerable justification, claim that they controlled much of the same territory.

SHARON AND ISMAILIA

A very different kind of operation had been going on north of Deversoir near Serabeum. On the 18th Sharon, over Gonen's and Bar Lev's objections, received approval from General Tal (presumably at Dayan's urging) to move Reshev's brigade to the west bank of the Canal. Gonen had wanted Sharon to use Reshev to widen the corridor east of the bridge by seizing the southern slopes of Missouri. Sharon insisted, however, that Egyptian resistance was so weakened that Raviv's brigade could assure security through the corridor, and Bar Lev accepted this.

Meanwhile, on Sharon's instructions, the preconstructed bridge, 170 meters long, was being inched down the Tirtur Road. It was pulled and pushed by ten or more tanks, with a ring of tanks, antitank guns and antiaircraft guns protecting the clumsy contraption from all sides. The bridge finally reached the edge of the Canal, just north of the yard, by early evening of October 18. Soon after midnight it was open for traffic.

By this time Egyptian artillery was causing heavy casualties on and near the original ponton bridge. The guns had the exact range to the bridge abutments, and occasional rounds hit the bridge itself. A substantial proportion of Israeli casualties suffered from the 18th to the end of the war were incurred on or near one of the bridges. Another ponton bridge was installed just north of the preconstructed bridge on the 19th. By this time repeated Israeli attacks had pushed the Egyptian right wing elements about 8 kilometers north of the original crossing point, about 4 kilometers north of the Chinese Farm.

On the west bank, on the 18th, Sharon ordered Colonel Matt to send a battalion of his paratroopers probing northward toward Serabeum. They ran into very strong resistance, and by nightfall withdrew to the bridgehead under severe Egyptian pressure.

The increasingly effective Egyptian resistance resulted from the arrival that day of the 182d Paratroop Brigade from the Second Army reserve. This brigade was commanded by Colonel Ismail Azmy. The Israeli attack, incidentally, was ordered before Sharon had received permission to launch an offensive in this direction; but Sharon was later able to justify the abortive probe as the same kind of battalion "patrol" that he had used seventeen years earlier at the Mitla Pass.

On the 19th, having received grudging approval for an offensive against, Ismailia, and having also shifted Reshev's brigade to the west bank, Sharon again ordered Matt to push northward through the green belt to Serabeum. But Matt's paratroopers encountered their match in the paratroopers of Azmy's 182d Brigade, and the attack was stopped completely. Sharon then sent Reshev to swing around Matt's left flank, and to seize the Orcha Hill, just west of the Serabeum. There the resistance was equally determined, but Reshev was able to use his superior maneuverability to seize the position before dark. The Israelis discovered that this was a major Egyptian radio intercept station. The Egyptian paratroopers withdrew to Touscan, and hastily organized a new defensive position.

On the 20th Sharon renewed the attack northward from Orcha and Serabeum toward Ismailia, attacking on a three brigade front, across the width of the green belt. Matt was on the right, Erez in the center, and Reshev on the left. After some intensive fighting, the Israelis sensed that the resistance of the 182d Brigade was weakening, but just as they began to roll forward the Israelis found themselves suddenly counterattacked.

Colonel Azmy, having received reinforcements, committed his reserve, and stopped the Israeli attack.

For the remainder of the day the battle seesawed back and forth, just south of Lake Timsah. During the afternoon the superior strength of the Israelis began to make itself felt, but they gained little more ground before nightfall. However, Israeli artillery fire had by this time made the main Ismailia-Cairo road almost unusable.

SHARON'S MISSOURI COMPROMISE

During the renewed battle on the 21st Sharon's troops again inched forward and surrounded the Touscan defensive position. But the Egyptians again counterattacked, and held the Israelis south of the Ismailia-Nile River Canal, just south of the city. The Egyptians believe that Sharon's failure to take Ismailia that day was due to their staunch defense. Sharon after the war insisted that his failure was due to interference from Southern Command headquarters.

Bar Lev and Gonen were concerned by the fact that the east bank corridor to the Deversoir bridgehead was only eight kilometers wide and that Israeli movements in the corridor were drawing fire from Egyptians on Missouri, and that Sharon was ignoring repeated instructions to reinforce Raviv to get the corridor widened. Finally, on the morning of the 21st Gonen issued a peremptory order to Sharon to send back troops, and to make a full scale attack on Missouri. Reluctantly Sharon complied—although he sent only five tanks back to reinforce Raviv—and at 3:00 p.m. Raviv began the long delayed attack on Missouri—specifically the Talia hill mass. The initial assault was successful, but counterattack by the Egyptian 16th Division retook Talia, and the Israeli offensive bogged down.

Gonen then issued another order to Sharon to attack Missouri. Sharon responded that all of his forces were engaged elsewhere—which was true—and thus he could not attack on the east bank. Bar Lev now took over from Gonen. He very slowly and clearly explained why a wider corridor was necessary, particularly in the light of the anticipated cease-fire. He ordered Sharon to make another attack, and to do so with adequate forces. A few minutes later, however, Gonen received a call from General Tal in Tel Aviv, to the effect that Minister of Defense Dayan had issued a direct order that Sharon was not to attack Missouri. After he received Bar Lev's order Sharon had telephoned direct to Dayan and had persuaded the minister to countermand the order.

Thus, on the 22nd Sharon was able to concentrate his attention and the efforts of three of his four brigades on the capture of Ismailia. But this time the Egyptians held completely firm, and, when the ceasefire went into effect at 6:52 p.m., the Israelis, on both sides of the Canal, were still about 10 kilometers south of the wrecked city.

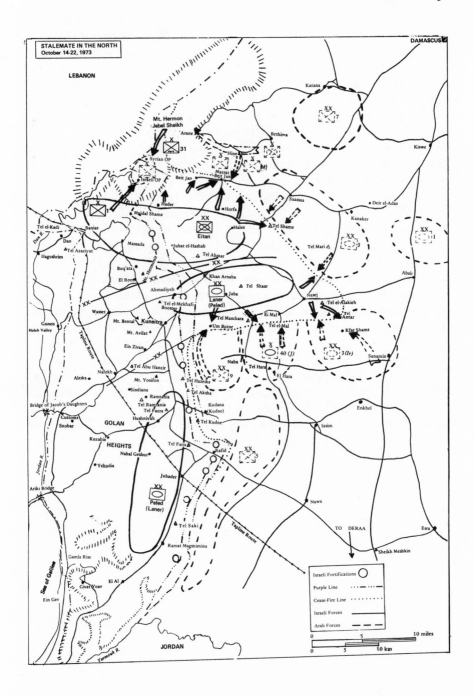

STALEMATE IN THE NORTH
October 14-22, 1973

16

Final Operations in Syria, October 14-23

KING HUSSEIN'S DILEMMA

On October 9 King Hussein of Jordan seems to have made his decision to enter the war against Israel. He and the Jordan Army General Staff had four obvious possible courses of action to consider: first, to launch a full-scale offensive across the Jordan River into Jordan's former West Bank territories, while Israel was totally committed in operations against the armies of Egypt and Syria; second, to contain a portion of the Israeli Army along the Jordan River front by massing the army in a threatening, but essentially defensive, posture east of the river; third, to commit a limited Jordanian force to the battle in Syria, where it could operate under the umbrella of the Syrian Air Force and SAM batteries; or fourth, to take no active part in the war.

On October 8, when Damascus Radio was confidently reporting that the Syrian Army was about to drive the Israelis into Lake Tiberias, it is not unlikely that Hussein and his General Staff were seriously tempted to adopt the first of these alternatives. But there were several reasons for caution. In the first place, the Jordanians did not have a modern air defense system; they had no SAMs at all, and only a small force of light AA guns. In addition Jordan did not have any antitank guided missiles, and the first newspaper reports, even though somewhat confused and confusing, made it very clear that such missiles were playing a major role in the ongoing battles in the Sinai and on the Golan. The Jordan Air Force was small and outmoded; even a minor diversion of Israeli aircraft from the other fronts could eliminate that air force as quickly as it did in 1967. And the Jordan Army, while possibly the best trained of all of the Arab forces, was short of manpower, had no reservoir of trained reserves, and even its conventional weapons were obsolescent and in short supply.

Furthermore, the Jordanian Director of Intelligence, as early as October 8, detected evidence that the Syrian attack had failed, and that the Syrians were already on the defensive on much of the Golan front.

This situation was confirmed on October 9, and so Hussein rejected the first alternative—if he had ever seriously considered it.

However, to retain respect among the other Arab nations, and in particular to assure continuing postwar financial support from King Feisal of Saudi Arabia, Hussein knew that he had to take some action. He felt reasonably certain that the Israeli Government would understand his situation, and that, if Jordan took no direct action on the Jordan River front, there would be no Israeli reprisals if a small contingent of Jordanian troops were to take part in operations in Syria. Accordingly Hussein adopted a mild version of the second alternative—threatening but defensive posture east of the Jordan River—and the third—commitment of a small Jordan Army contingent in Syria. He sent his principal personal military advisor, retired Lieutenant General Amer Khammash, former Chief of Staff, to Cairo to inform President Sadat of his decision and the reasons for it.

The 40th Armored Brigade, under the command of Colonel Haj Houj al Majali, was prepared as an expeditionary force to Syria. This unit consisted of about 4,000 men and 150 Centurion tanks. The Syrian Government was informed of the Jordanian decision, and on October 12 agreed to the entry of the Jordanian unit into Syria. On October 13 the 40th Armored Brigade marched north through Ramtha across the frontier, continued on the Damascus Road through Deraa, and thence northwestward toward the front.

By evening of that day the Syrian front began to settle down. Following their early morning victory over the Iraqi 3d Armored Division, the Israelis probed cautiously northward, found the Syrians well dug-in in front of and east of Saassaa, and seem to have decided to call a halt to their counteroffensive. The Israelis say that they had gone far enough to teach the Syrians a lesson, while avoiding overexpansion or the danger of costly involvement in the suburbs of Damascus. The Syrians are convinced that it was the staunchness of their defense that halted the Israelis. In any event, while there were minor fluctuations of the line in the immediate vicinity of Saassaa in the next few days—as a result of limited probes and counterattacks by each side—fundamentally the lines had reached their final delineation.

The Israeli left flank was firmly anchored in the foothills of Mt. Hermon near Beit Jan and Mazrat Beit Jan. From there the front extended southwest across the Damascus Plain for almost 30 kilometers in an almost straight line, passing just north of Tel Shams and south of Saassaa, to the vicinity of Kfar Shams, where it turned sharply west for about 25 kilometers, to the Purple Line. There it abruptly turned south, and followed the old ceasefire line to the Yarmouk Valley.

Although the line had stabilized, this does not mean that a lull pervaded the front. The first important new development on the 13th was the landing of an Israeli helicopter-borne commando force approximately 95 kilometers northeast of Damascus. The Israelis blew up a bridge and ambushed an Iraqi convoy, then returned to their helicopters for the trip back to the Golan Heights.

Also that evening long range Israeli artillery fire began to fall on the Damascus Military Airport, just southeast of the city. These harassing rounds, which would continue intermittently for the next ten days, were fired from American-made 175mm guns.

The Israeli Air Force also kept up its long range bombardment campaign against Syrian air bases and industrial facilities. During these attacks, two large Soviet cargo planes were hit and either destroyed or badly damaged at the Damascus civil airport, north of the city.

On the 14th the Jordanian 40th Armored Brigade entered the front lines on the south face of the Israeli salient, just north of El Hara, between the Iraqi 3d Armored Division and the 9th Syrian Division, holding the left shoulder of the salient. Jordanian Colonel Majali (who was on that same day promoted to Brigadier) was placed under the command of the 3d Iraqi Division commander, Brigadier General Lafta.

On October 15 the Iraqi 3d Armored Division—holding the eastern portion of the Arab line opposite the southern face of the Israeli salient —was ordered by General Chakkour to plan for a major counterattack west of Kfar Shams early the following morning. General Lafta was told to include the Jordanian brigade in his counterattack plans. He was told that the right flank brigade of the 9th Division would join in the attack at H-Hour—5:00 a.m. on the 16th. The Israelis noted the Iraqi preparations, and at 4:00 p.m. on the 15th General Laner launched a limited spoiling attack against the Iraqis in a wide envelopment of their right flank, driving them off Tel Antar, and forcing them to withdraw about five kilometers.

As scheduled, the Jordanians, an attached Saudi Arabian contingent, and a Syrian brigade near Um Butne launched their attacks at 5:00 a.m. on the 16th, only to discover that the Iraqis were not taking part. The attackers failed to gain any ground, and by 9:00 a.m. withdrew after suffering moderate losses. The opposing Israelis were impressed, however, by Jordanian tactical and technical performance, evidencing higher professional standards than the Syrians or the Iraqis.

At about 10:00 a.m. the Iraqis belatedly began their counterattack, and were stopped immediately by the waiting Israelis. A few hours later the Jordanian 40th Brigade was detached from the Iraqi Division, and placed under the Syrian 9th Division on its left. This created problems, however, since Brigadier Majali, the Jordanian commander, was senior in rank to Colonel Hassan Tourkmani, commanding the 9th Division. A general officer was rushed down from Damascus to act as liaison officer, and to transmit Colonel Tourkmani's orders to Brigadier Majali.

On October 17 and 18, for the first time since the war began, there was a lull all along the Syrian front. There was considerable artillery fire—mostly harassment and counterbattery—and some exchanges of tank fire, as well as patrol activity, but no significant maneuver effort by either side. Further north and east, however, the Israeli Air Force kept up its pressure on Syrian rear installations, seaports, and industrial plants. Syrian planes also struck at Ramat Magshimim and Gadat in upper Galilee, and at positions near the Druze village of Majdal Shams on the Golan.

The Israelis took advantage of this lull to send General Peled's rested division to relieve General Laner's tired troops on the eastern and southern faces of the Saassaa salient. Laner's troops moved back into Peled's old positions on the now quiet Purple Line. General Eitan's division remained in the bulge, however, holding the northeastern portion, and preparing for a renewed effort to assault Mt. Hermon to the north. Several battalions from all three divisions began to be shifted south to the Sinai front.

On the 19th the Syrian front again erupted into considerable activity with a series of Arab counterattacks. The principal Arab effort was against the south face of the Israeli salient, with Iraqi, Jordanian, and Syrian forces all taking part. There was little coordination, however, between these individual attacks, and the Israelis had little trouble in beating them back—despite the fact that some units had been pulled out to go to the Sinai front. Late the previous day the Israelis had occupied Um Butne; during this day of fighting they consolidated their hold on the town.

By October 20, with a lull over the battlefield, the Syrians believed that they were in a position to recover the initiative from the Israelis. They had substantially reequipped the divisions and brigades that had lost so heavily in the first four days of fighting, and had a firm ring around the Israeli Saassaa salient. The Moroccan Brigade and in independent brigade held the northern side of the salient, in the Mt. Hermon foothills. The 3d Division was firmly in control of the Saassaa line east of the salient, and an independent armored brigade held the southeast corner. On the south of the Israeli salient, from east to west, were the 3d Iraqi Division, the 40th Jordanian Brigade, and the 9th Syrian Division, which held the corner where the salient came back to the Purple Line. The 5th Division held the remainder of the Purple Line down to the Yarmouk Valley. To the right rear of the 3d Division were the reorganized and reequipped 7th Infantry Division and two independent armored brigades, in reserve and blocking the road to Damascus. Southwest of the 3d Division was the 1st Armored Division, providing both a reserve force and a potential second echelon for a counteroffensive which the Syrians were now planning.

Contributing to the Syrian confidence that they could regain the initiative was their realization that the Israelis had sent a number of battalions south to the Suez front, and had few reserves left in Israel to cope with a major Syrian success. At the same time another Iraqi division was on its way to join the northern battle, and contingents from several other Arab countries had arrived, with more due to come. It was this situation which had prompted the confident tone of President Assad in his communications with President Sadat.

The Syrian offensive was originally scheduled to begin on the 21st, and to be spearheaded by the 3d Iraqi Armored Division and the 40th Jordanian Armored Brigade. Once a breakthrough was acheived, the 1st Armored Division was to exploit northwestward toward the Kuneitra-Damascus Road, to cut the communications of the Israelis in front of Saassaa.

On the afternoon of the 20th, however, the Iraqis reported that they were not ready for an attack the following morning, so the offensive was postponed until the 22d. Nevertheless activity intensified that day as both sides began to try to improve their positions prior to an expected ceasefire. The major action that day took place on the flank of Mt. Hermon, but fighting was also heavy in the vicinity of Saassaa, where the Syrians attempted to push the Israelis back, unsuccessfully. Later that day, when it became clear that the ceasefire would go into effect the next day, General Chakkour called off the planned offensive.

On Mt. Hermon the Israeli Golani Brigade attempted to retake the former Israeli OP in a combined ground and helicopter assault. The effort failed, however. At about 4:00 p.m., as the Israelis were pulling back, they were hit by Syrian fighter bombers. Immediately, waiting Israeli fighters swept in to meet the attackers, and a spectacular air battle took place over Mt. Hermon.

After the Israelis withdrew, the Syrians carried out a well calculated helicopter reinforcement and resupply operation for the Syrian paratroop units which had been engaged by the Golanis on Mt. Hermon. By the time the Israeli Air Force reacted, the helicopters had moved in and flown out, and the Syrian fighters were waiting for the Israelis, leading to another late afternoon air battle over the mountain. There were losses on both sides in these dog fights, but the Israelis had somewhat the better of both.

On October 22 the Israelis made another attempt to retake their Mt. Hermon position. This was a larger and better planned attack, involving not only the Golanis, in another combined ground and helicopter assault, but also an airdrop of most of the 31st Paratroop Brigade.

While the Golanis focussed their efforts against the former Israeli OP, the paratroopers made a surprise drop beside the Syrian OP, higher up on the ridge, and close to the summit of Mt. Hermon. The Syrians, recognizing that their summit OP was about to fall, attempted a heliborne counterattack against the Israeli paratroopers. However, after three large Syrian helicopters—each capable of carrying 30 soldiers—were shot down, they called off the effort.

The Israeli paratroopers then quickly overran and secured the Syrian OP, and began to move down the ridge to assist the Golanis. By this time it was dark, and long after the time for the scheduled ceasefire—6:52 p.m.[1] The Israelis claim that Syria had not yet agreed to a ceasefire, and that they (the Israelis) were under no obligation to adhere to the ceasefire on this front. The Syrians respond that the ceasefire had been imposed by the UN, and that they were complying with it; the record suggests, however, that their official acceptance of the ceasefire did not reach New York until next day. In any event, the paratroopers discovered that the Golani units, on the ground and by helicopter, had surrounded their former OP and were beginning a final assault. This assault was successful. Between 7:30 and 8:00 p.m. the Israelis secured their old OP.

Both sides ceased further ground activity, lending credence to the Syrian position on this issue. However, artillery fire continued from both sides during the night and throughout October 23, as both received radio reports of continuing intensive combat on the Suez Canal front. After dark on the 23d the artillery fire began to slow down. Before midnight the front was completely quiet.

Thus, active combat operations on the Syrian front came to a close with the Israelis not only having recovered everything they had lost during the war, but also controlling a large additional portion of Mt. Hermon, as well as the Saassaa salient on the plain below.

COMPARATIVE ARAB PERFORMANCE

The performance of the Iraqis on the Syrian front is not given very high marks by any of the other three major participants: Israelis, Syrians, or Jordanians. The Syrians, for instance, note that the total number of Iraqis killed in action was only 278, and suggest that this was indicative of a less-than-all-out effort. Yet that figure of 278 dead translates into about 0.23% of committed strength per day of action, which is not terribly much lower than the Syrian figure of 0.29% per day, and is substantially higher than the Jordanian daily figure of 0.08%. An overall comparison of the casualty rates of the three major Arab forces on the Syrian front is interesting:

[1] In his book, Dayan confuses the Israeli efforts of October 21 and 22 against Mt. Hermon, merging them into one operation that he says was concluded by noon of October 22. *Op. cit.*, p. 441.

	Approximate ground force committed	Days of Operation	Killed		Total Casualties	
			Number	%/day	Number	%/day
Syrian	60,000	17	3,100	0.29	9,600	0.94
Iraqi	12,000	10	278	0.23	898	0.74
Jordanian ...	4,000	8	23	0.08	77	0.24

Thus, while there seems little doubt that the Iraqis were professionally less proficient than the Syrians (and therefore with a comparable level of effort would have been expected to have a higher casualty rate), their effort as evidenced by casualty rates was not disgracefully low. The generally-acknowledged professional superiority of the Jordanians would be expected to keep their casualty rates relatively lower than those of Syrians and Iraqis; however, their actual rates seem to have been so low as to confirm the postwar assessment of Israeli General Dan Laner, who gave the Jordanians high marks for professional competence, but low marks for effort.

Also, to the credit of the Iraqis was their rapid march from Iraq, across the Arabian Desert and through Jordan, to have their leading brigade arrive on the battlefield late on October 12. This was a highly creditable performance. And while they may not have been as combat effective as the Syrians, simply by occupying a substantial part of the line south of the Israelis' Saassaa salient, they permitted the Syrians to establish a solid defense, and also to release units for reserve.

On the basis of comparison of postwar observations of Israelis, Syrians, and Jordanians it is evident that the professional competence of other Arab contingents—such as Moroccans and Saudi Arabians—was less than that of Jordanians, Syrians, and Iraqis, and that none of them fought with a determination to match that of the Syrians.

17

The Battle for Suez,
October 23-25

THE ISRAELI DRIVE TO THE SUEZ GULF

Although Adan and Magen had secured the Geneifa Hills, and the area north of Deversoir, the intermingling of General Adan's units with those of the Egyptian 4th Armored and 6th Mechanized Divisions and a variety of Third Army rear area units made a fully-effective ceasefire impossible in the green belt between Kabrit and Shallufa.[1] Any effort by either side to establish contact with nearby friendly units was bound to be interpreted as a hostile action by an equally nearby foe. And yet both sides were under great compulsion to consolidate, as higher commanders tried to find out where their units were, and what condition they were in. Almost invariably, a chance encounter of opposing patrols would lead first to an expanding firefight, then to appeals for artillery support. There was little cessation of fire west of Shallufa the night of October 22-23.

Thus, if either side wished an excuse to blame a ceasefire violation on the other, it did not have to seek hard. The Israelis were anxious for such an excuse, since they had not yet succeeded in cutting off the Egyptian Third Army, the major objective of their southward drive from the bridgehead. In fact, they had not even secured a foothold on the Canal south of the Little Bitter Lake. Thus, sometime after the ceasefire went into effect, General Adan received an order from Southern Command which, in effect, authorized him to continue the offensive the following day.

The directive to Adan seems to have stated, very simply, that if the ceasefire was observed by the enemy, he was to observe it also. If there was no ceasefire, he was to continue with his mission. Apparently Magen got identical or similar orders.

---

[1] This and subsequent paragraphs reflect the author's effort to describe facts obscured by totally irreconcilable reports and comments from official and unofficial Egyptian and Israeli sources. Dayan (*op. cit.*, p. 441) clearly misrepresents what happened.

There was, of course, no ceasefire; so Adan pressed ahead without further orders or inquiry. His mission and Magen's was still to encircle the Third Army. Following the original plan, and closely coordinating their operations for the 23rd, Adan was to capture Suez, or isolate it, and push to the shores of the Gulf of Suez just south of the city. At the same time, to give depth to the encirclement, Magen was to continue on Adan's right, and to pass through the western portion of Adan's sector, his objective the village of Adabiya, at Ras (Point) Adabiya, about ten kilometers southwest of Suez, on the Gulf.

Adan decided that he had two major tasks. Obviously the first priority was for a thrust to Suez, either southeast along the Sarag Road, or south through the green belt along the Havit Road. At the same time, for reasons of security and logistical support, it was essential to clear the Havit Road and the green belt between Fayid and Shallufa. In fact, until this area was cleared, Adan felt that he could not concentrate sufficient force for a full-scale drive toward Suez.

During the night Adan received infantry reinforcements from other divisions, mostly from the Syrian front, rushed to him by helicopter and busses. However, he received no more military vehicles, either trucks, halftracks, or armored fighting vehicles. But he had captured a number of Egyptian APCs, which he assembled north of Shallufa. He combined the two battalions he had received a few days earlier with the new arrivals into a provisional brigade, under his second in command, General Dovic Tamari, and gave them the captured APCs. This gave him three armored brigades and a makeshift infantry brigade of five or six battalions.

By this time Adan's engineer battalion had cleared the Test Road as far south as Kabrit. To avoid dispersion of his forces, Adan decided that early on the 23rd he would concentrate all four of his brigades in clearing the Shallufa-Kabrit area, since he believed that this would facilitate a subsequent drive on Suez that afternoon with most of his division. At dawn on the 23d Adan's four brigades began to clear out their respective zones south of Kabrit. However, the terrain was difficult, and Egyptian resistance was tenacious; progress was slow in all brigade sectors. By noon Adan came to the conclusion that another ceasefire might be imposed by the UN or the superpowers before he had captured or isolated Suez. Accordingly, he left Baram's and Tamari's brigades to continue the mop-up operation north of Shallufa, and sent his other two armored brigades directly south toward Suez, with Amir on the right, west of the Havit Road, and Karen to the left, between the road and the Sweetwater Canal.

Employing the same kind of "charge" tactics that had been successful on the previous days, these two brigades fought their way through and around grim Egyptian defenders, to approach Suez. By dark after extremely hard fighting, both brigades had reached the outskirts of the city, and one battalion of Amir's brigade had pushed southwest of the town to reach the Gulf of Suez at the old oil refinery. Thus Suez was completely isolated from contact with Egypt to the west—and with Suez isolated, so too was most of the Egyptian Third Army.

Actually Amir's push across the Sarag Road just west of Suez was simply placing a double lock on the isolated Egyptians. About the same time the leading elements of Magen's division had stormed across the road a few kilometers farther west. A heliborne paratroop unit also seized an Egyptian electronic monitoring station in the northeast portion of Jebel Ataka.

With another ceasefire scheduled for the morning of the 24th, Brigadier General Dani Shomron, leading the 17 remaining tanks of Magen's leading armored brigade, was also making a traditional Israeli tank "charge" just west of Jebel Ataka with headlights on. His vehicles passed close to Amir's brigade, and reached Ras Adabiya and the shore of the Gulf of Suez just after midnight. Early the next morning, after a stiff fight, Shomron occupied most of Adabiya, while the rest of Magen's dangerously extended division was linking up with the paratroopers on Jebel Ataka, and blocking the Sarag Road near Kilometer 101, to stop Egyptian reinforcements pushing down the road from Cairo. The Israelis consolidated their newly-won positions as UNTSO observers arrived on the scene.

REPULSE AT SUEZ

The second ceasefire directed by the UN Security Council was to go into effect at 7:00 a.m. on the 24th. About 2:00 in the morning Adan received a radio call from Gonen, who asked if he could occupy Suez in the period of about two and a half hours between dawn and the ceasefire. Adan responded that this depended upon how many Egyptians were in the town, and how hard they fought. He thought, however, that he should be able to seize at least a portion of the town. Gonen hesitated a moment, then said: "Okay, if it's Beersheba, go ahead; if it's Stalingrad, don't do it!"[2] In other words, if the town could be taken as easily as Beersheba, in October 1948, Gonen approved the attack. If, however, Adan ran into resistance such as the Germans had encountered at Stalingrad, in 1942, then he should halt the attack. Adan accordingly gave his orders.

Amir's brigade would enter Suez from the west and southwest, and push into the center of the city. Karen would enter from the north and northwest, with his main effort on his right, along the Cairo Boulevard terminus of the Sarag Road; his converging drives would meet those of

[2] Interviews by the author with Generals Gonen and Adan.

Amir near the center of the city. To secure the town after it had been overrun by the tankers, two composite battalions of paratroopers and infantry, from Tamari's brigade, would follow Karen's rightmost battalion down the boulevard. The attack was to be preceded by a heavy artillery bombardment, followed by an air strike. Meanwhile Baram and the remainder of Tamari's brigade would continue the cleanup effort in the green belt between Suez and Shallufa.

About 5:00 a.m., as his artillery preparation was crashing into Suez, Adan received a call from Southern Command, ordering him to dispense with the rest of the artillery preparation and the planned air strike, and to move into Suez without delay. Even so, it is obvious that the attack did not begin until the second ceasefire was already supposed to be in effect.

Since up to this point there had been no evidence of any strong defensive determination on the part of the Egyptians, the Israelis did not expect much trouble, and presumably hoped to consolidate the city before the arrival of UNTSO observers. However, as the tanks moved into the city the Israelis found themselves under increasingly heavy fire. Ominously, also, the proportion of Saggers and RPG-7s was greater than they had been up to this time west of the Canal. Obviously their opponents included some elements of the 19th Division, shifted back west of the Canal with their antitank weapons to defend Suez.

Then another problem became evident. The infantry units had had no prewar training together, or with the tanks, and their past few days of combat experience had not prepared them for the kind of battle they found themselves in. They soon got held up behind the tanks, and in a few minutes realized that they were surrounded by Egyptians, who had plentiful artillery support from the east bank. The two battalions broke up into several company-size contingents, and they took up defensive positions in small perimeters in the apartment house area in the northwest corner of the town.

WITHDRAWAL FROM SUEZ

Meanwhile, despite heavy and effective Egyptian fire, elements of both Karen's and Amir's brigades had fought their way to the center of town, where they met in the early afternoon. Adan, keeping close touch with the operation by radio, decided that it would entail catastrophic losses if Karen's units in the center of the town were to try to retrace their steps to the northern edge of the city. He ordered Karen to have those units—about a battalion in strength—follow Amir out through the southwest portion of the city and the oil refinery.

Adan, meanwhile, had been trying to relieve the infantry surrounded in the northwestern portion of the city. He found, however, that Baram was also running into very intensive resistance in the green belt north of Suez, and could spare only one battalion. With this battalion and another battalion from Tamari's brigade, Adan spent most of the afternoon trying to extract the isolated infantry units from the town. By dark two contingents still remained in Suez. One of these, carrying a wounded battalion commander, followed Adan's advice, and slipped out of its perimeter and past the Egyptians in the dark.

The other contingent, more than a company in strength, was commanded by a young lieutenant who didn't know where he was and who was reluctant to leave the false security of the building walls despite all of Adan's urging.

Gonen, listening from his command post to the communications between this young officer and Adan, broke into the conversation. Revealing a side to his complex nature that few of his subordinates had ever before seen, Gonen calmly asked the lieutenant to describe the building he was in, and all nearby buildings. As the young officer responded, Gonen carried his handset over to a large-scale air photo of Suez, on the command post wall. Soon Gonen thought he had identified the building, and after the exchange of a few more questions and answers, he was certain of the identification.

The Southern Command commander quietly and soothingly described the situation to the lieutenant, assuring him that he had definitely identified his location on the air photomap. He then suggested that there was a nearby alley that was not likely to be blocked by the Egyptians. He recommended that the lieutenant lead his men to safety along that route, using of course all standard security precautions. He assured the lieutenant that he would keep contact by radio and guide him out of his predicament.

It worked! The lieutenant, having this personal, man-to-man attention from his theater commander, recovered his self-control and some confidence in himself, as well as in Gonen. Following the general's advice, and bolstered by a constant stream of radioed instructions, the young officer led more than 100 men out of the trap, and back to the safety of Karen's lines.

The Israelis made two more probes into Suez, one on the 25th and again on the 28th. Both times they were repulsed. By the 28th the United Nations observers were beginning to take up positions along the front west of Suez, along the line that Magen had established roughly from the center of Jebel Ataka north, across the Sarag Road near kilometer marker 101, and, continuing north, just west of the Vadaut Road, to the Nile Canal southwest of Ismailia. There were still frequent exchanges of artillery, infantry, and tank fire along that perimeter.

Inside the perimeter a wild and confused conflict was taking place.

The Israelis had bypassed many Egyptian units, and there were probably as many Egyptian soldiers within the Israeli perimeter as there were Israelis. On the 25th and 26th some of these Egyptian units fought their way out, particularly during the hours of darkness. But many surrendered with little or no resistance, and by October 27 the Israelis had captured about 8,000 Egyptian troops, most of them from logistical units.

PLIGHT OF THE THIRD ARMY

By this time the question uppermost in the minds of the Egyptian and Israeli High Commands was the plight of the Egyptian Third Army, completely isolated east of the Canal, except for its small—but equally isolated—bridgehead in Suez.

At this time the elements of the Third Army under siege were the 7th Infantry Division, commanded by Brigadier General Ahmad Badawy, holding the northern portion of the east bank bridgehead, and the 19th Infantry Division, commanded by Brigadier General Yussef Afifi, holding the southern half of the bridgehead, and also responsible for the city of Suez. Also in the bridgehead were two independent tank brigades, and miscellaneous other units. North of the main bridgehead an isolated force, about a battalion in strength, occupied the former Israeli stronghold of Botzer on the northeast shore of the Little Bitter Lake opposite Kabrit. In Suez there was a mixture of units, some from the 19th Division, some from the 4th Armored Division, some from the 6th Mechanized Division, and a number of rear area units, driven back into the city by Adan's advance on the 22d and 23d. All in all, the isolated force comprised about 40,000 troops.

One brigade of the 4th Armored Division had also been in the bridgehead, but this was ordered back across the Canal by Major General Mohommed Abd el Moneim Wassel, the Third Army Commander, on October 22. This brigade fought stubbornly in opposition to the Israeli drive south of the Geneifa Hills until, greatly reduced in strength, it fell back along the Cairo Road past Kilometer 101.

The Israeli thrust had severed communications between the bridgehead and the Third Army commander, General Wassel, who now had about the equivalent of two divisions on the west bank under his direct control. Following provisions of a planning contingency which the Egyptians had never expected to eventuate, General Badawy, commanding the 7th Division, had assumed command of the isolated portion of the Third Army as soon as the isolation became effective. Badawy's command was soon confirmed by radio order.

The Israelis were determined to cut off all supplies and reinforcements to the isolated portion of the Third Army, to force it to surrender. This eventuality, of course, would more than make up for the initial Israeli defeats and losses in the early days of the war. If the Third Army (meaning the portion of it commanded by General Badawy) did not surrender, or if it broke the tenuous ceasefire by trying to fight its way out of its trap, the Israelis were prepared to mount an all-out offensive to destroy the isolated Egyptians. In anticipation of such a resumption of hostilities, on October 28 General Adan was ordered to shift his division back to the east bank of the Canal, to make the main effort in a concentrated drive to smash the Third Army. In any event, the Israelis expected that without supplies the Third Army would collapse, or surrender, or offer itself for destruction within a few days after the ceasefire.

Strangely enough the United States and Soviet Governments not only had reached similar assessments of the threat to the Third Army, they also had a common—although not yet agreed—desire that this eventuality be avoided if at all possible. From the Soviet standpoint, it would mean a clearcut defeat for a client who had otherwise achieved a virtual military standoff with Israel. Russian prestige would suffer if Egypt, armed with Soviet weapons and equipment, were again to suffer a decisive military defeat.

Secretary of State Kissinger had quite different reasons for wanting the Third Army to survive. He saw the war (as did the Russians) as more or less a standoff, except for the Third Army situation. The Egyptians had been successful in the early stages of the war, the Israelis in the latter stage. But the Israeli success had not caused the Egyptians to abandon any of their early conquests east of the Canal, and these conquests more-or-less offset those of the Israelis west of the Canal. Thus the Egyptians could be proud of their accomplishments; they had wiped out the stigma of their 1967 defeat, they could possibly be prevailed upon to come to the bargaining table as equals, not inferiors, of the Israelis. To Kissinger this meant an opportunity for peace that must not be allowed to disappear. But it would disappear if the Third Army surrendered.

THE THIRD ARMY DIGS IN

The Egyptian Government, deeply concerned about the plight of the Third Army, had more confidence than the observing superpowers that neither collapse nor surrender was inevitable. In the first place, they believed that on the defense Egyptians were better than Israelis. And despite the failure of their defense against the thrusts of Adan and Magen west of the Canal, there was considerable evidence to support their confidence in their defensive capability. The units opposing Adan's drive up to October 23 were mostly rear-area units, and the combat elements were short of Saggers and RPG-7s; most of these had been transferred to the five infantry assault divisions which made the initial crossings. Second, the successful defense of the cities of Ismailia and Suez had helped retain or restore Egyptian self-confidence in the defense. Ismail also had confidence in Badawy, the acting Third Army commander east of the Canal—and, although Ismail didn't know it, the Israelis had also come to respect him as the ablest of the division commanders they had opposed.

Finally, the disruption created by the original Israeli breakout had disappeared, and the Israeli west bank salient was encircled by approximately five Egyptian divisions. The Egyptian line of encirclement was thin; but if the Israelis were to concentrate enough strength on the east bank to make a strong assault on the Third Army, their defensive line on the west bank would be far thinner. After Adan had moved back to the east bank, there were only two Israeli divisions deployed on the west bank. A major Israeli assault against the Third Army would have been countered by a major Egyptian assault against the Israeli salient, and the Egyptians believed (somewhat optimistically) they could punch through to Suez, and reopen communications to Badawy's command.

The one serious problem for Badawy's Third Army was supply, with three items crucial: ammunition, water, and food. Still there was a good reserve of food, there was considerable ammunition, and some water lines from wells in Suez were still available. Nevertheless, the supply problem was acute and was Ismail's most serious concern as he considered the future of the Third Army.

Meanwhile, on the east bank, and in Suez, Badawy and his men girded themselves for a struggle. Morale was heightened by the success of the Kabrit-Botzer enclave in repulsing repeated Israeli attacks between October 20 and 23. Entrenchments were deepened, antitank ditches were widened, heavier cover was thrown up on dugouts. And an intermittent night supply route across the upper Suez Gulf was opened.

In retrospect, it is clear that the position of the Third Army was nowhere near as vulnerable as the Israelis, Americans, and Russians believed. On balance, however, if the war had continued, or been renewed, and lasted for another week, it is likely that the combination of Israeli superiority in armored mobile warfare and their overwhelming air superiority would have overcome Badawy's command.

ON THE EAST BANK

Although the attention of both the Egyptian and the Israeli armies had been focused on the west bank of the Suez Canal, there had been no cessation of activity on the east bank.

In the north General Sassoon's division was responsible for the entire area from the Talisman Road north to the Mediterranean. He was able to reestablish permanent communications with Budapest, which was never again seriously threatened. There was constant patrol activity by both sides along the entire front south of the marshes, but neither made a serious attack in larger than battalion strength.

From Akavish Road to the southern approaches to the Mitla Pass a new division took over about October 15 when Magen's division prepared to move into the corridor. The commander was Brigadier General Granit Yisrael, the commander of Granit Force in the 1967 War. Almost immediately, however, he received word that his son had been killed on the Golan Front, and was given leave to be with his family in a time of sorrow. The new commander of the southern division was Brigadier General Menachim Meron, who retained the command until the end of the war. As in the north, this division was constantly active but neither undertook any major operations nor was subjected to a significant attack.

18

The Air and Air Defense War

Unquestionably the aspect of the 1973 October War which was most surprising not only to observers from other nations, but also to the Israeli participants, was the fact that—unlike the situation in the 1967 war—the Israel Air Force did not dominate the skies over the battlefield; conventional air superiority, as it had been known for half a century, was suddenly meaningless. This, of course, was due to the effective air defense umbrella which Russian-made surface-to-air missiles—SAMs— placed over the Egyptian and Syrian armies.

This does not mean that air operations were called off, or that this new development rendered airpower either impotent or unimportant. It did mean that from October 6, 1973, forward, the combat roles of air-power and of combat aircraft would be markedly different, and could be considered in the calculus of war only in relation to surface-based means of air defense.

EGYPTIAN AIR RECOVERY EFFORTS

After the disastrous destruction of Arab airpower in the opening hours of the June 1967 war, all of the Arab states in general, and Egypt in particular, had exerted extraordinary efforts to rebuild their air forces. For the Egyptians, Syrians, and Iraqis, this rebuilding process was done with assistance from the Soviet Union. For impecunious Jordan the re-building was more modest, and done with American (and some British) support.

The Egyptian Air Force, for instance, undertook a number of simul-taneous, parallel measures to rebuild and to recover. Pilot training both in the Soviet Union and in Egypt seems to have been the highest priority requirement, since on June 5, 1967, nearly one third of Egypt's trained pilots had been killed on or close to the ground when their aircraft were destroyed. Next, of course, was the procurement of aircraft from the Soviet Union—MiG-17s, Su-7s, MiG-21s, and, although reports are con-flicting, shortly before the war a few MiG-23s may have been delivered. There were also light and medium bombers: Il-28s and Tu-16s.

Hardly less important were measures to assure that the new planes would not be caught in any future surprise attack, and again destroyed on their airfields. One important aspect of the 1967 catastrophe was that while quite a few of the aircraft had survived the first wave of Israeli attacks, when the pilots of these planes had tried to get in the air to meet the subsequent strikes, they had been delayed, or unable to take off, because bomb craters had seriously damaged the runways; thus many of the planes and their pilots had become sitting ducks for the returning Israelis, and others were hit as they took off.

Thus the Egyptians built individual aircraft shelters for each plane, protecting the craft from anything short of a direct hit by a major bomb with a delayed action fuze. Similar shelters were built to protect operations centers and key ground installations. At the same time, several new runways were prepared for each Egyptian airbase. In some instances, where feasible, nearby roads were straightened and widened to serve as alternate runways; the alert traveler can see examples of this in the Nile Delta, on the main Cairo-Alexandria road. Additional air bases were also built, so that 35 were operational by late 1973.

Then came the process of rebuilding the confidence of the Air Force in general, and the pilots in particular, in their ability to engage the Israelis in the air. While considerable progress was made in this direction during the War of Attrition, 1968-1970, this effort was never completely successful, for several reasons. In the first place, the Israelis were not standing still, allowing the Egyptians to catch up with them. Israeli efforts to improve readiness, improve techniques, improve the fighting capabilities of their aircraft, and, above all, to improve the combat proficiency of their pilots, were just as intensive as those of the Arabs. The Israeli head start was so great that by 1973 there was little appreciable progress in closing the gap.[1] Furthermore, in addition to the skill and proficiency of the pilots was the fact that the Israeli's American- and French-made aircraft were bigger, sturdier, and more combat worthy than the lighter Russian aircraft, and the generally American-made Israeli weapons—air-to-air and air-to-surface—were more accurate and more powerful than those which the Soviets provided the Arabs.

Thus, the fact that Egyptian pilots regularly took to the air against the Israelis was a tribute to the leadership of the Egyptian Air Force, and to the gallantry and courage of the pilots. But the Egyptians did not try to deceive themselves—even though they may have tried to deceive others. General Mohommed Hosny Moubarak, Commander in Chief of the Egyptian Air Force, recognized that in 1973 the Israelis maintained a substantial superiority over the Egyptians in the air—even though the Egyptians had more planes. The Egyptians devised their strategy and tactics accordingly. Strategically, Ismail relied upon the

[1] See discussion p. 598 and Appendix B, p. 630.

Soviet-built air defense weapons to provide air cover for the ground forces against direct Israeli attack, thus leaving most of the Air Force free for missions in which Egyptian air inferiority would not be so marked or so serious.

Tactically, of course, Moubarak relied primarily upon hit-and-run air strikes, which would catch the Israelis unaware, while powerful air cover fighters overhead could engage the Israelis at a disadvantage, if they did have time to scramble to meet such a raid.

ISRAEL AIR FORCE PREPARATIONS

In the years after the Six Day War, the Israelis not only maintained their exceedingly high standards of training, performance, and maintenance, they reequipped their Air Force very largely with American planes. Up to 1967 the main high-performance aircraft of the Israel Air Force were French. But as a result of that war, French President de Gaulle shifted from support of Israel to sympathy for the Arabs, and stopped French armament sales to all participants in the 1967 war—which really only affected Israel. The Israelis, therefore, turned to the United States to acquire modern, sophisticated aircraft. They were able to get substantial numbers of rugged, fast, dependable A-4 fighter-bombers, particularly effective in the ground attack role, and also of F-4 fighter-bombers, probably at that time the most effective fighter plane and fighter-bomber in the world. They still had, of course, the French-made Super Mystères and Mirages, only slightly older and with air combat performance only marginally inferior to the F-4. For numerical comparisons of the respective air forces, see Table A, and for a qualitative comparison of the aircraft, see Table B (pages 606-607).

In several significant qualitative respects the Israelis maintained, or even increased, their edge over the Arabs. One of these areas of Israeli superiority was in aircraft maintenance. As a result the Israelis were able to achieve—in peace or combat circumstances—a higher in-commission rate of aircraft, were able to repair battle damage more rapidly, and in particular had a much higher turn-around rate for aircraft and pilots between missions. Thus, although the Arabs had more aircraft on hand at the outset of the war, in terms of available combat aircraft sorties per day, the Israelis actually had a quantitative superiority.

PERFORMANCE COMPARISONS

The Israel Air Force has not provided official figures on sorties flown, but it has reported casualties and a per sortie loss rate which indicate that approximately 10,500 sorties were flown. This is close to a theoretical maximum figure of about 11,000 sorties calculated on the assumptions of an 80% in-commission rate and a turn-around rate permitting four sorties per day for most missions. Of the sorties flown, about one half appear to have been air defense and long-range interdiction, one half close support.

Even less statistical information is available on Arab air operations. The available reports and comments indicate that the Arab in-commission rate was certainly lower than that of the Israelis, and probably about 65%. It is also clear that the normal sortie rate was about one per aircraft per day, although the Egyptians claim to have done better than that. The Egyptians have semiofficially reported[2] that they had 6,815 operational sorties during the war. Since the Syrians probably flew less than half as many, it is estimated that Arab aircraft flew fewer than 10,000 sorties during the war, about equally divided between defense and offense.

Newspaper accounts of the October War have emphasized the effectiveness of the Arab air defense umbrellas on both the Syrian and Egyptian fronts. Little notice has been given, however, to the fact that the Israelis supplemented the air-intercept efficiency of their Air Force with highly effective air defense weapons. Assessment of both Israeli and Egyptian comments about the American-made Hawk missiles —the SAM which the Israelis used to protect their key airfields and installations, particularly in the Sinai—suggests that these weapons had a hit and kill capability at least as high as any of the Arabs' Soviet-made SAMs, and were probably even more accurate. Also, the light, self-propelled Israeli multiple-mount 40mm antiaircraft guns provided very effective protection for the ground combat units.

THE ISRAELIS' FIRST-DAY PERFORMANCE

Possibly the most serious criticism of the Israel Air Force has been directed at its apparently slow and piecemeal commitment on the afternoon of October 6. It is known, for instance, that General Elazar, the Chief of Staff of the IDF, and Major General Benjamin Peled, commander of the IAF, both urged the use of the Israel Air Force in preemptive strikes against Egypt and Syria on the morning of October 6, as soon as the Israelis were convinced that war would break out that day. Why, it may be asked, if the Israelis were prepared to launch such a massive strike in the morning, did it take about 20 minutes for the first planes to react to the Arab offensive in the afternoon? Why was the Israeli effort a small-scale, uncoordinated series of ineffective, quite costly attacks? Why were so many lucrative targets—particularly on the Golan front—not taken under attack? If the Israelis could have mounted a massive preemptive strike, why could they not have mounted an

---

[2] Interview of author with Egyptian Major Generals Hassan el Badri and M.D. Zohdy; this figure appears in their *War of Ramadan,* Cairo, 1974.

equally massive counterblow within a few moments of the outbreak of the war?

There are several reasonable answers to these questions.

In the first place, anticipating the possibility of the preemptive strike, practically all of the fighter-bombers of the IAF—excepting a handful of air defense aircraft assigned to the protection of key installations—were armed for strikes against airfields, electronic installations, and SAM sites. When Prime Minister Golda Meir disapproved the Elazar-Peled recommendation, the IAF proceeded to get itself ready for a quick response to the expected Arab attack, with primary emphasis on ground support activities. The Israeli intelligence had assured the high command that this attack would come at 6:00 p.m. At 2:05 p.m., therefore, except for the air defense crews and aircraft, the entire IAF was in the process of shifting its readiness from one type of combat to an entirely different type, which would require different armament on most aircraft. At the same time, the pilots and ground crews had geared themselves to a 6:00 p.m. H-Hour. Like everyone else in Israel, they were caught flat-footed. This accounts largely for the slow reaction time, and partially for the relatively ineffective effort mounted that day.

The ineffectiveness, however, was in some measure the product of still another surprise shock. As the fighter-bombers were rushed to readiness and thrown into the battle, their pilots encountered a situation not unlike that which was creating confusion and causing high casualties among Israeli tank crews on the ground. Although the Israelis were well aware of the Arab SAM capabilities, they were completely surprised by the effectiveness of these weapons. A very high proportion of the first aircraft committed were either shot down or damaged by SA-2s, SA-3s, SA-6s, or ZSU-23-4s; a few were shot down or severely damaged by SA-7s.

Suddenly General Peled and his staff realized that they were incurring a totally unacceptable level of attrition. Egyptian sources claim that at 5:00 p.m. their monitors of the Israeli air command channels heard urgent radio orders issued in the clear, directing that pilots not approach closer than 15 kilometers from the old ceasefire lines (the Suez Canal and the Purple Line) until further instructions. And so, to the surprise of UN observers on the Golan Heights, the bumper-to-bumper columns of Syrian tanks, trucks, and miscellaneous armored vehicles were left totally untouched.

THE ISRAELI COUNTER-SAM EFFORT

During the next two or three days the Israel Air Force devoted frantic efforts to tactical and technical experimentation to cope with this totally unexpected situation. And in the process Israeli aircraft did begin to fly close support missions and to attack Arab airfields and lines of communications just behind the front lines—including the Egyptian bridges over the Suez Canal. But—except for truly sacrificial flights to slow down and help stop the Syrian breakthrough on the Southern Golan—these Israeli air attacks were made much more cautiously, and generally from considerably higher altitudes than had been the past practice. And so, while Israeli air casualties markedly declined because of longer ranges and more opportunity for evasive action, their air strikes were far less effective than in 1967. For instance, the Israelis claimed that they struck several of the Egyptian bridges over the Canal; the Egyptians say there was not one hit by Israeli aircraft, although they do admit some hits by Israeli long range artillery.

As earlier noted, an important element of the technical response to the SAM problem was the employment of chaff to "fox" the Egyptian radars. At the same time the Israelis were seeking tactical means of eluding the Arab SAMs by various kinds of evasive action. They had become quite expert at such tactics in the War of Attrition, but at that time they were not encountering such massive numbers of SAMs. Now they discovered that evasive action against one observed SA-2 or SA-3 would permit one or more others to lock on, with assured destruction the result. Furthermore, the tactics which had been effective against relatively slow SA-2s and SA-3s were not effective against the far faster and more deadly SA-6s. Experiments with helicopter spotters, also noted earlier, were not very successful.

Although the IAF was able to reduce its losses at the hands of the SAMs and in some instances (as on the Golan Front) to suppress SAM fire and reduce its effectiveness, the Israeli airmen did not find a real solution to the highly effective Arab mix of low-level and high-level air defense weapons. On both fronts the most effective action against the Arab air defense umbrella was a ground offensive that either overran the SAMs or forced them to displace. It was the ground offensive west of the Suez Canal, for instance, which enabled the IAF to operate with devastating effectiveness in support of the divisions of Generals Adan, Magen, and Sharon. A deep rip had been torn in the fabric of the Egyptian air defense umbrella, and the Israelis exploited this to the maximum. Thus the success of the Israeli west bank offensive of October 18-24 was very literally an achievement of combined arms coordination. The ground troops made the SAMs pull back; the IAF was then able to give air support which facilitated the continuing ground assault. Air defense efforts by the Egyptian Air Force did interfere with this support to some extent, but Egyptian air-to-air losses were severe.

This was true also on the Syrian front, although there the simultaneous Israeli strategic air offensive forced the Syrians to thin out the initially dense deployment of their SAMs; this in turn contributed to the Israeli breakthrough of the Purple Line positions on the 10th and 11th, and the widening of the front further contributed to the thinning out of the Syrian air defenses.

ISRAELI HELICOPTER PENETRATIONS

On at least two—and possibly four—occasions the Israelis made successful helicopter-borne raid penetrations of the Egyptian SAM umbrella. On about October 10 or 11, again on October 14, and probably on at least two other occasions, Israeli paratroops in helicopters, escorted by Israeli fighters, made demolition raids on the Egyptian electronic monitoring station or stations on Jebel Ataka, the hill mass southwest of Suez. At least one of these raids was made in daylight, probably that of October 14. Neither Israelis nor Egyptians will discuss either the electronic activities, the nature of the raids, or the manner in which the raiders "foxed" the Egyptian SAMs. That some such raids were made, however, is admitted by both sides, although the Egyptians minimize the significance, and the Israelis possibly exaggerate what was done and its effectiveness.[3]

Among possible theories of why the raids were made, and what they accomplished, two are particularly intriguing. One is that the major purpose of the electronic station (or one of the stations) was the coordination of the entire Egyptian air defense system, and that it thus was a major target of the Israel Air Force. (Egyptians categorize this theory as "nonsense.") Another, which has seemingly been indirectly confirmed by senior Israeli officers, but firmly denied by the Egyptians, is that Jebel Ataka was the principal (although not the sole) Egyptian monitoring station, where all Israeli radio communications were listened to, taped, and analyzed. If this theory is correct, it can help to explain why the Egyptian High Command was so confused by the Israeli crossing of the Canal between October 16 and 18. It would seem likely that if such monitoring stations were functioning properly on those days, the volume of Israeli radio traffic would have revealed the size and location of the effort, even if local commanders were inefficient (as they obviously were) in both reconnaissance and reports.

In any event, General Peled has confirmed that these raids were a successful effort of the IAF, and General Elazar has indirectly confirmed

[3] The Egyptians insist that there were no direct attacks on Jebel Ataka, and that the only comparable incident was the landing of a heliborne demolition group near the Cairo-Suez road north of Jebel Ataka for the purpose of destroying power lines and mining the road. (They also say the raiders were driven off before they could accomplish their mission.) The Egyptians say that a few other heliborne raiders—not at Jebel Ataka—had only reconnaissance missions.

that one objective, apparently successful, was to impede Egyptian electronic monitoring.[4]

There was only one reported Israeli helicopter penetration into Syria, other than several combat attacks on Mt. Hermon. On October 13 a helicopter-borne commando force landed about 100 kilometers northeast of Damascus. The Israelis destroyed a bridge, ambushed a convoy of Iraqi troops, then returned to Israel.

ISRAELI STRATEGIC AIR CAMPAIGN AGAINST SYRIA

The Israeli strategic air campaign against Syria was initiated on October 9, evidently in response to the firing of Syrian FROG surface-to-surface missiles throughout much of Galilee. The Israelis interpreted these missile attacks—which caused little damage and few casualties—as an indiscriminate antipopulation terror campaign by the Syrians. It is more likely, however, that the Syrian objective was to hit Israeli air bases in northern Galilee, and the widespread pattern of the explosions resulted from a combination of inherent inaccuracy of the weapons and poor Syrian targeting.

In any event, in responding to this presumed attack on the Israeli civilian population, the IAF initiated a very successful long-range strategic air campaign against Syrian economic targets as well as rear-area military installations. As noted earlier, the October 10 attack on the Syrian Ministry of Defense in Damascus resulted in a number of non-combatant and civilian casualties. Civilian casualties were also caused by attacks against industrial targets in Homs. For the most part, however, damage and casualties were limited to industrial and economic targets such as factories, fuel storage tanks, and power plants.

THE BATTLE IN THE AIR

Although the Israeli Air Force was never able to drive either the Egyptians or the Syrians from the skies, the IAF was able to establish clearcut air superiority in areas where the Arab SAM umbrella was not operative or was overextended. Regardless of any differential in pilot competence, the Arabs understandably avoided combat with the more powerful, and more effectively armed, Israeli aircraft. Yet surprisingly, there were more than 400 air-to-air battles. The Israelis had far the best of those aerial combats. They claim 334 Arab planes shot down in air-to-air combat, and admit the loss of only three of their planes in such encounters. This is a ratio of approximately one hundred to one. If pressed, however, they will admit that probably they lost six aircraft in aerial combat.

---

[4] In response to questions from the author.

The Arabs, attributing the difference entirely to equipment differential, admit that they lost more than the Israelis, but claim to have shot down fifty or more IAF planes in air-to-air combat.[5] When further pressed, Israelis will admit that at least some of the losses that they attribute to "unknown causes" may have been in air-to-air action. In fact, even if all such losses were so attributed the exchange ratio would remain better than twelve to one in the Israelis' favor, which is still very one-sided.

GROUND SUPPORT EFFECTIVENESS OF IAF

While Israeli ground soldiers will testify to the effectiveness of air support during their offensives on the west bank of the Suez Canal, in general they were disappointed with the assistance they got from the IAF, particularly during the first three critical days. Furthermore, to the intense frustration of General Peled and his airmen, the ground soldiers note that not a single Arab tank which came into their possession (more than 1,500) was unequivocally damaged or destroyed by air weapons.

Balancing this criticism from their own army, however, Israeli flyers can find some solace in a remark by an Egyptian division commander after the war: "When we tried to move out beyond the SAM umbrella, we took unacceptable losses from the Israel Air Force."[6] Even if there are no actual, confirmed tank kills to the credit of the IAF, its neutralizing effect upon Arab ground forces was obviously a major consideration in the ground battles.

On the other hand, the IAF contribution to the ground battles in this war was significantly less than it had been in the 1967 war. The quantitative analyses of the relative combat effectiveness of Israeli and Arab forces in the 1967 and 1973 wars, to which reference has previously been made, indicates that there was little difference in the relative combat effectiveness of the opposing ground forces (at least so far as the Egyptian-Israeli comparison is concerned) in the two wars. If anything the Israeli margin of superiority was greater in 1973 than in 1967. Yet in the 1973 war there was nothing like the collapse of the Arab armies which occurred in the 1967 war. Although there were reasons for this collapse other than the effectiveness of the Israeli Air Force, that nevertheless seems to have been one of the most important single contributing factors. It would seem, indeed, that both the Israeli ground forces and foreign observers failed to recognize the full extent of the devastating disruption which the air superiority of the IAF created in 1967. Thus, when comparable disruption did not occur in 1973, Israeli

---

[5] A total of more than 90 aircraft and helicopters is claimed.

[6] In an interview with the author.

and other observers tended erroneously to attribute this more to improvement in Arab ground forces' quality than to the effective neutralization of the IAF by the Arab air defense system.

ARAB STRATEGIC OPERATIONS

Neither the Egyptian nor the Syrian air forces made any serious effort to penetrate air space over Israel. The Syrians made an attack on the Haifa refinery on October 20, but failed to do any damage to the installation. Surprisingly, following the Syrian announcement of this attack, the Israelis made an ambiguous announcement in rebuttal, denying that the city of Haifa had been attacked. In fact, the attack had been made against the refinery some distance north of the city and the Israelis reported—in another announcement—that a Syrian Su-7 had crashed on the beach of Nahariya, not far from the refinery.

The Egyptians avoided such air raids against Israel, and insist that they deliberately avoided any action that could be considered an attack against populated areas. They kept their SCUD missiles ready, however, for retaliatory action in the event of an Israeli attack against Egyptian populated areas.

The Egyptians used their Tu-16 medium bombers as platforms for stand-off launching of AS-5, Kelt, missiles. They apparently launched about 25 such missiles from bombers flying over the Egyptian Mediterranean coast at targets deep inside Sinai, mostly radar sites. A number of these were shot down by Israeli fighters, including one which the Israelis claim was directed at Tel Aviv. Only five of the Kelts made clearly identifiable hits on Israeli targets, all in the Sinai, doing considerable damage to two Israeli radar sites and one supply base. Israeli fighters shot down one of the Tu-16s off the coast of Egypt.

The Israelis made no attempt to retaliate for the launching of the one Kelt which they claim was heading for Tel Aviv. Apparently they were not sure enough of the intended target to make this the basis for a dangerous and costly escalation of the war.

After the war, President Sadat stated that the Egyptians did not fire their SCUDs until just before the end of the war, keeping them as long range deterrent weapons threatening Israel's major population centers. The only combat use came just before the first ceasefire went into effect, on October 22, when they fired two SCUDs into the Israeli bridgehead on the west bank of the Suez Canal, near the southern Israeli bridge at Deversoir. This, said Sadat, was "a warning to let them know we had these weapons." There is some question whether the intended message was received by the Israelis, since Sadat's statement was the first unambiguous reference to these firings in the public press.[7]

[7] Herzog, *op. cit.*, p. 245, says that on October 22, "according to Sadat, a SCUD missile was launched against Israel. It landed in the desert of Sinai."

19

The Naval War

EGYPTIAN PREPARATIONS

Soon after President Sadat appointed General Ismail War Minister and Commander in Chief, he called out of retirement the former Commander of the Naval Forces, Admiral Ahmad Fuad Zekry, and reappointed him to his previous position. Ismail and Zekry were old friends and associates from the past, and Ismail was confident that they could work well together in the coming preparation for war.

In a process similar and closely related to that being performed by Ismail and his General Staff, Zekry and the Naval Staff began an intensive estimate of the situation, focussing particular attention on the new developments in the Israel Navy. As a result of this, early in 1973 the Egyptian Naval Staff reached a number of conclusions.

Israel's superiority in missile boats, supported as they were by a superb air force trained to cooperate in naval warfare, meant that Egypt should avoid close combat near the coast. In particular, Egypt's vulnerable destroyers should not be deployed in a coastal bombardment role, but rather were to be used for disrupting Israeli sea communications far from shore.

Neither the General Staff nor the Navy was happy about this conclusion, since the principal mission of the Egyptian Navy was considered to be the close support of ground forces. However, the Naval Staff pointed out that there were substantial light vessels with multiple rocket launchers that could perform the shore bombardment function, and could be used to supplement the initial bombardment by ground and air forces at the start of a surprise offensive.

Furthermore, there were a number of other useful missions which the Navy could perform, and for which it began preparations. Principal among these was blockade. The Navy could also employ mines to limit the effectiveness of the Israeli missile boats; and the Egyptians knew that the Israelis had no minesweepers. The Navy also had a well-trained and aggressive commando force; however, this force could not be deployed in the preparatory period for fear of alerting the Israelis.

557

The principal problem of the Egyptian Navy during the early months of 1973 was—as it was for the Army—to get ready for the conflict without revealing the purpose for which it was preparing. Since the war was likely not to last long, the Navy had to be prepared to use its resources as early as possible in the war. A very elaborate and effective deception plan was prepared, closely coordinated with the comparable plans of the Army and of the Ministry of Foreign Affairs. Gradually the blockading vessels were deployed to the vicinity of their wartime posts, making use of friendly ports, particularly in Libya and in Southern Yemen.

In the late summer, unostentatiously, but in such a way that the word would reach Israeli intelligence, arrangements were made with Pakistani shipyards for the refitting of two submarines. Parts for the refitting operation were sent to Karachi by merchant ship in September. On October 1 the two submarines put out to sea, presumably unfit for operations, with Karachi as their destination. They never arrived, of course, taking up their stations at Port Sudan. After the war Egypt quietly apologized to the Pakistanis for having made use of them in its deception plan.

While the Army was engaging in its "maneuvers" in the last days of September and the first days of October, the Egyptian Navy participated. On October 3 an announcement was made that General Ismail and Admiral Zekry had been dissatisfied with the fleet-wide mining maneuvers, and that the minelayers were going to practice again. During the night of October 5-6 they laid their minefields near Sharm el Sheikh, at the entrance to the Gulf of Suez.

OUTBREAK OF WAR

In the afternoon of October 6, shortly after the coordinated Egyptian and Syrian ground assaults began, Egypt issued a proclamation, warning all neutral ships away from designated areas of naval operations—including the regional waters of both Egypt and Israel, and the adjacent high seas—in the Mediterranean and Red Seas. Syria similarly proscribed ships of all nations from entering a zone of the eastern Mediterranean. The Democratic Republic of Yemen (South Yemen) declared the strait of Bab el Mandeb a war zone. There was no coordinated naval action between the Egyptian and Syrian navies. Both proceeded independently with their naval operations, the Egyptians with more success—but also more losses—than the Syrians. None of the combatants had sufficient naval forces or opportunity for a major naval engagement, and the naval story is one of raids, small unit actions, and blockade. The record of these activities is replete with claims and counterclaims and the exact toll paid by the combatants is impossible to determine.

THE ISRAELI-SYRIAN NAVAL CONFLICT

At around 10:00 p.m. on October 6 an Israeli flotilla consisting of four *Saar* class vessels and the *Reshef* (less than six months off the launching ramp) encountered and sank a Syrian K-103 torpedo boat five miles off Latakia. Two hours later the same unit engaged in a missile and gun battle with another Syrian force. During the two-hour battle, in which the Israeli Gabriel missile was first used in combat, the Israelis claimed that a Syrian T-43 minesweeper and three missile craft (either *Osas* or *Komars*) were sunk.

For the next three days there was a lull in the Israeli-Syrian naval war, as the Israeli Navy concentrated its efforts against Egypt. The Syrians, having received a costly demonstration of the prowess of the Israel Navy, and properly respectful of Israeli air surveillance and attack potentialities, also avoided action. On October 10, however, the Israel Navy again turned its attention northward.

As a preliminary, at noon Israeli planes attacked the Syrian naval command center, Minat al-Bayda, just north of Latakia. During the following night Israeli *Saar* craft also attacked Minat al-Bayda, and were active off Latakia, Banias and Tartus, shelling oil refineries and storage tanks as well as port installations with 76mm and 40mm guns. Syrian coastal batteries were very active, but scored no hits. Several Syrian missile boats came out to challenge at Latakia and two were sunk by three Israeli craft. Also sunk were a Greek merchantman, the *Tsiment-archios*, and a Japanese cargo vessel. The remaining Syrian vessels made their way safely to port.

The next night (October 11) Syrian vessels were engaged by four Israeli missile boats just before midnight near the entrance to Tartus harbor. During the ensuing hour and a half battle two Syrian vessels were sunk and Israeli missiles also sank a Russian freighter, *Ilya Merchnikov*, early in the morning of the 12th during this attack. A number of oil storage tanks were hit. Again Syrian coast defense batteries forced the Israelis to be cautious in approaching the coast.

The Israeli missile hits on freighters during these two actions seem to have resulted from a Syrian tactic developed when the effectiveness of the Gabriel missile was recognized during the first encounter. The Syrian missile boats darted out from between merchant ships only long enough to fire missiles and/or guns and then quickly retired among these merchantmen to foil the homing sensors of the Gabriel. Considering the consistent Syrian use of this tactic after the third day of the fighting, the Israelis believed that the fact that only three merchant vessels were hit was evidence of the excellence of the Gabriel's target discrimination.

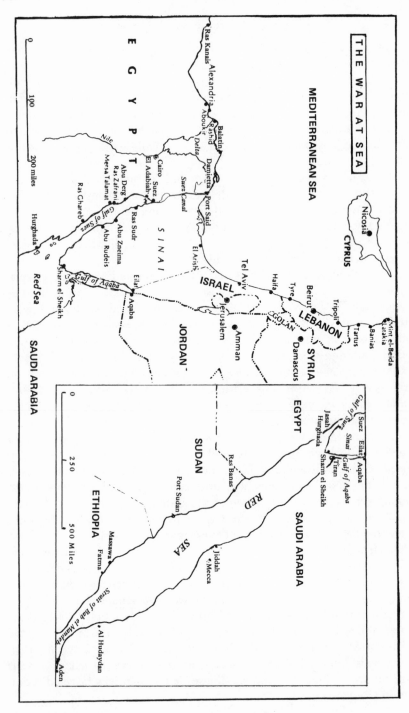

THE WAR AT SEA

There was another clash between Israeli and Syrian missile vessels north of Latakia before dawn on October 14. The Syrians, making a hit-and-run attack from Latakia, claim they destroyed two Israeli craft; the Israelis state that they suffered no losses but do not claim any hits either.

On October 19 Israeli *Saar* boats were back in action along the Syrian coast, shelling a bridge over the Al Abrash River, south of Tartus, during the night. On the 21st they shelled oil depots near Banias, starting large fires. They were not challenged by Syrian surface craft on either night, but were forced by intense Syrian coastal defense artillery fire to take evasive action.

There were no other major naval operations between Syria and Israel before the ceasefire.

THE SEPARATE WARS OF THE EGYPTIAN AND ISRAELI NAVIES

Israel and Egypt waged entirely different naval wars against each other, and thus there was no major confrontation between the two navies. Offensively, Egypt carried on naval blockade against Israel, and conducted a number of hit-and-run raids against Israeli Sinai coastal installations, in direct support of the Egyptian Army.

Defensively, the Egyptian Navy, ever aware of the deadly combination of the Israeli missile boats and the Israel Air Force, refused to be provoked into responses to Israeli threats and challenges except when major Israeli forces threatened important seaports or naval installations. Egyptian defensive tactics were to avoid large-scale encounters with Israeli missile craft beyond the range of their coastal batteries or of other missile vessels firing from ambush in coastal waters.

The Israel Navy, on the other hand, did not attempt to engage distant Egyptian blockading forces, since this would have meant long range diversion of limited surface strength, and the likelihood of distant surface encounters without air support. Further, they had no missile boats in the Red Sea, and the main Egyptian blockading force in the Mediterranean was beyond optimum operational range of the missile boats. Despite the highly successful tactics the Israelis had developed to overcome the range deficiency of the Gabriel missile, the Israelis were satisfied that in a short war—which they expected—the Egyptian blockade could not have a serious impact.

The Israeli surface craft, therefore, devoted their major attention to meeting and thwarting the Egyptian naval bombardments of military installations in the Sinai, and to seeking out the Egyptian missile craft and enticing them into action whenever possible. While this practice resulted in a number of surface engagements, in which the Israelis generally enjoyed success, the Egyptian defensive tactics frustrated the Israel Navy's hopes of winning significant surface victories against Egypt.

THE EGYPTIAN NAVAL BLOCKADE

Although Egypt had proclaimed large areas of naval operations, no blockade was officially declared, but in fact Israel was blockaded. Following the Arab war zone announcements, Israel stopped all of its own commercial traffic into and out of Eilat and its Mediterranean ports, and most neutral shipping also stayed away after the Egyptian announcement of dangerous areas. At the Strait of Bab el Mandeb Egyptian destroyers stopped neutral merchant ships, sometimes merely visiting them, sometimes searching them.

The Egyptian Navy did not risk any major vessels in the narrow waters of the Gulfs of Suez or Aqaba, but rather denied these areas to the Israelis—and particularly to tanker traffic—by minefields.

Egypt claims that it reduced commercial traffic to Israel's Mediterranean ports by more than 85% and to Eilat by 100%. These figures are denied by Israel, but there is reason to believe that the Israeli lists of entries and exits from Israeli ports, while probably not falsified, include naval ship movement.

SURFACE CLASHES OF THE EGYPTIAN
AND ISRAELI NAVIES

During the evening of October 6 an Israeli naval patrol in the Red Sea near Sharm el Sheikh intercepted and attacked several Egyptian landing craft believed to have been scouting preparatory to a commando landing. Some of the Egyptian craft were sunk. Later an Egyptian missile boat squadron made a rocket attack on Israeli positions along the northern Sinai coast; it was engaged by Israeli naval and air units. Israel claimed its aircraft sank at least one vessel. The Egyptians claim that the squadron successfully accomplished its hit-and-run bombardment and returned safely to Alexandria, but that Israeli aircraft sank one Israeli motor torpedo boat during the pursuit.

The Egyptians claim that during the night of October 7-8 two Egyptian missile boats sank an Israeli vessel 40 miles north of Port Said. The Israelis deny this.

The next night two Israeli fighter-bombers attacked and damaged two Egyptian missile boats, although no sinkings were confirmed, just off the southern tip of the Sinai Peninsula near Ras Muhammed. In the Mediterranean an hour after midnight that same night (October 8-9) six Israeli missile boats, supported by helicopters, cruising off the Egyptian port of Damietta in the Nile Delta, engaged four *Osa* and *Komar* boats. The Israelis called the resulting engagement the Battle of Damietta-Balatin; the Egyptians called it Damietta-El Burelos. Two of the Egyptian vessels were sunk by missiles within the first ten minutes, and 25 minutes later the Gabriels claimed a third Egyptian craft as it attempted to escape westward to Alexandria. The fourth successfully evaded the Israelis and reached Alexandria. Egyptians claim to have sunk four Israeli "targets;" three they believe were motor torpedo boats and one a missile boat. As a result of this engagement, the Egyptians became duly respectful of the combination of Israeli missile boats and Israeli helicopters.

Another action took place off Port Said during the night of October 11-12. The Israelis claim the sinking of two Egyptian missile boats, with no losses of their own. Two nights later, Israeli motor gunboats shelled the coast west of Damietta without opposition—and apparently without results. They were apparently laying an ambush for the Egyptians, who did not take the "bait."

Meanwhile, early on October 12, an Israeli commando group attempted a landing at Hurghada. However, their boat was sunk by artillery fire near Geiftan Island, and most of the Israelis drowned.

Early on October 14 the Egyptian Navy, in conjuction with the major offensive from the Sinai bridgeheads, landed commando units on the north Sinai coast, east of the northernmost Bar Lev Line stronghold, Budapest. The attack on the stronghold failed, and the Israelis claimed that all of the commandos were killed or captured. The Egyptians, however, claim that most of their commandos returned, bringing five POWs with them.

Also on October 14, troops of the Yemen Arab Republic (North Yemen) landed on several islands in the Red Sea to hold them against possible Israeli attempts to seize them preparatory to operations to break the blockade at Bab el Mandeb. (In fact the Israelis had no intention of any such operation.)

The Egyptian port of Ras Gharib in the Gulf of Suez was attacked by Israeli commandos and naval vessels early in the morning of October 15. The Israelis claim that munition dumps were blown up, and about 20 commando landing craft destroyed. The Egyptians insist that the "landing craft" were all fishing boats, and that there were no munitions dumps at Ras Gharib to be destroyed.

That same night Egyptian warships fired rockets against Israeli troops and defenses at Sharm el Sheikh. The Egyptians claimed a heavy loss in Israeli life and property, but the Israelis said that all rockets missed their mark. Meanwhile, in the Mediterranean, at coastal areas west and east of Alexandria, Israeli missile boats supported by helicopters conducted naval gunfire missions against Egyptian radar stations and military posts. Egyptian missile boats in Aboukir Bay responded.

When the Israelis attempted to close, they were also engaged by coastal defense guns, which drove them away. The Egyptians claim that one Israeli vessel, stuck on a sandbar, was destroyed by air attack the following morning.

The Israel Navy was busy in both the Mediterranean and Red Seas during the night of October 17, shelling coastal defense command centers at Port Said and at Ras Zafrana in the Gulf of Suez. After completing the shelling of Port Said, the Israelis landed frogmen in the port who set charges to a number of ships anchored there. This was the third straight night of Israeli frogman activity. The Egyptians claimed, however, that little damage was done in any of these raids, and that all Israeli frogmen were killed.

Israeli gunboats raked the Nile Delta coast with gunfire between Damietta and Rosetta during the night of October 19. At the same time Israeli naval commandos raided the Red Sea port of Al Gutdagah. The third Israeli frogman raid on Al Gutdagah took place two nights later. In this last Red Sea operation before the ceasefire the Israelis claimed they sank an Egyptian warship; the Egyptians have stated they had no warships in the port at that time.

The last Mediterranean activity before the ceasefire also took place during the night of October 21-22. Israeli *Saar* and *Reshef* boats patrolled off Aboukir Bay and Alexandria harbor, taking Egyptian shore installations under fire and claiming that two Egyptian reconnaissance boats were sunk. Egyptian batteries responded.

POSTWAR ACTIVITIES

After the second ceasefire a Greek freighter, *Chandois*, flying the Cypriot flag, was sunk by a ship whose identity could not be ascertained about 60 miles off Alexandria.

Egyptian destroyers, minelayers and submarines continued to patrol the strait of Bab el Mandeb some time after the truce. A Yemen Democratic Republic spokesman on November 5 declared the strait to be at Egyptian disposal.

SUMMATION

In summary the naval war was fought strategically by the Egyptians and tactically by the Israelis. Since they were fighting different wars, and neither side attempted very seriously to interfere with the principal activities of the other, both could quite honestly claim success. The Israeli missile boats had much the better of their few encounters with comparable Egyptian vessels, and were even more successful against the Syrians, virtually driving the Syrian Navy into its ports. Thus, in direct encounters at sea, the Israel Navy won its tactical war by a wide margin.

Meanwhile the Egyptians initiated a successful blockade of all seaborne traffic to the Israeli port of Eilat by closing the strait of Bab el Mandeb, and their blockade in the Mediterranean seems to have prevented most neutral and Israeli shipping from approaching Israel's coast. The Israelis' claim that they were simultaneously blockading Egypt's Gulf of Suez coast does not have comparable significance. In a short war the effects of blockade cannot be decisive. But the Egyptian Navy takes pride in an undeniable—if limited—naval success.

20

Involvement of
the Superpowers

THE RESUPPLY MYTHS

Some Israelis are convinced that Egypt and Syria could not have achieved their initial successes without planning assistance and operational advice from Soviet military advisors in those Arab countries. Probably an even higher percentage of Arabs believe that Israel was saved from total collapse after the successful Arab surprise attacks only through an American resupply effort which replaced Israeli losses—particularly of tanks, aircraft, and missiles of various kinds—and gave them confidence to move from defense to offense. These convictions are almost equally wrong.[1]

Despite what they may have learned from the Russians, and undoubtedly making use of earlier joint Arab-Russian plans, there is no doubt that the actual planning and organization of the Egyptian and Syrian surprise attacks were completely the responsibility of the Arabs. At the same time it seems clear that the Russians learned about these plans only about October 3 or 4.

Although the Israeli government was close to panic in the early days of the war, the Israel Defense Force did not have time to think about panic until both of the surprise assaults had been clearly halted. And while there was apparently serious concern in the Israeli High Command about consumption of ammunition, and some controls were placed upon firing rates, the plans for the Israeli counteroffensives were made long before it was known that there would be a massive American resupply effort. In fact, it was discovered after the war that, with the possible exception of one or two categories of ammunition, the Israelis never used up their prewar ammunition stocks and, thanks to the American resupply, actually ended the war with more ammunition on hand than when they started. As to tank resupply, while many tanks were sent to

---

[1] During the war, there were newspaper reports that North Korean fighter pilots —who reached Syria via the USSR—flew air defense missions in Syrian Air Force planes, and that Soviet advisors might have been active in directing Syrian air defense activities. There appears to be no validity to these reports.

Israel by ship (arriving long after the war) only one planeload of American tanks reached Israel during the war. This included fewer than five tanks; probably not one of these ever got into action before the end of the war.[2]

THE OPPOSING AIRLIFTS

Both the resupply efforts and myths that still surround them began in the war. Within two days of the beginning of the war, El Al passenger planes, stripped down to carry cargo, were arriving in the United States to pick up some urgently needed items of equipment. High in the priority of the items requested by the Israelis, and approved by the U.S. Government for inclusion in these emergency shipments, were chaff (to be used by Israeli planes to confuse the Egyptian SAM radars) and air-to-ground guided missiles (so-called "smart bombs," to be used to hit the SAM sites and the Egyptian bridges over the Canal at long range). But these few planes, with their very limited capacity, could not carry enough materials to have much effect on Israeli air operations. The first of these El Al flights that can be definitely identified left Norfolk, Virginia, on October 9.

Both American and Israeli radar had picked up a number of Soviet transport planes flying to Cairo and Damascus on October 4 and 5. At the time—before the outbreak of hostilities—little attention was paid to these flights; after the Arab attack, however, they seemed to provide solid evidence that the Soviets were in on the planning and were sending critical last-minute items in preparation for the attack on the 6th. It is now known, however, that these aircraft—which probably arrived empty at their destination—were sent to pick up the Russian technicians and their families, who were returning home when they were informed of the imminence of war by the Egyptian and Syrian Governments on October 4.

The first indication of a Soviet airlift to Syria was on October 9, when large numbers of aircraft were spotted flying to the Middle East from Russia by way of Budapest and Belgrade. This airlift was undoubtedly in response to Syrian appeals for help, beginning about October 7, when losses on the Golan Heights began to be catastrophic.

In Tel Aviv and Jerusalem reports on unexpectedly heavy losses and ammunition consumption from the two fronts in the first days of action were received by a government which had still not recovered from the

---

[2] Arabs, who have read misleading and erroneous reports on tank resupply in American and European newspapers and magazines, simply refuse to believe this fact. One Arab military man has commented that it is "almost a joke to send only five tanks; either more or nothing." He could not be convinced that this was mainly psychological warfare, and designed more to reassure Israelis than to worry Arabs.

disruption of the Arab surprise, and the unanticipated Arab successes. By October 11 the government of Israel had come to the conclusion that another week of such losses and consumption would so deplete Israeli stocks that Israel would be overrun. Early the next day a report to this effect was presented to the United States Government by the Israeli Ambassador, Simcha Dinitz, in a letter which asserted that "the future of the State of Israel is at stake."

It was now the turn of the United States Government to go into panic. At the direction of President Richard Nixon, Secretary of State Henry Kissinger convened the so-called Washington Action Group, the selected members of the National Security Council whose mission it was to deal with urgent national security crises. The Pentagon—the Joint Chiefs of Staff and the office of the Assistant Secretary for International Security Affairs—was unable to confirm or refute the Israeli prediction of doom. Accordingly, on October 13 President Nixon made the decision to provide the Israelis with virtually everything they asked for, even if this meant the depletion of US war reserves.

Following requests from Ambassador Dinitz on October 8, a small American airlift, semiofficially approved, had already begun about October 9 or 10. This effort delivered limited quantities of antitank ammunition, artillery shells, Sidewinder heat-seeking missiles and Sparrow air-to-air rockets, as well as chaff. Now this lift was to become official and greatly expanded.

On October 13 the official American airlift began; on October 14 the first planes of this airlift arrived in Israel. The effort operated under clearly defined ground rules established by the National Security Council. No US military men were to be sent to Israel, other than the minimum necessary to handle the technical ground arrangements for the airlift itself. And planes would not under any circumstances land in airfields outside the old 1967 boundaries of Israel; in other words, there would be no direct flights to air bases in the Sinai.

The American reaction to the Israeli request, under the circumstances in which it was made, would undoubtedly have been what it was regardless of the Arab oil embargo. However, the abrupt decision of the Arab oil-producing nations—including America's friend, Saudi Arabia—had already created a political and economic furor in the United States. America's increasing reliance upon petroleum imports made this country appear more economically vulnerable to the embargo than was in fact the case, arousing economic worries and resentments, mostly against the Arabs rather than against the Israelis. At the same time, the political affront demanded a response, such as that of the weapons airlift to Israel.

An unexpected complication in the planned airlift, however, was the abject surrender of America's NATO allies to the Arab oil embargo, which resulted in the closing of all west European air bases (except those of Portugal) to American supply planes. Using an intermediate base in the Azores, however, and shuttling some fighter planes by way of carriers in the Mediterranean, a highly efficient, massive airlift to Israel was soon in operation.

Meanwhile the Soviet airlift, first noticed on October 9, had also become massive. Most of the shipments were to Syria, to replace that country's catastrophic Golan losses. Some shipments were also made to Cairo—but only, as President Sadat later declared, with equipment that had been long on order from Russia.

The approximate size of these two emergency airlift efforts is shown in the chart below.

COMPARISON OF ESTIMATED US AND SOVIET RESUPPLY AIRLIFTS
October 9-24, 1973

| | October 9-15 | | October 16-22 | | October 23-24 | | Totals | | Combat |
	Sorties	Tons	Sorties	Tons	Sorties	Tons	Sorties	Tons	Aircraft
US Air Force	30	500	415	17,000	120	4,900	565	22,400	56
El-Al—Israel	90	1,600	125	3,000	35	900	250	5,500	—
Total to Israel	120	2,100	540	20,000	155	5,800	815	27,900	56
USSR	290	4,500	575	10,400	60	1,100	935	16,000	206

On October 16 the United States reinforced its Sixth Fleet in the Mediterranean Sea with a force of 2,000 Marines. Three days later President Nixon requested Congress to approve military aid to Israel in the amount of $2.2 billion, to include a number of direct military grants.

Some equipment was provided from US forces and reserve stocks in Germany. For the most part these weapons and equipment—including A-4 and F-4 aircraft—were shuttled to Israel via the aircraft carriers of the Sixth Fleet. Despite the US Government's prohibition on airlift landings in Israeli-occupied territory, there is evidence that some of the supplies sent by way of the Sixth Fleet were landed, by helicopter and possibly by plane, at the El Arish airbase, in the northeastern Sinai.

On October 19 or 20 Egyptian radar apparently picked up heavy helicopter traffic into El Arish, and sent two Mirages to investigate. The planes returned to report that they could not approach El Arish, because of the high density of American carrier fighters, flying air cover over the helicopter shuttle.

ARAB MISCONCEPTIONS OF SUPERPOWER ASSISTANCE

There is among the Arabs a curious ambivalence about the activities of the superpowers during the war. They accept as only right and natural the fact that they received support from Russia, which after all had incurred a moral commitment by providing them with most of their equipment, and with advice on how to use it. Yet they are quick to assert that, so far as the fighting of the war was concerned, Russia was not involved; the Arabs planned and fought their war without outside assistance.

On the other hand, the American support of Israel is castigated by Arabs as immoral aid to an aggressor, a kind of neo-colonialism, using the Israelis as an instrument of American expansionist policies. In fact, the Arabs contend, by providing arms and equipment to Israel the Americans were involving themselves in the war against the Arabs.

This line of reasoning is not only inconsistent and illogical, it is based on a wholly erroneous concept of what the superpower involvement was all about.

It is obviously in the interest of the USSR to gain a dominant position in the Middle East; and it is equally obvious that such dominance could be furthered by the military preeminence of Arab states that owed their military capabilities and accomplishments to Russia. It would be disastrous to Soviet interests, on the other hand, if their clients in the Middle East should again be ignominiously defeated. This was the motivation for their prewar assistance to Egypt and Syria, and for their emergency supply support to those nations during the war, as well as for their subsequent threatened involvement in the war. There is no reason to believe that the Soviets are motivated by a moral commitment to help the Arabs halt Israeli aggression, or to eject the Jews from Palestine.

US support for Israel, on the other hand, largely because of an empathy with the Jewish people, is based upon a belief that Israel deserves to exist as a nation. US policy also views a Soviet zone of influence in the Middle East as a potential source of danger to US national strategic interests. The provision of emergency assistance to the Israelis in this war, then, was neither an attempt to extend US power in the Middle East nor an effort to assist the Israelis in extending theirs. It was intended to provide support to a responsible and legitimate nation threatened by massive invasion while at the same time endeavoring to preclude an upset in the precarious Middle East strategic balance, since this could jeopardize world peace.

Thus, to the extent American assistance to Israel involved the United States in the war, so too Soviet assistance to the Arabs involved the USSR, and at least to an equal extent. Neither side became engaged directly or indirectly in the combat; both wanted to avoid such engagement. In light of the importance attached to this matter at the time, particularly by President Sadat, it is useful to examine the specifics of some Arab accusations regarding US assistance to Israel.

It has been asserted that without the US resupply effort, the Israelis could not have repelled the Egyptian offensive of October 14. A major contribution to that Israeli success, it is claimed, was the presence of new American antitank weapons, particularly the vaunted TOW. That assertion, while containing some elements of fact, simply cannot be substantiated. The American supply effort to Israel did not really start until the 14th. Actually, as noted above, it is doubtful if the total American effort, through October 25, influenced the outcome of a single engagement; the Israelis apparently never used up their prewar reserves of weapons or ammunition. The American supply effort probably did affect the way in which the Israelis fought the war, however, since they no longer had to worry about exhausting their reserves. Other items of equipment—spare parts, missiles, etc.—undoubtedly were valuable to the Israelis, but not crucial to the outcome. Thus the influence of the American effort was essentially moral and only marginally physical.[3]

There have also been assertions that only the American airlift of tanks to El Arish enabled Israel to continue the war. A respected American journalist has been one of those making this assertion. For propaganda purposes, at home and abroad, the Israelis made much of the one planeload of American tanks that reached Lod airport—*not* El Arish—and there were many photographs of tanks being unloaded. But no matter how many photographs, there was a moral value to this shipment, but little physical significance.

Much has been made in the Arab press of the passage of two American "spy planes" over the Suez-Sinai battlefront on October 13. The Americans are accused of giving the Israelis photographs from this mission, revealing the absence of Egyptian forces west of Deversoir, and it is said that this was the basis for the Israeli decision on time and place of crossing. Without access to highly classified sources, it cannot be proved that such photos were not given to the Israelis. However, the evidence does not substantiate the likelihood that American and Israeli intelligence cooperation would have included the transmittal of such photographs to Israel. But, even if the photographs were provided, there would not have been time to get them to Israel to influence the crossing decision on October 12. That decision was based upon operational and combat intelligence considerations that were compelling without any such photographs.

There is one critical fact, furthermore, that Arab complaints about the American supply airlift simply ignore. That is that a Soviet Russian airlift was supplying Israel's enemies with weapons, equipment, and ammunition on a scale comparable with that of the United States to

[3] As to the TOW, there is some reason to believe that a tiny number of these weapons reached a few Israeli units as early as October 14; however, most issues of the TOW seem to have been about the 24th or 25th. See p. 502.

Israel, and that an even larger Soviet sealift was beginning to reach Arab ports before the war ended. While the United States had also begun a sealift, not only was this probably smaller than that of the Soviets, it would not begin to arrive in Israeli ports until weeks after the end of the war. In other words, the American airlift support to Israel was at least offset by comparable Soviet resupply support to the Arabs.

THE SOVIET-AMERICAN CONFRONTATION

The most dramatic aspect of the involvement of the superpowers was the military and diplomatic confrontation between the United States and the Soviet Union just at the close of the war. This stemmed primarily from Soviet fears that the Israelis, violating a ceasefire that was jointly supported by the US and USSR, would destroy the isolated Egyptian Third Army. To prevent this the Russians apparently were prepared to send troops to Egypt. They were particularly upset by apparent American unconcern about the continuing Israeli offensive against Suez after the October 22 ceasefire, and the continuation of operations in Suez on the 24th and 25th after the second ceasefire.

Whether or not the collapse of the Third Army was imminent or likely is debatable, as has been noted earlier. But the Soviet motive, of course, was to avoid political and military defeat for Egypt, whose fortunes were so clearly identified with Soviet equipment and past military assistance. The Kremlin was also under considerable political pressure from the Egyptian Government, and failure to support Egypt adequately would have gravely undermined Soviet prestige in the Middle East and elsewhere.

The confrontation was in fact quite unexpected by both major participants. On October 19, in response to strong appeals from Egypt for help in arranging a ceasefire, the Soviet Government requested an urgent visit to Moscow by Secretary of State Kissinger. Kissinger arrived the next day, and in discussions in Moscow on October 20 and 21 the two governments reached agreement on the text of the ceasefire agreement that would become UN Resolution 338, approved by the Security Council early on the morning of the 22nd.

The first major complication—before the ceasefire was broken by the continuing Israeli offensive around Suez—was the apparent unwillingness of the Syrians to agree to the ceasefire. This reluctance, expressed in exchanges of telegrams between Presidents Assad and Sadat, was at least in part for the record, as far as Assad was concerned. He wished to avoid criticism by the Arab radicals, such as the Iraqis and Qadaffi of Libya, who were insisting that the war should continue. On the other hand, Assad demonstrated throughout the war considerable toughness and strength of character. However, Syria did comply with the ceasefire and formally accepted it sometime late on October 22 or early on the 23d.

On October 23 and 24 President Sadat of Egypt tried to get the two superpowers to agree upon the establishment of a joint Russian-American force to impose and maintain the ceasefire. He also tried to get the issue debated by the UN Security Council. The Soviets obviously liked this idea, but the United States was strongly opposed to the deployment of any Soviet forces to the Middle East. Therefore the Americans would not consider the inclusion of American troops in a United Nations ceasefire force, since this would mean that the Russians could not be excluded. The United States rejected the Sadat suggestion, but instead proposed the early establishment of a new United Nations Emergency Force to maintain the ceasefire.

American observers noted an unaccountable slackening of the Soviet airlift on October 23 and 24. American intelligence soon picked up these aircraft at Soviet paratroop bases in Russia, where something like seven Soviet parachute divisions seem to have been placed on alert. At the same time there came an ominous toughening in the tone of telegraphic exchanges taking place between President Nixon of the United States and Soviet Communist Party Secretary Leonid Brezhnev. Finally, on the 24th, Brezhnev included in a telegram words reported by one source to be as follows: "If the Israelis are not going to adhere to the ceasefire let us work together to impose a ceasefire, if necessary by force."[4] It has been suggested by some American observers that Brezhnev's words were even tougher, and more than hinted that the USSR was prepared to impose a ceasefire unilaterally if the United States was unwilling to cooperate. In any event, Brezhnev must have known that, in addition to the wording of his telegrams, the United States was receiving intelligence observations of the Soviet airborne alert.

Again the Washington Action Committee of the National Security Council met in Washington, and sometime after midnight on October 25 Secretary of State Kissinger informed President Nixon that the National Security Council recommended that a limited world-wide alert of United States military forces be put into effect, and announced. The President approved. Early on the 25th an astonished world, assuming that the Middle East crisis had been ended by the ceasefire, was informed by Mr. Kissinger of a "precautionary alert" in reaction to "ambiguous" signs suggesting the possibility of unilateral Soviet armed intervention in the Middle East.

The Soviets have professed to be surprised by this American reaction to their words and actions. It is possible that the American reaction was stronger than it needed to be. On the other hand, it clearly accom-

---

[4] Heikal, *op. cit.*, p. 254.

plished its purpose. On October 27 the United States and Soviet representatives at the United Nations cooperated in the establishment for six months of a 7,000 man United Nations Emergency Force (UNEF) to be placed between the Israeli and Egyptian armies, on a basis that would include forces from nations other than permanent members of the Security Council. Since Britain, France, and China had not in any way been involved, that meant that Russia was agreeing with the United States not to commit its forces in the Middle East.

The Soviet toughness had also accomplished *its* purpose. The United States, having announced its alert, could now in good faith put as much pressure as necessary on Israel to stop hostilities and to assure that emergency supplies of food, water, and medicines could be sent under UNEF sponsorship and control through the Israeli lines to Suez and the Third Army. In the next few days in negotiations in a tent at Kilometer 101 on the Sarag Road, Israeli and Egyptian representatives, meeting with the UNEF commander, Finnish Lieutenant General Ensio Siilasvuo, reached the necessary agreements to confirm the ceasefire and assure the emergency shipments to the Third Army.

Actually a small scale war of attrition continued along the Egyptian and Israeli front lines west of the Suez Canal for the next two months, and did not end until—as a result of the Kissinger "shuttle"—both sides reached a further disengagement agreement on January 17, 1974. Despite this, a trickle of vital supplies kept reaching the Third Army—under constant alert and considerable privation—and an overt breach of the ceasefire was avoided by both sides.

21

Attrition and Disengagement, October-May, 1973-1974

THE UNITED NATIONS AND THE CEASEFIRE AGREEMENTS

As has been noted, Secretary of State Kissinger's urgent visit to Moscow on October 20 resulted in a quick agreement between the American and Soviet governments on the text of a ceasefire resolution. On Sunday the 21st, Kissinger returned to the United States via Israel, where he explained the draft resolution to Prime Minister Golda Meir and the Israeli Cabinet. Shortly after he returned to the United States an emergency meeting of the UN Security Council was convened at 10:00 p.m. Sunday evening. By 12:52 a.m. on Monday morning UN Resolution 338 was approved unanimously, China abstaining. The resolution directed that a ceasefire go into effect within twelve hours (in other words, by 6:52 p.m. Suez Canal time). The opposing parties were directed to hold their positions and "immediately after the ceasefire" to implement Security Council Resolution 242 of 1967 in all of its particulars. At the same time, "negotiations should start between the parties concerned under suitable auspices for the establishment of a just and durable peace in the Middle East."

Both Egypt and Israel accepted the resolution; Syria did not until the 23d. But, of course, the ceasefire broke down when fighting continued in and around Suez.

The United States and the Soviet Union thereupon, on October 23, jointly presented to the Security Council another ceasefire resolution which reaffirmed Resolution 338 with the significant addition that the Secretary General was "to take measures for the immediate dispatch of UN observers to supervise the observance of the ceasefire, using for this purpose first of all the UN personnel now in Cairo," that is, members of the United Nations Truce Supervision Organization (UNTSO), which had been in existence since 1948. Resolution 339 was also passed unanimously, with China again abstaining. The new ceasefire was to go into effect at 7:00 a.m. Suez time, Wednesday, October 24. Again both Egypt and Israel accepted the ceasefire, Egypt reluctantly, since the resolution did not specify—as Egypt had demanded—a return to the lines of 6:52 p.m. on October 22. This time Syria also accepted; a *de facto* ceasefire had been in effect on the Syrian front since about midday on the 23d.

All day on the 24th, however, fierce fighting continued in Suez, as the Israelis first tried to sieze the city, then exerted all possible efforts to extract their battered units. It was this struggle in Suez which led directly to the superpower confrontation, and which in turn impelled the Soviet Union and the United States to resolve their differences quickly and amicably through another Security Council Resolution. There were two major provisions of this, Resolution 340 of October 25. First, the UNTSO was to be increased, so as to be able to define the ceasefire line precisely. Second, the new emergency force (UNEF) was to be established, to be interposed between the Egyptian and Israeli forces, and to police the ceasefire line as established by UNTSO.

General Siilasvuo, who had been Chief of Staff of UNTSO, relinquished that position in order to become Commander of the UNEF. By October 28 representatives of the Israeli and Egyptian armed forces were carrying out the provisions of Resolutions 338 and 339 by meeting at 1:45 a.m. in a tent set up near an Israeli check point at the Kilometer 101 marker on the Suez-Cairo Road (Sarag Road). On the same day, as has been related, the Israelis—under considerable pressure from the United States—agreed to the passage through their lines of limited amounts of nonmilitary supplies to the Egyptian Third Army.

Meanwhile fighting was continuing between the Israeli and Egyptian units cut off within their respective perimeters. There were also a number of skirmishes along the ceasefire lines around Suez, and Israeli aircraft attacked Suez, the Third Army bridgehead, and Egyptian positions west of Kilometer 101 and near Suez. The last of these skirmishes took place on October 27. Early the following morning United Nations troops began to arrive, and by 12:30 were finally able to establish themselves between the two opponents. Even so, minor hostilities erupted again the evening of October 31-November 1, and continued sporadically for several weeks.

The Egyptian-Israeli military negotiations at Kilometer 101 nevertheless continued, and on November 11 a six-point agreement was signed: (1) both sides would scrupulously observe the ceasefire; (2) both agreed to immediate discussions regarding the issue of a return to the October 22 lines; (3) the city of Suez would receive daily supplies of food, water, and medicine, and wounded civilians would be evacuated; (4) Israel would impose no impediment to continued movement of nonmilitary supplies to the Egyptian Third Army on the east bank of the Canal; (5) the Israeli checkpoints on the main Suez-Cairo Road would be replaced by UN checkpoints; and (6) there would be an exchange of all prisoners of war, including wounded, as soon as the UN checkpoints were established.

Although some portions of this agreement were soon implemented, others became bogged down. The first problem was that of the Israelis' withdrawal from the checkpoints; they were prepared to do this, but they refused to open the road completely, as the Egyptians insisted the agreement intended. The prisoners of war were exchanged between November 15 and 22, with the return of 241 Israelis and 8,031 Egyptians.

However, a fundamental stalemate soon occurred on the question of return to the October 22 lines. The Israelis insisted that at the time of the first ceasefire on October 22 they had held all of the Geneifa Hills, occupied a major portion of the northern Suez-Cairo Road (Asor) and had cut the main Suez-Cairo road (Sarag) in several places, thus effectively isolating Suez and those elements of the Egyptian Third Army on the east bank of the Canal. The Egyptians, however, claimed that they held most of the Geneifa Hills, that they had driven back Israeli spearheads from the northern road, and that up to the ceasefire the Israelis had interfered with traffic on the main road only by long range tank and artillery fire. They insisted that the Israelis reached their claimed positions more than 24 hours later, after a full day of attacks, in defiance of the ceasefire.

Those directly contradictory claims are still asserted with equal vehemence by both sides, and there is no objective way of assessing the validity of the opposing claims. Egyptian staff officers claim that they have seen copies of—but have never been given—an American satellite photograph which confirms their claims. The Israelis counter that argument by saying that they captured the logbook of the Third Army, which records the arrival of Israeli tanks at the road junction at Kilometer 109 on the main Suez-Cairo Road on October 22.

Morally the overall position of the Egyptians in this debate is slightly better than that of the Israelis because there is little doubt that the Israelis deliberately violated the ceasefire in order to improve their military position. On the other hand, on this particular issue—location of the front lines at 6:52 p.m. on October 22—General Adan's operation maps[1] make military sense, and there was no comparable Egyptian authority that was as precisely aware of the situation as was Adan.

On November 12, the Israelis stated that continued discussion of this issue was fruitless, and refused to consider it further. Instead, they suggested that they would withdraw from their bridgehead west of the Canal if the Egyptians withdrew from the east bank. This the Egyptians rejected immediately. On November 29 the discussions stopped.

[1] Which this author has seen.

A NEW "WAR OF ATTRITION"

There had been a number of ceasefire violations all along the Sinai-Suez front since October 31, most of them at Egyptian initiative. These were partly for the purpose of improving their positions, but mainly to keep constant pressure on the Israelis, to force them to continue their costly mobilization. Now that the military negotiations had broken down, the level of intensity of this new war of attrition increased, and artillery, tanks, and missiles became more frequently involved.

Nevertheless, in late November and early December, American diplomacy was able to bring about agreement that, pursuant to Resolutions 338 and 339, a peace conference would be held at Geneva. This was opened on December 21, under the cochairmanship of Secretary of State Kissinger and Soviet Foreign Minister Andrei Gromyko. In addition to US and Soviet delegations, there were representatives from Egypt, Jordan, and Israel. For reasons that will be discussed later, Syria refused to participate. The political conference adjourned on December 22, to reconvene after the Israeli elections on the 31st. The conference never reconvened in the three following years, for a variety of political reasons, of which the question of possible participation of representatives of the Palestinian people was the most important. Before adjournment, however, it was agreed that troop disengagement talks would resume at Geneva on December 26 between military representatives of Egypt and Israel.

These discussions—with Major General Mordechai Gur representing the Israel Defense Force and Major General Taha el Magdoub representing the Egyptian Armed Forces—continued into early January, but made little progress. Meanwhile, low-scale fighting continued along the so-called ceasefire lines on the east and west banks of the Suez Canal.

During this time—slightly more than three months in all—the two and a half divisions of the Third Army were isolated on the east bank of the Canal and in Suez. Under the terms of the original supply agreement of October 28, the Third Army was to receive about 150 tons of nonmilitary supplies every day, mostly food, water, and medicine. There had been a substantial reserve of water in Suez at the time it was cut off, and by exercising the strictest possible control of consumption, by the time the blockade was lifted, on January 24, 1974, General Badawy says that he had accumulated a 95-day reserve of food, water, and fuel.

Of course fuel was not included in the supply agreement, but the Third Army had discovered several underground tanks of Israeli fuel. Badawy had also discovered some Israeli ammunition, and during the exchanges of fire, he tried to use this as much as possible, to conserve his own supplies. By carrying out a strict training routine, by emphasizing sports and recreational activities of all kinds, and by responding vigorously to everything that he and his men considered to be Israeli provocations, Badawy maintained high morale in his isolated command.

KISSINGER AND THE DISENGAGEMENT AGREEMENT

A new element was introduced into the negotiaitng process on January 11: American Secretary of State Henry Kissinger. In a virtuoso diplomatic performance, shuttling by aircraft between Egpyt and Israel, Kissinger was able by the 17th to get both sides to accept a disengagement agreement. Under its provisions, Israeli forces within 40 days were to pull back from the west bank of the Suez Canal, and from the ceasefire line on the east bank for a distance of about 20 to 30 kilometers from the Canal. The Egyptians, with limited forces, were to retain on the east bank, in roughly the area they had occupied between October 6 and 15, a zone 8 to 12 kilometers deep. Between the two forces a buffer zone, 5 to 8 kilometers wide, was to be occupied by the UNEF. Both the Giddi and Mitla Passes remained well inside the Israeli lines.

The agreement was signed at Kilometer 101 on January 18 by Major General Mohammed el Gamasy, the new Chief of Staff of the Egyptian Armed Forces, and Lieutenant General David Elazar, Chief of Staff of the IDF. General Siilasvuo presided over the historic event.

The war of attrition at once ended, and by January 24 both sides had agreed upon detailed measures necessary to carry out the agreement. Israeli troops had begun to withdraw from their bridgehead on the 23rd, two days before the disengagement agreement deadline. On February 21, the Israelis completed their withdrawal from the west bank of the Canal. By March 4 the IDF had withdrawn to its new positions in the Sinai Desert.

THE SYRIAN "WAR OF ATTRITION"

During December and early January there had been somewhat less intensive exchanges of fire going on along the Israeli-Syrian ceasefire line on the slopes of Mt. Hermon and the Damascus Plain. However, when the Israeli-Egypt agreement of January 17 was announced, the firing ceased on that line as well as in the Suez-Sinai area.

This proved to be only a temporary lull. On January 26 Syrian artillery resumed firing on Israeli positions, but with considerably more intensity than before. The Israelis returned the fire, and—despite claims from both sides of inflicting many losses and incurring few—casualties were heavy. The firing was to continue almost every day, with varying intensity, for more than four months. On February 3 Syrian Foreign Minister

Abdel Halim Khaddam revealed that Syria was deliberately fighting a war of attrition along the ceasefire line with the objective of paralyzing the Israeli economy by forcing the continued mobilization of Israeli reserves.

There were two major issues which kept Israel and Syria from entering negotiations such as those which had brought about the disengagement in the Sinai Peninsula. Syria—offering the same reasons as for nonparticipation at Geneva—insisted that it would enter into negotiations only under two conditions: Israel must commit itself in advance to total withdrawal from occupied Arab territories and must also agree to respect the fundamental rights of the Palestinian people.

The Israeli Government not only refused to negotiate under any such preconditions, it also refused to enter into any discussions until Syria provided a list of all Israeli prisoners captured during the October War, and permitted representatives of the International Red Cross to visit the prisoners. In response to this, Syria said that the POW issue was separate from the peace issues involved in Resolutions 242, 338, and 339.

On February 26, in an effort to break the impasse, Secretary of State Kissinger visited Damascus and obtained a list of 65 Israeli prisoners from President Assad. The next day Kissinger flew to Israel, gave the list to Israeli Prime Minister Golda Meir, and told her that the Syrians had agreed that representatives of the International Red Cross could visit the prisoners after March 1.

However, intermittent firing continued along the ceasefire line, and Secretary Kissinger came to the conclusion that the two sides were still too far apart for him to consider the same kind of shuttle diplomacy that had broken the Israeli-Egyptian stalemate. He flew back to the United States.

In early March, after a brief lull, fighting on the ceasefire line again intensified. In response to a Syrian troop buildup behind the front, on March 7 Israel put its forces on full alert, and called up some reserves. The next day ground patrols skirmished in several places along the line. After a one-day lull in the fighting and exchange of fire on March 11, the next day tank gun and artillery duels erupted all along the line. The firing would continue every day for more than two and a half months.

Until early April the fighting was limited to sporadic, sometimes extensive, exchanges of tank and artillery fire and patrol activity along the ceasefire line. On April 13, however, the war of attrition escalated into active ground combat on Mt. Hermon. That day the Syrians mounted a major attack against Israeli troops holding the former Syrian observation post near the summit of the mountain. The Syrians used both ground and helicopter-borne assaults in their attacks. Israel called in its air force to provide close support to its fortified positions near the summit, and to suppress Syrian artillery fire supporting the attackers. The attack was repulsed, but by mid-April major air battles were taking place over the Mt. Hermon positions almost every day, and there were frequent patrol actions on the ground.

ISRAEL AND THE PALESTINIAN GUERRILLAS

The Syrian-Israeli tension was complicated by the increasing intensity of Palestinian guerrilla activity inside Israel, practically all of this from bases in Lebanon. In response to these guerrilla raids, the Israelis frequently raided into southern Lebanon, and on several occasions Israeli aircraft also attacked refugee camps in Lebanon where the guerrillas were supposedly based. While members of the Israeli government privately deplored the loss of civilian life that occurred during these retaliatory air raids, they pointed out that the guerrillas deliberately put their installations in civilian communities inside Lebanon so that Israel could not retaliate without endangering civilians, and that, furthermore, civilian lives were being lost in Israel from the guerrilla, or "terrorist," raids. The Israelis pointed out that they had no other means of deterrence or retaliation against the guerrilla raids, and that their air retaliation would cease at once if the provocations were ended.

On April 11 three guerrillas, infiltrating into Israel from Lebanon, created a brief reign of terror in Qiryat Shimona, in northern Galilee. They killed eighteen Israelis before they themselves lost their lives under attack by Israeli soldiers. The next day an IDF force crossed the border and raided six villages in southern Lebanon, in announced retaliation for the Qiryat Shimona raid. They also seized thirteen hostages to be held until Lebanon returned two Israeli airmen shot down over that country in early April.

On April 24 the United Nations Security Council, meeting at Lebanon's request, condemned Israel for its April 12 attack on southern Lebanon. Israel was called upon to return the thirteen hostages taken in the raids. The Israelis somewhat bitterly asked why the Security Council ignored the prior Palestinian attack on Qiryat Shimona, for which the Israeli operation was retaliation. The United States, after failing in an attempt to have the resolution include mention of the Qiryat Shimona raid, voted with the 13-0 majority.

KISSINGER AGAIN

In late April, as the Syrian-Israeli struggle on Mt. Hermon continued with undiminished ferocity, Secretary of State Kissinger again decided to attempt to seek a solution. After conferring at Geneva with

Soviet Foreign Minister Gromyko on April 28 and 29, and then at Algiers with President Houari Boumedienne of Algeria, and at Cairo with President Sadat, Kissinger began a new round of "shuttle diplomacy" between Israel and Syria on May 2. The fighting did not abate on Mt. Hermon or along the ceasefire line. At the same time violence was undiminished along the Israeli-Lebanon frontier, as guerrilla raids and Israeli ground and air retaliation continued.

On several occasions Kissinger became so discouraged by the refusal of the Israelis and Syrians to relax their bitter hostility and their mutually unacceptable demands that he threatened to return home. On such occasions, however, both sides seem privately to have assured the Secretary that they honestly did want to find some way to bring their costly, small scale war to end.

On May 15, Palestinian guerrillas, apparently hoping to assure the failure of the Kissinger mission, raided the Israeli border town of Maalot and seized a school; in subsequent fighting 20 schoolchildren were killed or mortally wounded before the Palestinians were killed in an Israel Army assault on the school. Beginning the next day Israeli jets attacked several guerrilla bases in southern Lebanon, including some in refugee camps. By the 21st Lebanese and Palestinian officials said that more than 50 people had been killed in these retaliatory raids.

Despite this incident, Kissinger was beginning to make progress with a Syrian-Israeli disengagement agreement. The two major issues which delayed the agreement were the Israeli refusal to give up several hills overlooking the city of Kuneitra—which town they were willing to return symbolically to Syria—and the size of the United Nations force which would patrol a buffer zone to be established between the two armies. Israel wanted a substantial force of about 3,000; Syria wanted only a nominal force of 300.

DISENGAGEMENT ON THE GOLAN

On May 30 finally both sides accepted an agreement drafted by Kissinger, and 81 days of uninterrupted shooting ended on the ceasefire line. The agreement was signed in Geneva on the 31st by Major General Herzl Shafir for Israel, and Major General Adnan Wajih Tayara for Syria. The principal points of agreement were as follows:

• Israel would withdraw completely from the Saassaa salient—about 770 square kilometers—occupied during October 1973.

• Israel would also withdraw from Kuneitra, occupied in 1967, to a new line about 300 meters from the town, thus retaining control of the three strategic hills overlooking the town.

• A buffer zone, varying in width from about 500 meters to four kilometers, would be established between the two armies; this would be on the Syrian side of the old Purple Line (except for a narrow zone just west of Kuneitra); this area—which included the former Syrian OP on Mt. Hermon—was to be completely demilitarized, except for UN troops, but was to be under Syrian civil administration.

• To patrol this buffer zone, a United Nations Disengagement Observer Force (UNDOF) of 1,250 troops was to be established. It would not include troops from any of the permanent members of the Security Council (thus, as in the UNEF, excluding Soviet and US troops).

• The two sides were to begin working out the details of the disengagement within 24 hours of signature of the agreement; the Israeli withdrawal was to be completed in 20 days.

• All prisoners of war were to be exchanged within 24 hours of signature of the agreement. Bodies of all dead soldiers within the opposing areas were to be returned in 20 days.

• There would be "thinned-out" areas on each side of the buffer zone; here the numbers of troops, guns, and tanks would be limited.

Both sides proceeded to carry out the terms of the agreement. The so-called October War had finally come to a conclusion, slightly more than seven months after the end of major operations.

22

Assessment

Rarely have the tides and fortunes of war shifted so frequently or so dramatically as in this brief conflict of less than three weeks. It began with stunning Israeli defeats and resounding Arab successes on both of its two fronts, yet the Israel Defense Forces soon regained the initiative and dominated the military operations for two full weeks. At the conclusion of the war on the Suez-Sinai front the Israelis were decisively repulsed by Egyptian forces at Suez and Ismailia, while they were simultaneously isolating and threatening the very existence of a major component of the Egyptian field army. At the same time, on the Syrian front, the Arab forces had sufficiently recovered from severe defeat to be seriously planning a major counteroffensive which they believed (probably overoptimistically) could drive the Israelis back to the Purple Line.

Involved in, and contributing to, these kaleidoscopic events were a number of issues, controversies, problems, ambiguities, or disputes—military, personal, and political. Some of these issues were major, some minor; some were resolved during the war, some later, and some are still unresolved.

Militarily the war has far greater significance than would normally be the case in a relatively brief, relatively limited regional conflict between nations which would normally be considered third-rank powers. This is largely because the opposing forces were equipped with quite modern weapons representing the effects of a significant modern revolution in military technology, with the opposing sides deploying and employing products of the two antithetical superpowers, the United States and the Soviet Union. Military observers—particularly those of the superpowers—were naturally interested in assessing the effectiveness of their weapons, the tactical implications of the new technologies, and the extent to which these developments have invalidated—or reaffirmed—traditional concepts of war. And, since the superpowers were at least indirectly involved, what were the global strategic implications of the war?

These topics will be assessed in the following paragraphs.

The Military Issues

ON THE ISRAELI SIDE

The first issue on the Israeli side was the question of the strategic and tactical value to Israel of building a line of defenses along the east bank of the Canal: the Bar Lev Line. In fact, the Bar Lev Line concept was not only theoretically sound, it worked. Even with the advantage of surprise, the Egyptian offensive was slowed sufficiently to let the Israeli local reserves, soon supported by mobilized reserves, first delay, and then stop, the Egyptian advance short of the goals hoped for by General Ismail. While this opinion is disputed by several Israeli and Egyptian generals, it is amply supported by the fact that the Egyptians—despite substantial initial success—failed to reach either the Giddi or the Mitla Pass.

The second issue is that of the failure of Israeli intelligence. This requires no detailed analysis. It was a classic failure, in which military intelligence was focussed on hostile intentions, while hostile capabilities were ignored because they were discounted; and this very discounting of Arab capabilities led to false assumptions about intentions. On the other hand, great credit must be given to Arab secrecy and security measures, which obscured the observable facts sufficiently to reinforce Israeli preconceptions.

The third issue is the dispute between General Sharon on the one hand, and Generals Gonen and Bar Lev on the other. Public attention was drawn to this by the outspoken utterances of General Sharon during and after the war. Sharon's part in these disputes, and his conduct during the war, were unorthodox, to say the least. On at least three occasions he deliberately disobeyed the orders of his commanding general. On one of those occasions (the order to attack the right flank of the Egyptian 16th Division at Missouri on October 21) he was probably right; on the others (two attacks to the Canal on October 9th and 14th) he was clearly wrong.

Right or wrong, Sharon should have been relieved of his command on all three occasions. In addition to instances of disobedience, he constantly argued about plans and tactics with his commanders (Gonen and Bar Lev); frequently he bypassed them by direct radio-telephone communications to IDF headquarters in Tel Aviv in efforts to get the High Command to change orders from Gonen and Bar Lev. On top of this, he acted like a prima donna by openly telling his subordinates and the press about his disagreements with, and criticisms of, his superiors. Surprisingly, this behavior was not only tolerated but was sometimes rewarded by changed orders from Tel Aviv, evidently mostly due to the personal intervention of Minister of Defense Dayan in Sharon's favor, after both Gonen and Bar Lev demanded Sharon's dismissal. This does not absolve General Gonen of some serious failures in his initial dispositions, or of his leadership errors on October 8. Under objective analysis, however, he shows up much better than Sharon.

In earlier wars and in this one Sharon revealed great tactical skill and an exceptional talent for command. He has earned a deserved place as an outstanding hero of modern Israel. These criticisms are in no way intended to denigrate his gallantry, skill, or courage. But in this war, even if he was right on the issues, he was wrong in his actions and attitude.

The fourth issue or controversy is another dispute between generals, this time Gonen and Adan. The principal question in this controversy is the orders Gonen gave Adan for the attacks on October 8. This seems to be largely a matter of differences of interpretation of what constitutes a "limited" attack, compounded by Gonen's apparent conviction that the Egyptians would collapse if the attack was not too limited. There is little doubt, in retrospect, that there was not enough Israeli force available to shake the Egyptians seriously. On the other hand, Adan's uncoordinated attacks did not test them severely. The postwar Agranat Commission[1] report apparently and correctly found completely in favor of Adan on the specific issues. This dispute appears, however, to have been in large measure a matter of good faith misinterpretations, and good faith blunders, by both men, with—in this instance—Adan showing up somewhat better than Gonen. General Elazar must also share the blame for the defeat of October 8. On the evening of October 7 he had issued the orders for the limited attack the next morning. He approved Gonen's change in those orders the following morning, in effect contradicting himself.

The fifth issue focusses on the effectiveness of Israeli mobilization. A number of criticisms of the mobilization have been made by Israeli observers. Unquestionably a number of things went wrong. But the ability of the Israelis to have substantial elements of four reserve divisions fighting actively on both fronts within 30 hours of the surprise Arab

[1] This commission, appointed by Prime Minister Golda Meir and her Cabinet on November 18, 1973, was given broad authority to investigate the failure of Israeli prewar intelligence, preparedness of the IDF for war, and its performance during the early period of Israeli defeats. Chairman was Shimon Agranat, President of the Supreme Court; members were Supreme Court Justice Moshe Landan, State Comptroller Dr. Yitzhak Nebenzahl, retired Lieutenant General N.B. Yigal Yadin, and retired Lieutenant General Haim Laskov. Its deliberations and findings were highly secret, but unclassified press releases of some elements of its report included: (a) severe criticisms of Generals Elazar, Zeira, and Gonen, (b) lukewarm praise for Prime Minister Meir and Defense Minister Dayan, (c) strong praise for the IDF mobilization and for its ability to perform well in combat under great adversity.

offensive is proof of the general efficiency of the system, and of its overwhelming success in this instance.

There is a sixth controversy, which is both military and politico-military rather than purely military. This is the question of censorship, and the extent to which the Israeli Government deceived its people by withholding or misrepresenting information. There is still bitterness in Israel about the Government's failure to tell the people the extent of the defeats in the first three days of the war. The symbol of this in the eyes of many Israelis was General Elazar's televised press conference, the evening of October 8, a few hours after the Israeli Army had suffered its worst defeat in history in Sinai, and was close to defeat on the Golan. Elazar promised an early Israeli victory, and in a dramatic scene asserted confidently: "We shall strike them, we shall beat them, we shall break their bones."

Israeli journalists also recall another dramatic incident, the following afternoon. Defense Minister Dayan addressed a meeting of Israeli editors, and for the first time gave them his unvarnished assessment of the defeats the IDF had suffered, as well as the continuing gravity of the situation. The editors were shocked, not only by the desperate picture portrayed for them by Dayan, but also by his obvious grim pessimism. Had Dayan lost his nerve, some wondered.

Dayan was scheduled to speak to the nation that evening on television, and he planned to give the general public the same picture he had given the editors. But word of the "shocking" meeting with the editors reached Prime Minister Meir, and she ordered him not to make his talk. In his stead there was retired General Aharon Yariv, who was recalled to active duty as the new IDF Spokesman. Yariv warned his countrymen that they faced a long war, but reaffirmed Elazar's prediction of eventual victory.

This issue of the right of a democracy to deceive—or at least not fully inform—its people in time of war was debated two years later in a symposium on the Israeli-Arab conflict, held in Jerusalem. The newsmen and university professors, who did most of the talking, made clear their opinion that the right of democratic citizens to know transcends the government's right of censorship. It is doubtful if any government, including that of Israel, will be greatly influenced by such debating points, for at least two reasons.

In the first place, neither the Army nor the Government was in a position to report confidently what was happening until late on the 8th, or early on the 9th. General Elazar's statement on the evening of the 8th was made before he became aware of the extent of the defeat that day. Second, if the survival of the nation was not in jeopardy, the lives of many of its men certainly were. Furthermore, the threat to the nation might have been substantially increased if Jordan entered the war. But above all, the war was not necessarily going too well for the Arabs; it would have been irresponsible to publish information that might have encouraged the Arabs to make renewed efforts.

Probably more significant than the issue is the question of the alleged loss of nerve by General Dayan. He does not seem to have been at his best on these days, and he was consistently more pessimistic than the military commanders. That, he suggests in his memoirs, was because he was more realistic. Certainly he demonstrated in his many visits to both fronts that his personal courage had not lessened a bit since 1967. He was probably more "realistic" than a Cabinet member should have been under the circumstances. But he had not lost his nerve.

ON THE EGYPTIAN SIDE

On the Egyptian side the first major controversy is the difference of opinion between Generals Ismail and Shazli as to exploitation after the successes of the 6th, 7th, and 8th. As discussed earlier, it seems clear that General Ismail was right, and General Shazli wrong, in the decision not to attempt to exploit. A fundamental element of the Egyptian plan was recognition of the great superiority of Israeli airpower, and the almost equally significant Israeli superiority in mobile armored warfare. Two other important generals in history had faced a problem similar to that of Ismail on October 7, 8, 9. One of these was American General Andrew Jackson at New Orleans in 1815. With a pick-up army he won a defensive victory against the best troops of the British Army, then wisely refused to pursue, recognizing that he would throw away his victory. British General Bernard L. Montgomery, similarly cautious, successfully fought a defensive battle at Alam Halfa in 1942, but did not pursue, refusing to give Rommel a chance to counterattack and retrieve victory from defeat. Any Egyptian offensive effort on the 9th, 10th, or later dates would probably have had the same result, even if possibly less decisive, as the attack that was launched on the 14th. At least one Egyptian division commander east of the Canal was convinced by losses incurred on these dates that it was not possible to advance beyond the SAM umbrella. Furthermore, those who suggest that the Egyptians lost an opportunity seem to forget that the Israelis were not close to collapse and were continuously counterattacking during this period.

The second Egyptian controversy has to do with the gap between the Second and Third Armies behind the Bitter Lakes and at Deversoir, and the surprisingly slow and inadequate Egyptian reaction to the Israeli penetration west of the Canal. Boundaries between units are always an invitation for hostile penetration. This fact should have been sufficiently recognized by the Egyptians—whose prior planning was otherwise impeccable—to warrant special efforts to provide security from surprise. Even so, had the Egyptians been alert after the crossing there is little doubt that a major counteroffensive on the 16th, or even the 17th, would have destroyed Sharon's force of less than two brigades on the west bank.[2] But the most serious deficiency was an inexcusably slow, piecemeal reaction by the Egyptian Second Army.

Third, on the Egyptian side, is the question of whether the Third Army could have been relieved or could have survived if the war had continued. It is not at all certain that if the Israelis had maintained a complete blockade of the Third Army elements east of the Canal, or had mounted an attack against them, General Badawy and his command would have been destroyed. This force was not on the verge of collapse, as some commentators have asserted. At the same time it is doubtful if Egyptian relief efforts, by the thin line of troops enclosing the Israeli bridgehead, could have been successful. It is no dishonor to Badawy and his gallant troops to suggest that an all-out Israeli offensive against the Third Army could not have been prevented by other Egyptian forces, and that it would probably have been successful.

ON THE SYRIAN SIDE

There has been no postwar controversy among the Syrians remotely comparable to those which rocked the Israeli and Egyptian forces. Or, if there has been, the close-mouthed Syrians have kept it to themselves. On the other hand the Syrians have been very much interested in the Egyptian Ismail vs. Shazli controversy about exploitation after the initial successes of October 6, 7, and 8. The Syrian interest, of course, is due to their feeling that it was lack of Egyptian pressure against the Israelis on October 9, 10, and 11 which permitted the Israelis to concentrate air support for their offensive toward Saassaa and Damascus.

Yet if there isn't a Syrian controversy, there should be. Because a reasonable case can be made that unlimited commitment of the 9th Division on October 7, and of the 3d Armored Division on October 7 or 8, might well have overwhelmed the Israeli defenses. As it was, the outcome was so close, and the issue was so long in doubt, that it is reasonable to suppose that an advance of the 9th Division toward Nafekh on the 7th, or of the 3d Armored Division between the 9th and 7th Divisions on the 7th or 8th, might have made the difference.

Colonel Ben Gal and Lieutenant Colonel Kahlny may well have been the "saviours of the people of Israel" on October 9. But would they have had a chance to be saviours if they had had to deal with between

[2] As noted on p. 553, Israeli raids on the Egyptian electronic monitoring station on Jebel Ataka on and after October 14 may have contributed to the Egyptian confusion regarding the Israeli operations of October 15-18.

250 and 350 additional Syrian tanks in the area between Nafekh and Tel Mekhafi on October 7 and October 8?

Another possible Syrian controversy could center about the failure of Syrian troops to move into Kuneitra. Israeli armor carefully avoided Kuneitra during the battle, for fear that the attackers would be ambushed by Syrian infantry. Had Syrian infantry—and there was plenty to spare in both the 9th and 7th Divisions—secured Kuneitra on October 7 or 8, the Israeli counterattacks in the central Golan would have been much more difficult, and the counteroffensives of October 10 and 11 would have been greatly delayed, and possibly thwarted.

Related to that failure of the Syrians to use their infantry in Kuneitra was the general failure of the Syrians to employ their infantry aggressively during the first two and a half days of the battle. On the 9th they committed paratroopers by helicopter north and west of Mt. Hermonit, while additional infantry of the 7th Division pushed into Buq'ata —north of Hermonit—from the east. But by that time it was too late. By a whisker the Israeli 7th Brigade held the saddle between Hermonit and Tel Makhafi, and without armored support the Syrian infantry near Buq'ata could not stand up against arriving Israeli reinforcements.

IMPLICATIONS OF THE NEW WEAPONS

There have been two quite different reactions by military commentators to the dramatic confrontation of the modern weapons systems of the Soviet Union, employed by the Syrians and Egyptians, and the modern weapons of the United States, with which the Israelis were largely armed. The first, somewhat hasty, reaction was that the new weapons had completely changed warfare. The second reaction, after a more sober appraisal of the events and their outcomes, was a confident reaffirmation by many critics that there was really nothing new, or even unexpected, in the October War experience.

These conflicting reactions will be assessed in terms of three weapons systems whose future value has been questioned: the tank, the airplane, and the helicopter.

The Tank

The first newspaper reports on the effectiveness of the Egyptian and Syrian Saggers and RPG-7s against Israeli tanks seemed to some people to mark the end of the tank in a manner reminiscent of the 16th century disappearance of the knight in armor after the revival of infantry and the advent of gunpowder weapons. This reaction has persisted to the extent that there is serious question by some authorities about the continuing value of the tank in warfare.

The other point of view is well stated by Israeli General Chaim Herzog in his book, *The War of Atonement*:

Contrary to the hasty conclusions published throughout the world after the Yom Kippur War, the tank still remains a dominant factor on the field of battle. . . . The results achieved by the Sagger antitank missile bore no proportion whatsoever to the publicity accorded it. In fact surveys published indicate that less than 25% of the Israeli tanks damaged were hit by such a missile.[3]

Yet the Egyptians insist that at least 70% of the Israeli tanks which were left behind the Egyptian lines had been hit by Saggers or RPG-7s. There are official US reports tending to confirm General Herzog's comment. No comparable Egyptian survey has been made available to the United States.

However, both sides are apparently right. The tanks that the Israelis inspected for damage were those that ended up inside the Israeli lines, most of them damaged in the Egyptian attack on the 14th and during subsequent operations in the Chinese Farm and Great Bitter Lake area, and on the west bank of the Canal. This damage was inflicted after the Israelis had learned from their bitter experience of the first three days how to deal with the AT missiles and rockets. This was also combat in which either the Israelis were on the defensive, after the effects of surprise had worn off, or they were on the offensive and the Egyptians were the ones who were disrupted. In the combat on the west bank, furthermore, the Egyptian units had fewer Saggers and RPG-7s than they had on the east bank.

The damage which the Egyptians claim was inflicted by missiles and rockets was to tanks that they inspected behind their lines after the war. These were mostly the victims of the first three days of fighting, when the Sagger and RPG-7 gained their reputations, which apparently were deserved, under the then existing circumstances of combat.

The conclusion that must be drawn from this is that both sides are right, and neither is completely right. There is no doubt that the Egyptian missiles inflicted serious damage on a lot of Israeli tanks. But there is also no doubt that the Israelis were successful to a considerable extent in defending their tanks against missile and rocket attacks late in the war. The Egyptian assessment, furthermore, seems to be more relevant for combat in central Europe, where tank and tank-antitank engagement ranges will be shorter than on the desert.

The end for the tank is not yet at hand. But the doctrine for its use must in the future recognize that alone it is currently more vulnerable, and consequently less valuable, than when employed as part of a combined arms team.

[3] Herzog, *op. cit.*, p. 272.

Manned Combat Aircraft

The argument against the future of airpower is very similar to that against the future of the tank. The success of the Arab SAM umbrella, complemented by the very effective low-level, automatic, multibarrelled 23mm cannon, has seemed to many to demonstrate that air superiority will no longer have a significant effect on the ground battle.

The counterargument is also similar to that in the tank-antitank debate. Israeli airpower was able at least partially to suppress the Syrian air defense umbrella. And airmen point out how effective Israeli air support was on the west bank of the Canal, in contributing to the success of the drive on Suez. Furthermore, it is argued, given more time, electronic countermeasures would undoubtedly have reduced the effectiveness of the SAMs.

The last argument is not persuasive; countermeasures lead to counter-countermeasures, and at this point it is impossible to predict if attack or defense is likely to be more successful.

It must be remembered that the reason the air defense umbrella was not fully effective against Israeli aircraft operating over the west bank was that Israeli ground troops had either destroyed the missile sites, or forced them to displace. On balance, however, particularly as part of an integrated combined arms team, the future of the combat aircraft seems about as bright as that of the tank: still one of the most powerful weapons of war, but no longer supreme in its element.

The Helicopter

The helicopter is another matter. Conclusions, however, must be tentative, since the helicopter did not play a major role in the war, and both sides used it with considerable caution. It was used quite effectively by the Egyptians to carry commando raiders to ambush Israeli troop movements behind the front in the Sinai, and it may have been used with comparable effectiveness by the Israelis in raids near or against the Egyptian electronic monitoring station at Jebel Ataka. Perhaps the most effective use of the helicopter was by the Israelis for evacuating wounded.

With one exception, neither side seems to have employed the helicopter in a combat support role, although both used them extensively as non-combat vehicles. The only known battlefield support use on the Suez-Sinai front was on October 18, when about five Egyptian helicopters attacked the Israeli-held bridges across the Sweetwater Canal west of Deversoir. These helicopters were evidently transport craft which merely dropped explosives or fuzed drums of napalm quite inaccurately; none hit their targets. However, they did disrupt a nearby division command post, and almost got Defense Minister Dayan, who was visiting the front at the time. All of the Egyptian helicopters were shot down by ground fire.

On the Egyptian front helicopters were used successfully for surprise raids by both sides: by the Syrians in their initial seizure of the Israelis' Mt. Hermon observation post, and by the Israelis in at least one deep commando penetration north of Damascus. They were also used with mixed results in the assault role by both Israelis and Syrians in subsequent fighting near the crest of Mt. Hermon, both during the war and during the "war of attrition" later. They were most successful in the surprise initiation of an attack, proving to be vulnerable to both ground and hostile aircraft fire when committing reinforcements during the course of an ongoing battle. They do not appear to have been used at all in the gunfire support role on the Syrian front.

There have been unverified reports, with no corroboration by either side, that on a few occasions the Israelis did use helicopter gun ships successfully. Until this can be verified, it must remain a rumor. Clearly the impact could not have been great. Sustained combat use of the helicopter in an environment that was deadly to the F-4 and A-4 seems highly unlikely. Its role in carefully planned raids, however, and as a noncombat support vehicle is assured.

Loss and Attrition Rates

There are two aspects of the employment of the new weapons that are much discussed. The first is their deadliness and the resultant high rates of personnel casualties and equipment losses. The second is the high rates of consumption of ammunition and fuel. There is a body of military opinion which believes that both loss and consumption rates were unprecedented, and very serious in their implications, at the very least suggesting that the loss planning factors of all General Staffs must be drastically changed.

There is no question that loss and consumption rates were high, but they have not yet been seriously studied in historical perspective, and judgment should be reserved on this issue. Preliminary examination suggests that the personnel losses on both sides were less than for comparable periods in the 1967 war, and that the 1967 rates were comparable to those for all fronts in World War II. As for tank loss rates, further preliminary examination suggests that they did not exceed those in similarly short periods in World War II, as at Kursk, Anzio, and Caen. Consumption rates, also, must be assessed in the context of a brief, high intensity period of combat.

The Future of Infantry and Artillery

Some observers have concluded from the available records of the war that neither infantry nor artillery played a very important role in operations in which the principal weapons were tanks and antitank missiles, and fighter bombers and antiair missiles. Others have taken the same evidence to demonstrate that both infantry and artillery played more significant roles than many American or Israeli officers had expected would be possible on the modern battlefield.

No such glib generalizations are possible, because evidence can be found to support either of these simplistic points of view. In fact, despite the traditional affinity of these arms, the issues of the importance of artillery and infantry need to be assessed separately.

One reason why artillery did not seem very important in the war is that both sides took it for granted, and principal attention was given to the more dramatic confrontations of tank and antitank weapons, and aircraft versus SAMs and ZSU-23-4s. There is no question that artillery cannot dominate forces in armored vehicles as it did the mainly infantry forces of World Wars I and II. Chances of direct artillery hits against moving tanks and APCs are relatively low, and those inside these vehicles are largely immune to shell fragments.

But both sides relied greatly on artillery both for traditional missions, and for some new ones. Artillery fire was pervasive and intense. Artillery probably caused more casualties on both sides than all other weapons combined. The value of artillery in combined arms coordination with both armor and infantry was clearly reconfirmed. And while artillery fire destroyed a relatively small number of tanks, it did seriously inhibit tank operations, by causing the tankers to "button up," by closing hatches and relying upon the less than fully satisfactory sighting and observation devices within tanks and APCs. Artillery was particularly effective in interdicting defiles—including bridges—as well as mountain passes and desert roads.

The most important new use of artillery was that by the Israelis in attacking the Egyptian and Syrian SAMs, thus permitting Israeli aircraft to approach the battlefield for close support. For this reason the Israelis pushed their long range 155mm and 175mm guns close to the front, to reach as far behind the hostile lines as possible, in order to make the deepest possible rent in the SAM umbrella.

Until this war there had been a debate among artillerymen about the value of self-propelled artillery weapons. Some artillerymen—including this author—had been disturbed by the almost complete conversion of artillery to self-propelled weapons. They knew that when a self-propelled gun has motor trouble, or has its engine hit, it is out of action.

When the prime mover of a towed weapon is deadlined, or hit by hostile fire, it is very easy to find another truck which can tow the gun into action.

However, the doubters were converted by the performance of Israeli self-propelled artillery in this war. Losses were higher, because engines were hit, and deadline troubles somewhat reduced the availability of guns that were needed. But the self-propelled artillery was never neutralized. If taken under fire, occasionally guns were put out of action, but the other weapons could move a short distance and fire again. On the other hand, Arab towed artillery was often neutralized by the Israelis. And once the firing positions were under fire, those weapons could neither move nor shoot until the fire lifted.

As to infantry, the defensive performance of both Egyptian and Syrian infantry demonstrated that well-dug-in infantry, in combined arms coordination with artillery and with tanks or antitank weapons in support, can effectively oppose armored forces on almost any kind of terrain.

Yet Israeli generals can continue to assert convincingly that infantry cannot survive on the modern battlefield. They are thinking, of course, of *their* kind of battle; one based upon mobility and tactical maneuver. They recognize that they didn't rely sufficiently upon infantry at the outset of the war, misled by the experience of the Six Day War. But in the pervasive presence of artillery fire as deadly as that encountered in this war, and with hostile armor a constant threat, the need for armor protection and mechanization of infantry in mobile warfare seems undeniable.

The overall Israeli assessment of the continuing importance of artillery and infantry in modern war was demonstrated by IDF reorganizational decisions immediately after the war. The proportions of artillery and infantry to armor were drastically increased.

TACTICAL IMPLICATIONS

Surprise

The overwhelming tactical fact is the Arab surprise achieved in the attacks on the Bar Lev Line and on the Golan Line on October 6. The Arabs on both fronts had the advantage of complete strategic and near complete tactical surprise. The strategic surprise was the result of clever planning and deception by both Syrians and Egyptians, as well as Israeli-self-delusion. Given this strategic surprise some tactical surprise was inevitable. This was enhanced, however, by the Israeli assumption, once the attack was anticipated, that it would not begin until 6:00 p.m., when in fact it came at 2:05 p.m. It was further enhanced—particularly on the Egyptian front—by the tactics of using man-portable antitank weapons in well-prepared ambush techniques, combined with massed waves of infantry assaults, along a broad front. Israeli traditional tank doctrine played directly into the hands of the Egyptians.

My colleagues and I have made preliminary and tentative qualified comparisons of the effects of surprise on the relative combat effectiveness of the opposing forces in both the 1967 and 1973 Wars, in comparison with the effectiveness of each in battles in which there was not surprise (see Appendices A and B). On the assumption that the effects of surprise were primarily in the relative mobility and relative vulnerability of the opposing forces, the combat capability of the side achieving surprise was—on the average—almost doubled.

These analyses show that surprise—although of lesser magnitude— had a comparable effect when employed by the Israelis in their crossing of the Canal on October 15-16.

The Arab Broad Front Offensives

Another notable tactical fact is that, rather than concentrating their forces in one or two overpowering assaults, both attacking Arab armies at the outset intentionally adopted a broad-front approach. This was intended to force the Israelis to disperse their forces and efforts and to dilute their defensive capabilities. This apparent violation of the basic military principles of *mass* and of *economy of forces* was an interesting use of another basic principle—*maneuver*—by the Arab side for the purpose of employing its numerical superiority in men and weapons effectively, as distinguished from the Israelis' conscious efforts to concentrate on quality (without ignoring quantity). There can be little doubt that (next to surprise) this application of the principle of maneuver was a major feature in the Egyptian successes of the 6th and 7th.

Strength of Defensive Warfare

The strength of defensive warfare was again clearly demonstrated, evidence that the concepts of Clausewitz and Moltke are still tactically valid. (Of course, both Prussian theorists recognized that although defense is the stronger form of combat, success in warfare can be achieved only with offensive action.) The Bar Lev and Golan fortified lines, even though not remotely comparable in defensive power to World War II fortified zones like the Maginot and Siegfried Lines, or to the massive Soviet defenses at Kursk, saved the Israelis from early and devastating defeat. The defensive ambushes of Israeli tanks by Egyptian infantry, armed with Saggers and RPG-7s, were further evidence, as was their defense of their bridgeheads against repeated Israeli counterattacks. So, too, was the comparable tactical concept of the Israelis in stopping the Egyptian assault of October 14.

The Egyptian Rangers

A look at the record of the Egyptian Ranger operations on October 6 and 7 does not convey the significance that both Egyptian and Israeli soldiers attach to these operations. The commandos were landed at a number of places far east of the Canal, and conducted operations against Israeli rear-area installations and set up ambushes for Israeli reinforcements arriving down main thoroughfares from the eastern Sinai and Israel. They did not accomplish much; they had high casualties, and inflicted relatively few; no Israel unit was knocked out or overrun by these units.

While Egyptian officers claim the results of these commando raids were greater than they actually seem to have been, they do admit that losses were high in comparison to results. Yet they insist that the psychological effect of the raids was great and was a significant addition to the disruption created by the initial surprise assault crossing of the Canal.

Interestingly, this assessment is indirectly confirmed by conversations with Israelis. There is ambivalence in Israeli comments about the raids. They are quick to point out that the results were insignificant; that many commandos surrendered without accomplishing anything; that there was no significant delay imposed upon the critical arrivals of Adan's and Sharon's divisions. Yet the Israeli officers also admit that they were worried by the raids, and that the damage could have been serious. The very vehemence of their remarks about the commando failures confirms the Egyptian assessment of the psychological importance of the raids.

The human element has always been important in war, and despite the technology available to both sides, the human element was undoubtedly the most significant feature in this war.

THE HUMAN ELEMENT IN WAR

Combat Effectiveness

The aspect of the Arab-Israeli wars that has most attracted the attention of all commentators, military specialists and others, has been the consistent ability of the Israelis to overcome far larger Arab forces in all kinds of combat—air-to-air duels, clashes of armored forces, night fighting, and conventional infantry combat—and in all kinds of terrain: flat desert, rugged desert, agricultural land, urban areas, and mountains. In fact, as has been noted earlier in this book, the Arab numerical superiority has never been as great as in popular imagination and Israeli propaganda, mostly because of the amazingly efficient Israeli mobilization system, and the lesser efficiency of the Arabs in mobilizing and utilizing their potentially vast manpower superiority. Nonetheless, the numbers, overall, have favored the Arabs, and yet the Israelis have consistently won, whether attacking or defending, and regardless of conventional military wisdom about force ratios required in different kinds of combat situations.

Of all of the results of the quantitative analysis mentioned above, and summarized in Appendices A and B, the most significant are the values obtained for the relative Israeli-Egyptian combat effectiveness comparisons for 1967 and 1973. In both instances the opponents were representative of the best military force the respective nations could at that time put in the field, with experienced officer corps, and with weapons of comparable quality and sophistication. In the 1967 war the Egyptians suffered the disruption resulting from moderate or substantial surprise; in the 1973 war the Israelis suffered disruption from practically complete surprise.

The average Israeli combat effectiveness value (CEV) with respect to the Egyptians in 1967 was found to be 1.75[4]; in other words, a combat effectiveness superiority of almost two-to-one. Following an identical procedure for the 1973 war, the average Israeli CEV with respect to the Egyptians for that war was 1.98, suggesting that the Israeli combat effectiveness superiority over the Egyptians had increased by about 13% in the intervening six years.

Two significant conclusions can be drawn from this. First, in the 1973 war as in 1967, the Israeli combat effectiveness superiority was nearly two-to-one. In other words: 100 Israelis, in effectively organized military units, were approximately the combat equivalent of about 200 Egyptians similarly organized. It is evident that a single Israeli soldier was not on the average twice as strong, or twice as intelligent, or twice as good a soldier as his Egyptian counterpart. In fact, on a man-for-man basis, there appears to be little qualitative difference between the opponents. So, the comparison is valid only in terms of organized units.

The second significant point to be noted is that while the differential between the Israeli units and the Egyptian units was close to the same in both wars—two-to-one—*the gap had not narrowed between 1967 and 1973; if anything it had widened.* This is completely contradictory to the conventional reasoning, which has suggested that the Arabs performed so much better in 1973 than in 1967 because they had learned from their 1967 lessons, and had utilized the time to improve themselves, while the Israelis, arrogant and overconfident, had not made comparable efforts.

[4] For an explanation of the CEV, see Appendix A.

Serious study of the matter, however, not only reveals that the conventional reasoning is wrong, it also reveals why it is wrong.

Demonstration that the 1973 performance is not an indicator of improved Arab performance is as follows:

1. In 1967, the Israelis started with surprise; the Arabs never recovered, in fact never had a chance to recover.

2. In 1973 the Arabs started with greater surprise than the Israelis achieved in 1967. Yet within three days the Israelis had recovered, and were fighting on equal terms with the Arabs. This is one of the most remarkable recoveries in military history.

3. One reason the initial Israeli frontier victories in 1967 were followed so quickly by Arab collapse is that the Israelis had eliminated the Arab air arm, and were able to use their own air in unchallenged, massive attacks that completed the demoralization of the Arab ground forces. Thanks to the acquisition of Soviet air defense weapons in great numbers between 1967 and 1973, in the latest war the Arabs were able to prevent the Israeli air from having a comparable field day.

4. In 1967 the overall Arab commander in chief, and the man directly responsible for the Sinai front, was a political appointee, believed by the Egyptian officer corps to have been a drunk and a drug addict. In 1973 the Egyptians (and also the Syrians) were led by men who, if not the equal of their Israeli opponents (Ismail probably can be compared not unfavorably with them), were at least competent soldiers who did not lose their heads either in victory or in adversity.

A comparison of the Israeli vs. Syrian performance in the two wars might, at first glance, appear to contradict these arguments. In fact, however, the Syrian situation was unique, and cannot be the basis for any comparison of this sort.

The Syrian performance in 1967 was very poor. One reason for this was Syria's history of frequent military coups d'etat. After each coup the successful upstart cleared out all potential rivals or enemies in the officer corps. This created turmoil in the armed forces, with inevitable incompetence of the sort demonstrated in the 1967 war. Another reason, of course, was that the Syrians did not seriously try to oppose the Israelis in 1967.

In 1970, following an equally dismal performance against Jordan, there had been one more coup d'etat, led this time by the then Minister of War, Air Force General Hafez al Assad. The new President again swept the senior commanders away (the evidence of the recent war suggests that this could not have done serious harm), and put in his own men, who have remained as the military leadership of the country ever since. Thus an improvement in Syrian performance, a major improvement, was inevitable, no matter what the Israelis, the Egyptians, or anyone else had also done in the meantime.

But if we focus on the conflicts between Israel and Egypt, it is evident that the Israelis had not only not fallen behind in the years between 1967 and 1973 but in fact had continued to widen the combat effectiveness gap between themselves and the Egyptians. The reasons for this which can be summarized as follows:

a. Continuous Israeli efforts to improve military performance at all levels and in all respects: training, schooling, mobilization plans and practices, etc.; thus the Israelis were improving themselves while the Arabs were essentially locked into an effort to defeat the Israelis of 1967;

b. A substantially higher research and development capability, and apparently a more intensive technological effort.

c. Sound, objective, Israeli professional military analysis of historical experience and current capabilities, in contradistinction to the Arab cultural tendency to allow emotion and wishful thinking to influence evaluation, planning and operational leadership, a tendency which has persisted, despite commendable Arab efforts to curb and control it.

The Leadership of General Ismail

As noted in the assessments of previous wars, a very significant element of the Israeli superiority in overall combat effectiveness was the higher quality of leadership at all levels. In 1973 this situation had not changed fundamentally since the 1956 and 1967 wars. Israeli leaders were more aggressive, more flexible, and were better able to coordinate their efforts with those of leaders at higher and lower echelons. Particularly important, of course, was the ability of higher commanders to get the most out of their subordinates through cooperation, direction, and example.

On the other hand, there was one important change in Arab leadership in this war, and this was the top-level command leadership of Egyptian General Ismail. He was not a military genius, but he was a sound, capable professional, in the best sense of the word. One Israeli general has compared Ismail to Russian Field Marshal Kutuzov, Napoleon's opponent at Borodino. "A competent, dogged commander who understood his men well, but not an outstanding leader." The comparison is apt; Kutuzov was possibly more responsible than any other man for Napoleon's most disastrous defeat. Ismail was more responsible than any other man for the most disastrous defeats the Israeli Army has suffered.

Ismail's principal accomplishment, which has assured him an honored place among successful generals of history, was his direction of the

Egyptian General Staff in the planning for the Suez Canal crossing of Operation Badr. That planning, including the achievement of near perfect surprise, was the fundamental basis for the principal Arab successes of the war.

Ismail made a serious error on October 14th, and others between October 15th and 17th when he could have smashed Sharon's division and assured an unqualified Egyptian victory in the war. On the other hand, he could have been less than perfect in his initial preparations and never have created the opportunity to win. Even more, he could have panicked in adversity, as Shazli panicked, and in a few hours have thrown away all that he had won in the previous days. He was cautious, yet he took great risks when his victory seemed to be crumbling, and in so doing he saved much that he had won. Above all, as the Israeli general said, he "knew his men," and got the most out of them.

Other Behavioral Considerations

Paramount among the behavioral considerations, of course, was the effect of the Arab surprise, already noted above. Surprise, which assured the magnitude of the Israeli victory in 1967, went far to redress the balance in 1973. This is given substantial attention in the analysis in Appendix B.

The evidence is overwhelming that behavioral considerations—such as combat effectiveness, leadership, and surprise—were considerably more important in 1973 than a purely material comparison of men, numbers, weapons, and technology.

If the October War proved anything, it demonstrated that the human element in war remains as important as it ever was. Men in combat in 1973 were governed by the same behavioral laws that affected men in combat in 1943, and 1863, and 1813. That is why it is at least as important to focus on the effects of tactics as it is to consider the effects of hardware on the battlefield outcomes.

STRATEGIC IMPLICATIONS

Surprise

Just as surprise was the overwhelming tactical fact of the war, so too it was the overwhelming strategic fact. This was not only because, as one Israeli scholar has written, "It enabled the Arabs to dictate the opening moves in the war and to secure their initial successes."[5] These

[5] Avi Shlaim, *op. cit.*

successes had political and psychological impacts on all participants, and on the rest of the world, that subsequent Israeli military successes were never able to offset completely.

The Role of the Superpowers

From a global standpoint the most important strategic implications of the war were those involving the superpowers. Each was at one time or another during the war faced with the possibility that the side it was supporting might be defeated. And each reacted firmly and positively to prevent such a catastrophe to its influence and prestige. Both, recognizing the danger that such reactions could conceivably bring them into conflict against each other, sought mutual cooperation to avoid either of two unacceptable alternatives: defeat for their clients, or World War III. On balance, in the interests of world peace, and of Middle East peace, the situation was probably more dangerous than most of us realized at the time.

Achievement of Sadat's Strategic Objectives

Possibly the most important single strategic result of the war was the accomplishment of President Sadat's basic war objective; the condition of "no peace, no war" was dramatically ended. The superpowers were forced to give serious attention to the question of Middle East peace, and to exert their substantial influence toward some kind of resolution of the stalemate that had existed since 1967. The impetus to resolution which this caused is still active. "Sadat's decision under the conditions of 1973 represented a subtle combination of force and diplomacy at the service of rational and limited aims."[6]

For several reasons, the war restored Egypt to a position of primacy among the Arab states. In the first place, President Sadat's bold leadership in ending the stalemate gave prestige to Egypt and its leadership. That prestige was further enhanced by the brilliant military success of the early part of the war, and by the fact that, despite later setbacks, the Egyptian armed forces ended the war intact with clearly one of the most powerful military machines in the world. In addition, the results of the war permitted Egypt to reopen the Suez Canal and thus to regain some of the economic resources as well as prestige lost in 1967.

As a result of the creditable showing of the Egyptian and Syrian armies, in marked contrast to earlier defeats, Arab pride and confidence were restored; this, combined with the evidence of the tremendous value of Arab oil as an economic instrument of strategy, generally enhanced Arab influence in world affairs.

[6] *Ibid.*

Thus, if war is the employment of military force in support of political objectives, there can be no doubt that in strategic and political terms the Arab states—and particularly Egypt—won the war, even though the military outcome was a stalemate permitting both sides to claim military victory.

The Shocks to Israel

On the other hand, even though the military outcome was on balance an Israeli military success, the war was a severe psychological shock to the people of Israel. Despite the very creditable showing of their armed forces, and their remarkable recovery from initial surprise and defeat, with almost unbroken successes in the final days of conflict, the war made the Israelis realize that their forces were not invincible. They also could see that their Arab foes were capable of coordinating at least some of their vast superiority in manpower and economic resources in a war effort against Israel. The use of the oil and money weapons to turn formerly friendly and neutral nations against Israel was particularly dismaying. These things made the Israelis realize something which they had previously generally ignored: in a hostile world, in which one superpower was willing to provide almost unlimited support to Israel's enemies, Israel could no longer self-confidently count on its own ability to preserve its security. Unpalatable though it is to many Israelis, they have had to accept the fact that, under these circumstances, their future security is dependent upon the continuation of American support and good will.

The physical shock to the Israeli population of nearly 3,000 dead and more than 11,000 total war casualties in 19 days of war cannot be overestimated. It is as though the United States had suffered 132,000 dead, or 543,000 total casualties, in a similar period of time in World War II. Since our total losses in that war, over a period of about 1370 days, were 292,000 dead, and 963,000 total casualties, the impact is clear. In the October War, the Israeli loss rate, with respect to population, was more than 30 times as great as the American loss rate in World War II. Even though the actual battlefield loss rates per day for Israeli units were substantially less than comparable American loss rates in World War II, this in no way alters the impact of such loss rates upon the population of a tiny state. Nor can the Israelis gain any significant comfort from the fact that their battlefield loss rates were less than half those of their Arab opponents. In terms of total population, the Israeli loss rate was about five times that of Egypt.

These were and are sobering thoughts for Israelis.

Unsettled Question: Arab Quantity
Versus Israeli Quality

One result of grim postwar assessments has been urgent Israeli measures to avoid future surprises, and to increase the readiness and military capabilities of the Israel Defense Force. As a result, Israel is probably relatively stronger today, with respect to its Arab neighbors, than ever before. But many Israelis are asking themselves how long this can last, in the light of the population disparity of Israel and its neighbors, as well as the recent evidence that the Arabs are also capable of effectively handling sophisticated military hardware.

The war did not provide a clearcut answer to the question of the relative validity of the basic strategic concepts of the opposing sides: the Arab employment of quantity against Israeli quality. That, of course, is an oversimplification, because the Arabs sought—and quite successfully—to assure reasonable military quality and sophistication in their essentially mass armies, and the Israelis sought—even more successfully— to provide substantial quantities of forces of high military quality.

CONCLUSIONS

One can draw a *short-term conclusion* from the results of the war, and of the postwar efforts of both sides to profit from the experience. There does not seem to be any possibility of any decisive Arab military success over the Israelis in the next ten or twenty years. Israeli quality, combined with an impressive marshalling of quantity by a small nation, will almost certainly retain military ascendancy for many years to come, so long as US support is available to offset any outside support to the Arabs.

On the other hand, there is a somewhat different *long-term conclusion.* Quantified analyses of World War II combat have demonstrated that the Germans had a combat effectiveness superiority over the Russians, even as late as 1944, in the range of 100%.[7] Comparable quantified analysis of the Six Day War and of the October War shows that the Israelis had a superiority in the range of 100% over the Arabs in both wars.[8] In World War II—despite the tremendous disparity in the capabilities of the Russians and the Germans—the Soviet Union, by employment of

[7] "A Study of Breakthroughs," Report by the Historical Evaluation and Research Organization (HERO), 1976, for the Defense Nuclear Agency and Sandia Laboratories.

[8] "Comparative Analysis, Arab and Israeli Combat Performance, 1967 and 1973 Wars," HERO Study Report, 1976. These are comparisons of combined arms formations of brigade and division size, and are not intended to suggest any inherent difference in the courage, skill, or determination of individual soldiers or officers. The results of these analyses are summarized in Appendices A and B, below.

its substantial manpower advantage, and by perseverance despite defeat (plus considerable help from the United States and Britain), eventually defeated the qualitatively superior German Army.

This example suggests that it behooves the Israelis to seek a lasting peace while their military quality is still preeminent. If they wait too long it may be too late.

Of course it is not just the relative fighting abilities of the confrontation states—Israel versus Egypt, Jordan, and Syria and their allies from such places as Iraq and Morocco—that are involved in the strategic equation. It is the relations between the superpowers and their efforts to achieve conflicting objectives which are most important. And in considering this superpower relationship it must not be forgotten that the Arab states—although not those in the confrontation position—can influence the superpower interaction both directly and indirectly by the important economic weapon of oil.

Table A
AIR FORCE STRENGTHS, OCTOBER WAR 1973

	ARABS								ISRAELIS		
	Egypt Inventory	Resupply°	Syria Inventory	Resupply°	Iraq	Other Arabs	Total Arab Inventory	Resupply°		Inventory	Resupply°
Fighters											
MiG-21	160	…	110	…	18	23	311	…	A-4, Skyhawk	150	20
MiG-19	60	…	—	…	—	—	60	…	F-4 Phantom	140	36
MiG-17	200	…	120	…	7	24	351	…	Mirage	50	
Su-7	130	…	45	…	32	12	219	…	Super Mystère	12	
Hunter	…	…	…	…	16	5	21	…			
						28	28				
Total Fighters	550	93	275	113	73	92	990	206		352	55
Bombers											
Tu-16	18	…	…	…	…	…	18	…	Vautour, lt bomber	8	
Il-28	30	…	…	…	…	…	30	…			
Total Bombers	48	—	—	—	—	—	48	—		8	?
Total Combat	598	—	275	—	73	92	1,038	—		360	
Transports											
An-12	30	…	…	…	…	…	30	…	C-130	6	
Il-14	40	…	12	…	…	…	52	…	C-47	12	
Il-18	…	…	4	…	…	…	4	…	C-97	10	
									Noratlas	30	
Total Transports	70	—	16	—	—	—	86	—		66	?
Helicopters											
Mi-6	12	…	6	…	…	…	18	…	Super Frelon	8	
Mi-8	70	…	30	…	…	…	112	…	CH-53	12	
									AB 205	30	
Total Helicopters	82	70	36	12	—	—	130	82		50	? ?
Total Noncombat	152		52		—	12	216			116	
Total Air Inventory	750		327		73	104	1,254			476	
Losses	265		131		21	30	447			109	
Resupply°	163		125		—	—	288			56+	
Total At End of War	648		321		52	74	1,095			423+	
Manpower	23,000		9,000		?	?	32,000+			17,000	

° October 9-23, inclusive.

Table B
FIGHTER AND FIGHTER-BOMBER CHARACTERISTICS, OCTOBER WAR 1973

	Gross Weight (lb.)	Length (ft.)	Span (ft.)	Max Speed (mach)	Combat Radius (mile)	Fixed Armament	Typical Bomb Load	Remarks
Arab Aircraft								
MiG-21	20,725	51¾	23¾	2.1	300	2 x 23mm cannon	2 x 1100 lb bombs or 64 x 57mm rockets	Apparently used only for air superiority tasks
Su-7	29,750	57	29¼	1.6	285	2 x 30mm cannon	2 x 550 lb bombs 32 x 57mm rockets	
MiG-17	12,500	36½	31	0.98	325	3 x 23mm cannon	2 x 550 lb bombs or 32 rockets	
Israeli Aircraft								
Mirage	29,760	49	27	2.2	745	2 x 30mm cannon	1 x AS30* (ASM) 2 x 1000 lb or 4 x 1000 lb or 72 rockets (prob 68mm)	
F-4	57,400	58¾	38½	2.27	656	1 x 20mm cannon	18 x 750 lb bombs 6 x Maverick PGM	Max load, 16,000 lbs Bombs and rockets
A-4	24,500	40¼	27½	0.94	340	2 x 30mm cannon	4 x 1000 lbs or 1 x 2000 lbs 4 x Bullpup	Max load 10,000 lbs bombs & rockets; only 4,000 lbs at 340 mile radius
Super Mystère	22,046	46	34½	1.73	250	2 x 30mm cannon	38 rockets (68mm) 2 x 1000 lbs or 38 rockets (68mm) 24 x 5" HVAR**	

* AS30 Air-to-Surface missile.
** HVAR High Velocity Aerial Rocket.

Table C

ESTIMATED GROUND STRENGTHS, OCTOBER WAR 1973

	Israel	Total Arab Committed	Egypt	Syria	Iraq Com-mitted	Jordan Com-mitted	Other Arabs	Iraq Total	Jordan Total	Total Arab Potential
Available Army Manpower[1]	310,000	505,000	315,000	140,000	20,000	5,000	25,000	95,000	75,000	650,000
Tank/Armored Divisions	7	5	2	2	1			2	2	8
Infantry/Mechanized Divs		11	8	3		1		4	3	18
Separate Brigades	18	47	20	21			5	?	?	46
Medium Tanks	2,000[2]	4,841	2,200[5]	1,820[9]	300	150	371	1,200	540	6,131
APCs	4,000[3]	4,320	2,400	1,300	300	200	120	1,500	550	5,870
Artillery (over 100mm)	570	2,055	1,210	655	54	36	100	600	320	2,885
Multiple Rocket Launchers		90	70	20	?	?		?		90
Mortars (over 100mm)	375	650+	350	300	?	?	?	?	?	650+
SSM Launchers		42	30	12						42
SAM Launchers	75	1,280	880[6]	360[10]	20		20	?		1,280
Strella		3,000	2,000	1,000	?		?	?		3,000
AA Guns	1,000	3,650+	2,750[7]	1,900[11]	?		?	?	?	3,650+
AT Missiles	280[4]	1,200	850[8]	350[12]						1,200
AT Rockets	650	5,300+	2,500	2,800	?	?	?	?	?	5,300+
AT Guns		2,200+	1,300	900	?	?	?	?	?	2,200+

[1] Only field army and direct support manpower; for instance, total Israeli mobilized strength was over 350,000, Egyptian over 1,000,000.

[2] Includes 150 captured T-54/55, modified.

[3] Includes 3,500+ half-tracks, 500 M-113.

[4] Includes SS-10 and SS-11, apparently not used.

[5] Includes T-62.

[6] Includes 80 SA-6.

[7] Includes 150 ZSU-23-4.

[8] Mostly Sagger, some Snapper.

[9] Includes T-62.

[10] Includes 60 SA-6.

[11] Includes 100 ZSU-23-4.

[12] Mostly Sagger, some Snapper.

Table D
ESTIMATED NAVAL STRENGTHS, OCTOBER WAR 1973

	Israel	Egypt	Syria
Manpower	4,000	17,000	2,000
Patrol & Torpedo Boats	18	34[2]	13[5]
Guided Missile Boats	14[1]	17[3]	9[6]
Destroyers & Frigates	0	8	0
Submarines	1	12	0
Amphibious Craft	0	14	0
Small Craft	10	24[4]	2[7]
Vessel Totals	43	109	24

[1] Includes 12 *Saar*, 2 *Reshev*.
[2] Lost 2 during war.
[3] Includes 5 *Komar*, 12 *Osa*; lost 2 *Osa* during war.
[4] Lost 2 during war.
[5] Lost 1 during war.
[6] Includes 6 *Komar*, 3 *Osa*; lost 2 *Komar* and 1 *Osa* during war.
[7] Lost 1 during war.

Table E
ESTIMATED AIR LOSSES, OCTOBER WAR 1973

	Egypt	Syria	Iraq	Other Arabs	Arab Total	Israel
A. By Type						
Fighter	222	117	21	30	390	103
Bomber	1				1	
Transport		1			1	
Helicopter	42	13			55	6
Totals	265	131	21	30	447	109
B. By Cause						
Air-to-Air					287	21
To SAM					17	40
To AAA					19	31
Misc or Unknown					66	15
Friendly Forces					58	2
Totals					447	109
C. Damage						
Damaged					125	236
Repaired in One Week					?	215

Table F
ESTIMATED LOSSES, OCTOBER WAR, 1973

	Israel	Arab Total	Egypt	Syria	Jordan	Iraq	Other Arabs
Personnel							
Killed	2,838[*]	8,528	5,000	3,100	28	218	100
Wounded	8,800[*]	19,549	12,000	6,000	49	600	300
Prisoners or Missing	508	8,551	8,031	500		20	?
Tanks[**]	840	2,554	1,100	1,200	54	200	?
APCs	400	850+	450	400		?	?
Artillery Pieces	?	550+	300	250		?	?
SAM Batteries		47	44	3			?
Aircraft	103	392	223	118		21	30
Helicopters	6	55	42	13		?	?
Naval Vessels	1	15	10	5			

[*] About 10% has been added to officially reported Israeli casualties to represent approximately the wounded who died of their injuries, and the fact that official Israeli figures apparently do not include those wounded not evacuated from aid stations and field hospitals.

[**] Tanks destroyed or put out of action for one or more days. For instance, the Israelis seem to have repaired and returned to operation about 400 of the tank losses shown here. They also recovered about 300 repairable Arab tanks.

Table G
CHARACTERISTICS: MISSILES AND ROCKETS, OCTOBER WAR 1973

Name	Designation	Length (cm)	Diameter (cm)	Wingspan (cm)	Max Speed (mach)	Launch Wt. (kg)	Warhead Wt. (kg)	Warhead Type
Air-to-Air Missiles—AAM								
Israel								
Shafrir		260.0	16.0	60.0	2.0	93.0	11.0	HE
Sidewinder	AIM-9	284.0	12.7	60.9	2.0	75.0	11.4	HE
Arab								
Atoll	K-13A	280.0	12.0	53.0	2.0	69.8	..	HE
Air-to-Surface Missiles—ASM								
Israel								
Walleye	GW-Mk-1	344.0	38.1	114.0	..	499.0	385.0	HE
Maverick	AGM-65	246.0	30.0	71.0	2.0+	209.0	59.0	HE-shaped
Bullpup	AGM-12	320.0	30.5	95.3	2.0	258.0	..	HE
Shrike	AGM-45	304.8	20.0	91.4	2.0+	177.0	..	HE frag
Standard ARM	AGM-78	457.0	30.5	139.7	..	826.0	..	HE
Arab								
Kelt	AS-5	940.0	..	460.0	..			HE
Surface-to-Surface Missiles—SSM								
Israel								
Jericho	MOD-660	..	..	..	..			..
Arab								
Frog°	..	900.0	55.0	105.0	..	2,000.0	..	HE
Scud°	..	1,100.0	85.0	..	5.0	6,300.0	..	HE
Surface-to-Air Missiles—SAM°°								
Israel								
Hawk	MIM-23A	512.0	35.0	122.0	2.5	580.0	..	HE
Arab								
Guideline°	SA-2	1,070.0	70/50	122.0	..	2,300.0	130.0	HE
Goa°	SA-3	670.0	60/45	122.0	..	..	..	HE
Gainful°	SA-6	620.0	33.5	..	..	550.0	40.0	HE
Grail° (Strella)	SA-7	125.0	7.0	..	..	..	..	HE
Antitank Rockets & Guided Missiles—ATR & ATGM°°°					(m/sec.)			
Israel								
TOW	BGM-71A	117.0	15.2	..	278.0	18.0	..	HE-shaped
LAW	M-72	65.3	6.6	..	145	1.25	..	..
Super Bazooka	M-20A1	153.0	8.9	..	148.9	3.31	..	HE-shaped
Arab								
Snapper°	AT-1	113.0	15.0	..	89.0	22.25	..	HE-shaped
Sagger°	AT-3	88.0	12.0	..	120.0	11.3	..	HE-shaped
	RPG-7	..	4/10	..	..	..	2.5	HE-shaped

° NATO nickname.
°° AA guns: Israel: 2 x 20mm, 4 x 20mm, 2 x 40mm, mounted on AML (Panhard) or M-42 chassis.
Arab: ZSU-23-4 (4 x 23mm), mounted on PT76 chassis; Su-57, twin 57mm on armored track chassis.
°°° AT guns: Israel: 106mm RR.
Arab: Su-100 (100mm, SP, armored); D-48 (85mm); 57mm, M-1943; B-10 (82mm recoilless rifle);

Table G (Continued)

CHARACTERISTICS: MISSILES AND ROCKETS, OCTOBER WAR 1973

Propulsion	Guidance	Homing	Range (km)	Launch Platform	Altitude
Solid fuel rocket	Infrared	Infrared		Mirage, F-4	
Solid fuel rocket	Infrared	Infrared	3.24	Mirage, F-4	
Solid fuel rocket	Infrared	Infrared	2.74	MiG-21	
Gravity	TV	Lock-on		A-4, F-4	
2-stage solid rocket	TV	TV		F-4	
Liquid rocket	Radio comd.	Radio comd.	17.00	A-4, F-4	
Solid rocket	Passive radar	Passive radar	16.00	A-4, F-4	
Dual-thrust solid rocket	Passive radar		25+	F-4	
			320.00	Tu-16	
			450.00	Not used, little info	
Solid rocket	Spin stabilizer	None	60.00	Tracked (PT-76)	
Liquid	Inertial		280.00	Wheeled transporter	
2-stage solid rocket	Radar	Radar	35.00	SP	11,600/30
2-stage liquid/solid	Radar	Radar	50.00		
2-stage solid	Radar	Radar	30.00		18,600/-
Integral rocket ram-jet	Optical		60/30	SP	18,000/4,000
		Heat seeking		Shoulder, BRDM	
2-stage solid rocket	Wire guided	Optical track	3.75/.065	M-113 APC	
Solid rocket	Aimed		.25	Shoulder	
Solid rocket	Aimed		.15	Shoulder	
Solid rocket	Wire guided	Visually guided	2.3/.5	(Hand-carried box)	
Solid rocket	Wire guided		3/.5	(BRDM, BMP)	
Solid rocket	Aimed	Visually guided	.3	Shoulder	

ISRAELI ORDER OF BATTLE[1]
October 1973

Minister of Defense	Moshe Dayan
Chief of Staff	LG David Elazar
Special Assistant to Chief of Staff	LG Haim Bar Lev
Deputy Chief of Staff, Operations	MG Israel Tal
Chief, Operations Division	MG Avraham Tamir
Assistant Chief, Operations Division	BG Arie Levi
Director of Intelligence	MG Eliahu Zeira
Assistant Director of Intelligence	BG Arie Shalev
Chief, Mossad (Secret Service)	MG Zvi Zamir
Southern Command	MG Shmuel (Gorodish) Gonen
252d Armored Division (Ugdah) (RA)[2]	MG Avraham (Albert) Mendler, BG Kalman Magen[3]
(460th Armored Bde[4]	Col. Gabi Amir)
(14th Armored Bde[4]	Col. Amnon Reshev)
(116th (16th?) Infantry Bde (Etzioni)	Col. Reuven Pinchas)
401st Armored Bde	Col. Dani Shomron
164th Armored Bde (c. 8-9 Oct.)[5]	Col. Avraham Barom
162d Armored Division (Res) (7 Oct.)	MG Avrahan (Bren) Adan
Deputy CG	BG Dovic Tamari
217th Armored Bde	Col. Arieh Karen
600th Armored Bde	Col. Natke Baram
460th Armored Bde (7 Oct.)	Col. Gabi Amir
(247th Armored Bde (16-17 Oct.)	Col. Tuvia Raviv)
(35th Para Bde (16-17 Oct.)	Col. Uzi Ya'iri)
(.... Armored Bde (c. 9-13 Oct.) (T-54/55 tanks)	Col. Yoel Gonen)
(Composite Inf Bde (21-25 Oct.)[6]	BG Dovic Tamari)
143d Armored Division (Res) (7 Oct.)	MG Ariel (Arik) Sharon
Deputy CG	BG Jacob Even
421st Armored Bde	Col. Haim Erez
247th Armored Bde	Col. Tuvia Raviv
14th Armored Bde	Col. Amnon Reshev
243d Para Bde (15 Oct.)	Col. Dani Matt
(116th (16th?) Inf Bde (8-13 Oct.)	Col. Reuven Pinchas)
146th Composite Division (c. 13 Oct.)	BG ? Sassoon
116th (16th?) Infantry Bde	Col. Reuven Pinchas
11th Mechanized Infantry Bde	Col. Jacob Peled
.... Bde	?
440th Composite Division[7] (c. 15 Oct.)	MF Granit Ysrael MG Menachim Meron
.... Bde	?
.... Bde	?
.... Bde	?
Southern Sinai Command	MG Yeshayahu Gavish
99th Infantry Bde	Col. Tili Shapira
.... Bde	?

ISRAELI ORDER OF BATTLE[1]
October 1973
(Continued)

Central Command	MG Yona Ephrat
. . . . Bde	?
. . . . Bde	?
Northern Command	MG Yitzak Hoffi
36th Mechanized Division (RA)	BG Raphael (Raful) Eitan
Deputy CG	BG Menachem Avirem
188th Armored Bde (Barak)	Col. Yitzhak Ben Shoham
7th Armored Bde	Col. Avigdor (Yanush) Ben Gal
1st Infantry Bde (Golani)	Col. Amir Drori
31st Para Bde	Col. Elisha Shelem
240th Armored Division (Res) (7 Oct.)	MG Dan Laner
Deputy CG	BG Moshe Bar Kochva
17th Armored Bde	Col. Ran Sarig
79th Armored Bde	Col. Uri Or
20th Armored Bde (c. 10 Oct.)	Col. Yossi Peled
14th Infantry Bde (c. 9 Oct.)	Col. Itzhak Bar
(19th Armored Bde	Col. Mir)
146th Armored Div (Res)[8] (8 Oct.)	MG Moshe (Mussa) Peled
Deputy CG	BG Arie Shakhar
19th Armored Bde (c. 10 Oct.)	Col. Mir
70th Armored Bde	Col. Yakob Pfeffer
9th Armored Bde	Col. Mordechai Ben Porat
(20th Armored Bde	Col. Yossi Peled)
Air Force	MG Benhamin Peled
Navy	MG (RAdm) Benjamin Telem

[1] Israel mobilized approximately 30 brigades, of which about half were armored brigades and the remainder about equally divided between mechanized infantry brigades and parachute/infantry brigades. This order of battle lists 30 separate brigades, plus one composite brigade. (See Note 4.) Eight brigades appear twice, one appears three times. Among the brigades not specifically identified were apparently the following: 205th Armored Brigade, 670th Mechanized Infantry Brigade, 240th Mechanized Infantry Brigade, 134th Armored Brigade, 23d Parachute Brigade, 3d Infantry Brigade, 210th Armored Brigade. At least four of the armored brigades listed above or in this note were probably mechanized brigades, incorrectly identified.

[2] Regular Army divisions are identified as RA, reserve divisions are Res.

[3] General Magen replaced General Mendler after the latter's death on October 13.

[4] Brigades shown in parenthesis were only temporarily under the indicated divisions. For instance, Colonel Gonen's brigade of captured T-54/55 tanks joined General Adan about October 9 or 10, and was transferred to either the 440th or 146th Division on about October 14. (Colonel Gonen was the younger brother of the Southern Command commander.) Colonel Matt's brigade joined Sharon's division on the 15th, and remained with that division for the rest of the campaign.

[5] Dates in parenthesis show dates a division or brigade was committed, joined, or was temporarily with a higher command.

[6] This brigade was created by General Adan, and placed under his second in command, as reinforcements were sent to him on October 21 or 22.

[7] The original commander of this division was BG Granit Ysrael, who was relieved for compassionate reasons after the death of his only son on the Golan.

[8] This division was transferred to the Sinai Front after the October 25 ceasefire.

EGYPTIAN ORDER OF BATTLE
October 1973

Minister of War and Commander in Chief	Col. Gen. Ahmed Ismail Ali
Chief of Staff	Lt. Gen. Saad el Shazli[1]
Chief of Operations	MG Mohommed el Gamasy
Chief of Intelligence	MG Ibrahim Fouad Nassar
Second Field Army	MG Moh. Saad el Din Mamoun[2]
Second Army Artillery	Brig. Abd el Halim Abou Ghazala
47th Artillery Bde	
57th Artillery Bde	
62d Mortar Bde	
18th Infantry Division	Brig. Fuad Aziz Ghaly
134th Infantry Bde	
135th Infantry Bde	
136th Mechanized Infantry Bde	
Artillery Bde	
15th Independent Armored Bde (attached)	
2d Infantry Division	Brig. Hassan Abou Seeda
4th Infantry Bde	
120th Infantry Bde	
117th Mechanized Infantry Bde	
59th Artillery Bde	
24th Armored Bde (23d Mczd Div) (attached)	
16th Infantry Division	BG Abd el Rab Nabi Hafiz
16th Infantry Bde	
112th Infantry Bde	
3d Mechanized Infantry Bde	
41st Artillery Bde	
14th Armored Bde (21st Armd Div) (attached)	
21st Armored Division (-14th Bde)	Brig. Ibrahim Oraby
1st Armored Bde	
18th Mechanized Infantry Bde	
51st Artillery Bde	
23d Mechanized Infantry Division (-24th Armd Bde) (attached from GHQ Reserve)	Brig. Ahmed Aboud el Zommor
116th Mechanized Infantry Bde	
118th Mechanized Infantry Bde	
67th Artillery Bde	
135th Independent Infantry Bde (Port Said area)	
182d Parachute Bde	Col. Ismail Azmy
9th Engineer Bde	Col. Gamel Talmei
90th Mechanized Infantry Bde	Col. Zalach Badir
129th Commando Group	Col. Moh. Abd el Kader Haikal

EGYPTIAN ORDER OF BATTLE
October 1973
(Continued)

Third Field Army	MG Moh. Abd el Moneim Wassel
Third Army Artillery	Brig. Moneir Shasli
53d Artillery Bde	
55th Artillery Bde	
60th Mortar Bde	
7th Infantry Division	Brig. Ahmad Badawy
11th Infantry Bde	
12th Infantry Bde	
8th Mechanized Infantry Bde	
49th Artillery Bde	
25th Independent Armored Bde	
(attached)	
19th Infantry Division	Brig. Yussef Afifi
5th Infantry Bde	
7th Infantry Bde	
2d Mechanized Infantry Bde	
69th Artillery Bde	
3d Armored Bde (4th Armd Div)	
(attached)	
4th Armored Division	Brig. Abd el Aziz Qabil
(-3d Armd Bde)	
2d Armored Bde	
6th Armored Bde	
6th Mechanized Infantry Bde	
4th Artillery Bde	
6th Mechanized Infantry Division	Brig. Abou el Fath Moharram
(attached from GHQ Res)	
1st Mechanized Infantry Bde	
113th Mechanized Infantry Bde	
22d Armored Bde	
43d Artillery Bde	
109th Engineer Bde	Brig. Fuad Muhammed Saletan
130th Mechanized Infantry Bde	Brig. Mohammed Shaib Shaliman
(3d Mczd Inf Div)	Col. Ramez Elgandi
127th Commando Group	
Red Sea Command	(not released)
Infantry Bde	
Infantry Bde	
133d Commando Group	
GHQ Reserve (-6th and 23d Mczd	
Inf Divs)	
3d Mechanized Infantry Division	Brig. Mohommed Nagaty Farahat
10th Mechanized Infantry Bde	
114th Mechanized Infantry Bde	
23d Armored Bde	

EGYPTIAN ORDER OF BATTLE
October 1973
(Continued)

39th Artillery Bde
140th Parachute Bde
150th Air Assault Bde
160th Air Assault Bde
Presidential Guard Bde
Nasser Independent Armored Bde
Independent Armored Bde
63d Artillery Bde (antitank)
64th Artillery Bde (FROG)
128th Commando Group
130th Commando Group
131st Commando Group
132d Commando Group
134th Commando Group

Artillery Department	MG Mohommed el Mahy
Engineer Department	MG Gamal Mohommed Ali
Ranger Command	Brig. Nabil Shoukry
Navy	VAdm Ahmad Fuad Zekry
Air Force	AVM Moh. Hosny Moubarak
Air Defense Forces	MG Mohommed Ali Fahmy

[1] Relieved of post October 20, replaced by MG Gamasy.
[2] Due to heart attack, October 14, replaced (October 16) by MG Abdul Moneim Khalil.

SYRIAN ORDER OF BATTLE
October 1973

Minister of Defense	MG Mustafa Tlass
Chief of Staff	MG Youssef Chakkour
Director of Intelligence	MG Jibrael Bitar
1st Armored Division	Col. Tewfiq Juhni
4th Armored Bde	
91st Armored Bde	Col. Shafiq Fayad
2d Mechanized Infantry Bde	
64th Artillery Bde	
3d Armored Division	BG Mustafa Sharba[1]
20th Armored Bde	
65th Armored Bde	
15th Mechanized Infantry Bde	
13th Artillery Bde	
5th Infantry Division	BG Ali Aslan
12th Infantry Bde	
61st Infantry Bde	
132d Mechanized Infantry Bde	
50th Artillery Bde	
47th Independent Armored Bde (attached)	
7th Infantry Division	BG Omar Abrash[1]
	BG Said Berakdar

SYRIAN ORDER OF BATTLE
October 1973
(Continued)

68th Infantry Bde	Col. Rafiq Hilawi
85th Infantry Bde	
1st Mechanized Infantry Bde	
70th Artillery Bde	
78th Independent Armored Bde	
(attached)	
9th Infantry Division	Col. Hassan Tourkmani
52d Infantry Bde	
53d Infantry Bde	
43d Mechanized Infantry Bde	
89th Artillery Bde	
51st Independent Armored Bde	
(attached)	
GHQ Forces	
Assad Independent Armored Bde	
30th Infantry Bde	
90th Infantry Bde	
62d Mechanized Infantry Bde	
88th Armored Bde	
141st Armored Bde	
1st Commando Group (5 battalions)	
82d Parachute Battalion	
Desert Guard Battalion	
(eastern Syria)	
.... Infantry Bde, Latakia	
.... Infantry Bde, Homs	
.... Infantry Bde, Aleppo	
Navy	BG (RAdm) Fadl Hussein
Air Force	MG Naji Jamil
Iraqi Contingent[2]	
3d Armored Division	BG Lafta
6th Armored Bde	
12th Armored Bde	
8th Mechanized Infantry Bde	
Artillery Group	
Jordanian Contingent[3]	
40th Armored Bde	Brig. Haled Hajhouj el Majali
Moroccan Contingent[4]	
Mechanized Infantry Bde	BG Safrawi
Saudi Arabian Contingent	
20th Armored Bde (King Abdul	
Aziz Bde)	
Palestine Liberation Army: two commando brigades	

---

[1] Graduates of the US Army Command and General Staff College.

[2] 6th Armored Division and elements of two infantry divisions also reached Syria but were not committed to combat.

[3] Headquarters 3d Armored Division and 192d Armored Brigade also reached Syria but were not committed to combat.

[4] Two additional independent infantry battalions were also apparently in Syria.

Epilogue:

Elusive Peace

Two facts have emerged from this pattern of wars and clashes of nationalist, religious, and philosophical beliefs:

First, the Arabs will not accept as an honorable peace anything that does not return to them (including the Palestinians) all of the territories occupied by the Israelis in 1967—with probably some slight room for bargaining on truly limited frontier changes. They will keep on fighting and persist in a state of war until this return is accomplished, or clearly in process in an irreversible form.

Second, Israel will not accept peace terms that do not provide unequivocal assurance that (a) Israel's frontiers are not vulnerable to infiltration by guerrillas (or fedayeen or terrorists, depending on the point of view); (b) hostile Arab armed forces cannot concentrate for invasion or threat of invasion in any of the territories occupied in 1967; and (c) Eilat is secure from blockade.

Any peace proposal which does not recognize these as *facts*, as *absolute conditions*, and not just as bargaining objectives, *is bound to fail*.

While these fixed positions are not completely mutually incompatible—bearing in mind such things as United Nations Forces, demilitarized zones, and neutral electronics surveillance possibilities—they do not leave much room for diplomatic maneuvering. And achievement of a formula which might offhand seem not to be terribly difficult is close to impossible because of a third fact almost (but hopefully not quite) as immutable as the first two: Mutual distrust between Arabs and Israelis is so strong and so deep-seated that neither will trust the other to abide by any agreement.

This also is currently absolute, but it is possibly susceptible to change over a long time. Until changed, however, this means that agreement under duress—in other words, an imposed settlement cannot satisfy the basic conditions of either party if it believes that it has been forced to accept the unacceptable. Since movement toward these objectives will be possible, however, only with some kind of outside pressures, which will be resented even if accepted, the room for diplomatic maneuvering is still further constrained.

619

Of the many examples that each side can marshal to demonstrate why the other is completely untrustworthy, just a few should be mentioned, to impress on the reader how strong is the existing feeling of antipathy and distrust.

On the Arab side:

The massacre of Deir Yassin, in April 1947, has never been forgotten, and resentment probably can be reduced only by public acts of atonement by Israel and Israelis such as West Germany has offered to the Jews in penance for the Nazi holocaust of the Hitler era. Such an act of atonement, however, is unthinkable in an atmosphere which is embittered by Israeli recollections of equally bloody Arab atrocities.

Much more recent was the senseless destruction of the previously undamaged buildings of Kuneitra by the Israeli Army before the city was evacuated in 1974, exacerbated by the looting of church and mosque, and the ghastly desecreation of the Arab-Christian graveyard by Israeli soldiers.

The Arabs will also require some kind of real assurance that they will not continue to be threatened by the Zionist policy of encouraging unlimited Jewish immigration to Israel, which, combined with the establishment of settlements in the Sinai, on the Golan, and on the West Bank, apparently confirm their assessments of Zionist expansionist intentions. How, they also ask, can this be reconciled with nominal Israeli acceptance of UN Resolution 242?

Finally, progress toward peace will probably never be possible as long as the Arabs detect Israeli condescension to them as less-civilized inferiors—the term "savages" can be found in Israeli literature. The Arabs, after all, have reason to be proud of a civilization which was for a long time intellectually superior to that of the Europe from which—as the Arabs see it—the Jews have come to Palestine.

The Israeli distrust and antipathy for the Arabs are just as firmly founded:

The slaughter of Jewish doctors and nurses at Sheikh Jarrach in April 1947 and the slaughter of men, women and children at Kfar Etzion a few weeks later are only two of the many bitter memories of Arab "savagery" which Israelis recall from the grim days before the War for Independence.

Israelis have particularly bitter memories of the deliberate desecration of Jewish graves on the slopes of the Kedron Valley between the Mount of Olives and the walls of Jerusalem, during the period of Arab occupation from 1947 to 1967.

The Israelis also remember the numerous instances in which, in their several wars against the surrounding, threatening Arab states, Jewish prisoners of war have been tortured and murdered; they can cite numerous specific instances which have been reported to the Red Cross and other international bodies.

Especially infuriating to Israelis, after recovery of the Mt. Hermon Observation Post on October 22, 1973, was the discovery of the bodies of the Israeli garrison, their hands tied behind their backs, obviously murdered in cold blood.

There are many documented instances of threats by presumably responsible Arab leaders of the Arab intentions to destroy Israel and to drive the Jews into the sea;[1] these threats have been muted in recent years because—the Israelis are convinced—the Arabs are seeking to calm Western public opinion. But how can the Israelis be convinced that this is not merely a propaganda tactic, since there are other evidences of the continuing and enduring Arab hatred that led to these threats in the first place? How can Arab assurances of willingness to accept the fact of Israel be reconciled with the Arabs' refusal to negotiate face-to-face, with their refusal to end the state of war, and with the frequent references to the Crusades (when the Arabs expelled the Christians, after a century of occupation of much of the Holy Land) as an inspirational example to their peoples today?

Helping to bridge this gap of mutual hatred and suspicion is the most important contribution any outsider can make to the future of peace in the Middle East. One important step in this direction was taken by Secretary of State Henry Kissinger in bringing about the 1975 Disengagement Agreement in the Sinai. Probably a majority of Arabs, and a majority of Israelis, consider this agreement a dangerous compromise favorable to the "enemy." But more responsible Egyptian and Israeli leaders see that it provides both sides with an opportunity to assess the intentions of the other in a remarkably fair and even-handed exchange, in which (should the other side choose to breach the agreement) neither side can be seriously worse off than it was before the agreement was made.

The conferences between Egyptian and Israeli officers working on the implementation of the agreement were, in themselves, another step toward removing suspicions, since both sides could see the other as human beings, with intellects, foibles, and professional pride remarkably similar to their own. Hopefully more such formal and informal meetings can be arranged, under circumstances in which both sides can increasingly see the potential benefits of true agreement, and true peace.

It is obvious to all that the nations and peoples of the Middle East need, and most of them are eager for, a stable situation with no threat of renewed warfare. At no time has the prospect for real peace been better, for in spite of their basic conflicting demands all but the most

---

[1] The author is aware of the publicized civil trial in England in 1975 as a result of an offer to pay a reward if it could be proven that such Arab threats had been made. When the offerers refused to pay the reward, the claimant sued and lost. But he lost on a technicality. The eivdence of Arab threats to destroy Israel is convincing to any objective observer.

radical on both sides seem ready to work for it. Even the Palestinians, who have suffered the most, seem prepared to accept less than they have been demanding. To what extent compromise is possible at present, however, is highly uncertain. Since peace in the Middle East is clearly in the interest of the major world nations, diplomatically imposed compromise may well be the only immediate solution to an enduring state of armed truce.

Quantitative Analysis of the June War, 1967

The Historical Evaluation and Research Organization (HERO) has recently undertaken quantitative analyses of the June War, or Six Day War, of 1967, and the October War of 1973. A summary of the results of that analysis, as it pertains to the 1967 war, is presented below.

THE DATA

Estimates of the overall strengths of the participating forces are included in the table on p. 337. Not included here are detailed listings of the principal varieties of weapons and combat equipment estimated to have been on hand in the field forces of the Israeli, Egyptian, Jordanian, and Syrian armies as of June 1, 1967, with the presumed allocations to major combat formations, such as divisions and brigades.

Figure A-1 is a listing of all major engagements on all three fronts between June 5 and June 10. The table on p. 333 provides total casualties and other losses for the war as best these can be estimated.

FIGURE A-1
ENGAGEMENTS, SIX DAY WAR, JUNE 1967

No.	WEST BANK FRONT Date	Engagement	No.	SINAI FRONT Date	Engagement
67-1	June 5	Rafah	67-21	June 5/7	Jerusalem
67-2	5/6	Abu Ageila-	67-22	5/6	Jenin
		Um Katef	67-23	6/7	Kabatiya
67-3	5/7	Gaza Strip	67-24	6/7	Tilfit-Zababida
67-4	5/6	El Arish	67-25	7	Nablus
67-5	5/6	Bir Lahfan			
67-6	6	Jebel Libni			
67-7	7	Bir Hamma-		GOLAN FRONT	
		Bir Gifgafa			
67-8	7	Bir Hassna-	67-31	9	Golan
	7	Bir el Thamada	67-32	9	Zaoura-Qala
67-9	7/8	Mitla Pass	67-33	9	Tel Fahar
67-10	8	Bir Gifgafa	67-34	9/10	Rawiya
67-11	8	Nakhl			

DATA ANALYSIS

Figure A-2, "Tentative QJM Analysis Summary, 1967 War, Sinai Front," provides a summation of analyses of the eleven engagements on that front by means of the Quantified Judgment Method of Analysis of Historical Combat Data (QJMA), a methodology developed by HERO.

FIGURE A-2
TENTATIVE QJM ANALYSIS SUMMARY, 1967 WAR, SINAI FRONT

1	2	3	4	5	6	7	8	9	10	11
	N_A/N_I	W_A/W_I	Basic P/P	Surprise/Disruption	Refined P'/P'	Effective PR/PR	Israeli CEV	CEV	Av.	
1. Rafah	1.00	0.65	0.84	0.50	0.43	0.25	1.73			
2. Abu Ageila	0.96	1.01	1.81	0.32	0.58	0.32	1.83			
3. Gaza Strip°	1.44	1.01	1.52	0.67	1.02	0.28	3.58°		(1.79)	
4. El Arish	1.84	0.63	0.77	0.67	0.52	0.34	1.52			(1.71)
5. Bir Lahfan	0.96	0.59	0.66	0.67	0.44	0.26	1.70	2.07		
6. Jebel Libni	0.96	0.65	0.80	0.67	0.53	0.31	1.72			
7. Bir Hamma	1.14	0.78	0.80	0.83	0.67	0.31	2.16			
8. Bir Hassna	1.24	0.55	0.49	0.83	0.41	0.28	1.46			
9. Mitla Pass	3.03	1.81	0.81	0.83	0.67	0.37	1.82			
10. Bir Gifgafa	0.97	1.02	0.58	—	0.58	0.38	1.54	1.78		
11. Nakhl	0.98	0.51	0.55	—	0.55	0.28	1.96	1.91		(1.75)

° Palestinian division under Egyptian command.

Column 1 is a list of the engagements.

Column 2 is a manpower strength comparison, Arab strength divided by Israeli strength. Thus for the Battle of Rafah the two sides were virtually identical in numerical strength, 19,500 Egyptians opposed by 19,520 Israelis; at Abu Ageila the Egyptians, 18,450 strong, were outnumbered by 19,280 attacking Israelis.

Column 3 is a firepower comparison; using a typical firepower score technique, the total Egyptian firepower inventory available for the battle (including airpower) is divided by the total Israeli firepower (also including airpower).

Column 4 shows a "basic" combat power ratio, which reflects the effects of terrain, weather, posture (offense vs. defense), mobility, vulnerability, and all other factors (except for factors directly related to troop and command quality and behavior) identifiable as possibly influencing the battle outcome.

Column 5 shows the effects of surprise or postsurprise disruption; in all of these instances in the 1967 war the effects of surprise favored the Israelis, and thus the factors degrade Egyptian performance. (Quantification of surprise effects in the QJMA is based upon assessment of World War II engagements in which surprise affected outcomes.)

Column 6 is a recalculated combat power ratio, to include the effects of the surprise factor.

Column 7 is a ratio reflecting an assessment of the actual force ratio demonstrated on the battlefield in terms of outcome, based upon a mathematical formula not shown here. The formula reflects (1) the extent to which each side accomplished its assigned mission, (2) the effectiveness of each side in gaining or holding ground, and (3) the relative effectiveness in terms of casualties incurred and inflicted.

Column 8, which shows the relative combat effectiveness values (CEVs) of the Israelis with respect to the Egyptians, is derived by dividing Column 6 by Column 7; i.e., by dividing the combat ratio which should theoretically have existed (from what we know of the battle) by the combat ratio which was actually demonstrated on the battlefield. For Rafah, for instance, the Israeli CEV of 1.73 means, in very rough terms, that on the battlefield 100 Israelis were the approximate combat equivalent of 173 Egyptians.

Column 9 shows the average Israeli CEVs for the first half of the campaign, for the second half, and overall.

Column 10, applying only to the Battle of the Gaza Strip, where the principal defending force was a Palestinian division, converts the CEV for troops other than "standard" on the basis of a conversion factor, in which the Palestinian division is assumed to be half as good as an Egyptian division of the same size and weapons strength. While this factor of 2.0 is arbitrary, it is consistent with substantial research into the relative quality of Arab forces, which is discussed further in Appendix B. Thus the Israeli CEV of 3.58 at Rafah is converted to a value of 1.79 in terms of "standard" Egyptian troops. That the conversion factor is reasonably accurate is demonstrated by comparing this 1.79 figure to the 1.73 and 1.83 figures for Rafah and Abu Ageila, and to the revised average in Column 11, 1.75.

Column 11, then, provides revised average Israeli CEV figures with respect to the Egyptians, allowing for the conversion in Column 10.

Figure A-3 shows similarly calculated Israeli CEV values for actions in which Israelis were opposed by Jordanians and Syrians. Column 10 applies a correction to allow for what would probably have been the CEV at Zaoura-Qala, had one Israeli column not taken the wrong road. These calculations show that the Israeli combat effectiveness superiority over the Egyptians was on the average 75%, or a CEV of 1.75; their superiority over the Jordanians was on the average 54%, or a CEV of 1.54; Israeli superiority over the Syrians was on the average 163%, or a CEV of 2.63; and Israeli superiority over the Palestinians was about 250%, or a CEV of 3.50.

FIGURE A-3
TENTATIVE QJM SUMMARIES, 1967 WAR
WEST BANK FRONT; GOLAN FRONT

1	2	3	4	5	6	7	8	9	10	11
	N_A/N_I	W_A/W_I	*Basic* *P/P*	*Surprise/ Disruption*	*Refined* *P'/P'*	*Effective* *PR/PR*	*Israeli* CEV	CEV *Av.*		
21. Jerusalem	0.49	0.41	0.77	0.83	0.64	0.40	1.61	1.61*		
22. Jenin	0.57	0.39	0.62	0.85	0.53	0.44	1.21			
23. Kabatiya	0.77	0.69	1.18	0.90	1.06	0.58	1.82	1.52		
24. Tilfit-Zababida	1.02	0.58	0.85	0.90	0.77	0.44	1.76			
25. Nablus	0.80	0.41	0.56	0.95	0.53	0.41	1.31	1.54		
								1.54		
* June 5-7; not included in partial averages.										
32. Zaoura-Qala	1.46	0.36	0.58	–	0.58	0.30	1.91**		(2.48)	
33. Tel Fahar	1.52	0.36	0.76	–	0.76	0.30	2.54			
34. Rawiya	0.80	0.74	1.76	0.54	0.95	0.33	2.88			
								2.44		(2.63)
** Israeli column takes wrong road.										

Normalizing these relationships on the Palestinian performance provides the following interesting comparisons:

Israelis	3.50	(1.54)	(1.75)	(2.63)			
Jordanians	2.27	(1.00)			(1.14)	(1.71)	
Egyptians	2.00		(1.00)		(1.00)		(1.50)
Palestinians	1.00						
Syrians	1.33			(1.00)		(1.00)	(1.00)

CONCLUSIONS

1. In battlefield combat performance the Israeli superiority over Arab opponents in the 1967 war was as follows:

a. Approximately 54% over the Jordanians; i.e., 100 Israelis in combat formations were the operational equivalent of about 154 Jordanians;

b. Approximately 75% over the Egyptians; i.e., a combat unit of 100 Israelis was approximately the operational equivalent of 175 Egyptians;

c. Approximately 163% over the Syrians; i.e., a combat unit of 100 Israelis was approximately the operational equivalent of a unit of 263 Syrians.

d. Approximately 250% over the Palestinians.

2. The poor Syrian showing was probably more due to the chaos and confusion in the Syrian armed forces as a result of frequent coups d'etat between 1949 and 1966 than a reflection of any inherent Syrian inferiority to the other Arab nations.

3. The relatively better showing of the Jordanians suggests that they were still benefitting from several decades of British leadership and military tradition.

4. Since Egypt was Israel's principal military opponent, Egyptian performance reflects a general Arab standard of relative combat effectiveness, roughly 75% that of the Israelis.

Appendix B

Quantitative Analysis
of the October War, 1973

Presented below is a summary of the HERO analysis of the 1973 war, comparable to that for the 1967 war as contained in Appendix A.

THE DATA

Tables C and F, pp 608-609, summarize the major statistical ground data of the 1973 October War, including overall strengths and losses of personnel and selected items of equipment for all major participants. Tables A and E provide comparable air strength and loss data.

Figure B-1 is a listing of all major engagements on the Suez-Sinai front from October 6 through 25. Figure B-2 is a similar listing for the Golan front.

FIGURE B-1
ENGAGEMENTS, 1973 WAR
SUEZ-SINAI FRONT

Number	Date	Engagement
73-01	Oct. 6	Suez Canal Assault (N)
73-02	6	Suez Canal Assault (S)
73-03	7	Second Army Buildup
73-04	7	Third Army Buildup
73-05	8	Kantara-Firdan
73-06	14	Egyptian Offensive (N)
73-07	14	Egyptian Offensive (S)
73-08	15-16	Deversoir (Chinese Farm I)
73-09	16-17	Chinese Farm II
73-10	18	Deversoir West
73-11	19-21	Jebel Geneifa
73-12	19-22	Ismailia
73-13	22	Shallufa I
73-14	23-24	Adabiya
73-15	23-24	Suez
73-16	23-24	Shallufa II

FIGURE B-2
ENGAGEMENTS, 1973 WAR
GOLAN FRONT

Number	Date	Engagement
73-21	Oct. 6-7	Ahmadiyeh
73-22	6-7	Kuneitra
73-23	6	Rafid
73-24	7-8	Yehudia-El Al
73-25	7-8	Nafekh
73-26	8-9	Mt. Hermonit
73-27	8	Mt. Hermon I
73-28	8-10	Hushniyah
73-29	8-10	Tel Faris
73-30	11-13	Tel Shams
73-31	11-12	Tel Shaar
73-32	13	Tel el Hara
73-33	15	Kfar Shams-Tel Antar
73-34	16	Naba
73-35	19	Arab Counteroffensive
73-36	21	Mt. Hermon II
73-37	22	Mt. Hermon III

DATA ANALYSIS

Figure B-3, "QJM Force Quality Analysis Summary, 1973 War, Suez-Sinai Front," is the same kind of overall summary of quantitative analysis of the 1973 war as is found in Figure A-2 for the 1967 war. There are some minor differences, however:

Column 5 is new. This provides a basis for assessing the extent to which an attacking force, qualitatively inferior to the defender, is able to improve itself by special prebattle preparations and rehearsals for what is called a "set-piece battle." This was the situation that existed when the Egyptians were crossing the Suez Canal, and continuing the attack, on October 6 and 7, and when they waited—fully prepared—for the expected Israeli counterattack, on October 8.

Column 6 is the same as Column 5 in Figure A-2, but includes the set-piece factor as well as the factor for surprise or postsurprise disruption; Column 7 is the same as Column 6 in A-2; Column 8 is the same as Column 7 in A-2; and so forth, through Column 10.

Columns 11 and 12 show the estimated effects of differences in force quality (as for Palestinians in Figure A-2) and command lapse (as the Israelis' taking the wrong road in Figure A-3).

Column 13 shows modified Israeli CEVs that take into consideration the factors of Columns 11 and 12.

Column 14 shows the averages of the modified Israeli CEVs.

FIGURE B-3

QJM FORCE QUALITY ANALYSIS SUMMARY, 1973 WAR, SUEZ-SINAI FRONT

1	2	3	4	5	6	7	8	9	10	11	12	13	14
	N_A/N_I	W_A/W_I	Basic P/P	Set Piece	Surprise/ Disruption	Refined P'/P'	Effective PR/PR'	Israel CEV	CEV Average	Quality[1] Arab	Quality[1] Israel	Mod Is CEV	Mod CEV Average
1. Suez Canal (N)	6.62	2.96	0.98	1.33	3.19	4.16	2.28	1.83		2	2	1.83	
2. Suez Canal (S)	7.57	2.98	1.06	1.33	3.14	4.43	2.30	1.92		2	2	1.92	
3. Egypt. Bldp. (N)	4.57	2.76	1.33	1.33	2.46	4.35	1.64	2.65		2*	2	2.04	
4. Egypt. Bldp. (S)	4.11	2.93	1.51	1.33	2.42	4.86	1.90	2.56		2*	2	1.97	
5. Kantara-Firdan	2.61	1.60	1.40	1.33	1.73	3.22	1.84	1.75		2	2	1.75	
6. Egypt. Off. (N)	1.87	1.42	0.82	—	—	0.82	0.36	2.30		2*	2	1.77	
7. Egypt. Off. (S)	2.03	1.93	1.34	—	—	1.34	0.42	3.20		2*	2	2.46	
8. Deversoir	1.34	1.43	2.08	—	0.35	0.73	0.55	1.34	2.19	2	2*	1.74	1.94
9. Chinese Farm	1.28	1.08	1.54	—	0.57	0.88	0.47	1.87		2	2	1.87	
10. Deversoir W.	1.12	0.70	0.97	—	0.78	0.76	0.43	1.76		2	2	1.76	
11. J. Geneifa	2.10	1.21	1.31	—	—	1.31	0.35	3.71		2-3	2	2.47	
12. Ismailia	1.40	0.91	1.16	—	—	1.16	1.06	1.09		1-2	2*	1.78	
13. Shaluffa I	1.58	1.01	1.14	—	—	1.22	0.27	4.48		3	2	1.82	
14. Adabiya	1.34	0.95	1.22	—	—	1.14	0.42	2.74		2-3	2	2.23	
15. Suez City	1.53	0.69	1.07	—	1.52	1.63	1.22	1.33		2	2*	1.73	
16. Shaluffa II	1.93	0.92	1.31	—	—	1.31	0.34	3.81	2.60	2-3	2	2.54	2.03
									2.40				1.98

* Command Lapse.

[1] Quality: 1=Elite; 2=Average; 3=Below Average.

FIGURE B-4
QJM FORCE QUALITY ANALYSIS SUMMARY, 1973 WAR, GOLAN FRONT

1	2	3	4	5	6	7	8	9	10	11	12	13	14
			Basic	Set	Sur-prise/ Disrup-	Refined	Effec- tive	Israel	CEV	Quality(1)		Mod Is	Mod CEV
	N_A/N_I	W_A/W_I	P/P	Piece	tion	P'/P'	PR/PR	CEV	Average	Arab	Israeli	CEV	Average
21. Ahmadiyeh	3.96	1.03	0.34	1.52	2.37	1.22	0.47	2.57		2	2	2.57	
2. Kuneitra	4.89	1.66	0.60	1.52	2.77	2.53	1.35	1.87		2	2	1.87	
23. Rafid	3.94	0.91	0.38	1.52	3.14	1.81	1.74	1.04		1-2	2(B)	1.95	
24. Yehudia-El Al	3.49	0.84	0.35	—	2.43	0.85	0.45	1.89		1-2	2	2.36	
25. Nafekh	1.80	0.80	0.51	—	2.30	1.17	0.45	2.60		2	2	2.60	
26. Mt. Hermonit	5.99	1.25	0.41	1.52	1.91	1.19	0.57	2.10		2	2	2.10	
27. Mt. Hermon I	0.59	0.36	0.85	1.52	1.91	2.47	1.65	1.50		1	2	2.25	
28. Hushmiyah	1.15	0.63	0.92	—	1.65	1.52	0.41	3.71	2.16	2	2	3.71	2.43
29. Tel Faris	1.33	0.84	1.32	—	1.68	2.22	0.43	5.17		2*	2	3.98	
30. Tel Shams	1.20	0.76	1.62	—	—	1.62	0.47	3.43		2	2	3.43	
31. Tel Shaar	1.46	0.83	1.46	—	—	1.46	0.45	3.26		2	2	3.26	
32. Tel El Hara	1.14	1.09	0.77	—	—	0.77	0.29	2.66		I*	2	1.52	
33. Kfar Shams	1.09	1.09	1.99	—	—	1.99	0.37	5.39		I*	2	3.07	
34. Naba	1.05	0.94	0.53	—	—	0.53	0.37	1.42		J	2	1.92	
35. Arab Cntroff.	2.22	1.84	0.94	—	—	0.94	0.39	2.40		2-J-I	2	2.40	
36. Mt. Hermon II	0.83	0.60	1.61	—	—	1.61	1.55	1.04		1	2	1.56	
37. Mt. Hermon III	0.42	0.37	0.95	—	—	0.95	0.36	2.63	3.05	1(B)	2	2.63	2.64
									2.63				2.54

* Command Lapse.

(1) Quality: Syrian: 1 = Elite; 2 = Average.

I = Iraqi; J = Jordanian; (B) = Broken.

Figure B-4 goes through the same process for the Golan front.

As with the 1967 war, the refined analyses show remarkably consistent values in relative combat effectiveness of the opponents in each of the two sets of data: that for the Suez-Sinai front, and that for the Golan front. The analyses show that the Israeli combat effectiveness superiority over the Egyptians was on the average 98%, or a CEV of 1.98; Israeli superiority over the Syrians was 154%, or a CEV of 2.54; superiority over the Jordanians was 88%, or a CEV of 1.88; superiority over the Iraqis was 243%, or a CEV of 3.43.

A normalized comparison, similar to that for the 1967 war, is shown below:

Israelis	3.43	(1.88)	(1.98)	(2.54)			
Jordanians	1.82	(1.00)			(1.35)		(1.05)
Egyptians	1.73		(1.00)			(1.28)	(1.00)
Syrians	1.35			(1.00)	(1.00)	(1.00)	
Iraqis	1.00						

CONCLUSIONS

1. In battlefield combat performance the Israeli superiority over Arab opponents in the 1973 war was as follows:

a. Approximately 88% over the Jordanians; i.e., a combat unit of 100 Israelis was approximately the operational equivalent of a unit of 188 Jordanians;

b. Approximately 98% over the Egyptians;

c. Approximately 154% over the Syrians;

d. Approximately 243% over the Iraqis.

2. The relative improvement of Syrian combat performance between 1967 and 1973 (still leaving them substantially behind the Egyptians) can be attributed primarily to politico-military stability in Syria between 1970 and 1973.

3. Except for the Syrians (for the reason noted above), the gap between the Israelis and their Arab opponents did not narrow between 1967 and 1973, and in fact it widened to some extent.

4. The apparent anomaly between this quantitative conclusion and the obvious fact that Egyptian performance was generally better in relation to Israeli performance in 1973 than in 1967 is readily explicable in terms of surprise (an Israeli advantage in 1967, an Egyptian advantage in 1973), limitations on Israeli air support in 1967 due to the Egyptians' Russian-made air defense system, and a marked improvement in the higher leadership of the Egyptian forces.

5. The reasons for the continuing, and slightly widened, gap between the Israelis and Egyptians, despite clearcut Egyptian improvement, are the higher quality of military professionalism in Israel, a substantially superior research and development capability and program, and the Arab cultural tendency toward self-delusion which, while declining as a result of Arab realization that there is such a tendency, nonetheless persists.

Bibliography

Allon, Yigal. *The Making of Israel's Army*. New York, 1971.
———. *Shield of David*. New York, 1970.
Badri, Hassan el, Taha el Magdoub, and Mohommed Dia el-Din Zohdy. *The Ramadan War*. Dunn Loring, Va., 1977.
Bell, J. Bowyer. *The Long War: Israel and the Arabs Since 1946*. Englewood Cliffs, NJ, 1969.
———. "National Character and Military Strategy: The Egyptian Experience." October 1973, *Parameters*, vol. 5, no. 1, 1975.
Ben-Gurion, David. *Israel: Years of Challenge*. New York, 1963.
Berkman, Ted. *Cast a Giant Shadow*. New York, 1962.
Bull, Odd. *War and Peace in the Middle East*. London, 1976.
Burns, E.L.M. *Between Arab and Israeli*. New York, 1963.
Churchill, Randolph, and Winston Churchill. *The Six Day War*. Boston, 1967.
Collins, Larry, and Dominique Lapierre. *O Jerusalem!* New York, 1977.
Dan, Uri. *Sharon's Bridgehead*. Tel Aviv, 1975.
Dayan, Moshe. *Diary of the Sinai Campaign*. New York, 1966.
———. "Israel's Border and Security Problems." *Foreign Affairs*, January 1955.
———. *My Life*. Tel Aviv, 1976.
Dayan, Yael. *Israel Journal: June, 1967*. New York, 1967.
Eden, Sir Anthony. *Full Circle: The Memoirs of Anthony Eden*. Boston, 1960.
Eisenhower, Dwight D. *Waging Peace, 1956-1961*. New York, 1965.
Fergusson, Bernard. *The Watery Maze; The Story of Combined Operations*. New York, 1961.
Gilbert, Martin. *The Arab-Israeli Conflict: Its History in Maps*. London, 1974.
Glubb, Sir John B. *A Short History of the Arab Peoples*. New York, 1969.
———. *A Soldier with the Arabs*. London, 1957.
———. "Violence on the Jordan-Israel Border." *Foreign Affairs*, July 1954.
Graves, William. "New Life for the Suez Canal." *National Geographic*, June 1975.
Gray, Colin S. "The Security of Israel." *Military Review*, October 1975.
Heikal, Mohamed. *The Road to Ramadan*. London, 1975.
Henriques, Robert. *A Hundred Hours to Suez*. New York, 1957.
Herzog, Chaim. *The War of Atonement*. Tel Aviv, 1975.
Howard, Harry N. *The Middle East: A Selected Bibliography of Recent Works*. Washington, 1970.
Hurewitz, J.C. *Middle East Politics: The Military Dimensions*. New York, 1969.
———, ed. *Soviet-American Rivalry in the Middle East*. Academy of Political Science, Columbia University. New York, 1969.
Hussein, King of Jordan, w/Vick Vance and Pierre Lauer; tr. by June P. Wilson and Walter B. Michaels, *My "War" With Israel*. New York, 1969.

Israel, Army Historical Branch. *The Sinai Campaign.* Tel Aviv, n.d.

Israel, IDF Spokesman's Office. *The Israel-Arab Wars.* Jerusalem, 1975.

Kahlny, Avigdor. *Fortress Seventy-Seven.* Tel Aviv, 1976. (Translated notes from this Hebrew book are available)

Kimche, Jon, and David Kimche. *A Clash of Destinies, The Arab-Jewish War and the Founding of the State of Israel.* New York, 1960.

Laqueur, Walter. *The Road to War: The Origin and Aftermath of the Arab-Israeli Conflict, 1967-8.* Baltimore, 1969.

London Times Insight Team. *The Yom Kippur War.* London, 1974.

Lorch, Nataniel. *The Edge of the Sword.* New York, 1961.

Love, Kennett. *Suez: The Twice Fought War.* New York, 1969.

Luttwak, Edward, and Dan Horowitz. *The Israeli Army.* New York, 1975.

Mansfield, Peter. *The Arab World; A Comprehensive History.* New York, 1976.

Marshall, S.L.A. *Sinai Victory.* New York, 1958.

————. *Swift-Sword; The Historical Record of Israel's Victory, June 1967.* New York, 1967.

Meir, Golda. *My Life.* Tel Aviv, 1975.

Murphy, Robert. *Diplomat Among Warriors.* New York, 1964.

Nutting, Anthony. *No End of a Lesson: The Story of Suez.* London, 1967.

O'Ballance, Edgar. *The Arab-Israeli War, 1948.* London, 1956.

Pajak, Roger F. "Soviet Arms and Egypt." *Survival,* July/August 1975.

Patai, Raphael. *The Arab Mind.* New York, 1976.

Pearson, Anthony. "A Conspiracy of Silence." *Penthouse,* May and June 1976.

Peres, Shimon. *David's Sling.* London, 1970.

Proceedings; International Symposium: Military Aspects of the Israeli-Arab Conflict (Louis Williams, ed). Tel Aviv, 1975.

Proceedings; International Symposium on the 1973 October War. Cairo, 1976.

Rabinovich, Abraham. *The Battle for Jerusalem, June 5-7, 1967.* New York, 1972.

Roosevelt, Kermit. *Arabs, Oil, and History.* New York, 1949.

Safran, Nadav. *From War to War.* New York, 1969.

————. "The War and the Future of the Arab-Israeli Conflict." *Foreign Affairs,* January 1974.

Schiff, Zeev. *A History of the Israeli Army (1870-1974).* San Francisco, 1974.

————. *October Earthquake.* Tel Aviv, 1974.

Schleifer, S. Abdullah. "The Fall of Jerusalem, 1967." *Journal of Palestine Studies,* vol. 1, no. 1, Autumn, 1971.

Shlaim, Avi. "Failures in National Intelligence Estimates: The Case of the Yom Kippur War." *World Politics,* April 1976, p. 348.

Stanford, Melvin J. "Middle East Strategic Factors." *Military Review,* December 1973.

Teveth, Shubtai. *The Tanks of Tammuz.* London, 1968.

U.S. Congress. House. Committee on Armed Services. Special Subcommittee on the Middle East. *Report.* H.A.S.C. No. 93-92. 93d Congress, 1st Session, December 13, 1973.

Van Creveld, Martin. *Military Lessons of the Yom Kippur War: Historical Perspectives.* Washington, 1975.

Von Horn, Carl. *Soldiering for Peace.* New York, 1967.

Yost, Charles W. "The Arab-Israeli War; How it Began." *Foreign Affairs,* January 1968.

Index

637